# WE ARE ALL CATAWBA

*COMPLETE GENEALOGY OF MY DADDY'S CATAWBA ANCESTORS*

**Judy Canty Martin**

**Published by Backintyme Publishing**
Crofton, Kentucky, U.S.A.

Copyright @ 2017 by Backintyme
ALL RIGHTS RESERVED
Backintyme Publishing
1341 Grapevine Rd.
Crofton, KY 42217
270-985-8568
Website: http://backintyme.biz
Email:backintyme@mehrapublishing.com
Printed in the United States of America
September 2017
ISBN: 978-0-939479-53-5
Library of Congress Control Number: 2017952578

**Cover Photo:**
Group Catawba Indians, Rock Hill, South Carolina
Photo edit by Aaron Nash

PART OF
THE AMERICAN BRED SERIES;
ODYSSEYS OF THE MIXED BLOOD PIONEER FAMILY
NUMBER IV
FROM BACKINTYME PUBLISHING

# We Are All Catawba

**By Judy Canty Martin**

**Edited by Shirley Hamblin**

Alma or Pete Canty

# Acknowledgements

People have asked me why I did this research and my only answer is that it grew on me. Anyone who begins to trace their genealogy looking for their ancestors is subject to Genealogist disease. We traverse grave yards, curse the mail, look at phone books and read the indexes of books more than we read them. Now we have many tools and a goodly amount of records to search. We have computers and programs to manipulate photos and put them into the text. When I started I literally had to cut and paste the photos into the pages.

Special thanks to Dr. Thomas Blumer for permission to use his photos and information. He has been with me for more than 30 years and we have yet to meet in person that is our goal for 2017. To Roger Trimnal and Fred Sanders who encouraged me all these years. My cousin Ben Garcia's wife Irene Beck Garcia who lent me her book on the Catawba by Brown, my late husband's friend John Neal who gave me the John Morgan book and my cousins Cindy Schneider Walsh and Wayne Head who bought me the Bulmer's Bibliography book so I didn't have to get it in the library. Thanks to Pony Hill a fellow researcher working in Northern Florida on similar bands and tribes.

Now to the members of each family, Harris both Hillary and Lillie Susan, the Galvez, Garcia, Sandoval, Canty, Watts both James and William, Georges, Harris's from South Carolina, and Cantys, I can't name you all, but I thank you.

Mandy Caponis Sisi, David Gunn, Paul and Mitchel Harris, John Brown, Bill Teaster, Geneva Gunton, and the rest of my Facebook friends who let me swipe photos. Too many to name but whom are all related. I hope I do justice to you, all tho you are too young to be in the book, you should find your ancestors.

For the photos besides Tom Blumer's, Rolaine Grant King , Monty McDonald Woodbury, Thora Watts Wright, Lucia Wright, Pat Canty Ramsey, Marna Canty Unruh, Mandy Sisi, Donald Williams, Paul and Mitchel Harris, Geneva Gunton, Marina Wahnetah and Frela Beck (two fine Cherokee Ladies), Lola Sandoval Ruybalid, Wayne Head, Tom Croasmun and all the rest of my relatives. I collected the rest of the news clippings and other photos myself. I have a new friend who has sent me journals and photos for this book and the next one Edrie Linn Cleaver. She has scanned and e-mailed me information that was well received in the eastern band and will be found in the next book about missionaries.

Last but certainly not least, my friend Shirley May Honey Hamblin. Without her work on this it would remain in Ancestry.com. She has worked tirelessly and without ceasing to put the information and photos into this book form. She now knows more about the Catawba than a good many of us, she corrected my mistakes, caught the duplicates and sent the books here and there for me.

We are all Catawba and we need to share our heritage with each other. This book only traces the Catawba blood; however, none of us would be here without our white ancestors and families. None of us are full blooded Catawba, but that is a strong enough blood line.

# About the Author

Judy Canty Martin, author

*Judy is author of this book and three other books on the Catawba Indian People.*

I was born April 15, 1946 in Alamosa Colorado. I am the only child of Alma (Pete) and Francis Clarabelle Payne Canty. My dad was Catawba and my mother was white.

Academically school was easy; I could read before I started and this gave me a head start, we didn't have kindergarten in those days. It wasn't until I was in the second grade that I began to face some prejudice because I was neither Spanish nor white. After that year my classmate's never gave me any grief about my Indian blood and the 5 of us who started school together, we lost one, there were 6, and the 2 later mates are still very close.

When we got into high school it was more difficult and I did not date anyone in school except my old playmate Nathan Wilson. I took all the hard classes at the time, had geometry before I had algebra etc. I graduated in May 1964 as valedictorian and won a bit of a scholarship to Adams state college in Alamosa. I found out that I would have to pay for much more and since I had no ambition to teach, I saw no reason to put financial stress on my dad.

I had trouble my senior year with anxiety and panic attacks, after I graduated I did not go to college. I became agoraphobic and it took me about a year to recover somewhat. I was approached by a drive in to work and I took it. I never had to apply for a job. The local lumber yard then hired me to be a bookkeeper and I went on to that for several years. I worked for two jewelry manufacturing businesses setting up bookkeeping systems, and then after a couple of years went back to the lumber company until I got married to Forrest Martin in 1970. I worked there until I had my first child, then after a time, I went to the construction company my dad worked for. After about 3 years, we moved from Sanford to Alamosa and I had my son Devin. Our daughter Tiffany started school and it became too difficult to work and drive 20 miles to get her to school so I became a stay at home mom.

Then because I needed the challenge I began my genealogy obsession. I collected my husband Forrest's genealogy, which was vast and mine was pitiful so I started my mother's side. After a move to Pueblo Colorado I began my pursuit of my Catawba genealogy. It was slow and i had to purchase pages, not books, which took money from the family so I did it a dollar at a time. After another move to Cortez, Colorado I could do more because I had unlimited access to the LDS church library, while I ran programs for the church. While I translated Mexican records, I collected my own genealogy. I found relatives, and my name got out and I could finally find enough to self-publish 3 books on my family and the whole Catawba Nation as I knew it. I became friends with Fred Sanders and then several South Carolina relatives; Jack and Dean Canty and Roger Trimnal and they helped me as much as they could. It turned out the one page naming parents etc. I had, was more than most had. I became acquainted with Dr Thomas Blumer who wrote Genealogy of the Catawba, which became the Catawba Genealogy Bible for me, and we were off.

At the time PCs and software had not quite gotten there and scanning hadn't been invented yet along with the internet. I muddled on collecting relatives, information and photos. By the time technology had caught up, I again had a head start. I was contacted by Dr Russell Judkins about the subject. I assisted him in his initial research and helped Ian Watson with his book and Wesley White and I shared information for several years. I did my own family first, Canty and Patterson, which led to Head and Tims and Hilary Harris and I had the 5 families that left Catawba in 1887-90. Then I was contacted by two other related families Watts and Lillie Susan Harris Ballard's and I had about half the tribe's genealogy. I obtained the missionary journal of Elder Joseph Willey and my great uncle Pinkney Head and transcribed and identified the people in it. I found other people had written about these people and since I knew them I could do a better job.

After the Missionary journals, I had collected so much genealogy and I was connected to nearly every Catawba in South Carolina, I decided to put everything I had into My Fathers People. This was the first attempt at genealogy of the whole tribe. This was before the internet and all the resources available now. Since I had access to the largest collection of genealogy in the world, the Church of Jesus Christ of Latter Day Saints the Mormons, and I was one, I used records no one else had used, except returned missionaries at BYU, and I put it together.

I also donated to the LDS Church collections the Family History Library as well as putting my own genealogy into the systems, so that a good deal of the information there, will be something I wrote or donated. I also donated to libraries and museums, Rock Hill Library got the first book, Genealogy of the Western Catawba, the APS American Philosophical Society in Philadelphia, PA, the Smithsonian, the University of South Carolina at Lancaster, all got both Genealogy of the Western Catawba and My Father's People. The Catawba Nation got those plus The Missionary Journals of Joseph Willey and Pinkney Head. I was approached by the Sanford Museum and although I offered to donate, Madge Perko insisted on buying all three for the museum. Sanford is the unofficial home of the Western Catawba, my home town. I was also approached by Dr. John Brandt to help with an exhibit for the Alamosa Colorado Museum, adding my Catawba Pioneers to the other pioneers of the San Luis Valley. I have my people listed as a Native American group in Colorado, and helped other writers to do papers on them. BYU students have asked for help for several Master's Thesis papers and I helped a researcher from Chappell Hill do a paper that is in their collections as well as one in the University of Colorado done by Dana Echohawk. I have donated photos and information all over the world, including a group of Western Catawba who moved to Brazil.

Heart of a researcher: 'My Father's People'
Adversity factor overcome as she finds her Catawba roots
By John L. Hart
Church News associate editor
Published: Saturday, Aug. 2, 2003
Judy Canty Martin has the heart of a family history researcher.

Family history research has captivated
Judy Canty Martin for 32 years, resulting
in three books and wider understanding of
her forebears.

        The slight, grandmotherly, part-Native American author has published three books of her ancestral
heritage. Most recent is "My Father's People," a complete history of the Catawba Nation. In the pages of
this copy-machine book assembled over a span of 30 years is captured personal histories and anecdotes
from three centuries. Each one gives evidence of the love of this labor by Sister Martin. Family history
research has captivated Judy Canty Martin for 32 years, resulting in three books and wider understanding
of her forebears. Photo by Tiffany Martin    "I have always been interested in history," she said. "I can't
describe what keeps me tied to it. I don't know." Sister Martin has been driven on the subject for 32 years,
representative of so many family history researchers who devote their lives to this area of study. Her
interest in family history spills over to her Cortez 4th Ward, Durango Colorado Stake, where for many
years she supervised Spanish name extraction.    As a youth she didn't think much about who she was until
someone used a racial slur and "adversity made me more determined." She would learn that overcoming
adversity was a family trait that went back many generations.    As she began her research, her husband

was a well-employed tractor mechanic in Alamosa, Colo. But during that time in the 1980s when many farmers lost their farms and were foreclosed on, he was laid off and without work for a year. They relocated from Sanford to Cortez, Colo. "We managed to keep it together, but it was tough financially," said Sister Martin. Her husband, Forrest L. "Frosty" Martin, continued to be a source of great encouragement to her regarding her Indian ancestry. "I can still see him standing in the background with a smile of understanding and pride," she said. "He loved Indians." She grew in understanding of her Catawba forebears who died before she was born: her grandfather, John Alonzo Canty; her great-grandfather, James Patterson; and great uncle, Pinkney Head. Her grandfather had died without talking about his history, a typical trait of this people, she was to learn. So she began to dig and found that a contingent of converts from Catawba, York County, S.C., had come to Colorado in the 1880s. She continued the search, but scraping up even enough change to pay for birth certificates was a challenge. She found a Catawba history book at the library and checked it out so many times that her cousins finally took up a collection and bought her a copy. Other hardships came with the loss of family members. The most recent was the most difficult with the death of her husband in 2002. But along the way, unexpected rewards of a spiritual nature came her way. She learned that the Catawba tribe dated back to the 16th-17th centuries. A conglomeration of smaller tribes, the Catawba never fought against the government, but fought with them in the Revolutionary War and assisted them in other skirmishes. She learned the Catawba were a spiritual people who had joined the Church in South Carolina against adversity in the 1880s. Such was the opposition that one journal noted: "The mobs are so bad that Elders Bingham and Cragun hid in the woods and were piloted through the swamps for 30 miles by [Catawba converts] James Patterson and James Watts." Between threats that sometimes materialized into mobs that shot at and once whipped a missionary, the Rock Hill Branch was organized in Catawba in 1884 with 25 Catawba among the 31 members. Two convert ancestors, Alonzo Canty and Pinkney Head, were called on a mission to the Cherokee in North Carolina. "We was glad to think we was worthy to go and teach others the gospel," wrote Elder Head in his journal. Elder Head's family was among five Catawba families who left South Carolina between 1885 and 1890 to settle in the West. They came by wagon to the Mississippi and then by train to Sanford, Colo. As Sister Martin researched on, she completed her Genealogy of the Western Catawba. She also found the missionary journals of Elders Joseph Willey and Pinkney Head, which she published. Other personal rewards included finding unknown cousins. Her grandfather had a half-brother in South Carolina with descendants. She also found many cousins in the West. Some of these often felt isolated in the community because of their Indian ancestry. The family started drawing closer as she contacted one and then another for information. They began to have more family connections and appreciate their roots more. "I have seen cousins who did not know the other existed 15 years ago go on vacations together and exchange letters," she said. "It has been a remarkable thing to watch. So not only are the genealogical requirements filled, but families have been reunited." Another source of support was her uncle, William Franklin "Buck" Canty, among the first Native Americans called as patriarch in 1962 in Sanford, Colo. "He was more than an uncle to me, more like the grandfather I had never known," said Sister Martin. In 1982, Sister Martin walked into his shop where he was working with a piece of wood and singing funeral songs, knowing his time was short. "I had not been able to hear him speaking of death," she said. "He knew it was near; I was not ready. I finally let him talk about it." They spoke of his eventual demise. He said he would discuss genealogy with their forebears. He promised "to send a COD letter." In just a few months, the aged patriarch died in that wood shop.   A few years later, Harvey Gardner, regional representative, came to the stake seeking Native American names for temple work, and announced a special temple day.   "I jumped at the chance and spent one whole night and day typing the forms and getting [names] ready for the temple," she said. On that special temple day, April 26, 1986, work was done for much of the Catawba tribe ancestry.   "April 26th was [Uncle Buck's] birthday," said Sister Martin. "There was my COD letter."

# LIVING

INSIDE
■ LIVING/See 2B
Mesa Verde recruits
'Graffiti Busters.'
■ TV LISTINGS/See 7-8B
Channel lineups for
Sunday, Monday & Tuesday.

**FOURTH WARD FAMILY** History Consultant Judy Martin poses inside the Cortez Family History Center on Wednesday afternoon at the Church of Jesus Christ of Latter-day Saints on East Empire Street.

JOURNAL/STEVE LEWIS

# Genealogy expert traces heritage

BY HOPE NEALSON
JOURNAL STAFF WRITER

A woman executed at the Salem Witch Trials, "the Anne," and Adam and Eve all have something in common.

They were all traced back in Forrest L. "Frosty" Martin's genealogy, a 35-foot long document started by his wife, Judy, in 1972, which she completed after his passing in 2002.

"I can trace him back to Adam and Eve through historical records. If you're a Christian, we all came from those two people," Judy Martin said, adding she discovered one of Frosty's ancestors, George Martin, to be among the passengers of the Anne when it sailed to Massachusetts in 1620, where he married a woman later accused of witchcraft.

"I traced my husband's family back to an executed witch (Susannah Martin) at the Salem Trials," she said. "She was 62 when they hung her. I kept thinking, how dangerous could a 62-year-old widow be?"

Martin said she became hooked on genealogy at 27, a couple years after the birth of her first son, and has continued it to this day.

"If you start working on something like that, it becomes addictive," she said. "I started doing my own. One of my aunts said it couldn't be done, and it just made me more determined."

Martin turned her attention toward her American Indian ancestry, starting with her Catawba grandfather, who came to the San Luis Valley with the Mormon Missionary in the 1880s.

"My Indians are back 12 or 13 generations," she said. "When I was little, I didn't pay any attention to it. I knew I was part, but I didn't know anything else about it."

Martin moved from Alamosa to Cortez in 1985 after she was called by the Church of Jesus Christ Latter-day Saints to head the Spanish Extraction project for the entire Durango Colorado Stake, an area that encompasses Cortez, Pagosa Springs, Red Mesa, Durango and Bayfield.

The Extraction Program was developed as part of LDS's Inter-

See HERITAGE on Page 2B

# Martin teaches ward people, librarian to do genealogy

*From Page 1B*

national Genealogical Index, started in 1969, to get records from around the world.

"I started taking the old baptismal records and translating them so they could put them into the computer. It's a big area. I was in charge of all of the work — all the people I had were translating Spanish into English," Martin said, adding she taught them how to recognize and transcribe names onto cards.

"My husband I looked at 150,000 cards," she said, noting they had two people doing the same job, and she was the fact checker when they didn't match.

Along with her 10 years in the Spanish Extraction program, Martin wrote three books about her Catawba relatives, finding records through the state, which was subsidizing the tribe.

"I had to buy them one paper at a time," she said, adding she could only afford the dollar per page fee since she was raising kids.

Martin said she eventually gathered enough information for three books.

"It didn't make me rich, but I got a call three weeks ago from a descendent that we've never been able to find. We knew the name and the parents, but we didn't know what happened to the kids. The guy called me, so we added a whole family."

Martin said what she loves about genealogy is connecting families, including her own, which held a reunion in 1993 in Sanford, in the San Luis Valley.

"It was neat," she said. "There were cousins there that didn't know each other existed until I made the list of who belonged to who."

To hunt down relatives, Martin recommends starting with LDS records, which include both member and nonmember documents, online and free of charge.

"Most everybody has a Mormon in the woodpile somewhere, someone you might not know about, a great aunt or cousin, so that may be someone to start with," Martin said. "Every time you look up, they'll refer you back to the Church of Jesus Christ of Latter-day Saints because we have the largest library in the world."

The library where Martin volunteers is in the Family History Center, located at 1700 E. Empire St., Cortez, in the Church of Jesus Christ of Latter-day Saints, open to the public.

Martin also recommends checking census records, which began in 1790 but didn't list household members until 1850.

Because of privacy laws that require the census to wait 72 years, the last one available to the public is from 1930 — all online.

Genealogy sites such as familysearch.com also provide access to all online legal documents, like birth, marriage, death, census, church and other indexes.

"Even where there are no obvious records, as in some marriages, records are still handed down, whether written in a Bible or whatever," Martin said.

"You start with the living — you and your parents."

Besides volunteering at the Family History Center, Martin has held both stake and ward callings in family history-genealogy in a leadership capacity for 20 years.

"I taught the ward people and librarians working in the libraries how to do genealogy, where to go, etc., and how to run the church programs. I'm the go-to person. If someone gets stuck, they call me, and then I try to unstick them if I can," she said, adding her research skills have also brought in some income.

"I do have somewhat of a business," she said. "If they've got more money than they have time, I will trace family trees for a fee. Even with a little bit of information, I'm dangerous."

*Reach Hope Nealson at hopen@cortezjournal.com.*

OCTOBER 19, 1993, VOL. 105, NO. 51          CORTEZ, COLORADO (USPS 360-960)

# Cortez woman looks back at forgotten tribe's history

**BY JEROME B. MAAG JR.**

A Cortez woman has spent the last twenty years tracking an almost forgotten chapter of American history — that of the Catawba Indian tribe.

Judy Canty Martin, a descendent of a group of Catawbas who settled in the San Luis Valley in 1885, has compiled a complex geneology of not only her own family, but of the other five families who settled in Colorado, of the white men who interbred with them and of several of the Catawba families still on tribal lands in South Carolina

**Tribal historian . . .**

JUDY CANTY MARTIN shows photos of her grandfather and grandmother, both members of five Catawba Indian families who settled in the San Luis Valley in 1885. Martin has spent twenty years tracing the families of Catawba Indians and even the white men who interbred with them back as far as 1581. The tribe was only recently granted recognition by the federal government after having been dropped during the Eisenhower administration.

as part of her efforts to get the western branch of the tribe added to the federal roles.

The tribe in August received federal recognition after having been removed from the list of federally recognized tribes by President Dwight D. Eisenhower. That recognition only took in the South Carolina Catawbas, Martin said.

"None of the Catawbas has ever been subsidized and never had any of the rights the rest of the Indian tribes had," Martin said.

According to Martin, however, those rights are beginning to be recognized both through federal recognition and a recent settlement with the state of Carolina over the Treaty of Nation Fords.

"The state of South Carolina was supposed to pay for (Catawba) lands and pay so much to each person and they never lived up to it," she said. "That was the third or fourth big treaty they had broken."

The Catawbas were am the most populace tribes of East Coast at about the [ that Columbus landed in Americas. A tribal tradi holds that Columbus carriCatawba back to Spain afte first landing. The tribe c prised several smaller digroups of the Siouan langfamily.

Over time, however, dwindled through wars, spox, measles and "the no pestilences," Martin said, about 1888 when the 60 maining Catawbas were vi by Mormon missionaries.

For about 100 years. state of South Carolina tried to move them off their itional lands, but no other would accept them.

When the missionaries c about two-thirds of the were converted to the Mo church. In 1885, five fami 25 people — left their tradi home in the Carolinas

moved to the San Luis Vall There they thrived, but move has caused something rift between the Colorado wabas and the South Car members of the tribe.

"There were some gr blings that they deserted a s ing ship, but I tend to thin got thrown overboard." M: said.

The five families were the tersons, the Cantys, the ? nuys, the Harrises and Tims. Martin's gre grandfather was James Pa son, head of that clan, and grandfather was John ACanty. She was also relat the Pinneeys and Harrises said. *HEADS*

21 April 1998

Mrs. Judy Canty Martin
921 N. Edith
Cortez, Colorado 81321

Dear Judy;

Your letter dated April 14th with the additional information
on the early Catawba settlers has been received.    You are
to be commended and congratulated on the terrific job you
have done on compiling all this extremely valuable historical
information.

The copy of the text you sent will be given to the San Luis
Valley History Museum here in Alamosa to keep in their
museum files and archives.    My thanks on their behalf.

I have developed two display frame for the museum.   One has a
short history of who the Catawbas are and who, and when and
what, about the early twenty six settlers that came to Sanford
and Manassa.    The second frame has the old historical
photographs that you gave me.    They should all be finished
in a few days and will be placed in the American Indian Exhibit
showcase in the museum.    I'm very grateful for your help
in assisting us with this matter.    I too am very surprised
that no one has recognized the Catawbas as "unique early
pioneers" in the Valley.    Hopefully we can now correct that
oversight.

I have ordered you a copy of Merrill's book on the Catawba
and will mail it as soon as it arrives.    I will be away
till mid-May but I'll send it as soon as I get back if it
doesn't arrive before I leave.

Best wishes to you and your husband.........

JOHN H. BRANDT, PhD

*[handwritten margin note:]* PS — just in opening the mail I got a note. The book is sold out. I'll locate another. I'll get it or us. Sorry.

FAMILY AND CHURCH HISTORY DEPARTMENT
50 East North Temple Street
Salt Lake City, Utah 84150-3800

November 14, 2003

Church History Library
50 E. North Temple Rm. 227F
Salt Lake City, Utah 84150-3420
(801) 240-4748

Judy Canty Martin
921 N. Edith
Cortez, Colorado 81321

Dear Sister Martin,

The Church News article of August 2, 2003, in which you were featured, mentioned that you had written three books about your ancestors, the Catawba Indians. I was particularly interested in the missionary work referred to in the article, both in the Catawba tribe and by Joseph Willey and Pinkney Head. I think that the books you have written about the history of Catawba Indians, as well as the published journals of Elders Joseph Willey and Pinkney Head, would be valuable additions to the Church History Library collection. Can you send me information on how we may obtain copies of each of these materials?

I appreciate your help and I look forward to hearing from you.

Sincerely,

Sarah Sorenson
Acquisitions Librarian

SS:jr

X

# JESUS CHRIST

OF LATTER-DAY SAINTS

FAMILY AND CHURCH HISTORY DEPARTMENT
50 E. North Temple St. Rm. 227E
Salt Lake City, Utah 84150-3420

May 17, 2004

Church History Library
50 E. North Temple Rm. 227 E
Salt Lake City, Utah 84150-3420
(801) 240-4748

Judy Canty Martin
921 N. Edith
Cortez, Colorado 81321

Dear Sister Martin,

We received the manuscript of *My Father's People*, which you sent to us last month, along with the other two volumes of Catawba Indian genealogy tjat were sent earlier. We have photocopied *My Father's People* and will bind it and add it to our collection. As we discussed on the phone, I am returning the original to you.

Thank you for sharing your work with us. These books will be valuable additions to the Church History Library collection. I wish you the best in your current projects as well as your future endeavors.

Sincerely,

Sarah Sorenson
Acquisition Librarian

SS:jr

HISTORICAL DEPARTMENT
East Wing
50 East North Temple Street
Salt Lake City, Utah 84150
Phone (801) 531-2745

November 3, 1981

Mrs. Judy Canty Martin
921 N. Edith
Cortez, Colorado   81321

Dear Sister:

I have been asked to answer your letter relating to my article on Chief Blue in the Church News. Your grandfather, John Alonzo Canty, was the first branch president of the Catawba Branch. Samuel T. Blue was made Branch president many years later. Brother Blue was president of the Branch during World War I and the Depression.

I am doing continued research on the Church's activities among the Catawba Indians and would be interested in any material relating to your own family. Please let me know if you have any information that would be of interest to the Church and I will be glad to help you in any way.

Sincerely,

Jeffery O Johnson
Historical Department
50 East North Temple
Salt Lake City, Utah  84150

## SHINING MOMENTS

# Giving to neighbors

"Love thy neighbor as thyself."

Sometimes this oft-repeated scripture is easier read than practiced. Judy Canty Martin admits that several years ago, she would have doubted that many people actually went out of their way to help others. But today her attitude is different. "I personally have seen this scripture put into practice," she stated.

Sister Martin is referring to members of the Sanford (Colo.) Ward and the Manassa Colorado Stake, where her parents, Pete and Clara Canty, have lived for many years.

"My 75-year-old father had a malignant brain tumor," she explained. Although he had the tumor surgically removed, the treatment required to complete his recovery would mean that the Cantys would have to rent an apartment in a town 100 miles away from their home because they were unable to drive that distance every day.

"Unfortunately, my parents couldn't afford this and their bishop, Preston Stanley, knew this," Sister Martin explained. "Before we could get my father home from the hospital, the Sanford (Colo.) Ward had two weeks of volunteers lined up to drive my parents back and forth to Pueblo (Colo.) every day. During the seven weeks of treatment, this town burned up the road five days a week."

Not only did willing volunteers drive the Cantys back and forth, they often fed them. Upon arrival home from the hospital, the older couple would often find dinner waiting for them, prepared by another member of the stake.

"The love these people have shown to me and my parents and family have strengthened my testimony," she continued. "Since I am an only child, the help they gave made it possible for me to stay with my own children for most of this stressful time."

Members continued to visit Brother Canty until his death a year ago. Many friends and neighbors came regularly, and the sacrament was taken to his home every week.

"Those members never did give up on my father, they were with him until the end," said Sister Martin.

"During this time of terrible troubles in the world, this stake of Zion has given much to their neighbors. I deeply appreciate the strength knowing these people has given me." — Kellene Ricks

(Another in a series of "Shining Moments." Illustration by Deseret News artist Reed McGregor.)

## Valley Courier

**THE CHRISTIAN SPIRIT IS ALIVE AND WELL**

DEAR EDITOR:

There is something very remarkable going on in the small town of Sanford, Colorado, that the rest of the valley is not aware of. In view of the questions asked second most often — "Are Mormans Christians?" — I felt that the actions of Mormons and non-Mormons alike in this small community answered that question.

My father and mother, Pete and Clara Canty, live in Sanford. Pete just had a malignant tumor removed from his brain and will require seven weeks of radiation treatment in Pueblo. The cost of staying in Pueblo is just too high for people with fixed income, so the people of Sanford decided to drive Pete and Clara to Pueblo five days a week for seven weeks. Not only does someone drive them over, but when they go home, someone else brings in food. People have given money, time, and food to help out in this terrible time. I am the only child and have family in Cortez, Colorado, so I can't stay with them all the time. Believe me, my parents are with their family, the town of Sanford, and I appreciate it very much. It certainly is a help to me.

Are Mormons Christians? Christ said, "Love one another." Sanford is living this scripture, freely giving of time and money, food and, most of all love, to the Canty family and my family here in Cortez. I would say that most definitely Sanford is full of Christians. Under the direction of Bishop Preston Stanley, these Mormons continue to give service to their fellow man.

Sincerely yours,

Judy Canty Martin, Forrest Martin, Tiffany Martin, and Devin Martin

Cortez

# Foreword

Russell A. Judkins, PhD

Anthropology Department, SUNY Geneseo, Geneseo, NY 14454

The world is doubtless a vast Oneness that only an unimaginable Omniscience could fully know. That is not a power given any of us. So I, like you, deal instead with this world in the mortal and very small scale perspectives of my own life. Thus, Cortez, Colorado, for instance, is – in my limited vision – the place that, when I think of it, calls forth images of two things – both Native American themed as it happens: (a) Blue Bird Flour (one of the veritable folk treasures of the Southwest – and of course the crucial necessity of Navajo fry bread artistry), and (b) Judy Canty Martin devotedly gathering and working away on her Catawba material. She, and you, will be thrilled to know that this little offering is not about Blue Bird Flour, but is, instead, an Appreciation for this contribution to the enduring Catawba story by Judy Mae Canty Martin of Cortez, Colorado.

Her work is a special contribution, offering an important and rather unique account of Catawba Indians – it is told "from the inside out," as it were. That is, every regular topic: politics, history, war, religion, land, economics, race and all the other standard, external factors are *in* this story, but, unlike other books, they are not *the* story. *The story is Catawba at its core*. It is a story of Catawba told by Catawba; it is not a story about Catawba told by others – with, ultimately, other agendas. The key to its proper appreciation is simply this: its perspective and its contribution are those of an account told by Catawba "from the inside out."

Oddly, or perhaps more accurately, fortuitously, Judy Canty Martin's perspective as a writer is fundamentally folk anthropological, i.e., it is ethnographic, giving, a whole, living view of the subject. Anthropologists are unique in their devotion to using an all-encompassing or "holistic" approach, linked firmly to a "synchronic" (integrated, single point in time) perspective. Because of that, this document you now hold and read has the fullness, the rich texture, the multiple perspectives and the utility of an account that simultaneously tells a story (or stories) and yet can still be mined later for other stories and other information as well. The difference and contrast is this. Historical accounts and focused genealogical publications are both deliberately honed types of publications which have fastidiously removed all content except that which highlights and rigorously documents some specific thesis or end goal. Thus, ultimately, they tell more constricted, more precisely focused stories, which then become accounts of those particular academic topics, no longer stories of whole, entire, living subjects. In contrast, meaningful, living wholeness is the intent of ethnography, and Judy Canty Martin's work is lodged firmly on that holistic, ethnographic side of this critical divide. Thus, this work is essentially an important, ethnographically informed Catawba story, told from the inside or "native" point of view..

By means of her method of following the stories of full, detailed family histories, the author has let the living movement and forward motion of Catawba people be recounted and experienced, not unlike following the motion of ocean wave energy and movement through its natural medium. It is always there, it is always visible, but it is never the same or in the same place. It's a "living process" more than it is a "something." In Judy Martin's account, the experience of being Catawba is not a situation one can physically take hold of. It is an onward-moving event; it is not a "thing." In this instance, Judy Martin's Catawba are viewed as a people in the midst of their own experience, much more than they are seen as a bounded entity, a static legality occupying an enclosed space, tossed and tumbled about by external historical forces made by others."

Viewing "people" as "history," some accounts have characterized the "Catawba" as a terminal, desperate gathering of displace and shattered peoples and tribes of the Southeast - a tiny, poverty-stricken, abused, almost forgotten, village world of refugees and remnant survivors, awaiting their final extinction at the hands of prejudice and economic and racial injustice.

But there is another way, a larger, more holistic or inclusive perspective, for visualizing this people and their experience. This one too begins with conjuring up the same image of that isolated core of Native peoples attracting other still-living and displaced elements of their world into an almost unnoticed setting, and that collection of remnant souls seemingly facing alone an unnoticed and apparently inevitable extinction. Except that is not what happens. Instead, "Catawba" emerge from their hiatus and historical bottleneck, to in fact survive, and beyond that to go on and expand and disperse across the continent into a future few could have guessed.

One can only wonder if there was not, perhaps, unwitting vision or actual prophecy at work, rather than mere irony, when Southeastern Indians - descendants of the Chesapeake peoples of Captain John Smith's day, now allied with the Catawba - were observed living in the far West, gazing out across the vast, interior salt sea of the Great Basin.

*"The last of the Powhatans or Pamunks are said to have followed some Mormon missionaries to Utah, and these lordly chiefs sit in lonely pride by the Great Salt Lake."(1)*

Surely still less did early authors have the gift of knowing what would take place subsequently, i.e., that among those very peoples, expanded into the Rocky Mountain and Great Basin West, would be perhaps the first Native American Patriarch (ordained Melchizedek Priesthood revelator in the LDS Church). That Patriarch would be Judy Canty Martin's own uncle, a Latter-Day Saint Catawba Indian of the San Luis Valley of Colorado. Meanwhile, in South Carolina, essentially the whole of "Catawba" remaining there would have embraced the Latter-day Saint faith as well.

My own, personal acquaintance with things Catawba dates back to undergraduate, college days when Roger Trimnal, a Catawba from South Carolina, was living in the same student apartment as I – along with a Navajo Indian and others too. We discussed little if anything that I recall regarding Catawba lore or topics. However, years later we briefly renewed our acquaintance and contact when I visited Catawba, SC, and benefited by his guidance and hospitality as I learned more of Catawba in their South Carolina world. Certainly, I came to appreciate their local physical setting, as well as the wonderful pottery tradition and artistry of the Catawba people in South Carolina.

In that period, I also read important ethnographic works on the Catawba by Frank G. Speck and came to further appreciate the accomplishments of that great anthropologist in general. However, on close inspection I also came to have a few questions about his Catawba work as well. Publications are in preparation to discuss some issues raised in that review of the Catawba work of Frank Speck.

As my growing awareness of the Catawba story continued, I became ethnographically interested in Catawba family history work, and where that might lead in terms of anthropological knowledge. Thus, inevitably I came across the name of Judy Canty Martin and began a correspondence with her. After more communication, visiting with her in Cortez, and realizing her vision was expansive and her resources great, though the process would be long, I watched by the sidelines as her project took form and grew. I was impressed and appreciative that her work would include much of ethnographic, as well as of family history, value  I felt it would be a unique and positive contribution to Catawba Studies.

At about the same time, Ian Watson, a then young (high school aged) son of a faculty colleague came to work in my college office on a genealogy project (in the sense of focused, precise, professional-style genealogy, in which he was already accomplished). Working initially with me, and starting with research resources I had begun to accumulate, Ian soon developed his own research project and became intently focused on doing the genealogy of the "Catawba of the East." His work proved to be extensive and ultimately highly important. After its completion and publication, he went on to Harvard and is now, years later, living in Europe with his own family. His Catawba genealogical research was published by the Anthropology Department at SUNY Geneseo, and after going out of print, later came to be available online under his name.

My own, budding interests in Catawba Studies seemed to be well covered – East and West - by these two dedicated, though very different approaches to the common topic. And each held the promise of benefiting the Catawba themselves, as well as benefiting the general archive of anthropological knowledge as well. Subsequently, primarily for these reasons, and with the illness and death of the editor with whom I had initiated a Catawba of the West publication myself, I stepped aside from active Catawba work, and turned to continued and more intensive work with the Seneca-Iroquois of Western New York, along with other research interests.

It is a joy now, however, to return to the topic of Catawba Studies and especially to have been asked to provide a perspective and appreciation to the work of Judy Canty Martin. This volume is both an account of and a tribute to the enduring and important Catawba people and it has the notable benefit of having been compiled and written by one who is a most dedicated Catawba person herself.

So now this work goes forth to the Catawba and all the people they truly are - and continue to become, in a future only the Omniscient can know.

(1) Quoted in "Anacostia and the Indian Tribes of the Potomac," in Katharine Mixer Abbott. *Trolley Trips in and about Fascinating Washington.* 1900:42

# Preface

This is an imperfect, probably error ridden project that has been my life's work. I have spent over 45 years collecting bits and pieces, photos and clippings to put this together. I know that there will be disagreements, and questions. My own family has their stories and information that do not agree with the facts. Unfortunately, those stories have been garbled with time, and each family will have a slightly different point of view. If everyone would have just written things down, my own family didn't and I have had to dig each photo or tidbit out myself. Those who knew things but didn't talk and the hoarders who won't share. Then you add the racial factors and you have a whole different set of problems.

I began this little project before the PC, before programs and word processors. I typed it all with an old Smith Corona typewriter my mom rescued from the dump. After the PC came about, I got a game Commodore with the big floppy disks, then another advance in computers and more programs. In all I retyped the first book 4 times, then technology caught up and I could buy a real computer and transfer it. So, I could do the other two books before I wore that one out.

I have fought computers, computer programs, and have decided to add everything I know about Catawba genealogy, Catawba people into this second to last book. I have one or two more that I need to do, I have collected missionary journals about 10 or so, and photos and I am trying to identify the individuals they are talking about. I learned quite a bit about my own grandparents thru these journals.

I consider that there are four books at this point, volume 1, Genealogy of the Western Catawba, volume 2, Missionary Journals of Joseph Willey and Pinkney Head, and volume 3, My Father's People. This is volume 4. I had to have the other 3 printed and then I bound them myself because I couldn't afford to have them done. The genealogy of the 2 Catawba branches is not bestselling material.

I hope that the reader learns something about their own ancestors, as I did about daddy and his folks as he called them. There are also the white men who are grandfathers etc. that I have information on. This book is specifically Catawba. As to the quotes and some of the language, I did not try to correct the original sources. I transcribed it exactly as it appears. I also will not call anyone illegitimate, as some of who have written about the Catawba. This interracial mixing of white and Catawba also added to the widening of the gene pool. Until very recently, intermarriage between races was against the law in South Carolina, so the 'marriages' entered between white men and Catawba women, I call marriages.

Briefly, the Catawba Nation was a conglomeration of smaller tribes who joined forces in the very early 1600-1700's. Once a very large and important tribe they had dwindled down to about 60 souls in the 1880's when the Church of Jesus Christ of Latter-day Saints began working amongst them. The reader can be the judge as to whether this was a good thing, or a bad thing. I think it saved the Nation. I also believe that the 'marriages' between whites and Catawba was a way of preserving the Nation, the gene pool was very small at about 60 people! I also believe that if the 26 in the 5 families and about 10 in the other 2 families had not come west in around 1887, the Nation's blood would have become even more diluted.

Those who left, did not give up their heritage, their identity, but they did leave an impoverished area to the other half. Most of the Catawba who left had homes and lands, what they came west with was trunks and small items. So, they left furniture and any equipment for the use of those left behind. I know from reading the Missionary Journals that my great grandfather and mother left a home and lands on which they grew cotton and other crops. I know that Alexander Tims home had a stable and house and lands. The rest that left had those things also, that is how they financed their trip west. When they got into the West, first into Colorado for the most part, they could marry who they pleased, vote, hold office etc. In other words, they were citizens of the United States, not like in the state of South Carolina.

While there were instances of racial prejudice, even murder here in the west, for the most part we all lived active lives. I faced a great deal of that growing up. My Uncle Buck also had his share, and probably some others, that I don't know about. There was prejudice among the Spanish speaking populations against the Indians. The Western Catawba were pretty much isolated from the other races. We outsider Catawba fought to retain our Catawba identity, most of us did that.

This is an attempt to explain names and other strange things I found. The Catawba most usually took their mother's names, especially the ones who were fathered by white men. So, the surname was somewhat incidental and could be either the mother or father or who they were living with at the time. An example is my own family. My grandfather John Alonzo Canty's mother was Eliza Scott Canty. She was married to Franklin Canty first and had several children the only ones we know of are William and George Washington Canty. She then had 3 children with the Indian agent Thomas Whitesides: Mary Jane who is usually called Watts because she married James Harvey Watts. Then came the twins Fannie and John Alonzo who appear as Fannie Whitesides Harris (wife of James Harris) and John Alonzo who took the Canty name.

Now we come to given names, they took on given names like putting on clothing. Lonzo Canty became John Alonzo and so forth. Betsy could become Elizabeth, Peggy would be Margaret etc. The more the white influence the more sophisticated the names. This is about clear as mud and the best I can do to explain.

## Introduction

At long last, my good friend Judy Canty Martin has sent her life's work to a publisher. For many years I had faith that this would happen, but I always wondered when this most important event would take place. At over 400 pages Judy's work will soon be with the publisher. Soon it will be available for the Catawba and those in the general public to use for important genealogical research. In fact I predict that it will serve as the key to much of the Catawba research for years to come.

Thank you Judy Canty Martin for your long dedication to a very difficult subject. The list of families contained in your research exhaustingly thorough to say the least; as far as I know, not one family has been omitted from this exhausting study. Again I have to say that this tome will be appreciated for many decades to come.

From this day and many years to come, a person who uses the material found in this work will be able to uncover the buried past and make a family link as far as it is possible. This country is dotted by documents concerning the Catawba who had fled their home of South Carolina and their Nation for economic and other varied reasons. This past history of the Catawba who fled has been buried in the sands of time. For many years the dream of serious Catawba researchers has been to be able to search for their ancestors. Mrs. Martin's valuable work will aid in their quest, while simultaneously putting doubt about the Western Band of the Catawba to rest.

One might suspect that Judy Canty Martin's volume will put Catawba research to an end; however, know that it is the nature of genealogical work to always strive for more depth. Judy Canty Martin's work is a large first step in the quest for Catawba history one that has been a long time in coming. Her work will allow a multitude of individuals who still live in the world that is outside the tribe in Rock Hill, South Carolina, to come into the light and find their roots as a Catawba Native American.

There shall never be an end to the many notes of gratitude for Mrs. Marin's effort. It will surely open the door for future important genealogical work.

I am proud and honored that I am the first of a long list of researchers, scholars, friends, and tribal members thanking Mrs. Martin for producing this volume.

As for me, I personally congratulate the work of Judy Canty Martin for her diligent work and scholarly effort on behalf of the Catawba Indian Nation.

Thomas J. Blumer, Ph.D.

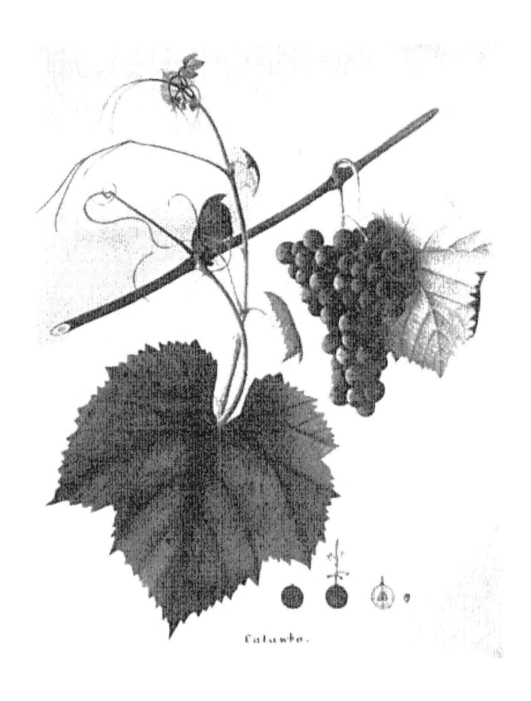

Catawba.

The Catawba grape is one of the earliest Native American grapes used in wine production, but can also be eaten or made into grape juice, jam, or jelly. The Vitis International Variety Catalogue gives credit to the Scholls and describes Catawba as a crossing of the North American species Vitis labrusca with the European species Vitis vinifera and list 1819 as its likely introduction. The Oxford Companion to Wine states the vine was identified in North Carolina even earlier, in 1802, but does not state who discovered the variety. British wine expert Oz Clarke also places the vine's origins in North Carolina but claims that it was first identified in 1801.

# Table of Content

# Chapter 1  Ears-Ayers Family

I. A William-Billy Ayers or Billy Ears, probably born around 1765, signed the petition of 1792, outlining the Catawba's grievances to the State legislature.[1] He is listed in the Indian Plat Books as having received payment or rent for lands between 1808 and 1829. General Billy Ayers, served with General Sumpter during the Revolution, according to D. G. Stinson, in a letter to Draper dated, July 27, 1874. He was listed as Colonel William Ayers in 1825, and continued signing leases as a headman until 1834, when he became Captain William Ayers.[2] Then in 1835 he signed a lease as Major William Ayers, along with General Jacob Ayers, Colonel John Ayers and Captain Samuel Scott. Billy was paid for Nanny or Nancy Keggs children in January 1819.[3] He is probably a brother to Jessie and John, because he did receive money for Kegg children, and John was married to a Kegg. He probably died after 1835, when the last mention of him is found; however, the Draper Manuscripts say he died about 1840.

\*\*\*\*\*\*\*\*\*\*\*\*\*\*\*\*\*\*\*\*\*\*\*\*\*\*\*\*\*\*\*\*\*\*\*\*\*\*\*\*\*\*\*\*\*\*\*\*\*\*\*\*\*\*\*\*\*\*\*\*\*\*\*\*\*\*\*\*\*\*\*\*

II. LT. Jessie Ayers born around 1750, signed leases from 1808 as Lt. Ayers along with General Jacob Scott and Colonel Lewis Canty.  In 1825, he is listed as Major Jesse Ayers.  He is reported to have died around 1835 and he does not appear to have signed leases after September 26, 1835.[4] Jessie shared the lease money with Sally New River, and he owned others, so that he received money from almost ten leases which was a great sum of money.[5]

\*\*\*\*\*\*\*\*\*\*\*\*\*\*\*\*\*\*\*\*\*\*\*\*\*\*\*\*\*\*\*\*\*\*\*\*\*\*\*\*\*\*\*\*\*\*\*\*\*\*\*\*\*\*\*\*\*\*\*\*\*\*\*\*\*\*\*\*\*\*\*\*

III. Captain-Major John Ears-Ayers -Airs-Hixayoura[6] was born around 1750, he was reported to have died around 1835, however he continued to sign leases through July 14, 1837, when he was scalped. John appears on Drennan's Pay Bill for the Revolutionary War, as 44 days and 22 pounds.  He also appears on a list for which there was no voucher. According to D. G. Stinson in a letter dated 1874; he served with General Sumpter.  John signed the petition of 1792 as Collo. John Ears. He married Betsy Kegg. Spratt says they both kept their own names "as usual".  Betsy was the daughter of Old James Kegg and Jenny Scott, so she could also appear as Betsy Scott. Spratt said in 1874 they were the parents of a "fine lot of boys, some of them about my age" but they were all dead by 1874.[7]  We know only of Jacob, and James and perhaps Edmund, as he fits in with the "lot of boys and being dead by 1874."

---

[1] Blumer, Thomas J., Bibliography of the Catawba, The Scarecrow Press, Inc., Metcuchen, NJ & London, 1987,    page 80, hereafter cited as Blumer.

[2] Blumer pages 122-147.

[3] Watson, Ian, Catawba Indian Genealogy, The Geneseo foundation, the Department of Anthropology, State University of New York at Geneseo, 1995, page 60, hereafter cited as Watson.

[4] Blumer pages 122-147.

[5] Merrell, The Indians' New World. Catawbas and their Neighbors from European Contact through the Era of Removal.  (3 parts) Institute of Early American History and Culture, Williamsburg, VA, University of North Carolina Press, Chapel Hill and London, 1989, pt. 3, page 231, hereafter cited as Merrell pt. 1, 2 or 3.

[6] Merrell, James H., part 3, page 235.

[7] Draper Manuscripts dated September 3, 1874 from Spratt to Draper.

1

Captain-Major John Ears-Ayers -Airs-Hixayoura, born around 1750, also called Col. John Ears - Colonel John Ears [8]   His Mark follows: [9]

A.  Edmund, (he was called Captain Edward Ayers in 1837)[10] was born around 1800, married Rebecca Marsh-Quash, daughter of John and Betsy Scott Quash Marsh.[11] Edmund was an adult and signed leases on Catawba land beginning in 18 July 24, 1827 through September 1837.[12] He does not live long enough to have been enumerated on any census, or any other petitions and papers. Rebecca began her marriage with Anthony George before 1840, so it safe to assume that Edmund either died or disappeared between September 1837 and 1839.

**Photo 1- Sarah Jane Ayers**

1.  Sarah Jane Ayers, born 1829, died 12 July 1917, married James Harris Sr., the son of David and Nancy George Harris.[13] When the Mormon Missionaries came to Catawba, Sarah's home was a frequent stop for them; many entries in Joseph Willey's Journal speak about stopping at her home and singing hymns with the Saints. One of his journal entries follows:

---

[8] Drennan's paybill
[9]  1792 petition
[10] Brown, page 299.
[11] Marsh genealogy.
[12] Blumer pages 132, 133 and 147.
[13] Watson page 27 and Catawba Branch Records.

"March 21 1885, Elder Cragun baptized Mrs. Sarah Harris, David Harris, and Franklin Canty. There was upwards of 25 Lamanites on the banks of the river. Had singing at 7pm at Bro. John Sanders, a good spirit was manifested." See their children under James Harris Sr.

**PHOTO 2 - SARAH JANE AYERS HARRIS AND HER GRANDDAUGHTER FANNIE HARRIS**

**PHOTO 3    SARAH JANE AYERS**           **PHOTO 4 SARAH JANE AYERS**

2.    Margaret Marsh-Ayers-George born 4 July 1837. Her Catawba name was E'ntini-hinowa, meaning Anthony George's daughter, she was actually his stepdaughter, and however he raised her. She married John William Brown, Joe Cherry and Sam Blue. Her children will be found in the Blue and Brown Chapters. She is the mother of Samuel Taylor Blue.

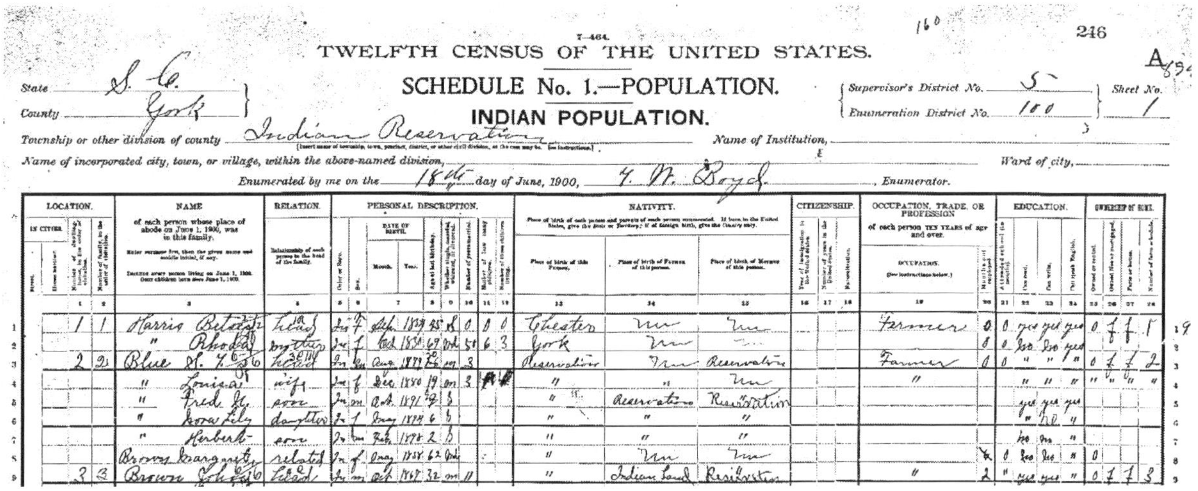

7-464. 160 246 A

TWELFTH CENSUS OF THE UNITED STATES.

SCHEDULE No. 1.—POPULATION.

INDIAN POPULATION.

State: S. C. — Supervisor's District No. 5 — Sheet No. 1

County: York — Enumeration District No. 100

Township or other division of county: Indian Reservation — Name of Institution,

Name of incorporated city, town, or village, within the above-named division, — Ward of city,

Enumerated by me on the 18th day of June, 1900, T. W. Boyd, Enumerator.

| Line | Dwelling No. | Family No. | Name | Relation | Color | Sex | Month | Year | Age | Marital | Years married | Mother of | Living | Birthplace | Father's birthplace | Mother's birthplace | Occupation | Months not employed | School | Read | Write | English | Owned/rented | Free/mortgaged | Farm/house | Schedule No. |
|---|---|---|---|---|---|---|---|---|---|---|---|---|---|---|---|---|---|---|---|---|---|---|---|---|---|---|
| 1 | 1 | 1 | Harris Betsey | head | In | f | Sep | 1839 | 55 | S | 0 | 0 | 0 | Chester | Un | Un | Farmer | 0 | 0 | yes | yes | yes | 0 | f | f | 1 |
| 2 | | | " Rhoda | mother | In | f | Oct | 1830 | 69 | Wd | | 6 | 3 | York | Un | Un | | 8 | 0 | no | no | yes | | | | |
| 3 | 2 | 2 | Blue S. T. | head | In | m | Aug | 1877 | 22 | m | 3 | | | Reservation | Un | Reservation | Farmer | 0 | 0 | " | " | " | 0 | f | f | 2 |
| 4 | | | " Louisa | wife | In | f | Dec | 1880 | 19 | m | 3 | | | " | " | Un | " | | | " | " | " | " | " | " | " |
| 5 | | | " Fred M. | son | In | m | Oct | 1891 | 8 | S | | | | " | Reservation | Reservation | | | | yes | yes | yes | | | | |
| 6 | | | " Nora Lily | daughter | In | f | Aug | 1894 | 6 | S | | | | " | " | " | | | | " | no | " | | | | |
| 7 | | | " Herbert | son | In | m | Feb | 1898 | 2 | S | | | | " | " | " | | | | no | no | " | | | | |
| 8 | | | Brown Margaret | related | In | f | Aug | 1838 | 62 | Wd | | | | " | Un | Un | | | 0 | no | no | " | 0 | | | |
| 9 | 3 | 3 | Brown John | head | In | m | Oct | 1867 | 32 | m | 11 | | | " | Indian Land | Reservation | " | 2 | " | yes | yes | " | 0 | f | f | 3 |

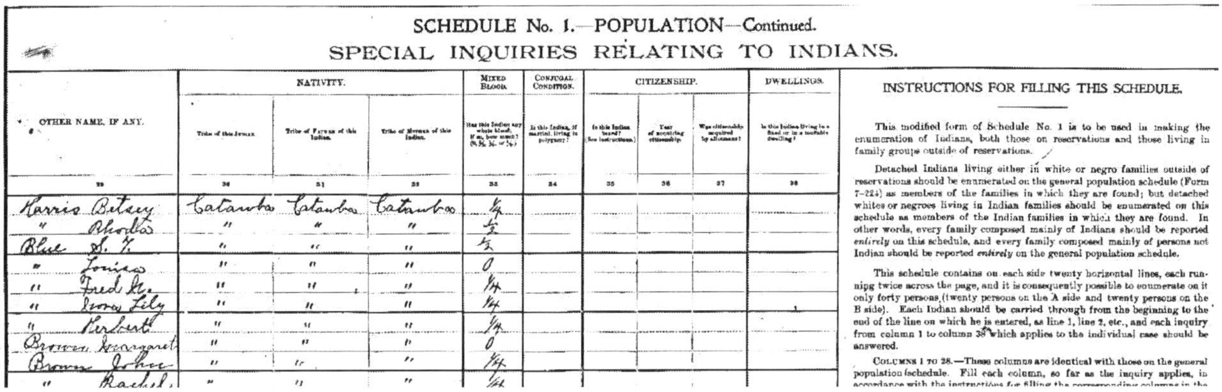

SCHEDULE No. 1.—POPULATION—Continued.

SPECIAL INQUIRIES RELATING TO INDIANS.

| Line | Other name, if any (29) | Tribe of this Indian (30) | Tribe of Father of this Indian (31) | Tribe of Mother of this Indian (32) | Has this Indian any white blood; if so, how much? (33) | Is this Indian, if married, living in polygamy? (34) | Is this Indian taxed? (35) | Year of acquiring citizenship (36) | Was citizenship acquired by allotment? (37) | Is this Indian living in a fixed or in a movable dwelling? (38) |
|---|---|---|---|---|---|---|---|---|---|---|
| 1 | Harris Betsey | Catawba | Catawba | Catawba | 1/4 | | | | | |
| 2 | " Rhoda | " | " | " | 1/2 | | | | | |
| 3 | Blue S. T. | " | " | " | 1/2 | | | | | |
| 4 | " Louisa | " | " | " | 0 | | | | | |
| 5 | " Fred M. | " | " | " | 1/4 | | | | | |
| 6 | " Nora Lily | " | " | " | 1/4 | | | | | |
| 7 | " Herbert | " | " | " | 1/4 | | | | | |
| 8 | Brown Margaret | " | " | " | 0 | | | | | |
| 9 | Brown John | " | " | " | 1/4 | | | | | |
| 10 | " Rachel | " | " | " | 1/4 | | | | | |

INSTRUCTIONS FOR FILLING THIS SCHEDULE.

This modified form of Schedule No. 1 is to be used in making the enumeration of Indians, both those on reservations and those living in family groups outside of reservations.

Detached Indians living either in white or negro families outside of reservations should be enumerated on the general population schedule (Form 7-224) as members of the families in which they are found; but detached whites or negroes living in Indian families should be enumerated on this schedule as members of the Indian families in which they are found. In other words, every family composed mainly of Indians should be reported *entirely* on this schedule, and every family composed mainly of persons not Indian should be reported *entirely* on the general population schedule.

This schedule contains on each side twenty horizontal lines, each running twice across the page, and it is consequently possible to enumerate on it only forty persons (twenty persons on the A side and twenty persons on the B side). Each Indian should be carried through from the beginning to the end of the line on which he is entered, as line 1, line 2, etc., and each inquiry from column 1 to column 38 which applies to the individual case should be answered.

COLUMNS 1 TO 28.—These columns are identical with those on the general population schedule. Fill each column, so far as the inquiry applies, in accordance with the instructions for filling the corresponding columns in the

**PHOTO 5 - 1900 CENSUS, MARGARET BROWN, LIVING WITH SAM BLUE'S FAMILY AS A RELATIVE (HIS MOTHER). AGE LISTED AS 62 AND SHE IS A WIDOW. SHE AND HER PARENTS ARE LISTED A BEING BORN ON THE INDIAN RESERVATION, YORK, SOUTH CAROLINA. SHE IS LISTED AS FULL BLOOD CATAWBA (0 WHITE BLOOD)**

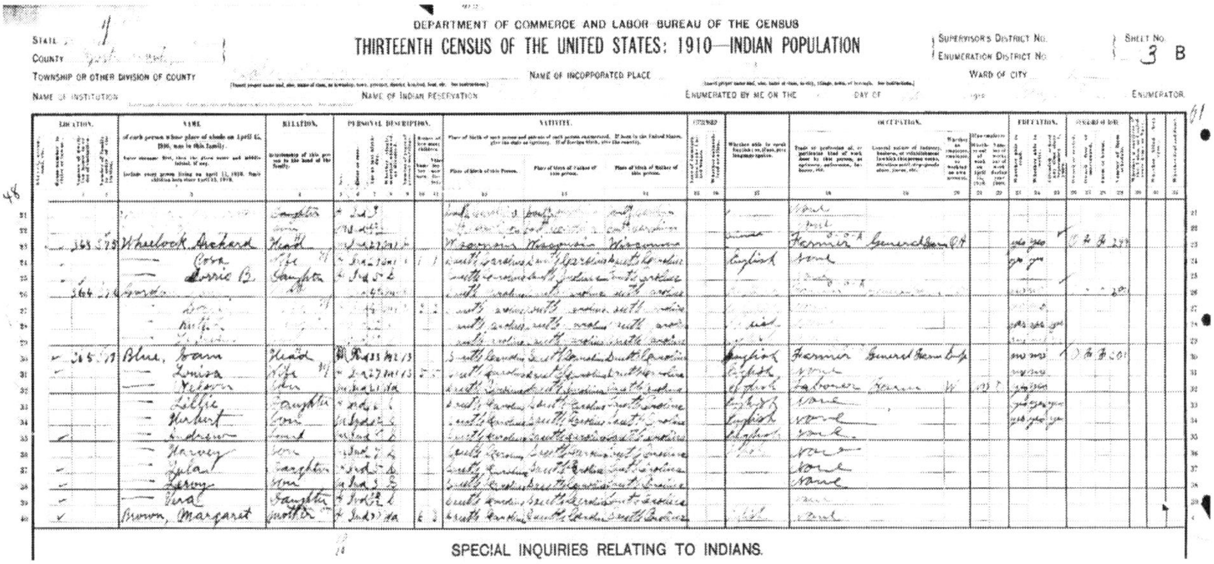

DEPARTMENT OF COMMERCE AND LABOR—BUREAU OF THE CENSUS

THIRTEENTH CENSUS OF THE UNITED STATES: 1910—INDIAN POPULATION

State — Supervisor's District No. — Sheet No. 3 B

County — Enumeration District No.

Township or other division of county — Name of incorporated place — Ward of city

Name of institution — Name of Indian reservation — Enumerated by me on the day of 1910 — Enumerator

| Line | Name | Relation | Birthplace | Father's birthplace | Mother's birthplace | Language | Occupation |
|---|---|---|---|---|---|---|---|
| 23 | Wheelock Richard | Head | Wisconsin | Wisconsin | Wisconsin | | Farmer |
| 24 | Cora | Wife | South Carolina | South Carolina | Indian | English | none |
| 25 | Dorrie B. | Daughter | | | | | |
| 30 | Blue, Sam | Head | South Carolina | South Carolina | South Carolina | English | Farmer |
| 31 | Louisa | Wife | South Carolina | South Carolina | South Carolina | English | none |
| 32 | Nelson | Son | South Carolina | South Carolina | South Carolina | English | Laborer |
| 33 | Lillie | Daughter | South Carolina | South Carolina | South Carolina | English | none |
| 34 | Herbert | Son | South Carolina | South Carolina | South Carolina | English | none |
| 35 | Andrew | Son | South Carolina | South Carolina | South Carolina | English | none |
| 36 | Harvey | Son | South Carolina | South Carolina | South Carolina | | none |
| 37 | Sylan | Daughter | South Carolina | South Carolina | South Carolina | | none |
| 38 | Leroy | Son | South Carolina | South Carolina | South Carolina | | none |
| 39 | Vera | Daughter | South Carolina | South Carolina | South Carolina | | none |
| 40 | Brown, Margaret | Mother | South Carolina | South Carolina | South Carolina | | none |

SPECIAL INQUIRIES RELATING TO INDIANS.

**PHOTO 6 - 1910 CENSUS MARGARET LIVING WITH THE SAMUEL BLUE FAMILY, LISTED AS HIS MOTHER, INDIAN, AGE 70, WIDOW AND HAD 6 CHILDREN WITH 3 STILL LIVING AND AS FULL BLOOD CATAWBA.**

**************************************************

Descendant List of Captain-Major John Ears-Ayers-Hixayoura

1-John "Ears" AYERS (abt 1750-1837)

+Betsey KEGG/SCOTT (abt 1750-aft 1800)

.... 2-Jacob AYERS (abt 1780-bef 1874)

.... 2-Edmund AYERS (1800-1837)

.... +Rebecca MARSH (1815-20 Jan 1882)

....... 3-Sarah Jane AYERS (31 Jul 1829-7 Dec 1917)

....... +James Thomas HARRIS (1828-23 May 1874)

.......... 4-Infant HARRIS (abt 1853-1853)

.......... 4-James Thomas HARRIS (27 Mar 1859-31 Aug 1912)

.......... +Nancy Elizabeth GORDON (9 Apr 1859-22 Nov 1929)

............. 5-Rachel HARRIS (1875-)

............. 5-Catherine Hester HARRIS (7 May 1889-26 Dec 1922)

............. +Margaret Elizabeth HARRIS (15 Aug 1879-8 Dec 1926)

............. 5-Jesse Allen HARRIS (25 Apr 1899-19 Nov 1977)

............. 5-Jacob HARRIS (1900-bef 1910)

............. 5-Eliza Jane HARRIS (30 Apr 1902-15 Nov 1960)

............. 5-Georgia Henrietta HARRIS (29 Jul 1905-30 Jan 1997)

............. 5-John Thomas HARRIS (30 Jul 1905-10 Jul 1912)

............. 5-Robert Lee HARRIS (16 Aug 1910-15 Jul 1912)

............. 5-George Furman HARRIS (7 Jan 1913-5 Jun 2006)

.......... +Fannie WHITESIDES (9 Nov 1859-1885)

.......... 4-Martha Jane HARRIS (25 Dec 1861-18 Dec 1898)

.......... +John Evins SANDERS (18 Feb 1862-30 Jul 1932)

............. 5-Robert Lee Jackson SANDERS (21 Sep 1881-29 Jul 1886)

............. 5-John William Thomas SANDERS (8 Sep 1885-20 Aug 1946)

............. 5-Joseph Hinson SANDERS (19 Jul 1886-13 Feb 1930)

............. 5-Dora Ann SANDERS (22 Dec 1888-18 Sep 1908)

............. 5-Loney Roy SANDERS (25 Dec 1890-25 May 1892)

............. 5-John Idle SANDERS (12 Dec 1892-27 Aug 1973)

............. 5-Lewis Ernest SANDERS (18 Jul 1895-5 Feb 1936)

............. 5-Sarah Ann SANDERS (22 Dec 1897- )

. . . . . . . . . . . . . . . 5-Andrew Behrman SANDERS (10 Sep 1898-27 Oct 1898)

. . . . . . . . . . 4-Anthony "Andy" HARRIS (abt 1862-bet 1920 and 1930)

. . . . . . . . . . 4-Mattie HARRIS (abt 1871- )

. . . . . . . . . . 4-David Adam Toad HARRIS (15 Jun 1872-1 Sep 1930)

. . . . . . . . . . +Margaret Della GEORGE (4 Dec 1879-28 Feb 1917)

. . . . . . . . . . . 5-Hoyt Sidney HARRIS (8 Nov 1901-19 Mar 1955)

. . . . . . . . . . . . 5-Isabelle HARRIS (7 Feb 1904-15 Mar 1989)

. . . . . . . . . . . . 5-Dennis HARRIS (4 Aug 1907-14 Sep 1973)

. . . . . . . . . . . . . 5-Chester Gilbert HARRIS (15 Aug 1909-30 Dec 1970)

. . . . . . . . . . . . . 5-Floyd Raymond HARRIS (17 Nov 1913-23 Jan 1952)

. . . . . . . . . . +Lizzie Jane WATS-PATTERSON (23 Apr 1874-Feb 1917)

. . . . . . . . . . . 5-Edith Bertha HARRIS (13 Jun 1893 - 12 Jun 1985)

. . . . . . . . . . . . 5-Wade V. HARRIS (Nov 1895-abt 1905)

. . . . . . . . . . . . 5-Lavinia M HARRIS (18 Nov 1896-25 Jul 1916)

. . . . . . . . . . . . . 5-Richard Jackson HARRIS (13 Feb 1897-4 Feb 1985)

. . . . . . . . . . . . . 5-Fannie HARRIS (6 Jul 1900-15 Dec 1951)

. . . . . . . . . . +Dorothy Minerva PRICE (1893-22 May 1961)

. . . . . . . . . . . 5-Sarah Lee HARRIS (22 Aug 1919-25 Nov 2002)

. . . . . . . . . . . . 5-Florence Rebecca HARRIS (28 Apr 1922-12 Apr 2017)

. . . . . . . . . . . 5-James Loran HARRIS (10 Jun 1924-5 Aug 1958)

. . . . . . . . . . . 5-David Adam HARRIS jr (12 Jul 1927-13 Sep 1988)

. . . . . . . . . . 4-Isabella HARRIS (abt 1876- )

. . . . . . . 3-Margaret MARSH-AYERS-GEORGE (4 Jul 1837-9 Aug 1922)

. . . . . . . +Samuel BLUE (1838-abt 1878)

. . . . . . . . . 4-Samuel Taylor BLUE (15 Aug 1873-16 Apr 1959)

. . . . . . . . . +Louisa Hester Jane CANTY (7 Feb 1883-9 Jul 1963)

. . . . . . . . . . . 5-Herbert BLUE (25 Apr 1898-10 Apr 1979)

. . . . . . . . . . . 5-Samuel Andrew BLUE (16 Oct 1900-18 Sep 1960)

. . . . . . . . . . . 5-Joseph Harvey BLUE (3 Mar 1903-10 Jan 1914)

. . . . . . . . . . . 5-Lula Henrietta BLUE (3 May 1905-11 May 1996)

. . . . . . . . . . . 5-Henry Leroy BLUE (14 Aug 1907-11 Jul 2002)

. . . . . . . . . . . 5-Vera Louise BLUE (21 Aug 1909-16 Mar 1991)

. . . . . . . . . . . 5-Guy Larson BLUE (3 Dec 1911-7 Feb 1984)

. . . . . . . . . . . 5-Elsie Inez BLUE (3 Mar 1914-25 Nov 2013)

. . . . . . . . . . . 5-BLUE (abt 1915- )

. . . . . . . . . . . 5-Arnold Lee BLUE (23 Nov 1917-31 Oct 1962)

. . . . . . . . . . +Minnie Hester GEORGE (19 Sep 1871-1897)

. . . . . . . . . . . 5-Frederick Nelson BLUE (25 Oct 1889-8 Aug 1980)

. . . . . . . . . . . 5-Nora Lily BLUE (12 Nov 1893-26 May 1915)

. . . . . . . . . . . . 5-Rhoda Cornelia BLUE (abt 1895-abt 1895)

. . . . . . . +John William BROWN (1837-Sep 1867)

. . . . . . . . . . . 4-Mary Victoria BROWN (25 Dec 1856-11 Apr 1952)

. . . . . . . . . . 4-H A BROWN (abt 1861- )

. . . . . . . . . . 4-Emily BROWN (1863- )

. . . . . . . . . . 4-Wade Hampton BROWN (1865-bef 1867)

. . . . . . . . . . 4-Sally Rebecca BROWN (25 Dec 1865-20 Sep 1952)

. . . . . . . . . . +Lewis Harris GORDON (Aug 1869-13 Oct 1926)

. . . . . . . . . . . . . 5-Ruth Lucinda (Rhett) GORDON (29 Apr 1898-)

. . . . . . . . . . . . . 5-Lewis Ervin GORDON (9 Apr 1900-23 Mar 1954)

. . . . . . . . . . +John BOARCH (-)

. . . . . . . . . . . . 5-Nora Elvina BOARCH BROWN (8 Sep 1884-17 Oct 1918)

. . . . . . . . . . 4-John William BROWN (21 Oct 1867-20 Jun 1927)

. . . . . . . . . . +Rachel Wysie GEORGE (21 Aug 1874-20 Sep 1960)

. . . . . . . . . . . . . 5-Early Burly Morgan BROWN (26 Jan 1889-16 Mar 1963)

. . . . . . . . . . . . . 5-Sallie Rebecca BROWN (22 Sep 1893-27 Jan 1993)

. . . . . . . . . . . . . 5-Arzada BROWN (3 Jul 1896-20 Mar 1989)

. . . . . . . . . . . . . 5-Cora BROWN (13 Aug 1898-9 Oct 1918)

. . . . . . . . . . . . . 5-Maggie Abbie BROWN (17 Mar 1901-5 Oct 1918)

. . . . . . . . . . . . . 5-John William BROWN (15 Apr 1903-4 Oct 1918)

. . . . . . . . . . . . . 5-Roy BROWN (28 Jan 1905-22 Nov 1979)

. . . . . . . . . . . . . 5-Mary Rachal BROWN (11 Jul 1907-22 Feb 1955)

. . . . . . . . . . . . . 5-Henry BROWN (31 Mar 1909-12 Jan 1911)

. . . . . . . . . . . . . 5-Ethel Alberta BROWN (6 Oct 1911-8 Oct 1918)

. . . . . . . . . . . . . 5-George BROWN (16 Sep 1914-29 Jun 1985)

**********************************************************************************

I. Big-Town-Jacob Ayers born around 1770, he continued signing leases through March 1837, so he died after that date and was buried near Providence Church, in Mecklenburg County, North Carolina. [14] His rank in the Catawba government went from Colonel, to General then King and even Emperor at one time.[15] In December 1820, Jacob was confirmed as Brigadier General of the Catawba Nation.[16] He married the daughter of King Hagler, who had children by William (Billy) Scott during the Revolution. This Ms. Hagler, for want of a better name, also had a child by Matthew Toole, a white Indian trader, that child was Sally Scott-Toole New River.[17]

Jacob, then a Colonel, succeeded King Hagler upon his death in 1763. He ruled from 1763-1764. He led 27 Catawba on a second expedition during Forbe's campaign against Fort Duguesne in 1759. He

---

[14] T.D. Spratt letter dated September 3, 1874.

[15] Brown page 250.

[16] Blumer page 115.

[17] Brown page 228.

is also on Drennan's Pay Bill with 44 days and 22 pounds.[18] He was also called upon to settle a dispute with the Cherokee over the death of a Catawba woman.

"His land was spoilt, he had lost a great deal both by scarcity of Buffaloes and deer. The white men have spoiled him 100 miles every way and never paid him, his hunting lands formerly extended to the Pedee and Broad River, but now he is driven quite to the Catawba Nation, if he could kill any deer he would carry the meat to his family and the skins to the white people, but no deer are now to be had and he wants 15 miles on each side his town free from any encroachments of the white people who will not suffer him to cut trees to build with but keep all to themselves."[19]

**Article Four of the Treaty of Augusta concerned the Catawba**:

"We the Catawba Head Men and Warriors in confirmation of an agreement heretofore entered into with the White People declare that we will remain satisfied with the tract of land of fifteen miles square a survey of which by our consent and at our request has been already begun and the respective Governors and Superintendent on their parts promise and engage that the aforesaid survey shall be completed and that the Catawba's shall not in any respect be molested by any of the King's subjects within the said lines but shall be indulged in the usual manner of hunting elsewhere." Colonel Ayers signed it. This set aside 144,000 acres in the counties of Lancaster, York and Chester, South Carolina for a reservation.

Jacob was not the loved leader that King Hagler had been. In fact, one time when he was drunk, he sold some official presents. In 1764, the Catawba begged Charles Town to depose him. The white government wisely declined to interfere, however, Samuel Wyly supervised an election and Captain Frow-Prow-Joe was chosen Chief.[20]
Jacob accepted rents from the lands of Billy Canty around 1813, and is associated through Billy with the Kennedy's.
Jacob Ayers signed the lease of David Hutcheson along with Major Thos. Brown, Henry Whyte and Genl. Jacob Scott, in 1817.
Colonel Jacob Ayers, born around 1770. He signed the lease of David Hutcheson along with Major Thos. Brown, Henry Whyte and Genl. Jacob Scott, in 1817 and his mark follows:

Jacob and Ms. Hagler had three known children: Betsy, Sally, and Polly Ayers.

---

[18] Brown pages 268 & 269
[19] Brown page 251.
[20] Brown page 252.

A. Betsy Ayers, born around 1789, married first, John Scott son of Jacob Scott.[21] The only identifiable child of Betsy and John is found here. Betsy Ayers Scott then married second Major George Canty; the son of William Canty; and after 1813, she married for the third time, John Kennedy.

> 1. Jacob Scott Jr. born around 1800 called Jacob Jr. in honor of his grandfathers, Jacob Ayers and Jacob Scott. He received payments on lands with Indian Lands between 1808 and 1829.[22]

B. Sally Ayers, born 1799, married first Jamey Clinton probably around 1819; second William Harris who died in 1838 and she married third Lewis Canty, by August 1825.[23] Sally Ayers collected payments from leaseholders on the East Side of the Catawba River. Jamey Kegg leased lands belonging to Sally and Betsy on February 7, 1822 to Capt. John Hutcheson, for 800 dollars and 3 dollars rent each year for 99 years. Sally and one of these men had Jacob Ayers.[24] She had seven children by Lewis Canty. She also married William Nelson George[25] Only the Ayers children appear here. The Canty children will be found in the Canty Chapter.

> 1. Jacob Ayers. Probably born around 1800, took his Mother's name. This person also collected rents on the mill place for Katty Scott (Joe). [26]

C. Polly Ayers[27] born around 1812 or 1814,[28] is probably the Polly Tims, who with John Marsh had Mary E. Whitesides, born February 7, 1848 in Wait County, Georgia.[29] Why she would be a Tims is unknown, however, most probably because she had a relationship with John Alexander Tims who fathered John Alexander or Alec Tims, who removed to Sanford, Colorado. I think that even though a Polly Ayers and a Polly Harris are listed twice in the 1849 census, they are one and the same individual.

She was probably called Polly Ottis, Polly Oders in 1875 when she received $4.50 from R. L. Crook the Indian Agent, and in 1881, Polly Otis received $6.66. There is also a listing for Polly Brown who received $2.00 on April 10, 1875. I think that they are all the same person. Only one child is known, I believe that Jenny Ayers was her child

> 1. Jenny Ayers born around 1830, married John "Mush" Harris born 1831, son of David and Nancy George-Marsh, there were no children. She is dead by 1857.[30]

---

[21] Brown page 251.
[22] Indian Piatt Books.
[23] Watson, page 27
[24] Indian Piatt Books.
[25] Catawba Branch Records.
[26] Ibid
[27] Brown page 295.
[28] 1849 Catawba census.
[29] Church of Jesus Christ of Latter Day Saints International Genealogical Index, hereafter cited as, LDS International Genealogical Index or IGI.
[30] John's wife was Jenny. A Jenny Ayers signed a petition in 1847; she is not on the 1849 Catawba census, nor the

2.    Jefferson Ayers, born 1840 married first Emily Elizabeth Cobb, daughter of Lucy Marsh-Quash and John D. Cobb a white man.[31] Jefferson Ayers, enlisted in the Confederate Army, December 9, 1861 in Company K. 17th South Carolina Infantry. He is listed as one of the Lacy Guards in a letter from L. P. Sadler, Captain commanding the guard, along with Alec Tims and William Canty. Jefferson is listed, along with Alec Tims as men absent without leave, AWOL in January 1863. He was wounded at the Battle of Boonesboro on September 14, 1862, and the Battle at Hatcher's Run in March 1865, listed as prisoner of war on May 6, 1865.[32]

In 1865, he was listed among the wounded, stating that he was wounded in the head in the Battle of Petersburg. Jefferson died July 2, 1865 at Point Lookout, Maryland,[33] and just 5 months before the birth of his last child Alice.

## Civil War Records

Jefferson Ayers – war the husband of Emily Cobb. At the time of his enlistment, he was the father of Jefferson (Buddy) Ayers and Alice Ayers. He was wounded at the battle of Boonsboro on Sept. 14, 1862 and was sent home to recover. He returned to service on Oct 3, 1862, and fought in the battles of Kingston (Dec. 14,1862), Goldsboro (Dec. 17, 1862), Sumter James Island (Nov 1863), and Petersburg (Summer 1864). He was wounded again on March 25, 1865, at the battle of Hatcher Run. He was captured on May 6, 1865, and war sent to point lookout, Maryland, where he died as a prisoner of war on July 2, 1865.

---

1854 census.
[31] Catawba Branch Records.
[32] Civil War record of Jefferson Ayers.
[33] Blumer page 178.

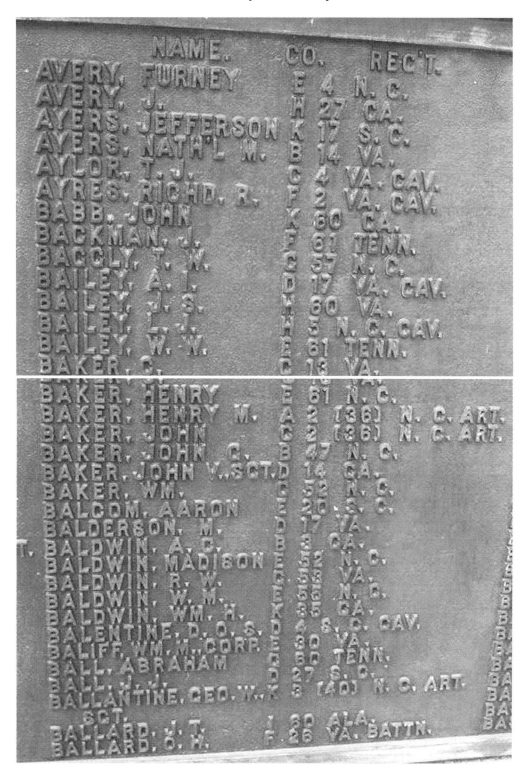

POINT LOOKOUT, MD., 3.

| Name. | Rank. | Co. | Regiment. | Date of Death. | Locality of Grave. | |
|---|---|---|---|---|---|---|
| Ashley, Richard S., | Pvt. | G | 1 S. C. Rifles. | Aug. 24, 1864. | Confederate Cemetery | |
| Ashworth, W. O., | " | C | 24 Va. Inf. | Feb. 10, " | " | " |
| Askew, Jno., | " | B | 30 N. C. Inf. | Aug. 25, " | " | " |
| Askew, Thomas P., | " | H | 2 Battn. N. C. Inf. | Feb. 4, " | " | " |
| Atkin, Thomas S., | Sgt. | K | 11 N. C. Inf. | Jan. 8, 1865. | " | " |
| Atkins, John H., | Pvt. | G | 22 Battn. Va. Art. | Dec. 24, 1863. | " | " |
| Atkins, Samuel, | " | D | 26 N. C. Inf. | Oct. 23, 1864. | " | " |
| Atkins, Wm., | " | I | 57 N. C. Inf. | Feb. 14, " | " | " |
| Atkinson, W., | " | C | 37 N. C. | July 25, " | " | " |
| Atphin, Calvin, | " | A | 38 N. C. Inf. | Feb. 27, 1865. | " | " |
| Attaway, T. G., | " | F | 27 S. C. | June 18, " | " | " |
| Austin, A., | " | H | 55 N. C. Inf. | Nov. 5, 1863. | " | " |
| Austin, D. A., | " | F | 22 N. C. | March 8, 1865. | " | " |
| Austin, J., | " | B | 4 N. C. Inf. | Dec. - 1863. | " | " |
| Austin, J. L., | " | D | 37 N. C. Inf. | Nov. 19, " | " | " |
| Autry, Newsome, | " | A | 36 N. C. | March 2, 1865. | " | " |
| Avant, J. R., | " | A | 21 S. C. | Jan. 15, " | " | " |
| Avant, J. W., | " | A | 5 S. C. Cav. | Feb. 22, " | " | " |
| Avery, Furney, | " | E | 4 N. C. Inf. | Nov. 21, 1863. | " | " |
| Avery, J., | " | H | 27 Ga. Inf. | June 24, 1865. | " | " |
| Ayers, Jefferson, | " | K | 17 S. C. | July 2, " | " | " |
| Ayers, Nathaniel M., | " | B | 14 Va. | April 6, 1864. | " | " |
| Aylor, T. J., | " | C | 4 Va. Cav. | Feb. 22, 1865. | " | " |
| Ayres, Richard R., | " | F | 2 Va. Cav. | Jan. 22, 1864. | " | " |

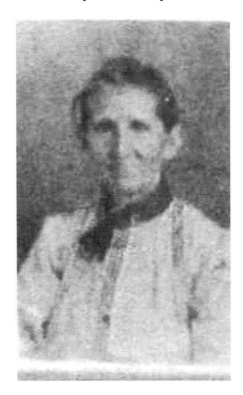

**PHOTO 7 - EMILY ELIZABETH COBB GEORGE**

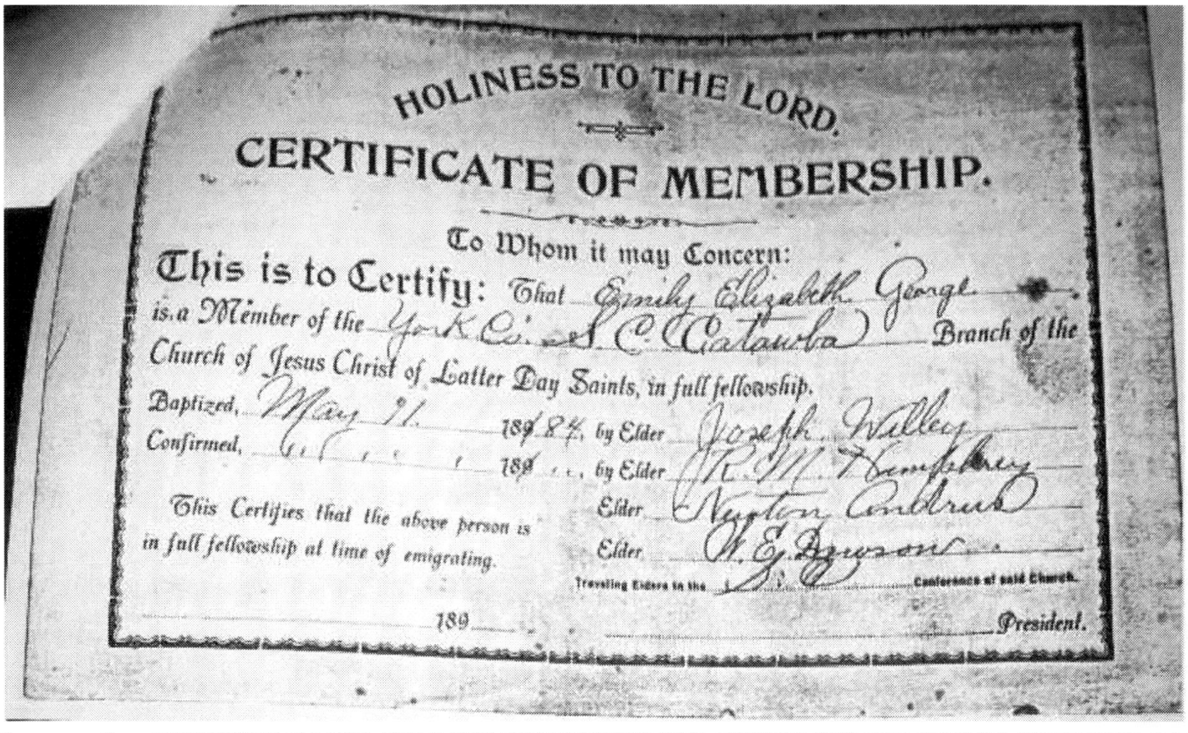

HOLINESS TO THE LORD.

CERTIFICATE OF MEMBERSHIP.

To Whom it may Concern:

This is to Certify: That Emily Elizabeth George is a Member of the York Co. S. C. Catawba Branch of the Church of Jesus Christ of Latter Day Saints, in full fellowship.

Baptized, May 11 1884, by Elder Joseph Willey

Confirmed, " " 189 , by Elder R. M. Humphrey

This Certifies that the above person is in full fellowship at time of emigrating. Elder Newton Andrus

Elder W. E. Dawson

Traveling Elders in the S. C. Conference of said Church.

189 President.

**PHOTO 8 – CERTIFICATE OF MEMBERSHIP TO CHURCH OF JESUS CHRIST OF LATTER DAY SATINS**

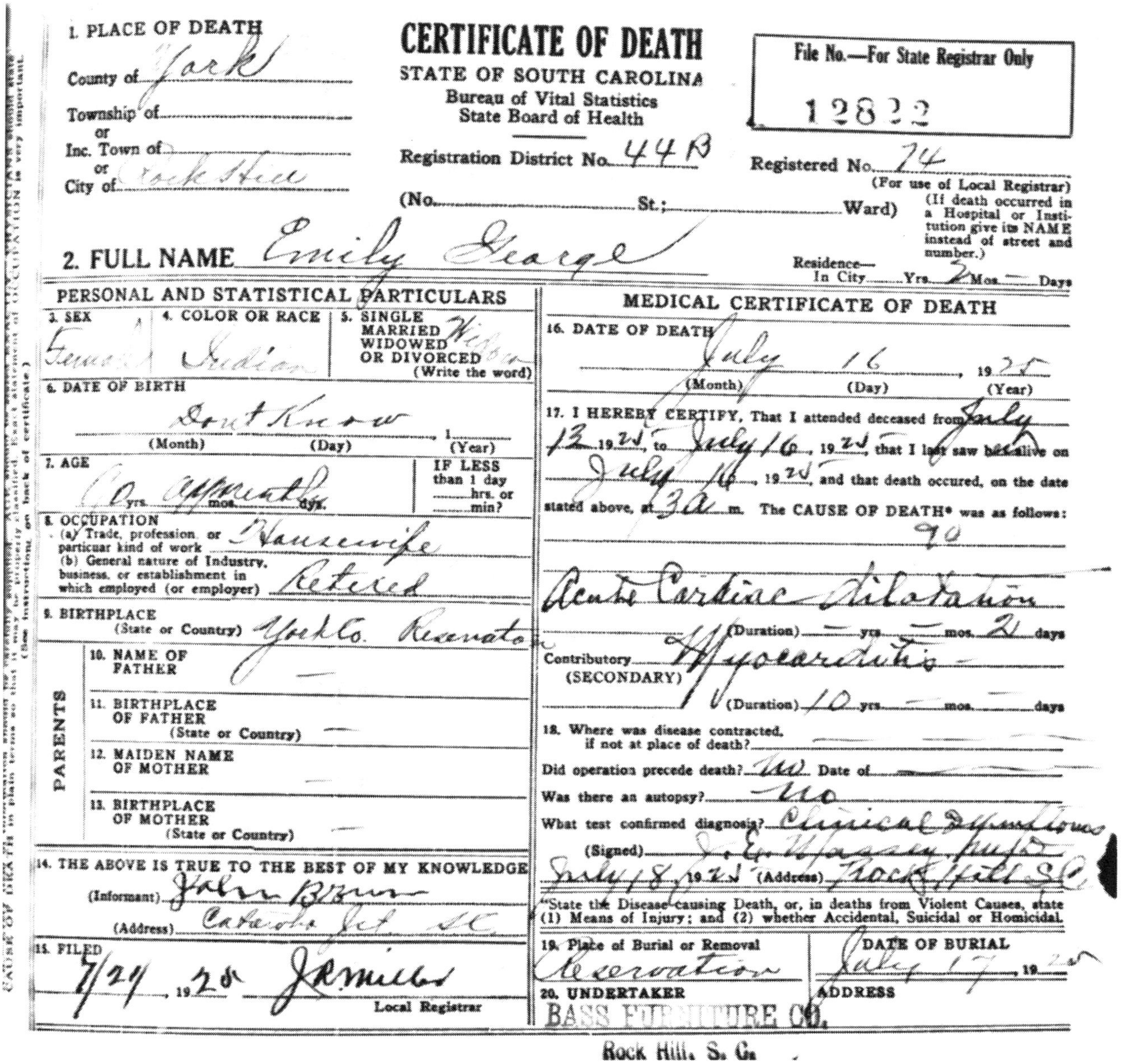

1. PLACE OF DEATH
County of York
Township of
or
Inc. Town of
or
City of Rock Hill

CERTIFICATE OF DEATH
STATE OF SOUTH CAROLINA
Bureau of Vital Statistics
State Board of Health

File No.—For State Registrar Only
12822

Registration District No. 44B
Registered No. 74
(For use of Local Registrar)

(No. St.; Ward) (If death occurred in a Hospital or Institution give its NAME instead of street and number.)

2. FULL NAME Emily George
Residence—In City Yrs. 2 Mos. — Days

PERSONAL AND STATISTICAL PARTICULARS

3. SEX Female
4. COLOR OR RACE Indian
5. SINGLE MARRIED WIDOWED OR DIVORCED (Write the word) Widow
6. DATE OF BIRTH Dont Know (Month) (Day) 1 (Year)
7. AGE 60 yrs. approximately mos. dys. IF LESS than 1 day hrs. or min?
8. OCCUPATION (a) Trade, profession, or particular kind of work Housewife
(b) General nature of Industry, business, or establishment in which employed (or employer) Retired
9. BIRTHPLACE (State or Country) York Co. Reservation

PARENTS
10. NAME OF FATHER —
11. BIRTHPLACE OF FATHER (State or Country) —
12. MAIDEN NAME OF MOTHER
13. BIRTHPLACE OF MOTHER (State or Country) —

14. THE ABOVE IS TRUE TO THE BEST OF MY KNOWLEDGE
(Informant) John Brown
(Address) Catawba Jct. S.C.

15. FILED 7/21, 1925 J.R. Miller Local Registrar

MEDICAL CERTIFICATE OF DEATH

16. DATE OF DEATH July 16, 1925 (Month) (Day) (Year)
17. I HEREBY CERTIFY, That I attended deceased from July 13, 1925, to July 16, 1925, that I last saw her alive on July 16, 1925, and that death occured, on the date stated above, at 3 a. m. The CAUSE OF DEATH* was as follows:
90
Acute Cardiac Dilatation
(Duration) — yrs. — mos. 2 days
Contributory (SECONDARY) Myocarditis
(Duration) 10 yrs. — mos. — days
18. Where was disease contracted, if not at place of death? —
Did operation precede death? no Date of —
Was there an autopsy? no
What test confirmed diagnosis? Clinical Symptoms
(Signed) J. E. Massey, M.D.
July 18, 1925 (Address) Rock Hill S.C.
*State the Disease causing Death, or, in deaths from Violent Causes, state (1) Means of Injury; and (2) whether Accidental, Suicidal or Homicidal.

19. Place of Burial or Removal Reservation
DATE OF BURIAL July 17, 1925
20. UNDERTAKER BASS FURNITURE CO. Rock Hill, S.C.
ADDRESS

PHOTO 9 – CERTIFICATE OF DEATH FOR EMILY ELIZABETH COBB GEORGE

**Only two children are known, Jefferson and Alice.**

Jefferson is buried in Laurelwood Cemetery, near Rock Hill, South Carolina.[34]

   **a.** Jefferson Davis Ayers, born December 21, 1861,[35] he received $6.66 from the Indian Agent R. L. Crook in 1881. He married as her third husband Harriet Berry Sidney, born 1865; (white) who already had a child, Gertrude Dye who took the surname Ayers.[36]
In 1889, Jeff Davis Ayers applied for money that was to be distributed to his children by the Indian Agent, Wm. Whyte. The children were denied because they were half-white, the mother being the person from whom inheritance could be obtained.[37]

"Finding this was the condition of affairs Thursday morning, Ayers made demand upon the Indian agent through his attorney, W. B. Wilson, Esq. for his children's part of the fund, but the agent has not yet made the distribution, as the Indians threaten to hold his bondsmen responsible if he pays any money to the Ayers children. Thus matters stood Thursday. When Ayers approached a number of his comrades who were standing on mainstreet, they denounced him for delaying the payment of the money. One burly fellow, John Brown, became furiously mad and assaulted Ayers when the women interfered and a general fight was imminent." The fight was averted, and Brown was jailed.[38]

He stated he was a widower in the 1920 census then died October 12, 1920. Harriet L. Berry Ayers married second Nephi Lehi Sidney, together they had an infant: Jefferson Davis Ayers, born February 3, 1887, he died April 6, 1887. Therefore, Harriet Berry Dye Sidney Ayers had children by three different men; a man named Dye, Jefferson Davis Ayers, and a Sidney.

Wednesday 7

Engaged in settling the difficulty between Bro. Sydney Berry and family about working part of Mr. John Black's Farm. Took dinner with Sydney Berry & stayed all night with Alonzo Canty. (From the missionary journal of Elisha Clark.)

---

[34] Blumer page 231.
[35] Catawba Branch Records.
[36] Catawba Branch Records.
[37] Rock Hill Herald, May 5, 1894, page 3.
[38] Ibid

### Indian War in Rock Hill.

War has been declared among the Catawba braves, with a probability that the whole tribe will become involved.

Each year the State of South Carolina appropriates $800 to the remnant of the Catawba Indians in this county. This money is distributed among the members of the tribe by Capt. A. E. Smith, the agent. The tribe now numbers 68 Indians and half breeds, and the custom has been to distribute the fund among the pure bloods and such of the half breeds as have Indian mothers, never among the half breeds whose fathers only are Indians. Under the rules of the tribe as they have existed for generations, so we are informed, children only inherit from their mothers, never from their fathers. This fact is the cause of the present trouble. Jeff Davis Ayers is a member of the tribe. About seven years ago he was lawfully married to a white woman, who has borne three children by her Indian husband. Of these children one is six years old, another four years, and the youngest one year.

Thursday all the Indians came to town to draw the money appropriated by the State, but before the distribution could be effected Ayers learned that the agent would observe the rules of the tribe and not apportion the money among the children of any white woman who was the wife of an Indian, inasmuch as no part of the fund was appropriated for a white woman, and under the tribal regulation children could only inherit from their mother. If she had no claims upon the fund, the children would have none. This regulation deprived Ayers' children of any part in the distribution. Finding this was the condition of affairs Thursday morning, Ayers made demand upon the Indian Agent, through his attorney, W. B. Wilson, Esq., for his children's part of the fund, but the agent has not yet made the distribution, as the Indians threaten to hold his bondsmen responsible if he pays any money to the Ayers children. Thus matters stood Thursday when Ayers approached a number of his comrades who were standing on Main street. They denounced him for delaying the payment of the money. One burly fellow, John Brown, became furiously mad and assaulted Ayers, when the women interfered and a general fight was imminent. The Chief of Police happened to be on hand and nabbed Brown, but he resisted and jerking the Chief's walking stick out of his hand threw it into the street. About this time Policeman Carroll reinforced the Chief and the two hurried Brown off to the guardhouse. He was subsequently taken before the mayor and fined $15 or thirty days. He failed to pay up and is now in the jug.

**Jefferson Davis Ayers's children are Annie, Wade, Rossalino, Mary, John Jefferson, Robert Herbert and Alice Ayers.**[39]

1). Annie Ayers, born June 1888, a student of Mrs. Dunlap in 1899/8.[40] Only one child can be identified.

**PHOTO 10 – PEARLY RUTH C AYERS**

a). Pearly Ruth C. Ayers, born 14 February 1909, Catawba, South Carolina and died 16 September 2000, Rock Hill, York, South Carolina. Father unknown; Pearly married first James A Strickland[41] and her second husband was Luther Price or Luther Noah C. Harris, the adopted son of Ed Harris and the natural son of Ruthie Price Harris, he was not Catawba.

**Children of Pearly Ayers and Luther Price or Noah C Harris**

---

[39] Catawba Branch Records.
[40] Ibid
[41] Ibid

**PHOTO 11 – LILLIAN HARRIS**

(1) Lillian Harris born 27 August 1925 married Arnold Lee Blue, son of Samuel and Louisa Canty Blue.[42] She passed away 9 February 1991 - Catawba, South Carolina.

**PHOTO 12- BURIAL: CHURCH OF JESUS CHRIST OF LATTER-DAY STS CEMETERY, CATAWBA, YORK COUNTY, SOUTH CAROLINA,**

---

[42] 1958 membership rolls.

**PHOTO 13 – CHRISTINE HARRIS**

(2) Christine Harris born 3 September 1930, Catawba, South Carolina and died 31 January 1999, Rutherfordton, Rutherford, North Carolina1930. She married Otis Samuel Petty (1917-1983).

**PHOTO 14 - BURIAL: ALVERSON GROVE BAPTIST CEMETERY, INMAN, SPARTANBURG COUNTY, SOUTH CAROLINA –**

(3) Luther Morgan Harris born 8 August 1933,[43] South Carolina and died 28 August 2016, Rock Hill, South Carolina

(4) Jefferson W.C. Harris born 23 September 1936, South Carolina.

(5) Lottie Harris born 15 June 1942, South Carolina.

(6) Charlotte Ann Harris born 13 June 1944,[44] South Carolina. She married a Branham.[45]

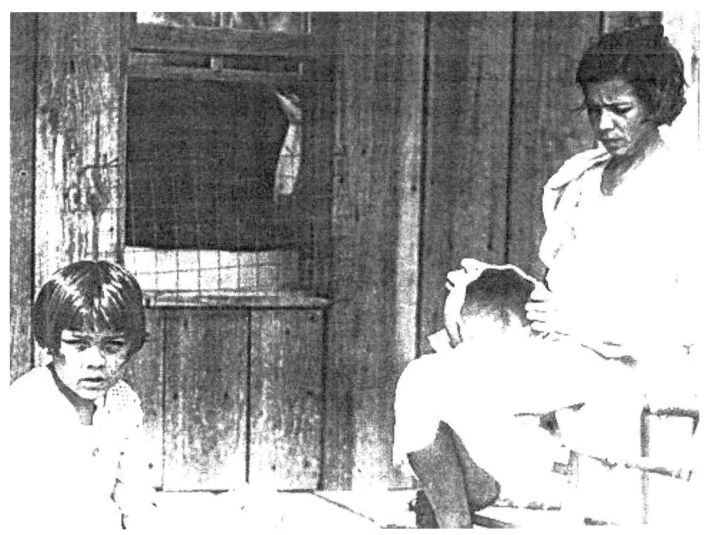

**PHOTO 15 - PEARLY AND DAUGHTER CHARLOTTE ANN AYERS. PEARLY IS THE DAUGHTER OF ANNIE AYERS.[46]**

---

[43] 1961 membership roll
[44] Catawba membership rolls, 1943-1961.
[45] Blumer page 439 article 3637.
[46] South Carolinian Library # 288, from files of The Writers program of WPA 1930 sent by Wes White

**Jefferson Davis Ayers's children continued:**

2). Wade Ayers, born 16 September 1890, also listed as a student in Mrs. Dunlap's school in 1899.[47] He died in 1904, as a reaction to a small pox vaccination.

3). Rossalino Ayers, born February 27, 1893 dead by 1900.

4). Mary Evelyn Ayers, born 24 December 1895, married William B. (Squirrelly) Foxx, born in New York, the son of Italian immigrants.[48] She passed away 27 January 1973, Rock Hill, York, South Carolina.

**PHOTO 16 – HEADSTONE OF MARY EVELYBN AYERS FOX**

[47] Evening Herald, March 12, 1973, page 18.
[48] Evening Herald, November 6, 1962, page 2.

(a) Mary Ethel Foxx born 1 February 1910, Rock Hill, South Carolina, Death July 1980, Norfolk, Norfolk City, Virginia. She married Lewis A. Wright

(b) Antonio B Foxx Sr. born 21 August 1915, Catawba, York, South Carolina, Death 30 January 1979, Rock Hill, York, South Carolina, married Beadie R (1918–1985), white.

(c) Ernest Basile Foxx born 16 July 1917, Catawba, York County, South Carolina, Death 26 June 1994, Gastonia, Gaston, North Carolina, He married Grace Creasum,[49] (1919-1998), (white), on 28 Dec 1935 Gaston, North Carolina.

(d) Joe Basile Foxx born 23 April 1924, Columbia, Richland, South Carolina, Death 22 February 1993, Rock Hill, York, South Carolina. He married Carolyn Doris Monroe (1925–1989), (white).

(e) Josephine Foxx born 10 August 1929[50] married Perry Branham, (white); Children are Betty Joe born 1947 and Barbara Jean Branham born 1954.[51]

(f) Jimmy Coy-Cox Foxx born 18 May 1937 married Doris Rae, (white). Two children: Ronald Guy Foxx, born 1957. Kimberly Dinesi Foxx born 1959

**Jefferson Davis Ayers's children continued:**

5). John Jefferson "Johnnie" Ayers, born September 1898, married Ruth Lucinda "Rhett" Gordon, daughter of Louis and Sallie Brown Gordon, and died September 16, 1929. LDS records show Lucinda Harris as the mother of John J. Ayers. John had six children: Mary Ann, John Junior, Hazel-Foxx, Ruby, Robert and Joseph.

---

[49] Blumer page 338 article 2698
[50] All Fox information from membership rolls.
[51] 1958 membership roll.

Blackmon

1. PLACE OF DEATH
County of York
Township of Ebenezer
or
Inc. Town of
or
City of

CERTIFICATE OF DEATH
STATE OF SOUTH CAROLINA
Bureau of Vital Statistics
State Board of Health

File No.—For State Registrar Only 16758

Registration District No. Registered No.
(No. St.; Ward) (For use of Local Registrar.) (If death occurred in a Hospital or institution give its NAME instead of street and number.)

2. FULL NAME Johnnie Ayers
Residence— In City Yrs. Mos. Days

PERSONAL AND STATISTICAL PARTICULARS
3. SEX Male
4. COLOR OR RACE Indian
5. SINGLE MARRIED WIDOWED OR DIVORCED (Write the word) Married
6. DATE OF BIRTH (Month) (Day) (Year)
7. AGE 30 yrs. mos. dys. IF LESS than 1 day hrs. or min.
8. OCCUPATION (a) Trade, profession, or particular kind of work Textile (b) General nature of Industry, business, or establishment in which employed (or employer)
9. BIRTHPLACE (State or Country) S. C.
PARENTS
10. NAME OF FATHER Dan Ayers
11. BIRTHPLACE OF FATHER (State or country) S. C.
12. MAIDEN NAME OF MOTHER Harriet Berry
13. BIRTHPLACE OF MOTHER (State or country) S. C.
14. THE ABOVE IS TRUE TO THE BEST OF MY KNOWLEDGE
(Informant) Lorne Blue
(Address)
15. FILED 9/16 1929 J. R. Miller Local Registrar

MEDICAL CERTIFICATE OF DEATH
16. DATE OF DEATH 9/14 (Month) (Day) 1929 (Year)
17. I HEREBY CERTIFY, That I attended deceased from 9/5/29 19 to 9/14 1929 that I last saw him alive on 9/14 1929 and that death occurred, on the date stated above, at 4 P.m. The CAUSE OF DEATH* was as follows:
Bronchial Pneumonia
(Duration) yrs. mos. 4 days
Contributory (SECONDARY) Influenza
(Duration) yrs. mos. 6 days
18. Where was disease contracted if not at place of death?
Did operation precede death? no date of
Was there an autopsy? no
What test confirmed diagnosis?
(Signed) W. R. Blackmon M.D.
9/16 1929 (Address) Rock Hill S.C.
*State the Disease causing Death, or, in deaths from Violent Causes, state (1) Means of Injury; and (2) whether Accidental, Suicidal or Homicidal.
19. Place of Burial or Removal Indian Nat
DATE OF BURIAL Sept 15, 1929
20. UNDERTAKER W. Reid & Son
ADDRESS Rock Hill SC

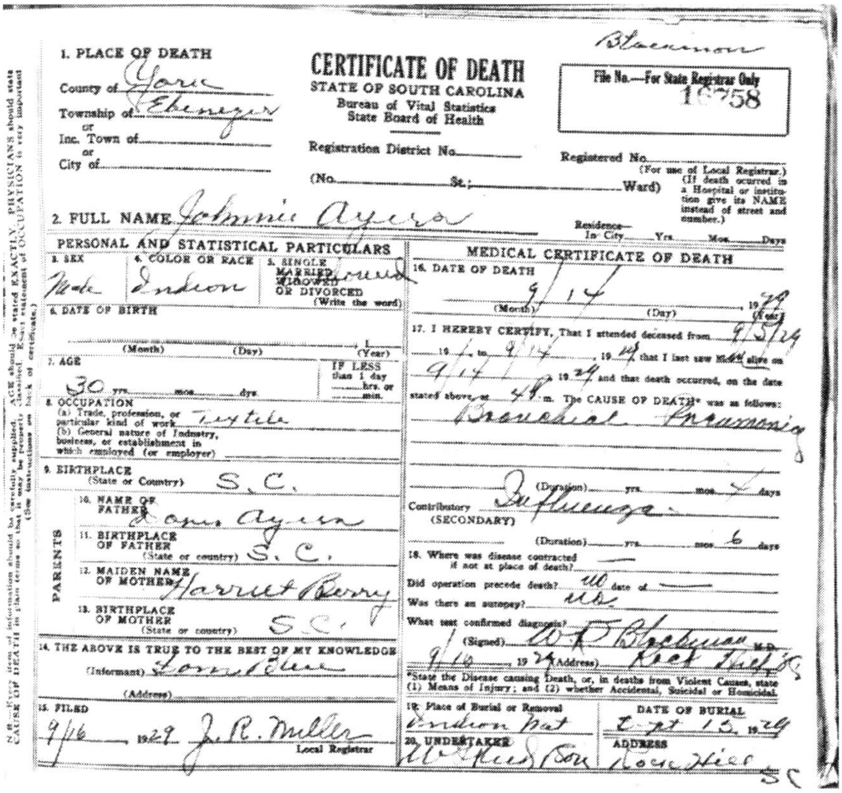

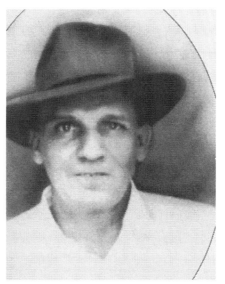

**PHOTO 17 – CERTIFICATE OF DEATH FOR JOHN JEFFERSON AYERS**

**PHOTO 18 - ROBERT HEBER AYERS**

6) Robert Heber Ayers, born 5 October 1901, Catawba, York, South Carolina and died 15 March 1996, Rock Hill, York, South Carolina. He married first Daisy Henrietta Starnes (1904-1971), daughter of James Starnes Lucy George; married second Iva, a white woman.

**PHOTO 19 - ROBERT AYERS WITH CHILD**     **PHOTO 20 - DAISY HENRIETTA STARNES**

**Robert Ayers and Daisy Henrietta Starnes Ayers'- children:**

> a. Claude or Clyde Ayers born 15 October 1922, Catawba, York South Carolina and died 19 January 1935, Richland, South Carolina. He passed away in the Baptist Hospital, Columbia, Richland, South Carolina from appendix abscess at age 12 years 3 months and 4 days.

**PHOTO 21 – CERTIFICATE OF DEATH FOR CLYDE AYERS**

**PHOTO 22 – WILLIAM FRELL AYERS AND WIFE FLORENCE AGNES WALKER AYERS**

b. William Frell Ayers born 22 January 1925, Rock Hill, York, South Carolina and died 22 April 1988, Blacksburg, South Carolina (Buried in Rock Hill). He married Florence Agnes Walker (1931–2010).

c. Earnest Wade Ayers born 12 March 1927, Rock Hill, South Carolina and died 3 March 1982, Rock Hill, South Carolina. He married Betty Greene (1933–1996).

**PHOTO 23 - BURIAL:  CHURCH OF JESUS CHRIST OF LATTER-DAY STS CEMETRY CATAWBA, YORK COUNTY, SOUTH CAROLINA**

**Ernest and Betty had a son Robert H Ayers born 20 May 1955 and died 21 May 1955.**

NORTH CAROLINA STATE BOARD OF HEALTH
BUREAU OF VITAL STATISTICS
CERTIFICATE OF DEATH

Birth No. 132
JUN 7 1955
REGISTRATION DISTRICT NO. 36-80 REGISTRAR'S CERTIFICATE NO. 11443

This is a legal record and will be permanently filed.
Type or write legibly. Use black ink.
All items must be complete and accurate.

1. PLACE OF DEATH a. COUNTY Gaston b. TOWNSHIP Gastonia c. LENGTH OF STAY (in this place)
d. CITY OR TOWN Gastonia Is Place of Death Within City Limits? YES [x] NO [ ]
e. FULL NAME OF HOSPITAL OR INSTITUTION Garrison General Hospital
2. USUAL RESIDENCE a. STATE N C b. COUNTY Gaston
c. CITY OR TOWN Gastonia Is Place of Residence Within City Limits? YES [x] NO [ ]
d. STREET ADDRESS 1913 E Hemlock Street
3. NAME OF DECEASED a. (First) Robert b. (Middle) H c. (Last) Ayers
4. DATE OF DEATH (Month) May (Day) 21 (Year) 1955
5. SEX M 6. COLOR OR RACE W 7. MARRIED, NEVER MARRIED, WIDOWED, DIVORCED (Specify) Child
8. DATE OF BIRTH May 20, 1955 9. AGE (In years last birthday) IF UNDER 1 YEAR Months Days 1
10a. USUAL OCCUPATION 10b. KIND OF BUSINESS OR INDUSTRY
11. BIRTHPLACE (State or foreign country) Gastonia, N.C. 12. CITIZEN OF WHAT COUNTRY? USA
13. FATHER'S NAME Ernest Wade Ayers 14. MOTHER'S MAIDEN NAME Betty May Green
15. WAS DECEASED EVER IN U.S. ARMED FORCES? No 16. SOCIAL SECURITY NO. None
17. INFORMANT'S NAME AND ADDRESS Ernest W Ayers, Gastonia, N.C.

The undertaker, or person acting as such, is responsible for filing the completed certificate with registrar of the district where death occurred.

18. CAUSE OF DEATH — MEDICAL CERTIFICATION
I. DISEASE OR CONDITION DIRECTLY LEADING TO DEATH (a) Anoxia
ANTECEDENT CAUSES DUE TO (b) Probable blockage
DUE TO (c) of bronchi c mucous
II. OTHER SIGNIFICANT CONDITIONS
INTERVAL BETWEEN ONSET AND DEATH

The physician last in attendance is required to state the cause of death and sign the medical certification.

19a. DATE OF OPERATION 19b. MAJOR FINDINGS OF OPERATION 20. AUTOPSY? YES [x] NO [ ]
21a. ACCIDENT SUICIDE HOMICIDE 21b. PLACE OF INJURY 21c. (CITY, TOWN, OR TOWNSHIP) (COUNTY) (STATE)
21d. TIME OF INJURY 21e. INJURY OCCURRED 21f. HOW DID INJURY OCCUR?

If there was no doctor in attendance, medical certification to be completed by local Health Officer (or Coroner, if inquest was held).

22. I hereby certify that I attended the deceased from May 20, 1955, to May 21, 1955, that I last saw the deceased alive on May 21, 1955, and that death occurred at 12:15 P m., from the causes and on the date stated above.
23a. SIGNATURE [signature] M.D. 23b. ADDRESS Clover, S.C. 23c. DATE SIGNED 5/23/55
24a. BURIAL, CREMATION, REMOVAL Burial 24b. DATE 5-21-55 24c. NAME OF CEMETERY OR CREMATORY Hollywood Cemetery 24d. LOCATION Gastonia N C
DATE REC'D BY LOCAL REG. 5-27-55 REGISTRAR'S SIGNATURE J. Q. [illegible] M.D. 25. FUNERAL DIRECTOR Carothers Funeral Home, Gastonia, N.C.

FORM 8 Rev. 1/49

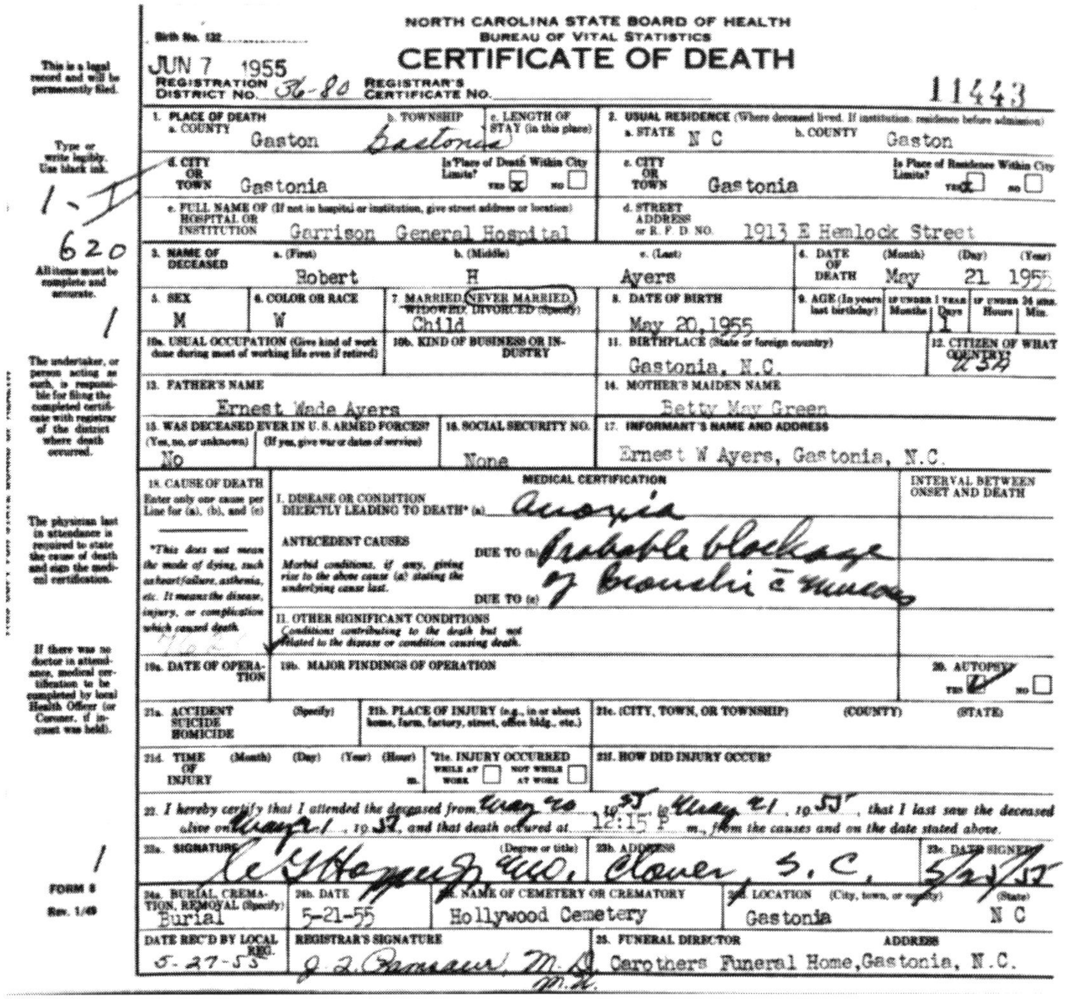

**PHOTO 24 – CERTIFICATE OF DEATH FOR ROBERT H AYERS**

**Jefferson Davis Ayers's – children continued**

7) Joseph Ayers born 1905, Catawba Indian Reservation died before 1954.[52] He is the son of Jefferson Davis Ayers and Harriett Lucinda Berry.

1910 US, Catawba township, York County, South Carolina, 10 May 1910 Census
Has the Ayers family of. J Davis Ayers - 48, Mary - 14, John - 11, Heber- 8 and Joseph -5.

[52] Ibid

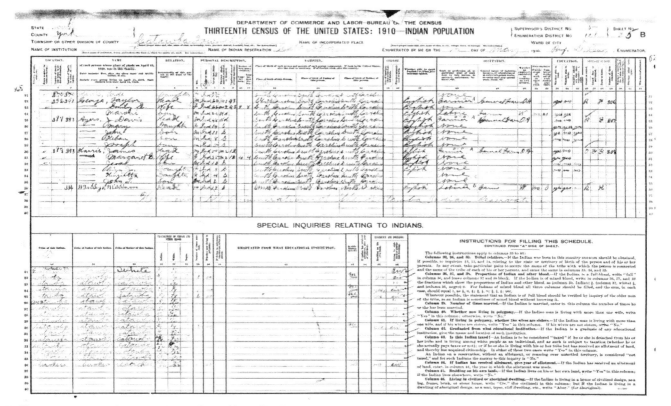

Jefferson Ayers 1840–1865 and Emily Elizabeth Cobb Ayers 1843–1925 daughter Lusy Alice Ayers.

b. Lucy Alice Ayers, born December 17 1866, Catawba Indian Reservation, South Carolina, United States and died After 1893, Catawba, York, South Carolina. She married Wesley Harris, son of John and Lucinda Harris Harris.

"Miss Alice Ayers, March 6, 1884 baptized by Elder Joseph Willey, along with her brother Jefferson Davis Ayers on March 6, 1884." She died after 1893.[53] Her children will be found under Lucinda Harris's son Wesley in the Lucinda Harris.

\*\*\*\*\*\*\*\*\*\*\*\*\*\*\*\*\*\*\*\*\*\*\*\*\*\*\*\*\*\*\*\*\*\*\*\*\*\*\*\*\*\*\*\*\*\*\*\*\*\*\*\*\*\*\*\*\*\*\*\*\*\*\*\*\*\*\*\*

James Eayrs-Ayers probably born around 1760, and died after 1839. He is listed on Drennan's Pay Bill of 1780, and appears as Jammy Ears in the petition of 1792. James Ayers signed leases in 1838 along with General William Harris, Colonel Samuel Scott, Major James Ayers and Captain David Harris, through the year 1840. He disappears after the lease of November 1, 1839.[54] The Plat Books list a Col. Jacob Scott and Jimmy; this is probably James Ears.

Major John Ears, probably born around 1760, signed the petition of 1792, along with Colonel John Ears, showing that they were two separate individuals.

[53] Catawba Branch Records.
[54] Blumer page 154.

UNKNOWN AYERS
Nancy Ayers received rents along with a Scott Ayers.[55]

Moses-Mosy Ayers, served in Revolution, and received rents, but no other records have been found.[56]

A Sarah Ayers married William George sr., born around 1790.[57]

Rosa-Rosie Ayers, born 1813,[58] had married a Canty by time of the 1849 census. She removed to Cheraw of North Florida in 1851-53.

Betsy Ayers, born 1830, went to Cheraw of North Florida.
Sophronia Ayers, child of one of these women. All removed in 1851-53

Juliana Ayers, born 1834,[59] (may have become Julia Harris by 1875 when a Julia Harris received money from the Indian Agent R. L. Crook)

Mary Ayers, born 1837[60]

---

[55] Ibid
[56] Drennan's pay bill and Indian Piatt books
[57] Catawba Branch Records, LDS Film #0001983-86, hereafter cited as Catawba Branch Records.
[58] 1847 Petition, 1849 census.
[59] 1849 census
[60] 1849 census

## Chapter 2   Beck Family

I. Fletcher John Beck (Cherokee) born 11 March 1893 in Clayton, Georgia, son of Jefferson Swafford, white and Lillie Florence Beck (Cherokee). Lillie Florence was the daughter of Samuel Beck and Arah Powell Beck of Clayton, Georgia.[61] Fletcher married on December 24, 1914, Sallie Rebecca Brown, daughter of John William and Rachel Wysie George Brown.[62] Sallie was a student of Mrs. Dunlap in 1899. Fletcher is listed as the child of Joseph Hinson Sanders and Lillie Florence Beck. (Therefore, Lillie married second Joseph Hinson Sanders, son of John Evins Sanders and Joseph Hinson Harris evidently raised Fletcher.)  Fletcher died 27 January 1979 in Rock Hill and Salley died 27 January 1993.[63]

**PHOTO 25 - SALLY REBECCA BROWN BECK AND SON SAMUEL JOHN BECK**

---

[61] LDS Ancestral File and IGI and Catawba Branch Records.

[62] Catawba Branch records.

[63] Obituary of Sallie in the Herald, January 28, 1993.

**PHOTO 26 – THE THREE PICTURES ARE OF
FLETCHER JOHN BECK AND WIFE SALLIE REBECCA BROWN**

**PHOTO 27 - BURIAL: CHURCH OF JESUS CHRIST OF LATTER-DAY STS. CEMETERY, CATAWBA, YORK COUNTY, SOUTH CAROLINA.**

**PHOTO 28 - FLETCHER JOHN BECK AND SALLIE REBECCA BROWN BECK WITH THREE OF THEIR CHILDREN, SAMUEL, FANNIE AND BABY EUGENE.**

# Sallie Beck, oldest Catawba, dies

By KENNETH A. GAILUARD
Herald Staff Writer

CATAWBA - Sallie Rebecca Brown Beck, who had a reputation as one of the best potters on the Catawba Indian reservation and was known as the oldest living Catawba, died Wednesday. She was 99.

Beck's son Fletcher Beck said she died of pneumonia at Magnolia Manor nursing home in Rock Hill, where she lived.

Several friends and relatives described Beck as gentle, caring, fun and a wealth of information.

"She was a remarkable lady, and a lot of history went with her and is gone forever," said Wenonah Beck Haire, a Catawba Indian and chairwoman for the Catawba Cultural Preservation Project. The group was formed by tribal members to keep the Catawba heritage. Haire said she recently had discussed meeting with Beck to record some of the tribe's oral history, in the words of Beck and other elder Catawba's.

"She was a remarkable lady," Haire said. "She was a wealth of information — the stories that she could tell and the humor that she added to it was just great.

"She was a link to a part of our history that was way back, and that most of us younger ones don't have a good grasp of," Haire said, adding that many people looked up to Beck. "She was the true individual who could keep you captivated with history and facts."

Catawba Indian Chief Gilbert Blue said: "Sallie Beck was one of the stalwarts of our tribe." He described her as a good potter and said he often visited her and reminisced about "the old days," when Catawba's would sell their pottery at Winthrop to earn extra money. Some of her pottery is on display in the Smithsonian Museum, as well as at the Museum of York County. "We will definitely miss her," said Blue, who remembered Beck as the church piano player when he was just a child.

Beck was born in York County and was a member of the Catawba Ward of the Church of Jesus Christ of Latter Day Saints.

The funeral will be 2 p.m. Saturday at the Church of Jesus Christ of Utter Day Saints in Catawba, with Bishop Michael Broadhead and Patriarch Benjamin W. Wilkerson officiating. Burial will be at the Catawba Baptist Church Cemetery.

Surviving are two sons, Eugene Beck of Rock Hill and Fletcher "Russ" Beck of the Catawba Indian Reservation; three daughters, Rachel Yates, of Potomac, Md., Ethel Warner of Bolivar, Ohio and Irene Garcia of Pueblo, Colo.: 39 grandchildren; 36 great-grandchildren and 11 great-great grandchildren.

The family will receive friends at the home of her son Fletcher Hi. K, 2030 Reservation Road in Rock Hill. Greene Funeral Home is in charge of arrangements.

Rock Hill Herald, sent in by Fave Dodds.

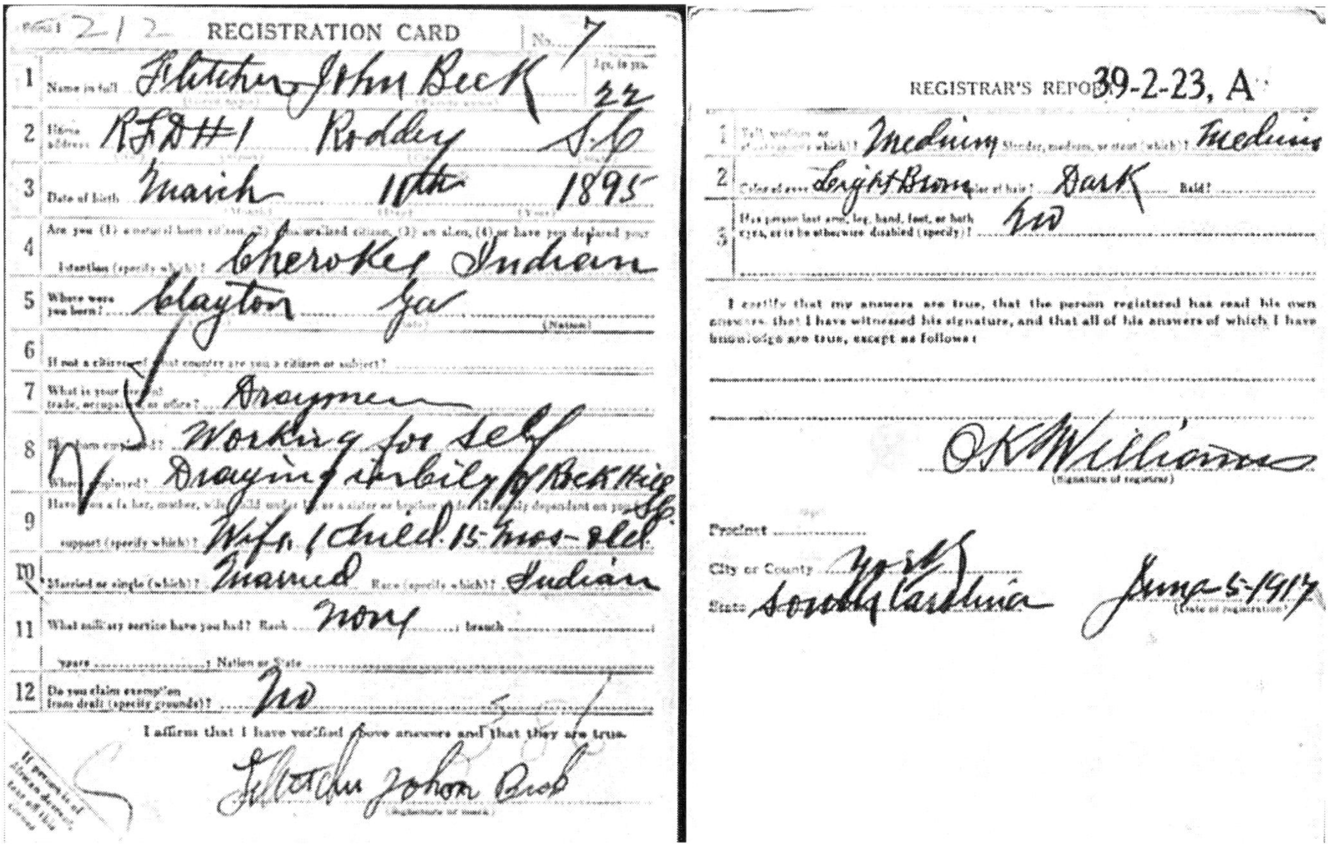

212 REGISTRATION CARD No. 7

1 Name in full Fletcher John Beck Age, in yrs. 22

2 Home address RFD #1 Roddey S.C.

3 Date of birth March 10th 1895

4 Are you (1) a natural born citizen, (2) a naturalized citizen, (3) an alien, (4) or have you declared your intention (specify which)? Cherokee Indian

5 Where were you born? Clayton Ga (Nation)

6 If not a citizen, of what country are you a citizen or subject?

7 What is your present trade, occupation or office? Draymen

8 By whom employed? Working for self Where employed? Draying in vicinity of Rock Hill S.C.

9 Have you a father, mother, wife, child under 12, or a sister or brother under 12, solely dependent on you for support (specify which)? Wife & Child 15 mos old

10 Married or single (which)? Married Race (specify which)? Indian

11 What military service have you had? Rank none ; branch ; years ; Nation or State

12 Do you claim exemption from draft (specify grounds)? No

I affirm that I have verified above answers and that they are true.

Fletcher John Beck (Signature or mark)

REGISTRAR'S REPORT 39-2-23, A

1 Tall, medium, or short (specify which)? Medium Slender, medium, or stout (which)? Medium

2 Color of eyes Light Brown Color of hair? Dark Bald?

3 Has person lost arm, leg, hand, foot, or both eyes, or is he otherwise disabled (specify)? No

I certify that my answers are true, that the person registered has read his own answers, that I have witnessed his signature, and that all of his answers of which I have knowledge are true, except as follows:

O K Williams (Signature of registrar)

Precinct

City or County York

State South Carolina June 5-1917 (Date of registration)

**PHOTO 29 - FLETCHER JOHN BECK – WWI – DRAFT REGISTRATION CARD**

W #227

A P P L I C A T I O N

Richard + for Sallie Downing

Enrollment with the Eastern Band of Cherokee
Indians of North Carolina

(See instructions on last page) *Mill Co*
*Roll # 166*

I hereby make application for enrollment with the Eastern Band of
Cherokee Indians of North Carolina. My name is Fletcher John Beck,
in York County, S.C.
and I reside at Catawba, S.C. R.F.D. I also make application for the
enrollment of my minor children as follows:

*Samuel John Beck, Irene Beck*
*Eugene Beck and Ethel Beck*

State of S. C.........)
                      ) ss
County of ...York......)

I, the said Fletcher John Beck, of lawful age, being first duly
sworn, depose and say:- That my full and correct name is Fletcher John Beck;
that I am ...53...... years of age, and that I now reside at Catawba, S. C.
and (in case of married female) that my name prior to my marriage was

........................; that I was born at ........................, and that I have

resided at the following places for the periods of time herein stated:

I resided in Rabun County, Georgia, from birth until 1909;
                    Swain
resided in Cherokee County, N. C., on the Government land
                    from 1909 to 1912
and attended the Cherokee Indian School;/ I resided in York
County, S. C., from 1912 until now, this February 1926.

2. That I am of Eastern Cherokee Indian blood of 1/16 degree, and
I claim lineal descent from ...Mother....., who was my *Lillie Beck*

(state the relationship), and that my descent from said ancestor is as

follows: Richard Downing married Nellie. To them were born Sallie
Downing a full Cherokee Indian; Allie Downing married James Blythe
who had no Indian blood (white) to them were born Stacy Blythe,
who married Berry Beck (white man), to them were born Sam Beck
et al., Sam Beck being the Father of Lillie Beck, who is the
mother of Fletcher John Beck

**Obituary Sallie Beck**

Birth: Sep. 22, 1893 Death: Jan. 27, 1993
Charlotte Observer, the (NC) - Thursday, January 28, 1993
CATAWBA POTTERY PIONEER SALLIE BECK DIES


Sallie Rebecca Brown Beck - one of the most famous potters in the history of the Catawba tribe - died Wednesday, Jan. 27, 1993, in Rock Hill. She was 99.

Mrs. Beck is credited with introducing Catawba pottery into local museums as well as acting as one of the tribe's first official pottery instructors in 1976. Historian Thomas Blumer notes she is also thought to be the person responsible for introducing the "wedding jug" to tribal potters in the 1930s. The two-spouted jar, which is Cherokee in origin, is among the most popular pottery forms made by the tribe, Blumer said. "'She was a master potter of note," Blumer said. "Her work was popular for years with private collectors and museums who would seek her out to buy pottery."

Born in York County, Mrs. Beck survived a 1918 influenza epidemic that killed five of her seven siblings.

She later became one of the first to attend the Catawba Indian School in Rock Hill, Blumer said. Beck's pottery won a blue ribbon at the second annual Catawba Fair in 1939, and later earned similar honors at various county fairs. In 1952 she participated in the first exhibit of Catawba pottery held at the Museum of York County, which now has several of her pieces in its permanent collection. Family members also say her work is included in the Smithsonian.

Her funeral is at the Church of Jesus Christ of Latter-day Saints in Catawba, with Bishop Michael Broadhead and Patriarch Benjamin Wilkers officiating. Burial will be in Catawba Baptist Church Cemetery in Catawba.

Survivors are her sons, Fletcher Beck of Catawba and Eugene Beck of Rock Hill; daughters, Ms. Rachel Yates of Potomac, Md., Ms. Ethel Warner of Bolivar, Ohio, and Ms. Irene Garcia of Pueblo, Colo.; 39 grandchildren; 56 great-grandchildren; and 11 great-great-grandchildren.


**Fletcher and Sallie had seven children and they are listed below.**

**PHOTO 30 – SAMUEL JOHN BECK**

A. Samuel John Beck born 12 February 1916 married Margaret Helen Canty, daughter of Alonzo George and Fannie Harris Canty. Her biological father was Ernest Givens (white) but Alonzo George Canty raised her and she considered him her father. In November of 1985, Samuel represented the Catawba nation at a forum of concerned citizens.[64] He was an electrician working in the printing and finishing plant.[65]

---

[64] Blumer page 500 article 4265.

[65] 1958 membership roll.

PHOTO 31 - THESE TWO PICTURES ARE OF SAMUEL JOHN BECK

PHOTO 32 - CHURCH OF JESUS CHRIST OF LATTER-DAY STS CEMETERY -- BURIAL OR CREMATION PLACE CATAWBA, YORK COUNTY, SOUTH CAROLINA, UNITED STATES OF AMERICA

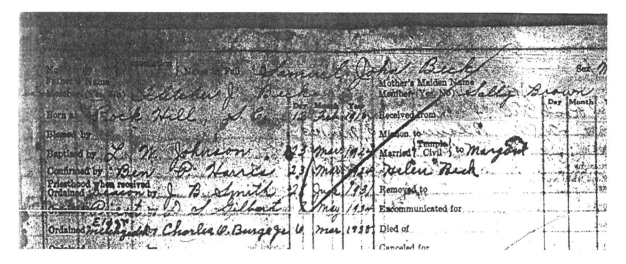

**PHOTO 33 – L.D.S. BAPTISM RECORD FOR SAMUEL JOHN BECK**

**Charlotte Observer, the (NC) - Monday, May 8, 1989**

Samuel John Beck, Indian Leader 73, a former leader of the Catawba Indian tribe, died May 6, 1989, at his home. Funeral is at the Church of Jesus Christ of Latter-day Saints (Catawba Ward), with Bishop Kenneth Harris and President Benjamin Wilkerson officiating. Burial will be in the church cemetery.

Mr. Beck was a retired employee of the Rock Hill Printing and Finishing Co. in the Electrical Department. He was self-employed electrical contractor and was part owner of Beck and Beck Electric Co.

Mr. Beck was secretary and treasurer for the executive committee for the Catawba tribe for 50 years. He was a former member of the Catawba Regional Planning Commission and a lifetime farmer. He was also a member of the American Legion, VFW, and the York County Fair Association.

Surviving are his wife, Helen; sons, Joel Beck Sr., Samuel Mitchell Beck and Roderick Beck; daughters, Mrs. Shasta Proxel of Richland Center, Wis., and Mrs. Phyllis Williams; mother, Mrs. Sallie Brown Beck; brothers, Eugene Beck and Fletcher Beck; sisters, Mrs. Irene Garcia, Pueblo, Colo., Mrs. Ethel Warner, Bolivar, Ohio, Mrs. Rachel Yates, Pontiac, Md.; 20 grandchildren, and nine great-grandchildren.

**PHOTO 34 – FANNIE MINERVA IRENE BECK**

B. Fannie Minerva Irene Beck born 19 May 1918 in Catawba, South Carolina, married Ben. E. Rich Garcia, son of Rufus and Abbie Patterson Garcia.[66] She died 16 April 2013, Pueblo, Colorado.[67]

**PHOTO 35 - – FANNIE MINERVA IRENE BECK AS A SMALL CHILD**

---

[66] Patterson Genealogy.
[67] Patterson genealogy.

### Miss Me, But Let Me Go

When I come to the end of the road
And the sun has set for me
I want no rites in a
gloom-filled room,
Why cry for a soul set free?
Miss me a little but not
too long,
And not with your
head bowed low,
Remember the love that we once shared.
Miss me . . . but let me go.
For this is a journey that we all must take,
And each must go alone.
It's all a part of the master plan
A step on the road to home.
When you are lonely and sick of heart,
Go to the friends we know
And bury your sorrow in doing good deeds,
Miss me . . . but let me go.

### IN LOVING MEMORY OF
### Irene Garcia

**SUNRISE**
May 19, 1918
Rock Hill, South Carolina

**SUNSET**
April 16, 2013
Pueblo, Colorado

**FUNERAL SERVICE**
Wednesday, April 24, 2013
Ten O'clock in the morning
Imperial Funeral Home Chapel

**OFFICIATING**
Brother Joe Musso

**MUSIC SELECTIONS**
"Amazing Grace"
"This World is Not My Home"
"Memories"

Following the service a reception will be held
at the Church of Jesus Christ of Latter Day Saints
1411 Fortino Blvd.

**INTERMENT**
Imperial Memorial Gardens

**ARRANGEMENTS BY**
Imperial Funeral Home
5450 Hwy 78 West, Pueblo, Colorado

**Fannie Minerva Irene Beck's children are:**

**PHOTO 36 – BEN E RICH GARCIA JR.**

1. Ben E Rich Garcia Jr."Doc" born 25 August 1935, Catawba Now Rock Hill, York, South Carolina, Died 27 October 2009, Pueblo, Pueblo, Colorado.

**PHOTO 37 - BONNIE GARCIA**

2. Bonnie Garcia born 1937 in South Carolina.

**PHOTO 38 - CALVIN FLETCHER GARCIA**

3. Calvin Fletcher Garcia born 12 May 1941, in Colorado.

\*\*\*\*\*\*\*\*\*\*\*\*\*\*\*\*\*\*\*\*\*\*\*\*\*\*\*\*\*\*\*\*\*\*\*\*\*\*\*\*\*\*

**PHOTO 39 – EUGENE BECK**

C.  Eugene Beck born 30 July 1920, Rock Hill, York County, South Carolina – died 9 August 1993, Rock Hill, York, South Carolina, United States.  His wife was Evelyn Mae Simmers (white) (1926-2010).

**Obituary: The Charlotte Observer - Thursday, August 12, 1993**.

-- ROCK HILL - Mr. Eugene Beck 73, construction worker, died Aug. 9, 1993, at home. Funeral is Friday at Church of Jesus Christ of Latter-Day Saints where he was a member. Bishop Glen Spurling and Elders Garth Reed and Steve Whitesell will officiate. Burial will be in Grand View Memorial Park.

# Beck Family

Mr. Beck, a World War II Army veteran, had been an asbestos installer. He was a member of Veterans of Foreign Wars Post 2889 and National Asbestos Workers in Charlotte and Charleston, West Virginia.

Survivors are his wife, Mrs. Evelyn Simmers Beck; sons, Ronald Beck, Duane Beck; daughters, Ms. Sandra Corbridge of American Falls, Idaho, Ms. Tammy Beck of Catawba; brother, Fletcher Beck; sisters, Ms. Irene Garcia of Pueblo, Colo., Ms. Ethel Warner of New Philadelphia, Ohio, Ms. Rachel Yates of Potomac, Md.; seven grandchildren.

**PHOTO 40 - EUGENE BECK WHEN YOUNG**

**PHOTO 41 - GRANDVIEW MEMORIAL PARK - BURIAL OR CREMATION - PLACE, ROCK HILL, YORK COUNTY, SOUTH CAROLINA**

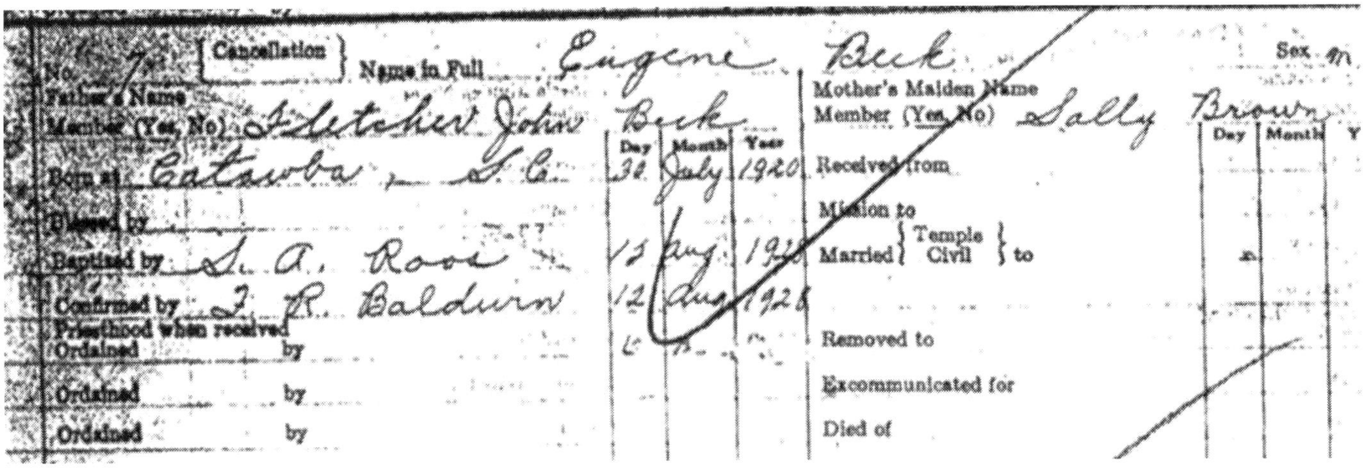

**PHOTO 42 – L.D.S. BAPTISM RECORD FOR EUGENE BECK**

**PHOTO 43 – MAGGIE CORA ETHEL BECK**

D.  Maggie Cora Ethel Beck born 14 October 1924, Rock Hill, York, South Carolina and died 18 November 1999, Dover, Tuscarawas, Ohio. She married a white man named Oliver Warner (1916-1993)

| Ordained | by | | | | Canceled for | | | |
|---|---|---|---|---|---|---|---|---|
| No. *{* Cancellation *}* | Name in Full | *Maggie Cora Ethel Beck* | | | | | Sex *J.* | |
| Father's Name Member (Yes No) *Fletcher John Beck* | | | | | Mother's Maiden Name Member (Yes No) *Sally Brown* | | Day | Month |
| Born at *Catawba, S.C.* | | 14 | Oct. | 1924 | Received from | | | |
| Blessed by *H. W. Biesinger* | | 16 | Nov. | 1924 | Mission to | | | |
| Baptised by *J. C. Davis* | | 23 | Oct. | 193_ | Married *{* Temple *}* Civil *}* to | | | |
| Confirmed by *{* *Herbert Blue* | | 23 | Oct. | 1932 | | | | |
| Priesthood when received Ordained by | | | | | Removed to | | | |
| Ordained by | | | | | Excommunicated for | | | |
| Ordained by | | | | | Died of | | | |

**PHOTO 44 – L.D.S. BAPTISM RECORD FOR MAGGIE CORA ETHEL BECK**

**PHOTO 45 - FLETCHER BROWN BECK**

E. Fletcher Brown-Buck Beck born 3 June 1927, Catawba, York, South Carolina and died 24 September 2010, Catawba, York, South Carolina. He is listed as Jr. on 1961 census and married Gwendolyn Jewel Parks (White).

**Obituary: From the Herald rock Hill South Carolina 26 September 2010**

ROCK HILL Mr. Fletcher Brown Beck, 83, passed away on Friday, Sept. 24, 2010, at his home.

The funeral will be held at the Church of Jesus Christ of Latter Day Saints-Catawba Ward. Burial will be in the church cemetery.

A native of Rock Hill, Mr. Beck was the son

of the late Fletcher John Beck and the late Sallie Brown Beck. He was a very proud U.S. Navy veteran of WWII. He was retired from Rock Hill Printing & Finishing with over 45 years of service and was president of the Local 710 Union. He was a member of the Church of Jesus Christ of Latter Day Saints-Catawba Ward and also a member of the Catawba Tribe and the tribe baseball team. Buck was a loving father and grandfather who always put others first. He was the widower of Gwendolyn Parks Beck and was also preceded in death by his daughter, Dianna Marthers; his brothers, Samuel John Beck and Eugene Beck; and his sister, Ethel Warner.

Surviving are his son, Mitch Beck and his wife, Melodie, of Rock Hill; his daughters, Angela Beck Varnadore and her husband, Tim, of Rock Hill and Deborah Beck Mason of Clover; his sisters, Rachel Beck Yates and her husband, John, of Columbia and Irene Garcia of Pueblo, Colo.; ten grandchildren; two great-grandchildren; and his very dear friend, Doris Yesersky of Rock Hill.

**PHOTO 46 - FLETCHER BROWN BECK**

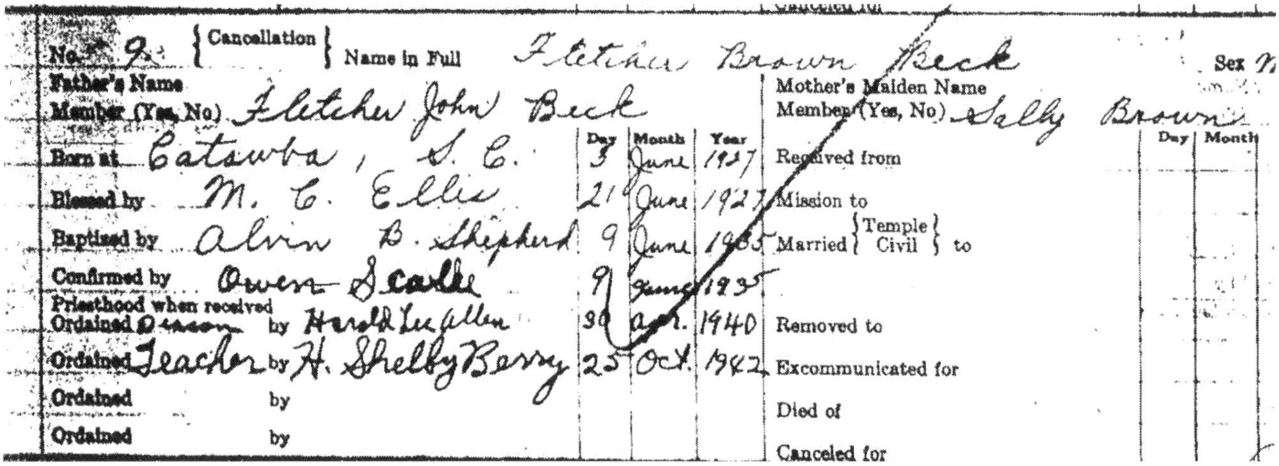

No. 9 {Cancellation} Name in Full Fletcher Brown Beck Sex M
Father's Name
Member (Yes, No) Fletcher John Beck
Mother's Maiden Name
Member (Yes, No) Sally Brown

| | | Day | Month | Year |
|---|---|---|---|---|
| Born at | Catawba, S. C. | 3 | June | 1927 |
| Blessed by | M. C. Ellis | 21 | June | 1927 |
| Baptised by | Alvin B. Shepherd | 9 | June | 1935 |
| Confirmed by | Owen Searle | 9 | June | 1935 |
| Priesthood when received Ordained Deacon | by Harold Lee Allen | 30 | Apr. | 1940 |
| Ordained Teacher | by H. Shelby Berry | 25 | Oct. | 1942 |
| Ordained | by | | | |
| Ordained | by | | | |

Received from
Mission to
Married {Temple / Civil} to
Removed to
Excommunicated for
Died of
Canceled for

**PHOTO 47 – L.D.S. BAPTISM RECORD FOR FLETCHER BROWN BECK**

F. Lillie Rachel Beck born 16 October 1934, Catawba, York, South Carolina. She married a white man named John Michael Yates.[68]

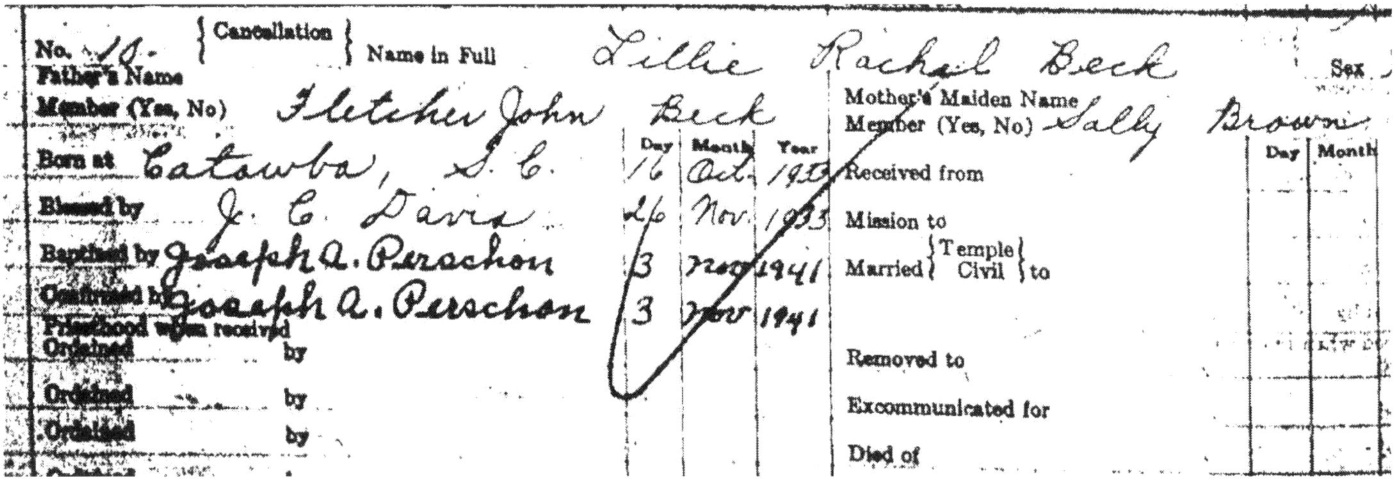

No. 10 {Cancellation} Name in Full Lillie Rachel Beck Sex
Father's Name
Member (Yes, No) Fletcher John Beck
Mother's Maiden Name
Member (Yes, No) Sally Brown

| | | Day | Month | Year |
|---|---|---|---|---|
| Born at | Catawba, S. C. | 16 | Oct. | 1934 |
| Blessed by | J. C. Davis | 26 | Nov. | 1933 |
| Baptised by | Joseph A. Perschon | 3 | Nov | 1941 |
| Confirmed by | Joseph A. Perschon | 3 | Nov | 1941 |
| Priesthood when received Ordained | by | | | |
| Ordained | by | | | |
| Ordained | by | | | |

Received from
Mission to
Married {Temple / Civil} to
Removed to
Excommunicated for
Died of

**PHOTO 48 - L.D.S. BAPTISM RECORD FOR LELLIE RACHEL BECK**

*******************************************************************

[68] Ibid

I. Major John Beck (Cherokee) married first Lula Samuel Henrietta Blue born May 3, 1905, daughter of Samuel Taylor and Louisa Canty Blue; second Fannie Harris Canty, daughter of David Adam and Lizzie Patterson-Watts Harris, first wife of Alonzo George Canty.[69]

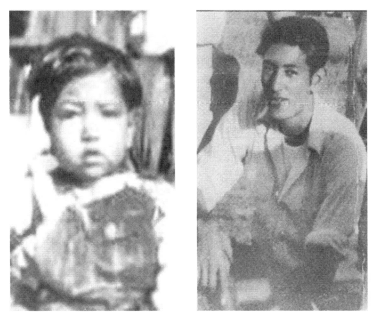

**PHOTO 49 - SAMUEL NELSON BECK**

A. Samuel Nelson Beck born 17 December 1926,[70] Catawba, South Carolina. Samuel was killed in an automobile accident on January 23, 1950, Rock Hill, South Carolina. Fletcher Beck Jr. was driving and Albert Sanders Jr. was a passenger. The accident occurred at 1:30 Sunday morning and all were taken to St. Philips Hospital.[71] The inquest into the death was postponed on January 26, because of a coroner delay. Samuel was buried January 26, 1950.[72]

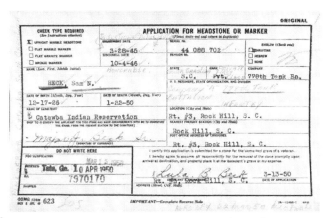

**PHOTO 50 – SAMUEL NELSON BECK – APPLICATION FOR HEADSTONE**

---

[69] Membership rolls.

[70] Catawba Branch Records.

[71] Blumer page 349.

[72] Blumer page 349

**PHOTO 51 – CATAWBA INDIAN RESERVATION CEMETERY,
LANCASTER COUNTY, SOUTH CAROLINA**

**PHOTO 52 - MAJOR W HUEBANK JOHN BACK**

B. Major W. Huebank John Beck born 27 August 1929, Catawba Indian Reservation, Rock Hill, York, South Carolina, known as Jr. He married Beatrice Wallace (1931-2008) (white).[73]

---

[73] Membership rolls

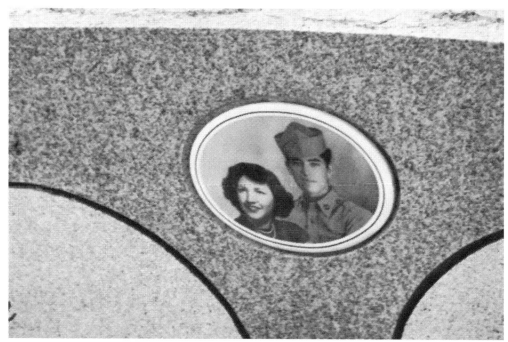

**PHOTO 53 – MAJOR W HUBANK JOHN BECK 1929- AND WIFE BEATRICE WALLACE 1931-2008**

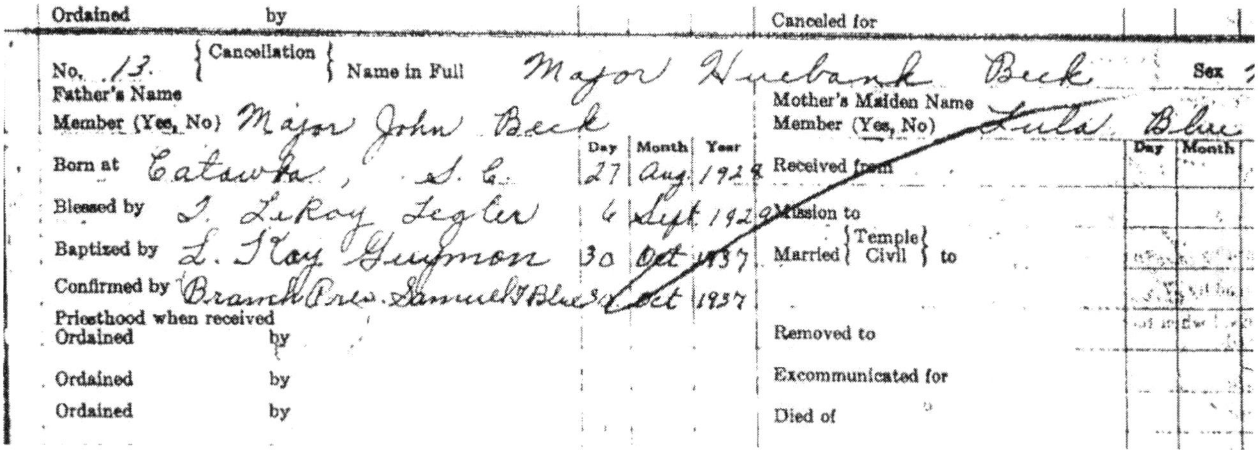

Ordained by
Canceled for
No. 13. {Cancellation} Name in Full Major Hucbank Beck
Sex
Father's Name
Member (Yes, No) Major John Beck
Mother's Maiden Name
Member (Yes, No) Lula Blue

| | | Day | Month | Year |
|---|---|---|---|---|
| Born at | Catawba, S. C. | 27 | Aug. | 1928 |
| Blessed by | I. LeRoy Zegler | 6 | Sept. | 1929 |
| Baptized by | L. Roy Guymon | 30 | Oct | 1937 |
| Confirmed by | Branch Pres. Samuel T Blue | | Oct | 1937 |

Priesthood when received
Ordained by
Ordained by
Ordained by

Received from
Mission to
Married {Temple / Civil} to
Removed to
Excommunicated for
Died of

**PHOTO 54 – L.D.S. BAPTISM RECORD FOR MAJOR HUBANK JOHN BECK**

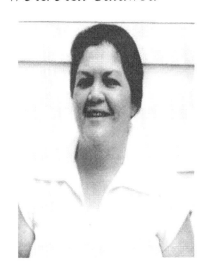

**PHOTO 55 - THELMA LOUISE BECK**

C. Thelma Louise Beck born 15 August 1931, Catawba, South Carolina and died 25 February 1987, Rock Hill, South Carolina. She married Dennis Leroy Bryson, (white) Born 1934.

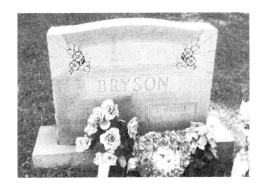

**PHOTO 56 - CHURCH OF JESUS CHRIST OF LATTER-DAY STS CEMETERY - BURIAL PLACE, CATAWBA, YORK COUNTY, SOUTH CAROLINA**

No. 14. Cancellation Name in Full Thelma Louise Beck Sex

Father's Name Member (Yes, No) Major John Beck

Mother's Maiden Name Member (Yes, No) Lula Blue

| | | Day | Month | Year |
|---|---|---|---|---|
| Born at | Catawba, S. C. | 15 | Aug | 1931 |
| Blessed by | M. F. McBride | 25 | Aug | 1931 |
| Baptized by | Howard C. Tate | 7 | Oct. | 1939 |
| Confirmed by | Willard M. Hayes | 7 | Oct. | 1939 |
| Priesthood when received Ordained by | | | | |
| Ordained by | | | | |
| Ordained by | | | | |
| Ordained by | | | | |

Received from

Mission to

Married {Temple / Civil} to

Removed to

Excommunicated for

Died of

Canceled for

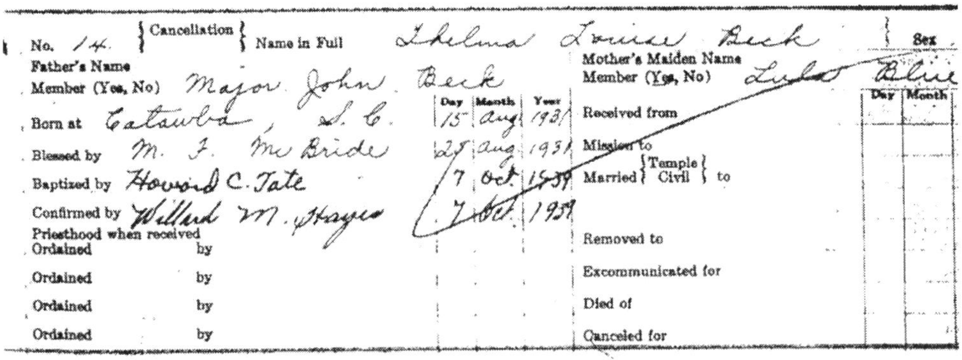

**PHOTO 57 – L.D.S. BAPTISM RECORD FOR THELMA LOUISE BECK**

## Chapter 3   Blue Family

I.   Margaret Ayers-George, born 4 July 1837,  Catawba Indian Nation, York, South Carolina and died 9 August 1922, Catawba Reservation, Rock Hill, York, South Carolina. Daughter of Edmund and Rebecca Mush - Mursh-Marsh Ayers. Margaret was one of two stepdaughters of Anthony George, that is the reason she us called by alternately Ayers and George.[74] She married first Joe Cherry a white man; second John William Brown and third Samuel Blue a white man.[75]  Margaret died 9 August 1922.[76]

She had the following children: Sally Brown, John Brown and Samuel Taylor Blue. See the others under Brown.

Margaret George Brown - Catawba Elder

July 4, 1837 - August 9, 1922
      Margaret George Brown was one of the last person in South Carolina to raise her children to speak the Catawba language. Born in 1837, Margaret lived on the Catawba Indian Nation reservation near Rock Hill her entire life.
      Her status as one of the last speakers of the Catawba language led her to become an invaluable source of information for numerous linguist and anthropologist. She was the daughter of Edmund and Rebecca Marsh George.
      Margaret's son, Samuel Taylor Blue, was the chief of the Catawba tribe from 1931 to 1959 and was considered the last native speaker of the Catawba language.
      Margaret was known as a master potter, making pots and pipes with tools inherited from her mother and grandmother. She would trade her pots for cornmeal, flour and food.
      Margaret used innovative methods to sell her pottery, barteringing from door-to-door in a covered wagon and meeting trains at Catawba Junction to sell to the passengers.
      She is buried at the Catawba Indian Nation Cemetery, Rock Hill, York County, South Carolina

---

[74] NOTE; JOHN SCOTT JR WAS THE UNCLE OF CHIEF SAM BLUE. SAM BLUE'S FATHER WAS WHITE, SO THE RELATIONSHIP HAD TO BE ON HIS MOTHER'S SIDE. REBECCA MUSH-MARSH HAD BOTH JOHN SCOTT AND THIS MARGARET; THUS, THIS MARGARET IS THE MOTHER OF SAM BLUE. MAKING JOHN SCOTT, SAM'S UNCLE.

[75] I call the union between white and Catawba married, although the white man most likely was married to a white woman at the time. I will not call any child illegitimate.

[76] Watson pages 16, 17, and 18.

**PHOTO 58 - MARGARET AYERS-GEORGE BROWN SAMUEL T BLUE'S MOTHER**

**PHOTO 59 – SAMUEL TAYLOR BLUE**

# Blue Family

A. Samuel Taylor Blue was born 15 August 1872. He married first, Minnie Hester George, daughter of Taylor and Emily Cobb George, and 2nd Louisa Jane Canty, daughter of George Washington and Mary Jane Elizabeth (Betsy Mush)-George Canty. Samuel had a great many children and the numbers are debatable.[77]

"One of the sterling men of the tribe and during the past 100 years was one of the significant men in the Nation. Even when others held the title, he was the Chief to outsiders because of his unique personality and friendly cooperation with white friends or others seeking information.[78]

His Catawba name was Nam'e Patki, meaning Big Bear.[79] Many things can be said of Chief Blue, and many have been said. A few things have not been printed in anything other than religious books. He was the Branch President of the Catawba Branch for 40 years, and was chief of the tribe for 20 years. The most compelling things about Chief Blue are told in his own words a story about the killing of his young son, Joseph Harvey in 1914.

"The following account given in his simple words by the late Chief Blue of the Catawba Indian Nation graphically reveals the power of self-control induced by his testimony of the Gospel. 'One day, my eleven year old son went hunting with six other Indians. They were hunting squirrels. A squirrel started up a pine a tree and my son climbed up the tree to scare him out on a limb. Finally the squirrel ran out where he could be seen. My boy called to the hunters to hold their fire until he could get down out of the tree. Now one of these Indians in the hunting party had always been jealous of me and my position as chief. He and his son both shot deliberately at my boy. He was filled with buckshot from his knees to his head. One blast was aimed at his groin and the other hit him squarely in the face. The Indians carried my boy towards our home and found a cooled spot under a pine tree. They laid him down and ran for a doctor. A friend came to me in Rock Hill where I had gone to buy goods and said, "Sam, run home at once: your boy has been shot." I thought it was one of my married sons. I ran all the way home and found it was my little boy near death. The doctor was there. He had put the boy to sleep with morphine so he wouldn't be in such pain. He said my boy would not live. He was right, the boy died in a few minutes. Now the man and his son who had done the shooting were out in my front yard visiting with members of the crowd that had gathered. They did not appear to be upset at their deed. My heart filled with revenge and hatred. Something seemed to whisper to me, "If you don't take down your gun and kill that man who murdered your son, Sam Blue, you are a coward.' Now I have been a Mormon ever since I have been a young lad, and I knew it would not be right to take revenge.

I decided to pray to the lord about it. I left the house and walked to my secret place out in the timber where I always have gone to pray alone when I have a special problem, and there I prayed to the Lord to take the revenge out of my heart. I soon felt better and I started back to the house. When I approached, I heard something inside of me whisper, 'Sam Blue if you don't kill that Indian who shot your boy, you are a coward.' I turned around and went back to my place of prayer and prayed until I felt better. Then on my way back to the house, the same spot along the path, I heard the voice say again, 'Sam Blue, you are coward.' I

---

[77] Ancestral File of Samuel Blue, sent by Priscilla Johnson.
[78] Brown, page 349.
[79] Ibid

turned again and went back to pray and this time I told the Lord he must help me or I would be a killer. I felt good when I got up from praying, I went back to the house a third time and when I reached the house I went out and shook hands with the Indian who had killed my boy. There was no hatred or desire for revenge in my heart."[80]

**The news account states:**

"A Catawba Indian lad named Blue, about 12 years old son of Sam Blue was killed yesterday by being accidentally shot by some of his companions. The accident occurred about noon and the boy died during the afternoon, having never regained consciousness. Coroner L. W. Louthian of Yorkville was summoned to the reservation by Indian Agent S. H. White. The coroner came over this morning and went down to the reservation accompanied by Constable F. C. Allen and Dr. J. E. Massey." The news account goes on, "The coroner empaneled a jury consisting of J. A. Waters, foreman; Billy Harris,[81] Robert Harris, David Harris, Lewis Gordon,[82] Taylor George, Farris Blankenship,[83] W. B. Rawlinson, William Sawyer,[84] Henry Canty, Frank Chantey and B. Harris.[85] The investigation disclosed the fact that the shooting was done by Walter,[86] Harris, son of Wesley Harris, a boy of about eleven years old. The details of the shooting were to be substantially as outlined above, with the exception that it was found that Wesley Harris, father of the boy, was in the hunting party and that he fired the shot that killed the Squirrel. The Harris boy fired at the squirrel about the same time and the load of shot from his gun struck the Blue boy."[87]

**PHOTO 60 - CHIEF SAM BLUE IN "OFFICIAL GARB" WORN WHEN REPRESENTING THE TRIBE AT PAGEANTS OR VISITING THE STATE CAPITAL. HIS GRANDSON IS CARRYING THE "CHIEF'S STANDARD" (1937) IN THE ROLL OF "STANDARD BEAR"**

---

[80] Romney, Marion G., The Power of God Unto Salvation, Speeches of the Year, Provo, Utah, Extension Publication, Brigham Young University, 1960 pages 6-7.
[81] Nephew of Wesley Harris.
[82] Son in Law of Samuel Blue
[83] Son-in-law of Samuel Blue.
[84] Brother of Wesley Harris
[85] Benjamin Perry Harris
[86] One of the sons of Lucinda Harris.
[87] Evening Herald, September 30, 1917, page 1.

**PHOTO 61 - SAMUEL TAYLOR BLUE AND HIS WIFE LOUISA JANE CANTY BLUE - CATAWBA INDIANS**

**PHOTO 62 - SAMUEL TAYLOR BLUE AND HIS WIFE LOUISA JANE CANTY BLUE - CATAWBA INDIANS**

**PHOTO 63 - CHIEF SAMUEL TAYLOR BLUE AND HIS WIFE LOUISA JANE CANTY BLUE**

**PHOTO 64 – CHIEF SAMUEL TAYLOR BLUE**

**PHOTO 65 - SAMUEL TAYLOR BLUE AND HIS WIFE LOUISA JANE CANTY BLUE**

**PHOTO 66 - SAMUEL AND LOUISA WITH FAMILY - CATAWBA INDIANS**

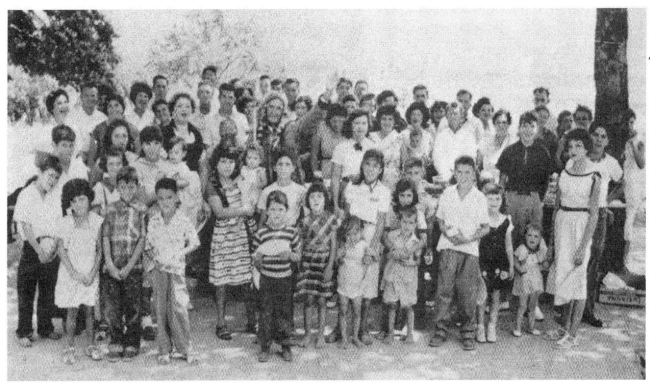

**PHOTO 67 - CHIEF SAMUEL TAYLOR BLUE'S FAMILY**

No. 22 {Cancellation} Name in Full Samuel Taylor Blue
Father's Name
Member (Yes, No) Samuel Blue
Mother's Maiden Name
Member (Yes, No) Margaret
Born at York Co., S. C. Day 15 Month Aug. Year 1873
Received from
Blessed by
Mission to
Baptized by J. A. Gordon 7 May 1897
Married {Temple Civil} to Louisa Canty
Confirmed by J. W. Parker Not Given
Priesthood when received
Ordained by
Removed to
Ordained by
Excommunicated for
Ordained by
Died of
Ordained by
Canceled for

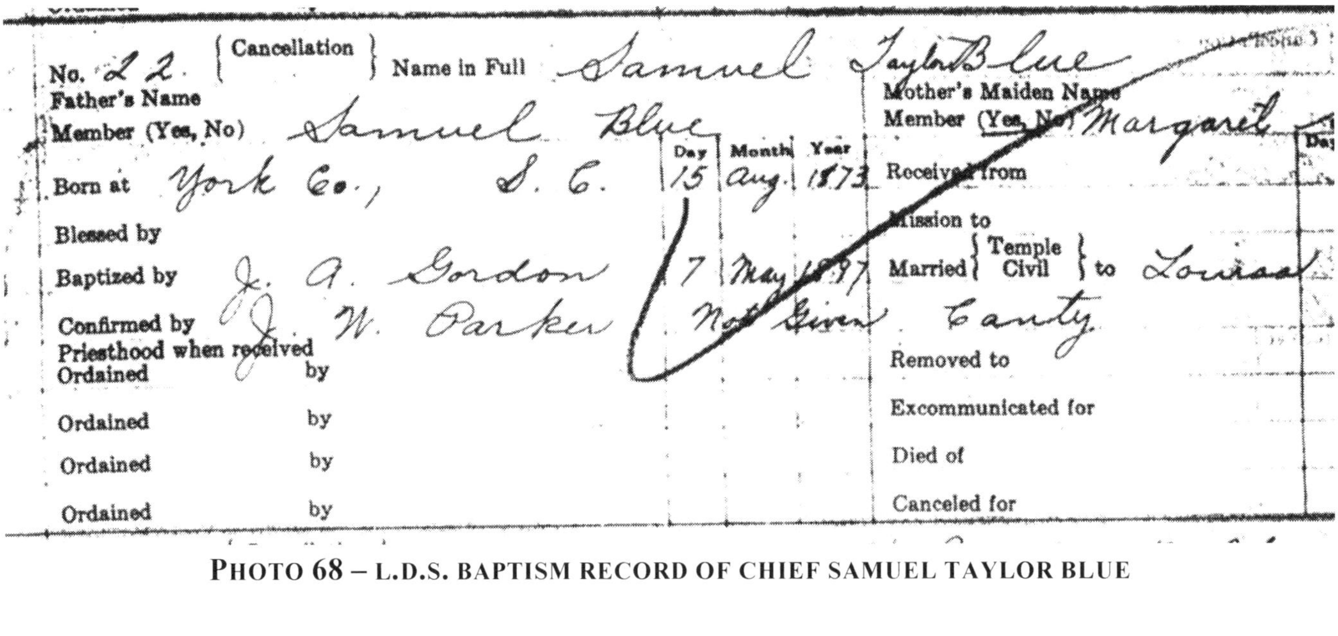

**PHOTO 68 – L.D.S. BAPTISM RECORD OF CHIEF SAMUEL TAYLOR BLUE**

# Bill McDermott shaves off mustache for role of Chief Blue in Indian drama

## By WILLETTE GAULT

The theatre sometimes demands great sacrifices of an actor.

Witness the offering required of William L. McDermott, who plays the role of Chief Sam Blue in "Kah-Woh, Catawba," Sept. 21-24, in Winthrop's auditorium.

"I've had that mustache off and on for 18 years," said McDermott.

## Chief Blue's son dies

The eldest son of a Catawba chief has died.

Samuel Andrew Blue, 59, of Rt. 3, Rock Hill, died at his home yesterday after an illness of about five months.

He was the eldest son of the late Chief Samuel T. Blue and Louisa Canty Blue.

Funeral service will be tomorrow at 3 p.m. at the Church of the Latter Day Saints. Burial will be in the church cemetery.

Survivors include his mother; the widow, Mrs. Doris Wheelock Blue; two sons, Harvey and Andrew; two daughters, Mildred of the home and Mrs. Guy Garcia; five brothers Nelson Herbert La

"But everybody knows that Chief Blue didn't have a mustache, and I wanted to be as authentic as possible."

Mrs. Emma Jane McDermott, wife of the Winthrop Fine Arts Department head, tells an interesting story connected with her husband's mustache.

"When we were dating, Billy Mack wore a mustache. He shaved it off for our wedding, but decided to grow another one after we were married. I objected and he agreed that he would not grow a mustache if I would prepare a dish of fried hash brown potatoes and onions once a week.

"I kept this up for about three

## Nature Museum to show Artist Guild's paintings

The York County Children's Nature Museum will host the art showing of the Artist Guild of York and Chester Counties beginning tomorrow.

J. Lee Settlemyre Jr., director of the museum, said today that approximately 33 paintings will be on display for throughout the rest of September.

months, but one week, I forgot. He re-grew the mustache. And he's had it ever since."

McDermott is one of the few actors in the Catawba Indian drama who is doing his own make-up job.

"I gathered up several pictures of the late Chief Blue, some taken from different angles."

By using these to go by, I tried to achieve as near a likeness as possible."

McDermott built up his nose with theatrical putty to resemble the late chief's.

"I feel a little like Cyrano de Bergerac with this new nose," he said.

The make-up process takes McDermott about two hours.

"I feel that I can improve on my make-up still," he said.

In last night's first dress rehearsal for "Kah-Woh, Catawba," McDermott appeared with white hair, a handsome new nose and no mustache.

No newcomer to community drama, McDermott was director of Rock Hill Little Theatre in 1948-49. Two of his productions were "Antigone" and "Arsenic and Old Lace."

"I would like to see another Little Theatre group begun in Rock Hill," said McDermott.

**PHOTO 69 – CHURCH OF JESUS CHRIST OF LATTER-DAY STS CEMETERY
BURIAL OR CREMATION PLACE CATAWBA, YORK COUNTY, SOUTH CAROLINA**

**Photo 70 - Sam Blue in front, back row 2ⁿᵈ
From left Lydia Harris and 6ᵗʰ from left Walter Harris. 1932**

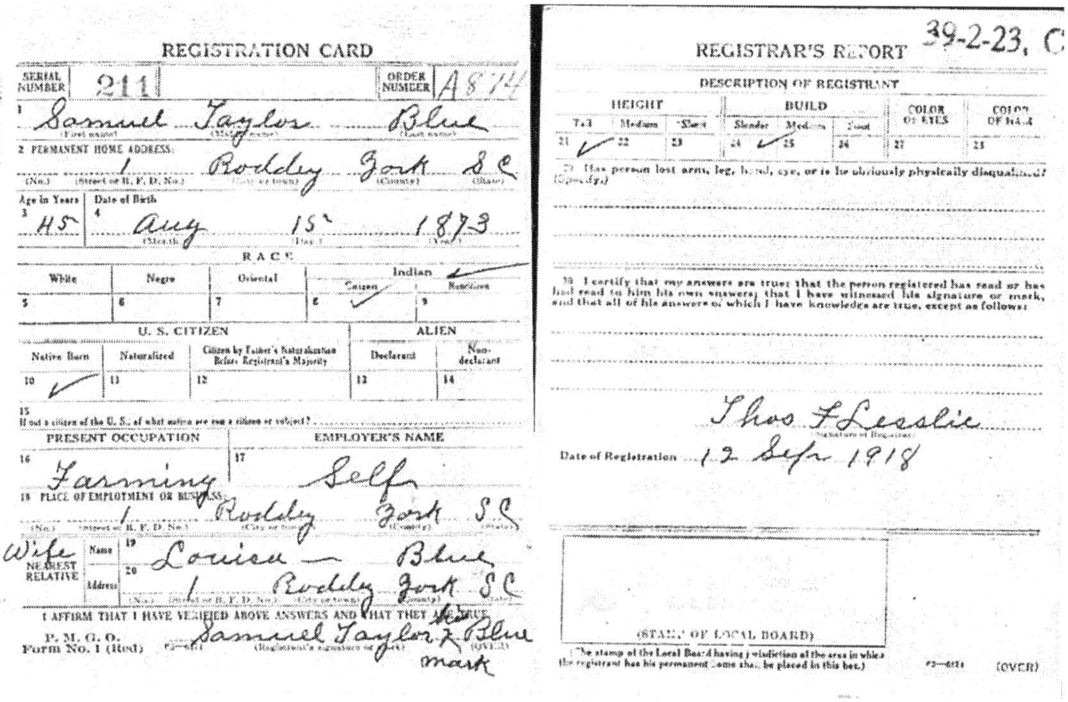

**PHOTO 71 - SAMUEL TAYLOR BLUE WWI DRAFT REGISTRATION CARD**

The Deseret News - August 22, 1959, page 5

# Catawba Indians Carry On Despite Loss Of Chief Blue

The Catawba Indian tribe continues to operate a successful branch of the South Carolina Stake despite the recent death of their veteran chief and branch president, Chief Samuel Taylor Blue.

Chief Blue was president of the Catawba branch for 40 years.

His tribe, which numbered 10,000 members in the year 1701, had diminished through wars and disease to some 300 when the first Mormon Elders, Charles Robertson and Henry Miller, began holding meetings with them in 1883. Since that time 95 per cent of the Cataw-

bas joined the Church.

Chief Blue was 14 years old when he married his first wife, Minnie George. She died seven years after their marriage.

According to information supplied by his granddaughter, Margaret Blue Sanders, Chief Blue remarried in 1896 and 54 years later took his second wife, Louisa Hesta Canty, to Salt Lake City for a Temple marriage. He died April 16, 1959, in his home on the reservation.

Obituaries carried in South Carolina papers credited Chief Blue with 119 grandchildren. Two great-grandchildren,

Roger and Gloria Trimmsal, are attending the BYU.

Funeral services for the 86-year-old Chief were held in the attractive white chapel erected on the banks of the Catawba river, 10 miles from Rock Hill, S.C., for the use of the Catawba Branch. The building was dedicated in 1952 by President David O. McKay with Chief Blue taking part as a speaker in the dedicatory services.

**PHOTO 72 – NEWSPAPER ARTICLE ABOUT DEATH OF SAMUEL TAYLOR BLUE**

**From the missionary journal of Sister Mary Barrus**

"Bro Blue told us of having his leg broken & blood poison (sic) setting in. It turned purple & the Dr said it much be cut off above the knee. He refused to have it done but prayed for the elders to come. Without any appointment two elders were impressed to come to his home & administered to him. He was healed & went to church the next Sunday walking all the way. Truly a miracle.

Bro Blue used to haul wood to Rock Hill abt once a week. He was sort of a father to the whole tribe the main chief. The Indians used to send for little & big items by him to the stores & he felt that he owed it to them to do this for them. One time they had given Bro blue several dollars & since he could not read or write he used his wonderful memory to buy & bring to the Indians the needed items. As he jolted along the money dropped out of his pocket. He prayed Lord show me where to find that money. After his prayer he took a few steps & found every cent of it in a pile – dollars at the bottom then halves, quarters & nickels & dimes just as neatly as tho they had been done by human hands.

I heard him bear this testimony & I know he tol-1927d the truth. Bro Blue is a man God loves. An Indian but a good upright one. when our mission was over he took us to the train & cried like a child to see us leave.

He said I love the very ground they walk on."

**"Bro Blue's cotton**

Bro Samuel T. Blue was the main man in the Catawba tribe. He owned three mules & a cow. He pd. his tithing strictly – kept the commandments in every way. At one time after he had taken his bales of cotton to market, he discovered that they had pd. him 10.00 too much. The next day he called on the buyer at Rock Hill and handed the money back. The mistake had not been discovered. In answer to the question of surprise about his honesty he explained the stand of the Mormon people.

Everybody trusted Bro Blue. He was healed by the administration of the elders when his leg had been broken and crushed. It became infected – turned black & Drs said it must be cut off. His family had great faith. They were fine characters Bro Blue's testimony."

**Chief Blue's testimony**

In 1883, Mormon missionaries found refuge among the small log cabins on the Catawba Indian Reservation near Rock Hill, South Carolina. The missionaries had received hostile treatment from the Catawbas' white neighbors, who tarred- and feathered them and threatened their lives. The Catawbas' hospitality was a welcome relief. They provided missionaries with food and shelter, and the missionaries shared with them the gospel's truths. His missionaries' sincere interest in these people soon bore fruit, and Catawba baptisms were performed regularly.

# Blue Family

One of the early converts was 15-year-old Samuel Taylor Blue, who lived with his mother and several younger brothers and sisters. His 25-cents-a-day job kept the family clothed and fed, and he later shared his meager belongings with many missionaries. Samuel Blue readily accepted the gospel and became the Church's chief spokesman to the tribal leaders.

Brother Blue was an outgoing person, who represented his tribe in their dealings with government officials. On all these occasions, he spoke eloquently in his people's behalf. His leadership was soon recognized, and be was elected chief of the tribe —a position he held for over 20 years. When the Church organized a branch on the reservation after the turn of the century, Brother Blue became its first president The branch flourished under his leadership and by 1984, most of the Catawba's were Church members.

Brother Blue received no formal education, so he could neither read nor 'write. His children and grandchildren read him the scriptures, and be memorized the passages he needed for his talks. By the end of his life, he had memorized much of the Bible. In 1960, he and his wife traveled to Salt Lake City to be sealed in the temple. They also attended general conference, where the First Presidency called on him to speak extemporaneously, and his unwavering testimony was broadcast to thousands. His unfaltering faith sustained him until his death at the age of 84. — Jeffery O Johnson

## PROFILES FROM THE PAST

In September of 1953, Samuel Taylor Blue spoke at the Catawba Baptist Church, which had a non-Indian congregation. At the time, Samuel was still Branch President of the Catawba Branch of the LDS Church.[88] Samuel opened a class on Catawba crafts at the Rock Hill Museum in 1953.[89]

**Samuel Taylor Blue and Minnie Hester George had two children:**

**PHOTO 73 – FREDERICK NELSON BLUE AND WIFE LUCY LEOLA WATTS**

---

[88] Blumer paae 357 article 2873
[89] Ibid

1. Frederick Nelson Blue, born October 25, 1889, Catawba Indian Reservation, South Carolina. He married Lucy Leola Watts. She died in July 1969 in Salt Lake City. Nelson was a student in Mrs. Dunlap's school in 1899. Nelson was charged with slashing H. N. Baley of the Industrial Community in 1927.[90] He served as Chief from 1950-1952 and a few months in 1958. Fred died 8 August 1980,[91] Rock Hill, York, South Carolina.

**PHOTO 74 – WWI DRAFT REGISTRATION CARD FOR FRED NELSON BLUE**

**PHOTO 75 - CHURCH OF JESUS CHRIST OF LATTER-DAY STS CEMETERY -- BURIAL PLACE - CATAWBA, YORK COUNTY, SOUTH CAROLINA**

---

[90] Blumer page 294.
[91] Blumer page 468 articles 3938, 3940, 3944.

**Frederick Nelson Blue and wife Lucy Leola Watts – their six children are:**

PHOTO 76 – MAMIE AZALEE BLUE

a. Mamie Azalee Blue born 18 September 1912, Catawba Nation, South Carolina and died 8 November 1999, Rock Hill, York, South Carolina, United States. She married Roddey Benjamin Adams, not Catawba.

PHOTO 77 - TWO PICTURES OF MAMI AZALEE BLUE

b. Lucile Freddie Blue born 13 November 1915,[92] Catawba, York, South Carolina and died 1 September 1987, Rock Hill, York, South Carolina, United States . She married Carl Walter McGhee, white. A stepchild, Wayne, is listed as white.

> Lucille B Mcghee- in the Web: Columbia, South Carolina, Obituary Index, 1892-1994
> Lucille B Mcghee  Publication Date: 2 Sep 1987
> Publication Place: Columbia, Richland, South Carolina, United States  -
> Death Date:    Abt 1987
> U.S., Social Security Death Index, 1935-2014
>  Name Lucille McGhee   --   SSN     251-16-9211
> Last Residence   --   Rock Hill, 29730, York, South Carolina
> Born    13 Nov 1914,   Died    Sep 1987
> State (Year) SSN issued       South Carolina - Before 1951

**PHOTO 78 - BURIAL: CHURCH OF JESUS CHRIST OF LATTER-DAY STS CEMETERY, CATAWBA, YORK COUNTY, SOUTH CAROLINA**

---

[92] 1920 census York County, page listing Nelson & Leola's family.

**PHOTO 79 - LILLIAN"LILLIE" VIOLA BLUE**

c. Lillian (Lillie) Viola Blue born 10 September 1919, Catawba Reservation, York, South Carolina and died 15 May 2002, Kaysville, Davis, Utah, United States and she married Horace Hunter, white.

U.S., Social Security Death Index, 1935-2014
Name Lillie V. Hunter - SSN ,249-12-3348 - Last Residence , Kaysville, 84037, Davis, Utah, Born 10 Sep 1918, Died 15 May 2002
State (Year) SSN issued - South Carolina - Before 1951

**Obituary**

Birth: Sep. 10, 1918 - Death: May 15, 2002
Standard-Examiner (Ogden, UT) - Sunday, May 19, 2002

Lillie Viola (Blue) Hunter, age 83, passed away peacefully at her home in Kaysville, UT on Wednesday, May 15, 2002 and has been reunited with her beloved Horace, who preceded her in death in 1976. On the Sunday before her passing, Lillie had an enjoyable Mother's Day with her family, surrounded by all of her grandchildren and great-grandchildren.

She was born on Sep 10, 1918 in Catawba, SC to Fred Nelson Blue and Lucy Leola (Watts) Blue. She is survived by a sister (Mary Jane Elkins of Rock Hill, SC), a daughter (VaLoy Walsh of Chehalis, WA), a son (Calvin Hunter of Layton, UT), four grandchildren, and six great-grandchildren.

She was preceded in death by three sisters: Mamie Azalea Adams, Freddie Lucille McGhee, and Margaret Alberta Blue; and two brothers: Marion Nelson Blue and Clarence Taylor Blue.

Lillie was a Native American of the Catawba Indian Nation and was born on the Reservation. She and Horace Calvin Hunter were married August 8, 1942 in Lancaster SC and lived in Rock Hill, SC until they and their children moved to Utah in 1959. They solemnized their marriage in the Salt Lake City Temple, on March 28, 1960. She was a life-long member of The Church of Jesus Christ of Latter-Day Saints. Her most frequent calling was working with children in the Primary, where she served faithfully and touched the lives of several generations.

She and Horace served a Church mission in the Salt Lake Stake, where they were instrumental in bringing the truth to people that they came to know and love. The extent of the influence of that service and the number of lives that have been affected is difficult to measure and has now extended into the third generation. Lillie was loved by her family and friends will be deeply missed.

The Funeral Service will be held on Tuesday, May 21, 2002 at Wasatch Lawn Memorial Park Mortuary, 3401 Highland Dr, SLC, UT.

**PHOTO 80 – MARY JANE BLUE**

d. Mary Jane Blue born 6 February 1921, Catawba Reservation, York, South Carolina and died 29 October 2011, Rock Hill, York, South Carolina. She first married Ernest DaNiel (Buck) Rogers and then married an Mr Elkins.

> Mary Jane Blue Rogers Elkins in the U.S., Obituary Collection, 1930-2015
> Name: Mary Jane Blue Rogers Elkins  -  Gender:  Female
> Birth Place:   Rock Hill, York, South Carolina

Residence (at time of death): Rock Hill, South Carolina

Death Date: 29 Oct 2011 --- Obituary Date: 30 Oct 2011

Spouse: Mike

Parents: Fred Nelson and Leola Watts Blue

Children: Mary Beth Spell and husband, Mike, of Rock Hill and Wanda Pryor and husband, Sanford, of York; Mary Beth Spell

**PHOTO 81 - FOREST HILLS CEMETERY --
BURIAL PLACE- ROCK HILL, YORK COUNTY, SOUTH CAROLINA**

e. Clarence Blue born in 13 April 1923, Catawba,York,South Carolina and died before 1958, He is 18 in 1943. He served in the armed forces and is listed in 1944; however, he is not listed in the 1958 membership roll.

**PHOTO 82 - MARGARET ALBERTA BLUE**

f. Margaret Alberta Blue born 20 December 1924, married first Gene Medlin and had William Lamon, Nora Jean and Charles Robert Medlin; she married second Fred

Sanders, son of John Idle and Arzada Brown Sanders, and they had Freda and Sonji Nell Sanders. Those children will be found under Fred Sanders, in Lucinda Harris Chapter.

Obituary --- Birth: Dec. 20, 1924 --Death: Mar. 13, 1992
Charlotte Observer, The (NC) - Sunday, March 15, 1992
Margaret Blue, Homemaker 67, died March 13, 1992, at Piedmont Medical Center. Funeral is Monday at Greene Funeral Home, with the Rev. David Sealy officiating. Burial will be in Church of Jesus Christ of Latter-day Saints Cemetery in Catawba.
        Mrs. Blue, a homemaker and member of Park Baptist Church, was born in Rock Hill, South Carolina.

**PHOTO 83 - CHURCH OF JESUS CHRIST OF LATTER-DAY STS CEMETERY --
BURIAL PLACE - CATAWBA, YORK COUNTY, SOUTH CAROLINA**

\*\*\*\*\*\*\*\*\*\*\*\*\*\*\*\*\*\*\*\*\*\*\*\*

**PHOTO 84 – NORA LILLIE BLUE**

2. Nora Lillie Blue, born November 12, 1893. Lillie was also a student of Mrs. Dunlap in 1899.[93]  She was ill in 1914 and a picnic was postponed because of her illness. She married Farris Blankenship a white man and died May 26, 1915 in childbirth.[94]  Four children died in infancy.

**PHOTO 85 - INSCRIPTION: SHE IS BURIED WITH FOUR CHILDREN WHO DIED IN INFANCY.  SHE WAS THE DAUGHTER OF SAMUEL T. BLUE AND MINNIE HESTER GEORGE BLUE.**
**BURIAL:  CATAWBA INDIAN NATION CEMETERY, ROCK HILL, YORK COUNTY, SOUTH CAROLINA**

---

[93] Blumer page 213 article 1555
[94] Watson page 18

**PHOTO 86 – CERTIFICATE OF DEATH FOR NORA LILLIE BLUE BLANKENSHIP**

**PHOTO 87 – BOTTOM OF HEADSTONE FOR NORA LILLIE BLUE BLANDENSHIP**

3. Rodah Conneila Blue born around 1895 died in infancy.[95] Child of Samuel T blue and Minnie Hester George Blue

**Samuel married second Louisa Canty, daughter of George Washington and Mary Jane Elizabeth (Betsy) Mush-George Canty.**

**PHOTO 88 - HERBERT BLUE**

4. Herbert Blue born April 25, 1898 married first Lavinia Harris, on February 1915,[96] daughter of David Adam and Lizzie Patterson-Watts Harris; she died in 1916 of TB.[97]

They were married by Benjamin Perry Harris. Herbert married second Lula Addie Mae Blankenship, on 2 May 1918. Lula was white. Herbert was the Branch President of the LSD Church during the years when the Termination Roll was published in 1960-61 and he was made supervisor of the Catawba lands.

Daddy eating watermelon.

**PHOTO 89 – HERBERT BLUE EATING WATERMELON**

---

[95] Ibid, Ian Watson gives birth year as around 1890
[96] Announcement of marriage, March 1, 1915 page 2.
[97] Obituary of Lavina Harris Blue, listing family, Record, July 27, 1916.

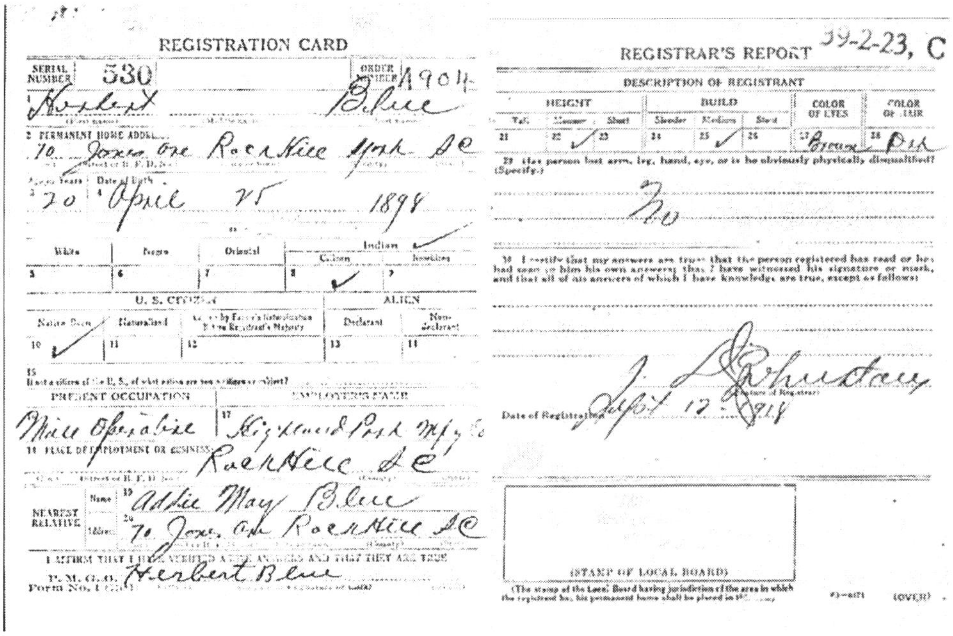
REGISTRATION CARD

SERIAL NUMBER 530 ORDER NUMBER A904

Herbert Blue

2 PERMANENT HOME ADDRESS
70 Jones Ave Rock Hill York SC

Age in Years 20 Date of Birth April 25 1898

Indian ✓

U. S. CITIZEN — Native Born ✓

PRESENT OCCUPATION: Mill Operative
EMPLOYER'S NAME: Highland Park Mfg Co
PLACE OF EMPLOYMENT OR BUSINESS: Rock Hill SC

NEAREST RELATIVE — Name: Addie May Blue — Address: 70 Jones Ave Rock Hill SC

I AFFIRM THAT I HAVE VERIFIED ABOVE ANSWERS AND THAT THEY ARE TRUE
Herbert Blue

P. M. G. O. Form No. 1

REGISTRAR'S REPORT 39-2-23, C

DESCRIPTION OF REGISTRANT

| HEIGHT | | | BUILD | | | COLOR OF EYES | COLOR OF HAIR |
|---|---|---|---|---|---|---|---|
| Tall | Medium | Short | Slender | Medium | Stout | | |
| 21 | 22 ✓ | 23 | 24 | 25 ✓ | 26 | 27 Brown | 28 Blk |

29 Has person lost arm, leg, hand, eye, or is he obviously physically disqualified? (Specify.) No

30 I certify that my answers are true; that the person registered has read or has had read to him his own answers; that I have witnessed his signature or mark, and that all of his answers of which I have knowledge are true, except as follows:

Date of Registration Sept 12 1918

(STAMP OF LOCAL BOARD)

(OVER)

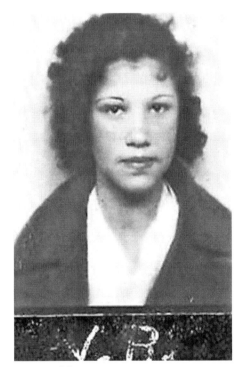

**PHOTO 90 – WWI REGISGTRATION CARD FOR HERBERT BLUE**

**PHOTO 91 – VIRGINIA LOUISE BLUE**

a. Virginia Louise Blue born 4 December 1920, Catawba, York, South Carolina and died 27 November 1992, Everett, King, Texas, United States. She married Thomas Woodrow Trimnal, white.

**Photo 92 - Burial: Laurelwood CEMETERY - Rock Hill, York County, South Carolina**
**Plot: Section 7, lot 62, A**

**U.S., Social Security Death Index, 1935-2014**
Name  Virginia B. Trimnal     SSN    251-38-8342
Last Residence  - Rock Hill, 29730, York, South Carolina
Born    4 Dec 1920  ---   Died   Nov 1992
State (Year) SSN issued         South Carolina - Before 1951

**Virginia Louise Blue and Thomas Woodrow Trimnal had three children"**

**Photo 93 – Gloria June Trimnal**

(1). Gloria June Trimnal born 5 July 1938, Catawba, South Carolina and she died 22 March 1981, Fullerton, Orange, California, United States. She married Wayne Fay Bales. Utah, Select Marriage Index, 1887-1985

**Utah, Select Marriage Index, 1887-1985**
Name:　　　　　Gloria June Trimnal - Gender: Female:
Marriage Date:　29 May 1964
Marriage Place: Utah, UT - Spouse: Floyd Wayne Bales

**PHOTO 94 - BURIAL: LOMA VISTA MEMORIAL PARK -- FULLERTON, ORANGE COUNTY, CALIFORNIA PLOT: ENDURING FAITH LAWN**

**PHOTO 95 - ROGER SNOW TRIMNAL**

(2). Roger Snow Trimnal born 23 January 1940, Catawba, South Carolina. He married Rene Merrill.

**PHOTO 96 - ROGER SNOW TIRMNAL**

**PHOTO 97 – MAE CAROL TRIMNAL IN 1959-1960**

(3). Mae Carol Trimnal born 1943 and she married Gary Dean Williams.

\*\*\*\*\*\*\*\*\*\*\*\*\*\*\*\*\*\*\*\*\*\*\*\*\*\*\*\*\*\*\*\*\*\*\*\*\*\*\*\*\*\*\*\*\*\*\*\*\*\*\*\*\*\*

b. Marcile Elizabeth Blue born 15 January 1924, Catawba, South Carolina and died 22 April 2006, Catawba, South Carolina, United States. She married William Forest Cabaniss, white.

**U.S., Social Security Death Index, 1935-2014**
>   Name: Marcile Blue Cabaniss
>   Last Residence:   29730 Rock Hill, York, South Carolina
>   BORN: 15 Feb 1924  ---  Died:  22 Apr 2006
>   State (Year) SSN issued:      South Carolina (1952)

**PHOTO 98 - BURIAL:  GRANDVIEW MEMORIAL PARK -- ROCK HILL, YORK COUNTY, SOUTH CAROLINA**

**PHOTO 99 - HERBERT ROOSEVELT BLUE WITH  UNKNOWN CHILD**

c. Herbert Roosevelt Blue born 3 February 1927,[98] Catawba, South Carolina and died 11 October 2009,  Fort Lawn, Chester, South Carolina. He never married.[99]

---

[98] Ibid
[99] Ibid

**Obituary:**

Herbert Roosevelt Blue (February 3, 1927 - October 11, 2009) ROCK HILL - Herbert R. Blue, 82, of 261 S. Herlong Ave., died Sunday, Oct. 11, 2009, at Unihealth PAC of Rock Hill. A graveside service will be 3 p.m. Wednesday at Laurelwwod Cemetery. He is survived by several nieces and nephews.

**PHOTO 100 - BURIAL:  LAURELWOOD CEMETERY, ROCK HILL, YORK COUNTY, SOUTH CAROLINA
PLOT: SECTION -- 7, LOT 62, A**

\*\*\*\*\*\*\*\*\*\*\*\*\*\*\*\*\*\*\*\*\*\*\*\*\*\*\*\*\*\*\*\*\*\*\*\*\*\*\*\*\*\*\*\*\*\*

**PHOTO 101 - SAMUEL ANDREW BLUE**

5. Samuel Andrew Blue born October 6, 1900, Rock Hill, York, South Carolina. He married Doris Belle Wheelock, daughter of Archie and Rosa Harris Wheelock. In 1929, Andrew was involved in a shooting over chickens, and Burt Thatcher was injured. Andrew died 19 September 1960 in Rock Hill, York, South Carolina after a five month illness.[100]

**PHOTO 102- BURIAL: CHURCH OF JESUS CHRIST OF LATTER-DAY STS CEMETERY CATAWBA, YORK COUNTY, SOUTH CAROLINA**

---

[100] Blumer page 396 article #3216

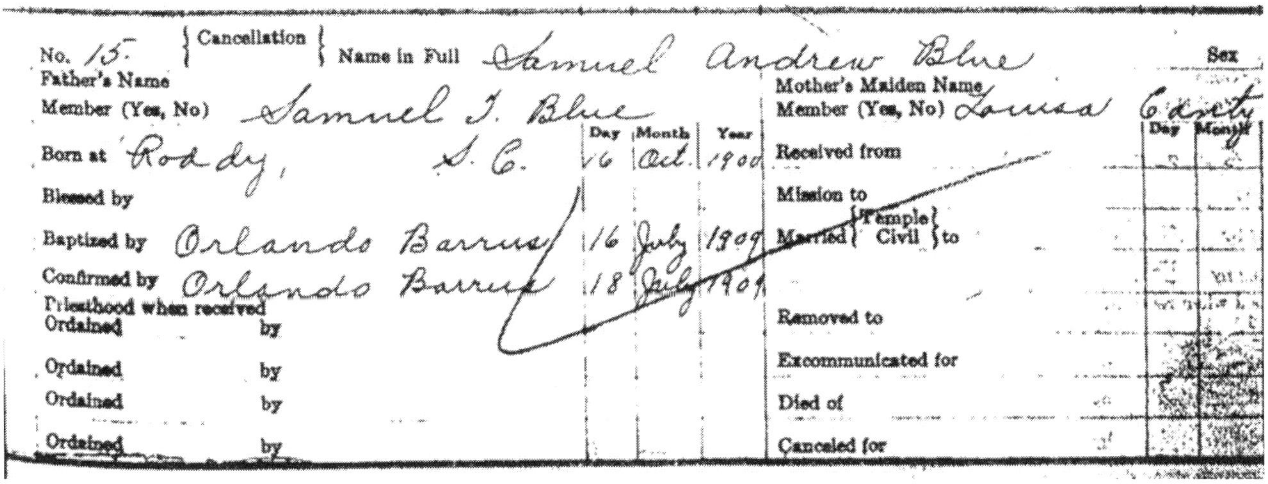
No. 15 Cancellation Name in Full Samuel Andrew Blue Sex
Father's Name Member (Yes, No) Samuel T. Blue
Mother's Maiden Name Member (Yes, No) Louisa Canty
Born at Roddy, S. C. Day 16 Month Oct. Year 1900
Received from
Blessed by
Mission to
Baptized by Orlando Barrus 16 July 1909
Married Temple Civil to
Confirmed by Orlando Barrus 18 July 1909
Priesthood when received
Ordained by
Removed to
Ordained by
Excommunicated for
Ordained by
Died of
Ordained by
Canceled for

**PHOTO 103 – L.D.S. BAPTISM RECORD FOR SAMUEL ANDREW BLUE**

# Chief Blue's son dies

The eldest son of a Catawba chief has died.

Samuel Andrew Blue, 59, of Rt. 3, Rock Hill, died at his home yesterday after an illness of about five months.

He was the eldest son of the late Chief Samuel T. Blue and Louisa Canty Blue.

Funeral service will be tomorrow at 3 p.m. at the Church of the Latter Day Saints. Burial will be in the church cemetery.

Survivors include his mother; the widow, Mrs. Doris Wheelock Blue; two sons, Harvey and Andrew; two daughters, Mildred of the home and Mrs. Guy Garcia; five brothers, Nelson, Herbert, Leroy, Guy, Arnold; three sisters, Mrs. Albert Sanders, wife of the current Catawba chief, Mrs. Major Beck, Mrs. Landrum George; and two grandchildren.

Blue was employed at the Rock Hill Printing and Finishing Co. for 30 years.

The body will be taken to the home late this afternoon.

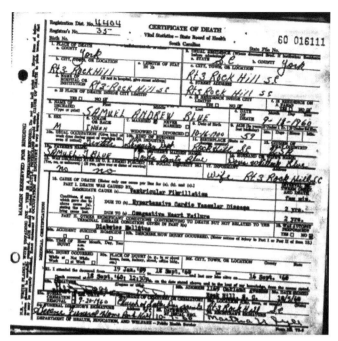

PHOTO 104 – CERTIFICATION OF DEATH FOR SAMUEL ANDREW BLUE

**Samuel Andrew Blue and Doris Belle Wheelock's children are Mildred, Betty, Harvey & Andrew Blue.**

PHOTO 105 - MILDRED LOUISE BLUE

a. Mildred Louise Blue born 4 August 1922, Catawba, South Carolina and died 16 October 1997, Rock Hill, York, South Carolina, United States. She was the first member of the South Carolina Catawba to graduate from high school. Members of the Western Catawba had graduated before this time in Colorado and Utah. Mildred was not married in 1958, and she died in 1997. Mildred was considered a master potter.

**PHOTO 106 - CHURCH OF JESUS CHRIST OF LATTER-DAY STS. CEMETERY - BURIAL OR CREMATION PLACE CATAWBA, YORK COUNTY, SOUTH CAROLINA**

**PHOTO 107 - BETTY JUANITA BLUE**

b. Betty Juanita Blue born 13 December 1924. She married Guy Garcia, son of Rufus and Abbie Patterson Garcia a Western Catawba.

Edward Guy Garcia Birth 15 September 1912 in Sanford, Conejos, Colorado and he died 1 October 2000, Catawba Reservation, South Carolina. More about him will be under Patterson, Abbie Ellen.

**Edward G. Garcia in the U.S., Social Security Death Index, 1935-2014**
Name: Edward G. Garcia          SSN:   524-09-0883
Last Residence: 29730 Rock Hill, York, South Carolina
BORN:          15 Sep 1912          Died:   1 Oct 2000
State (Year) SSN issued:       Colorado (Before 1951)


c.  Harvey Wheelock Blue born 26 April 1930, Catawba Indian Nation, York, South Carolina and died 27 April 1985, Camden, Kershaw County, South Carolina. He married Mildred Lillian Davis.
Burial: Forest Lawn Memorial Park, Camden, Kershaw County, South Carolina

d. Andrew Gene Blue born 20 July 1938, Catawba, York, South Carolina and he married Margaret De Lillion Kennedy,

e. Harry Reid Blue born 23 August 1947,  Catawba Nation, York, South Carolina

\*\*\*\*\*\*\*\*\*\*\*\*\*\*\*\*\*\*\*\*\*\*\*\*\*\*\*\*\*\*\*\*\*\*\*\*\*\*\*\*\*\*\*\*\*\*\*\*

**Samuel Taylor Blue and Louisa Hester Jane Canty's children continued**

**PHOTO 108 - JOSSEPH HARVEY BLUE**

6. Joseph Harvey Blue born March 3, 1903, died January 1914. See the account of his death below.

# CATAWBA INDIAN BOY
# KILLED BY ACCIDENT

## Son of Sam Blue Shot by Companion While Squirel [Hunting—Coroner Louthian Investigating the Matter Today.

A Catawba Indian lad named Blue, about 12 years old, a son of Sam Blue, was killed yesterday by being accidentally shot by some of his companions. The accident occurred about noon and the boy died during the afternoon, having never regained consciousness.

Coroner L. W. Louthian of Yorkville was summoned to the reservation by Indian Agent S. H. White. The coroner came over this morning and went down to the reservation, accompanied by Constable F. C. Allen and Dr. J. E. Massey. The gentlemen are expected to return to the city this afternoon, when it will be learned more definitely how the accident occurred.

From the best information obtainable by Indian Agent White it seems that the Blue boy and several other Indian lads were hunting squirrels on the Barber lands, probably a mile and a half from the reservation. The Blue lad climbed a tree to get at a squirrel nest, and when one of the animals ran out on a branch of the tree two of the boys standing on the ground fired at the squirrel. The squirrel was killed, but a good portion of two loads of shot struck the boy in the face and side. It seems that the boys who did the shooting were Walter Harris and Early Brown. This fact, however, has not been definitely ascertained, as the boys in the crowd are still much excited and have told conflicting stories. However there appears to be no doubt that the shooting was an accident, caused by the boys becoming excited and firing at the squirrel while the Blue boy was still within range of their guns.

#### Later Details of Accident.

Coroner Louthian, Dr. Massey and Constable Allen returned to the city this afternoon at 2:30 o'clock, after having made an investigation of the killing of Harvey Blue, as that was the name of the boy killed. The coroner empanelled a jury, consisting of J. A. Waters, foreman; Billy Harris, Robert Harris, David Harris, Lewis Gordon, Taylor George, Farris Blankenship, W. B. Rawlinson, William Sawyer, Henry Cantey, Frank Cantey and B. Harris.

The investigation disclosed the fact that the shooting was done by Walter Harris, son of Wesley Harris, a boy about eleven years old. The details of the shooting were found to be substantially as outlined above, with the exception that it was found Wesley Harris, the father of the boy, was in the hunting party and that he fired the shot that killed the squirrel. The Harris boy fired at the squirrel about the same time, and the load of shot from his gun struck the Blue boy.

Dr. Massey stated to a representative of the Herald that the charge of shot must have been a very heavy one as it struck the boy in the side of the face and eyes and in the arm and left side. Both eyes were destroyed, and there was no possible chance for the boy to recover. He lived, however, about six hours after being shot.

The verdict of the jury in the case was that the boy came to his death after being shot by Walter Harris and that the shooting was accidental.

**PHOTO 109 - LULA HENRIETTA BLUE**

7. Lula Henrietta Blue, born 3 May 1905, Rock Hill, York County, South Carolina and died 11 May 1996, Rock Hill, York County, South Carolina. She married Major John Beck. Children will be found under John Beck.

**PHOTO 110 - LULA HENRIETTA BLUE AND SON SAMUEL BECK**

**PHOTO 111 - CHURCH OF JESUS CHRIST OF LATTER-DAY STS CEMETERY - BURIAL PLACE CATAWBA, YORK COUNTY, SOUTH CAROLINA**

**PHOTO 112 - HENRY LEROY BLUE**

8. Henry Leroy Blue, born 14 August 1907, South Carolina and died 11 July 2002, Rock Hill, York County, South Carolina. He married January 21, 1933, Era Mae Bodiford, daughter of Dock and Lou Ella Holley Bodiford, white.[101]

---

101

**PHOTO 113 - HENRY LEROY BLUE AND ERA MAE BODIFORD WITH CHILDREN AND HENRY SETTING ON A CANOE**

**PHOTO 114 - HENRY LEROY BLUE AND ERA MAE BODIFORD**

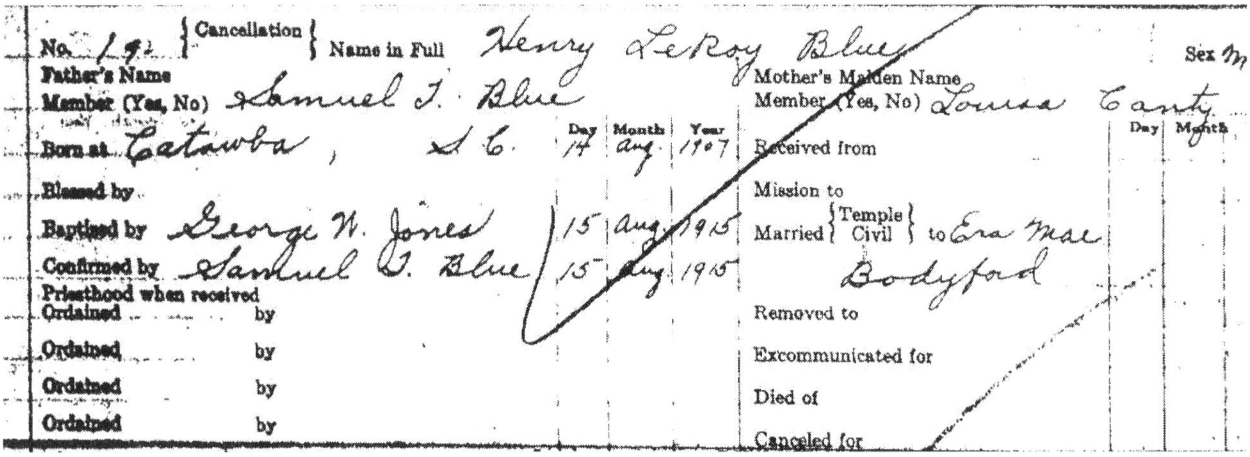

No. 19 {Cancellation} Name in Full Henry LeRoy Blue Sex M
Father's Name
Member (Yes, No) Samuel T. Blue
Mother's Maiden Name
Member (Yes, No) Louisa Canty
Born at Catawba, S.C. Day 14 Month Aug Year 1907
Received from
Blessed by
Mission to
Baptized by George W. Jones 15 Aug 1915
Married {Temple / Civil} to Era Mae Bodyford
Confirmed by Samuel T. Blue 15 Aug 1915
Priesthood when received
Ordained by
Removed to
Ordained by
Excommunicated for
Ordained by
Died of
Ordained by
Canceled for

**PHOTO 115 – L.D.S. BAPTISM RECORD FOR HENRY LEROY BLUE**

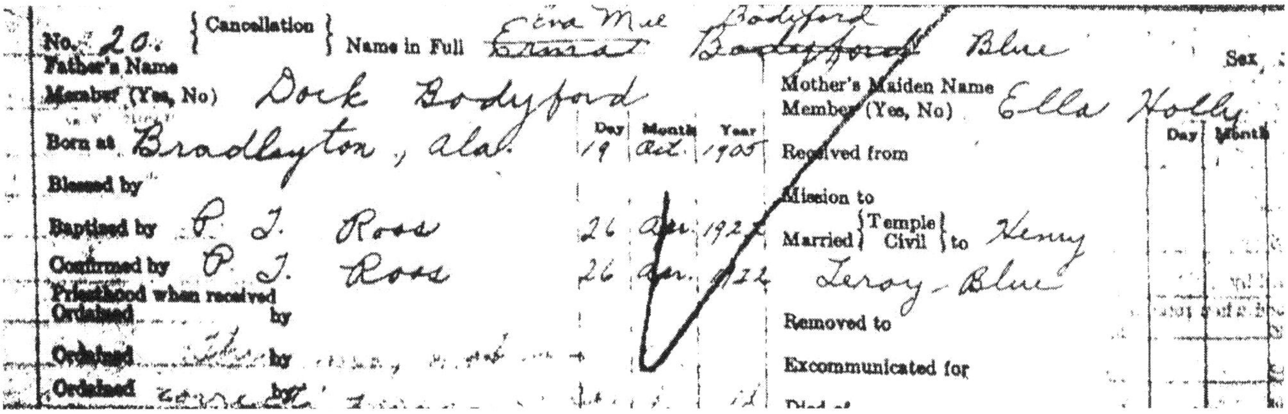

No. 20. {Cancellation} Name in Full Era Mae Bodyford Blue Sex
Father's Name
Member (Yes, No) Dock Bodyford
Mother's Maiden Name
Member (Yes, No) Ella Holly
Born at Bradlayton, Ala. Day 19 Month Oct Year 1905
Received from
Blessed by
Mission to
Baptized by P. T. Ross 26 Apr 1922
Married {Temple / Civil} to Henry Leroy Blue
Confirmed by P. T. Ross 26 Apr 1922
Priesthood when received
Ordained by
Removed to
Ordained by
Excommunicated for
Ordained by

**PHOTO 116 - L.D.S. BAPTISM RECORD FOR ERA MAE BODIFORD**

**State, The (Columbia, SC) - Saturday, July 13, 2002**

ROCK HILL - Services for Henry "Leroy" Blue, 94, will be held at the Church of Jesus Christ of Latter-Day Saints - Catawba Ward with burial in the church cemetery.

Mr. Blue, widower of Era Mae Bodiford Blue, died July 11, 2002. Born in Rock Hill, he was a son of the late Chief Samuel Blue and the late Hester Canty.

Surviving are sons, Randall Sr., Bobby, Carson and Harry Blue; daughters, Patsy Sloat, Priscilla Johnson, Shirley Francisco; sister, Elsie George; 30 grands; 45 great-grands; five great-great-grands.

**The Herald** | Sunday, July 14, 2002

## Deaths & funerals

### Leroy Blue

ROCK HILL — Mr. Henry "Leroy" Blue, 94, of 1851 W. Baskin Road died Thursday, July 11, 2002, at home.

The funeral will be 3 p.m. Monday at the Church of Jesus Christ of Latter-day Saints-Catawba Ward, with Bishop Pieter Reynders officiating. Burial will be at the church cemetery.

A native of Rock Hill, Mr. Blue was a son of the late Catawba Indian Chief Samuel Taylor Blue and Hester Louisa Canty Blue. He was a member of the Church of

**Leroy Blue**

Jesus Christ of Latter-day Saints-Catawba Ward, where he was a high priest and was the Sunday school superintendent. He was retired from the Rock Hill Printing & Finishing Co. plant. He worked at the Rock Hill Feed & Seed and Smith Enterprises after his retirement. He was the oldest living male member of the Catawba Indian tribe. He was the widower of Era Mae Bodiford Blue.

Surviving are four sons, Randall L. Blue Sr., Bobby E. Blue and Carson T. Blue, all of Rock Hill, and Harry R. Blue of Mooresville, N.C.; three daughters, Shirley A. Francisco

Fund, 2767 Shand... Hill, SC 29730.

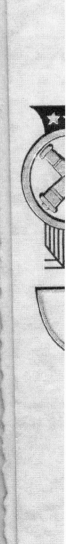

**Henry Leroy Blue and Era Mae Boniford had seven children:**

**PHOTO 117 – RANDALL LAVON BLUE**

a. Randall Lavon Blue born 20 December 1933, Catawba, South Carolina, United States and he died 15 September 2011, Rock Hill, York, South Carolina. He married first Mildred Luena Ballard; second Betty Jo Suthpin.

**Obituary**:
Our loving and compassionate husband, Daddy, Pawpaw, brother, son, and friend, Randall LaVon Blue, Sr., 77, of Rock Hill, passed away Thursday, September 15, 2011, at his home surrounded by loved ones. Randall was born Dec. 20, 1933 on the Catawba Indian Reservation in Rock Hill, SC, to the late Henry LeRoy Blue and Era Mae Bodiford Blue. As a Sergeant in the United States Marines Corps, he served in the Korean War. He retired from Continental General Tire with over 30 years of service, and York County with over 10 years of service. Randall was an active member of The Church of Jesus Christ of Latter-day Saints. He served in the Columbia, SC Temple. He was also a High Priest and Home Teacher among other

callings in the church. Randall enjoyed gardening, working, and his family. Randall is survived by his wife of 33 years, B.S. Blue; his son, Randall LaVon (Tania) Blue, Jr. of Frederick, MD; his daughters MaLinda Blue (Mark) Swett, of Hardeeville, SC; Kathy Blue (Phil) Griffis, of Ridgeland, SC; Crystal Blue (Mike) Casler, of Rock Hill, SC; one stepson, Roy (Karen) Helms, of Rock Hill, SC; two stepdaughters, Rehna (Dane) Loflin, of Rock Hill, SC; Yvonne (Donnie) Wood, of Corbin, KY; three brothers, Bobby (Betty) Blue, Carson (Susan) Blue of Rock Hill, SC and Harry (Debra) Blue, Troutman, NC; two sisters, Patsy Sloat, Midwest City, OK and Shirley (Eldon) Francisco, Laguna, NM; 16 grandchildren; 12 great-grandchildren and many nieces and nephews; Special Aunts Ella Mae Bodiford Kelley, Montgomery, AL and Elsie Blue George, Rock Hill, SC; Special Uncle, Dewey Bodiford, Highland Home, AL. In addition to his parents, he was preceded in death by his grandparents, Chief Samuel Taylor and Louisa Canty Blue; Dock and Ersie Malenda Hammond Bodiford and Lou Ella Holley Bodiford; sister, Priscilla Blue Johnson and brother-in-law, Lamar Johnson.

Funeral services will be held at 2 p.m. Monday, Sept. 19, 2011, at the Church of Jesus Christ of Latter-day Saints Catawba Ward, 1989 Reservation Road, Rock Hill, SC, with Bishop Benjamin Gleason officiating. The family will visit with friends from 5 p.m. to 7 p.m. Sunday, Sept. 18, 2011 at Bass-Cauthen Funeral Home, in Rock Hill. Burial will be in Rock Hill Memorial Gardens Veterans Section.

Memorials may be made to Hospice & Community Care, 2275 India Hook Road, Rock Hill, SC 29732.

**PHOTO 118 - BURIAL: ROCK HILL MEMORIAL GARDENS - ROCK HILL, YORK COUNTY, SOUTH CAROLINA**

PHOTO 119 – BOBBY EVERETTE BLUE

b. Bobby Everette Blue born 16 December 1934, South Carolina and he died 12 August 2003, Sanford, Lee, North Carolina. He married Betty Lou Harris, daughter of Floyd Ramond[102] and Nola Harris Harris.

PHOTO 120 – BOBBY EVERETT BLUE

---

[102]Watson page 41.

**PHOTO 121 - PATRICIA "PATSY" LOUNETTE BLUE**

c. Patricia[103] (Patsy) Lounette[104]  Blue born 5 June 1937 married Porter Lee Graves, white.

**PHOTO 122 - PRISCILLA LANE BLUE**

d.  Priscilla Lane Blue born 24 September 1939, Rock Hill, York, South Carolina  and died 9 February 2011, Bonneville, Idaho, United States. She married first - Irvin Francis Jose' in 1963, divorced, married second, LaMar John Johnson 1978.

---

[103] 1943 membership roll
[104] Priscilla Johnson genealogy

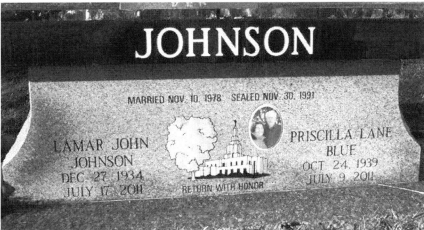

**PHOTO 123 - RIRIE SHELTON CEMETERY - BURIAL PLACE - BONNEVILLE COUNTY, IDAHO**

**PHOTO 124 – SHIRLEY ANN BLUE**

e. Shirley Ann Blue born 28 September 1941, Catawba, York, South Carolina. She married Eldon Anthony Francisco.

**PHOTO 125 – CARSON TAYLOR BLUE**

f. Carson Taylor Blue born March 17, 1944, Catawba, York, South Carolina. He married Susan Drennan Tennant.

**PHOTO 126 - HARRY REID BLUE**

g. Harry Reid Blue born 23 August 1947 married first Jo Ann Maples, second ? Scharlett, third Pamela Elizabeth Richards. The child is by Jo Ann Maples

PHOTO 127 – VERA LOUISE BLUE

      9. Vera Louise Blue born 21 August 21, 1909, Roddy, York, South Carolina and died 16 March 1991, Rock Hill, York, South Carolina, She married Albert Henderson Sanders, son of William and Nora Boarch-Brown Sanders. Children would be found under Albert H Sanders.

PHOTO 128 – VERA LOUISE BLUE AND FAMILY

**Charlotte Observer, The (NC) - Sunday, March 17, 1991**

# Blue Family

Vera Sanders, Homemaker 81, died March 16, 1991, at home. Funeral is Tuesday at the Church of Jesus Christ of Latter Day Saints, where she was a member. Elder Albert Sanders Jr., Elder Randall Sanders and Bishop Kenneth Ayers will officiate. Burial will be in the church cemetery.

Born in York County, Mrs. Sanders was the daughter of the late Chief Samuel T and Louisa Canty Blue. She was a homemaker.

Survivors are her husband, Albert Sanders Sr.; sons, Albert Sanders Jr. of Greenville, S.C., Randall Sanders, daughters, Leona Watts of Fort Mill, Susan Campbell of Catawba, Ada Sanders, Marilyn Sanders, Lois Thompson, Laura Varnadore, Brenda Ball and Ann Morris; brother, Leroy Blue; sisters, Lula Beck, Elsie George; 28 grandchildren; 55 great-grandchildren; five great- great-grandchildren.

**PHOTO 129 – GARY LARSON BLUE**

10. Guy Larson Blue born, 3 December 1911, Rock Hill, York, South Carolina and died 7 Feb 1984, Catawba Indian Reservation, York, South Carolina. He married Eva Bell George, daughter of J. C. Starnes (white) and Lucy George.

**PHOTO 130 - BURIAL: CHURCH OF JESUS CHRIST OF LATTER-DAY STS CEMETERY - CATAWBA, YORK COUNTY, SOUTH CAROLINA**

**Gary Larson Blue and Eva Bell George had seven children:**

**PHOTO 131 – GILBERT BILLY LARSON BLUE**

a. Gilbert Billy Larson Blue born 5 December 1933, Catawba, York, South Carolina and died 11 June 2016, Catawba Indian Nation, York, South Carolina. He married Elizabeth Lavern Sharpe, white. He was the former Chief.

**Obituary**
Gilbert Billy Blue

ROCK HILL – Gilbert Billy Larson Blue, 82, of 1480 Hopewell Road, died Saturday, June 11, 2016, at the Wayne T. Patrick Hospice House.

Funeral services will be 3:00 PM Wednesday, at The Church of Jesus Christ of Latter-Day Saints, Catawba Ward. Burial will follow in the church cemetery. The family will receive friends from 6-8 PM Tuesday, at Whitesell Funeral Home.

Born in Rock Hill, Gilbert was the son of the late Guy and Eva George Blue. The family is truly thankful that they were taught by their Dad to live life to the fullest, spend as much quality time with your family and be sure to let them know that you love them. He taught them to give to others and you will be blessed. He also taught them it does not take money to be happy.

He truly loved working with wood, always making things for his kids and grand-kids and that gave him great joy at Christmas. He always had a joke to make people laugh. He also enjoyed sitting outside watching all the different birds eating in the yard. His best quality was making others happy. He will be truly missed and never replaced. He is our Hero.

He is survived by his wife, Libby Sharpe Blue; two sons, Chris Blue (Cathy) and Glenn Blue (Michelle); a daughter, Denise Gilbert (Steve); two sisters Jeannette Largo and Gail White; 10 grandchildren and 13 great grandchildren. He was preceded in death by a brother, Guy Lesslie Blue; and two sisters, Sylvia Caudle and Toy Murray.

**PHOTO 132 – GILBERT BILLY BLUE**

b. Sylvia Deloris Blue born 2 April 1936, Catawba, York, South Carolina and died 26 August 2005, Rock Hill, York, South Carolina. She married Edward Caudle, a white man.

c. Guynell Blue born 1937.

d. Jeanette Blue born 31 August 1938, Catawba, York, South Carolina. She married Jimmie Roper Largo.

e. Guy Lesslie Blue born 8 January 1941, Catawba, York, South Carolina and 4 July 1966, Catawba, York, South Carolina. He married Linda Sue Lynn.

f. Toy June Blue born 21 December 1943, Catawba, York, South Carolina. He married a Fowler,

g. Gail Beatrice Blue born 30 November 1947, Catawba, York, South Carolina. She married

\*\*\*\*\*\*\*\*\*\*\*\*\*\*\*\*\*\*\*\*\*\*\*\*\*\*\*\*\*\*\*\*\*\*\*\*\*\*\*\*\*\*

**PHOTO 133 - ELSIE INEZ BLUE**

11. Elsie Inez Blue born 3 March 1914, Catawba Township, York, South Carolina and died 25 November 2013, Catawba Indian Nation, York, South Carolina. She married Landrum Leslie George, son of James Cloyd Starnes, white, and Lucy Jane S. George, they had no children.

PHOTO 134 – ELSIE INEZ BLUE

12. Infant Blue born 1916 died as an infant

**PHOTO 135 – ARNOLD LEE BLUE**

13. Arnold Lee Blue (Donny) born 23 November 1917, Rock Hill, York, South Carolina and died 31 October 1962, Rock Hill, York, South Carolina. He married Lillian Harris, daughter of Pearly Ayers Harris.

**PHOTO 136 – ARNOLD LEE "DONNY" BLUE**

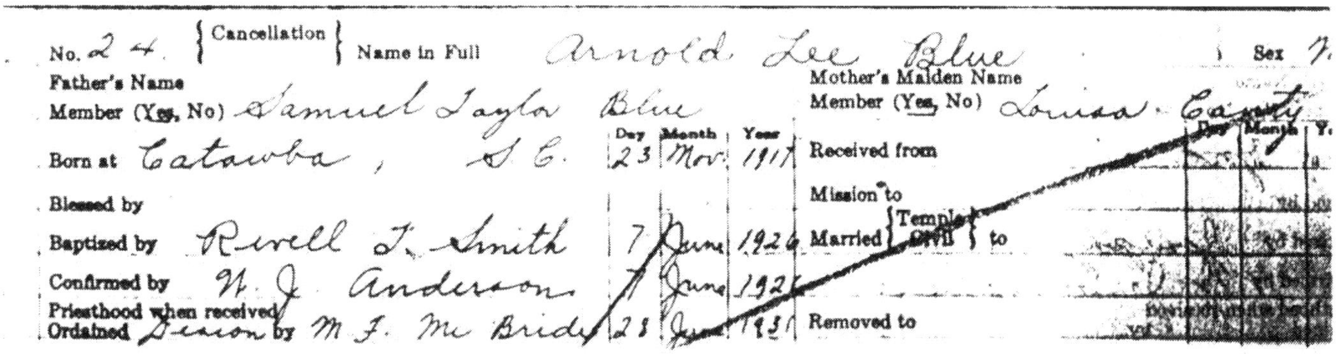

No. 24 | Cancellation | Name in Full Arnold Lee Blue | Sex M
Father's Name
Member (Yes, No) Samuel Taylor Blue | Mother's Maiden Name Member (Yes, No) Louisa Canty
Born at Catawba, S.C. | 23 | Nov. | 1917 | Received from
Blessed by | | | | Mission to
Baptized by Revell T. Smith | 7 | June | 1924 | Married {Temple/Civil} to
Confirmed by W. J. Anderson | 7 | June | 1924
Priesthood when received
Ordained Deacon by M. F. Mc Bride | 23 | June | 1931 | Removed to

**PHOTO 137—L.D.S. BAPTISM RECORD FOR ARNOLD LEE BLUE**

**Group Photo: Blue Family Reunion**

## Chapter 4  Brown Families

I. Patrick Brown, white trader, born around 1690, he was associated with his brother Thomas Brown and Alexander Kilpatrick. Patrick bought the tracts of Dr. Daniel Gibson and Henry Gignilliat and three hundred acres at the bend of Congaree Creek, the site of the old fort.

II. Thomas Brown, white man of northern Irish origin,[105] said to be the greatest Indian trader in the Nation.[106] He was probably born around 1690; his will was dated December 4, 1745. He states William Brown, "My natural son born of a free Indian Woman of the Catawba's Nation," and that William was 15 years old. In 1735, Thomas bought land between the Congaree and Wateree Rivers. Thomas served as executor of Alexander Kilpatrick's will.[107] After Thomas's death, George Haig served as his executor and took care of William.[108]

He was the Indian Agent as early as 1743 and died shortly thereafter.

A. William Brown born 1729,[109] was abducted by a band of Indians in 1748 on a trip William was sent by Governor Glen to Charles Town to smoke the peace pipe with the Chickasaws.[110] William was kidnapped along with George Haig, who was killed; however, a George Haig signed the 1759 letter along with King Halger. Therefore, the George who was killed must have been white, or it was just a mistake altogether. The Indians moved very fast and often with their captives and George Haig was ill. They were held for nearly a year before he begged his captors to put him out of his misery. They did, by killing him with a tomahawk.[111] William eventually found his way back home.

**Only two children are identified; John and Patrick Brown.**

1. John Brown-Major John Brown born around 1750, he was a Major by 1785.[112] He signed leases from 1785 to 1796.[113] His Revolutionary service with the Catawba reads, 98 days, 49 pounds.[114] Only one child can be identified, John Genet Brown.

a. John Genet-Gennett-Jennett Brown alive in 1810, born around 1780, died around 1824. He signed leases in May 1809, signing as Major John Gennet Brown.[115] The next time he signed leases was in July of 1813.[116]

---

[105] Brown page 164
[106] Brown page 108.
[107] Merrell page 341 from SC Public Treasurer's Accounts, Ledger A., Folio 57, 1726; Folio 100, 1727; Folio 134, 1729; Folio 135.
[108] Merrell page 341, Court of Common Please, Judgement Rolls. 1755, 151A, and 1765 359A. SCDAH; SCCJ. 29 Mar 1748; SC Wills Book LL, 1737-1740, 231, SCDAH.
[109] Watson page 18.
[110] Brown page 225.
[111] Brown page 168.
[112] Watson page 19.
[113] Ibid
[114] Brown page 225.

He then does not sign again until July of 1815, and he is absent until May 22, 1817 when he again signed the Miller lease.[117] He is again signing regularly from 1817 to July of 1824, when his title is Colonel John G. Brown.

In December 1820, he was named a colonel by the tribe, but signs the lease the same year as Major John J. Brown.

Prissy Bullen, wife of Peter Harris willed her rents to "him. He is associated with the Redhead family and the Harris family, in the Plat Books. Since his wife is unknown, most likely he married a woman from either or both the RedHead and Harris families.

        (1). Nancy Brown, born around 1810, married Richardson

B. Patrick Brown, born around 1755. He and an interpreter went back with Tiagadarughurah (Thomas King, the Oneida Chief) in 1771, after receiving gifts, on a peace mission. Patrick died before the mission was completed, presumably in 1771. He served in the Revolutionary War and is listed with John Nettles and others not listed in Drennan's paybill.[118]

    1. Thomas Brown, born around 1730, he signed leases in 1808 along with John Nettles and General Jacob Scott. This Thomas had to have been a Catawba because law required that four Catawba sign each lease. In a lease dated July 1811, he has become Captain Thomas Brown. Thomas became Major Thomas Brown in a lease dated May 1813. He signed the lease dated 12 August 1817 renting land to David Hutcheson. He signed for the Catawba, along with Henry White-Whyte. The last lease he signed was on 2 September 1825, along with Gen. Jacob Scott and Col. Jacob Ayers.

III. A Matthew Brown born around 1750, served with the Catawba during the Revolution, he is listed as white on Drennan's Pay bill and as having 20 days. Matthew was most probably the father of three children: Billey, Jamey and Thomas. He married a Catawba and William becomes a Catawba in this fashion, through his mother.

    A. William -Billey Brown probably born around 1780, was a Captain in 1805. He did not live long after 1818. Billy's rents went to Gemmima Joe the stepdaughter of his wife. Ian Watson states that he is strongly associated with John Joe and it would be through Gemmima Joe. One theory that can be drawn is that John Joe had a daughter; this daughter married an unknown man who had a daughter named Gemmima Joe. Then daughter Joe married Billy Brown. Billey Brown signed a petition in 1805 as Captain Billy Brown.[119]

---

[115] Blumer, page 85 article 672.
[116] Blumer page 98 article 748-753.
[117] Blumer page 105 article 791-796.
[118] Blumer page 502 article 1339.
[119] Watson page 20.

# Brown Family

    1. Nancy Brown born around 1800

    2. Harriet Brown born around 1802. Harriet married Daniel Patterson who was alive in May 1824.[120]

B. Jamey Brown born probably around 1770 and Sally or Susy Ayers,[121] daughter of General Jacob Ayers. Jamey Brown is in the plat book in 1810-1819, and he died in 1820.[122] Jamey was also married to Sarah Mursh, daughter of Robert and Elizabeth Mursh Mush, Pamunkey Indians around 1820. Jamey could be the son of either Patrick or William, the half-Catawba sons of Thomas Brown. He is most likely the brother of Thomas Brown below.

C. Thomas Brown born around 1780, he begins signing leases in 1801 as a Captain, then in 1822 as a Major.[123] He married Jinney-Jenny Patterson,[124] first, and she was living 1813-1826, so was she was probably born around 1779; he married Betsey[125] George second, around 1814, because she began to receive rents then as Betsy Brown. She probably was born around 1770 and was the mother of Anthony and Patsy Brown George. Thomas died in the 1820's. Betsey's maiden name is unknown; she married William George SR, as his first wife. Thomas had two children, Anthony and Patsey that are identifiable; they both used the surname George.[126]

\*\*\*\*\*\*\*\*\*\*\*\*\*\*\*\*\*\*\*\*\*\*\*\*\*\*\*\*\*\*\*\*\*\*\*\*\*\*\*\*\*\*\*\*\*\*\*\*\*\*\*\*\*\*\*\*\*\*\*\*\*\*\*\*\*\*\*\*\*\*\*\*\*\*

Unknown Browns

Polly Brown is Polly Tims, Polly Harris then Ayers see Ayers.

Rebecca Brown

Betsy or Mary Brown

    1.

    2. 1854 census [127]

Esther or Easter Scott[128] Brown, born 1820 married Peter Harris, son of David and Nancy

---

[120] Merell page 234

[121] Sally took Billy Ayers rents because she was his sister.

[122] Watson page 18

[123] Watson page 24

[124] Watson pages 20&21

[125] Ibid

[126] Watson pages 20 & 21.

[127] 1849 census, Watson pages 20 & 21.

[128] Petition dated 1848, October 4, relative to their removal and the appointment of Samuel Sherrill as agent lists Easther Scott. 1849 census lists her as Esther Brown.

Quash Harris as his first wife.

> 1. child in 1854 census.

> 2. Ditto [129]

Franky Brown, born 1821[130]

> 1.

> 2.

\*\*\*\*\*\*\*\*\*\*\*\*\*\*\*\*\*\*\*\*\*\*\*\*\*\*\*\*\*\*\*\*\*\*\*\*\*\*\*\*\*\*\*\*\*\*\*\*\*\*\*\*\*\*\*\*\*\*\*\*\*\*\*\*\*\*\*\*\*\*\*\*\*\*\*\*\*\*\*\*\*\*\*\*\*\*\*\*\*\*\*\*

William -Billy Brown born 1829 [131] married. William is more than likely the father of John William Brown. No proof exists, other than the proximity of each other on the census records and the naming patterns.

I. John William Brown SR, born around 1800 married Sallie Rachel who was born 1813. [132] Her parents are unknown. Sallie Rachel married Joe Cherry first a white man who is John William's actual father. Rachel then married second John William Brown SR who raised the boy as his own.[133] Joe Cherry is most likely of the family of James Milton Cherry, who were very prominent in the early days of Rock Hill.

**PHOTO 138 – JOHN WILLIAM BROWN**

---

[129] 1854 census.
[130] 1849 census
[131] 1849 census
[132] 1849 census
[133] Catawba Branch Records, Watson page 22, 23.

A. John William Brown Jr, born 1837,[134]York, South Carolina and died September 1867. He married Margaret.Ayers-George born 12 November 1845, daughter of Edmund Ayers and Rebecca Mursh-Quash.[135] John served in the Confederate Army during the Civil War and died September 1867.[136] Margaret then had a child by Sam Blue, a white man.

**John William had five children: Sallie Brown, an unnamed child, Wade Hampton Brown, an Unnamed Twin to Wade, and John William Brown Jr.**

1. Sallie Brown, born 1862.[137] Sallie was a student of Mrs. Dunlap in 1899. She had a child, Nora Elvina, by a man called John Boarch.[138] Sallie married Louis Gordon, son of Stell Gordon, a white man and Lucinda Harris. She died 20 September 1952.[139] White calls her a potter and states that she and her brothers John Brown and Samuel T. Blue used English as an acquired second language, and used Catawba exclusively when speaking to each other. She used the pottery in cooking during 1929-34. See other children under Gordon, Lucinda Harris.

(a) Nora Elvina Boarch-Brown was born September 1884, married William Sanders, son of John and Martha Harris Sanders.[140]

2. unnamed child who died, probably a stillborn.

3. Wade Hampton Brown born around 1865 in Catawba, York, South Carolina.  He died as an infant, must have lived a little while to be given a name.

4. Unnamed twin to Wade Hampton probably died as an infant.[141] 1849 census

---

[134] 1849 census, Catawba Branch Records.
[135] Catawba Branch Records.
[136] Catawba Cemetery Inscriptions.
[137] 1880 census York county, SC.
[138] LDS Ancestral File, she went by Nora Brown.
[139] Obituary of Sallie, 1952.
[140] Watson, pages 29,30,77,78.
[141] LDS Ancestral File

**PHOTO 139 – JOHN WILLIAM BROWN**

5. John William Brown, born 21 October 1867, Catawba, York, South Carolina and died 20 June 1927 • Rock Hill, York, South Carolina. He married Rachel Wysie George, daughter of Zacariah Taylor and Emily Elizabeth Cobb Ayers George.[142] He ran a ferry on the Catawba River, and was a potter.

Some news clippings and other notations, which mention John William follow:

The first from the Diary of Elder Joseph Willey, a Mormon Missionary to Catawba in 1885

"March 26, I accidentally through Mr. Brown out of the boat. I was somewhat excited but I handed him my pole and he got in the boat safe."

---

[142] Catawba Branch Records.

Others in which he is mentioned also have been found, and give John a more full character, rather than just a name.

"May 5, 1894, One burly fellow, John Brown, became furiously mad and assaulted Ayers, when the women interfered and a general fight was imminent. The Chief of Police happened to be on hand and nabbed Brown, but he resisted and jerking the Chiefs walking stick out of his hand threw it into the street. About this time Policeman Carroll reinforced the chief and the two hurried Brown off to the guardhouse. He was subsequently taken before the mayor and fined $15 or thirty days. He failed to pay up and is now in the jug"[143]

These other items were found in news clippings.

3 July 1889, "State vs. John E. Ballard (white) assault and battery with intent to kill. Prosecutor, John Brown a Catawba Indian, verdict, Not Guilty."[144] (This is the reason that Lillie Susan Harris and her husband John E. Ballard fled to Oklahoma.)

There is a strange notation in the Dunlap letters, referring to the fact that John Brown gave R. E. Dunlap an opossum for Christmas in 1900. Wes White states that he only spoke Catawba conversationally.

In 1913, John and Early Brown were accused of inflicting wounds upon William Sanders. They were arrested by F. G. Allen on July 8, 1913 and faced trail on July 14, 1913. No indication of whether or not they were acquitted or convicted is found.[145]

Daily Journal of Mrs. Orlando Barrus - Feb. 1st, 1909 -- Roddey, S.C.

1908 to 1910

Thoughts written while on my mission to the Southern States with my husband. From the missionary journal of Sister Mary Barrus

---

[143] Blumer page 204.
[144] Yorkville Enquirer, Circuit Court, July 3, 1889 page 2
[145] Blumer Page 250 articles 1879 & 1880.

"We had a special program on July 4th and gave talks abt Declaration of Independence. The Indians helped us to prepare a barbacue (sic) and they all joined in a picnic around a long table under the shade trees. Xmas time fire crackers are their great delight.

They have what they call a "play" sometimes. Someone plays a fiddle or mouthorgan & they all join in a reel & enjoy it. Lunch & C. They love to sing & are good singers.

Before we were there it was customary for them to get on a drunk at Xmas day fun. We arrived there just a short time before Xmas and were shocked to hear a big racket over to the neighbor's home. The Sanders boys had a quarrel and used knives & guns. We were very frightened.

John Brown, was sober & tried to get Mr. Whellock to his home. Wheellock chocked Brown & in the scramble Bro Brown bit off Wheellocks ear. When Bro Brown came in with his hands covered with blood, we were surely filled with horror.

The next day Orlando took Bro B. over to Wheellock's to see if he could make peace between them, not knowing what the outcome might be for him. Bro B. was willing to be peaceable (sic) but Wheellock was not a Mormon

A peace maker

I was pretty anxious but Orlando came back in less than an hour.

The first thing Bro Brown said to his foe was – "I'm sorry I bit off your ear Arch."

Wheelock said, "I deserved it & if I get drunk again, I wish you would bit the other one off." When they got acquainted with our ideals – they refrained entirely from that drinking habit while we were there."

"Bro. John Brown is assistant to Bro Blue. He is a firm believer in the church and has reformed greatly since the elders have brought the gospel message here. He loves the gospel well enough to leave off tobacco and liquor and is trying to overcome what he calls his bad temper."

John Brown was Chief in the years 1923-1927 and he died June 20, 1927. [146] John Brown had Early Morgan, Sallie Rebecca, Arzada, Cora, Addie, John William, Roy, Mary Rachel, Henry, Ethel Alberta, and George.

---

[146] Ibid

**PHOTO 140 - JOHN AND RACHEL POUNDING CLAY.**

**PHOTO 141 - JOHN AND RACHEL AND KIDS DIGGING CLAY**

**Photo 142 – John Brown making pottery**

**PHOTO 143 - JOHN W BROWN WITH HIS CHILDREN**

**PHOTO 144 JOHN AND RACHEL WYSIE BROWN AND CHILDREN**

**Photo 145 - John W Brown on Ferry**

**PHOTO 146 - FERRY 1916**

**PHOTO 147 - HEADSTONE OF JOHN BROWN**

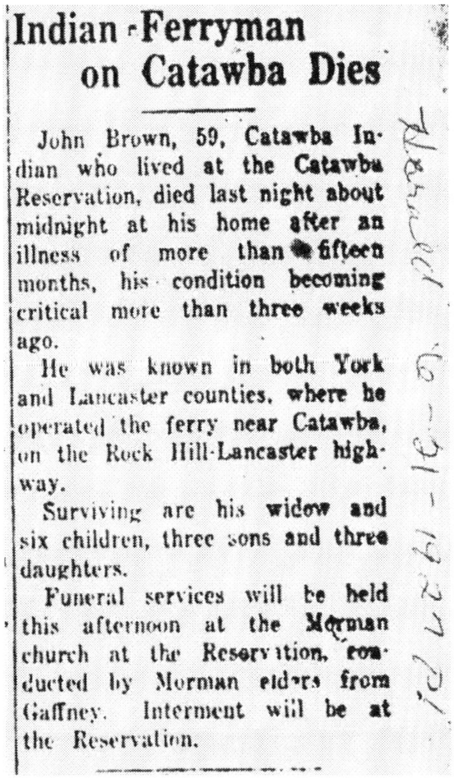

# Indian Ferryman on Catawba Dies

John Brown, 59, Catawba Indian who lived at the Catawba Reservation, died last night about midnight at his home after an illness of more than fifteen months, his condition becoming critical more than three weeks ago.

He was known in both York and Lancaster counties, where he operated the ferry near Catawba, on the Rock Hill-Lancaster highway.

Surviving are his widow and six children, three sons and three daughters.

Funeral services will be held this afternoon at the Mormon church at the Reservation, conducted by Mormon elders from Gaffney. Interment will be at the Reservation.

Form No. 10

CERTIFICATE OF DEATH
STATE OF SOUTH CAROLINA
Bureau of Vital Statistics
State Board of Health

File No.—For State Registrar Only. 10404

1. PLACE OF DEATH
County of York
Township of Catawba
Registration District No. 4404
Registered No. 40

2. FULL NAME John Brown

PERSONAL AND STATISTICAL PARTICULARS
Sex: Male
Color or Race: Indian
Single, Married, Widowed or Divorced: married
Date of Birth: Oct 15, 1867
Age: 59 yrs 8 mos 5 ds
Occupation: Farming & Ferryman
Birthplace: SC
Name of Father: John Brown
Birthplace of Father: SC
Maiden Name of Mother: Marguerite Harris
Birthplace of Mother: SC

Filed July 8 1927 J. R. Miller, Local Registrar

MEDICAL CERTIFICATE OF DEATH
Date of Death: June 20, 1927
I hereby certify, that I attended deceased from April 14, 1927, to June 17, 1927, that I last saw him alive on 19 June 1927, and that death occurred, on the date stated above, at 11:30 p.m. The cause of death was as follows:
Carcinoma of Stomach & Pancreas
Duration 2 yrs mos 2 ds

Place of Burial or Removal: Indian Reservation
Date of Burial: June 21, 1927
Undertaker: Friends
Address: Catawba

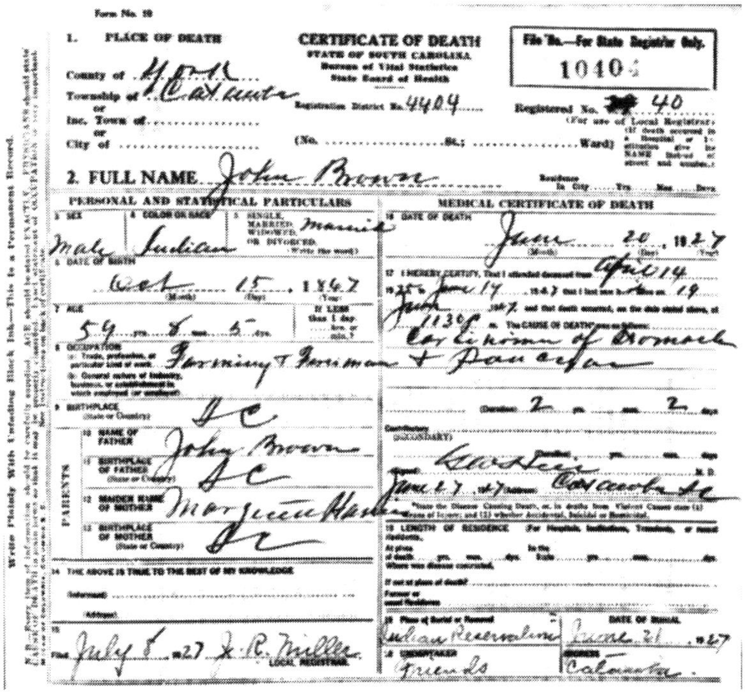

**PHOTO 148 – CERTIFICATE OF DEATH FOR JOHN BROWN 1867-1927**

**John and Rachel's children were**:

**PHOTO 149 – EARLY MORGAN BROWN**

a. Early Morgan Brown, born January 26, 1891.[147]  He was a student of Mrs. Dunlap in 1899.[148] He married 4 July 1910, Edith Bertha Harris, daughter of D.A. and Lizzie Patterson-Watts Harris. He later married Emma Harris Canty, daughter of Wesley and Alice Ayers Harris, and widow of Henry Canty.[149]

Early was in the hunting party with Wesley and Walter Harris when Harvey Blue, son of Samuel Taylor and Louisa Canty Blue was shot and killed. See the Samuel Blue Chapter.

Early was the operator of the Ferry over the Catawba River in 1944

He served in World War I [150] and he died on June 20, 1927.[151]

| Father  Early Bearly Morgan BROWN | |
|---|---|
| Birth        26 Jan 1889 | Catawba Indian Reservation, York, South Carolina, United States |
| Residence 1900 | Age: 9Relation to Head of House: Son; Catawba Indian Reservation, York, South Carolina |
| Residence 1910 | Age in 1910: 19Marital Status: Single; Relation to Head of House: Son; Catawba, York, South Carolina |

[147]Catawba Branch Records.
[148] Brown page 345.
[149] Watson pages 22 and 46.
[150] Brown page 352.
[151] Catawba Cemetery inscriptions.

| Residence 1920 | Age: 29Marital Status: Married; Relation to Head of House: Son; Waxhaw, Lancaster, South Carolina |
|---|---|
| Residence 1930 | Age: 40Marital Status: Married; Relation to Head of House: Head; Waxhaw, Lancaster, South Carolina |
| Burial          Mar 1963 | Catawba, North Carolina, United States |
| Death           16 Mar 1963 | Age: 74; Catawba, York, South Carolina |
|  |  |
| Publicatio 18 Mar 1963 n Date | Richland, South Carolina, United States |
| Residence | York, South Carolina |
| Marriage    4 Jul 1910 | Catawba, York, South Carolina, United States |
| Father       John William BROWN (1867-1927) | |
| Mother      Rachel Wysie GEORGE (1874-1960) | |
| Other spouse      Annie AYERS (1888-1910) | |
| Other spouse      Emma Jane HARRIS (1888-1961) | |

**Mother  Edith Bertha HARRIS**

|  |  |
|---|---|
|  |  |
| Birth           13 Jun 1893 | Catawba Indian Nation, York, South Carolina, United States |
|  |  |
|  |  |
|  |  |
| Residence 1900 | Age: 6Marital Status: Single; Relation to Head of House: Daughter; Catawba Indian Reservation, York, South Carolina |
| Residence 1910 | Age in 1910: 16Relation to Head of House: Daughter; Catawba, York, South Carolina |
| Residence 1930 | Age: 36Marital Status: Widowed; Relation to Head of House: Head; Catawba, York, South Carolina |
| Residence 1935 | Industrial Aragon Mills, York, South Carolina |
| Residence 1 Apr 1940 | Age: 46Marital Status: Widowed; Relation to Head of House: Head; Industrial Aragon Mills, York, South Carolina, United States |
|  |  |
| Death          12 Jun 1985 | Rock Hill, York, South Carolina, United States |
|  |  |
|  |  |
|  |  |
| Burial |  |

| Father | David Adam HARRIS (1872-1930) |
|---|---|
| Mother | Lizzie Jane (Elizabeth) WATTS-PATTERSON (1818-1917) |

| **M** | **Edward Alford BROWN** | |
|---|---|---|
| | Birth | 8 Dec 1911 | Catawba, York, South Carolina, United States |
| | Residence 1920 | Age: 8Marital Status: Single; Relation to Head of House: Son; Catawba, York, South Carolina |
| | Residence 1930 | Age in 1930: 19Marital Status: Single; Relation to Head of House: Lodger; Rock Hill, York, South Carolina |
| | Residence 1935 | Industrial Aragon Mills, York, South Carolina |
| | Residence 1 Apr 1940 | Age: 28Marital Status: Single; Relation to Head of House: Son; Industrial Aragon Mills, York, South Carolina, United States |
| | Death | 17 Mar 1969 | Age: 57; Rock Hill, York, South Carolina, United States |
| | Civil | South Carolina |
| | Burial | |
| | Marriage | |

| **F** | **Evelyn Lucille BROWN** | |
|---|---|---|
| | Birth | 7 Feb 1914 | Catawba Indian Nation, York, South Carolina, United States |
| | Residence 1920 | Age: 6Marital Status: Single; Relation to Head of House: Daughter; Catawba, York, South Carolina |
| | Residence 1930 | Age: 16Marital Status: Single; Relation to Head of House: Daughter; Catawba, York, South Carolina |
| | Residence 1935 | Industrial Aragon Mills, York, South Carolina |
| | Residence 1 Apr 1940 | Age: 26Marital Status: Married; Relation to Head of House: Wife; Industrial Aragon Mills, York, South Carolina, United States |
| | Residence 1994 | Age: 80; Rock Hill, SC |
| | Burial | Dec 2007 | Catawba, York, South Carolina, United States |
| | Death | 9 Dec 2007 | Age at Death: 93; Rock Hill, York, South Carolina, United States |
| | Civil | South Carolina |
| | Spouse | John Marvin GEORGE (1909-1999) |
| | Marriage | 28 Jul 1930 | |

| **M** | **Richard BROWN** | |
|---|---|---|
| | Birth | 21 Apr 1916 | Catawba, York, South Carolina, United States |
| | | |
| | Residence 1920 | Age: 4Marital Status: Single; Relation to Head of House: Son; Catawba, York, South Carolina |
| | Residence 1930 | Age: 14Marital Status: Single; Relation to Head of House: Son; Catawba, York, South Carolina |
| | Residence 1935 | Industrial Aragon Mills, York, South Carolina |

| | |
|---|---|
| Residence 1 Apr 1940 | Age: 24Marital Status: Married; Relation to Head of House: Head; Industrial Aragon Mills, York, South Carolina, United States |
| Death 19 May 1979 | Age: 63; Rock Hill, York, South Carolina, United States |
| | |
| Civil | South Carolina |
| Burial | Rock Hill, York County, South Carolina |
| Spouse Mary Ann AYERS (1918-2008) | |

**M William John Henry BROWN**

| | |
|---|---|
| Birth 5 Nov 1919 | Catawba Indian Nation, York, South Carolina |
| Birth | |
| Residence 1920 | Age: 0Age: 4/12; Marital Status: Single; Relation to Head of House: Son; Catawba, York, South Carolina[14] |
| Residence 1930 | Age: 10Marital Status: Single; Relation to Head of House: Son; Catawba, York, South Carolina |
| Residence 1935 | Industrial Aragon Mills, York, South Carolina |
| Residence 1 Apr 1940 | Age: 20Marital Status: Single; Relation to Head of House: Son; Industrial Aragon Mills, York, South Carolina, United States |
| Death 24 Mar 2000 | Age: 80; Rock Hill, York, South Carolina, United States |
| | |
| Civil | South Carolina |
| Burial | South Carolina |
| Spouse Ruby Alberta AYERS (1929-1997) | |
| Marriage 16 Sep 1948 | Rock Hill, York, SC |

**F Lizzie BROWN**[11,18,26]

| | |
|---|---|
| Birth 21 May 1928 | Catawba, South Carolina |
| Residence 1930 | Age: 3Age: 2 6/12; Marital Status: Single; Relation to Head of House: Daughter; Catawba, York, South Carolina |
| Residence 1935 | Industrial Aragon Mills, York, South Carolina |
| Residence 1 Apr 1940 | Age: 12Marital Status: Single; Relation to Head of House: Daughter; Industrial Aragon Mills, York, South Carolina, United States |
| Death | |
| Burial | |
| Marriage | |

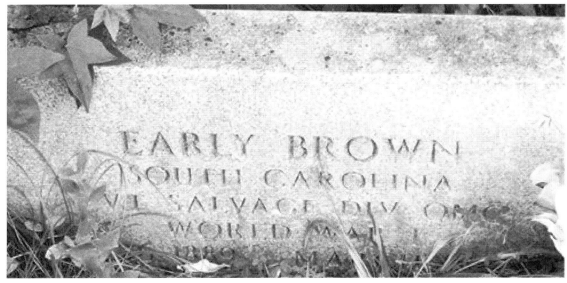

**PHOTO 150 - CHURCH OF JESUS CHRIST OF LATTER-DAY STS CEMETERY -- BURIAL PLACE - CATAWBA, YORK COUNTY, SOUTH CAROLINA**

Red
Form 1 208 REGISTRATION CARD No. 5

1 Name in full Early Brown (Given name) (Family name) Age, in yrs. 26

2 Home address R. F. D #1 Roddey S.C. (No.) (Street) (City) (State)

3 Date of birth January (Don't know) 1891 (Month) (Day) (Year)

4 Are you (1) a natural-born citizen, (2) a naturalized citizen, (3) an alien, (4) or have you declared your intention (specify which)? Catawba Indian

5 Where were you born? Reservation S.C. Catawba (Town) (State) (Nation)

6 If not a citizen, of what country are you a citizen or subject? Ward of S.C.

7 What is your present trade, occupation, or office? Farming

8 By whom employed? Working for self
Where employed? on Reservation

9 Have you a father, mother, wife, child under 12, or a sister or brother under 12, solely dependent on you for support (specify which)? Wife + 3 children oldest 5 yrs

10 Married or single (which)? married Race (specify which)? Indian

11 What military service have you had? Rank none; branch
years; Nation or State

12 Do you claim exemption from draft (specify grounds)? no

I affirm that I have verified above answers and that they are true.

Early Brown (Signature or mark)

If person is of African descent, tear off this corner.

REGISTRAR'S REPORT 39-2-23

1 Tall, medium, or short (specify which)? Short Slender, medium, or stout (which)? Slender

2 Color of eyes? Brown Color of hair? Black Bald?

3 Has person lost arm, leg, hand, foot, or both eyes, or is he otherwise disabled (specify)? No

I certify that my answers are true, that the person registered has read his own answers, that I have witnessed his signature, and that all of his answers of which I have knowledge are true, except as follows:

O. K. Williams (Signature of registrar)

Precinct
City or County York
State South Carolina June 5-1917 (Date of registration)

an exact copy.

LOCAL BOARD. NO. 1
YORK CO. SOUTH CAROLINA

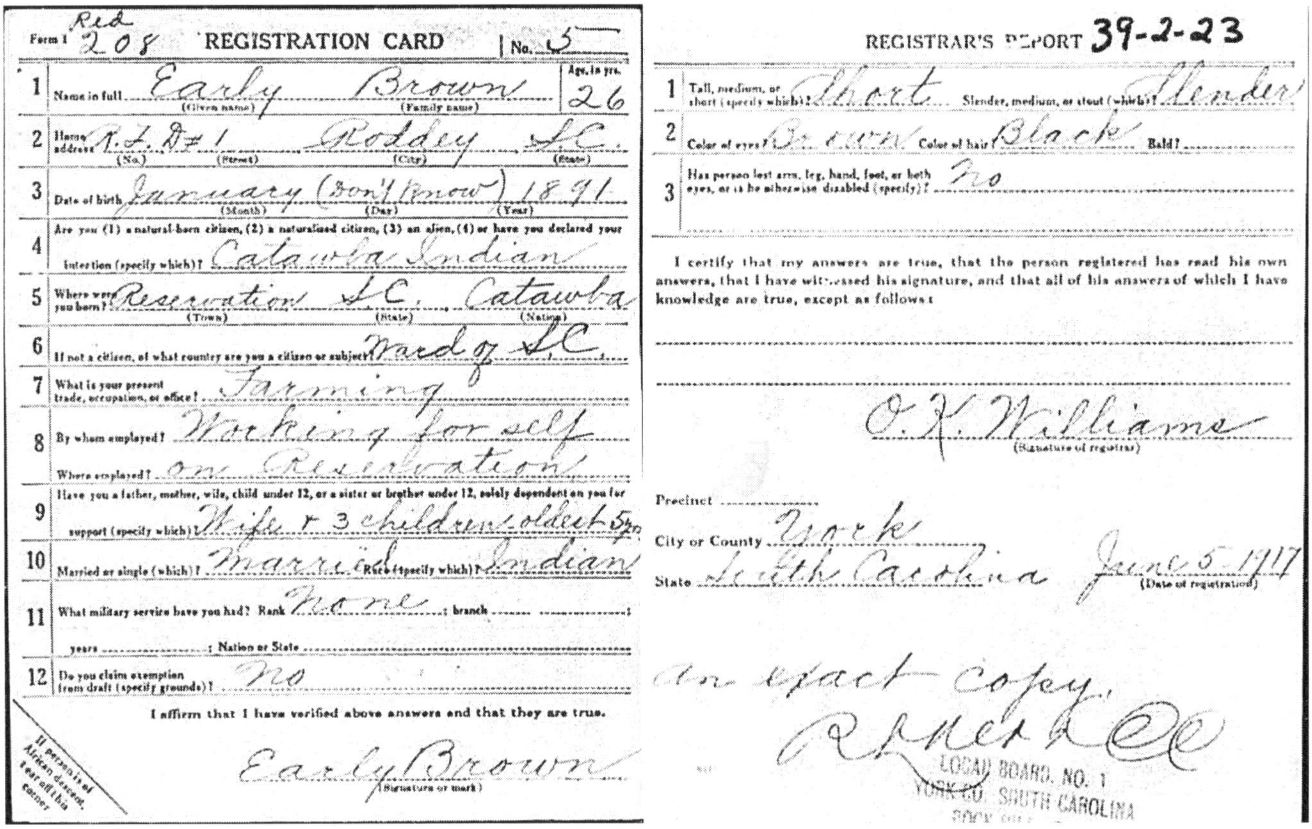

**PHOTO 151 – WWI REGISTRATION CARE FOR EARLY BROWN**

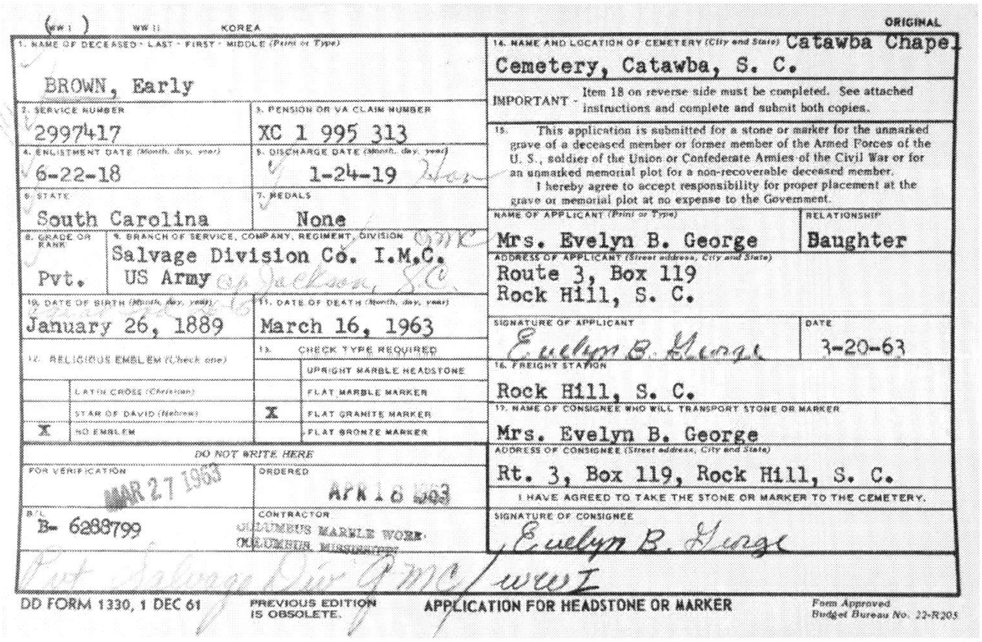
(WW I) WW II KOREA ORIGINAL

1. NAME OF DECEASED - LAST - FIRST - MIDDLE (Print or Type): BROWN, Early
2. SERVICE NUMBER: 2997417
3. PENSION OR VA CLAIM NUMBER: XC 1 995 313
4. ENLISTMENT DATE (Month, day, year): 6-22-18
5. DISCHARGE DATE (Month, day, year): 1-24-19
6. STATE: South Carolina
7. MEDALS: None
8. GRADE OR RANK: Pvt.
9. BRANCH OF SERVICE, COMPANY, REGIMENT, DIVISION: Salvage Division Co. I.M.C. US Army
10. DATE OF BIRTH (Month, day, year): January 26, 1889
11. DATE OF DEATH (Month, day, year): March 16, 1963
12. RELIGIOUS EMBLEM (Check one): LATIN CROSS (Christian); STAR OF DAVID (Hebrew); X NO EMBLEM
13. CHECK TYPE REQUIRED: UPRIGHT MARBLE HEADSTONE; FLAT MARBLE MARKER; X FLAT GRANITE MARKER; FLAT BRONZE MARKER

DO NOT WRITE HERE
FOR VERIFICATION: MAR 27 1963
ORDERED: APR 18 1963
B/L: B- 6288799
CONTRACTOR: COLUMBUS MARBLE WORKS COLUMBUS, MISSISSIPPI

14. NAME AND LOCATION OF CEMETERY (City and State): Catawba Chapel Cemetery, Catawba, S. C.
IMPORTANT - Item 18 on reverse side must be completed. See attached instructions and complete and submit both copies.
15. This application is submitted for a stone or marker for the unmarked grave of a deceased member or former member of the Armed Forces of the U. S., soldier of the Union or Confederate Armies of the Civil War or for an unmarked memorial plot for a non-recoverable deceased member. I hereby agree to accept responsibility for proper placement at the grave or memorial plot at no expense to the Government.
NAME OF APPLICANT (Print or Type): Mrs. Evelyn B. George
RELATIONSHIP: Daughter
ADDRESS OF APPLICANT (Street address, City and State): Route 3, Box 119 Rock Hill, S. C.
SIGNATURE OF APPLICANT: Evelyn B. George
DATE: 3-20-63
16. FREIGHT STATION: Rock Hill, S. C.
17. NAME OF CONSIGNEE WHO WILL TRANSPORT STONE OR MARKER: Mrs. Evelyn B. George
ADDRESS OF CONSIGNEE (Street address, City and State): Rt. 3, Box 119, Rock Hill, S. C.
I HAVE AGREED TO TAKE THE STONE OR MARKER TO THE CEMETERY.
SIGNATURE OF CONSIGNEE: Evelyn B. George

Pvt Salvage Div QMC / WWI

DD FORM 1330, 1 DEC 61 PREVIOUS EDITION IS OBSOLETE. APPLICATION FOR HEADSTONE OR MARKER Form Approved Budget Bureau No. 22-R205

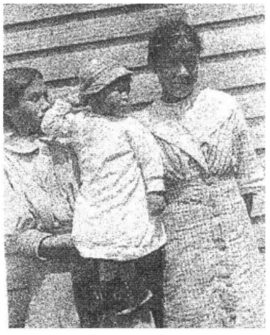

**PHOTO 152 - U.S., HEADSTONE APPLICATIONS FOR MILITARY VETERANS, 1925-1963 FOR EARLY BROWN**

Edith Bertha Harris - born 13 Jun 1893 in Catawba, York, South Carolina, United States and died 12 Jun 1985 in Rock Hill, York, South Carolina, United States. Daughter of David Adam Harris and Lizzie Jane Watts-Patterson. Wife of Early Brown.

**PHOTO 153 – EDITH BERTHA HARRIS BROWN**

**Early and Edith had five children, Edward, Evelyn, Richard, William and Lizzie.**

PHOTO 154 – EDWARD ALFORD BROWN

(1). Edward Alford Brown born 8 December 1911, Catawba, York, South Carolina and died 17 March 1969, Rock Hill, York, South Carolina. He married Edna Lucille Smith (1925-1991).[152]

PHOTO 155 – EDWARD ALFORD BROWN

---

[152] 1920 Census York County, SC

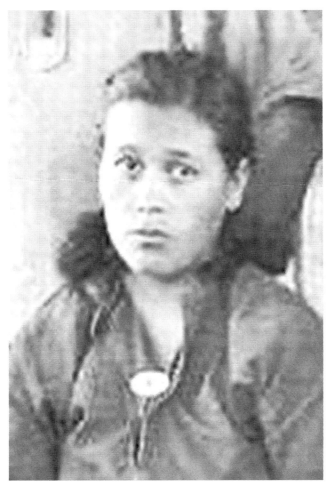

**PHOTO 156 – EVELYN BROWN**

(2). Evelyn Brown born 7 February 1914, Catawba Indian Nation, York, South Carolina and died 9 December 2007, Rock Hill, York, South Carolina. She married John Marvin George (1909-1999), son of Johnny P. and Hester Catharine Harris George. Evelyn married Moroni James Joseph George Jr. as his second wife.[153] Children will be found under George.

Evelyn Brown George was one of the most generous potters the Catawba Indian Nation ever produced. She received the Jean Laney Harris Legislative Award from South Carolina for her contributions in 2004. She was a leader in the revival of Catawba dance in the 1990s.

Rock Hill - Evelyn Brown George, 93, of 2545 John Brown Road, died Sunday, December 9, 2007, at her home.

---

[153] Catawba Branch Records.

**PHOTO 157 - EVELYN BROWN**

**PHOTO 158 – EVELYN BROWN AT HOUSE**

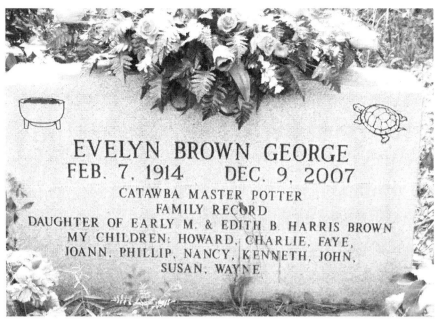

**PHOTO 159 - BURIAL: CHURCH OF JESUS CHRIST OF LATTER-DAY STS. CEMETERY, CATAWBA, YORK COUNTY, SOUTH CAROLINA**

**PHOTO 160 - HEADSTONE OF RICHARD BROWN 1916-1979**

(3). Richard Brown born 21 April 1916, Catawba, York, South Carolina and died 19 May 1979, Rock Hill, York, South Carolina. He married Mary Ann Ayers (1918-2008), daughter of John J. and Ruth Lucinda "Rhett" Gordon Avers.[154] Daughter Ayers.

---

[154] 1920 census

**PHOTO 161 – HEADSTONE OF WILLIAM JOHN HENRY PETE BROWN**

(4). William John Henry Pete Brown born 5 November 1920, Catawba Indian Nation, York, South Carolina and died 24 March 2000, Rock Hill, York, South Carolina. He married Ruby Ayers (1929-1997), daughter of John Jefferson and Ruth Lucinda (Rhett) Gordon Brown.

**Obituary:**

State, The (Columbia, SC) - Saturday, March 25, 2000

ROCK HILL - Services for William Pete Brown, 80, will be held at the Church of Jesus Christ of Latter Day Saints - Catawba Ward, with burial in the church cemetery.

Mr. Brown died Friday. Born in Rock Hill, he was a son of the late Early Morgan and Edith Bertha Harris Brown.

Surviving are his sons, Bobby, Owen, William, and Patrick Brown, all of Rock Hill; daughters, Nancy Brown of Seneca, Reba Sigmon of Sharon, Vanessa Troublefield, Velma Whitesides, Anna Branham, Myra Brindle, all of Rock Hill; two sisters; ten grandchildren; three great-grandchildren.

Burial:  Church of Jesus Christ of Latter-day Sts Cemetery   - Catawba, York County, South Carolina

**PHOTO 162 – LIZZIE BROWN**

(5). Lizzie Brown born in 21 May 1928, Catawba, South Carolina.

**********************************

**The rest of John and Margaret's children.**

**PHOTO 163 – SALLIE REBECCA BROWN**

b. Sallie Rebecca Brown, born 22 September 1893, Catawba Indian Reservation, Rock Hill, York, South Carolina and died 27 January 199, Rock Hill, York, South Carolina. She was a student of Mrs. Dunlap in 1899. She married December 24,

1914, Fletcher John Beck, son of Jefferson Swafford, white, and Lillie Florence Beck, part Cherokee.[155] They had six children and they will be found under Beck.

**Obituary:**

Charlotte Observer, The (NC) - Thursday, January 28, 1993

## CATAWBA POTTERY PIONEER SALLIE BECK DIES

Sallie Rebecca Brown Beck - one of the most famous potters in the history of the Catawba tribe - died Wednesday, Jan. 27, 1993, in Rock Hill. She was 99.

Mrs. Beck is credited with introducing Catawba pottery into local museums as well as acting as one of the tribe's first official pottery instructors in 1976. Historian Thomas Bloomer notes she is also thought to be the person responsible for introducing the "wedding jug" to tribal potters in the 1930s. The two-spouted jar, which is Cherokee in origin, is among the most popular pottery forms made by the tribe, Bloomer said. "'She was a master potter of note," Bloomer said. "Her work was popular

for years with private collectors and museums who would seek her out to buy pottery."

Born in York County, Mrs. Beck survived a 1918 influenza epidemic that killed five of her seven siblings.

She later became one of the first to attend the Catawba Indian School in Rock Hill, Bloomer said. Beck's pottery won a blue ribbon at the second annual Catawba Fair in 1939, and later earned similar honors at various county fairs. In 1952 she participated in the first exhibit of Catawba pottery held at the Museum Of York County, which now has several of her pieces in its permanent collection. Family members also say her work is included in the Smithsonian.

Her funeral at the Church of Jesus Christ of Latter-day

Saints in Catawba, with Bishop Michael Broadhead and Patriarch Benjamin Wilkers officiating. Burial will be in Catawba Baptist Church Cemetery in Catawba.

Survivors are her sons, Fletcher Beck of Catawba and Eugene Beck of Rock Hill; daughters, Ms. Rachel Yates of Potomac, Md., Ms. Ethel Warner of Bolivar, Ohio, and Ms. Irene Garcia of Pueblo, Colo.; 39 grandchildren; 56 great-grandchildren; and 11 great-great-grandchildren.

---

[155] Watson page 22.

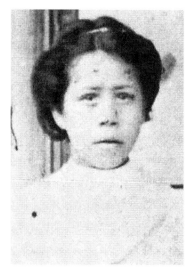

**PHOTO 164 – ARZADA BROWN**

c. Arzada Brown, born 3 July 1896,[156]on Catawba Indian Reservation, York, South Carolina and died 20 Mar 1989, in Rock Hill, York, South Carolina, United States. She is also listed as a student of Dunlap. She married John Idle Sanders on 5 July1912, son of John and Martha Harris Sanders.[157] Wes White states "she was an extremely prolific Catawba potter, only recently inactive due to age" Children will be found in the Allen Harris Chapter.

**PHOTO 165 – ARZADA BROWN**

---

[156] Ibid
[157] Catawba Branch Records.

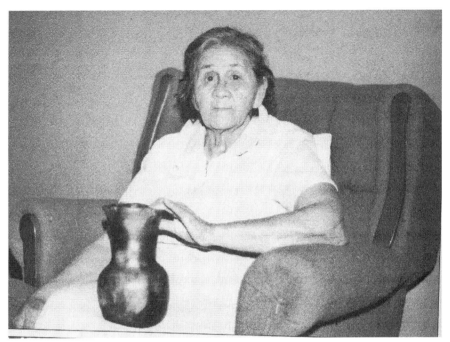

**PHOTO 166 - ARZADA BROWN**

# Sanders' married 61 years ago

**MR. AND MRS. JOHN IDLE SANDERS**
.... were married in 1912 on Catawba Indian Reservation

ROCK HILL — Arzada Brown married John Idle Sanders, later to become a Catawba tribal chief, two days after her sixteenth birthday. Married July 5, 1912, they observed their 61st anniversary last week.

Mr. and Mrs. Sanders had 12 children, nine of whom are living. They include Catherine Sanders Canty, Thomas Sanders, E. Fred Sanders, William E. Sanders, Roberta Sanders Honeycutt, Vivian Sanders Williford and Mohavie Sanders Brewton, all of Rock Hill; Eula Wanders Watts, Salt Lake City, Utah; and John Jack Sanders of Belmont, N.C.

Their oldest children, now deceased, were Blanche, Kirk and Herman Sanders. The couple also has 35 grandchildren and 36 great-grandchildren.

An anniversary celebration planned by their children was marred by the death of a grandson, Earl H. Honeycutt Jr., in a car accident June 29.

Mr. Sanders, 80, worked in textile mills and at Roy Neely Lumber Co. before his retirement. As a tribal committee member, he spoke before the U.S. Congress prior to the division and sale of parts of the Catawba Reservation near Lesslie.

Mrs. Sanders is one of the few remaining Catawba Indians who still fashion handmade pottery. Her pottery is sold at the Nature Museum of York County and in area craft shops. She was ten years old when she began learning the craft from her mother.

Mr. and Mrs. Sanders still reside on Rt. 3 at the Catawba Indian Reservation.

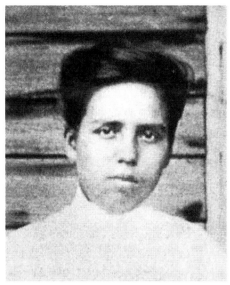

**PHOTO 167 – CORA BROWN**

d. Cora Brown, born 13 August 1898, Catawba, York, South Carolina and died 9 October 1918, Rock Hill, York, South Carolina. She married Lewis Ernest Sanders, son of John Sanders on 22 April 1917. She died (one day before their infant son died). [158] More can found in the Lucinda Harris chapter.

**PHOTO 168 – CERTIFICATE OF DEATH CORA BROWN SANDERS**

---

[158] Ibid

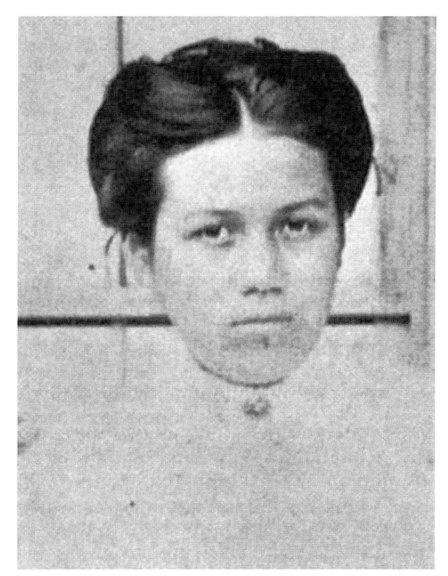

**PHOTO 169 – ABBIE OR MABBIE BROWN**

e. Abbie or Maggie or Mandy Brown, born 17 March 1901, Catawba Indian Reservation, Rock Hill South Carolina and died 5 October 1918, Catawba Indian Reservation, Rock Hill South Carolina. [159] She married Richard J. Harris on April 6, 1916, the son of David Adam and Lizzie Patterson Harris. Children will be found under David Adam Harris. She was a victum of the Spanish Influenza.

---

[159] Catawba Branch records.

Brown Family

PHOTO 170 - HEADSTONE FOR MAGGIE BROWN HARRIS –
BURIAL: CATAWBA INDIAN NATION CEMETERY - ROCK HILL –YORK, SOUTH CAROLINA

PHOTO 171 - CERTIFICATE OF DEATH FOR MAGGIE BROWN HARRIS

**PHOTO 172 -** HEADSTONE FOR JOHN WILLIAM BROWN - BURIAL: - CATAWBA INDIAN NATION CEMETERY ROCK HILL, YORK COUNTY, SOUTH CAROLINA
**Inscription:** Son of John Brown and Rachel George Brown. Died in influenza epidemic

f.  John William Brown was born 15 April 1903, Catawba Indian Reservation, Rock Hill South Carolina and died 4 October 1918, Catawba Indian Reservation, Rock Hill South Carolina, a victim of the influenza epidemic.[160]

**PHOTO 173 - CERTIFICATE OF DEATH JOHN W BROWN**

---

[160] Catawba Cemetery inscriptions.

**PHOTO 174 - ROY BROWN**

g. Roy Brown, born 28 January 1905, Rock Hill, York, South Carolina and died 22 November 1979, Rock Hill, York, South Carolina. He married Edna Mae Wheelock, daughter of Archie and Rosa Harris Wheelock on May 23, 1931.[161] The Thatcher children are living with them in 1943

**PHOTO 175 – ROY BROWN**

---

[161] Watson page 22

**PHOTO 176 – HEADSTONE FOR ROY BROWN AND HIS WIFE EDNA M WHEELOCK BROWN**

**PHOTO 177 - MARY RACHEL GROWN PLYLER -- CATAWBA INDIAN NATION CEMETERY, BURIAL PLACE - ROCK HILL, YORK COUNTY, SOUTH CAROLINA**

h. Mary Rachel Brown, born July 11, 1907,[162] Catawba Indian Reservation, Rock Hill South Carolina and died 22 February 1955, Catawba Indian Reservation, Rock Hill South Carolina. She married Olin Flow Plyler, (white) on December 9, 1924.

---

[162] Ibid

**PHOTO 178 – HEADSTONE FOR HENRY BROWN - BURIAL: CATAWBA INDIAN NATION CEMETERY, ROCK HILL, YORK COUNTY, SOUTH CAROLINA**

i. Henry Brown, born 31 March 1909, Catawba, York, South Carolina and died 12 January 1911, Rock Hill, York, South Carolina. He was also a victim of influenza.[163]

**PHOTO 179 - HEADSTONE OF ETHEL ALBERTA BROWN -BURIAL: - CATAWBA INDIAN NATION CEMETERY - ROCK HILL, YORK COUNTY, SOUTH CAROLINA**

j. . Ethel Alberta Brown, born 6 October 1911, Catawba, York, South Carolina and died 8 October 1918, Rock Hill, York, South Carolina.

---

[163] Watson page 22 and cemetery inscriptions.

Form No. 10

CERTIFICATE OF DEATH
STATE OF SOUTH CAROLINA
Bureau of Vital Statistics
State Board of Health

File No.—For State Registrar Only. 24386

1. PLACE OF DEATH
County of York
Township of Catawba
Registration District No. 4400
Registered No. 81

2. FULL NAME Ethyl Brown

PERSONAL AND STATISTICAL PARTICULARS

3 SEX Female
4 COLOR OR RACE Indian
5 SINGLE, MARRIED, WIDOWED, OR DIVORCED Single
6 DATE OF BIRTH
7 AGE 9 yrs.
8 OCCUPATION
9 BIRTHPLACE (State or Country) South Carolina
10 NAME OF FATHER John Brown
11 BIRTHPLACE OF FATHER (State or Country) South Carolina
12 MAIDEN NAME OF MOTHER
13 BIRTHPLACE OF MOTHER (State or Country) South Carolina
14 THE ABOVE IS TRUE TO THE BEST OF MY KNOWLEDGE
(Informant)
(Address)
15 Filed 11/1 1918 LOCAL REGISTRAR

MEDICAL CERTIFICATE OF DEATH

16 DATE OF DEATH Oct 9, 1918
17 I HEREBY CERTIFY, That I attended deceased from Oct 3 1918, to Oct 8 1918, that I last saw h... alive on Oct 8 1918, and that death occurred, on the date stated above, at ... m. The CAUSE OF DEATH* was as follows:
Influenza complicated with malarial fever
Contributory (SECONDARY) Pneumonia
(Signed) M.D.
Oct 9 18 (Address) Catawba
18 LENGTH OF RESIDENCE
19 PLACE OF BURIAL Nation
DATE OF BURIAL Oct 10 1918
20 UNDERTAKER
ADDRESS

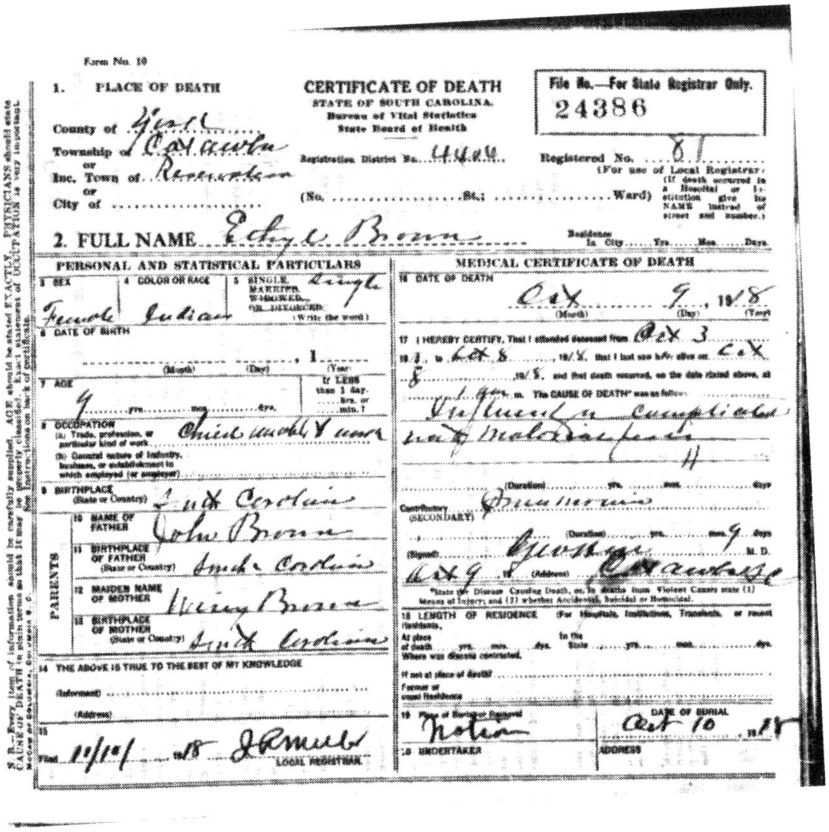

**PHOTO 180 - CERTIFICATE OF DEATH FOR ETHEL ALBERTA BROWN**

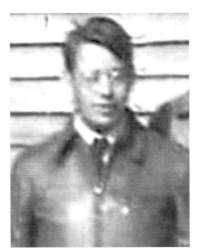

**PHOTO 181 - GEORGE BROWN**

k. George Brown, born September 16, 1914, married Mildred Tomlinson, (white) and Viola Adams. George died June 30, 1985.[164] No children are listed in 1958.

[164] Ibid

**PHOTO 182 - EARLY, ROY, SALLIE, ARZADA AND
GEORGE BROWN - 1958**

## Chapter 5   Bullin or Bullen Family

I. Spanaw[165]-Jemey-Jimmy James Bullin-Bullen probably born around 1720 died around 1757. He fought in the French and Indian War.   He was said to be a half-breed, son of a Colonial trader named James Bullen and a Catawba Woman.[166] In November of 1756, a party of Catawba joined George Washington at Winchester, Virginia.  In April and May of 1757, they were part of a campaign at Fort Cumberland and Fort Loudoun, in which James Bullen was said to be one of the bravest.  The Catawba had sent 124 men to fight, however, most returned home and Bullen was sent to try to get them to come back.  Twenty-five Catawba did return, joining Washington at Fort Cumberland.[167]

   He was said to have been a rival of King Hagler, and received his commission from Governor Dobbs of North Carolina as ruler of the Catawba.[168]   In 1756, James greeted 80 Mohawks.[169]   Shortly before his death, it was thought that he was a spy for the British.  He was involved in the capture of 10 Cherokee for spying.  He tried to enlist the help of the Chickasaw and Creeks, and Washington approved; however, Bullen died before the plans could be carried out.  Colonel Bouquet wrote, to Washington, "I regret extremely the loss of poor Bullen, which very truly is a great one at this juncture.  He was the Indian I had the greatest opinion of for his truth to the English Nation.[170] James died around 1757 or 1758.

A. Prissy Bullen-Bullin probably born around 1750 married Peter ThusSeeWontSee or Thus Saw Wontree Harris, Birth 1752, Broad River, Catawba Indian Land and died 6 December 1823, Fort Mill, South Carolina.  She collected payments for land of the East side of the Catawba River between 1808 and 1829.

   1.  David (D Bullin) Harris was born in 1805.[171] He married Nancy George, daughter of Nancy George.  David collected rents[172] and according to Spratt, Prissy Bullen was the mother of David Harris.   Prissy bequeathed all her rents to John Genet Brown, except for a small bit that James Miller and James Moore had, for a little boy.[173]   The Indian agent called David, D. Bullin; however, unlike most Catawba; he went by Harris, which was his father's name.  Children will be found under Peter Harris.

---

[165] Merrell page 139
[166] Merrell page 123
[167] Brown 108 & 109
[168] Brown page 234
[169] Blumer page 49.
[170] Milling, Chapman James, Red Carolinians, University of North Carolina Press, Chapel Hill, 1940, page 248 hereafter cited as Milling.
[171] 1849 census
[172] Indian Platt Books
[173] Brown, Douglas Summers' reprint of Platt Books, from A City without Cobwebs, page 297.

## Group Photo

Photo 183  - Catawba    Branch – 1926

## Chapter 6   Canty Family

William Canty was probably born around 1680, he was the first trader, and is the earliest documented trader, in the years 1707-1711.[174]   In those years, he brought gifts of deerskins for the governors to the government in Charles Town, Virginia. Expenses of 4:12:6 pounds were allowed to William for entertaining the Catawba.[175]   He is most likely the father of Captain John Canty.[176]   In those early years, a Catawba host often offered the white traders and officials the services, so to speak, of Catawba women. In a good many cases, the white traders actually "married" the women, and reared their children. Some of the rich plantation owners and government men just used the women, leaving a half-white Catawba child, as well as white families and some cases black families. In a great many cases of white-Catawba relations, the fathers' parents and grandparents and other genealogical information was known by the women. Most likely William had a Catawba woman, and that is how the Canty name came to be in Catawba.

I. Captain John Canty[177]  was a white Indian fighter. He was probably born around 1700 but he was definitely alive in 1712.[178]   Since the traders took Catawba wives, this is most likely the first Catawba Canty. He most likely was the father of George Canty since there are no Catawba Canty's between John and Major George. John commanded 41 Catawba during the Yamassee War.[179]

 A.  George Canty, probably born around 1730, signed leases in 1757 as Captain Canty. He became Major Canty in 1784 on Drennan's Pay bill, and is Major George Canty on leases dated July 20, 1810-through September of 1810.[180]

Major George Canty fought in Revolution and is on the listing of Drennan in 1780 as George Canty, 44 days and 22 pounds.[181]   He signed the petition of 1792. George most likely married first Betsy Ayers Scott Kennedy Canty, daughter of Col. Jacob Ayers. She was the first wife of John Scott. Betsy then married, as his second wife, John Kennedy.

George probably died around 1813, since Jacob Ayers received George's rental accounts in 1813 for "one horse for seven years, the above rent was paid on a/c of the heirs of the late Major Canty and is to be paid hereafter to them"[182] rents on that lease were paid to Nancy and Johnston Kennedy and the family of Billey Canty. George is described by Howell in the Draper Manuscripts as "small of stature and not under a very bad character," and that he died about the year 1820.

---

[174] Brown page 107
[175] Brown pages 110, 126,271 and 330.
[176] Brown page 132
[177] Blumer page 55 article 436.
[178] Watson page 26.
[179] NOTE: The Yamassee War was during 1715-16 when the Catawba joined other Indian tribes in an attempt to wipe out the white settlements. Nearly every tribe from Cape Fear, NC to Florida and Alabama were in revolt. This was the only time the Catawba ever fought the whites
[180]Blumer pages 85 article 673, page 86, 87, 88.
[181] Watson page 26.
[182] Ibid

Stinson gave Revolutionary War information to Draper about General Jacob Canty, since Jacob Ayers received George's rentals 1813; it is probable that Stinson meant Jacob Ayers.

1. William-Billy Canty born around 1760. Captain Billy Canty began signing land leases on August 18, 1813, and signed the first two as Captain Billy Canty. He then became Captain William Canty, in October of 1813.[183] William alternated between Captain William and Billy Canty on leases through 1816.[184] He served in the Revolution, as Major William Canty. According to Hutchison, a resident of the area, and one time Indian Agent, Major William Canty served along with Billy Ayers, Captain Gilbert George. Captain Kelly, John Scott, Catawba George and Mosey Ayers (Moses-Mosy Ayers, served in Revolution, and received rents, but no other records have been found).

William-Billy was last known to be living in 1816, when he received rents. His wife is unknown, however since Nancy, Richard and Johnston Kennedy received rents after Billy's death around 1810-13, it is likely, that Billy married the daughter of John Kennedy. Mentioned in the Plat Books are Betsy, Johnston, Nancy and Richardson Kennedy. All are accounted for except the Betsy Kennedy. The ties between Jacob Ayers, Sally New River, Canty and Kennedy, would be through Billy Canty's marriage with the Kennedy daughter, he would have married the daughter of John Kennedy and her unknown mother, she would have been a step daughter to his own mother. The relationship sounds terribly complicated, but not unlike many other such interrelationships and marriages. William-Billy's mother being Betsy Ayers Scott Canty Kennedy would explain the ties between Jacob Ayers, Sally New River and Billy Canty

2. Old Nancy Canty born 1779[185] married William George Sr., she then was known as Old Nancy George in the remaining censuses. Children will be found under George.

3. Lewis Canty born around 1780. He was strongly connected with the Spratts, dropping by for visits often.[186] He was a Captain by 1821, and continued signing leases beginning from the year 1808, through 1835 as one of the headmen of the Nation. He was a Colonel about 1825.

He was able to read and write, and considered literate. Spratt described him in a letter of September 3, 1874 as being in the company of Sally New River and was "Intelligent and was about as good a specimen of the Catawba physically and mentally as I ever saw."

" Governor Spotswood's fort included the creation of an Indian School. He personally paid the salary of the schoolmaster, Charles Griffin. At the school, the students were taught English and Religion. A visitor in 1716 reported that the Indian students knew the Lord's Prayer and could recite the Anglican catechism. As many as 100 students were in the Indian School at Fort Christanna. Having Indian children within the walls of the fort was a strategy to prevent an Indian attack. However, by 1717 the fort and the school at Christanna had lost its support in London and

---

[183] Blumer page 99 article 756.
[184] Blumer page 103 article 780.
[185] 1849 census
[186] Merrell page 213

Virginia. The Indian School closed, and it schoolmaster went back east to teach Indian students at the College of William and Mary"[187]

Lewis married first, Jenny Scott, daughter of General Jacob Scott. This would explain the relationship between Lewis, General Scott and Sally New River, that Spratt headspoke of when Jenny died before 1825, and her rents were given to Lewis Canty. She is listed in the Piatt book as J. Canty.

They were the parents of seven children. Lewis married second, Sally Ayers Clinton Harris, the daughter of Jacob Ayers, around 1825. The Plat books intimate that Lewis and Sally may have had children. Lewis probably died around 1838. Lewis and Jenny Scott had Harriot, Henry, Leroy, Lewis, Billy, Peggy and Franklin Canty.[188]

> a. Harriot Canty, born 1805, married Lewis Stevens, born 1804. Harriot last received rents on June 25, 1827. There is some association with John Joe, and a Billy Kelley, according to the Plat Books. Children will be found under Stevens-Stephens.
>
> b. Henry Canty born around 1806, had some kind of relationship with a Lucy Canty, as rents were assigned to Henry Canty and Lucey Canty, to take rents on the lands of Robert Marsh around 1820.
>
> c. Leroy Canty born around 1807
>
> d. Lewis Canty born around 1808
>
> e. Billy Canty born around 1809. Billy left his leases to his sister Harriet in his will. He was evidently considered quite well off, when he and Rebecca Marsh both received their rents between 1810 and 1830.[189]
>
> f. Peggy Canty born 1819 and Chancy Evans,[190] probably a white man, had only one child that can be identified
>
>> (1) unidentified child in 1854
>>
>> (2) also an unidentified child

---

[187] http://wwwbrunswickco.com/ftchris.asp
[188] Watson pages 26, 27
[189] Watson page 26.
[190] Catawba Branch Records.

**PHOTO 184 – SARAH ANN LOUSIE CANTY-EVANS**

(3) Sarah Ann Louise Canty-Evans born July 1, 1845, married first Robert Henry Head, son of Lucy Marsh and unknown Head. Robert died because of the Civil War, and Sarah remarried, Alec Tims around 1886. She was a widow for many years. She then came west with Alec. While in South Carolina, the Mormon missionaries stayed with Alec and Sarah many times. The following is found in Joseph Willey's Diary of his mission, it is one of the most interesting, to think of the fear and terror Sarah must have faced.

"June 6, On May 25 at Elder Cragun and Fraughton was visiting one of our Lamanite friends, Mr. Alexander Tims and Elder Cragun had his shoes off ready to go to bed for the night. When a mob of about 20 men rushed on them. Mr. Tims said to the Elders, 'Run.' Elder Cragun ran out the back door. Some 10 or 12 shots was fired at him. He fell but rose again and got in the woods. He received a slight wound on the chin. Several fine shot hit him on the right side of the chin. The wound was not serious. Elder Fraughton concealed himself under the bed but was brought out at the point of several pistols. They took him about one mile out of the Nation and found men whipped him, giving him 10 lashes each, 40 lashes in all. He returned to the house and they spend the night in the woods. "

**Pinkney Head wrote in his journal:**

"I heard they was some Saints going to Colorado so I though I would go then and the 3rd day of April I quit work to fix up to go. I left and walked 10 miles that evening. Come to Martinsville, P.O. SC and there I got a letter from home stating that my mother was sick, bad off, no life expected for her. She said that she wanted me to come home and see her one more time so I went on to Bro. Russells got there about sundown. I staid there till 12 o'clock that night getting ready to go home. One of my cousins went with me down to Mr. Blacks, which was about 10 miles. We got there just at daylight, went to Grandmothers house and had breakfast and then went with my Uncle J. H. Watts to Gaffney Station, which was 10 miles. I check my bundle and started a foot on home, 35 miles that night. Next day late I travel all night on the railroad until about one hour before day. I went out in the woods a little ways and made me a little fire. I awoke next morning about daylight and started on the Catawba Nation which was 10 miles. I call at some five houses along the railroad for something to eat. At last I got a little to eat and then I went and with haste to get home. I got in about 1/2 mile half of home. I met up with one of my old friends. He told me my mother was a little better. I then began to feel better. I went on home and saw my mother very low and there I met with Elders Joseph Willey and W. E. Cragun again."

**Joseph Willey describes the same incident:**

"March 29, held meeting at Bro. Wm. Georges. March 30, Mrs. Sarah Head was taken very sick. She sent us to come and administer to her. We did so; she was a very sick woman. She seemed to rest better after she had been administered to." Sarah died and in 1919 and is buried in Kirtland, New Mexico.

**Sarah married Robert Henry Head; they had only one child, Pinkney.**

**PHOTO 185 – PINKNEY HENRY HEAD**

(a). Pinkney Henry Head, born 26 October, 1862, married Martha    Jane Patterson, daughter of James Goodwin and Elizabeth Missouri White Patterson. In the 1854 census, Sarah has three children, so there are two unknown children. Pinkney Henry Head family is continued in Head Chapter.

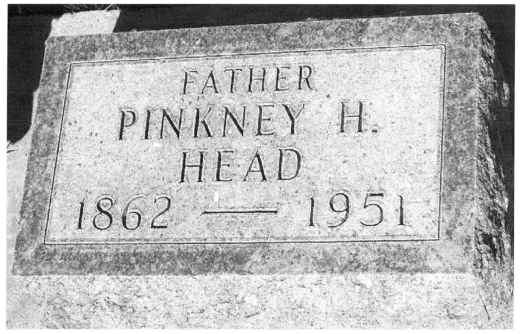

**PHOTO 186 - HEADSTONE OF PINKNEY H HEAD**

g. Franklin Canty born 1826, Catawba, York, South Carolina and he died in 1885, Catawba, York, South Carolina. He married Eliza Scott born 1826, daughter of Caty Scott Joe and most likely John Joe. Eliza did not live very long. He married in 1843 Eliza Scott Canty had three children in the 1854 census and one is unknown.[191]

**1849 Census of the Catawba**

NUMBER IN SOUTH CAROLINA. Greenville District.
MALES. AGE. MALES. AGE.
**Franklin Canty, 23** John Scott, 23
John Brown, 12 David Harris, 40

List of the Catawbas in connection with the Church at Echota Mission.

SHOAL CREEK CAMP GROUND, Sept. 17th, 1849.

Mr. MASSEY,

Dear Sir : At your request I furnish you with the number and names

of the Catawbas, in connection with the Methodist Episcopal Church South,

at the Echota Mission, viz :

William Morrison, John Scott,

---

[191] Catawba Branch Records.

Mary Morrison, John Hart,

Betsy Hart, Lewis Stevens,

Nancy George, Allen Harris,

Polly Stevens, Rhoda Harris,

Cinthy Kegg, **Franklin Canty**,

Betsy Brown, David Harris,

**Eliza's Scott Canty's children by Thomas Whitesides, the Indian Agent. John Alonzo, Fannie and Mary Jane will be found under Scott, since the three were not true Canty's but Whitesides-Scott. She married Frank Canty**

(1) William Canty born 1845, Catawba Indian Reservation, York, South Carolina and died 15 January 1865, Richmond, Madison, Virginia. He enlisted in the Confederate army on December 9, 1861. He fought at Manassas. Sharpsburg and Boonesboro. William is listed as one of the Lacy Guards in 1862. He was discharged on February 3, 1863; he re-enlisted on March 11, 1864 in Company H, 12th South Carolina Infantry with Nelson George. He is called Billy Canty on the 1863 petition for John R. Patton. William does not ever appear anywhere else. He was last paid July 7, 1864 in Richmond, Virginia. William Canty was wounded on May 5, 1864, and died of disease in January 1865.

**U.S. Civil War Soldiers, 1861-1865**

William Canty – Side - Confederate

Regiment State/Origin - South Carolina

Regiment - 17th Regiment, South Carolina Infantry

Company – K    Rank In – Private    Rank Out - Private

Film Number - M381 roll 5

Other Records

17th Regiment, South Carolina Infantry

U.S., Civil War Soldier Records and Profiles, 1861-1865

William Canty

Rank at enlistment - Private

State Served - South Carolina

Service Record - Enlisted in Company K, South Carolina 17th Infantry Regiment.

Sources - Index to Compiled Confederate Military Service Records

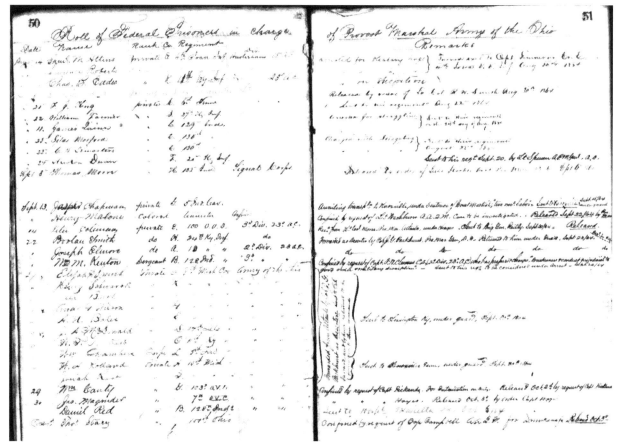

**PHOTO 187 - U.S., CIVIL WAR PRISONER OF WAR RECORDS, 1861-1865**

(2). George Washington Canty born January 16, 1851 in Union County, South Carolina and died 20 July 1893, Catawba Indian Reservation, South Carolina. He married Mary Jane Elizabeth (M. J. E. -Betsy Mush-George) who was born 1857, daughter of William and Betsy Mush George.[192]  George received money from the Indian Agent R. L. Crook on April 10, 1875 in the amount of $10.00. In 1881 from the new agent William White, he received $26.64, and his wife got $13.50 at the same time. On June 19, 1875, M. J. Canty received $4.50. George signed a Petition in 1877 asking that Crook be removed as Indian Agent. He also signed one naming William White as agent.

George and the rest of the Catawba then began their investigations of the Mormon Church.

---

[192] Catawba Branch Records.

**Elder Joseph Willey writes in 1885:**

"Mr. John Sanders and Mr. George Canty was baptized on the next nite after baptism we held meeting and confirmed them in meeting. March 19, 1 baptized four young women, two married and two single namely Mrs. Betsy Canty and Martha Sanders and Miss Rachel Tims and Betsy Crofford."

Pinkney Head, another Catawba writes of the Mormon Elders having to hide in the stable of Alec and Sarah Head Tims because of the persecution of the Mormons at the time.

"One morning Brother George Canty came to our house and was surprised to see Elders there and to hear them say they had been there all the time."

"Sunday March 8, Mr. John Sanders and Mr. George Canty was baptized on the next nite after baptism we held meeting and confirmed them in meeting." George Washington and Mary Jane Elizabeth (Betsy) Mush-George Canty had 6 children, John William, Franklin, Henry Alonzo Washington, Louisa Jane, Sarah A., Peggy, and Hester Canty.

George took his father's surname, not his mother's, which is unusual.

George died July 20, 1893.[193]

| Father  George Washington CANTY | | |
|---|---|---|
| Birth | 16 Jan 1851 | Union, Union, South Carolina, United States |
| Residence | 1880 | Age: 30Marital Status: Married; Relation to Head of House: Self; Catawba, York, South Carolina, United States |
| Burial | Jul 1883 | ,,, United States |
| Death | 20 Jul 1893 | Catawba Indian Reservation, Rock Hill, York, South Carolina, United States |
| Marriage | 1875 | Catawba Reservation, , South Carolina |
| Father | Franklin CANTY (1826-1854) | |
| Mother | Eliza SCOTT JOE (1826-1869) | |
| **Mother  Mary Jane Elizabeth-Betsy MUSH GEORGE** | | |
| Birth | 27 Dec 1856 | Catawba Indian Reservation, York, South Carolina |
| Residence | 1880 | Age: 23Marital Status: Married; Relation to Head of House: Wife; Catawba, York, South Carolina, United States |
| Death | Oct 1898 | Catawba Indian Reservation |
| 0 | | 46KG-D9 |
| AFN | | CKJF-4N |
| Burial | | |
| | | |

---

[193] Blumer 202 article 1473.

| | | |
|---|---|---|
| M | Franklin "Frank" CANTY | |
| | Birth | 21 Mar 1875 | Catawba Indian Reservation, York, South Carolina, United States |
| | Residence 1880 | Age: 5Marital Status: Single; Relation to Head of House: Son; Catawba, York, South Carolina, United States |
| | Residence 1910 | Age: 33Marital Status: Married; Relation to Head of House: Head; Catawba, York, South Carolina |
| | Death | 24 Jun 1933 | Age at Death: 59; Catawba Reservation, York, South Carolina, United States |
| | Burial | Rock Hill, York County, South Carolina |
| | AFN | 46KG-NN |
| | Spouse | Dorothy Minerva PRICE (1893-  ) |
| M | Henry Alonzo William CANTY | |
| | Birth | 27 Jan 1877 | Catawba Reservation, York, South Carolina |
| | Residence 1900 | Age: 28Relation to Head of House: Lodger; Catawba Indian Reservation, York, South Carolina |
| | Residence 1910 | Catawba, York, South Carolina |
| | Residence 1930 | Age: 56Marital Status: Married; Relation to Head of House: Brother-in-law; Catawba, York, South Carolina |
| | Death | 12 Mar 1934 | Age at Death: 57; Catawba Indian Reservation, York, South Carolina, United States |
| | Residence | York, South Carolina |
| | Burial | Rock Hill, York County, South Carolina |
| | AFN | 46KG-PT |
| | Spouse | Emma Jane HARRIS (1888-1961) |
| M | Robert Lee CANTY | |
| | Birth | abt 1878 | Catawba, York, South Carolina |
| | Residence 1880 | Age: 2Marital Status: Single; Relation to Head of House: Son; Catawba, York, South Carolina, United States |
| | Residence 1910 | Age: 41Marital Status: Single; Relation to Head of House: Boarder; Catawba, York, South Carolina |
| | Death | |
| | Burial | |
| | Marriage | |
| F | Louisa Jane Hester CANTY | |
| | Birth | 7 Feb 1883 | Catawba Reservation, York, South Carolina |
| | Residence 1900 | Age: 19Marital Status: Married; Relation to Head of House: Wife; Catawba Indian Reservation, York, South Carolina |

| | | |
|---|---|---|
| Residence 1910 | | Age in 1910: 27Marital Status: Married; Relation to Head of House: Wife; Catawba, York, South Carolina |
| Residence 1920 | | Age: 37Marital Status: Married; Relation to Head of House: Wife; Catawba, York, South Carolina |
| Residence 1930 | | Age: 47Marital Status: Married; Relation to Head of House: Wife; Catawba, York, South Carolina |
| Death | 9 Jul 1963 | Catawba Reservation, York, South Carolina |
| Burial | | |
| Spouse | | Samuel Taylor BLUE (1872-1959) |
| Marriage | 8 May 1897 | Lancaster, Lancaster, South Carolina, United States |

| F | Peggy "twin" CANTY | |
|---|---|---|
| Birth | 27 Jun 1886 | Catawba Reservation, York, South Carolina |
| source | | Peggy is listed on the LDS Branch Records. |
| Death | | |
| Burial | | |
| Marriage | | |

| F | Sarah A "twin" CANTY | |
|---|---|---|
| Birth | 27 Jun 1886 | Catawba Reservation, York, South Carolina |
| Residence 1935 | | Sumter, Sumter, South Carolina |
| Residence 1 Apr 1940 | | Age: 54Marital Status: Widowed; Relation to Head of House: Head; Sumter, Sumter, South Carolina, United States |
| Death | | |
| Burial | | |
| Marriage | | |

**Children of George Washington Canty and Mary Jane Elizabeth-Betsy Mush George.**

**PHOTO 188 - JOHN WILLIAM FRANK CANTY**

1. John William Frank Canty was born, March 21, 1876, Catawba Reservation, York, South Carolina and died 25 June 1933 (age 59), Catawba Reservation, York, South Carolina. He married Dorothy Minerva Price a white woman, the marriage ended in divorce. She then married David Adam Harris as his third wife. The son of George Washington and Margaret Elizabeth Marsh-Mush Canty.

On his death certificate and in the census he is listed as Frank. But on his WWI Draft Registration Card he is listed as John William. On the 1930 census Frank, Kirk Sanders and Arthur and Albert Thatcher were all in the Rock Hill City jail at the same time. The census states he is full blood Catawba Indian. He died of acute alcoholism that is probably why he was in jail. The Thatcher's are connected to the Catawba through marriage later on. "Kirk Sanders was the son of John Idle and Arzada Brown Sanders. He was involved in mischief some how.

Burial: Catawba Indian Nation Cemetery, Rock Hill, York County, South Carolina

**PHOTO 189 - WWI REGISTRATION CARD FOR JOHN WILLIAM CANTY**

**Frank and Dorothy Minerva Price Canty's three children were:**

(a). Jennie Canty born 2 June 1908, married first Lewis Ernest Sanders, son of John Idle and Martha Harris Sanders; she married second Jessie Allen Harris, son of James and

Margaret Elizabeth Harris Harris; she married third Floyd Brindle, a white man. There were no children and she died October 1986.[194]

(b). William H. Canty born 30 October 1911 he died as an infant.

(c). George Canty born around 1913. He died as an infant.

**PHOTO 190 - HENRY ALONZO WILLIAM CANTY**

2. Henry Alonzo William Canty, born 27 January 1877, Catawba Tribe, Native American and he died 12 March 1934, Catawba, York South Carolina (Henry was accidentaly burned to death when trapped in a strawfield fire)   He married Emma Jane Harris, daughter of Wesley and Alice Ayers Harris

From Jerry D Lee's paper: "The church and the Catawba continued to grow and prosper during the next few years with little outside interference. In 1911 the chapel was found to be too small and was enlarged by twelve feet. The tribe now possessed a school house, a chapel and a well. With the heop of Sister Barrus the relief society was organized on Marth 7, 1910 with sisters Mary C Barrus, Mary J Watts and Eliza Blue as the presidency and Sister Lucy George as secretary. The Sunday School was operating very smoothly with upwards to sisty pupils and an efficient teaching core under the able direction of Elder Sam Blue assisted by John Brown and Henry Alonzo Canty, Elder Robert Harris presided over the branch."[195]

He is listed as Henry on the census records and his death certificate; on his WWI Draft Registration Card he is listed as Henry William Canty and on Find a Grave as Henry Alonzo William Canty.

**He had five children: Alonzo George, Ollie Mae, Allen Barnes, Henry, and Billy Columbus Canty.**

**PHOTO 191 - EMMA JANE HARRIS WIFE OF HENRY ALONZO WILLIAM CANTY. BORN JUNE 1888, GAFFNEY, CHEROKEE, NORTH CAROLINA AND DIED 19 JANUARY 1961, ROCK HILL, YORK, SOUTH CAROLINA.**

---

[195] Paper from Jerry D Lee – byuhttp://scholarsarchive.byu.edu/cgi/viewcontent.cgi?article=5870&context=etd

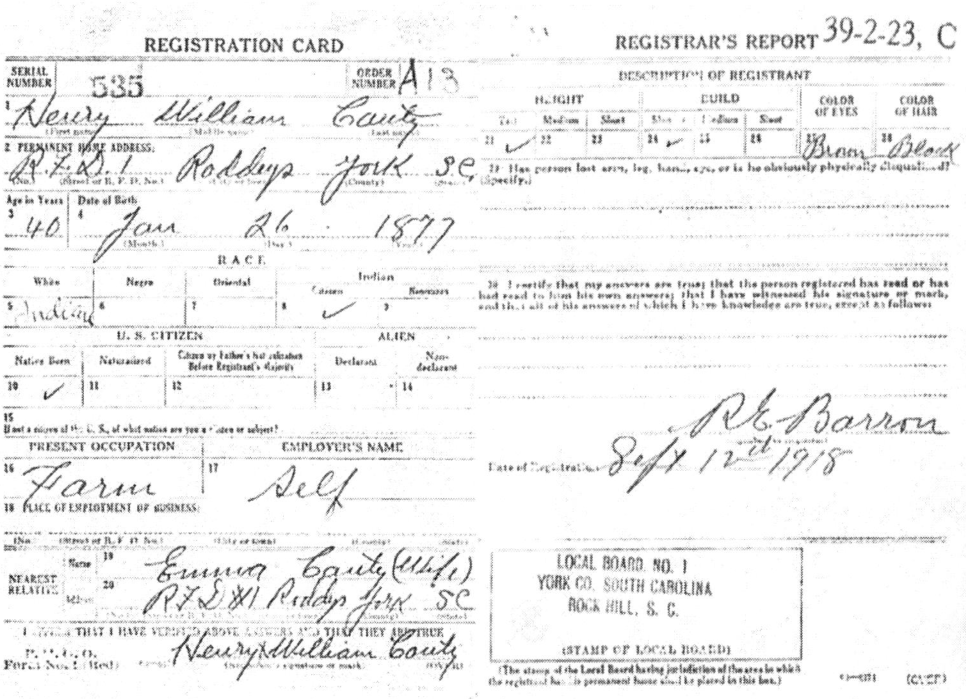

REGISTRATION CARD

REGISTRAR'S REPORT 39-2-23, C

SERIAL NUMBER 535 ORDER NUMBER A13

1 Henry William Canty (First name) (Middle name) (Last name)

2 PERMANENT HOME ADDRESS: R.F.D.1 Roddeys York S.C.

Age in Years 3 40 Date of Birth 4 Jan 26 1877

RACE: White, Negro, Oriental, Indian (Citizen, Noncitizen) — 5 Indian; 8 ✓

U. S. CITIZEN: Native Born 10 ✓; Naturalized 11; Citizen by Father's Naturalization Before Registrant's Majority 12. ALIEN: Declarant 13; Non-declarant 14

15 If not a citizen of the U. S., of what nation are you a citizen or subject?

PRESENT OCCUPATION 16 Farm EMPLOYER'S NAME 17 Self

18 PLACE OF EMPLOYMENT OR BUSINESS:

NEAREST RELATIVE: Name 19 Emma Canty (Wife) Address 20 RFD#1 Roddeys York SC

I AFFIRM THAT I HAVE VERIFIED ABOVE ANSWERS AND THAT THEY ARE TRUE

Henry William Canty

DESCRIPTION OF REGISTRANT: HEIGHT Tall, Medium ✓, Short; BUILD Slender ✓, Medium, Stout; COLOR OF EYES Brown; COLOR OF HAIR Black

29 Has person lost arm, leg, hand, eye, or is he obviously physically disqualified? (Specify)

30 I certify that my answers are true; that the person registered has read or has had read to him his own answers; that I have witnessed his signature or mark, and that all of his answers of which I have knowledge are true, except as follows:

R E Barron

Date of Registration Sept 12th 1918

LOCAL BOARD NO. 1 YORK CO. SOUTH CAROLINA ROCK HILL, S. C.

(STAMP OF LOCAL BOARD)

**PHOTO 192 - WWI REGISTRATION CARD FOR HENRY WILLIAM CANTY**

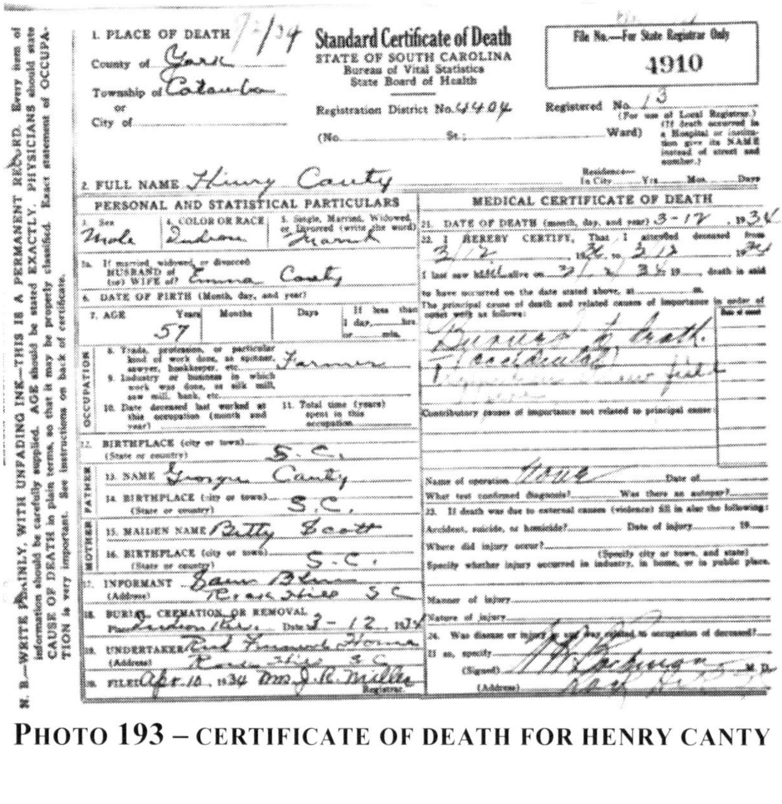

N. B.—WRITE PLAINLY, WITH UNFADING INK—THIS IS A PERMANENT RECORD. Every item of information should be carefully supplied. AGE should be stated EXACTLY. PHYSICIANS should state CAUSE OF DEATH in plain terms, so that it may be properly classified. Exact statement of OCCUPATION is very important. See instructions on back of certificate.

1. PLACE OF DEATH 7/34 County of York Township of Catawba or City of

Standard Certificate of Death STATE OF SOUTH CAROLINA Bureau of Vital Statistics State Board of Health

File No.—For State Registrar Only 4910

Registration District No. 4404 Registered No. 13

2. FULL NAME Henry Canty

PERSONAL AND STATISTICAL PARTICULARS

3. Sex Male 4. Color or Race Indian 5. Single, Married, Widowed, or Divorced Married

5a. If married, widowed, or divorced HUSBAND of (or) WIFE of Emma Canty

6. DATE OF BIRTH (Month, day, and year)

7. AGE 57

8. Trade, profession, or particular kind of work done Farmer

12. BIRTHPLACE (city or town) S.C.

13. NAME George Canty

14. BIRTHPLACE S.C.

15. MAIDEN NAME Betty Scott

16. BIRTHPLACE S.C.

17. INFORMANT Sam Blue (Address) Rock Hill S C

18. BURIAL, CREMATION, OR REMOVAL Place Indian Res. Date 3-12 1934

19. UNDERTAKER Red Funeral Home (Address) Rock Hill S C

20. FILED Apr. 10 1934 Mrs. J. R. Miller Registrar.

MEDICAL CERTIFICATE OF DEATH

21. DATE OF DEATH (month, day, and year) 3-11 1934

22. I HEREBY CERTIFY, That I attended deceased from 3/12 1934 to 3/12 1934

The principal cause of death and related causes of importance were as follows: Burned to death (accidental)

Name of operation None

**PHOTO 193 – CERTIFICATE OF DEATH FOR HENRY CANTY**

**Henry and his wife had five children:**

**PHOTO 194 - ALONZO GEORGE CANTY**

(1). Alonzo George Canty, born February 26, 1905, married Fannie Harris, daughter of David Adam and Lizzie Jane Patterson Harris, evidently they divorced, and by 1958 he had married a white woman, Virginia. Alonzo died June 16, 1979. Alonzo had 14 children: Margaret Helen,[196] Edith Francis, Heywood Jackson, Laviania Alberta, Thelma, Geneva Geraldine and Joyce, Lynne, Alonzo George jr., Judith Patricia, Edward Bruce, Betty, Wallace Lee and Eric Jerome.

**PHOTO 195 - FANNIE HARRIS WIFE OF ALONZO GEORGE CANTY**

---

[196] Biological father was Ernest C

(2). Ollie Mae Canty born 1908 died in childbirth 20 June 1928.[197]

Columbia, South    Carolina, Obituary Index, 1892-1994

Name   Ollie May Canty

Publication Date        20 Jun 1928  -  Publication Place      Columbia, Richland, South
Carolina,

Death Date      Abt 1928

Household Members    Name          Age

Ollie May Canty

**PHOTO 196 - HEADSTONE OF ALLEN BARNES CANTY**

(3). Allen Barnes Canty born December 8, 1911, a twin, married Ella Saunders, daughter of
William and Nora Brown-Boarch Saunders-Sanders.[198] Their children are: Cecil A Canty
1935– , Lawrence Laverne Canty 1942–2011, Jane Canty, Ollie Canty, Rosemary Canty,
Elaine Canty, Edward Eddie Canty.

**PHOTO 197 - HENRY CANTY AND HEADSTONE OF HENRY**

---

[197] Watson pages 26 & 27

[198] Catawba Branch records.

(4). Henry Canty born December 8, 1911, a twin, married Artie Jane George, daughter of Moroni James Joseph and Hattie J. Millings George. Henry died January 9, 1984. Their children are: James Edward Canty 1937–2008, Nellie Faye Canty 1939–2003, Louella Canty 1941–2000, Alva Bernard Canty 1944–2001, Emily Canty 1952– , Roger Bradford Canty 1955–1993, Theresa Canty, Stella Canty, Marion Canty, Leonard Canty.

**PHOTO 198 – BILLY COLUMBUS CANTY**

(5). Billy Columbus Canty born March 26, 1914 married Catherine Sanders, daughter of John Idle and Arzada Brown Saunders. Billy died February 1968.[199]

**PHOTO 199 - BILLY C CANTY WITH GRAND CHILDREN**

---

[199] Catawba Branch records.

**PHOTO 200 - BILLY WITH WIFE CATHERINE AND CHILDREN – SADIE ILENE, BILLIE ANN, CLIFFORD TROY, KIRK ROBERT AND ENMMA GERALDINE.**

*Back row. Dad, mom, & me.*

*...row Billie anne, Troy Geraldine & Kirk.*

*...is picture was made a coupl...*

*...rs. ago, it ~~isn't~~ wasn't good.*

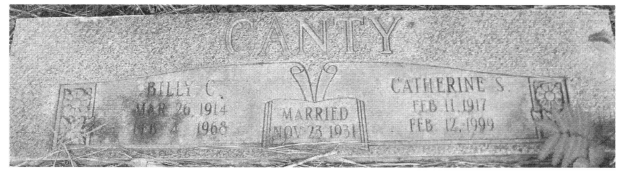

**PHOTO 201 - BILLY C CANTY AND WIFE CATHERINE SANDERS CANTY**

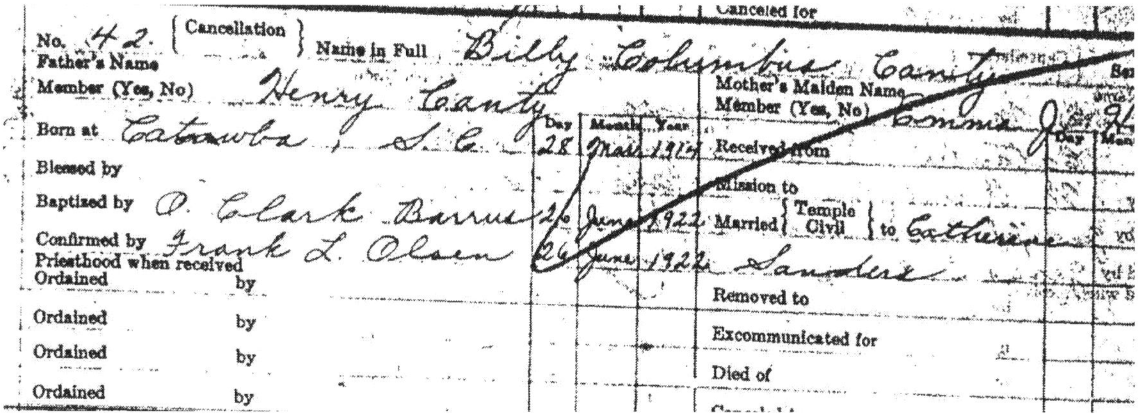

No. 42. Cancellation — Name in Full: Billy Columbus Canty
Father's Name / Member (Yes, No): Henry Canty
Mother's Maiden Name / Member (Yes, No): Emma J. H
Born at: Catawba, S. C. — Day 28, Month Mar, Year 1914
Received from
Blessed by
Mission to
Baptized by: O. Clark Barrus — 26 June 1922
Married (Temple / Civil) to Catherine Sanders
Confirmed by: Frank L. Olsen — 26 June 1922
Priesthood when received
Ordained by
Removed to
Ordained by
Excommunicated for
Ordained by
Died of
Ordained by
Canceled for

**PHOTO 202 – L.D.S. BAPTISM RECORD FOR BILLY COLUMBUS CANTY**

## Children of Billy Columbus Canty and Catherine Sanders

a). Alvin Huey Canty born August 12, 1933 in Catawba, York, South Carolina. He married Lee, a white woman and died on July 28 2012 in Rock Hill, South Carolina.

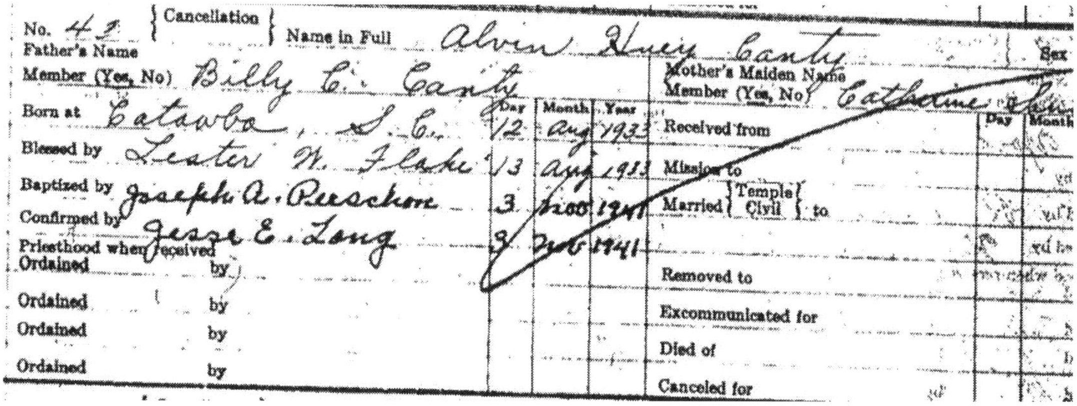

No. 42 Cancellation — Name in Full: Alvin Huey Canty
Father's Name / Member (Yes, No): Billy C. Canty
Mother's Maiden Name / Member (Yes, No): Catherine
Born at: Catawba, S. C. — Day 12, Month Aug, Year 1933
Received from
Blessed by: Lester W. Flake — 13 Aug 1933
Mission to
Baptized by: Joseph A. Peeschon — 3 Nov 1941
Married (Temple / Civil) to
Confirmed by: Jesse E. Long — 3 Nov 1941
Priesthood when received
Ordained by
Removed to
Ordained by
Excommunicated for
Ordained by
Died of
Ordained by
Canceled for

**PHOTO 203 – L.D.S. BAPTISM RECORD FOR ALVIN HUEY CANTY**

b). Sadie Ilene Canty born 28 April 1936, Catawba, South Carolina and died 1 February 2000, Catawba, South Carolina

**State, The (Columbia, SC) - Friday, February 4, 2000**

ROCK HILL - Services for Sadie Canty Whitlock, 63, will be held at the Church of Jesus Christ of Latter Day Saints, Catawba, with interment in the church cemetery.
Mrs. Whitlock died Tuesday. She was a daughter of the late Billy C. and Catherine Sanders Canty and member of the Church of Jesus Christ of Latter Day Saints.
Surviving are her sons, Paul M. and Chris S. Carpenter Jr.; daughters, Glenda C. Martin, Sandra C. Edgar; brothers, Huey A. and Clifford T. Canty; sisters, Billie Anne McKellar, Geraldine C. Tinker; four grandchildren.

c). Billie Ann Canty 12 Oct 1945 in Catawba, York, South Carolina –

d). Clifford Troy Canty 28 October 1946, Rock Hill, York, South Carolina –

e). Kirk Robert Canty 21 Dec 1947, South Carolina –27 Feb 1997, Huntersville, Mecklenburg, North Carolina.

f). Emma Geraldine Canty 6 Feb 1949, Rock Hill, York, South Carolina – 6 Aug 2006, Rock Hill, York, South Carolina

3. Robert Lee Canty, born 1878, Catawba, York, South Carolina. Son of George Washington Canty and Mary Jane Elizabeth-Betsy Mush George listed on the 1880 census as their son 2 years of age. In 1910 living with Hester Canty as a boarder occupation – carpenter, he was single. Died sometime after 1910. Can find no more records of him after the 1910 census.

**PHOTO 204 - LOUISA HESTER JANE CANTY**

4. Louisa Hester Jane Canty, born February 7, 1883, married Samuel Taylor Blue as his second wife. She died 9 July 1963. See the Blue family in the Blue Chapter.

**From the Missionary Journal of Mary Baruss**

"A dream of seeing the Indians

Another night I dreamed we were at our journeys end a house full of the Indians were out to meet us. I heard them singing a song where two voices led and in duet (sic) and the rest joined in chorus. I also saw very plainly four Indian women.

Jesus Lover of my soule (sic)

I also told Orlando this dream & that I was sure I could recognize them if I ever saw them. Both these dreams or manifestations were proven to my satisfaction to have been given me by the spirit of the Lord for sure enough after we arrived at the Indian Nation the first night there were the people I had seen assembled. Only three of the women were there but I saw the fourth one a few days after. Their features were familiar when I met them. They were sisters Watts, Blue, Gordon & Brown. They sang many songs that night but they did not sing "Jesus Lover of my soule (sic)" with duet (sic) and chorus till I taught it to them & I recognized it just as soon as they sang it as the one I had heard in my dream. This was a very strong testimony to me and I thanked my heavenly

Father for the same. These dreams were a source of comfort to me since I of course dreaded the thoughts of taking our family among the Indians. My idea of an Indian was of course the ones I had seen who wore their long unkept (sic) hair – male & female – and with blankets & moccasins. I was thoroughly surprised tho to find a people speaking the English language & natural songsters –"

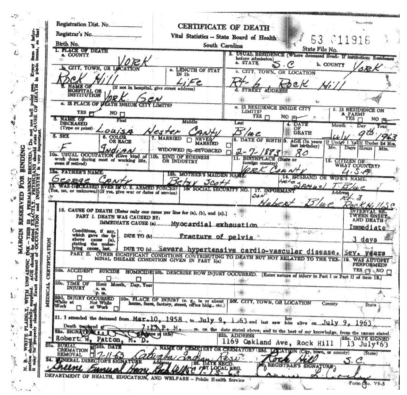

**PHOTO 205 – CERTIFICATE OF DEATH FOR LOUISA HESTER CANTY BLUE**

5. Sarah A. Canty, born June 27, 1886, twin

6. Peggy Canty, born June 27, 1886, twin

*****************************************************

Hester Canty born 1890

1. Marvin Canty born 1910, known as John Marvin Canty

Billie Canty born 1856

Robert Lee Canty born 1869.[200]

On the 1910 These Canty's are found US census, Catawba, York, South Carolina.

*******************************

---

[200] 1910 census York County, SC

Eliza Scotts forth child:

John Alonzo Canty - He was the son of a white man, named Thomas Patrick Whitesides who was the Indian Agent and a Catawba woman Eliza Scott.

| **Father  John Alonzo CANTY**[1-8] | | |
|---|---|---|
| Birth | 9 Nov 1859 | Catawba Reservation, York, County, South Carolina |
| Residence | 1880 | Age: 22Marital Status: Married; Relation to Head of House: Self; Catawba, York, South Carolina, United States |
| Residence | 13 Jun 1900 | Sanford, Conejos, Colorado |
| Residence | 1910 | Marital Status: Married Relation to Head of House: Head; Precinct 14, Conejos, Colorado |
| Residence | 1920 | Marital Status: Married Relation to Head of House: Head; Sanford, Conejos, Colorado |
| Residence | 7 Apr 1930 | Sanford, Conejos, Colorado |
| Burial | Feb 1938 | Sanford, Conejos County, Colorado |
| Death | 1 Feb 1938 | Age at Death: 79; Sanford, Conejos County, Colorado |
| Marriage | 17 Feb 1886 | John Black Place, Spartanburg, South Carolina |
| Father | Major Thomas Patrick WHITESIDES (1825-1904) | |
| Mother | Eliza SCOTT (1826-1869) | |
| Other spouse | Harriet HARRIS (1856-    ) | |

| **Mother  Georgia Henrietta PATTERSON** | | |
|---|---|---|
| Birth | 4 Jul 1870 | Catawba Reservation, York, South Carolina |
| Residence | 13 Jun 1900 | Sanford, Conejos, Colorado |
| Residence | 1910 | Marital Status: Married Relation to Head of House: Wife; Precinct 14, Conejos, Colorado |
| Residence | 1920 | Marital Status: Married Relation to Head of House: Wife; Sanford, Conejos, Colorado |
| Death | 27 Feb 1925 | Sanford, Conejos, Colorado[3] |
| Burial | 28 Feb 1925 | Sanford, Conejos, Colorado[3] |
| | | |
| Father | James Goodwin PATTERSON (1849-1931) | |
| Mother | Elizabeth Missouri WHITE (1849-1934) | |

| **Children** | | |
|---|---|---|
| **M Wilford Marion CANTY** | | |
| Birth | 26 Jan 1893 | Manassa, Conejos, Co |
| Residence | 1900 | Marital Status: Single Relation to Head of House: Son; Sanford, Conejos, |

| | | |
|---|---|---|
| | | Colorado |
| | Residence 1910 | Marital Status: Single Relation to Head of House: Son; Precinct 14, Conejos, Colorado |
| | Residence 1917–1918 | Conejos, Colorado |
| | Residence 1920 | Sanford, Conejos, Colorado |
| | Residence 1930 | Sanford, Conejos, Colorado |
| | Residence 1 Apr 1940 | Sanford, Conejos, Colorado, United States |
| | Death        28 May 1949 | Pueblo, Colorado |
| | Burial | Sanford, Conejos, Colorado |
| | | |
| | Residence | Not Stated, Conejos, Colorado |
| | Spouse        Florence JOHNSON (1901-1980) | |
| | Marriage   21 Sep 1917 | Alamosa, Alamosa, Colorado, United States |
| **M** | **John Henry CANTY** | |
| | Birth        13 Aug 1895 | Sanford, Conejos, Colorado |
| | Death        1897 | Sanford, Conejos, Colorado |
| | Burial        1897 | Sanford, Conejos, Colorado |
| | | |
| | Marriage | |
| **M** | **Eddie Archie CANTY** | |
| | Birth        20 May 1898 | Sanford, Conejos, Colorado |
| | Residence 1900 | Marital Status: Single Relation to Head of House: Son; Sanford, Conejos, Colorado |
| | Residence 1900 | Sanford, Conejos, Colorado |
| | Residence 1910 | Marital Status: Single Relation to Head of House: Son; Precinct 14, Conejos, Colorado |
| | Residence 1917–1918 | Conejos, Colorado |
| | Residence 1920 | Marital Status: Single Relation to Head of House: Son; Sanford, Conejos, Colorado |
| | Residence 1930 | Marital Status: Married Relation to Head of House: Son; Sanford, Conejos, Colorado |
| | Burial        Apr 1980 | Sanford, Conejos, Colorado |
| | Death        4 Apr 1980 | Alamosa, Alamosa, Colorado |
| | | |
| | Residence | Not Stated, Conejos, Colorado. |
| | Residence | Not Stated, Conejos, Colorado |
| | Spouse        Lena Elsie TOWNSEND (1903-1942) | |
| | Spouse        Bernice Evelyn WESTBROOK (1899-1970) | |
| **M** | **William Franklin CANTY** | |

| | | |
|---|---|---|
| Birth | 26 Apr 1901 | Sanford, Conejos, Colorado |
| Residence 1910 | | Marital Status: Single Relation to Head of House: Son; Precinct 14, Conejos, Colorado. |
| Residence 1920 | | Marital Status: Single Relation to Head of House: Son; Sanford, Conejos, Colorado |
| Residence 1930 | | Marital Status: Single Relation to Head of House: Son; Sanford, Conejos, Colorado |
| Burial | Jul 1982 | Sanford, Conejos, Colorado |
| Death | 23 Jul 1982 | Sanford, Conejos, Colorado |
| | | |
| Residence | | Sanford, Colorado |
| Spouse | Alice WRIGHT (1913-2006) | |
| Marriage | 5 Aug 1931 | Sanford, Conejos, Colorado |

**M | Lazell CANTY**

| | | |
|---|---|---|
| Birth | 28 Mar 1904 | Sanford, Conejos, Colorado |
| Residence 1910 | | Marital Status: Single Relation to Head of House: Son; Precinct 14, Conejos, Colorado. |
| Residence 1910 | | Precinct 14, Conejos, Colorado |
| Residence 1920 | | Marital Status: Single Relation to Head of House: Son; Sanford, Conejos, Colorado |
| Residence 1930 | | Age: 25 Marital Status: Married; Relation to Head of House: Head; Sanford, Conejos, Colorado |
| Residence 1930 | | Sanford, Conejos, Colorado |
| Residence 1 Apr 1940 | | Yavapai, Arizona, United States |
| Death | 12 Nov 1988 | Parks, Arizona |
| Death | 13 Nov 1988 | Parks, Coconino, Arizona, United States of America |
| Burial | | Williams, Coconino County, Arizona |
| Spouse | Inda Locile DUKE (1908-1930) | |
| Marriage | 11 May 1929 | Lordsburg, New Mexico |
| Spouse | Anita GONZALES SCOTT (1914-2013) | |

**M | Alma (Pete) CANTY**

| | | |
|---|---|---|
| Birth | 19 Jun 1912 | Sanford, Conejos, Colorado |
| Residence 1920 | | Sanford, Conejos, Colorado |
| Residence 7 Apr 1930 | | Sanford, Conejos, Colorado |
| Residence 30 Apr 1940 | | Sanford, Conejos, Colorado, United States |
| Death | 27 Jan 1989 | Alamosa, Alamosa, Colorado, United States |
| Burial | Feb 1989 | Sanford, Conejos, Colorado |
| Residence 1935/1993 | | Sanford, Colorado |
| Spouse | Frances Clarabelle PAYNE (1924-2002) | |

**PHOTO 206 – JOHN ALONZO CANTY**

4.   John Alonzo Canty born 9 November 1858 married Georgia Henrietta Patterson, daughter of James Goodwin and Elizabeth Missouri White Patterson. John Alonzo died 1 February 1939 in Sanford, Colorado. John Alonzo Canty the son of Eliza Scott, she was born in 1826 and died after 1860, leaving the children to be raised by their grandmother Katy Scott Joe. [201] Eiza married first Franklin Canty. [202] She then had three children by Thomas Whitesides. (It should be noted that not only was Thomas Whitesides a rich man, but that he supported the tribe out of his own money, when, after the Civil War, a Carpetbagger was named Indian Agent and the Catawba were starving. Also the Catawba potters used a special type of clay from the Waxhaw swamp near Twelve-Mile Creek, but that some clay was called "Whitesides" and "Stewart", coming from land owned by those persons. [203]

Alonzo's half-brother, George Washington Canty, whose father was Franklin Canty, remained in the Nation, and his descendants and grandmother still reside there.  Alonzo had a twin Fannie Whitesides who died in 1885 and she had no children. There are no known relatives except Katy Scott Joe the grandmother, born 1799 and died after 1860. There are also no known reason why

---

[201] Blumer,p age1 72.
[202] CatawbaB ranch ' Records.
[203] Ward, Bob, T he Children of  King Hagler, The Catawba press, Rock H ill. SC., 1940, page 4

Mary Jane and Fannie went by Whitesides, while John Alonzo went by his mother's previous husband's name, Canty, he should have taken the Scott name. He had have taken his mother's maiden name of Scott instead of Canty. Alonzo received money from then Indian Agent R. L. Crook on June 19, 1875 in the amount of $4.50 and in 1881, he received $33.30.[204]

**Joseph Willey states in his journal:**

"Sunday February 24, 1884. Sunday school was held Bro. Evans Watts. This was the first Sunday school the Lamanites had ever attended. They seemed to take a lively interest. After Sunday School a young man by the name of John Alonzo

John Alonzo Canty was also called as the first Branch President of the Catawba Branch after it had been disbanded and moved to Spartanburg, South Carolina.[205] It had originally been the Rock Hill Branch, led by James Goodwin Patterson.[206]

. He was called 24 February 1884 to 1 June 1884, when on 1 June, James Patterson was presiding. John was the President when the Catawba moved up to John Black's land in Spartanbury in November 1884. John Alonzo was called on his mission August 2, 1885 along with Pinkney Head, according to Jerry D Lee's thesis. The mission was just from December 1885 to June 1886.

**Elder John Morgan states, as the reasons for the need to resettle the Catawba in the West:**

"Among those that the Elders have come in contact with are the remnants of the once numerous and powerful Catawba Tribe of Indians now numbering only 93 souls. They live on a reservation consisting of 660 acres of land and receive an annuity of $800 per annum from the State of South Carolina. About two-thirds of the tribe embraced the Gospel with very fair prospects of all or nearly all being baptized. They seem earnest and zealous and are endeavoring to make good Latter-Day Saints.

At the coming session of the Legislature we shall endeavor to secure an act empowering them to sell their lands with a view of gathering them out to the appointed gathering place and we trust we shall be successful in so doing.

During our visit, two of their numbers, quite intelligent young men were called and sent on a mission to a remnant of the Cherokee natives in North Carolina, numbering about 1,500 and it was trusted that through their acquaintance with the Cherokees, formed in previous visits, that access could be obtained to their hearts and confidence and that in due season Elders could follow after and much good be done in their midst." These two young men were John Alonzo Canty and Pinkney Head.

---

[204] A. E. Smith Statement No. 6. Report of the Catawba Indian Agent, Report of the Comptroller General, Reports and Resolutions , South Carolina 1893, Charles A Calvo, 1894, page 607
[205] Letter from LDS, Church Historian, Jeffery O. Johnson to Judy Canty Martin, dated November 3, 1981.
[206] Joseph Willey Diary.

**Pinkney Head writes in his Journal of his Mission to the Cherokee:**

"October 31, 1885, me and Brother Alonzo Canty received a letter from Elder W E. Bingham stating that our names had been suggested that we were worthy young men to take a mission among the Cherokee Lamanites in South Carolina, Swain county and Jackson county. He told us that we could gather our crops before we started but we was willing to go at any time. We was glad to think that we was worthy to go and teach others the Gospel. So I left my home at Catawba Nation, South Carolina and on the first day of December 1885, to go to the Cherokee Nation. Brothers John Sanders and B. P. Harris accompanied us 12 miles. We all stopped and staid all night at Lucinda's[207] house 6 miles above Rock Hill. Next morning started for Kings Mountain."[208]

Alonzo and Rehet had 6 sons, all born in Colorado. He was a farmer in South Carolina, and in Colorado, he turned to carpentry.

**PHOTO 207 – CANTY FATHER AND SON ON HAYSTACK**

**PHOTO 208 - JOHN ALONZO CANTY AND SON PETE ON HAYSTACK**

---

[207] B. P. Harris is Benjamin Perry Harris, sone of John and Nancy Harris and Lucinda Harris.
[208] Pinkney Head journal, by date instead of page.

Alonzo did not read nor write, it is told; however, his mother taught school on the reservation, so he probably just did not do much of it. (1910 census says he can read but not write-1920 census says he can both read and write.) He could "figure" as the old times put it, and must have had a bit of mechanical ability, because the Canty's had an adobe making machine. This machine went from the rough box, where the barefoot boys, to a mechanized version that resembled an old fashioned cement mixer mixed the mud. Alonzo used his hands to test the adobe and turn it out into the molds, squatting on his haunches, all day long. In spite of this work, Alonzo's hands were never rough, nor did he wear gloves, in spite of his work "he soaked them in mutton fat at night," in order to do the day after day, in cold weather.[209] His hands were also very large and the boys had very large hands also.

The ingredients for the adobe were the earth on the site and which the building was to be built no other ingredients were used, such as straw. Pete Canty, as well as Quinn Morgan explained the workings of this machine.

The box of the adobe machine was about 3 feet square. It had a hole in the middle, from which a horse was tethered. The box had blades or fingers, some wide and some longer and some round. There was a hole in the front that the mud came out of, after being mixed. Behind this box, they had a pit of mud. One man would shovel mud in the box. The horse would go around and around, and turn the pole with the fingers on it. After the mud was mixed, they would lift the gate that blocked the hole, and let the mud out into molds. The man in front would fill the molds, which made three dobies at a time, then they were dipped in water, and then in sand, to keep them from sticking together. They were then taken to a field to dry. This machine and men could make about 3,000 dobies a day. The original mixers were barefooted boys, instead of the blades. A couple of molds were used, one small one so a small boy could carring the dobies, usually Pete, and a larger one making 3 at a time was used by a larger boy. Building and insulation was accomplished in a couple of steps. The adobe was laid in a double wall, with sawdust in between, then a roof with sawdust on top and to finish it off, tin, and a building that was capable of holding a temperature of 40 degrees year round was achieved.

See the rough prints of what the machine looked like, from descriptions of Pete Canty and Quinn Morgan, drawn by Tiffany M. Martin about 1989, on the following page.

---

[209] Quinn Morgan tape, recorded March 1995 by Judy and Forrest Martin. Quinn's personal knowledge.

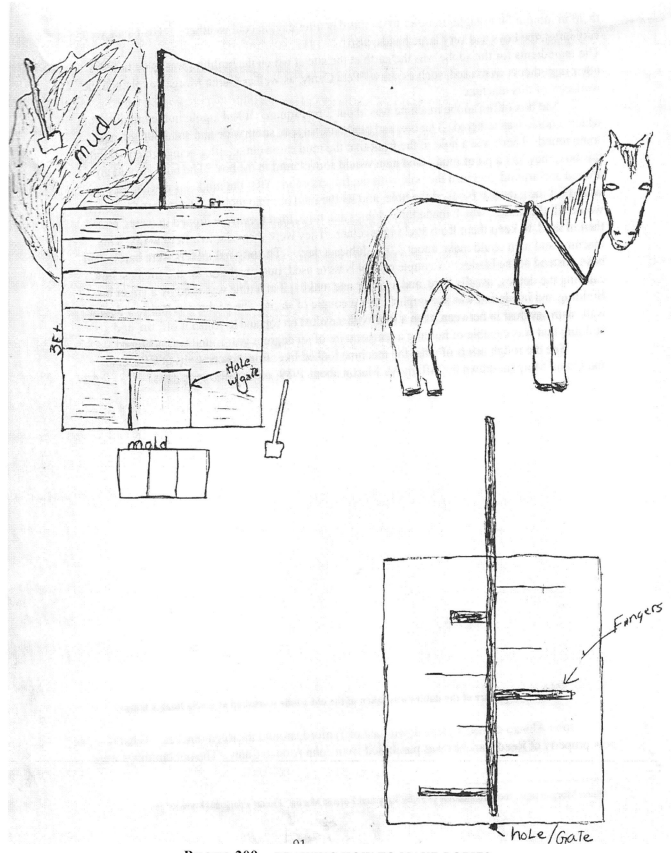

**PHOTO 209 – DRAWING HOW TO MAKE DOBIES**

# Canty Family

John Alonzo owned a place down East of Sanford, around what is now property of Reed Ranches was purchased by Reeds from John Alonzo Canty. The out buildings were of the Canty adobe. The house of Quinn's father in Sanford was made of those dobies. Peter Christensen sold the dobies.

Although Alonzo was very active in the LDS Church in South Carolina, I have found very little about his activity in religious matters in Colorado. Although Branch president of the Catawba Nation Branch, but apparently did not serve in any sort of leadership capacity in Colorado.

About three years prior to his death, John Alonzo had a stroke, which left him unable to speak.

Alonzo and Alma lived in the well house at the house in the south end of Sanford, after Ed's marriage to Lena, until Alonzo died on 1 February 1938. He is buried in Sanford, as well.

Georgia Henrietta "Rhett" Patterson Canty was born 4 July 1870 in Catawba, South Carolina. The following passage is found in Joseph Willey's diary of his Mission:

"February 20th, 1884. My companion led two young women down in the waters of baptism, viz. Martha and Heneretta Patterson confirmed them at Bro. Evans Watts and we blessed two of Brother Patterson's children, Eldora and Emma Patterson. I being the mouth on Emma. This was the first child I ever blessed"

**PHOTO 210 - JOHN ALONZO FAMILY, ED, ALONZO, WILLIAM "BUCK", ZELL AND GEORGIA H CANTY**

**PHOTO 211 – HEADSTONE OF JOHN ALONZO AND GEORGIZ H CANTY**

**PHOTO 212 - FOUR GENERATION PICTURE, JOHN ALONZO, HIS MOTHER IN LAW ELIZABETH MISSOURI WHITE PATTERSON, HIS SON EDDIE ARCHIE "ED" AND GRANDSON EDDIE WILLIAM "SLIM" IN ABOUT 1933**

**The children of John Alonso Canty and his wife Georgia Henrietta Patterson Canty**

**PHOTO 213 – WILFORD MARIAN CANTY**

1. Wilford Marion Canty was born on January 26, 1893 in Manassa, Colorado. He married Florence Johnson in 1927. Floss and Wilford then built a small house and moved to the south end of Sanford. Floss and Wilford had one son who died in infancy. He was a carpenter by trade. When he was younger, he was quite a horse-man, and broke horses for riding.

He once bragged, in jest, that there wasn't a horse he couldn't ride, and got up on his horse, then promptly ended up in the dust. Wilford was a man who was very likeable. He played a set of bells, and played for dances around the area. Evidently, he was part of some sort of band. These bells, is a portable xylophone, with two sets of keys, played with wooden mallets were given to Judy Canty Martin after she played them in Stake Conference. Floss said they were put to good use then. In 2001, Judy gave these valuable mementos to Wilford's youngest daughter Patricia. Wilford died as a result of an accident while the

Canty family was working on the present Church of Jesus Christ of Latter Day Saints chapel in Sanford, Colorado.

**PHOTO 214 – WILFORD MARIAN CANTY WITH HORSES**

**PHOTO 215 – WILFORD MARION CANTY BEEN FISHING AND RABBITT HUNTING**

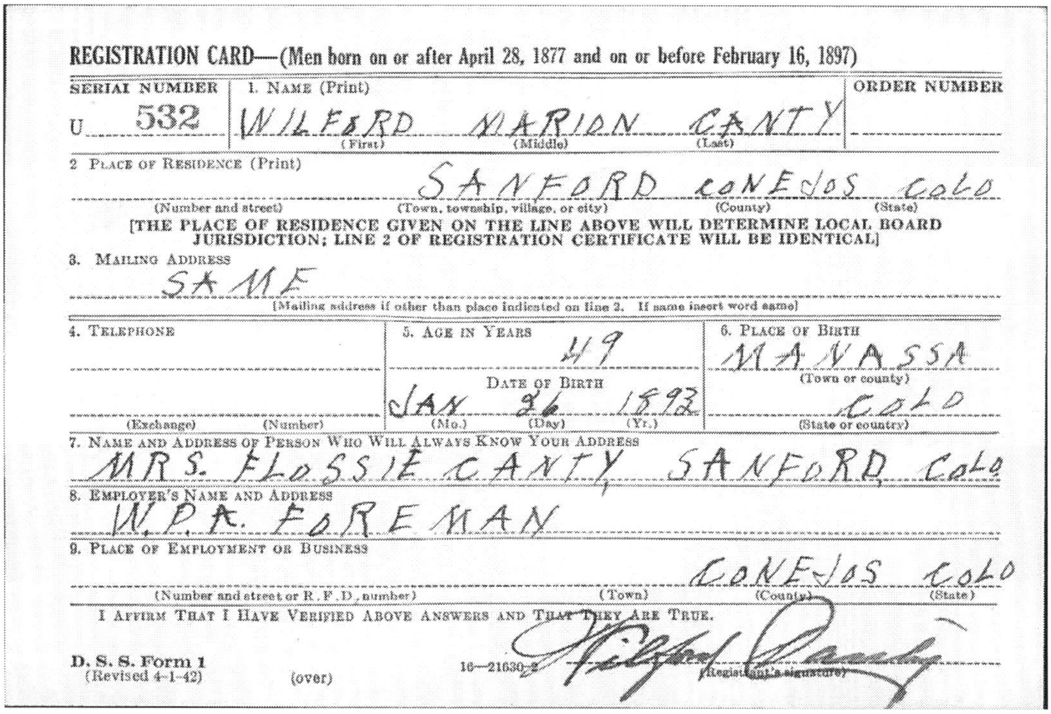

**PHOTO 216 - MILITARY REGISTRATION CARD FOR WILFORD MARION CANTY**

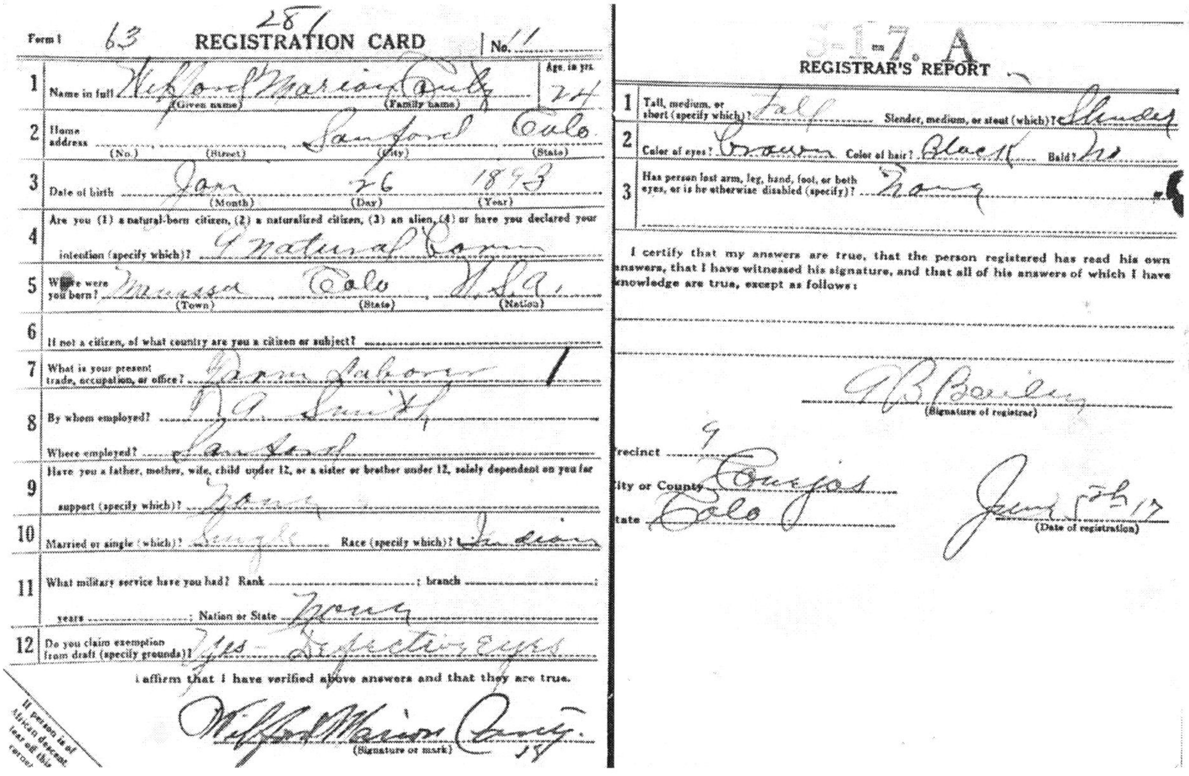

**PHOTO 217 - WWI REGISTRATION CARD FOR WILFORD MARION CANTY**

| State of Colorado | | 219 |
| Division of Vital Statistics | No. | |

**MARRIAGE RECORD REPORT**

County ............ ALAMOSA

Husband's Name ...... CANTY, WILFORD M.  Age 23  Race W

Wife's Name ...... JOHNSON, FLORENCE  Age 19  Race W

Place of Marriage ... ALAMOSA COLO  Date 9/21/17

Name of Official who Performed Ceremony ..... T L WILCOXON

Title ............ JP  Address ...... ALAMOSA COLO

Reported by ........... G W HATCH

Address ........... ALAMOSA COLO

**PHOTO 218 - FLORENCE JOHNSON CANTY WIFE OF WILFORD M CANTY**

**Wilford and Floss lost their first baby, Robert, in infancy.[210]**

(1). Robert Alonzo born 18 February 1925, died 9 March 1925.

**PHOTO 219 – DORIS CANTY**

(2). Doris Canty born 15 May 1921, Sanford, Conejos, Colorado, United States and she died 14 February 2008, Monte Vista, Colorado. She met her husband during her

---

[210] Canty Genealogy.

military service and married Hillis P. Ravlin. They had two children: Michael and Peggy Ann and she raised hillis's boys Larry and Vaughn. Doris attended nursing school at Sage Memorial Hospital, Ganado Arizona at the same time that her cousin Viola Garcia was training there.

Both joined the Army Nurse Corps, during World War II. Doris's tour of duty was from March 1945, to April 1946. She was a 2nd Lt. Basic training was taken at what was then Camp Carson, later Fort Carson, Colorado. Then she was assigned to O'Rielly General Hospital in Springfield, Missouri. She worked in the Nuero-surgical unit, and later in the Paraplegic unit. The friends that she made there, have lasted her lifetime. She and Hillis moved to Hampton, Iowa, where Doris continued her nursing career. She also worked in the Monte Vista, Colorado hospital for a time, and that is where she died. Doris has been the Relief Society present in Monte Vista. She and Hillis had two children:[211]

## Obituary

Monte Vista Doris C. Ravlin, 86, of Monte Vista, died Feb.14, 2008 at the Juniper Village in Monte Vista.

She was born May 15, 1921 in Sanford, Colo. to Wilford Marion and Florence Johnson Canty. She married her husband of 42 years, Hillis P. Ravlin, on Jan. 17, 1946 in Springfield, Mo. and their marriage was sealed in the Albuquerque N.M. Temple of the Church of Jesus Christ of Latter-day Saints on November 12, 2004.

Doris attended school at the Presbyterian School of Nursing in Ganado, Ariz., worked as a Registered Nurse and served in the United States Army Nurses Corps. She also volunteered in the Church Library for a time.

She enjoyed traveling, knitting, crocheting and sewing and especially liked spending time with her family. She also loved her loyal dogs.

Her parents, her husband in 1988, her infant brother, Robert Alonzo Canty and her step-son Larry Ravlin all preceded her in death.

Survivors include her children, Peggy Anne (Roger) Skarie of Custer, S.D., and Michael (Corinne) Hillis of Pahrump, Nevada; one step-son, Vaughn (Mary) Ravlin of Oregon; her sister, Patricia Ann Ramsey of Young, Ariz.; 5 grandchildren and numerous great-grandchildren.

The Funeral Service was held Monday, Feb. 18, at the Rio Grande Ward of the Church of Jesus Christ of Latter-day Saints in Monte Vista. Burial was in the Sanford Cemetery.

---

[211] Doris Canty Ravlin genealogy, photo courtesy Clara Canty, Doris in uniform, courtesy Doris Ravlin.

**PHOTO 220 HEADSTONE OF DORIS CANTY AND HUSBAND HILLIS P RAVLIN**

Doris Canty Ravlin passed away Feb. 14, 2008, Monte Vista, Rio Grande County, Colorado --- Burial: Sanford Cemetery, Sanford, Conejos County, Colorado, Plot: 159-B

**PHOTO 221 PATRICIA ANN CANTY**

3. Patricia Ann Canty, born 3 August 1938, Sanford, Conejos, Colorado. She married Roger Ramsey, they were divorced. Patricia also turned to nursing, and graduated from St. Mary's in Denver, Colorado. Pat has been working for Indian Health Services on Indian Reservations for the past 18 and 1/2 years. She has worked in Keams Canyon, Az., and has now purchased land near Payson, AZ, for her retirement she is now retired. Pat has received a promotion recently, and is now working directly under the Hospital

Administrator in the hospital and Whiteriver, Arizona. Since the last addendum, Pat has retired to her home in Young, Arizona, working on projects for the Service all over the United States.

**Bernalillo County, New Mexico, Marriage Index, 1888-2011**

    Name   Patricia Ann Canty
    Birth Place     Albuquerque, NM
    Marriage Date     Abt 1962
    Marriage Place -- Bernalillo, New Mexico, United States
    Household Members  Name  Age
      Roger W Ramsey
      Patricia Ann Canty

**The Second son of John Alonzo and Georgia Henrietta Patterson Canty was John Henry**

**PHOTO 222 – HEADSTONE OF JOHN HENRY CANTY**

2. John Henry Canty was born 13 August 1895 in Sanford, Colorado. He died in 1897 and nothing more is known of his short life.

**PHOTO 223 - EDDIE ARCHER CANTY**

3. Eddie Archer Canty was born May 20, 1898 in Sanford, Colorado. Ed was a quiet man, not speaking much of the past. The few things that he did tell us helped in research greatly. He told of grandpa Canty, Alonzo, talking about a twin sister Fannie and an older sister Jane. He also told of Alonzo having an older half-brother, who served in the Civil War. Ed's child Ed and his younger brother William were playing a game. The game consisted of pushing an egg through a hole and the other catching it in his hat. When William (Buck) got tired of playing, he broke the egg and pushed it through the hole into Ed's hat.

He used to visit the old folks in the nursing homes, and laughed, because he was older than most of them at the time. Ed purchased an old truck, this old truck figured into Canty building. Ed built benches in the back, and it was used as the first Sanford School bus. Ed married Lena Townsend, who he met while working near Luna, New Mexico, with his brothers. [212]Lena and Ed did not have good luck with their family, and must have faced terrible times when they lost baby after baby.

**PHOTO 224 – EDDIE ARCHER CANTY AND WIFE LENA TOWNSEND**

**PHOTO 225 – HEADSTONES FOR EDDIE ARCHER AND LENA TOWNSEND CANTY -- BURIAL: SANFORD CEMETERY, SANFORD, CONEJOS COUNTY, COLORADO, PLOT:62-A, 62-C**

**The six children of Eddie and Lena Canty**

1. John A. Canty, born June 14, 1927, died as an infant.

2. Agnes Canty, born May 12, 1928, died as an infant.

---

[212] Memories of Judy Canty Martin.

3. Eddie W. (Slim) Canty, born October 25, 1932 died May 2, 1944.

4. James A. Canty, born April 8, 1934, died as an infant.[213]

5. Charles Curtis Canty, bora February 17, 1936. He had three living children, Eve Marie died in infancy, Charles Eddie, Maxine and Erica.

6. Lois Canty, born September 6, 1938. Lois married first, Clarence Broyles, whom she divorced. Her second husband was the brother of Jolean Winters Canty, Terry Winters. Lois had 3 children: Connie Broyles, Teddy and Terry Wayne Winters.

After the death of Lena, Bernice Westbrook Ottesen Clark helped Ed look after Slim, Chuck and Lois. They married after the death of Slim and they had one final child together - Marna Louise Canty.

**The fourth son of John Alozno and Georgia Henrietta Patterson Canty was William.**

PHOTO 226

4. William Franklin Canty was born 26 April 1901 in Sanford, Colorado. He married Alice Wright on August 5, 1931, and died on July 23, 1982. William was nicknamed "Buck" at an early age, and according to his youngest brother, Alma, this was a racial slur at the beginning

William purchased an old truck, about a 1930 and built sideboards to haul the sand and gravel in it. He worked with his brother Zell, working all over the west, building bridges and High Rise Buildings of steel.

---

[213] Canty genealogy.

Although he was relatively unschooled, he was an avid reader, especially religious books.

He was a carpenter by trade, and specialized in finish work, that is making the fine details in woodwork and trims. When he became unable to work after his heart attack that is what he did to help support Alice and himself. He was very inventive, making furniture and items out of scrap.

He played the harmonica, and had a beautiful singing voice, although his speaking voice was very deep, he did not sing a true base.

His father and grandfather had been very active in bringing the Catawba into the LDS Church in South Carolina, but his sons never knew this. Alonzo was the first branch president of the Catawba Branch.

William became active in the Church, serving in various teaching and other positions, until 1962. It was then that he was called to one of the most prestigious positions in the church, that of Patriarch. This was the first time an Indian had been called to such a position, and he became quite famous within the Church. He spoke at 174 funerals, blessed uncounted babies and gave countless blessings to the sick, gave over 1000 Patriarchal Blessing and spoke at many, many meetings. As a result of his Church position, he began speaking at the graduation of the Indian School, at Brigham Young University, in Provo, Utah. He also traveled around the area, speaking to Indians about his experiences, even traveling to Anadarko, Oklahoma, to speak at a Pow Wow for the Cherokee there.[214]

**PHOTO 227 – WILLIAM "BUCK" CANTY**

---

[214] Personal knowledge of Judy Canty Martin.

**PHOTO 228 - A. MCLNTIRE, BUCK CANTY, KIT CARSON III, LYLE VALENTINE**

**PHOTO 229 - WILLIAM FRANKLIN "BUBK" CANTY AND WIFE ALICE WRIGHT CANTY 50TH**

## WILLIAM "BUCK" CANTY FIRST LAMANITE PA TRIARCH 1962

WILLIAM CANTY, A CATAWABA INDIAN, was called as patriarch of the San Luis Colorado Stake in 1962, and he was the first Lamanite to ever hold such a position. It was at Brigham Young University's Indian Week that I first met Brother Canty. We had many hundreds of LDS Seminary students present when he bore such a strong testimony of how he knew that he was a child of God. This is his story:

"As a youth I always thought of myself as a 'dirty Indian' I would get in the wrong crowd but the Church would always find me, I could not get away from the church. The Church always followed me wherever I went. Whenever possible the Church would find me and teach me that I was a child of God. I was called to be a counselor in a bishopric, and later a member of the High Council, and then later as the first Lamanite Patriarch in the Church. Why was the Church so interested in me, a "dirty Indian'? Students, I have always thought of myself as a dirty Indian, but the Church always sought me out, and the Church has helped me all these years. . . I was ordained a patriarch to the Church and I want to tell you about that first blessing! Offered upon the head of a young man, that became the testimony of all testimonies to me. I put my hands upon this man's head, and said, 'Brother So-and-So, by the authority of the holy Melchizedek Priesthood and in the name of Jesus Christ I lay my hands upon your head to give you a patriarchal blessing. It took me only a few seconds to say this little sentence, and I felt as though I was standing in the air off the floor It was during these few seconds that I received a revelation that has sustained me these years and has helped me to know that I am indeed a child of God. During those few seconds I was permitted to see a revelation of that person's life from his pre-earth life, his life of mortality and into his eternal future existence. All pertaining to that man was revealed to my mind's eye. I saw it! I saw his whole life pass before my eyes and now all I had to do was to put into words what I saw.... What a beautiful testimony of revelation of God's love to me, your Lamanite Brother." I, Gerald Ray Hall, testify to the fact that his testimony as written is as close as I remember it given.

I know that the Holy Ghost bore witness to me on that day of the truth of the words of that great Patriarch, Brother William "Buck" Canty,

 Signed Gerald Ray Hall

"A deep voiced, soft spoken and humble man, Brother Canty delivered speeches. At one of his engagements at BYU, the students lined up three deep to shake his hand. Two hours later, he shook the hand of the last student."

This statement puts one in the mind of another Catawba preacher, Robert Quash-Marsh.

"Robert Marsh, became a Baptist minister, and preached "sincerely" at Hopewell Baptist Church, but not effectively enough to convert many Catawba's. He had a melodious voice and used natural gestures.[215]

Robert Mush-Mursh-Marsh was also a great-grandfather of William Canty.

---

[215] Brown, pages 271 & 272.

When he and his wife Alice, toured the Scandinavian Countries with Brigham Young University's Indian group, the Lamanite Generation, he was even recognized there. One little girl came up to him and said she knew him. When asked how she knew him, she referred to a Deseret Church News article that was written about him in 1978, just prior to the trip.

In speaking of his experiences at BYU, he said; "Here was this old uneducated Indian, sitting in the Deans desk.' He never did realize exactly what impact he had upon anyone who knew him.

"In true Catawba-Indian fashion, on the evening of July 23, 1982, his spirit just walked away from his body." He died almost exactly how and where he wanted, in his workshop, with a hammer within reach. This was his desire.

These pictures were taken when Buck and Zell were working in Luna, New Mexico. More pictures can be seen in Lazell Canty's chapter.

**William and Alice had only one son: John Marvin Canty.**

a.    John Marvin Canty, born December 25, 1932, in Sanford, Colorado. He married Janeen Johnson, daughter of Ren and Clara Johnson. He attended Sanford High School, and then Adams State College. He was a good student and athlete. After attending Adams State College, where he was a Cage Star, he joined the Marine Corps. According to him, to emulate his favorite uncle, Pete (Alma). He had orders for Korea, but did not have to serve there. When he returned, he and Janeen were married, and they began a new Canty family.

John has been featured in the newspapers frequently through the years, first for his sports accomplishments and later when he was the Assistant Superintendent of Schools for Alamosa, Colorado. He was also featured one time, for the size of his shoes, a remarkable size 20, big for that time, another time for his prowess with the bow and arrow. He brought down a cow elk with a single arrow. It was remarked that he was Indian. He also was forced to kill a black bear with the bow, when it charged his sons on a camping trip. [216]

**John and Janeen's children are Martha, Michael, Kyle, Kip, Blake, Bret & Brock.**

SANFORD—Coach Francis Dahm, Leon Johnson, Lyle Espinosa, Wallace Peterson, Frank Christensen, Donnie Crowther, Robert Crowther, Kurt Cornum, Kay Faucette, Norman Crowther, John Canty.

---

[216] Photos and information collected by Judy Canty Martin.

## Sanford Man Gets Elk With Arrow

Most hunters consider themselves fortunate if they are able to take an elk with a rifle. But John Canty, Sanford, did it the hard way — with a bow and arrow.

Canty took a large cow elk Tuesday evening at Osier, in the Cumbres Pass area, with a single arrow.

It is reported that Canty made the shot about 6:30 p.m. at an approximate range of 50 yards.

Lt. John M. Canty

Graduated from the five month officer Basic Course at the Marine Corps Schools here February 26, Marine 2nd Lt. John M. Canty, son of Mr. and Mrs. William F. Canty of Sanford, Colo., has been transferred to the 1st Marine Division.

He is a graduate of Adams State College.

**PHOTO 230-NEWSPAPER ARTICLE –LT. JOHN M CANTY**

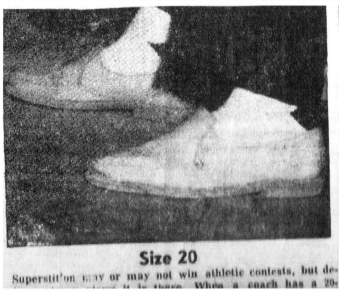

## Size 20

Superstition may or may not win athletic contests, but de-

**The fifth son of John Alonzo and Georgia Henrietta Patterson Canty was Zell.**

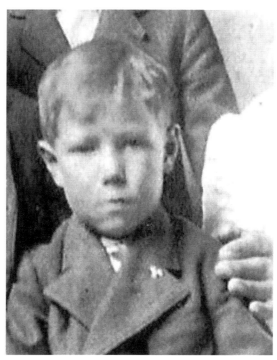

**PHOTO 231 – LAZELL "ZELL" CANTY**

5. Lazell "Zell" Canty was born March 28, 1904, in Sanford, Colorado. The stories he always told at reunions were that he was this innocent person, but he was just as ornery as the others, even as he protested his innocence, with the most disarming smile, and gleam in his eye, you knew he was mischievous, to say the least. One time Zell made his little brother Pete mad and Pete picked up a pair of shears and threw them at him. They stuck into a bucket that Zell was smart enough to put in front of him. Of course, he never told why Pete was so mad. Zell would elaborate, showing how far the shears stuck into the bucket; sometimes they went clear through it. Another time he and Buck were arguing, and Zell threw a grubbing hoe at Buck that stuck in the side of the door. Another time they were target shooting, the only problem was that they were shooting flies off the walls and ceilings with 22's.

Buck and Zell were walking home one time, when Buck told Zell that he was so fast, he could out run a rock. Zell sat down and picked a good one. Buck came running down the road, barefooted, and Zell pegged him right in the side of the head with his rock. Then they started to make up stories about how Buck got such a goose egg on his head. Grandpa Canty was no fool, and didn't believe them for a minute. Zell said "dad picked up a board, it looked like a 2x6 and hit him in the rear end, it was so big he had to cut it to get it in the door. When he'd hit me, I'd lift off the ground and yell, and as soon as I hit the ground, he'd let me have it again."

Another time Zell was cleaning out the chicken coop. Pete and Guy Garcia were harassing him, hitting him with horse manure etc. Zell saw a shadow coming up to the house and got a big old shovel full of the softest manure he could find. When the shadow got up to the door, he let it fly around the door. Guess who the shadow was not?  Pete and Guy. Now, guess who it was, dad (grandpa Canty). Zell said he was not amused! Zell worked around Luna, New Mexico and around the West with Buck and some of their cousins, the Heads and Garcia's. They built bridges and worked the high steel jobs, building high-rise buildings and bridges in Phoenix, AZ. When they worked on a job, they camped out in tents while on the job. Buck lost the top half of his ear to an angry boyfriend, who thought he was Zell; he swore it was Zell's fault, Zell swore it wasn't. [217]

**PHOTO 232 – INDA LOCIL "RED" DUKE**

Zell married Inda Locile "Red" Duke on 11 May 1929, Lordsburg, New Mexico. She was born 24 Autust 1908, Kelly, Caldwell, Louisana and she died 24 May 1930, Sanford, Conejos, Colorado (in child birth).

**U.S., Find A Grave Index, 1600s-Current**
Name  Inda Locile Canty
Spouse  LaZell Canty
Mother  Charlotte Jane Duke
Father  James Pat Duke

**PHOTO 233 - HEADSTONE INDA LOCILE DUKE CANTY**

Lazell and Inda had a daughter Johnnye (Inda died in child birth)

---

[217] Canty genealogy, memories of Zell, Buck and Pete Canty.

199

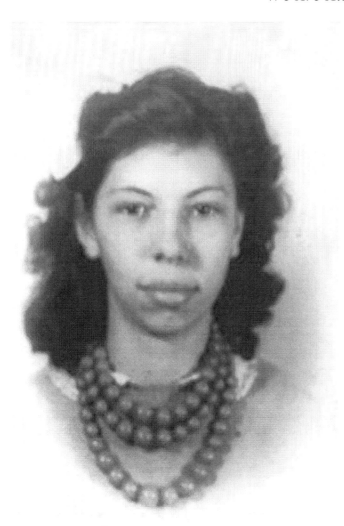 

**PHOTO 234 – JOHNNYE RUTH CANTY**

    a.  Johnnye Ruth Canty was born on May 24, 1930. Her mother died in childbirth and Johnnye Ruth was raised by her Aunt and Uncle Willard and Ethel Humble Nethery in Kelley, Louisiana. The family already had two children Thomas and Virginia, which gave Johnnye Ruth a sister and brother.

She was always told that Ethel was her aunt and the family told stories of her mother, so she grew up in a loving home. Daddy Zell visited her often while she was young, but, as she grew older, visits became shorter, although she did spend summers with him.

After graduation from Kelly High School in 1947, she went to business school and then to work at Guy H. Alford Drug Company in Columbia, Louisiana. Here she met and married Hulon Parrish. She was outgoing and he was shy, but finally, taking the initiative, she introduced herself, and the rest is history. He always thought of her as the most beautiful woman he had ever seen.

The only problems they faced in the beginning were Hulon's family who did not like the fact Hulon married an Indian girl. The old family joke came when his family told him, "Marrying that Indian you are going to wake up with knife in your back." Johnnye Ruth responded in a typical spunky way, "If I was going to stab him, he's not going to wake up."

She was a kind-hearted woman, but believed in speaking her mind and Hulon faced that fact early, when he attempted to take his brothers advice and "slap a little sense into her." He soon found out he had bitten off more than he could chew. Hulon said, "Her black eyes popped." and she proceeded to slap a little sense right back into his head. When he turned to walk away, he heard a funny sound. When he turned back, he saw a butcher knife was sailing in his direction and it stuck in the wall right beside his head. Hulon's mother was horrified, telling Johnnye Ruth, 'You might have killed my baby." In typical Johnnye Ruth fashion, she said, "No, if I had wanted to kill him, I would have hit him with it." That was the end of the arguments, and Johnnye Ruth and Hulon had a very happy, loving relationship.

They had 5 children together. While in Fort Smith, Arkansas, Johnnye Ruth found out that she had cancer of the lymph gland. She died in Fort Smith, in 1964. She is buried in Kelley, Louisiana, about 30 miles north of Jonesville.

**PHOTO 235 – HEADSTONE OF JOHNNYE RUTH CANTY PARRISH**

**Zell married the second time to Anita Gonzales Scott and they had 4 more children.**

PHOTO 236 – ZELL AND ANITA GONZALES SCOTT CANTY

**Zell and Anita Canty's children:**

a. Leroy Ellsworth Canty was born in Kingman, Arizona on March 21, 1938 and ne died 29 March 1999, Portland, Multnomah, Oregon.

b. Carolyn Anne Canty was born 23 February 1943, in Kingman, Arizona.

c Georgia Sue Canty was born 5 February 1946.

d. Diana Lee Canty was born 2 August 1950.

PHOTO 237 - 1ST LAZELL AND HIS PET CHICKEN AND 2ND ZELL AND HIS FRIENDS

**PHOTO 238 - ZELL AND VIRGIE SAPP, ELIAS GIBSON AND UNCLE BUCK IN ST JOHNS**

**PHOTO 239 - ZELL AND VIRGIE AND FRIENDS**

**PHOTO 240 - ZELL AND ANITA WITH THEIR CHILDREN**

**PHOTO 241 - ALICE CANTY, DORIS RADLIN, ANITA AND ZELL CANTY, PETE AND CLARA CANTY, AND ZELL'S GRANDKIDS**

**PHOTO 242 – HEADSTONE OF LAZEL AND ANITA CANTY BURIAL: MOUNTAIN VIEW CEMETERY, WILLIAMS, COCONINO, ARIZONA- PLOT: SEC 8**

**The sixth son of John Alozno and Georgia Henrietta Patterson Canty was Pete.**

**PHOTO 243 – ALMA OR PETE CANTY**

6. Alma or Pete Canty, was born June 191, 1912, the last child of the Canty family, he attended school in Sanford, until 1925, when his mother died. He was in the 7th grade at the time. During the school

months after the Canty's moved into the country, Pete stayed with his grandparents, the Patttersons, so he would be close to school.

Pete was much smaller than his brothers were, but he was just as mischievous as they were, and got into his share of trouble. He was a fairly good student, and was good in math. When his mother died, William promised her he would look after the baby, Alma, who was 13 at the time.

Alma and his grandfather, James Patterson both had small pox during an epidemic between 1915 and 1919. Very few died during that epidemic, even though a great many people had it that time. "How Grandpa Patterson and Pete got it, without anyone else in the family getting it, remains a mystery, especially when it was so devastating to the Indian tribes and the Catawba in particular.

John Alonzo had a stroke, about 1935; Pete and he were living in John Alonzo's house. When Ed married Lena Townsend, and moved into the house. After a time, Pete and his father slept in the well house. After William (Buck) settled down and married and John Alonzo died, Pete lived with Buck and Alice."

During the depression, Pete and several of his cousins, primarily Guy, Ben and Elbert Garcia all went to South Carolina. I do not know if they went together, all I know is that Guy and Pete stayed pretty much together, when they hitchhiked and rode the rails. At some point they also traveled with Elbert and Ben, because Pete always told of someone, I wonder who, put watermelon rinds in Elbert's boots. I imagine that feeling in the morning, was a shock. They also took out the picture of Elbert's girl and replaced it with a picture of a bulldog. Guy and he spent the night in the Walsenburg jail, and it was by choice, and a welcome warm bed for a change. The only drawback, Pete said, was it was lousy. They traveled with an Indian, a Navajo, they called Hosteen. I have never been sure if this was his real name, but that is what they called him. He had lice so bad; they held him down and sprayed him with Flit, the strong insect killer of that time. On their way down, they ate sugar cane for the first time, and they saw Blacks. They were going by, and two black fellows were fishing, and they had caught an eel. Daddy always said, the old man said, "Lordy, Lordy, What we do now?" They stayed with several blacks, families, I suppose. One in particular had such strong coffee; daddy said you could pave a road with it. Apparently, the blacks were pretty friendly to two hitchhikers, in the South.

Coming back, they caught a ride with a scissors salesman, and convinced him that Alamosa was such a large city that he would make a killing there. When they got there, in the dark, they got away quickly, before he found out how large it actually was not. Another time he and Guy got separated on the railroad. Later, from another car he heard, "Let's sing. You sing high and I'll sing terrible." He had found Guy.

Ben, Elbert and Guy eventually married Catawba girls, although as Elbert said, his didn't take.

Pete joined the Marine Corps during World War II. He was too old for the draft, but he enlisted on 2 March 1942. He served in the 278th Platoon, U.S.M.C. He saw action at Guadalcanal, Bougainville and Iwo Jima. After reading accounts of these battles, I wonder what he saw. All he ever told about was digging, or trying to dig, fox holes. Since the islands were fine sand over lava rock, foxholes were not very deep, a few inches at most. One night, they had a black out, because of snipers. All of a sudden the

# Canty Family

Sergeant struck a match in his foxhole. He said he would take his chances with the snipers, he was not going to share the hole with a snake. That is about the size of the war stories he told. He just did what had to be done. Pete was a cook with the heavy artillery, and did some carpentry work as well. When he was discharged it was as Staff Sergeant in San Diego, California in March of 1946.

On a leave, just before discharge, he came home and met Francis Clarabelle Payne and they were married after a long courtship of 2 weeks, on May 18, 1945 in Taos, New Mexico.

They moved into the home that the Canty boys and others helped him build of cement and cinder blocks on the same place that Clara lives today. It is the last house on the East Side of Main Street, in Sanford, Colorado. This completed Canty corners, Ed Canty's house, originally John Alonzo and Rhett's, just north of Pete's, Wilford's just east of Ed, and Buck, just north of Wilford in Sanford.

Pete and Ed worked together for many years. He also worked with Buck for several years, always doing carpentry. He worked with Whitney Construction, owned by Larry Whitney, and his last employer was Clad Christensen. Here he helped many houses around La Jara and Alamosa, and they perfected a construction system using red perlite, pouring it like cement, making storage units and other buildings. The perlite is very porous, and these were very well insulated.

Pete was a young 74 years old when a malignant tumor was discovered on his brain. Bishop Preston Stanley, Paul Jackson and Ferrell Coley came to give him a blessing the night before surgery. As they knelt beside the couch to bless this old man, Paul stated that the cancer would not kill him. The sight of those good men, on their knees, administering to my father, is a sight I still see today. The tumor lay on his motor nerve, and made communication difficult even after surgery.

He was operated on in Pueblo, where the family was given the bad news. News reached Sanford that he would need 35 radiation treatments, and that meant a long commute from Pueblo to Sanford every day, because they couldn't afford to stay in Pueblo. Before the 5-day stay in the hospital in Pueblo was over, Bishop Preston Stanley and Sanford had lined up all 35 trips with different people volunteering. Some took them more than once, and most often, the driver, also

bought them lunch. Supper was brought in also.

This frustrated him badly. He began deteriorating badly when he could see no improvement, and stopped eating. Clara, dutifully and loving, tried her best to nurse him, but he, even in deteriorating health, was a great deal larger than she, at about 4'9", and shrinking. His extended family, Judy, Frosty, Tiffany and Devin made trips to Alamosa every two weeks. Pete's first love was his grandchildren, and he wouldn't hear of Judy staying away from them. He also dearly loved his son-in-law Frosty. He tried to be a good patient, but patience was never one of his virtues, and he grew tired of not being independent. When he lost control of his bodily functions, and had to be changed like a baby, he just gave up. Clara nearly killed herself, trying to keep him alive, and in the end, he went to the nursing home in Alamosa, to live the last three months of his life.

The grandchildren and Judy and Frosty still traveled from Cortez, Colorado every 2 weeks, taking him out of the home. Devin would get him in his wheelchair, and they would run through the mud puddles. These were pleasures for Pete. We would take him to see the cranes; he loved cranes, and took him home for both holidays. Holidays have never been the same for any of us. Pete baptized both his grandchildren, and they were the first and only baptisms for him.

He lived every moment of his life, the best he could, and the last picture we took of him shows a big smile, when his heart must have been breaking.

Looking back at his nursing home stay, I can smile a bit, because he got out of every kind of restraint they tried. This was a major thing for him, and he would always be found looking out the windows. There was this little old lady in the home, she was in a wheelchair, and she would grab you if you got close enough. She was alone, and had few, if any visitors, and always wanted to see her son. I saw mom do something that will always stick with me, as the most unselfish thing a person could do. One day, that little old lady caught her by the sleeve. Mom bent down, not very far, since she is so tiny, and the lady put her hands on mom's face. She said, "Would you kiss me?" Mom did not hesitate one moment, she kissed this little old stranger, and the stranger went away, feeling loved. She was with daddy every day until he died on January 28, 1989. It seemed that he almost waited until she went out to her sister's home to rest, and he slipped away. He came into the world alone, and he went out the same way, but both ways, he was loved.

He taught lessons that will never be forgotten. After his death, I spoke to Paul Jackson.

With tears in his eyes, he apologized for saying the cancer would not kill daddy, but that is what he felt. I told him that I felt that daddy's doctor had killed him, by not trying to give him physical and speech therapy because he was an old man. I believed this blessing that Heavenly Father can heal, and would have, and I still do.

**PHOTO 244 - PETE CANTY AND HIS BIG FISH**

**PHOTO 245 - ALMA "PETE" AND HIS WIFE FRANCES CLARABELLE PAYNE CANTY**

**PHOTO 246 – 1ST - FRANCES CLARA PAYNE CANTY -- 2ND ALMA "PETE" AND CLARA CANTY**

**PHOTO 247 – HEADSTONE OF ALMA "PETE" CANTY  -   BURIAL  AT  SANFORD CEMETERY -
SANFORD, CONEJOS COUNTY, COLORADO**

**PHOTO 248 – HEADSTONE OF FRANCES CLARA PAYNE CANTY -
BURIAL AT SANFORD CEMETERY  -  SANFORD, CONEJOS COUNTY, COLORADO**

**PHOTO 249 - JUDY CANTY WITH FATHER PETE AND MOTHER CLARA – CHRISTMAS 1969 --- PETE CANTY**

**PHOTO 250 - JUDY CANTY MARTIN, CLARA AND PETE CANTY AND GRANDSON DEVIN**

**Pete and Clara Canty had only one child a daughter Judy Canty.**

**PHOTO 251 - JUDY CANTY WITH WILLIAM FRANKLIN CANTY -- HER UNCLE BUCK**

**PHOTO 252 - JUDY CANTY MARTIN**

1. Judy Mae Canty born April 15, 1946 in Alamosa, Colorado. I married Forrest L. Martin, son of Gale and June Martin of La Jara, Colorado and we moved into a trailer house just east of mom and dad's. After a few years there, we bought a house in Alamosa, Colorado.

While in Alamosa, I became interested in Genealogy, because Forrest's was so vast, and when I completed collecting all his, I found my own sadly lacking. I went to his great aunt Gladys Shawcroft, and she began trying to help me work on my Catawba lines. That was the one that interested me the most, because I had been told it couldn't be done. Gladys did what she could to help, and mostly to encourage me, by her work in the field.

After a move to Pueblo, Colorado, I reacquainted myself with some of daddy's cousins, Ben and Irene Beck Garcia, Lee and Dorothy Garcia Ong and May Croasmun, as well as their children. Irene, being a Catawba, had a book on the tribe, called The Catawba Indians, People of the River, by Douglas Summers Brown. I borrowed the book, and then ended up buying a copy. It has been the basis for all my research, while not always being correct, it was a good beginning, and Brown cared for the people. This book mentioned my family, the Patterson, Canty's, Heads and so forth by name.

Books I have contributed to are "The Wild Garlic Isles" about the Ramsey line, "Vale, Thomas, Frazier, Mankin and Moreland," biographical information about the above mentioned families, "The Burger and Amish Families of Johnson County, Iowa" and "Catawba  Indian Genealogy" by Ian Watson, and contributed information to Dr. Thomas

**Blumer and Dr. Wesley White of the Smithsonian, on Catawba genealogy.**


BOOK REVIEW BY DR. THOMAS BLUMER

Editor: Dr. Thomas Blumer has been the official Catawba Tribal Historian for some thirty years. A longtime friend of the Catawba's who has tirelessly volunteered his professional expertise in supporting, protecting, and promoting Catawba Tribal interests and culture. Dr. Blumer has frequently lectured at the Catawba Nation on Catawba history. In recent times, he has been on weekly radio discussions on Catawba history and culture. We are fortunate to have Dr. Blumer's contribution to the Newsletter and for his professional reviewing of Judy Canty Martin's work

_Genealogy of the Western Catawba_- by Judy Canty Martin, (1998), 215 pages, $50. -  Available through the author.

Recently I received my copy of Judy Canty Martin's long anticipated genealogical study. It presents a record of the five Catawba families who migrated to Colorado in the 1880s from the Catawba Nation in South Carolina: the Patterson, Head, Canty, Harris, and Tims. Delighted to see the wide scope of this first genealogy done by a Catawba, I dove right into its offerings.

In each chapter devoted to a specific family, Martin discusses the origin of the name within the Catawba Nation. The volume contains numerous photographs, some documents of interest, short biographical sketches of key family members, and even contemporary news articles. The author quotes frequently from the pages of the Joseph Wiley Diary, and Pinkney Head's journal.

The first chapter is devoted to the Patterson Family (page 1). Biographical sketches are provided key individuals such as James Patterson who led the family to Colorado, Martha Jane Patterson, George Henry Garcia (grandson), and Edward Guy Garcia (grandson). The Head Family follows (page 53) and appropriately begins with a short biography of Robert's son, Pinkney H. Head. Pinkney is remembered for his efforts to see the State of South Carolina settle with the Catawba. He first took an interest in this old problem in 1889 and lived to see the Catawba obtain Federal recognition in 1943, but the Head family was not put on the Catawba roll. Biographical sketches are provided for Heber Jackson Head and Guilherme Albert Marcelino.

Chapter three belongs to the Canty Family (page 84). The patriarch here is John Alonzo Canty. The author begins with a valiant attempt to unravel the complicated history of this family in the mid- 19th Century and immediately provides a lengthy biographical sketch of John Alonzo's life. The discussion sheds additional light on the Catawba migration movement. Other biographies are provided for William Franklin Canty, John Marvin Canty, Lazell Canty, and Pete Canty.

The Harris Family is the subject of chapter four. Two related branches of this family are descended from Nancy Harris (Texas) and Lillie Susan Harris Ballard (Oklahoma). Again the links to South Carolina remain strong. In 1892, Nancy Harris wrote a letter to the governor of South Carolina complaining about the loss of her share of the propriations money.

The second key member of the Harris family, Lillie Ballard, does not have an extensive biographical sketch; but, this section is rich in genealogical data. The balance of Martin's effort contains short genealogical notes on the Mush-Mursh-Marsh family (Pamunkey Indian origin), the Tims family, the Watts-Wats family, the White family, followed by a short essay "Religion of the Catawba Indians " and a bibliography.

Judy Canty Martin has worked for many years to produce the Western Catawba. "This fact is obvious. The book contains a wealth of information. Martin's effort, however, is more than just a genealogy. It is the first full-length effort made by a Catawba Indian to explain the tribe's history. It will also prove to be a crucial document in the on-going struggle to place the names of the "western" (Editor: or "should have been") Catawba on the Catawba Nation Tribal Rolls. This volume will help realize Pinkney Head's dream. Martin has done her part to see justice done. When a group approaches the Bureau of Indian Affairs in search of recognition, the most formidable task is the production of a genealogy. Such records prove each individual's Indian lines. Judy Canty Martin has done most of this work for the "Western" Catawba and deserves applause for her many years of research.

Genealogy of the Western Catawba also points to the continued history needs. While the "Western" Catawba continue to prove that their names "...should have been on the 1943 Catawba Tribal Roll.." work should be done to tell the migration story. This volume is a must for the library of every Catawba family. It not only contains a wealth of information on the Western Catawba but provides ample evidence regarding the bridges between the South Carolina Catawba and their western cousins.** '" [722]

Judy and Forrest Martin have two children: Their daughter Tiffany Michelle Martin 1970– and their son Devin Layne Martin 1974–

## Chapter 7   Dudgeon Family

I. John Dudgeon, probably born around 1720, probably took the name of a white man named John Dudgeon who was said to be related to King Hagler.[218] Around 1751 or 2, John and an unnamed Negro caught King Hagler while he was intoxicated. They beat him up and caused him to lose his sight for a time. This act of violence caused the Chief to be adamantly against alcohol.[219]

II. Betsy Dudgeon, probably born around 1750 married Peter Harris,[220] ThusSee- WontSee. Only one child is identified, William Harris. Peter also had a child with

Prissy Bullen, that child is David Harris.[221]

1. William Harris, was born around 1800, he married Sally Ayers, born 1799 the daughter of General Jacob Ayers. In 1759 Reverend Richardson tried to convince Captain Harris that a school was need for the children. Captain Harris declined the urgings, because he was not the Chief at the time, Haggler was.[222] He succeeded General Jacob Ayers around 1837. After the death of the two great Jacobs, Ayers and Scott, William and Sally finally let go of Kings Bottoms.

Children will be found in the Peter Harris Chapter.

---

[218] Brown page 230.
[219] SC Indian Affairs Documents pages 128, 129 and 201.
[220] Watson page 31.
[221] Watson page 32.
[222] Brown page 249.

**Group Photo**

Photo 253 -   Catawba Branch, 1932, South Carolina

## Chapter 8   George Family

The Catawba name for George is Yawe'i.[223]

I.  Peter George, probably born around 1700 is alive around 1750. Reverend John Rooker, told of the catechism of Peter George, who when asked about the Resurrection, had replied "It was not so that dry bones rose again and put on flesh, he saw their bones lays in the graves all the time."[224] (It does not make sense to me either.) Peter is also listed on the pay bill of Drennan for Revolutionary service in 1780.

II. Catawba George probably born around 1720. He is listed as a Revolutionary War soldier, and a separate individual from Gilbert George.

III. Gilbert George-Captain Gilbert George & Widow George.[225] He was probably born around 1720, thus being an adult in the 1759 petition.

According to T. D. Spratt, Gilbert was the same person as the one on Drennan's pay bill of the Revolution as Catawba George; however, lists of Catawba in the Revolutionary War list both a Catawba George, and a Gilbert George.

Gilbert George[226] and Captain Gilbert George.   He was probably born around 1720, thus being an adult in the 1759 petition.      His marks follow:

A. B (Betsy?)  Jamey, daughter of the widow of Gilbert George.

IV. Pinetree George, Pinetree Robbin and Robbin, was probably born around 1760. He is listed on Drennan's Pay Bill of 1784 and on the Petition of 1792. It is most likely that Pinetree and Peter are brothers.

V. Gilbert George served in Civil War, probably born around 1840. He also signed a petition on July 15, 1868, along with Nelson George SR and William George, showing there were three separate individuals.

---

[223] Merrell page 259
[224] Merrell page 243.
[225] Brown 2 page 297.
[226] 1759 Smallpox Petition.

He was never been picked up on any Catawba census and nothing more has been found about him. It would be my guess that Gilbert is a descendant of Gilbert George above.

A note about the 1868 petition, the signature reads George, Gilbert, while the others read William George etc.

\*\*\*\*\*\*\*\*\*\*\*\*\*\*\*\*\*\*\*\*\*\*\*\*\*\*\*\*\*\*\*\*\*\*\*\*\*\*\*\*\*\*\*\*\*\*\*\*\*\*\*\*\*\*\*\*\*\*\*\*\*\*\*\*\*\*\*\*\*\*\*\*\*\*\*\*\*\*\*\*\*\*

I. Sally George born 1814,[227] she was alive in 1854, when she is mentioned as having received provisions from B. S. Massey, Indian Agent. She had three children. It is possible, and seems likely that this Sally might be Sally Screech Owl or Sally Wahoo. Sally Wahoo would have been born around this time. She is mentioned in the 1847 petition of Catawba; however, she is not identified anywhere else. In 1881, Gatschet mentions "that Mooney states - that Sally Screech Owl, the old Catawba potter here (Quallatown reserve, NC) has died leaving Sampson Owl's wife, (Susannah Harris Mush Owl) the only full Catawba on the reservation."[228]

Mooney states further, "about the same time (about 1841) a number of Catawba, dissatisfied with their condition among the whites, removed to the eastern Cherokee in western North Carolina, but finding their position among their old enemies equally unpleasant, all but one or two soon went back again. An old woman, the last survivor of this emigration, died among the Cherokee in 1889. Her daughter and a younger full-blood Catawba (Susannah Owl) still reside with that tribe."[229] On August 9, 1870, the Indian agent paid M. Wahoo and G. George for Sally's rents.[230] The connection between Sally and the Georges are explained if this is Sally George Wahoo-Screeh Owl. Moses and a daughter would account for two of the three unknown children of Sally George.

A. Moses Wahoo was paid by the Indian agent in 1870 and M. Wahoo and G. George were paid on August 9, 1870.

B. Daughter Wahoo-George..

C. [231]

\*\*\*\*\*\*\*\*\*\*\*\*\*\*\*\*\*\*\*\*\*\*\*\*\*\*\*\*\*\*\*\*\*\*\*\*\*\*\*\*\*\*\*\*\*\*\*\*\*\*\*\*\*\*\*\*\*\*\*\*\*\*\*\*\*\*\*\*\*\*\*\*\*\*\*\*\*\*\*\*\*\*

I. William  Nelson George born around 1766-1776 and Sarah Ayers born around 1790.[232] Nelson died around 1836-1846. This explains why he was not picked up on any of the Catawba censuses, however, a Nelson George SR, indicates there must be a Nelson George Jr. Nelson Jr. signed a petition in 1868 concerning the resignation of Thomas Whitesides as the Catawba Indian Agent.

---

[227] 1849 census of the Catawba.
[228] Letter to AS Gatschet, Cherokee, NC, July 19, 1888.
[229] Watson page 81.
[230] Watson page 82
[231] 1854 census of Catawba.
[232] Catawba Branch Records.

# George Family

A. Nelson George probably born about 1800[233] served in the Civil War, along with Gilbert George. Nelson George, "March 11, 1864, served with Company H, 12 South Carolina Infantry, enlisted with William Canty.[234] Nelson was paroled as a prisoner of war on May 16, 1865 at Charlotte, North Carolina.[235] He also signed the petition of 1868 concerning the resignation of Thomas Whitesides as Indian Agent. He signed the petition Nelson George senior, died about 1826.

B. William "Billy" Joseph George, Captain William George, Corrichee, -Karitici [236] meaning "I was There" was born in 1816,[237] was married to first Betsy[238] Mush Scott, they had 3 children, only one is identified, Mary Jane Elizabeth. Billy's second wife was Margaret Jane Peggy McClure, daughter of Robert McClure, a white man and Lucy Quash-Mush-Mursh-Marsh.[239]

Elder Joseph Willey says in his journal, "January 27, 1884. Started to the Nation. Staid all night to Bro. Taylor Georges which was on the main roads. Next morning we started on to fill our appointments. We had a good meeting a good spirit prevailed. Walked nine miles after meeting. Mr. William George & Peggy Jane Marsh was united in marriage. I performed the ceremony. Witnesses J. J. Humphreys & John Gandy." [240]

Billy served as chief in 1877 and in that capacity wrote a letter to the Roman Catholic Priest, A. M. Folchi who wished to start a mission.[241]

According to William-Billy Bowlegs, the son of Nelson Sr., and Sarah Ayers[242] in an account given to Scaife, reprinted by Bob Ward in 1940: "I was born in York County on Cowans plantation, above Ebenezer.

My people would go out from the reservation to work a year or two that's when I was born. I came to the reservation when only a boy. I remember my father. He's dead now and was buried in Union County, N.C. He was like the old Indians-talked Indian better than English.

Our People talked differently then than now. They ought to keep the language the Lord gave them. The language they speak now is changed a great deal. I was 10 or 12 years old when my father died. I have heard him talk about the Revolutionary War. Some of his people were in it, he was not. My father was 50 or 60 when he died. The foreign Indians used to come here and fight with the old Indians. The last fight

---

[233] Samuel Blue tells of his existence; however, he does not say Nelson was a brother to Margaret, or does he say he was Rebecca's son. Catawba Folk Tales by Frank Speck, from Chief Sam Blue page 38.
[234] Civil War Records. Blumer page 177 article 1268.
[235] Ibid
[236] Ward, page 5.
[237] 1849 census.
[238] Patterson genealogy.
[239] Catawba Branch Records.
[240] John was Peggy's half brother.
[241] Brown page 335.
[242] Catawba Branch Records.

was close to Rock Hill and we went upon them and killed them out-that was before I was born. My father was in it.

He said that the foreign Indians slipped in and killed some of our people and when he saw them he went upon them and killed them. We have been cheated out of our land. I was living during the war of 1812, was only a boy; I heard talk of the fighting while it was going on in the late war, the Civil War, other Indians were though, a good many went, about 20. I have married twice and have five children in all. We can't have but one wife and that ain't right." (Billy told the LDS Missionaries that he was born in 1816 and that agrees with the Catawba censuses in 1847, so the birth year was after the War of 1812.)[243] He must have been telling stories he had heard so often, he believed them, not an uncommon action of the old.

Elder Joseph Willey mentions Billy several times.

> "Sunday, Jan. 6th 1884. Held meeting at Mr. William George's. The weather was so cold there was only about twelve out to our meeting. They kept good order and we had a good time together. We staid there three days, reading the Book of Mormon and explaining to them. Also we read several sermons from the Deseret News."

August 29, 1884. Went in the woods where was fed by Bro. Wm George.[244]

Of Uncle Billy, Dr. Scaife wrote

"I ended my tour at the house of Uncle Billy George, who has the universal good will not only of the Indians but of the white people in the neighboring country." Scaife also stated that "only several members of the tribe who are far from being deceitful and thievish, and among the few who bear good reputations are Bob Harris and Uncle Billy George."

Billy died May 12, 1896.

Billy and 1st wife Betsy Mush had three children.

1. child on 1854 census

2. child on 1854 census]

3. Mary Jane Elizabeth (Betsy Mush-George), born December 27, 1856, married

George Washington Canty, son of Franklin and Eliza Scott Canty. More on this family is in the Canty Chapter.

Billy and 2nd wife Margaret Jane Peggy Marsh had two children:

---

[243] Ward Bob, The Children of King Hagler, 1940 page 5, hereafter cited as Ward.
[244] Joseph Willey Journal.

4. John Pierce Nelson George born 20 September 1879, Catawba Indian Reservation, York, South Carolina and died 8 September 1950, Rock Hill, York County, South Carolina  He married Hattie Ella Starnes (1878-1909), a white woman.[245] His second marriage was to Catherine Hester Harris (1889–1922  He is sometimes in LDS Records listed as Johnny George.[246] In the Dunlap letter of 1902, it states that the Johnny George family had small pox, and the Catawba would rather be shot than be vaccinated. This proved to be prophetic, because in 1903-04, Wade Ayers, died because of the vaccination.

**PHOTO 254 - JOHN PIERCE NELSON GEORGE -- BURIAL: LAURELWOOD CEMETERY, ROCK HILL, YORK COUNTY, SOUTH CAROLINA - PLOT: SECTION 13, LOT 334**

**PHOTO 255- WWI REGISTRATION CARD FOR JOHN PIERCE GEORGE**

---

[245] 1910 census of York County, SC
[246] Catawba Branch Records.

9-J10-1-4-7-570-1-046

Registration Dist. No. 442

Registrar's No. 116

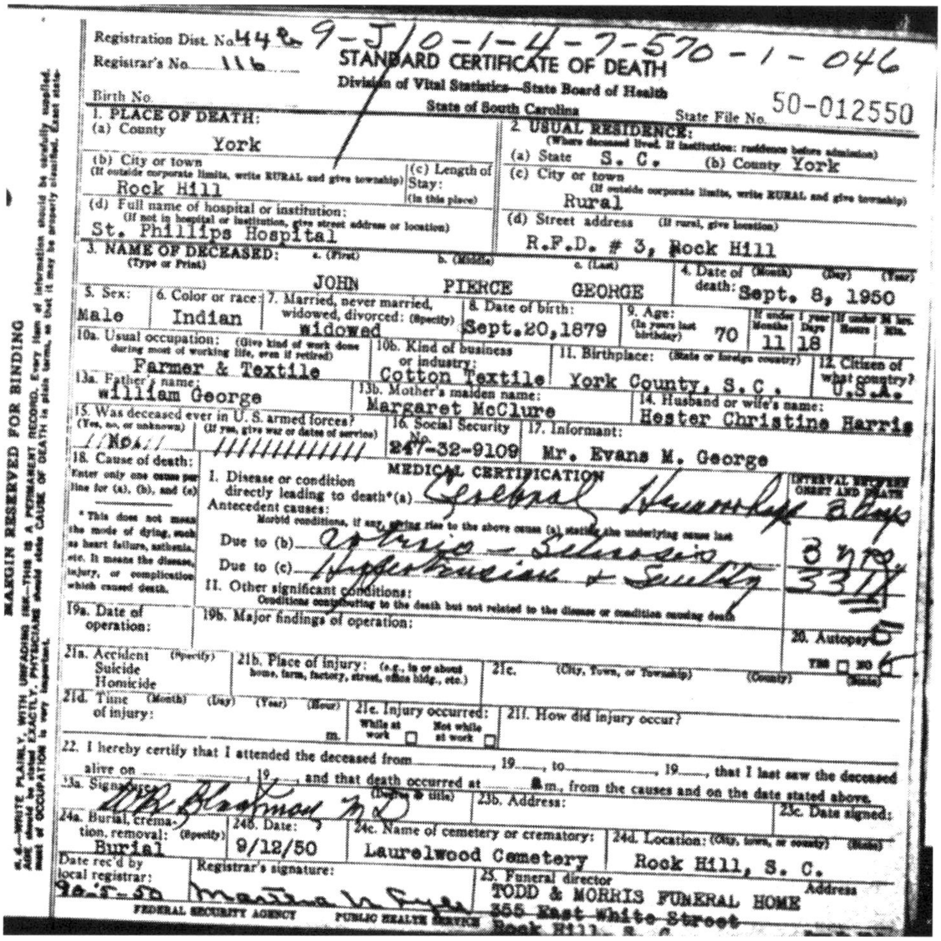

STANDARD CERTIFICATE OF DEATH

Division of Vital Statistics—State Board of Health

State of South Carolina

Birth No.

State File No. 50-012550

1. PLACE OF DEATH: (a) County York

(b) City or town (If outside corporate limits, write RURAL and give township) Rock Hill

(c) Length of Stay: (in this place)

(d) Full name of hospital or institution: (If not in hospital or institution, give street address or location) St. Phillips Hospital

2. USUAL RESIDENCE: (Where deceased lived. If institution: residence before admission)

(a) State S. C. (b) County York

(c) City or town (If outside corporate limits, write RURAL and give township) Rural

(d) Street address (If rural, give location) R.F.D. # 3, Rock Hill

3. NAME OF DECEASED: (Type or Print) a. (First) JOHN b. (Middle) PIERCE c. (Last) GEORGE

4. Date of death: (Month) (Day) (Year) Sept. 8, 1950

5. Sex: Male

6. Color or race: Indian

7. Married, never married, widowed, divorced: (Specify) widowed

8. Date of birth: Sept. 20, 1879

9. Age: (In years last birthday) 70; If under 1 year: Months 11, Days 18; If under 24 hrs.: Hours, Min.

10a. Usual occupation: (Give kind of work done during most of working life, even if retired) Farmer & Textile

10b. Kind of business or industry: Cotton Textile

11. Birthplace: (State or foreign country) York County, S. C.

12. Citizen of what country? U.S.A.

13a. Father's name: William George

13b. Mother's maiden name: Margaret McClure

14. Husband or wife's name: Hester Christine Harris

15. Was deceased ever in U. S. armed forces? (Yes, no, or unknown) No (If yes, give war or dates of service)

16. Social Security No. 247-32-9109

17. Informant: Mr. Evans M. George

18. Cause of death: Enter only one cause per line for (a), (b), and (c)

MEDICAL CERTIFICATION

I. Disease or condition directly leading to death* (a) Cerebral Hemorrhage — 8 days

Antecedent causes: Morbid conditions, if any, giving rise to the above cause (a) stating the underlying cause last

Due to (b) Arterio-Sclerosis — 3 yrs.

Due to (c) Hypertension & Senility — 3 yrs.

*This does not mean the mode of dying, such as heart failure, asthenia, etc. It means the disease, injury, or complication which caused death.

II. Other significant conditions: Conditions contributing to the death but not related to the disease or condition causing death

Interval between onset and death

19a. Date of operation:

19b. Major findings of operation:

20. Autopsy? Yes ☐ No ☐

21a. Accident Suicide Homicide (Specify)

21b. Place of injury: (e.g., in or about home, farm, factory, street, office bldg., etc.)

21c. (City, Town, or Township) (County) (State)

21d. Time of injury: (Month) (Day) (Year) (Hour) m.

21e. Injury occurred: While at work ☐ Not while at work ☐

21f. How did injury occur?

22. I hereby certify that I attended the deceased from ______, 19__, to ______, 19__, that I last saw the deceased alive on ______, 19__, and that death occurred at ______ m., from the causes and on the date stated above.

23a. Signature W. R. Blackmon M.D. (Degree or title)

23b. Address:

23c. Date signed:

24a. Burial, cremation, removal: (Specify) Burial

24b. Date: 9/12/50

24c. Name of cemetery or crematory: Laurelwood Cemetery

24d. Location: (City, town, or county) (State) Rock Hill, S. C.

Date rec'd by local registrar: 9-15-50

Registrar's signature: Martha W. Fyer

25. Funeral director: TODD & MORRIS FUNERAL HOME Address 355 East White Street Rock Hill, S. C.

FEDERAL SECURITY AGENCY PUBLIC HEALTH SERVICE

MARGIN RESERVED FOR BINDING

WRITE PLAINLY, WITH UNFADING INK—THIS IS A PERMANENT RECORD. Every item of information should be carefully supplied. AGE should be stated EXACTLY. PHYSICIANS should state CAUSE OF DEATH in plain terms, so that it may be properly classified. Exact statement of OCCUPATION is very important.

PHOTO 256 -- CERTIFICATE OF DEATH FOR JOHN PIERCE GEORGE

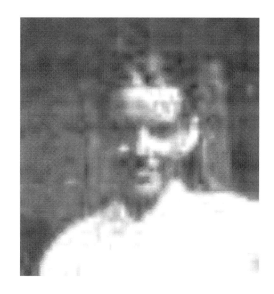

PHOTO 257 - HATTIE ELLA STARNES GEORGE FIRST WIFE OF JOHN PIERCE NELSON GEORGE

**Children for John Pierce Nelson George and Hattie Ella Starnes are Buela and Evans .**

**PHOTO 258 – BUELAH B GEORGE**

a. Beulah B George, born August 31, 1900.[247] In Catawba, South Carolina, United States and died March 1966 in South Sioux City, Iowa.  Buela married a man by the name of Guy Arrow (a Yanktonai Sioux) and she went to Haskell Institute. They had four children: Lloyd, Elaine, Anna, Robert and Darlene.

**PHOTO 259 – HEADSTONE FOR BEULAH B GEORGE ARROW
-- BURIED AT LOGAN PARK CEMETERY –
SIOUX CITY, WOODBURY COUNTY, IOWA,**

---

[247] Ibid

**PHOTO 260 - JAMES EVANS MCCLURE "BUCK" GEORGE**

b. James Evans McCIure (Buck) George sr. born 29 December 1905, Lancaster Co, South Carolina and died 22 October 1969, Rock Hill, York, South Carolina, . Buck married a white woman, Phoebie Lucinda Messer 1912-1995.[248]

**U.S., Social Security Death Index, 1935-2014**

Name   Evans George
SSN    247-03-2193
Last Residence   -- Rock Hill, 29730, York, South Carolina
Born, 29 Dec 1905 – Died, Dec 1969
State (Year) SSN issued
South Carolina - Before 19

---

[248] Obituaries, Evening Herald, December 8, 1969, page 10.

**PHOTO 261 – HEADSTONE FOR EVANS M GEORGE AND WIFE PHOEBIE LUCINDA MESSER GEORGE**

Mount Hope Cemetery.

### E. M. GEORGE SR.

ROCK HILL — Evans M. George Sr., 63, died Saturday.

He was the son of the late John P. and Hattie Starnes George.

Funeral services will be at 4 p.m. Sunday in the Greene Funeral Home.

Surviving are his widow, Mrs. Phoebia M. George; two sons, Buck and La Verne George of Rock Hill; two daughters, Mrs. Frances Davis and Miss Elaine George of Rock Hill; and two brothers, Marvin George of Rock Hill and Hiram O. George of Chicago, Ill.

**PHOTO 262 - NEWSPAPER CLIPPING - E M GEORGE SR.**

**PHOTO 263 - CATHERINE HESTER HARRIS**

Catherine Hester Harris born 7 May 1889, Fort Mill, York, South Carolina and died 26 December 1922, Rock Hill, York, South Carolina. She is the daughter of James Thomas Harris (1858–1912) and Nancy Elizabeth Gordon (1859–1929). (Watson calls her Easter instead of Hester). She is the second wife of John Pierce Nelson George. Their children are John Marvin, Hiram Qually-Quelly and Hazel George.

**PHOTO 264 JOHN MARVIN GEORGE**

c. John Marvin George born 16 August 1908, Van Wyck, Lancaster, South Carolina and died 6 November 1999, Rock Hill, York, South Carolina. He married Evelyn Brown George, daughter of Early and Edith Bertha Harris Brown.[249] Their children: Hiram Quella George 1913–1989, Charles Lewis George 1933–2007, Hazel Faye George 1935–, Joann George 1938–, Baby George 1939–, John E George 1940–, Howard George 1941–, Nancy Eileen George 1943–1944, Kenneth Neil George 1944–1946, Roger Wayne George 1948–2016, Susan George

**PHOTO 265 – JOHN MARVIN GEORGE**

[249] Catawba Branch Records.

**PHOTO 266 - JOHN MARVIN GEORGE'S HOUSE IN CATAWBA, SOUTH CAROLINA**

**PHOTO 267 HEADSTONE OF JONG MARVIN GEORGE – IN CHURCH OF JESUS CHRIST OF LATTER-DAY STS CEMETERY   -   BURIAL PLACE - CATAWBA, YORK COUNTY, SOUTH CAROLINA**

# George Family

**State, The (Columbia, SC) - Monday, November 8, 1999**

ROCK HILL - Services for John Marvin George, 90, will be held at the Church of Jesus Christ of Latter Day Saints, Catawba Ward, with interment in the church cemetery. The casket will be placed in the home.

Mr. George died Saturday. He was a son of John Priece and Easter George.

Surviving are his sons, Howard, Charlie, Phillip, John and R. Wayne George; daughters, Faye Greiner, Jo Ann Bauer, Susan George; nephews, Evans and Laverne George; niece, Frances Davis; 37 grandchildren; 60 great-grandchildren.

d. Hiram Qually-Queely George born 14 February 1913, Catawba, York, South Carolina and died 10 November 1989, Richland, South Carolina, United States.

**Obituary from Find a Grave**: Charlotte Observer, The (NC) - Thursday, November 16, 1989 ROCK HILL - Mr. Hiram Q. George 76, died Nov. 10, 1989, at VA hospital in Sacramento. Funeral is Friday at the Church of Jesus Christ of Latter-day Saints in Catawba. Survivors are his brother, Marvin George; half sister, Mrs. Hazel Wilson of Austin, Tex.

Burial: Church of Jesus Christ of Latter-day Sts Cemetery, Catawba, York County, South Carolina.

**PHOTO 268 – HEADSTONE FOR HIRAM QUEELY GEORGE - BURIAL AT CHURCH OF JESUS CHRIST OF LATTER-DAY STS CEMETERY -- CATAWBA, YORK COUNTY, SOUTH CAROLINA**

e. Hazel George born 3 May 1915, Catawba, South Carolina and she died 26 September 1999, Irving, Dallas, Texas. Married a Wilson and lived in Austin Texas in 1989 at the time of her ½ brother Hiram's death.

### U.S., Social Security Death Index, 1935-2014

Name  Hazel I. Wilson
SSN    456-20-9323
Last Residence          Irving, 75061, Dallas, Texas

Born    3 May 1915
Died    26 Sep 1999
State (Year) SSN issued        Texas - Before 1951

5. Margaret (Della) George born March 1880, father of her two children is unknown at this time, 2017. She married David Adam Toad Harris (1872–1930) and they had 5 children making 7 total for Margaret Della. She is listed on the 1900 US Census, 20 June, Indian Reservation, York, South Carolina, born Mar 1880, Catawba Indian with ¼ white blood.

**PHOTO 269 – ARTIMISA (MISSIE) H GEORGE**

1. Artimisia (Missie) H  George born 6 September 1896, Rock Hill, York, South Carolina and died 18 December 1959, Catawba Indian Reservation, South Carolina. She was listed as a student of Mrs. Dunlap in December 1899. She married Robert Theodore Harris (1893-1972) and they had 11 children. She is found on the 1900 US Census, 20 June, Indian Reservation, York, South Carolina, along with her sister Cora and mother Della. She is listed as born Sep 1896, Catawba Indian with 1/8 white blood.

(This picture identified by Billie Ann Canty McKellar)

2. Cora George born December 1899,[250]Catawba, York, South Carolina and died 1910, Catawba, York, South Carolina. She is found on the 1900 US Census, 20 June, Indian Reservation, York, South Carolina, along with her sister Missie and mother Della. She is listed as born Dec 1899, Catawba Indian with 1/8 white blood.

---

[250] 1900 census of York County transcribed by Dr. Wesley White.

6. Lucy Jane S. George born 16 November 1885.[251] Lucy is shown in Mrs.

Dunlap's school in 1899. In 1909, the newspaper states that she has married a white man named Lay Porter.[252] Lucy is married to James Starnes, a white man in the 1920 census. Lucy, (who was called the daughter of Peggy Watts and Billy George) burned to death on February 10, 1960.[253]

**PHOTO 270 – EPHRIAM DAVID GEORGE**

a. Ephriam David George, born 1 June 1902, his father was Julius M. Nesbit, white.[266] Ephriam married first Fannie Harris Canty, daughter of David Adam and Lizzie Patterson- Watts Harris, (she was married to Alonzo Canty first.) Ephriam married second Isabell Harris Harris, daughter of David Adam and Della George Harris. (Isabell was the first wife of Robert W. Harris, son of Benjamin Perry and Mary Dovie George Harris.) Ephriam was chief in the years 1952-54. He died June 14, 1965. Ephriam was the biological son of white land owner Julius Nesbitt and Lucy George, a Catawba Indian. Lucy married James Starnes. Ephriam was raised as a George.

---

[251] Catawba Branch Records
[252] Blumer page 237 article 1765
[253] Evening Herald, February 10, 1960 page 2, "Indian Woman Fatally Burned."

**PHOTO 271 -** HEADSTONE FOR EPHRAIM D GEORGE - BURIED AT CHURCH OF JESUS CHRIST OF LATTER-DAY STS CEMETERY - CATAWBA, YORK COUNTY, SOUTH CAROLINA

**PHOTO 272 – LANDRUM LESLIE GEORGE**

b. Landrum Leslie George born 21 March 1909, Catawba, York, South Carolina and died 1 August 1995, Rock Hill, York, South Carolina. He married Elsie Inez Blue, daughter of Samuel Taylor and Louisa Canty Blue. No children are listed anywhere. Landrum Leslie George, was the biological son of white land owner Julius Nesbitt and Lucy George, a Catawba Indian. Lucy married James Starnes. Landrum was raised as a George and married Elsie Blue.

## LANDRUM GEORGE: MOST DECORATED WWII CATAWBA VETERAN
### By Dr. Thomas Blumer
Catawba Tribal Historian and Author

When Landrum George died a couple of years ago, the Catawba Nation lost its most highly decorated veteran, with the possible exception of King Hagler of the Indian Wars and General New River of the American Revolution. For his service on the European Front during World War II, Landrum was the recipient of a Presidential Citation, a Bronze Star, and an Oak Leaf Cluster. In spite of these honors Landrum George was an extremely modest man. He was the first man to agree to be interviewed as part of the Catawba Memory Book Project (1989).

He was born on March 21, 1909, on a morning when (according to his mother Lucy George

Starnes) a rooster stood on the fence and crowed for the longest time.

He grew up on the reservation and attended the Catawba Indian School. During the 1930s he was a star player for the celebrated Catawba Indian Baseball Team. Perhaps his excellence at sports is

part of the reason his military career was marked by so many honors. When World War II broke out, he did his duty. War service brought out the best in Landrum George. When his squad leader was shot and killed, Landrum was given the task to write the dead man's grieving mother:

"He [the squad leader] raised up and he had his stripes on—that was the onliest place-he had his stripes on his helmet. He raised up and said, "I see him" [a German soldier]. " I'm going to get him." And when he raised his head up again, that German shot him and it went right through that

helmet. Our helmets wouldn't help, wouldn't turn a bullet.

"We got a letter from, his mother. 1 forget where she was at, New York or New Jersey or somewhere. She was up in a northern state. She wanted to know how he got killed. So I wrote her a letter back and told her."

His compassion also extended to the enemy. During the Battle of the Bulge, Landrum's company took a German machine gun position that was tying down the entire unit. The solitary soldier who had been manning the position surrendered:

"It wasn't but a little bit and that German came trotting out of there. Some of the fellows took him on back [behind the lines] and there was one of them fellows in my squad who wanted to (take?) him back. He told that German, said, "You could have been the one that killed my brother." And you know, he shot him. I told him, I said, "Boy, I have a good notion to shoot you."** I said, "I ain't in love with them, but," I said, "that man was helpless."

Landrum George's tapes are also laced with humor. On one occasion his eyes danced as he talked about how the Germans had infiltrated the American chow lines. No one could tell a German soldier from an American. He was also as stoical as any Indian can be. This trait came out when he talked about digging out a fox hole in the dead of the coldest winter he had ever experienced.

"That was the coldest country I've ever been in. I'll tell you what, I dug all night digging a fox hole. Me and a boy got behind [a stack of sugar beets]. We was out in an apple orchard and dug and dug. And that ground was froze. Looked like it was froze [three feet deep]. It was just as hard as cement. We dug and dug all night, just about got our fox hole dug, thro wed a blanket in there - got a little stiff on [the blanket) and dog gone we was just ready to go to sleep, crawling in there and the man ordered us, "all right, let's move out" Man I was sleep tired.'

But he followed orders and went on to dig another fox hole in another frozen field. He gathered commendations and medals all along the way including a Good Conduct Medal.

At the end to the War, Landrum George returned to the Nation and resumed life with his wife, Elsie George, the daughter of Chief Samuel T. Blue. He worked for J.P. Stevens textile company. But Landrum's real passion in life was hunting, particularly hunting birds. This sport was so important to him; he would often spend a few hours hunting birds before working.

Ironically, Laudrum George and the over 40 other Catawba veterans who freely volunteered to

serve in World War II were not citizens of the State of South Carolina.. Although one might assume that the Catawba came under the general American Indian Citizenship Bill of 1924, South Carolina refused to recognize this federal legislation. The S.C. Legislature finally passed the Catawba Citizenship Bill on March 1, 1944. This Bill was passed under Bureau of Indian Affairs pressure. In spite of the passage of this legislation, the Catawba were denied the right to vote for several years after 1944.[254]

---

[254] 7th Generation News

**PHOTO 273 – 1ST LANDRUM AND ELSIE GEORGE – 2ND HEADSTONE FOR LANDRUM AND ELSIE GEORGE – BURIED AT CHURCH OF JESUS CHRIST OF LATTER-DAY STS CEMETERY, CATAWBA, YORK COUNTY, SOUTH CAROLINA**

**The last children of Lucy George were Janette, Nancy and Eva Bell.**

c. Janette Starnes George born 3 September 1905, Lancaster County, South Carolina and died 2 June 1925, Catawba Indian Nation, York, South Carolina. She married Walter Beauregard Harris 1902–1969.

b. Nancy Starnes born 1906

e. Eva Bell George was born 7 June 1910-1911.[269] In LDS Church records, she is listed with her mother only, and her birth date is given as 7 June 1909 in Vanwyck, Lancaster, South Carolina. She married Guy Blue, son of Samuel Taylor and Louisa Canty Blue. Children will be found in the Blue Chapter. She died 5 September 1982, Rock Hil, York, South Carolina.

**PHOTO 274 - HEADSTONE OF EVA BELL GEORGE AND HUSBAND GUY L BLUE – BURIAL: CHURCH OF JESUS CHRIST OF LATTER-DAY STS CEMETERY - CATAWBA, YORK COUNTY, SOUTH CAROLINA**

**Eva Blue in the U.S., Social Security Death Index, 1935-2014**
Name: Eva Blue                    SSN:   250-03-3669
Last Residence:  29730 Rock Hill, York, South Carolina
BORN:        7 Jun 1910   Last Benefit:      29730, Rock Hill, York, South Carolina, United States of America
Died:   Sep 1982
State (Year) SSN issued:       South Carolina (1952)

\*\*\*\*\*\*\*\*\*\*\*\*\*\*\*\*\*\*\*\*\*\*\*\*\*\*\*\*\*\*\*\*\*\*\*\*\*\*\*\*\*\*\*\*\*\*\*\*\*\*\*\*\*\*\*\*\*\*\*\*\*\*\*\*\*\*\*\*\*\*\*\*\*\*\*\*\*\*\*\*\*\*\*\*

I. William George Sr. born around 1779 died around 1827. He married first Betsey Brown; she received rents from June of 1814 to October of 1824 as Betsy Brown. She probably was born around 1770 and was the mother of Zacariah Taylor Anthony George. Later he married Old Nancy Canty and they had Patsey Brown George.[255] Betsy then married Major Thomas Brown around 1814, when she began to receive rents as Betsy Brown; Thomas died in the 1820's.[256]

William George and Betsy's child is Anthony and William and Old Nancy Canty's child is Patsy. Dr. Frank T. Siebert stated that Anthony and Uncle Billy George were brothers.[257]

    A. Anthony-Yeku- (Zacariah Taylor) George born 1799,[258] died 1862.[259] From Thomas's list at Qualla Town, an entry appears Anthana George, Patsey George, and Anthana's daughter. (Anthana

---

[255] Watson page 20. Miscellaneous Notes. June 2-12, 1913. In 1917 the newspaper states
[256] Ibid
[257] Smithsonian records, Bureau of American Ethnology, negative #55, 023, remarks, on a photo of Margaret George Brown. Uncle Billy was Gatschet's informant.
[258] Brown page 328.
[259] 1849 census of Catawba.

is Anthony.) In the 1850 census there is a Nancy Poag born 1784 in York district, with a large bunch of children, but no husband.

Anthony then married Rebecca Quash-Mush-Marsh, daughter of John Mursh and Betsy Quash- Scott. This further complicates records, because he came into this marriage with a daughter called Margaret George, and Rebecca had two daughters by Edmund Ayers, one that was named Margaret, and one named Sarah Jane Ayers. The two Margarets are constantly mixed up in nearly all records. Together Rebecca and Anthony had Zacariah Taylor George.

1. Zacharia Taylor George Jr., born 1824.[260]  Zacharia's children follow his unknown sibling.

2. unknown child

Children of Zacharia Taylor George

(a) Zacariah [261] Taylor George jr. born 1 February 1849. The birthplace is

Swain County or Kings Mt. Branch, Cleveland, North Carolina.[262] Taylor received money from the Indian Agent R. L. Crook on April 10, 1875 in the amount of $31.50, on July 29, 1875, he received $8.00 and in 1881, he received $53.28. This was not a good year for Taylor, he was assaulted[263]  by William Harris and William was tried in June of 1881. In November 3, 1881, William Harris was convicted of the assault. Taylor was a contributor to Truman Michelson's book Catawba Linguistic Notes, Texts. Vocabularies And

"Indian Woman Succumbs From wounds Inflicted by her Husband, Delia George Dies." This must have been heart wrenching for Taylor and Emily. Taylor married Emily Elizabeth Cobb Ayers, and Zacariah Taylor George's children follow. Emily was married first to Jefferson Ayers, her children by him will be found in the Ayers chapter.

(1) Nancy Jane George, born13 July 1869,[264] Rock Hill, York, South Carolina.  She is listed on the 1880 census with Taylor George and Emily as being 10 years old. She died in South Carolina but we don't know just when.

(2) Minnie Hester George, born September 21, 1871, married in July 1887 to Samuel Taylor Blue, as his first wife, son of Margareth McLonah and Sam Blue,[265] a white man. Children will be found under Blue.

---

[260] LDSIGIpre-1970.

[261]  One Catawba record gives the name of Moroni's father as Zacharia, he is called Taylor George on the rest of the children. Therefore since more was better he is Zacharia Taylor George

[262] Old LDS International Genealogical Index pre-1970.

[263] Blumer page 189, articles 1365 and 1366.

[264] Catawba Branch records

(3) Willie W. George, born 1873. Willie is dead by the 1900 census.

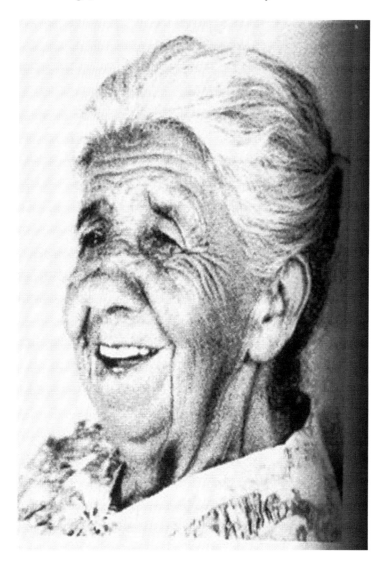

**PHOTO 275 – RACHEL WYSIE GEORGE**

(4) Rachel Wysie George, born August 21, 1874 in , Catawba Indian Reservation, Rock Hill, York, South Carolina and died 20 September 1960 in Rock Hill, York, South Carolina, United States. She married John William Brown, son of Sallie Rachel Brown and Joe Cherry.[266] Children will be found in the Brown chapter.

---

[265] Catawba Branch records
[266] Ibid

**PHOTO 276 – RACHEL WYSIE GEORGE**

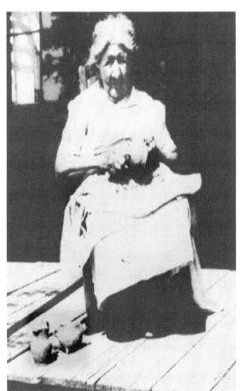

**PHOTO 277 – 1ST RACHEL WYSIE GEORGE BROWN – 2ND JOHN WILLIAM AND RACHEL WYSIE BROWN WITH FAMILY**

**From the Missionary Journal of Mary Barus**

"A dream of seeing the Indians

Another night I dreamed we were at our journeys end a house full of the Indians were out to meet us. I heard them singing a song where two voices led and in duet (sic) and the rest joined in chorus. I also saw very plainly four Indian women.

Jesus Lover of my soule (sic)

I also told Orlando this dream & that I was sure I could recognize them if I ever saw them. Both these dreams or manifestations were proven to my satisfaction to have been given me by the spirit of the Lord for sure enough after we arrived at the Indian Nation the first night there were the people I had seen assembled. Only three of the women were there but I saw the fourth one a few days after. Their features were familiar when I met them. They were sisters Watts, Blue, Gordon & Brown. They sang many songs that night but they did not sing "Jesus Lover of my soule (sic)" with duet (sic) and chorus till I taught it to them & I recognized it just as soon as they sang it as the one I had heard in my dream. This was a very strong testimony to me and I thanked my heavenly Father for the same. These dreams were a source of comfort to me since I of course dreaded the thoughts of taking our family among the Indians. My idea of an Indian was of course the ones I had seen who wore their long unkept (sic) hair – male & female – and with blankets & moccasins.

I was thoroughly surprised tho to find a people speaking the English language & natural songsters "

**PHOTO 278 - JOHN AND RACHEL BROWN AND SON EARLY MORGAN BROWN**

**PHOTO 279 – MARY DOVIE GEORGE**

(5) Mary Dovie George, born 23 May 1874, married Benjamin Perry Harris, son of John "Mush" and Nancy Harris Harris. She died 12 September 1972 [267] Children will be found under Benjamin Perry Harris in the Peter Harris chapter.

**PHOTO 280 -  HEADSTONE OF MARY DOVIE GEORGE HARRIS -  BURIAL:   CHURCH OF JESUS CHRIST OF LATTER-DAY STS CEMETERY  -  CATAWBA, YORK COUNTY,  SOUTH CAROLINA**

---

[267] Catawba Branch records

(6) Margaret Della George, born December 1881, married David Adam Harris, as his second wife, he was the son of James & Sarah Jane Ayers Harris sr.[268] Delia was shot by her husband David Adam Harris, or was accused by her, on her deathbed, on March 1, 1917.[269] She told Dr. Theo Neely that David Adam had shot her not by accident. Accordingly, David Adam was held for murder. The trial was supposed to have been held in July 1917, and in November, he was acquitted.[270] Their children will be found under David Adam Harris in the Peter Harris chapter.

**PHOTO 281 – MORONI JAMES JOESPH GEORGE AND WIFE**

(7) Moroni James Joseph George, born 21 August 1884, Catawba Nation and died 4 September 1979 in York, South Carolina. He was a student of Mrs. Dunlap in 1899.

Moroni married Martha Mattie Price born 9 October 1893, South Carolina and died 1 March 1910, Catawba Reservation, York, South Carolina. They married 9 Feb 1909 and one child: Mabel George born 13 February 1910, South Carolina and 20 February 1910, South Carolina.

Second he married Hattie J. Millings, a white woman born 20 February 1893, South Carolina and died 4 July 1993, York, York, South Carolina. They were married 5 Aug 1912, Charlotte, Mecklinburg, North Carolina and they had thirteen children,[271]

---

[268] Ibid
[269] Blumer page 261 articles 1986, 87 & 88.
[270] Blumer page 264-65 article 2021.
[271] Catawba Branch Records.

Below -Moroni George at Carlisle, (their uniform)

**PHOTO 282 – MORONI JAMES JOSEPH GEROGE**

**PHOTO 283 - 1ST HATTIE** [272]   **HATTIE J. MILLINGS GEORGE**

**PHOTO 284 – MORONI AND HATTIE GEORGE**

[272] Hattie photos are from Mandy caponis Sisi.

This certificate is not valid until it has been entered in the Branch District Record.

Entered in the Branch District Record, line No. *So Carolina 6-1112*

By _Maude Bird_ Date *2 October 1939*

Branch Clerk
District Clerk

Asst Recorder

Name in full _Moroni James Joseph George_

Father's Name _Taylor George_

Mother's Maiden Name _Emily Taff_

| | DAY | MONTH | YEAR |
|---|---|---|---|
| Born at _York York South Carolina_ | 21 | Aug | 1884 |
| Baptised by _R A Barry_ | 24 | Feb | 1894 |
| Confirmed by _Hyrum Carter_ | 24 | Feb | 1894 |

**PHOTO 285 – L.D.S. BRANCH DISTRICT RECORD – SOUTH CAROLINA FOR MORONI JAMES JOSEPH GEORGE**

# Marriage Certificate

STATE OF NORTH CAROLINA. **Greeting:**

MECKLENBURG COUNTY

I, *John R. Renfrow, Register of Deeds for the above named State and County,* do hereby certify that ___M. J. George (age 25)___ and ___Addie Millen (age 19)___ were married by ___Rev. H. M. Pressly___ on the ___5th___ day of ___August___ 19_12_, as appears of record in the office of the Register of Deeds for said County and State.

Witness my hand and official seal, this ___6th___ day of ___April___ 19_51_

_John R. Renfrow_

REGISTER OF DEEDS

BY _____ DEPUTY

**PHOTO 286 – MARRIAGE CERTIFICATE FOR MORONI J GEORGE AND ADDIE MILLEN**

**State of North Carolina**
Mecklenburg County

OFFICE OF REGISTER OF DEEDS

*August 5'' 191 2*

To any Ordained or Authorized Minister of any Religious Denomination, or any Justice of the Peace of said County:

*M. A. Frazier* having applied to me for a LICENCE for the Marriage of *M. J. George* of *Roddey, S.C.* aged *2 5* years; race *White* the son of *Taylor George* and *Emily George* the father now *living* the mother *living* resident of *Catawba County* and *Addie Millon* of *Charlotte, N.C.* aged *19* years; race *White* daughter of *M. R. Millon* and *Margaret Millon* the father the mother *dead* resident of *not known*

I. *M. A. Frazier*, do solemnly swear that the statement rendered above is true, that the parties to the proposed Marriage are of legal age, and that there is no legal impediment to the said Marriage.

*M. A. Frazier*

Sworn and subscribed before me, this the *5th* day of *August* 191 2

*W. M. Moore*
By *R. S. Long D.R.*
Register of Deeds.

And with the written consent of the of the said to the proposed Marriage having been filed with me.

And there being no legal impediment to such Marriage known to me you are hereby authorized at any time within one year from the date hereof, to celebrate the proposed Marriage at any place within the said County.

You are required within two months after you shall have celebrated such Marriage, to return this License to me at my office, with your signature subscribed to the certificate under this License, and with the blanks therein filled according to the facts, under the penalty of forfeiting two hundred dollars to the use of any person who shall sue for the same.

*W. M. Moore*
By *R. S. Long, D.R.*
Register of Deeds.

**State of North Carolina**
Mecklenburg County

I. *H. M. Pressly* a *Presbyterian Minister* united in matrimony *M. J. George* and *Addie Millen* the parties licensed above, on the *5''* day of *August* 191 2 at *Charlotte* in *Charlotte* township in said County, according to law.

Witnesses Present at Marriage:

*C. Witte Queen* of *Charlotte*
*Mrs Mary C. Pressley* " "
of

(Minister or Magistrate Please Sign here) *H. M. Pressly*

**PHOTO 287 – MARRIAGE RECORD OF M J GEORGE AND ADDIE MELLON (MILLINGS) 5 AUG 1912**
**Moroni and Hattie J. Millings George's children are Roberta, Bertha, Artie Jane, Leola, Missouri, Moroni, Margaret, Etta, and Leonard.**

a. Roberta George born 12 March 1911, Catawba, York, South Carolina and died after 1940

**PHOTO 288 – BERTHA MAE GEORGE**

b. Bertha Mae George born 29 June 1913, Lancaster, Lancaster, South Carolina and died 11 October 2014, Catawba, York, South Carolina. She married George Furman Harris (1913-2006), the son of James JR and Margaret Harris Harris. Children will be found in the Peter Harris chapter.

From Thomas Blumer

"Bertha grew up watching her elders making pottery. After her marriage to Furman Harris, the lived with his grandmother Martha Jane White Harris. This is where she came under the tutelage of the master potter Martha Jane. She was also close with her sister in law, another great potter, George Harris and they often made pottery together. She often demonstrated her skills for the Church of Jesus Christ of Latter Day Saints (Mormons). She retired at one time, but came back in 1976, perhaps to enjoy the fact that prices had gone up and it was more profitable."

**PHOTO 289 – ARTIE JANE GEORGE**

c. Artie Jane George born 21 March 1915, Catawba, York, South Carolina and died 15 January 1985, Catawba, York, South Carolina. She married Henry Canty Jr (1911-1984), son of Henry Alonzo and Emma Jane Harris Canty. Children will be found under Canty. She died one day after her husband Henry on the 16th.[273]

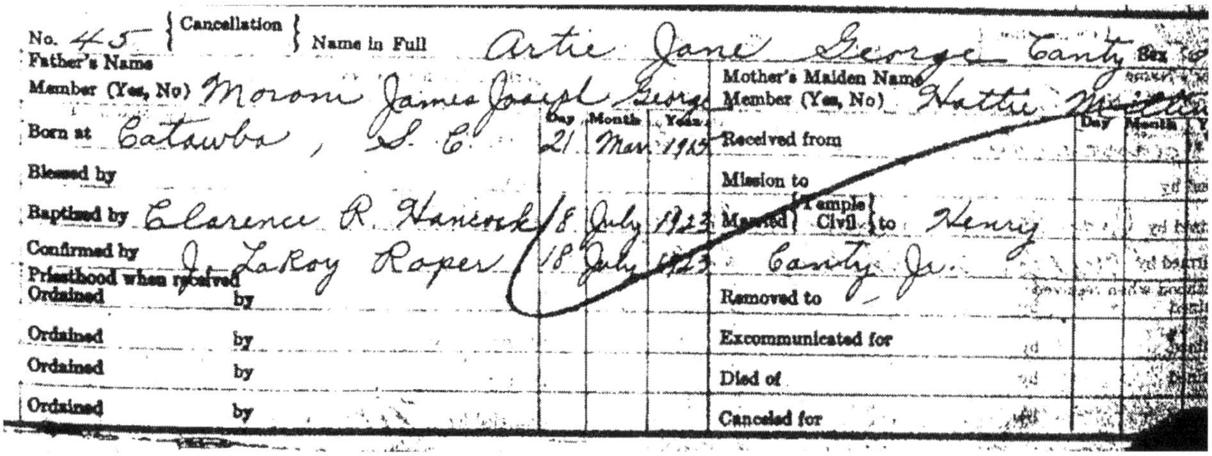

**PHOTO 290 L.D.S. BAPTISM RECORD FOR ARTIE JANE GEORGE**

d. Ida M. George born 11 May 1915, York, York, South Carolina died 31 August 1992, Latta, Dillon, South Carolina.

---

[273] Catawba Branch Records and Membership records

**PHOTO 291 – REINA A GEORGE**

e. Reina A George born 17 May 1917, York, York, South Carolina and died 23 January 2003, Rock Hill, York, South Carolina, United States. She Married Angelo Caponis (1897 Italy – 1980 Florida).

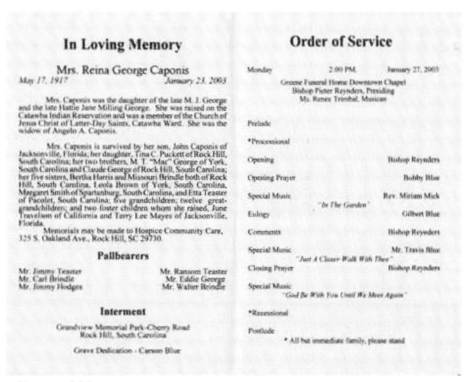

**PHOTO 292 - FUNERAL CARD FOR REINA GEORGE CAPONIS**

**PHOTO 293- LEOLA GEORGE BROWN WITH HUSBAND AND CHILD**

f. Leola George born 23 August 1919, York, York, South Carolina and died 6 October 2008, York, York, South Carolina. She married Samuel Brown (1921-2003), white.

From her Obituary: Burial will be at Lakeview Memory Gardens.

A native of Lancaster, S.C., Leola Brown was a daughter of the late Maroni George and Hattie Jean Millins George. She was the widow of John Samuel Brown. She was a member of the Jesus Christ of Latter Day Saints Church.

She is survived by three daughters, six sons, a brother, two sisters, 26 grandchildren; 40 great-grandchildren; and two great-great-grandchildren.

**PHOTO 294 – ELIZABETH MISSOURI GEORGE**

g. Elizabeth Missouri George born 23 April 1921, Rock Hill, South Carolina and died 5 July 2008, York, York, South Carolina. She married first a Frank Henry Brindle (1919-1945), who was not a Catawba and second a Teaster.

h. Elmer George born about 1924, South Carolina and died before 1940, South Carolina. He was listed on the 1930 census as 5 but not on the 1940 census.

**PHOTO 295 – MORONI TAYLOR "MAC" GEORGE**

i. Moroni Taylor "Mac" George JR born 28 April 1925, Rock Hill, York, South Carolina and died 3 November 2009, York, York, South Carolina. He served in World War II, and married Evelyn Lucille McAbee, white.

**PHOTO 296 - MAC, HATTIE AND CLAUDE GEORGE**

YORK, S.C. - Moroni Taylor "Mac" George, 84½, of 17 Georgia Ave., went to his heavenly home on Nov. 3, 2009, at Wayne T. Patrick Hospice House on India Hook Road in Rock Hill, S.C.

Funeral will be 2 p.m. Friday at Bratton Funeral Home, 1455 Filbert Highway in York. Pastor Lee Teal will have charge of the services and will be assisted by Pastor James Erle. Burial will be at Union Baptist Church in Filbert, S.C.

Mac was a Native American Indian of York Co. (Catawba Tribe) and was the son of the late Moroni James & Hattie Milling George.

Mac retired from the City of York Police Dept. after 23 years of service in May 1987. He was a veteran of the U.S. Navy in World War II. He is a lifetime member of the Veterans of Foreign Wars. He is a former wrestler in 1957 known as Chief Yellowbird. He was a former member of the Indian Beagle Club and a former volunteer of the York Fire Dept. in York , S.C.

Mac is survived by his wife of 64½ years, Evelyn McAbee George; one son, Eddie Mac George and his wife, Jackie of York, S.C.; two sisters, Bertha G. Harris, of Rock Hill , S.C. and Margaret G. Smith of Moore , S.C.

Mac enjoyed his grandchildren, Tige, Megan, & Amanda George also his great grandchildren, Brooklyn, Hayley & Clarklyn George, Chase "Stitch" Brown, Aden Faulkenberry. Also he had five step grandchildren & three step great grandchildren.

He leaves behind two special people in his life, who he loved and cared about as a daughter, Diane & Steve McNeely.

# George Family

He was predeceased by son, Thomas Clark (T.C.) in 2005, grandson, Taylor George, great grandson, Colby Brown, one brother and 5 sisters: Claude George, Reina G. Caponis, Artie Canty, Etta G. Teaster, Missouri G. Brindle, Leola G. Brown.

The family will receive friends at Bratton Funeral Home on Thursday night November 5, 2009 from 6pm to 8pm, and other times at the home of his son Eddie & Jackie George, 42 Oklahoma St.York.

Instead of flowers please send donations to Cornerstone Family Worship Center Bldg. Fund Po Box 38 York, SC 29745, Wayne T. Patrick Hospice House, P.O. Box 993, Rock Hill , SC 29731 or Sharon Baptist Church Elevator Acct. PO Box 6 Sharon, SC 29742.

Bratton Funeral Home in York is serving the George family.

Published in Gaston Gazette from November 4 to November 5, 2009

j. Kieth George born 1927, South Carolina and died before 1940, York, York, South Carolina. He appears on the 1930 census as 3 but is not on the 1940 census.

**PHOTO 297 – MARGARETT REBECCA GEORGE**

k. Margarett Rebecca George born 24 September 1927, Rock Hill, York, South Carolina and died July 1985, Spartanburg, Spartanburg, South Carolina. She married John Earl Smith (1925-2005).

**PHOTO 298 – ETTA DELVINA GEROGE**

l. Etta Delvina George born 17 April 1929, York, York, South Carolina and died 26 June 2006, Pacolet, Spartanburg, South Carolina. She married Glen Teaster (1928-), white.

**Obituary: PACOLET, SC--** Etta George Teaster, 75, of 4014 Pacolet Highway, went home to be with the Lord on Tuesday, June 27, 2006 at her residence.

A native of Rock Hill, SC, she was the wife of Glenn Teaster and daughter of the late M. J. George and Hattie Millens George. She was a retired LPN and was a member of Goucher Baptist Church.

In addition to her husband, surviving are five daughters, Debbie McCraw, Diane Price, Elaine Price all of Gaffney, Libby Hodge and Claudette Thompson both of Pacolet; three sons, Ransom Teaster and Bill Teasterboth of Gaffney, and Jimmy Teaster of Pacolet; one brother, M. T. George of York; four sisters, Bertha Harris and Missouri Brindle both of Rock Hill, SC, Leola Brown of York, SC, and Margaret Smith of Spartanburg, SC; thirteen grandchildren; and ten great grandchildren. She was preceded in death by a brother, Claude George; two sisters, Rena Caponis and Artie Canty; and a grandson, Adam Thompson.

# George Family

The family will receive friends from 6:00 until 8:00 p.m. on Thursday, June 29, 2006 at Blakely Funeral Home. Funeral services will be held at 2:00 p.m. on Friday, June 30, 2006 at Goucher Baptist Church conducted by Rev. Norman Gardner and Mr. Ashby Blakely. Interment will follow in the church cemetery.

Memorials may be made to Adam Thompson Fund, c/o Goucher Baptist Church, 415 Goucher Creek Road, Gaffney, SC, 29340 or to American Diabetes Association, 16-A Brozzini, Greenville, SC, 29615.

**PHOTO 299 – LEONARD CLAUDE GEORGE**

m. Leonard Claude George born 30 June 1933, Rock Hill, York, South Carolina and died 31 December 2003, Rock Hill, York, South Carolina. He married a white woman named Sally Grace.

**PHOTO 300 - MRS. HARRIS, HATTIE, UNCLE MAC AUNT MARGARET, AUNT MISSOURI, AUNT REINA, AUNT ETTA, (UNCLE CLAUDE AND AUNT LEOLA NOT PICTURED)**

Patsy is the daughter of William George and Old Nancy Canty.

B. Patsy Brown George, born 1819, also called Patsy Brown. Patsy was named a model mother of the year in 1860; it is unknown which Patsy this was. A Patsy George received $4.50 in April 1875. She had one identifiable child, Mary.

    1. Mary George born May 1835 married Absolum (Epps) Harris, son of Sallie Harris, as his first wife. Mary received funds from R.L. Crook Indian Agent on April 10, 1875 in the amount of $22.50 and from W. M. Whyte, Indian Agent, she received $6.66. She is still living around 1884, when Pinkney Head and John Alonzo Canty visited the Cherokee. She had two children who were deceased by the 1900 census.

• • • • • • • • • • • • • • • • • • • • • • • • • • • • • • • • • • • • • • • • • • • • • • • • • • • • •

William George sr. born around 1779, married second Old Nancy Canty- George born 1779, daughter of William-Billy Canty of Revolutionary War fame. Only one child is found for the couple. Little Nancy George.

    1. Little Nancy George born 1805, was involved with an Alexander George somehow,

she married David Harris later. Evidently, Nancy George born 1825 is the product of

Alexander George. She is always listed as George, while the Harris children used their father's name.

The Harris children will be found under Peter Harris.

    (a). Nancy George born 1825. Proof of this relationship between Rhody and Nancy is the 1880 census where Nancy is called Allen Alston Harris's aunt. Nancy George collected funds from the Indian Agent, W. M. Whyte in the amount of $6.66 in 1881.

    (b.)

    (c)

Rhoda a white foundling was raised by this Catawba family. She married Allen Harris, her children etc. will be found in his chapter.

## Chapter 9  Hagler Family

I.        Nopkehea-[274] King Essetaswa -Arataswa-King Hagler, probably born around 1725, ruled from 1750 to 1763.

He was known to be a great leader. Much has been written about his life and his discretion in settling disputes. One such dispute arose when a musician was killed for his violin. When the whites complained, King Hagler, sitting upon a high piece of ground took his gun and shot the murderer dead in his tracks. Governor Bull had given him the rifle that he used, and it was silver-mounted.[275]

In 1750, the Iroquois and Catawba were at war, and the Catawba had sworn to "fight them whilst there was one of them alive, and that after their Death their very bones shall fight the Six Nations."

On May 23, 1751, the King and five other Catawba went to New York to make peace with the Iroquois. During the meeting, a Tree of Peace was planted in Albany.[276]

One of his most eloquent speeches occurred at a council meeting on August 29, 1754, King

Hagler said:

"As to living on these lands we possess, we expect to live on these lands we now possess during our time here, from when the Great Man above made us he also made this island. He also made our forefathers and of this colour and hue. He also fixed our forefathers and us here and to inherit this land, and ever since we lived after our manner and fashion.

We in those days had not instruments to support our living but our bows which we completed with stone. Knives we had none. It was our custom in those days to cut our hair, which we did, burning it off our heads and bodies with coals of fire. Our axes we made of stone. We bled ourselves with fish teeth. Our clothing was skins and furs, instead of which we now enjoy these clothes which we get from the white people. And ever since they first came among us we have enjoyed all these things that we were then destitute of for which we thank the white people. To this day we have lived in a brotherly love and peace with them and more especially with these three governments and it is our earnest desire that love and friendship which has so long remained shall ever continue.[277]

King Hagler "was made drunk" in the middle of the year 1751, beaten and temporarily blinded by a Negro trader and John Dudgeon, who was said to be related to Hagler.[278] After this incident, Hagler was very much against alcohol making the following statement to the North Carolina commissioners on August 29, 1754:

---

[274] Brown page 229.
[275] Ward, page 3.
[276] Brown page 172.
[277] Ward page 3.
[278] Brown pages 229 & 230.

"Brothers here is one thing you yourselves are to blame very much in, That is you rot your grain in tubs, out of which you take and make strong spirits. You sell it to our young men and give it to them many times; they get very drunk with it and this is the very cause that they oftentimes commit those crimes that is offencive to you and us and all thro' the effect of that drink. It is also very bad for our people, for it rots their guts and causes our men to get very sick

and many of our people has lately died by the effects of that strong drink, and I heartily wish you would do some-thing to prevent your people from dareing to sell or give them any of that strong drink, upon any consideration whatever for that will be a great means of our being free from being accused of those crimes that is committed by our young men and will prevent many of the abuses that is done by them thro' the effects of that strong drink. "

In March of 1757, King Hagler was expected by the Government to take 100 men to Canada to fight the French.

In 1758, 33 Catawba warriors went to Virginia, where they served for 7 months, in the campaign of Fort Duquesne, 27 of their men served under General Forbes.

On January 3, 1759, King Hagler wrote:

"Dear Brother: Agreeable to our promise to you and Mr. Atkin, I and my Warriours went out against the Enemys of our Father the Great King George, whom we shall be always ready and willing to serve. Upon our return we found the dry weather had interely destroyed our crop and unless our good Brother, the Governor will supply us with a little com, our wives and children will perish for want."

Unfortunately, small pox struck the tribe, while Hagler was away leaving only 60 warriors alive.

On his way home on Twelve-Mile Creek from the Waxhaw, Shawnee raiders, suddenly fired upon him and he was killed on August 30, 1763. [279]He was killed instantly; however, he was scalped. Even parties of whites were unable to find the killers, and the Catawba took their revenge upon seven Shawnee, and, likely accidentally, including one of the party who killed Hagler. King Prow and his warriors took the scalps of the Shawnee to Charles Town, where the Catawba were rewarded.

He was said to have been buried beneath a tree near Newton, Virginia. The grave was said to be ten feet wide, ten feet deep and ten feet long. In the grave was placed his silver mounted rifle, powder flash, gold and silver money, pipes, tobacco and enough possessions to fill the grave. A guard of sixteen warriors was to keep watch for a moon, or four weeks, however, Virginia gambiers who were present at the Kings funeral, took all the valuables.[280]

> 1. Son died in infancy born around 1750. "King Hagler needs a new flag, because he has covered his dead son with his old one."

---

[279]  Brown pages 247.
[280] Brown page 214& 248

2. Daughter married one waters, born around 1750.

3. Daughter married William Scott born around 1750 and Matthew Toole, a white trader. Matthew was such an important man in the area, that a trail through the territory was called Matthew Tool's Path. Matthew died in 1757. This daughter had three children.

a. General Jacob Scott was born around 1778, died 1858.

b.

c. Sally Scott-Toole born around 1780. The center of the Nation at this time was about Sugar Creek, and Sally spent her early years at King's Town, on the western bank of HorseShoe Bend. Some said that in her youth she was very beautiful. [281] She claimed to have watched the Red Coats build the North Carolina fort that was near the present site of Fort Mill. She was called a half blood by a Professor Blackburn in 1816, "intelligent and of inquiring mind". She was interested in his compass and it did not take long for her to figure that a knife made the needle turn. Evidently, the Professor had told the Indians he was a magician, and Sally took the steel she made fires with, and did the same trick, thus proving the Catawba were smarter than people thought they were. He made the statement that, "These Indians are shrewd, what a pity it is they are not wise." Maybe they were smarter than he was, and knew when to play dumb.

Sally would not ride a horse the "proper" way. She rode astride; not sidesaddle like a "lady". The settlers were not able to make her see the sense in riding sidesaddle, because, Sally, being a Catawba was straightforward. The best way, the most practical way, to ride a horse would be astride like the men.[282]

In her speaking English, one old settler said, "she always put the horse before the saddle," when constructing her sentences.

Sally married first. Little Aleck-Allik; and second. General New River.

She is described on a visit to Kings Bottoms:

"Seated on a jet-black Indian Poney, with six of the most attractive maidens of her people as attendants, she rode with grace and dignity of mien (men) to the principle town, near King's Bottoms".

She was an esteemed person and commanded great respect. Once when a hair pulling fight broke out between two Indian women at a general meeting with the

---

[281] Brown page 278

[282] Merrell page 546.

Indian Agent, just her appearance at the meeting broke the fight up and calmed the women.

She was also known as a prankster. A newly emigrated Irishman, who had a great fear of rattlesnakes, visited Sally. It was a very cold day, and was snowing with an accumulation of about 2 inches on the ground. Obviously, any rattlesnakes out then would have to have long underwear on. As he left the store this Irishman followed her out of the store to ask her something about the country and about rattlesnakes and what he could do to defend himself if attacked by one of the "varments". Sally told him she would tell him how to act if attacked by one or more rattlers. He said he would be very grateful for the information as he was going to settle in one of the Irish settlements. She told him he must take a long pole and put it upon his shoulders and whoop and sing as loud as he could and the snakes looking out of their holes would see the long pole and then would draw back their heads. The thought of this Irishman doing what Sally had told him, caused her to laugh for years afterwards. It also gives present day Catawba a laugh. Sally was an individual, riding her horse, her way, a straddle, instead of sidesaddle, like the white women.

She owned an old slave named Jon only because she had received him instead of rents due her husband.[283]

It was said that her husband General New River ruled, because of the fondness of the people for her. She was very close to the Spratts and was said to have spent many of her last years in their home. Thomas Spratt said that his grandfather Thomas Spratt raised Sally.

Sally died around 1824 in the same cabin that the General had died in 1804.

Three children can be identified, Jane, Jacob and Jenny.

> a. Jane Allik born around 1800, no more information.
>
> b. Jacob Scott born around 1790, died around 1825, son of Sally.
>
> He collected rents. See more information under the Scott Chapter.
>
> c. Jenny Scott born around 1785 married Jamey -James Kegg born 1785. The Children will be found under Kegg.

II.     The sister of King Hagler married Big Town-Colonel Jacob Ayers, born around 1730; her children were probably called Ayers-Ears..

---

[283] Merrell page 587.

**PHOTO 301 – KING HAGLER**

## King Hagler, Catawba Chief, Conference with Peter Henley 1756

Posted on February 4, 2013 by Roberta Jestes

Many times the only glimpses we have of the Native people as individuals are through documents like this. I sure wish the names of his warriors had been recorded.

Colonial and State Records of North Carolina

Report by Peter Henley concerning his conference with King Hagler and the Catawba Nation

Henley, Peter, 1725-1758

May 26, 1756 – May 28, 1756

Volume 05, Pages 579-584

[B. P. R. O. North Carolina. B. T. Vol. 12. C. 106.]

Copy of a Conference held with the King and Warriors of the Cataubas by Mr. Chief Justice Henley at Salisbury in North Carolina in May 1756.

Salisbury Thursday 26 May 1756.

At two o'Clock this afternoon King Hagler of the Catawba Nation of Indians with 15 of his principal Warriors and about 30 of his young

Men painted and armed in the manner that they are when going to War and in great Order and regularity marched through this Town, and encamped a small distance from it, about an hour after he waited upon Peter Henley Esqre Chief Justice at the House of Edward Cusick, and by an Interpreter expressed himself as follows.

I and my people are Brothers and fast friends to the English and intend always to be so: Having heard of some Injuries lately done to my Brethren it has given me great concern, and being told that you and many more of them were to be here at this time I am come to talk with you about these Matters, and to endeavor to make all things straight.

To which the Chief Justice answered: King Hagler I have a sensible pleasure in seeing you and my other Brothers the Catawba's here. As I don't know the particular Articles upon which you desire this Conference when you please to communicate yourself upon that subject, I will hear you with the greatest attention.

To which the King replied. I thank you, but as it is now late I will defer doing it to 9 o'clock to-morrow morning if that time be agreeable to you, which being answered by the Chief Justice in the Affirmative on Friday May 27th the Chief Justice and principal Gentlemen in Town with King Hagler 15 of his Warriors and the rest of his people went to the House of Peter Arran and being seated round a Table, the King spoke as follows—

The Cherokees We and the White People have been Brothers, and I desired that the path between us might be kept clear but the Cherokees have been playing the Rogue at which I am extremely concerned.

All the White People from South to North as far as New York nay beyond the great Waters under the great King are our Brothers, should the French come we will stand by our Brethren the English or go down into the Grave with them.

The Cherokees have told me that they would enter into a Friendship with the French but be assured that the White People shall still be my Brothers and I will assist them, these men I have brought here (pointing to his Warriors) are all come freely and voluntarily to acquaint the English that they will stand by them as long as they live, Mine is a small Nation yet they are brave men, and will be fast friends to their Brothers the White people as long as the sun endures.

I always advise my Men to be kind and obliging to the White People, as they are their Brothers and I shall continue to do so and remain their Brother 'till a sharp thing pierces my Breast so that I die, when that happens they must do as they please.

As I suppose there will soon be a War, I desire the Governor of North Carolina as this Land belongs to him to send us some Ammunition as soon as possible, and that he will build us a fort for securing our old men women and children when we turn out to fight the Enemy on their coming and as we love to wear silver plates on our Breasts and Arms I should be glad he would send us some of them with some Wampum.

Colo. Alexander Colo. Harris and Capt. Berry told me they would make my Warriors a small present for assisting the White People in retaking their Goods Horses &c: from the Cherokees which they had plundered them of.

I go very much among the White people and have often my Belly filled by them and am very sorry they should at any time be distracted.

I return the Governor thanks for his care in purchasing Corn for my people which has saved the lives of many of our old men women and children.

As my people and the White people are Brethren I desire that when they go to their houses they may give them victuals to eat, some of the White People are very bad and quarrelsome and whip my people about the head, beat and abuse them but others are very good.

I desire a stop may be put to the selling strong Liquors by the White people to my people especially near the Indian Nation. If the White people make strong drink let them sell it to one another or drink it in their own Families. This will avoid a great deal of mischief which otherwise will happen from my people getting drunk and quarrelling with the White people. Should any of my people do any mischief to the White people I have no strong prisons like you to confine them for it, Our only way is to put them under ground and all these men (pointing to his Warriors again) will be ready to do that to those who shall deserve it.

I desire to know what is to be done with the White Woman I took from the Cherokees: I hope she will not be put to death, she is but a Woman and can do no great harm and I think she was compelled by the Cherokees to do what she did.

To which the Chief Justice answered, Nothing has hitherto appeared against her that will affect her life. I am informed she is an indented servant to a man in Virginia, if that be the case and she should not be charged with any offence I shall direct her to be conveyed to her proper owner.

To which King Hagler replied, I am glad of it. I am always sorry to lose a Woman. The loss of one Woman may be the loss of many lives because one Woman may be the mother of many children. At which the audience smiling, he added I believe I have spoke nothing but Truth.

263

I look upon the English and ourselves as many good things put into one pocket as Brothers that have issued from one Womb.

When the Gentlemen from Virginia were in this Nation they told me to get a house built for myself and they would repay me the expense when they saw me in Virginia but having lately acquainted Colo. Alexander and Colo. Harris with this they said No they would as I lived in Carolina get it done at their own Expense by workmen that resided near us.

After this the King informed the Chief Justice he had nothing more to say to him but had something to observe to his Warriors and thereupon addressed himself to them and then to his young men and desired them to declare whether in what he had said to his Brethren the English he had expressed their Sentiments as well as his own to which they unanimously answered that he had. Then he added that should his Brethren of Carolina be engaged in a War as he feared they soon would. He would have his Men already on the first notice to march to their assistance. He desired them to fight on such an occasion as became Catawba's and do nothing that might lessen the great Character they had obtained by their Military achievements He added they were under the greatest Obligations to do this for two reasons. First because the English had clothed them naked and fed them when hungry secondly because the White people were now seated all round them and by that means had them entirely in their power.

To which the Warriors and young men all answered they would remember what he had given them in charge.

On this the King presented the pipe of Peace to the Chief Justice who as well as the rest of the company accepted it in the usual manner. The King was then informed that the Chief Justice would answer his Speech the next morning and they met accordingly, as before, when he spoke as follows.

King Hagler, Brethren and Friends Sachems and Warriors of the brave Catawba Nation.

It can't help giving me vast satisfaction to see here so many great Indian Warriors who are as remarkable for their conduct and Intrepidity in Battle as their brotherly affection for the English I look upon your coming here upon this occasion as a fresh instance of the inviolable friendship you have for our common Father and Benefactor the King of Great Britain as well as for us his children and your brothers.

Your expressions of concern in regard to the Behavior of the Cherokees your determined resolution to stand by and assist us against the French or go down into the Grave with us and the Willingness with which your Warriors have embraced the same resolution require the particular acknowledgement of us all.

Let the Cherokees behave as they will I hope We and our Brethren the brave Catawba's shall stand firm together like a large mountain which cannot be moved.

The Station our Great King has been pleased to place me in will in many Instances enable me to be assisting in the Preservation of that Peace and Harmony which subsists between us and if any Injuries or offences should again be committed against you by the White People I will take care upon a proper Application to me that they shall not go unpunished.

You have our Thanks for the resolution you have taken of punishing such of your young people as shall commit any Injuries upon us your Brethren, but we hope you will not have occasion to make any Examples of that kind.

Your Observation in respect to the White peoples selling Liquor to the Indians is very just as there is no Law at present to prevent it I will mention to the Governor the necessity of making one to restrain these pernicious practices for the future.

I will also take the first opportunity of representing to him in the strongest manner I can the singular services you have done us in compelling the Cherokees to deliver up the White Woman and in obtaining restitution of the Goods they had unjustly taken from us.

The application of the public money, belongs to the Governor and Assembly with the advice of the Council, over that I have no power but I will use all the Interest I have to obtain a present from them as a small acknowledgement of the Obligations we think ourselves under to you upon that account.

I shall also faithfully represent the request you have made by me to your Brother the Governor to have a speedy supply of Ammunition to have a fort built as soon as possible for the protection of your old men your wives and children and some silver plates for your Breasts and arms with some Wampum.

In the meantime as a Testimony of the great regard we have for our brave friends and Brethren the Catawba's we have procured at our own Expense such a supply of powder and lead as we could get to supply your present necessities which we now present you with.

Colo. Alexander and Colo. Harris assure me they will build the house they promised as soon as conveniently they can.

To which the King answered. I look upon you as my elder Brother and what you told me to day I shall not forget tomorrow but remember as long as I live. If any of the English shall at any time be attacked by the Enemy let me know it as soon as possible by any hand and I and my people will immediately come to your assistance.

The Chief Justice observed to him that their Brethren the White people of Virginia and the Nottoway Indians were now fighting to the Northward against the French and their Indians and had long expected their joining them and were surprised they had not yet done it.

The King replied that when the Gentlemen of Virginia were in their parts, his Warriors were all willing and desirous to go with them, but when they were gone Governor Glenn sent an express to him and forbad him to let them go unless he should order it, and that he had sent the said Govr for answer that he would wait till he had further considered of the Matter but that he had taken up the Hatchet against the French and could not lay it down without using it.

N. B. There were two Interpreters sworn Mr. Giles and Mr. Tool.

Posted on February 4, 2013 by robertajestes

Many times the only glimpses we have of the Native people as individuals are through documents like this. I sure wish the names of his warriors had been recorded.

Colonial and State Records of North Carolina

Report by Peter Henley concerning his conference with King Hagler and the Catawba Nation

Henley, Peter, 1725-1758
May 26, 1756 – May 28, 1756
Volume 05, Pages 579-584

**PHOTO 302 - KING HAGLER, CATAWBA CHIEF, CONFERENCE WITH PETER HENLEY 1756**

**Descendants List of King Hagler - Nop-ke-hea (6 generations)**
1-King Hagler-Nop-ke-hea HAGLER (abt 1725-30 Aug 1763)
+SCOTT (-)
. . . . 2-Daughter - two HAGLER (abt 1750-)
. . . . +William-Billy SCOTT  (whiteman) (abt 1720-abt 1817)
. . . . . . . . 3-General Jacob SCOTT (1770-1858)
. . . . . . . . +Sally Scott Tool (Sally NEWRIVER) (abt 1780-abt 1824)
. . . . . . . . . . . 4-Jacob SCOTT (abt 1790-died around 1825)
. . . . . . . . 3-Sally Scott Tool (Sally NEWRIVER) (abt 1780-abt 1824)
. . . . . . . . +Little Alek  (abt 1770-)
. . . . . . . . . . . 4-Jane ALEC (abt 1800-)
. . . . . . . . +General Jacob SCOTT (1770-1858)
. . . . . . . . . . . 4-Jacob SCOTT (abt 1790-died around 1825)
. . . . . . . . 3-Jenny-Jinny SCOTT (abt 1785-)
. . . . . . . . +General James KEGG (abt 1785-1852)
. . . . . . . . . . . 4-Phillip KEGG (1815-)
. . . . . . . . . . . +Cynthia  (1818-)
. . . . . . . . . . . . . . . 5-Jamie KEGG (abt 1860-aft 1886)
. . . . . . . . . . . 4-Betsy-Quatsie or Quatsy KEGG (1820-)

. . . . . . . . . . . +Da-Wee-Gun-skar-lee-skior WILL (-)

. . . . . . . . . . . . 5-Rebecca WILL (1839-)

. . . . . . . . . . . . 5-James WILL (1841-)

. . . . . . . . . . . . 5-William WILL (1844-ca 1860)

. . . . . . . . . . . 4-Susy KEGG (1820-1852)

. . . . . . . . . . . 4-Jamey KEGG (-)

. . . . . . . 3-Samuel SCOTT (1799-killed beteen 1849-1880)

. . . . +Jacob AYERS-EARS (abt 1770-1838)

. . . . . . . 3-Betsey AYERS (1794-abt 1867)

. . . . . . . +John KENNEDY (-)

. . . . . . . . . . . 4-Johnson KENNEDY (alive from 1812-1820-)

. . . . . . . . . . . 4-Richardson KENNEDY (1813-)

. . . . . . . +John Jacob SCOTT (1790-1825)

. . . . . . . . . . . 4-Edmund AYERS (1800-1837)

. . . . . . . . . . . +Rebecca MARSH (1815-20 Jan 1882)

. . . . . . . . . . . . 5-Sarah Jane AYERS (31 Jul 1829-7 Dec 1917)

. . . . . . . . . . . . +James Thomas HARRIS (1828-23 May 1874)

. . . . . . . . . . . . . . 6-Infant HARRIS (abt 1853-1853)

. . . . . . . . . . . . . . 6-James Thomas HARRIS (27 Mar 1859-31 Aug 1912)

. . . . . . . . . . . . . . 6-Martha Jane HARRIS (25 Dec 1861-18 Dec 1898)

. . . . . . . . . . . . . . 6-Anthony "Andy" HARRIS (abt 1862-bet 1920 and 1930)

. . . . . . . . . . . . . . 6-Mattie HARRIS (abt 1871-)

. . . . . . . . . . . . . . 6-David Adam Toad HARRIS (15 Jun 1872-1 Sep 1930)

. . . . . . . . . . . . . . 6-Isabella HARRIS (abt 1876-)

. . . . . . . . . . . . . 5-Margaret MARSH-AYERS-GEORGE (4 Jul 1837-9 Aug 1922)

. . . . . . . . . . . . . +Samuel BLUE (1838-abt 1878)

. . . . . . . . . . . . . . 6-Samuel Taylor BLUE (15 Aug 1873-16 Apr 1959)

. . . . . . . . . . . . . +John William BROWN (1837-Sep 1867)

. . . . . . . . . . . . . . 6-Mary Victoria BROWN (25 Dec 1856-11 Apr 1952)

. . . . . . . . . . . . . . 6-H A BROWN (abt 1861-)

. . . . . . . . . . . . . . 6-Emily BROWN (1863-)

. . . . . . . . . . . . . . 6-Wade Hampton BROWN (1865-bef 1867)

. . . . . . . . . . . . . . 6-Sally Rebecca BROWN (25 Dec 1865-20 Sep 1952)

. . . . . . . . . . . . . . 6-John William BROWN (21 Oct 1867-20 Jun 1927)

. . . . . . . . . . . 4-Jacob SCOTT (1810-)

. . . . . . . . +Major George CANTY (1730-aft 1810)

. . . . . . . . . . . 4-William-Billy CANTY (abt 1760-)

. . . . . . . . . . . . 5-Nancy CANTY (abt 1779-)

. . . . . . . . . . . . +William GEORGE (abt 1770-)

. . . . . . . . . . . . . . 6-Nancy QUASH-MARSH (abt 1800-)

. . . . . . . . . . . . . 5-Lewis CANTY (abt 1780-abt 1838)

. . . . . . . . . . . . . . . +Sally AYERS CLINTON HARRIS (abt 1799-)

. . . . . . . . . . . . . . 6-Harriet CANTY (1805-)

. . . . . . . . . . . . . . 6-Henry CANTY (abt 1806-)

. . . . . . . . . . . . . . 6-Leroy CANTY (abt 1807-)

. . . . . . . . . . . . . . 6-Lewis CANTY (1808-)

. . . . . . . . . . . . . . 6-Billy CANTY (1809-)

. . . . . . . . . . . . . . 6-Peggy CANTY (1820-)

. . . . . . . . . . . . . . 6-Franklin CANTY (1826-aft 1885)

. . . . . . . 3-Sally AYERS CLINTON HARRIS (abt 1799-)

. . . . . . . +William HARRIS (1792-1838)

. . . . . . . . . . 4-Nancy HARRIS (May 1835-Jun 1908)

. . . . . . . . . +John "MUSH" HARRIS (1831-1874)

. . . . . . . . . . . . 5-William Billy Bowlegs HARRIS (1 Apr 1857-1925)

. . . . . . . . . . . . 5-Thomas Wesley HARRIS (14 Oct 1858-24 Oct 1915)

. . . . . . . . . . . . 5-Angeline HARRIS (abt 1858-bef 1900)

. . . . . . . . . . . . 5-Johnny HARRIS (1862-abt 1900)

. . . . . . . . . . . . 5-Fanny HARRIS (1865-bef 1900)

. . . . . . . . . . . . 5-Robert "Red Cloud" Lee HARRIS (15 Sep 1867-11 Nov 1954)

. . . . . . . . . . . . +Martha Elizabeth COLLINS (17 Oct 1884-1966)

. . . . . . . . . . . . . . 6-Wynona Estella HARRIS (20 Jan 1927-7 Jun 2000)

. . . . . . . . . . . . +Nettie Frela HARRIS (1 Apr 1875-9 Mar 1923)

. . . . . . . . . . . . . . 6-wynona HARRIS (-)

. . . . . . . . . . . . 5-Benjamin Perry HARRIS (Feb 1871-15 Dec 1930)

. . . . . . . . . . . . +Mary Dovey Cornelia GEORGE (27 May 1877-15 Sep 1972)

. . . . . . . . . . . . . . 6-Sallie Hester HARRIS (28 Apr 1895-21 Nov 1990)

. . . . . . . . . . . . . . 6-Robert H. William HARRIS (15 Aug 1897-13 Jul 1956)

. . . . . . . . . . . . . . 6-Nancy Cornelia HARRIS (17 Oct 1899-17 Feb 1975)

. . . . . . . . . . . . . . 6-Melvin HARRIS (aft 1900-)

. . . . . . . . . . . . . . 6-Martha H HARRIS (14 Jan 1902-11 May 1983)

. . . . . . . . . . . . . . 6-Cora Ida HARRIS (17 Apr 1904-23 Jun 1983)

. . . . . . . . . . . . . . 6-Benjamin Joseph HARRIS (15 Apr 1906-9 May 1967)

. . . . . . . . . . . . . . 6-Irene Evelyn HARRIS (1908-)

. . . . . . . . . . . . . . 6-Minnie Florence HARRIS (23 Dec 1909-24 Jun 1979)

. . . . . . . . . . . 4-Absolom Epp HARRIS (Jun 1837-9 Jul 1916)

. . . . . . . . . . +Martha Jane WHITE (3 Jul 1854-3 Jul 1936)

. . . . . . . . . . . . 5-Margaret Elizabeth HARRIS (15 Aug 1879-8 Dec 1926)

. . . . . . . . . . . . +James Thomas HARRIS (27 Mar 1859-31 Aug 1912)

. . . . . . . . . . . . . . 6-Jesse Allen HARRIS (25 Apr 1899-19 Nov 1977)

. . . . . . . . . . . . . . 6-Jacob HARRIS (1900-bef 1910)

. . . . . . . . . . . . . . 6-Eliza Jane HARRIS (30 Apr 1902-15 Nov 1960)

. . . . . . . . . . . . . . 6-Georgia Henrietta HARRIS (29 Jul 1905-30 Jan 1997)

. . . . . . . . . . . . . . . . . . 6-John Thomas HARRIS (30 Jul 1905-10 Jul 1912)

. . . . . . . . . . . . . . . . . 6-Robert Lee HARRIS (16 Aug 1910-15 Jul 1912)

. . . . . . . . . . . . . . . . . 6-George Furman HARRIS (7 Jan 1913-5 Jun 2006)

. . . . . . . . . . . . +Mary GEORGE (May 1835-aft 1900)

. . . . . . . . +Lewis CANTY (abt 1780-abt 1838)

. . . . . . . . . . 4-Harriet CANTY (1805-)

. . . . . . . . . . +Lewis STEPHENS (1804-)

. . . . . . . . . . . . 5-Polly STEPHENS (1823-)

. . . . . . . . . . . . . 5-Thomas STEPHENS (1831-14 Dec 1905)

. . . . . . . . . . 4-Henry CANTY (abt 1806-)

. . . . . . . . . . 4-Leroy CANTY (abt 1807-)

. . . . . . . . . . 4-Lewis CANTY (1808-)

. . . . . . . . . . 4-Billy CANTY (1809-)

. . . . . . . . . . 4-Peggy CANTY (1820-)

. . . . . . . . . . +Chancy EVANS (1818-)

. . . . . . . . . . . . 5-Sarah Ann EVANS-CANTY HEAD (1 Jul 1845-29 Dec 1919)

. . . . . . . . . . . . . +Alec John Alexander TIMS (15 Jul 1845-20 Apr 1941)

. . . . . . . . . . . . . +Robert Henry HEAD (12 Jan 1841-26 Jul 1864)

. . . . . . . . . . . . . . . 6-Pinkney Henry HEAD (26 Oct 1862-25 May 1951)

. . . . . . . . . . 4-Franklin CANTY (1826-aft 1885)

. . . . . . . . . . +Eliza SCOTT (1826-aft 1869)

. . . . . . . . . . . . 5-William CANTY (1844-15 Jan 1865)

. . . . . . . . . . . . . 5-George Washington CANTY (16 Jan 1851-20 Jul 1893)

. . . . . . . . . . . . . +Mary Jane Elizabeth-Betsy MUSH GEORGE (27 Dec 1856-Oct 1898)

. . . . . . . . . . . . . . . 6-John William Frank CANTY (21 Mar 1876-25 Jun 1933)

. . . . . . . . . . . . . . . 6-Henry Alonzo William CANTY (27 Jan 1877-12 Mar 1934)

. . . . . . . . . . . . . . . 6-Robert Lee CANTY (abt 1878-aft 1910)

. . . . . . . . . . . . . . . 6-Louisa  Hester Jane CANTY (7 Feb 1883-9 Jul 1963)

. . . . . . . . . . . . . . . 6-Sarah CANTY (27 Jun 1886-)

. . . . . . . . . . . . . . . 6-Peggy CANTY (27 Jun 1886-)

. . . . . . . . . . . . . . . 6-Hester CANTY (1890-)

. . . . . . . . +Jamey CLINTON BROWN (abt 1770-1825)

. . . . . . . . 3-Polly AYERS-EARS (abt 1812-)

. . . . . . . . . . 4-Jenny AYERS (abt 1830-bef 1857)

. . . . . . . . . . +John "MUSH" HARRIS (1831-1874)

. . . . . . . . . . 4-Jefferson AYERS (21 Dec 1840-2 Jul 1865)

. . . . . . . . . . +Emily Elizabeth COBB AYERS (4 Dec 1843-16 Jul 1925)

. . . . . . . . . . . . 5-Jefferson Davis AYERS (21 Dec 1861-12 Oct 1920)

. . . . . . . . . . . . . +Harriett Lucinda BERRY (Feb 1871-abt 1905)

. . . . . . . . . . . . . . 6-Annie AYERS (23 Jun 1888-bef 1910)

. . . . . . . . . . . . . . 6-Wade AYERS (16 Sep 1890-1904)

. . . . . . . . . . . . . . . . . . 6-Gertrude Dye AYERS (Aug 1892-)

. . . . . . . . . . . . . . . . . . 6-Rossalina AYERS (27 Feb 1893-bef 1900)

. . . . . . . . . . . . . . . . . . 6-Mary Evelina AYERS (24 Dec 1895-27 Jan 1973)

. . . . . . . . . . . . . . . . . . 6-John Jefferson AYERS (20 Oct 1898-14 Sep 1929)

. . . . . . . . . . . . . . . . . . 6-Robert Heber AYERS (5 Oct 1900-15 Mar 1996)

. . . . . . . . . . . . . 5-Lucy Alice AYERS (17 Dec 1866-aft 1893)

. . . . . . . . . . . . . . +Wesley Allen HARRIS (15 Sep 1857-24 Oct 1915)

. . . . . . . . . . . . . . . . . 6-Emma Jane HARRIS (7 Jun 1888-19 Jan 1961)

. . . . . . . . . . . . . . . . . 6-Allen Spencer HARRIS (Aug 1891-25 Jun 1918)

. . . . . . . . . . . . . . . . . 6-Robert Theodore HARRIS (27 Mar 1893-2 May 1972)

. . . . +Matthew TOOLE (abt 1710-)

. . . . . . . . 3-Sally Scott Tool (Sally NEWRIVER) (abt 1780-abt 1824)

. . . . . . . +Little Alek  (abt 1770-)

. . . . . . . . . . . 4-Jane ALEC (abt 1800-)

. . . . . . . +General Jacob SCOTT (1770-1858)

. . . . . . . . . . 4-Jacob SCOTT (abt 1790-died around 1825)

. . . . +William SCOTT (-)

. . . . . . . 3-John SCOTT (1790-1849)

. . . . . . . 3-Catey Or Katie SCOTT (1799-abt 1869)

. . . . . . . +John JOE (abt 1795-Jul 1843)

. . . . . . . . . . 4-Eliza SCOTT (1826-aft 1869)

. . . . . . . . . . +Thomas Patrick WHITESIDES (14 Jan 1825-16 Feb 1904)

. . . . . . . . . . . . 5-Mary Jane WHITESIDES (13 Feb 1855-8 Nov 1910)

. . . . . . . . . . . . +James Harvey WATTS (8 Apr 1858-21 Mar 1926)

. . . . . . . . . . . . . . 6-Lucy Leola WATTS (29 Apr 1892-22 Jul 1969)

. . . . . . . . . . . . 5-John Alonzo CANTY (9 Nov 1858-1 Feb 1938)

. . . . . . . . . . . . +Georgia Henrietta (Rhett) PATTERSON (4 Jul 1870-27 Feb 1925)

. . . . . . . . . . . . . 6-Wilford Marion CANTY (26 Jan 1893-28 May 1949)

. . . . . . . . . . . . . 6-John Henry CANTY (13 Aug 1895-1897)

. . . . . . . . . . . . . 6-Eddie Archie CANTY (20 May 1898-4 Apr 1980)

. . . . . . . . . . . . . 6-William Franklin CANTY (26 Apr 1901-23 Jul 1982)

. . . . . . . . . . . . . 6-Lazell CANTY (28 Mar 1904-12 Nov 1988)

. . . . . . . . . . . . . 6-Alma (Pete) CANTY (19 Jun 1912-27 Jan 1989)

. . . . . . . . . . . . +Harriet HARRIS (1856-deceased)

. . . . . . . . . . . . 5-Fannie WHITESIDES (9 Nov 1859-1885)

. . . . . . . . . . . . +James Thomas HARRIS (27 Mar 1859-31 Aug 1912)

. . . . . . . . . . +Franklin CANTY (1826-aft 1885)

. . . . . . . . . . . . 5-William CANTY (1844-15 Jan 1865)

. . . . . . . . . . . . 5-George Washington CANTY (16 Jan 1851-20 Jul 1893)

. . . . . . . . . . . . +Mary Jane Elizabeth-Betsy MUSH GEORGE (27 Dec 1856-Oct 1898)

. . . . . . . . . . . . . . 6-John William Frank CANTY (21 Mar 1876-25 Jun 1933)

. . . . . . . . . . . . . . . . . . 6-Henry Alonzo William CANTY (27 Jan 1877-12 Mar 1934)

. . . . . . . . . . . . . . . . . 6-Robert Lee CANTY (abt 1878-aft 1910)

. . . . . . . . . . . . . . . . . 6-Louisa  Hester Jane CANTY (7 Feb 1883-9 Jul 1963)

. . . . . . . . . . . . . . . . 6-Sarah CANTY (27 Jun 1886-)

. . . . . . . . . . . . . . . . 6-Peggy CANTY (27 Jun 1886-)

. . . . . . . . . . . . . . . . 6-Hester CANTY (1890-)

. . . . . . . . . . . 4-Joseph JOE (abt 1840-)

. . . . . . . . . . 4-Samuel SCOTT (1799-)

. . . . . . . 3-Samuel SCOTT (1799-)

. . . 2-Daughter - one HAGLER (abt 1750-)

. . . +WATERS (1750-)

. . . 2-Son HAGLER (abt 1752-INFANT)

**PHOTO 303 - KING HAIGLAR TOWER MARKER**

## Chapter 10   Allen Harris Family

(Nanny-Nancy Kegg born around 1780, daughter of James SR and Jinny Scott Kegg. Nancy had married and had children by January 1819. [284] By January 1819 Billy Ayers was paid for her (Nancy Kegg) children.[285] She received rents from 1816 to 1821 as Nancy Harris. This is a possibility, not proven.) Nancy Harris-(Kegg?) and Sam Evans had a son they named Allen Harris.[286] Sam Evans was most likely a white man and connected to the Evans family who had been Indian traders in the area for years. A Chancy Evans appears as children of other Catawba babies and John Evans was an interpreter.

I. Allen or Alan Harris was born in 1813.[287] He married Rhoda (a white foundling)[288] who was raised by Sally George. Allen died in July of 1860. He signed leases for several years, using various titles. One signature shows Allen signing leases as Major Allen Harris in August 1837,[289] and yet in September 1837 he signs as a Captain.[290] In September 1839, he signs as Lieutenant Allen Harris [291]while in November 1839; he signed as a Captain.[292] In 1859, Allen was paid for making a coffin.

He was a signer of the Treaty of Nation Ford in 1840, signing as a Lieutenant. Allen did not use a mark, but signed his name, showing his ability to read and write. This put him in the company of just four other Catawba who were considered literate.

In 1860 he wrote to A. Whyte asking him to inform former South Carolina governor Robert Allston that Allen had "named his only son after Allston." Whyte did not copy the letter, instead he forwarded it to the governor to show how much some of the Catawba had advanced. He also remarked that "ingratitude does not constitute any part of Allan's character.[293]

"After this Treaty,' it is said, "Allen Harris became for all practical purposes, Chief Man. He settled upon the land and a part of those here have collected round him, and a part will not. Harris with a reasonable portion of labor would support his own family, which consists of but three persons,[294] but the others collected around him will eat up all that is made, and will then be traveling about the rest of the year, living on the bounty of the people as heretofore.[295]

---

[284] This is not proven, just a guess

[285] Watson pages 60-62.

[286] Merrell page 236, information came from Draper Manuscripts 6 VV, 291.

[287] 1849 census

[288] Blumer columns.

[289] Blumer page 150 article 1077.

[290] Blumer page 147 article 1062.

[291] Blumer page 152 article 1091.

[292] Blumer page 153 article 1102.

[293] Watson page 43.

[294] Allen, Rhoda and Susannah

[295] Brown page 330.

In 1849, the Indian Agent took Allen Harris and his 9-year-old daughter to meet Nancy George in an attempt to gather the tribe.[296] Unless Lucinda Harris was a daughter of Allen then a mistake, because his oldest child Susannah would have been only 3 years old.

**Life of Lucinda Harris after Allen Harris is finished.**

A petition from the 1850's shows him as chief. A petition signed by Allen, Nancy White and Nancy George, requested land in the State of Arkansas, and he and John Harris went to see it. Unfortunately; Allen died soon after his arrival at their destination, around July 1860, at the age of 45or46.[297]

Allen was reported to have served in the Civil War, however no records have been found to prove it, and his death in 1860 make it seem unlikely. In 1875, Rhoda received $ 10.00 from the Indian Agent Crook and in November 1881, she received $13.32.

"The best house in the nation by all odds in the home of Rhoda Harris, widow of Chief Allen Harris. I called at this house, which has been built three years. It has a piazza and four rooms, is surrounded by fruit trees and several outhouses, and has a very nice looking garden at its back. This was the most intelligent household that I visited among the Indians. Rhoda is a dignified pleasant old lady who is something over 60 and who shows the white blood strongly.[298] She has two granddaughters at the Carlisle Indian School in PA, one Cammie Owl, and lives with the Cherokees."[299] This differs a great deal from the visit of Scaife in 1893 who stated that Rhoda was living in a "one-room corn crib."[300] It is possible that this is not Rhoda, but one of her daughters or someone else entirely.

Rhoda became blind in her old age and very frail, according to Sallie Wade. She called her "Well worn."[301] Rhoda died in March 1919. She had six children, with three who died before 1900 and 1910. The children were Susannah, Nancy, Harriet, Allen Allston and Betsy Harris

---

[296] Blumer page 161, article 1155.
[297] Watson page 43 & 44.
[298] Nothing has been shown to prove that she was white at all.
[299] Watson page 35.
[300] Watson page 44.
[301] Ibid.

# Allen Harris Family

## Rohda George - Harris -- 1830-1919

**PHOTO 304 – 1ST RHODA GEORGE HARRIS – 2ND RHODA IN ROCKER – 3RD RHODA SETTING AND ROSA HARRIS WHEELOCK STANDING**

Rhoda Harris in rocker left to right. Margaret Harris Harris with son George Furman. Betsy called Betsy Bob because she was briefly married to Robert Lee Harris, Nellie Harris Owl and Martha Jane White Harris called Aunt Jane –Original photo from Faye Dodds

# Blood line

The rumor was that Rhoda was a white foundling that the Catawba took and raised as their own.  The George family raised her. .

**Story**: The legend has it that Rhoda was a white foundling baby, found by the Catawba George family and raised. Susannah, her daughter lists herself as 1/2 Catawba, on her death certificate, making the story true.

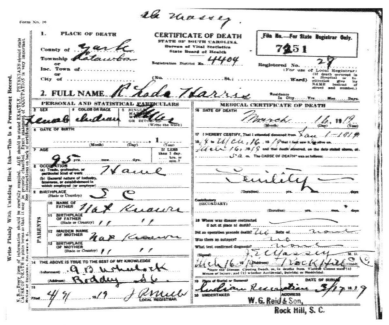

**PHOTO 305 – CERTIFICATE OF DEATH FOR RHODA HARRIS**

A. Susannah Harris was born in 1 July 1847, Catawba, York, South Carolina,[302] and died 26 February 1934, Cherokee, Swain, North Carolina.  She was one of Speck's informants, telling folk tales and so forth. She signed a petition in 1872 asking that Solomon Harris be made Indian Agent.[303] She participated in James Mooney's Book " Indian Tribes of the District of Columbia" in 1889.[304] In April of 1875, she received $10.00 from the Indian Agent R. L. Crook. In November of 1881, she received $23.23. Her family and that of Lula Harris Owl were censused as Eastern Cherokee in June of 1898. [305]  Susannah married first. Robert Mush, son of Robert Alexander and Betsy Quash- Mush-Marsh, [306] as his second wife. They had three children, only one is identified, George Marsh.

---

[302] 1880 census York County, SC. Patterson genealogy and Harris genealogy.
[303] Blumer page 183 article 1313
[304] Blumer page 200 article 1455.
[305] Blumer page 210 article 1539.
[306] Patterson genealogy identifies Susannah as the second wife of Robert Mush-Marsh.

1.

2.

3. George Marsh was born 1862. George was said to be idiotic in the 1880 census.

Robert died in 1864 from his wounds inflicted during the Civil War. Susannah married as her second husband Sampson-Samson Owl a Cherokee. Susannah signed a petition in 1863 as Susannah Mush.[307]  A petition where the Catawba were attempting to remove R. L. Crook from the office of Indian agent, written in 1877

Susannah Harris Owl --1837-1934 – 1st daughter of Allen and Rhoda George Harris

**PHOTO 306 - SUSANAH HARRIS OWL**

---

[307] Patton petition of 1863.

Susannah Harris Owl (1837–1934),
the daughter of Rhoda Harris, comes
in second after Martha Jane only
because she spent most of her life
among the Cherokee Indians. Every
major collection possesses some of
her work; it is identified as hers by
records. One of her favorite forms
was the traditional snake pot. She
was popular among linguists,
particularly Frank G. Speck, and
spoke Catawba all her life. Susannah
is credited with starting the North
Carolina mountain trade with her
husband, Sampson Owl. She made
many small pieces for this trade.
(Courtesy of the National Museum
of the American Indian.)

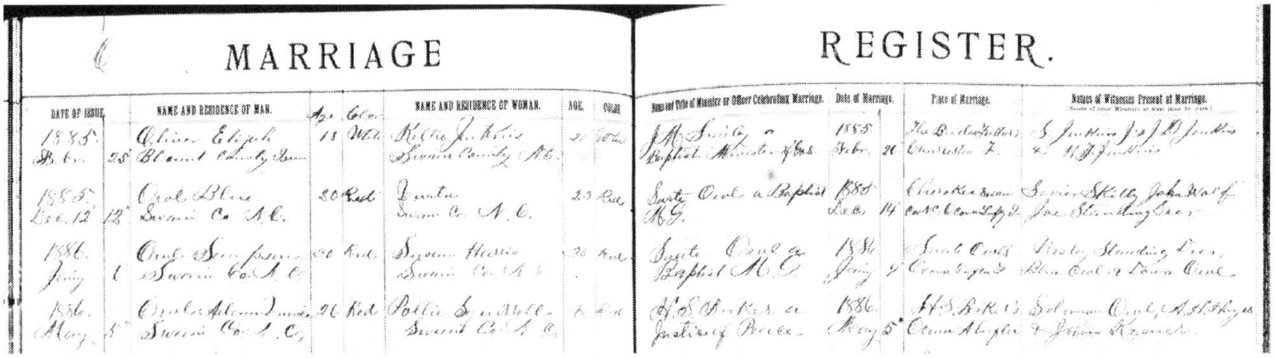

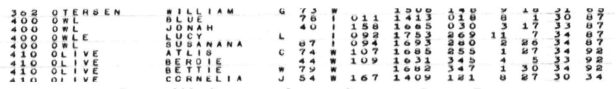

**PHOTO 307 - SAMPSON OWL AGE 30  AND SUSANNAH HARRIS  AGE 35 – MARRIAGE JAN 1886**

**PHOTO 308 - SUSANNAH OWL ON CHERAKEE INDIAN ROLL**

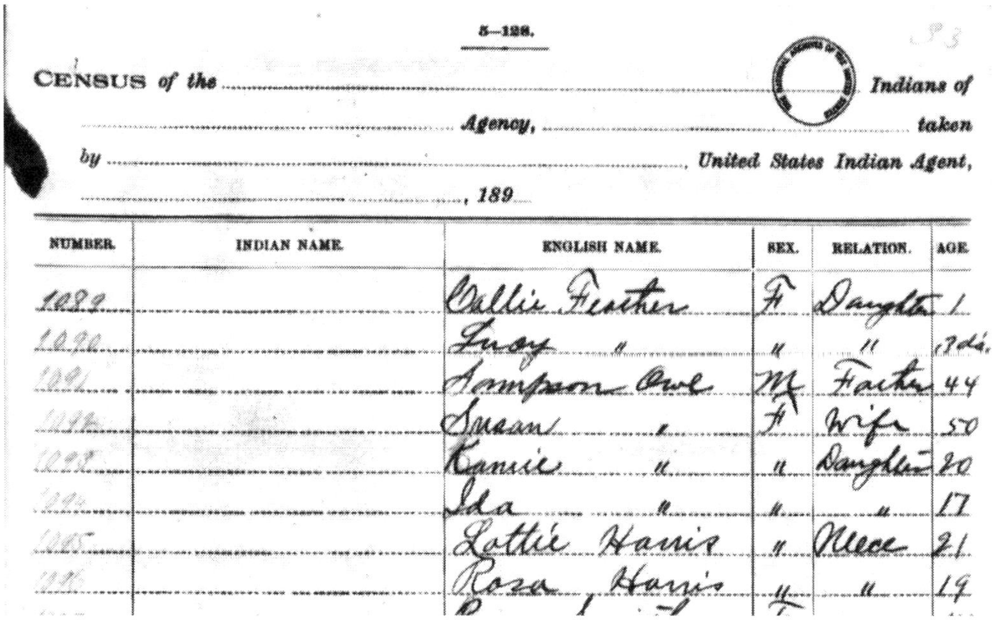

5—128.

CENSUS *of the* ............ *Indians of* ............ *Agency*, ............ *taken by* ............, *United States Indian Agent*, ............, 189

| NUMBER. | INDIAN NAME. | ENGLISH NAME. | SEX. | RELATION. | AGE. |
|---|---|---|---|---|---|
| 1089 | | Callie Feather | F | Daughter | 1 |
| 1090 | | Lucy " | " | " | 3 ds. |
| 1091 | | Sampson Owl | M | Father | 44 |
| 1092 | | Susan " | F | Wife | 50 |
| 1093 | | Karrie " | " | Daughter | 20 |
| 1094 | | Ida " | " | " | 17 |
| 1095 | | Lottie Harris | " | Niece | 21 |
| 1096 | | Rosa Harris | " | " | 19 |

**PHOTO 309 - SAMPSON OWL, WIFE - SUSAN, DAUGHTERS KARRIE AND IDA ON CHEROKEE INDIAN ROLLS IN CHEROKEE NORTH CAROLINA**

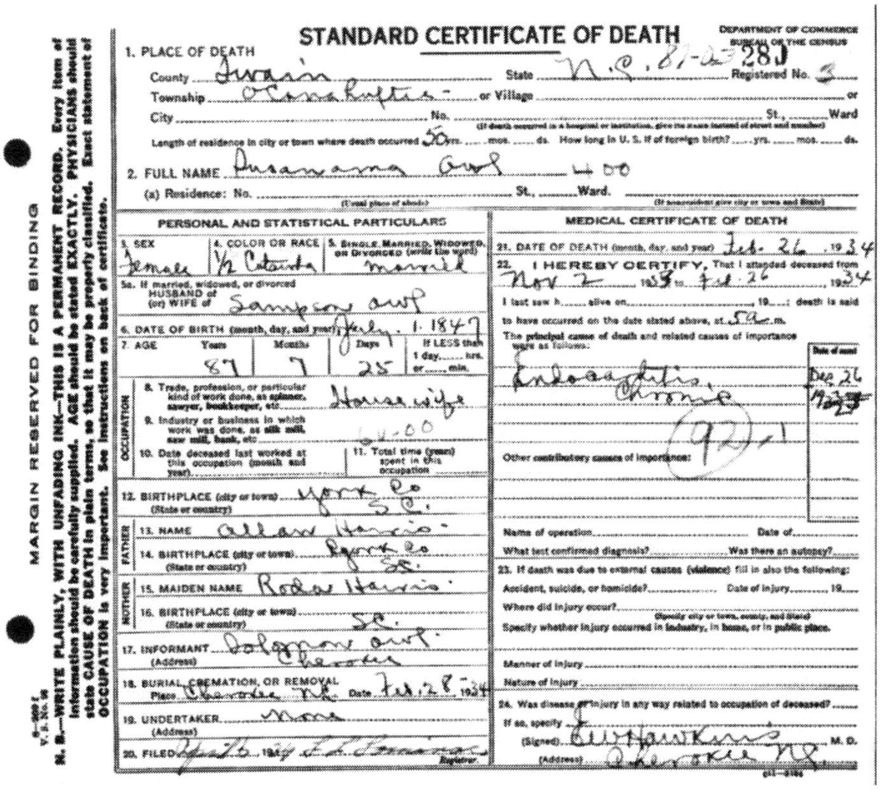

STANDARD CERTIFICATE OF DEATH

1. PLACE OF DEATH County Swain State N.C. Registered No. 3
Township Oconaluftee
Length of residence in city or town where death occurred 50 yrs.
2. FULL NAME Susannanna Owl

PERSONAL AND STATISTICAL PARTICULARS
3. SEX Female 4. COLOR OR RACE 1/2 Catawba 5. SINGLE, MARRIED, WIDOWED, OR DIVORCED married
5a. HUSBAND OF Sampson Owl
6. DATE OF BIRTH July 1. 1847
7. AGE 87 Years 7 Months 25 Days
8. Trade, profession, or particular kind of work done Housewife
12. BIRTHPLACE York Co. S.C.
13. NAME (FATHER) Allan Harris
14. BIRTHPLACE York Co. S.C.
15. MAIDEN NAME (MOTHER) Roda Harris
16. BIRTHPLACE S.C.
17. INFORMANT Solomon Owl, Cherokee
18. BURIAL Place Cherokee N.C. Date Feb. 28 1934
19. UNDERTAKER none

MEDICAL CERTIFICATE OF DEATH
21. DATE OF DEATH Feb. 26 1934
22. I HEREBY CERTIFY, That I attended deceased from Nov 2 1933 to Feb 26 1934
The principal cause of death: Endocarditis, Chronic
(Signed) E. W. Hawkins M.D. (Address) Cherokee N.C.

**PHOTO 310 - CERTIFICATE OF DEATH FOR SUSANNAH HARRIS OWL**

*************************************************************************************

B. Nancy Harris was born 16 January 1851, Catawba Reservation, York, South Carolina[308] and she died 16 December 1919, Bradley, Grady, Oklahoma. She received an allotment with Susannah Harris in 1870. Nancy married Thomas Kilpatrick, son of Alexander Kilpatrick.[309] They had three children; twins, Hillery and Agnes and Lillie Susan Harris.[310]

She received $19.98 in November 1881 and also $26.64 from the Indian Agent. Nancy had her children by a white man named Kilpatrick.[311] In July, 1860 in the Yorkvill Enquirer, Ex-Governor Allston awards five Catawba women as model mothers; Sallie Harris, Nancy Harris, Patsy George, Rhoda George Harris and Caty Joe.

Yorkville Enquirer, July 3, 1889, page 2; "State Vs Samuel B. Brady and Nancy Harris, adultery. No. Pros. entered on motion of the solicitor."

Nancy Starkey is buried in the Bradley Cemetery with the Starkey and Foster families.

The following is a true history for Nancy: "Nancy Harris Starkey was born in South Carolina, she was a Catawba Indian. Her parents were Chief Allan Harris and Rhoda George Harris. Her first 'husband", the father of the Harris Children was a white man named Kilpatrick. She later married Samuel Brady a white man, before moving to Gainesville, Texas where she married John Starkey. Since she was beyond the years to bear children, we know of none.

**PHOTO 311 – NANCY HARRIS STARKEY - HEADSTONE – BURIED AT BRADLEY CEMETERY, BRADLEY, GRADY, OKLAHOMA, PLOT: W1-1**

---

[308] Harris genealogy.

[309] The will of Alexander, one of the traders who had been in the Nation for years, asks that his "executors to try to get his son Thomas down from the Catawbas."Meriwether, page 53, quoted in Brown page 164. The Harris genealogy lists the father as a Kilpatrick.

[310] Harris genealogy from Donna Tanner, Cortez, Colorado and Wanda Williams from New Mexico.

[311] My guess would that it was Thomas Kilpatrick, Alexander's, and (his father) will asked that some one go to the Catawbas and bring son Thomas down.

Continued.

State vs. Samuel B. Brady and Nancy Harris; adultery. Nol. pros. entered on motion of the solicitor.

In all the above continued cases the defendants have not been arrested.

**PHOTO 312 - YORKVILLE ENQUIRER, JULY 3, 1889, PAGE 2; "STATE VS SAMUEL B. BRADY AND NANCY HARRIS, ADULTERY. NO. PROS. ENTERED ON MOTION OF THE SOLICITOR."**

Journal History, May 28, 1883, Bro. D Osborn. LDS Church, SLC: "In 1883, Mormon Elders Henry Miller and Charles E Robison met with a number of other missionaries at King's Mountain, North Carolina. It was there that the pair discerned an opportunity in York County South Carolina to work among the Catawba tribe. They first visited the Catawba Reservation in May and held a meeting at the home of a Catawba woman, Mrs. Nancy Harris Brady, where they sang the Mormon hymn, "We Thank Thee O God for a Prophet" and expounded on their Beliefs.

From the missionary journal of Sister Mary Barrus she states:

Nancy Harris

"Pres Callis advised me to use my influence to get them to make yeat (sic) bread as so many of them had stomach trouble due he said partly to so much bad bread & not enough vegetables in the diet. I believe I succeeded somewhat. Nancy Harris a white woman used to bring a slice of her bread over as proud as can be. She made good bread.

Nancy married an Indian – had a firm testimony and had faith to be healed many timesc while we were there.

One day she came over and ask me if I would pour some oil – she called it aile (sic) on her sore finger. After I saw it had proud flesh in I advised her to wash it with a good disinfectant instead of oil.

her faith

The next day she came over again and said "Sister Barrus wont (sic) you please let me have just a little aile." I could see that I had made a mistake so I said of course I will. As I poured it on I saw her lips move and I knew she was praying. in abt three days she held her finger up and said I knew the Lords holy consecrated oil would heal it. Ordinarily it would have taken at least 10 days or more. it was an awful looking finger. Those saints were most interesting and sincere. We used to buy oil quarts of it and never charge them for it. They had faith to use it for every kind of illness. We were glad to fill their bottles.

When I was sick she brot (sic) me a bowl of mulligan stew. In it was – a squirrels

Upper jaw – part of a possum – bacon & c & c. I thanked her and didn't eat it. They liked it, and are anxious to help make us feel at home.

I heard her tell of having an awful toothache and after being administered to they never did ache again and they were rotted & worn to the roots. I found that she lived up to the light she had quite perfectly.

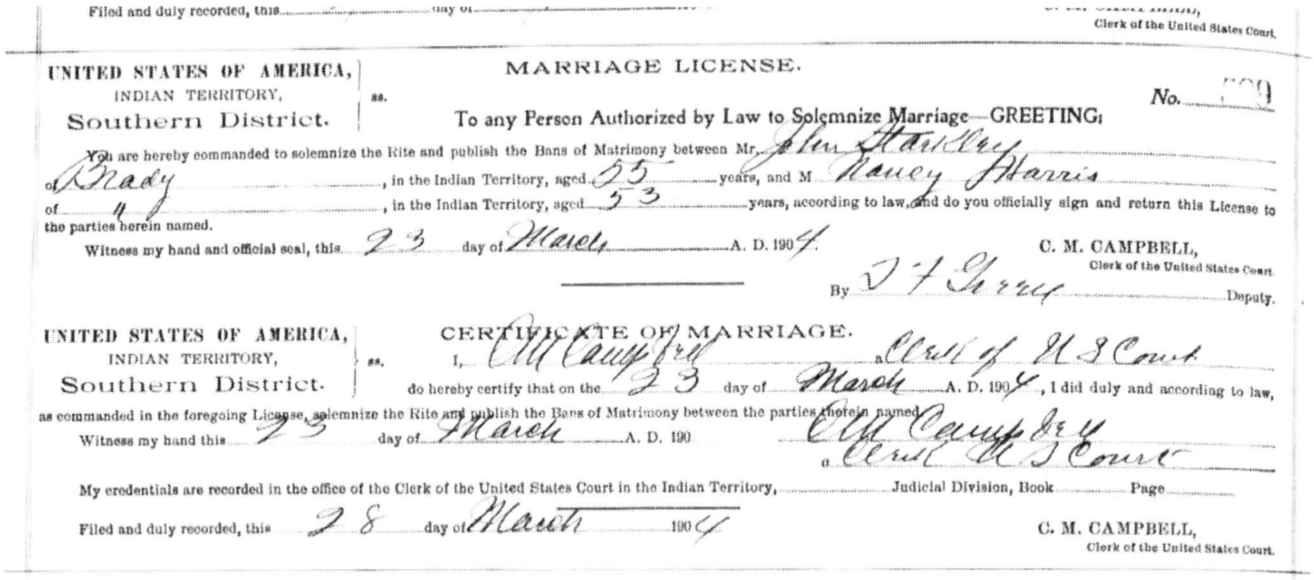
Filed and duly recorded, this ... day of ...
Clerk of the United States Court.

UNITED STATES OF AMERICA, INDIAN TERRITORY, Southern District. ss.

MARRIAGE LICENSE.

No. ...

To any Person Authorized by Law to Solemnize Marriage—GREETING:

You are hereby commanded to solemnize the Rite and publish the Bans of Matrimony between Mr. John Starkey of Brady, in the Indian Territory, aged 55 years, and M Nancy Harris of " in the Indian Territory, aged 53 years, according to law, and do you officially sign and return this License to the parties herein named.

Witness my hand and official seal, this 23 day of March A. D. 1904.

C. M. CAMPBELL,
Clerk of the United States Court.
By ... Deputy.

UNITED STATES OF AMERICA, INDIAN TERRITORY, Southern District. ss.

CERTIFICATE OF MARRIAGE.

I, ... Clerk of U S Court do hereby certify that on the 23 day of March A. D. 1904, I did duly and according to law, as commanded in the foregoing License, solemnize the Rite and publish the Bans of Matrimony between the parties therein named.

Witness my hand this 23 day of March A. D. 190

... Clerk U S Court

My credentials are recorded in the office of the Clerk of the United States Court in the Indian Territory, ... Judicial Division, Book ... Page ...

Filed and duly recorded, this 28 day of March 1904

C. M. CAMPBELL,
Clerk of the United States Court.

**PHOTO 313 - MARRIAGE LICENSE JOHN STARKEY AND NANCY HARRIS**

In 1892, she was in Gainesville, Texas where she sent a letter to the Governor Benjamin Tilman, dated 1892. Nancy Harris, Gainesville, Texas.

"A.E. Smith & Co.
GENERAL MERCHANDISE.

Gov. Benjamin R. Tillman's
Papers, Box 9, folder 22,
S.C. Archives

"Rock Hill, S.C., January 16, 1892

"Nancy Harris
Gainesville, Texas

"Your letter of 8th instant duly received. I am told by our member to the Legislature this year, that I am not allowed to pay any of the money appropriated by the state for support of Catawba Indians to those who are outside the state. This of course will bar my paying anything to you from that source. Of course it will give those Catawbas in the state a larger share — and I would advise Agnes, if she thinks of going to you, to wait, until after the money for present year is disimbursed; that if she saves it all, will go far toward paying her way to you, as her children are too small to pay Rail Road fare, and will draw from State as any others........ Your friend, A.E. Smith"

"Gainesville, Texas, February 10th, 1892

"Mr. Governor Tillman, Sir, to your honor;

I have been inform by our agent A.E. Smith of Rock Hill, South Carolina, that the last session of legislature has passed an act of law to cut out me & my children of our just rights. And if it be so, God help them and perserve better heart in them, for trampling our old fore-father.

"George Washington's flat farm: he set apart 15 miles square of land for us Catawba Indians on the Catawba river in the state of South Carolina. And now our

150

old forefather & the white people together has share us down to the sum of 750 acres of land & a small sum of $800 in money a year, to be divided among 90-some-odd heads of us. — And simply because we don't all set serenely down inside of that little boundary, we are deprive of our just rights.

"Governor, if you was to move over in Georgia or North Carolina, would the members of the legislature have a right to take your home from you? I think not justly. I am a little feard that our Agent, Mr. A. E. Smith, has had some little influence over some one of your members of the legislature in order so they can keep the small bulk of $800 in a pile together, so they can have a good picnic over it. I have studied it over & I can't see no just cause for it, only the picnic.

"Our Agent, Mr. Smith, sent me & my children & grandchildren last year the small sum of $50 to Gainesville, Texas where I live now. Now Governor, if you please, look into this matter for me. I would thank you very kindly if you will do so, to say whether we outside Catawbas ought to be deprived of our money & our rights there in the state of South Carolina. If we are, it is the first time since the flat farm has been laid down to us by George Washington. So I will close, wishing to hear direct from you.

Yours respectfully,
NANCY HARRIS, Catawba
Indian, Gainesville, Cooke
County, Texas

"P.S. Don't take my word, but read this letter of Mr. A. E. Smith, our Agent."

**Father  Thomas KILPATRICK**

| | | |
|---|---|---|
| Birth | | |
| Chr | | |
| Death | | |
| Burial | | |
| Marriage | 1869 | Rock Hill, York, South Carolina, United States |
| Father | | |
| Mother | | |

**Mother  Nancy HARRIS**

| | | |
|---|---|---|
| Birth | 16 Jan 1851 | Catawba Reservation, York, South Carolina, United States |
| Residence | 1880 | Age: 30 Marital Status: Widowed; Relation to Head of House: Self; Catawba, York, South Carolina, United States |
| Residence | 1900 | Age: 49 Marital Status: Widowed Relation to Head of House: Mother; Justice Precinct 1, Cooke, Texas |
| Residence | 1910 | 56 Age in 1910:  Marital Status: Widowed; Relation to Head of House: Mother; Turnbull, McClain, Oklahoma, United States |
| Burial | Dec 1919 | Bradley, Grady, Oklahoma, United States |
| Death | 16 Dec 1919 | Age: 68; Bradley, Grady, Oklahoma, United States |
| Father | Allen HARRIS (1813-1880) | |
| Mother | Rhoda GEORGE (1830-1919) | |
| Other spouse | John STARKEY (1846-1907) | |
| Marriage | 23 Mar 1904 | Bradley, Grady, Oklahoma, United States |
| Other spouse | Samuel S BRADY (1850-   ) | |

**Children**

**F  Agnes HARRIS**

| | | |
|---|---|---|
| Birth | 8 Mar 1870 | Catawba Reservation, South Carolina |
| Residence | 1880 | Age: 10  Marital Status: Single   Relation to Head of House: Son; Catawba, York, South Carolina, United States |
| Residence | 1920 | Age: 50 Marital Status: Widowed Marital Status: Widow; Relation to Head of House: Mother; Cherokee, Spartanburg, South Carolina |
| Death | | |
| Burial | | |
| Spouse | | |

**M  Hillard Josiah "Hillary" HARRIS**

| | | |
|---|---|---|
| Birth | 8 Mar 1870 | Catawba  Reservation, York Co., South Carolina |

| | |
|---|---|
| Residence 1880 | Catawba, York, South Carolina, United States |
| Residence 1900 | Age: 29Marital Status: Married; Relation to Head of House: Head; Justice Precinct 1, Cooke, Texas |
| Residence 1910 | Turnbull, McClain, Oklahoma |
| Residence 1920 | Age: 45Marital Status: Married; Marital Status: Widow; Relation to Head of House: Head; Caney, Atoka, Oklahoma |
| Residence 1930 | Age: 60Marital Status: Married; Relation to Head of House: Head; Caney, Atoka, Oklahoma |
| Residence 1935 | Rural, Atoka, Oklahoma |
| Residence 1 Apr 1940 | Age: 70Marital Status: Married Relation to Head of House: Head; Caney, Atoka, Oklahoma, United States |
| Burial        Jul 1941 | Carney, Atoka, Oklahoma, United States |
| Death         18 Jul 1941 | Carney, Oklahoma |
| Spouse      Rachel Jane TIMS (1866-1946) | |
| Marriage   20 Apr 1886 | |
| Spouse      May Tuck JOHNSON (1895-    ) | |
| Marriage | Oklahoma, United States |

**F   Lillie Susan HARRIS**

| | |
|---|---|
| Birth         21 Apr 1872 | Catawba, Catawba, North Carolina, United States |
| Residence 1880 | Catawba, York, South Carolina, United States |
| Residence 1900 | Justice Precinct 3, Cooke, Texas |
| Residence 1920 | Turnbull, McClain, Oklahoma |
| Residence 1930 | Age: 58Marital Status: Widowed Relation to Head of House: Mother-in-law; Turnbull, McClain, Oklahoma |
| Residence 1935 | Rural, Mcclain, Oklahoma |
| Residence 1 Apr 1940 | Age: 68Marital Status: Widowed; Relation to Head of House: Head; Leeper, Murray, Oklahoma, United States |
| Burial        1955 | McClain, Oklahoma, United States |
| Death         21 May 1955 | Age at Death: 83; Lindsey, Oklahoma, United States |
| Spouse      John Ephriam BALLARD (1867-1907) | |
| Marriage  1889 | |

**PHOTO 314 – HILLERY (JOSIAH HILLARD) HARRIS**

1. Hillery (Josiah Hillard) Harris was born 8 March 1870 in Catawba, South Carolina and died 18 July 1941 and is buried in Oklahoma. He married on April 20, 1886, Rachel Jane Tims, daughter of John Alexander (Alec) and Martha Cottsky-Scott Tims.330 This family moved to Colorado in the mid 1880's. Hillary left his wife Rachel in Sanford where she is buried and eventually moved to Oklahoma where he remarried Mae "Tuck" Johnson. He died in 1941 and is buried beside Mae in Carney, Oklahoma. Rachel is buried in Sanford, Colorado along with her parents and brother. More can be found in, Genealogy of the Western Catawba. Hillary and Rachel had four children, Josiah, Allan, Evalena and Ellis Harris.

**PHOTO 315 - HILLERY (JOSIAH HILLARD) HARRIS**

**PHOTO 316 – JOSIAH HILIARD ALEXANDER HARRIS**

a. Josiah Hiliard Alexander Harris born 17 October 1887, Catawba, South Carolina and died 17 February 1953, Alamosa, Alamosa, Colorado. He married Malinda Augusta Wood (1892–1923). They had 4 children: Ruby Ella (1909–1959, James Harvey (1912–1987), Raymond Henry (1913–2002), Evelyn Odell (1916–1983). He was also married to Vernice Lucille Shawcroft (1900–1959) and Ida Odell Wood(1888–1963). His second wife was Ida Odell Wood 1888–1963 – they were married 9 Jun 1923 • Durango, La Plata, Colorado.His third marriage was to Vernice Lucille Shawcroft 1900–1959 on 2 December 1943, La Jara, Conejos, Colorado, United States

b. Allen Harris born 15 January 1891, Gainsville, Cooke, Texas and he died 20 January 1891, Cooke, Texas.

**PHOTO 317 - EVELYN J HARRIS**

c. Evalina J Harris born 6 December 1891, Gainsville, Cooke, Texas, and died 1944 , Cooke, Texas. She married Joseph Murray (1880–1940).

**PHOTO 318 - HEADSTONE FOR EVALINA J HARRIS MURRAY - BURIAL: KIRTLAND CEMETERY, KIRTLAND, SAN JUAN COUNTY, NEW MEXICO**

d. Ellis Nelson Harris born 17 March 1893, Sanford, Conejos, Colorado, and died 29 August 1966, Phoenix, Maricopa, Arizona. He married Ruth Rebecca Carico (1896–1972).

\*\*\*\*\*\*\*\*\*\*\*\*\*\*\*\*\*\*\*\*\*\*\*\*\*\*\*\*\*\*\*

2. Agnes Harris was born 8 March 1870 in Catawba, a twin to Hillary. She went to Cook County Texas where Nancy wrote a letter to the governor asking that her allotment money be sent to her there. She is with her mother in Gainsville, Texas in 1890. Nothing more is known of Agnes.

Lillie Susan (Harris) Ballard
Grand-daughter of Rhoda and Allen Harris
Daughter of Nancy Harris

**PHOTO 319 - LILLIE SUSAN HARRIS**

3. Lillie Susan Harris was born April 21, 1872 in Catawba. She died on May 21, 1955 in Oklahoma (she was only 34 years old). Lillie married John Ephriam Ballard a white man from Catawba who was born 5 January 1867. When he was 21 years old and Lillie was 2 months shy of her 16 birthday, they married on 2 March 1888. John got into an altercation with a Catawba, John Brown. He was charged with assault in Circuit Court in July, 1889,[340] but because he was white, he was acquitted. Several of the Indians decided to take matters into their own hands and tied John to a tree at night. They planned to kill him the next morning, they didn't want to do it at night, something about spirits wandering. Lillie slipped out in the night and took a hunting knife and cut the ties and brought him a saddle horse with which to escape. John Ballard's tombstone states that "he was a Woodman of the World. He died of an infection, a mule had bitten him on the leg, and since there were no antibiotics, the infection killed him. This left Lillie with 8 children to raise, the last one not even 2 years old. She was on 34 years old, what a woman. I am sure it was a hard life for her. I know that she farmed in Bradley, Oklahoma after she was widowed. Their children: Alfred Hawkins (1889–1966), Daisy Irene (1890–1970),

Richard Ephraim (1893–1957), Bevard Vardy (1895–1972), Bulah Vera Lee (1897–1991),

Lillie May (1900–1991), Corene (1903–1957), Lula Bell (1905–1936).

\*\*\*\*\*\*\*\*\*\*\*\*\*\*\*\*\*\*\*\*\*\*\*\*\*\*\*\*\*\*\*\*\*\*\*\*\*\*\*\*\*\*\*\*\*\*\*\*\*\*\*\*\*\*\*\*\*\*\*\*\*\*\*\*\*\*\*\*\*\*\*\*\*\*\*

**PHOTO 320 – BETSY HARRIS**

C. Betsy Harris was born in Sep 1854. Betsy died in October 1921, being proclaimed the oldest member of the Catawba tribe. She married Robert Lee Harris and they had no children..

Name: According to Dr. Thomas Blumer, he calls her Betsy Crawford Harris from his book Catawba Indian Pottery, 2003. Joseph Willey calls her Betty Estridge, when he baptized her on 19 March 1885.

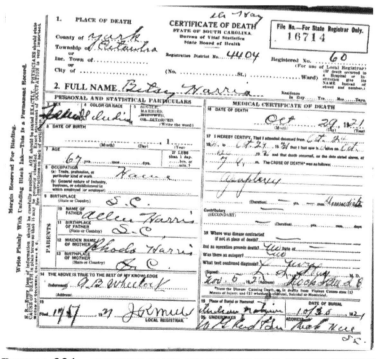

**PHOTO 321 - CERTIFICATE OF DEATH FOR BETSY HARRIS**

**PHOTO 322 - HARRIET HARRIS**

D. Harriet Harris was born 1856. Harriet received $10.00 from the Indian Agent Crook in 1875. She was living with Alonzo Canty in 1880, with her children identified as his children. Her children were actually fathered by a white man named Frank Collins. She is alone in 1883. The story in the Patterson family is that John Alonzo left his old wife and married a new, young one, George Henrietta Patterson.

**PHOTO 323 - ALLEN ALLSTON HARRIS -- HEADSTONE -**
**BURIAL: CATAWBA INDIAN NATION CEMETERY, ROCK HILL, YORK, SOUTH CAROLINA**

E. Allen Allston Harris was born in 1857. He married first according to Thora Wright's genealogy, Nancy Christine Watts Patterson, daughter of James A. and Charlotte Tomson Watts. No proof exists of this marriage and there were apparently no children. Not much proof of any of these marriages exists, so I use the information anyway. Allen married second Nancy White daughter of George and Margareth-Peggy Quash-Marsh White. He was murdered on $26^{th}$ of February 1881. [Son of Chief Allen Harris and Rhoda George Harris; stabbed to death in an altercation with white men in Rock Hill; his attackers were acquitted.]

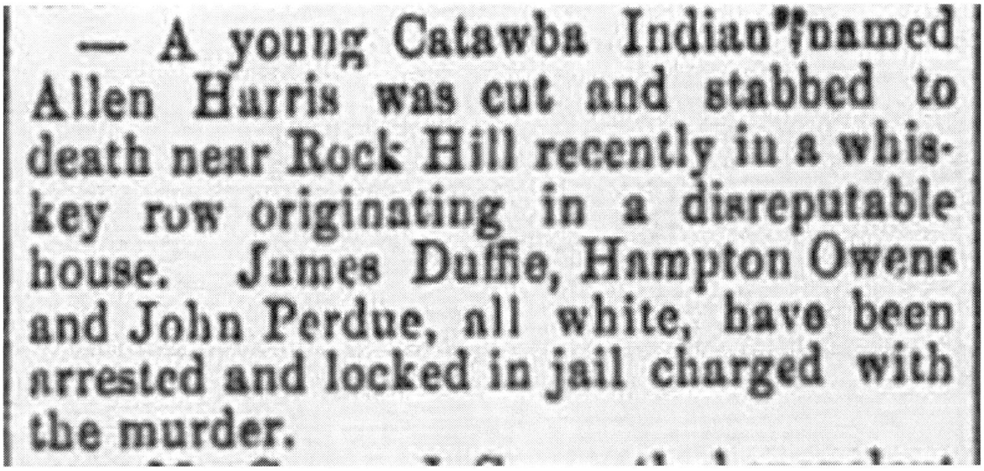

— A young Catawba Indian named Allen Harris was cut and stabbed to death near Rock Hill recently in a whiskey row originating in a disreputable house. James Duffie, Hampton Owens and John Perdue, all white, have been arrested and locked in jail charged with the murder.

**PHOTO 324 - THE HERALD NEWSPAPER, ROCK HILL, SOUTH CAROLINA. 1881**

"James Duffie or McDuffie and H. B. Owens, charged with the murder of the Indian Allen Harris on the 26'1 of February, began at Yorkville on last Thursday and continued until Saturday. The greater portion of the first day was consumed in obtaining a jury, of which Mr.
J. D. Guian was made foreman. It is not necessary to state the names of the lawyers engaged in the case, as this was done in our last issue. The strongest testimony for the state was that given by the Indians who were present or nearby at the time of the killing. They swore that the defendants followed them and provoked the difficulty. This was broken down by testimony to the effect that the defendants acted in self-defense. Duffie testified to the Indians holding a knife in one hand and grasping him by the throat with the other when he did the cutting. Co.W. B. Wilson sr., Col. I. D., Witherspoon and Capts. J. C. Witherspoon made splendid speeches in behalf of the defendants and Solicitor Gaston did his duty well for the state. The Judge explained the law bearing upon the case and it was then given to the jury. After remaining out a short time, the jury returned to the court room and rendered a verdict of Not Guilty."
Allen's funeral expenses were paid in November 1881 by the Indian Agent W. M. Whyte in the amount of $18.30.

**PHOTO 325 – NANCY WHITE**

Nancy White wife of Allen Allston Harris, born April 1860, Catawba, South Carolina, United States, died 1900, Catawba.

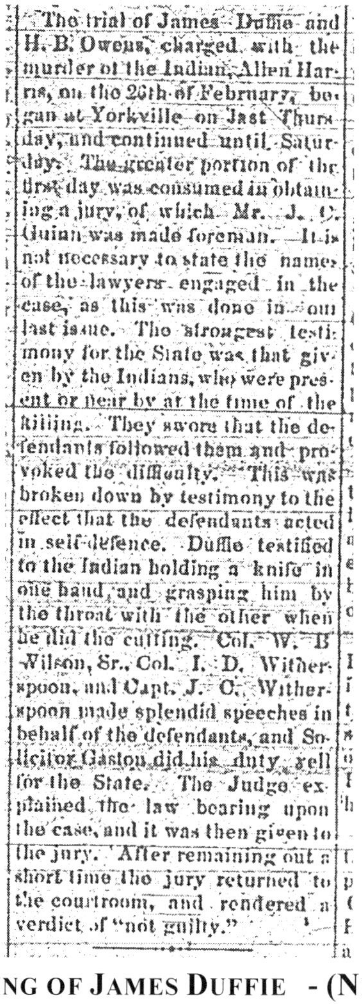

The trial of James Duffie and H. B. Owens, charged with the murder of the Indian, Allen Harris, on the 20th of February, began at Yorkville on last Thursday, and continued until Saturday. The greater portion of the first day was consumed in obtaining a jury, of which Mr. J. C. Quinn was made foreman. It is not necessary to state the names of the lawyers engaged in the case, as this was done in our last issue. The strongest testimony for the State was that given by the Indians, who were present or near by at the time of the killing. They swore that the defendants followed them and provoked the difficulty. This was broken down by testimony to the effect that the defendants acted in self-defence. Duffie testified to the Indian holding a knife in one hand, and grasping him by the throat with the other when he did the cutting. Col. W. B Wilson, Sr., Col. I. D. Witherspoon, and Capt. J. C. Witherspoon made splendid speeches in behalf of the defendants, and Solicitor Gaston did his duty well for the State. The Judge explained the law bearing upon the case, and it was then given to the jury. After remaining out a short time the jury returned to the courtroom, and rendered a verdict of "not guilty."

**PHOTO 326 - NEWSPAPER CLIPPING OF JAMES DUFFIE - (NEWS CLIPPING OF TRIAL, DATED FEBRUARY 188, HERALD, ROCK MILL, SC PAGE 3.)**

**LUCINDA HARRIS**

Sarah[312] Lucinda Harris was born in 1840.[313] She received supplies in 1853, and is listed on both the 1849 and 1854 census of the Catawba. Lucinda died November 1888, at which time the Indian Agent paid the funeral expenses.[314] Lucinda had four children, Wesley Harris[315] by Bob Crawford a white man; John Sanders-Saunders by John Evins Sanders, a Catawba; Louis Gordon by Stell Gordon a white man; and William Sawyer by another white man named Sawyer.

Wesley Harris is the son of Lucinda Harris and Bob Crawford.

**PHOTO 327 - WESLEY HARRIS**

A. Wesley Harris was born 15 September 1857[316] Rock Hill, York, South Carolina and died 24 October 1915, York, South Carolina. He married L. C. A. (Alice) Ayers, daughter of Jefferson and Emily E. Cobb Ayers.[317] Alice died around 1895, and was never enumerated on the Catawba census records. Watson and other writers called her Alice George; however, Jefferson Ayers was her father. Jefferson did not live to see her birth, and by the time of Alice's birth, Emily was

---

[312] Catawba Branch records call her Sarah Lucinda
[313] Catawba Branch Records.
[314] Watson, pages 55 & 56.
[315] Watson page 56 states makes the statement that "McDavid said Bob Crawford or Joe Hagan was Wesley's father.'
[316] Catawba census records and Branch Records.
[317] Catawba Branch Records

married to Taylor George, who raised the children. Wesley was involved in the shooting of Harvey Blue, son of Chief Samuel Blue. More information will be found in the Blue Chapter.

"The investigation disclosed the fact that the shooting was done by Walter Harris, son of Wesley Harris, a boy of about eleven years old. The details of the shooting were found to be substantially as outlined, with the exception that is was found that Wesley Harris, father of the boy was in the hunting party and that he fired the shot that killed the squirrel. The Harris boy fired at the squirrel about the same time and the load of shot from his gun struck the Blue boy.[318] Wesley was blamed for shooting Harvey Blue, however they were best friends.. Wesley had four children, Emma, Allen, Theodore and Walter and possibly an Easter Hester Harris, according to Priscilla Blue Johnson.

FORM NO. 

CERTIFICATE OF DEATH
STATE OF SOUTH CAROLINA
Bureau of Vital Statistics
State Board of Health

File No.—For State Registrar Only 20857

1. PLACE OF DEATH
County of York
Township of Catawba
or Inc. Town of
or City of
Registration District No. 4404
Registered No. 56 (For use of Local Registrar)
(No. St.; Ward) (If death occurred in a Hospital or Institution give its NAME instead of street and number.)

2. FULL NAME Wesley Harris
Residence In City Yrs. Mos. Days.

PERSONAL AND STATISTICAL PARTICULARS
3 SEX Male
4 COLOR OR RACE Indian
5 SINGLE, MARRIED, WIDOWED, OR DIVORCED (Write the word) Married
6 DATE OF BIRTH Sept 15, 1857 (Month) (Day) (Year)
7 AGE 58 yrs. 1 mos. 15 dys. If LESS than 1 day, hrs. or min.?
8 OCCUPATION (a) Trade, profession, or particular kind of work (b) General nature of Industry, business, or establishment in which employed (or employer) Farming
9 BIRTHPLACE (State or Country) York
PARENTS
10 NAME OF FATHER Rob Crawford
11 BIRTHPLACE OF FATHER (State or Country) York
12 MAIDEN NAME OF MOTHER Harris
13 BIRTHPLACE OF MOTHER (State or Country) York
14 THE ABOVE IS TRUE TO THE BEST OF MY KNOWLEDGE
(Informant)
(Address)
15 Filed 11/27, 1915 J. J. Smith LOCAL REGISTRAR

MEDICAL CERTIFICATE OF DEATH
16 DATE OF DEATH Oct 24, 1915 (Month) (Day) (Year)
17 I HEREBY CERTIFY, That I attended deceased from Sept 1915 to Oct 24, 1915, that I last saw him alive on 24 Oct 1915, and that death occurred, on the date stated above, at 12 P.M. The CAUSE OF DEATH* was as follows:
Mitral insufficiency
(Duration) yrs. mos. dys.
Contributory (SECONDARY)
(Duration) yrs. mos. dys.
(Signed) M. D.
Oct 24, 1915 (Address) Catawba Jc
*State the Disease Causing Death, or, in deaths from Violent Causes, state (1) Means of Injury; and (2) whether Accidental, Suicidal or Homicidal.
18 LENGTH OF RESIDENCE (For Hospitals, Institutions, Transients, or recent Residents)
At place of death yrs. mos. dys. In the State yrs. mos. dys.
Where was disease contracted, if not at place of death?
Former or usual Residence
19 Place of Burial or Removal Catawba
DATE OF BURIAL Oct 25 1915
20 UNDERTAKER
ADDRESS

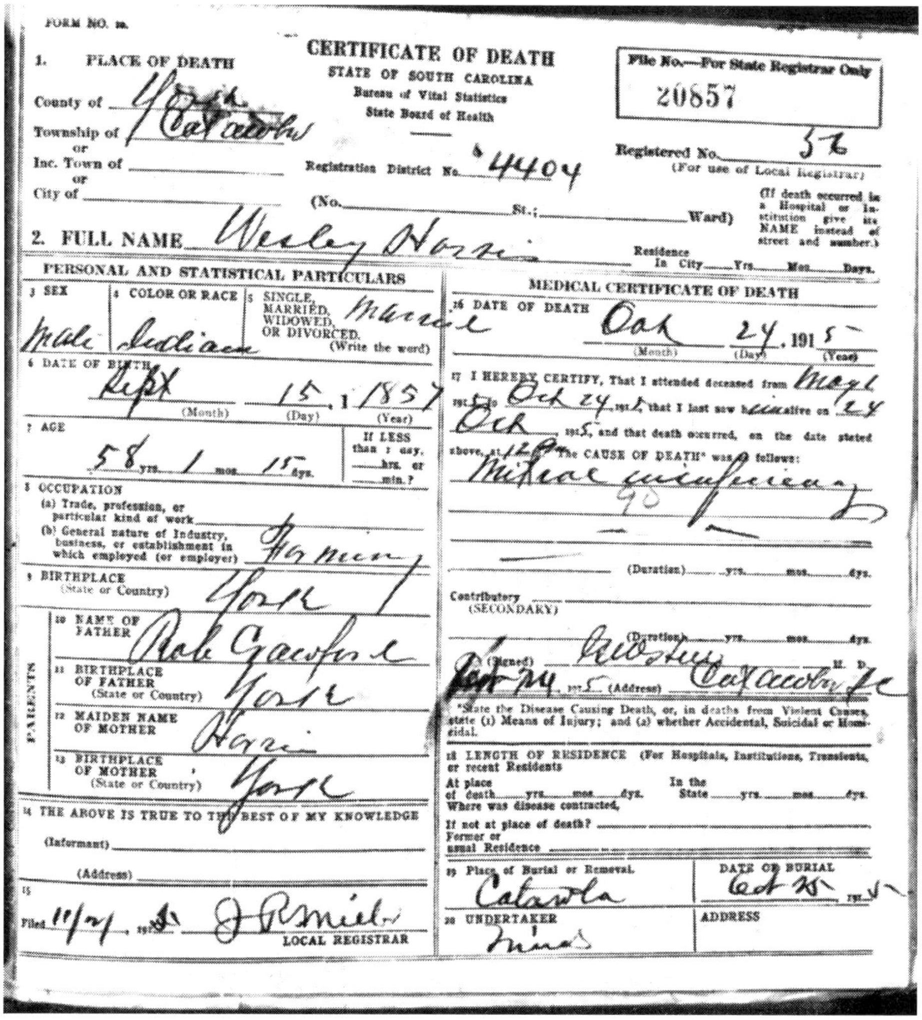

**PHOTO 328 – CERTIFICATE OF DEATH FOR WESLEY HARRIS - HE'S BURIAL: CATAWBA INDIAN NATION CEMETERY , ROCK HILL, YORK COUNTY, SOUTH CAROLINA**

[318] Evening Herald, January 9, 1914 page 1.

**PHOTO 329 - EMMA JUANE HARRIS**

a. Emma Jane Harris was born 7 June 1888 in Gaffney, Cherokee, North Carolina and she died 19 January 1961in Rock Hill, York, South Carolina. She married first Henry Canty, son of George Washington and Mary Jane Elizabeth Mush-George Canty.[319] Emma married second Early Morgan Brown, son of John and Rachel Wysie George Brown.[320] Children would be found in the Brown and Canty chapters.

---

[319] Catawba Branch Records.
[320] Ibid

**PHOTO 330 - HEADSTONE OF EMMA JANE HARRIS – BURIAL AT CHURCH OF JESUS CHRIST OF LATTER-DAY STS CEMETERY, CATAWBA, YORK COUNTY, SOUTH CAROLINA**

**PHOTO 331 - EMMA JANE HARRIS**

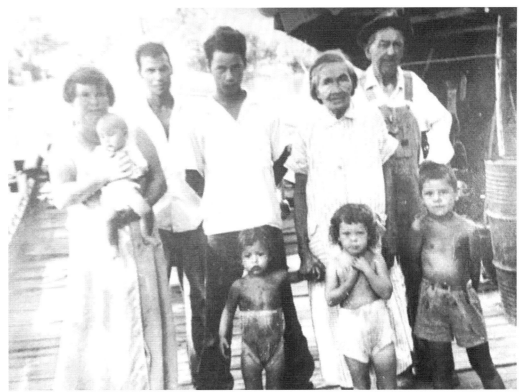

**PHOTO 332 - LEFT TO RIGHT, AILEEN GEORGE, HOWARD GEORGE, PHILLIP, EMMA HARRIS BROWN, AND EARLY BROWN. KIDS RIGHT TO LEFT, TOMMY, FLONNIE, RITA AND SHAWN GEORGE**

Registration Dist. No. 11405
Registrar's No. 22
Birth No.

STANDARD CERTIFICATE OF DEATH
Division of Vital Statistics – State Board of Health
State of South Carolina

State File No. 61 002893

1. PLACE OF DEATH: (a) County York
(b) City or town Rock Hill SC
(c) Length of Stay:
(d) Full name of hospital or institution: York County

2. USUAL RESIDENCE: (a) State SC (b) County York
(c) City or town Rock Hill SC
(d) Street address Rt 3 Rock Hill SC

3. NAME OF DECEASED: EMMA HARRIS BROWN

4. Date of death: 1-19-1961

5. Sex: F
6. Color or race: Indian
7. Married, never married, widowed, divorced: Married
8. Date of birth: 6-22 1889
9. Age (in years last birthday): 72

10a. Usual occupation: Domestic
10b. Kind of business or industry: House wife
11. Birthplace: Rock Hill SC
12. Citizen of what country? USA

13a. Father's name: Wesley Harris
13b. Mother's maiden name: Alice George
14. Husband or wife's name: Early B Brown

15. Was deceased ever in U.S. armed forces? no
16. Social Security No.
17. Informant: Husband

18. Cause of Death.
MEDICAL CERTIFICATION
I. Disease or condition directly leading to death (a) Acute Pulmonary Edema (Dead on Arrival) — Interval between onset and death: few hrs.
Due to (b)
Due to (c)
II. Other significant conditions: Hypertensive Cardio Vascular Disease — 2 yrs.

19a. Date of operation:
19b. Major findings of operation:
20. Autopsy? YES ☐ NO ☒

21a. Accident, Suicide, Homicide
21b. Place of injury:
21c. (City, Town, or Township) (County) (State)
21d. Time of injury:
21e. Injury occurred: While at work ☐ Not while at work ☐
21f. How did injury occur?

22. I hereby certify that I attended the deceased from 12 July 1958 to 19 Jan. 1961, that I last saw the deceased alive on 17 Jan. '61, and that death occurred at 4:00 A.m., from the causes and on the date stated above.

23a. Signature: M.D.
23b. Address: 1169 Oakland Avenue, Rock Hill, S. C.
23c. Date signed: 23 Jan. '61

24a. Burial, cremation, removal: Burial
24b. Date: 1-21-1961
24c. Name of cemetery or crematory: Latter Day Saints Church cemetery
24d. Location: Rt 3 Rock Hill SC

Date rec'd by local registrar: 1-25-61
Registrar's signature:
25. Funeral director: Greene Funeral Home, Rock Hill SC

FEDERAL SECURITY AGENCY — PUBLIC HEALTH SERVICE

MARGIN RESERVED FOR BINDING

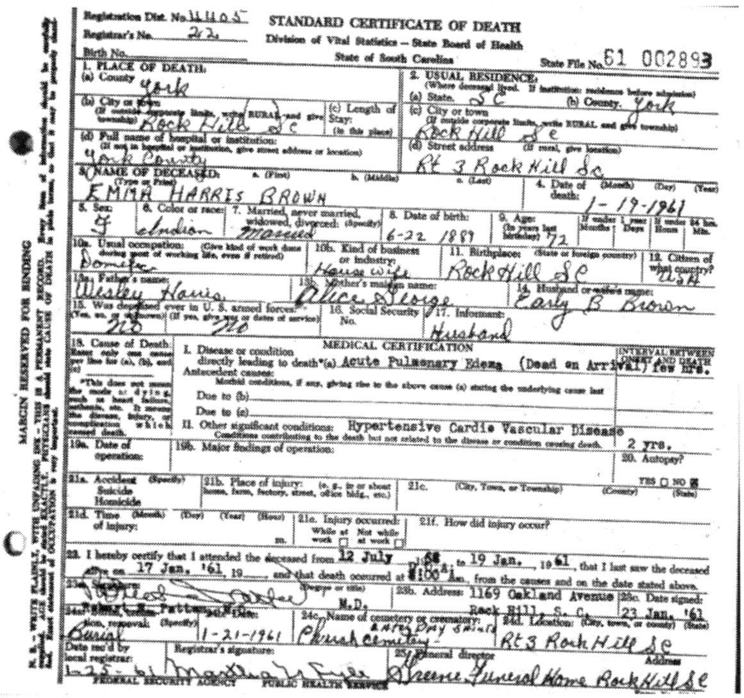

**PHOTO 333 – CERTIFICATE OF DEATH FOR EMMA HARRIS BROWN**

b. Allen Spencer-Allen S. Harris was born August 1891, South Carolina and died 25 June 1918 Catawba, York, South Carolina. He married Minnie Florence Harris born 23 December 1909, Rock Hill, South Carolina and deid 24 June 1979, Rock Hill, York, South Carolina. Daughter of Benjamin Perry Harris 1871–1930 and Mary Dovey Cornelia George 1877–1972.

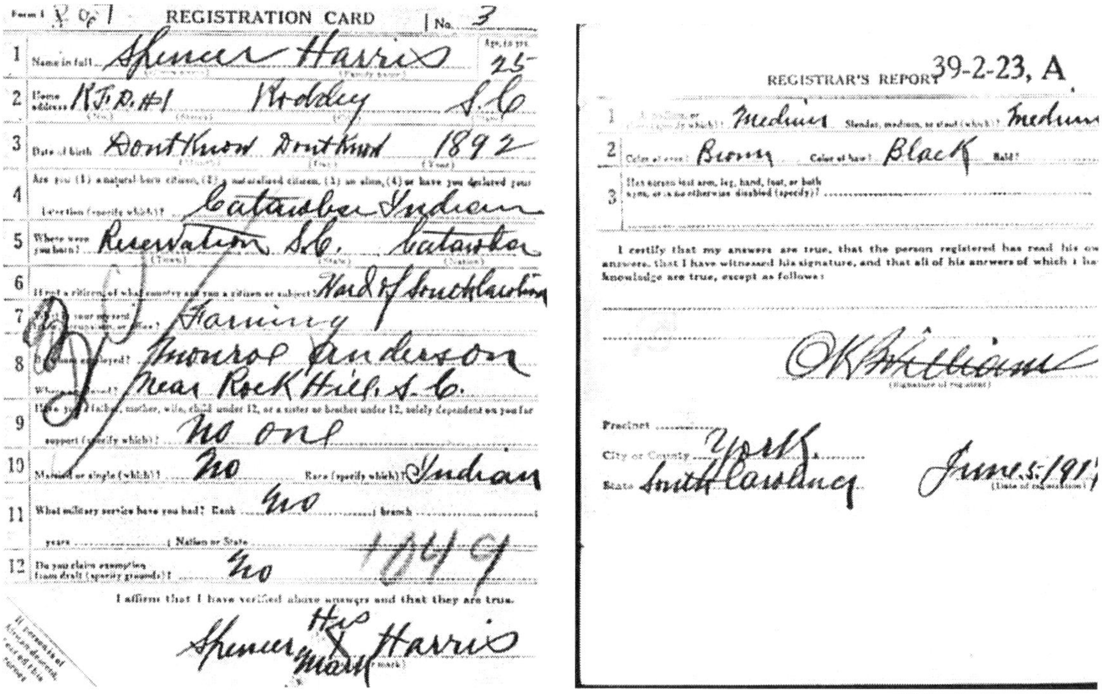
REGISTRATION CARD No. 3

1 Name in full: Spencer Harris. Age in yrs: 25
2 Home address: R.F.D. #1 Roddey S.C.
3 Date of birth: Dont Know Dont Know 1892
4 Are you (1) a natural-born citizen, (2) a naturalized citizen, (3) an alien, (4) or have you declared your intention (specify which)? Catawba Indian
5 Where were you born? Reservation S.C. Catawba
6 If not a citizen, of what country are you a citizen or subject? Ward of South Carolina
7 What is your present trade, occupation, or office? Farming
8 By whom employed? Monroe Anderson. Where employed? Near Rock Hill, S.C.
9 Have you a father, mother, wife, child under 12, or a sister or brother under 12, solely dependent on you for support (specify which)? No one
10 Married or single (which)? No. Race (specify which)? Indian
11 What military service have you had? Rank No
12 Do you claim exemption from draft (specify grounds)? No

I affirm that I have verified above answers and that they are true.

Spencer His Mark Harris

REGISTRAR'S REPORT 39-2-23, A

1 Tall, medium, or short: Medium. Slender, medium, or stout (which): Medium
2 Color of eyes: Brown. Color of hair: Black. Bald?
3 Has person lost arm, leg, hand, foot, or both eyes, or is he otherwise disabled (specify)?

I certify that my answers are true, that the person registered has read his own answers, that I have witnessed his signature, and that all of his answers of which I have knowledge are true, except as follows:

O K Williams (Signature of registrar)

Precinct
City or County: York
State: South Carolina. June 5, 1917 (Date of registration)

**PHOTO 334 – WWI REGISTRATION CARD FOR ALLEN SPENCER HARRIS**

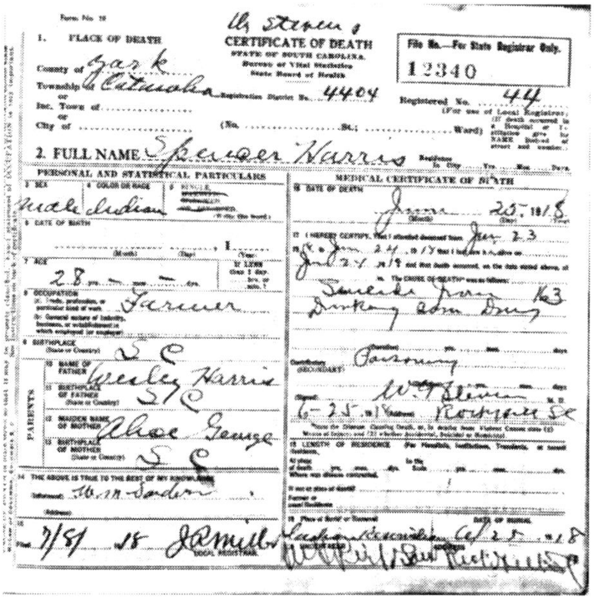
CERTIFICATE OF DEATH
STATE OF SOUTH CAROLINA
Bureau of Vital Statistics
State Board of Health

File No.—For State Registrar Only. 12340

1. PLACE OF DEATH
County of York
Township of Catawba. Registration District No. 4404. Registered No. 44

2. FULL NAME Spencer Harris

PERSONAL AND STATISTICAL PARTICULARS
Sex: Male. Color or race: Indian. Single
Age: 28
Occupation: Farmer
Birthplace: S C
Name of father: Wesley Harris
Birthplace of father: S C
Maiden name of mother: Alice George
Birthplace of mother: S C

MEDICAL CERTIFICATE OF DEATH
Date of death: June 25, 1918
Cause of death: Suicide from drinking ... Poisoning

**PHOTO 335 - CERTIFICATE OF DEATH FOR ALLEN SPENCER HARRIS**

c. Robert Theodore "Ted" Harris was born 27 March 1893, Catawba Indian Reservation, York, South Carolina and died May 1972[321] in Catawba Indian Reservation,

[321] Blumer page 311 and page 416.

York, South Carolina. He married first Artemis Harris, daughter of David Adam and Della George Harris. Ted enrolled in the armed services in 1917 and was among the first eight hundred men called from Eastern York, County.[322]. In April 1936, he and Hoyt-Hoy Harris along with Joseph Harris were all tried for larceny. Ted was later sentenced to 30 days and fined $100 for stealing 22 chickens.[323]

Form 2 - Rev. 7-1-63
KEYS PRINTING

**STATE OF SOUTH CAROLINA**
**APPLICATION FOR CERTIFICATE OF BIRTH**
(With Instructions)

17-275

Full Name. Robert Theodore Harris

Date of Birth. March 27, 1893

Male. X. Female.

Where Born:

Race. White Indian. Nationality. American.

City. Indian Reservation

Present Address. Indian Reservation.

County. York

State. South Carolina

Full Name of Father. Wesley Harris

Age Last Birthday, if living.

Nationality. American.

If Dead, Age at death. 55

Race. White Indian.

Where Born:

City. Indian Reservation

Present Address. Deceased

County. York

State. South Carolina

Maiden Name of Mother. Alice George

Age Last Birthday, if living.

Nationality. American.

If Dead, Age at death. --

Race. Indian.

Where Born:

City. Indian Reservation

Present Address. Deceased

County. York

State. South Carolina

A. If family Bible is used as proof. Yes, as exhibited to me this 7th day of Feb. 1958.

PHYSICIAN'S CERTIFICATE:
B. I hereby certify that I attended the birth of the above named person on the date given and that I am ____ years of age.

Tom L. Wilson
Tom L. Wilson
Clerk of Court
Attending Physician or Midwife

Day of ____ 19 ____ (Signed) ____

Address ____

Notary Public.

(OVER)
Filed Feb. 7, 1958

115

**PHOTO 336 - STATE OF SOUTH CAROLINA APPLICATION FOR CERTIFICATE OF BIRTH**

---

[322] Blumer page 263.
[323] Blumer page 311.

**PHOTO 337 – GRAVE MARKER FOR ROBERT THEODORE HARRIS - BURIAL:**
**CHURCH OF JESUS CHRIST OF LATTER-DAY STS CEMETERY,**
**CATAWBA, YORK COUNTY SOUTH CAROLINA**

**Robert T and Artemis had 11 children: Carrie, Garfield C, David S, Martha L, Theodore W, Wilford P, Blanche M, Alice E, Edna, Cleadous O and Ralph.**

**PHOTO 338 –HEADSTONE FOR CARRIE HARRIS 1911-1913 - INSCRIPTION:**
**DAUGHTER OF THEODORE HARRIS AND ARTEMIS HARRIS - BURIAL: CATAWBA INDIAN NATION**
**CEMETERY, ROCK HILL, YORK COUNTY, SOUTH CAROLINA**

(a) Carrie Harris was born 8 December 1911, Catawba Indian Reservation, Rock Hill South Carolina and died 4 May 1913, Catawba Indian Reservation, Rock Hill South Carolina.[324]

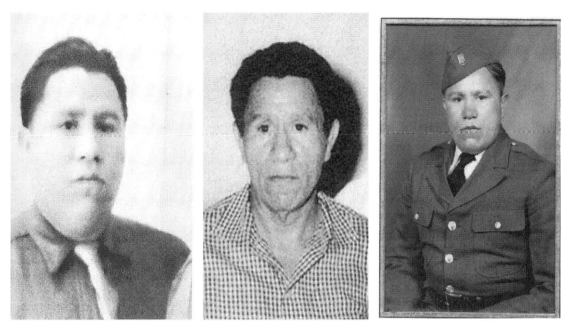

**PHOTO 339 - GARFIELD CRAWFORD HARRIS**

(b) Garfield Crawford Harris was born 1 February 1914 in Catawba Indian Reservation, York, South Carolina and died 20 January 1994 in Lancaster, Lancaster., South Carolina. He married Olga Louise Hill (1913–1992)

## Dr. Thomas Blumer after the death of Garfield Harris

Biographical Note:

"Catawba Indian Autobiographer Passes"

"I was born March 14, 1914, between midnight and day." Thus begins the direct opening statement of Garfield Harris, who for many years had planned to write "his story." Actually begun in September 1993, his autobiography preserves bits and pieces of Catawba history in a way uniquely his own.

He was the son of Theodore and Artemis Harris, both Catawba Indians. His father was a sharecropper and his mother, a graduate of Carlisle Indian Industrial, kept the home and made Catawba pottery. The family totaled 11 children in all.

School began for Garfield at age seven in 1921. He was always studious and liked the learning process, but school was difficult for him, for early in life he faced adult chores around the house and in the cotton

---

[324] Catawba cemetery inscriptions.

fields. He received his schooling at the Catawba Indian School, founded in 1896 and closed in 1966. While hundreds of Indian children there learned to read, write and calculate, only Garfield Harris aspired to write his autobiography. His spotty attendance record however, surely impressed his teachers negatively. Chores came first:

"I only have seven grades in school. My dad was a farmer, and he didn't believe in kids going to school. When farming time came, it was in March. If I was in school, I had to stay out to clear up the field and to plant, cut sprouts and briars, corn stalks and cotton stalks to start plowing. Next, cotton had to be hoed. When we finished, I was able to go back to school for two weeks. We took our exams in May."

When Garfield had time left for study, it was often late at night. And the family often didn't have money for kerosene to fuel the lamps. His solution was found in pine knots. He gathered them for their steady, bright light. Then after dinner, he would light one and study by it "until one or two in the night."

His formal schooling ended in 1929 at the age of 15. He went to work on the nearby Sullivan farm for 50 cents a day in summer and 40 cents a day in winter, working from "Sunday to Sunday." He knew he was fortunate to have even this meager income because the family could do much with so little. His earnings made his 1933 marriage to Ruthie Harris possible. After two years, they separated.

In 1936 he joined the Civilian Conservation Corps and left the Catawba nation for the first time.

"I remember the day we left. We met a bus in front of People's Bank in Rock Hill and left early in the morning for Columbia…I kind of got homesick but stayed."

From Columbia, the group was sent to Pennsylvania where Garfield was impressed by the "hard winter." In the spring he was transferred to Salina, California. His last written statement concerns the joy of seeing the country:

"I learned a lot about traveling and it was a wonderful experience which came in handy in later years."

While Garfield's personal account ends with this brief comment, the historical documentation picks up at this point. When WWII broke out, Garfield joined the US Army and served in North Africa. Upon returning home, he went to work for the Rock Hill Printing and Finishing Company (the Bleachery). In 1950 he was elected to the Catawba Indian Nation Tribal Council and served several terms under Chiefs Nelson Blue and Ephraim George. In 1958 he was again elected to the Council under Chief Nelson Blue whose task it was to guide the Catawba Nation through the termination of Federal status. Chief Blue resigned, and Garfield continued to serve under Chief Albert Sanders. Frustrated by the way Catawba assets were being terminated, he resigned in June 1959. Some months later, he married Olga Fowler.

The last years of Garfield's life were spent nursing his wife and preparing his autobiography. While he did not live to complete the story, his brief contribution to Catawba written history is important for its deep sincerity. Perhaps this is most evident in his description of a house his parents rented from fellow tribal member Davis Ayers:

"The floor was fit together with rough timber, and you had cracks in the floor. You could feed chickens through the cracks. You got plenty of wind from them. We had to put sacks on the floor to keep the wind out…The shingles were made out of oak. When it rained, you had to set pots around to keep your bed from getting wet. As soon as the shingles got wet and swelled, the leaking stopped...I enjoyed my life and was as happy as anybody. We lived through it all, and I am still going on."

Scope and Content Notes

The collection consists of 3.75 linear feet of material. The journals begin in 1950 and span 45 years. They are a chronicle of daily life on the Catawba Indian Nation and are filled with accounts of the weather and events that Garfield found interesting. Many journals resemble scrapbooks, containing clippings, obituaries, and other ephemeral items.

The 1983 journal contains Garfield's "Remembrances", autobiographical accounts of reservation life between the World Wars and Garfield's military experiences. Of special note are his California experiences. Garfield, a Native American is a guard at a Japanese American internment camp. He also talks about seeing the Navajo (the Navajo wind talkers) practice their signals across the valley.

Garfield was a devoted husband, and Olga the great love of his life. The two fell in love but separated due to the South Carolina ban on interracial marriage. They married in 1959, when the law was abolished. A long and happy marriage ensued with Olga predeceasing Garfield. From this point, almost all journal entries are addressed to his "dearest, darling."

Many journals contain handwritten indexes created by Dr. Blumer.

The collection also contains some of Garfield's personal effects such as marriage certificates, an honorable discharge from the Civilian Conservation Corps and various clippings. Of special interest is the unique family blood type shared by his family. The Harris variant was so rare the American Red Cross created a special category for it, and researchers around the world requested samples for study. Further folders include a small correspondence file, and Mormon Church materials.

Folder List of Contents of the Garfield Crawford Harris Papers 1936-1995

(c) David Spencer Harris born16 June 1916, Catawba,York, South Carolina and died 30 OCtober 1963, Rock Hill North, South Carolina. He married Minnie Florence Harris 1909–1979 and they had 5 children: Woodrow Benjamin, Ann, Viola, Jeff and Morgan.

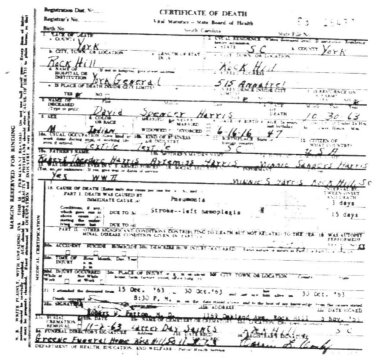

PHOTO 340 - CERTIFICATE OF DEATH FOR DAVID SPENCER HARRIS

FIGURE 1 – MARTHA LEE HARRIS

(d) Martha Lee Harris was born 1 May 1919, Catawba, South Carolina[325] and died 1 July 1940, Rock Hill South Carolina. She married Harry White.[326] Martha and Harry had a son, Eber Walter Harris born 5 June 1940.[327]

---

[325] Ibid

(e) Theodore Wesley-Westly Harris born 27 August 1921, Catawba Indian Nation, York, South Carolina and died 9 July 1991, York County, South Carolina. He married Roela Wade, daughter of William and Sally Hester Harris Wade.- They had; Roger born 1943, Lynette born 1945, Walter born 1946, Dessa born 1947, Wesley Garland born 1950, Nannie Lyda born 1951, Lester born 1953, Cora born 1954 and Audrery born 1957.

**PHOTO 341 – WILFORD PHILLIP HARRIS**

(f) Wilford Phillip Harris born 7 February 1924, South Carolina and died 14 March 1997[328], Rock Hill, York, South Carolina. He married Buleah Thomas, daughter of Emory and Cleo Blanch Sanders Thomas.[329] He and Buleah had; Loretta born 1947, Teresa born 1948, Barry born 1949 and Donald Wilford born 1950.[330]

---

[326] Ibid
[327] Membership rolls.
[328] The Catawba Spirit, a part of the Catawba Cultural Preservation Project. Volume 4, Issue 3, September 1997, pages 1,2 & 3
[329] Membership rolls 1943-58.
[330] Ibid

**Charlotte Observer, The (NC) - Saturday, March 15, 1997**

ROCK HILL - Mr. Wilford Phillip Harris 73, died March 14, 1997 at Piedmont Medical Center.
Funeral is at Jesus Christ Church of Latter Day Saints-Catawba Ward.

Mr. Harris was a native of Rock Hill, SC, son of the late Theodore and Artimis Harris. He was a member of the Jesus Christ Church of Latter Day Saints-Catawba Ward. He was a United States Army Veteran and served in World War II. He was an executive committee member for the Catawba Indian Nation since 1975. He retired from Display Fixtures of Charlotte, NC.

Survivors include his wife, Beulah Thomas Harris of the home; two sons, Barry Phillip Harris and Donald Wilford Harris both of Charlotte, NC; two daughters, Alice Loretta Harris of Gastonia, NC; and Teresa Harris Sox of Rick Hill; one brother Cletus Harris of Rock Hill; and one sister, Blanche Bryson; six grandsons and two great-grandchildren.

**PHOTO 342 – HEADSTONE FOR WILFORD PHILLIP HARRIS -**
**BURIAL: CHURCH OF JESUS CHRIST OF LATTER-DAY STS CEMETERY, CATAWBA, YORK COUNTY, SOUTH CAROLINA**

**PHOTO 343 – BLANCHE MYRTLE HARRIS**

(g) Blanche Myrtle Harris, born 22 November 1926, Catawba South Carolina and died 30 December 2006, Rock Hill, South Carolina. She married Sanford A Bryson.

**Obituary for Myrtle Blanche Bryson**

Mrs. Myrtle Blanche Bryson, 80, died Saturday Dec. 30, 2006, at Piedmont Medical Center. The funeral will be at the Church of Jesus Christ of Latter-day Saints, Catawba Ward, with Kenneth Harris and

Samuel Beck officiating. Burial will be at Catawba Cemetery.

A native of Rock Hill, Mrs. Bryson was a daughter of the late Theodore Harris and Artimiss Harris Harris. She was a homemaker, was a member of the Church of Jesus Christ of Latter-day Saints, Catawba Ward, and was a member of the Catawba Indian Nation.

Surviving are her husband, Sanford A. Bryson Sr. of Rock Hill; her granddaughter; four great-grandchildren; and four great-great-grandchildren. She was preceded in death by her son, Stanley A. Bryson.

**PHOTO 344 GRAVE MARKER FOR BLANCHE MYRTLE HARRIS BRYSON - CHURCH OF JESUS CHRIST OF LATTER-DAY STS CEMETERY, CATAWBA, YORK COUNTY, SOUTH CAROLINA**

**PHOTO 345 –HEADSTONE ALICE E HARRIS - BURIAL: CATAWBA INDIAN NATION CEMETERY, ROCK HILL, YORK COUNTY, SOUTH CAROLINA INSCRIPTION DAUGHTER OF THEODORE HARRIS AND ARTEMIS HARRIS**

(h) Alice E Harris was born in 1929 and died 1929 the same year.

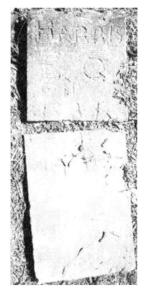

**PHOTO 346 – HEADSTONE FOR EDNA O HARRIS 1931-1932**

(i) Edna O Harris was born in 1931 Catawba Indian reservation, Rock Hill South Carolina and died 30 October 1932, Catawba Indian Reservation, Rock Hill South Carolina.

(These children were born a long time a part, information comes from their Cemetery inscriptions.) Burial: Catawba Indian Nation Cemetery, Rock Hill, York County, South Carolina. Inscription: Daughter of Theodore Harris and Artemis Harris

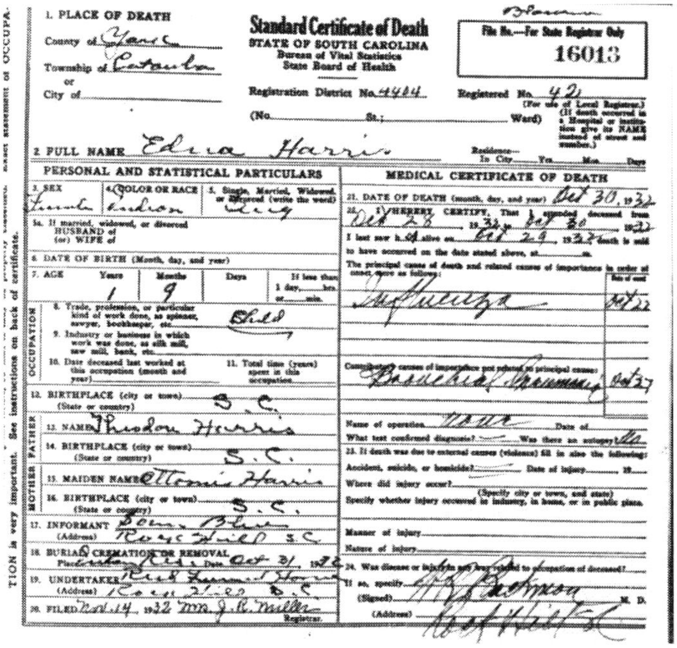

Standard Certificate of Death
STATE OF SOUTH CAROLINA
Bureau of Vital Statistics
State Board of Health

File No.—For State Registrar Only 16013

1. PLACE OF DEATH
County of York
Township of Catawba
or City of

Registration District No. 4414
Registered No. 42

2. FULL NAME Edna Harris

PERSONAL AND STATISTICAL PARTICULARS

3. SEX Female
4. COLOR OR RACE Indian
5. Single, Married, Widowed, or Divorced (write the word) Single
5a. If married, widowed, or divorced HUSBAND of (or) WIFE of
6. DATE OF BIRTH (Month, day, and year)
7. AGE Years 1 Months 9 Days
8. Trade, profession, or particular kind of work done Child
9. Industry or business in which work was done
10. Date deceased last worked at this occupation
11. Total time (years) spent in this occupation
12. BIRTHPLACE (city or town) (State or country) S. C.
13. NAME (Father) Theodore Harris
14. BIRTHPLACE (city or town) (State or country) S. C.
15. MAIDEN NAME (Mother) Ottemis Harris
16. BIRTHPLACE (city or town) (State or country) S. C.
17. INFORMANT Sam Blue
(Address) Rock Hill S. C.
18. BURIAL, CREMATION OR REMOVAL Place Catawba Res. Date Oct 31, 1932
19. UNDERTAKER
(Address) Rock Hill S. C.
20. FILED Nov. 14, 1932 Mrs. J. R. Miller Registrar.

MEDICAL CERTIFICATE OF DEATH

21. DATE OF DEATH (month, day, and year) Oct 30, 1932
22. I HEREBY CERTIFY, That I attended deceased from Oct 22, 1932, to Oct 30, 1932
I last saw her alive on Oct 29, 1932; death is said to have occurred on the date stated above, at ___ m.
The principal cause of death and related causes of importance in order of onset were as follows: Influenza Oct 22
Contributory causes of importance not related to principal cause: Bronchial Pneumonia Oct 27
Name of operation None
Was there an autopsy? No
23. If death was due to external causes (violence) fill in also the following:
Accident, suicide, or homicide? Date of injury
Where did injury occur? (Specify city or town, and state)
Specify whether injury occurred in industry, in home, or in public place.
Manner of injury
Nature of injury
24. Was disease or injury in any way related to occupation of deceased?
If so, specify
(Signed) Robinson M. D.
(Address) Rock Hill S.C.

**PHOTO 347 – CERTIFICATE OF DEATH – SOUTH CAROLINA – FOR EDNA HARRIS**

**PHOTO 348 – GRAVEMARKER FOR CHARLES – CLEADOUS ONEAL HARRIS -
BURIAL: CHURCH OF JESUS CHRIST OF LATTER-DAY STS CEMETERY, CATAWBA, YORK COUNTY,
SOUTH CAROLINA**

(j) Charles-Cleadous Oneal Harris born 13 July 1935.[331] Catawba, South Carolina
and died 6 December 2008, Rock Hill, York, South Carolina.

**U.S., Social Security Death Index, 1935-2014**
Name   Cleodous O. Harris
Last Residence         Rock Hill, 29730, York, South Carolina
Born    13 Jun 1935
Died    6 Dec 2008
State (Year) SSN issued        South Carolina - Before 1951

---

[331] Westly, Wilford, Blance & Cloatus from 1941 membership roll.

**PHOTO 349 - HEADSTONE FOR RALPH HARRIS - BURIAL: CATAWBA INDIAN NATION CEMETERY, ROCK HILL, YORK COUNTY, SOUTH CAROLINA -- INSCRIPTION: SON OF THEODORE HARRIS AND ARTEMIS HARRIS.**

(k) Ralph Harris was born in 1938 and died in 1940, Catawa Indian Reservation, York, South Carolina. Inscription: Son of Theodore Harris and Artemis Harris

Wesley Harris second marriage was to Nancy Elizabeth Gordon born 9 April 1859, York, South Carolina and died 22 November 1929, South Carolina. They had one child (Wesley's 4th child) Walter B Harris. Wesley and Nancy are shown on the 1900 US census in Morgan, Cherokee, South Carolina and 1910 US Census Catawba, York, South Carolina.

**PHOTO 350 - NANCY ELIZABETH GORDON HARRIS**

**PHOTO 351 – CERTIFICATE OF DEATH FOR NANCY ELIZABETH GORDON HARRIS**

**PHOTO 352 – WALTER BEAUREGARD HARRIS**

d. Walter Beauregard Harris the final child of Wesley Harris was born in 16 September 1902, Gaffney, Cherokee, South Carolina and died 7 July 1969, Chubuck, Bannock, Idaho. He married twice, first to Jeanie George (1905-1925) and the second Lyda Melda Haney(1909–1986) a white woman. On the 1930 census they were in Rock Hill, York, South Carolina but on the 1940 census they were in Chubbuck, Bannock, Idaho.

He lived in Idaho and had two children who died young.[332] Walter was involved in the shooting of Harvey Blue in 1914.

He was accused of being the one who shot the boy. See more information on this incident in the Blue chapter. His life story is below.

**PHOTO 353 – WALTER BEAUREGARD HARRIS**

**Walter Harris in the U.S., World War II Army Enlistment Records, 1938-1946**

Name: Walter Harris -- Birth Year: 1902 -- Race: White, citizen (White)
Nativity State or Country: Utah -- State of Residence: Utah - County or City: Weber
Enlistment Date: 19 Aug 1942 -- Enlistment State: Idaho
Enlistment City: Pocatello
Branch: Branch Immaterial - Warrant Officers
Branch Code: Branch Immaterial - Warrant Officers
Grade: Private -- Grade Code: Private

---

[332] Information from Dr. Thomas Blumer.

Term of Enlistment:   Enlistment for the duration of the War or other emergency, plus six months, subject to the discretion of the President or otherwise according to law
Component:   Selectees (Enlisted Men) -- Source: Civil Life
Education:  2 years of high school -- Civil Occupation:   Carpenters
Marital Status: Separated, without dependents
Height:  64 -- Weight:  130

Lyda Melda Haney Harris and Walter B Harris

Walter B Harris

LIFE SKETCH OF WALTER BEAUREGARD HARRIS

Born Sept. 16, 1902   *Written by: Mamie Andersen*  *Read by: Eurilla Dunn*   Passed away July 7, 1969

As the first streak of daybreak stretched across the autumn sky on the morning of Sept. 16, 1902 at Gaffney in Cherokee County, South Carolina, a bouncing baby boy was born to Westley and Nancy Elizabeth Goyden Harris. He was a beautiful baby with big, dark eyes and lots of black hair, weighing 12 pounds, an especially big baby for such a tiny 100 lb. mother. How her heart did swell with pride as she saw Westley just about burst off his vest buttons when he placed his big, healthy son in the arms of his dear little wife.

The important task now was finding a name suitable for such a special one. Walter sounded just right for the first name and what could be more appropriate for a middle name than Beauregard (a nice southern name). Thus the final choice remained Walter Beauregard Harris. He was the only child born to this couple as his mother was now 43 and his father 45 years of age. Each had children by a previous marriage. Nancy had three daughters but two had died in childhood. Westley had two sons and one daughter. Since these half brothers and sisters were years older, they soon were all married and in homes of their own. Needless to say, Walter was adored and received much love and attention from his parents.

When he was three years of age the family moved to Catawba, a small reservation near Rock Hill, South Carolina. His father belonged to the Catawba tribe, but his mother was of English decent. Here Walter spent his childhood, living a carefree life with the other Indian braves - fishing for catfish and swimming in the Catawba River - the two favorite sports of all the boys. He learned to play a good game of baseball and was still an ardent fan, watching the games on TV and making a milk shake bet with Millie Roueche.

His mother loved him so much and was very proud of her son. He often told how she would scrub him until his face just shone, comb his black wavy hair until it was so perfectly in place, then dress him in his Sunday best and put him right up on the front bench in the chapel so everyone could see him. He didn't like this very well, but it was one of those things that one must accept and endure.

Walter's father always walked wherever he went and never did look back, which is a typical Indian trait. Every time he would start out he would say to his son, "Now you stay here." Walter, being an obedient son, always stayed - until his father would get just around the bend of the road and then his little feet just had to take one "little ole" step - he wouldn't really follow him - then another little step; and another, until pretty soon they weren't so little and got faster until before long he was just a step behind the big fellow in front. Then, without looking back, his father would say, "Boy, didn't I tell you to stay there?" Then Walter knew everything was right and he would go skipping along with his dad to the store or to the neighbors to play.

Then, too suddenly and too soon, this carefree life came to an end. All his schooling, which was haphazard at best, also ended. His father died leaving Walter at the age of 12. Walter was the sole support of his mother and himself. 17 He worked at odd jobs at the saw mills and also for farmers in the neighborhood to earn enough for the bare necessities of life. But he really did a fine job being "man of the house."

At the age of 16 he started working for the cotton mills in the summer of 1918. This was a steady job with a little better pay. Not once did he let his mother go cold or hungry.

When Walter was nearly 20, he married a little Indian maid, Jeannette George. They had been married about two years when Jeannette became very ill with a severe case of flu causing her to give birth to premature twin girls who only lived a few hours. Jeannette never recovered and in about 5 months followed the little girls in death. This was a trial for Walter but his mother was still with him and encouraged him to seek a new life in Rock Hill.

Walter had always loved his church and had been taught from birth to uphold the standard of the gospel. The first branch of the church in South Carolina was organized in the home of Moses M. Gorden, his maternal grandfather. Walter enjoyed the missionaries and often helped them. His home was always headquarters for them when they were in Rock Hill. He never accepted any pay for what he did for them, always seeing that they had food to eat and a clean bed to sleep in. He took them places in his wagon, and later car. His mother washed and ironed their clothes for them. He often protected them from angry mobs at the peril of his own life. At that time the church wasn't organized in Rock Hill so he had to attend the little branch at Catawba. He would tell how he and a friend, Herbert Blue, would board the train at Rock Hill and ride to a little stop called Leslie, get off and walk the remaining few miles to the church (this was before he owned a car). He just loved to go to conference and attended many in the mission field.

It was at one of these in Greenville, South Carolina that he met a beautiful girl who was to completely change his life. They both knew that it was fate that led them to that particular pew in church that day. She was hunting a nice corner where she could relax during the two-hour meeting. He was just ready to seat himself when he heard her tell her three sisters, "I'm going to get me a corner this time." Well, being the gentleman he was, Walter bowed, slightly, and asked, "Here, would you like this one?" Just one look into those twinkling eyes and one flash of that mischievous smile, and she was a goner for sure, but it would never do to let him know. After conference they introduced themselves and he found out her name was Lyda Haney from Westminster, Oconee County, about 50 miles northwest of Greenville, where she was working as bookkeeper for a furniture store. That was the beginning of a beautiful romance that has lasted for 40 years. At last he had found what he had been looking for. A year after they met he decided to find out for sure if she would marry him so he told his mother he was going over to Greenville to see her and propose marriage. He still wasn't sure she would say yes. His mother informed him that he had better not come home without her. Of course, he didn't know this, but Lyda wasn't about to let _him_ get away. So, on October 26, 1929, they were married by, and in the home of, the president of the Greenville branch, Bro. Pinkney Aiken. Walter's cup of joy and happiness was overflowing. He had a lovely wife who adored him and she was, indeed, his queen. They were sealed for time and all eternity in the temple April 8, 1935. It was a joyous occasion

when he took his bride home to his mother. One morning his mother told
Lyda many things about her son - her pride and joy - her son - how kind
and gentle he was and how well he had assumed responsibilities when he
was still a child and how she had taught him to respect people. Then she
said, "I've prayed to my Heavenly Father to let me live to see my son
married to a good girl worthy to be his wife. Now, my prayers are answered
and he has one who even exceeds my hopes. Now I can leave him with peace
of mind anytime the Lord sees fit to take me." Soon after that Lyda heard
a little gasp and ran to her side. Nancy, Walter's beloved mother passed
away happily in the arms of her loving daughter-in-law just four weeks
after they were married.

The depression was on. Everyone was out of work, and Walter was no exception. The missionaries were living in his home as usual with Lyda caring
for their needs as his mother had always done. They would hold cottage
meetings, inviting their neighbors to help with the singing and prayers.
Life went on this way for another year. Then they decided to go to Pocatello, Idaho, where Lyda's two brothers, four sisters, and her mother
were living. They gave away most of their belongings and packed what
they could in the old Model T Ford and with their life's savings of $35
started out for Pocatello. At nights they slept out on the grass secluded
from the road as much as possible. Finally, they arrived in Pocatello
in June, 1931. Their folks here were so happy to have them near.

Walter worked at anything he could get to do - helping the farmers (who had
no money to pay), working on W.P.A., as thousands of others did, and he worked
also in the CCC camp. Finally on September 8, 1935, he started to work for
the Union Pacific Railroad where he worked until his death.

Walter loved children. He and Lyda have spent their lives making things
easier for others. Not having children of their own, they practically
adopted their many nieces and nephews. Walter loved to entertain them
with jokes and stories of his childhood on the reservation and show them
little tricks. In his younger days he played the accordian and guitar.
The kids enjoyed this very much. They would go to him with their problems
and he never was too busy to help them. He was always their second father.
They knew they could depend on him when they needed something for school,
such as tuition or books when dad was short of cash. He kept a watchful
eye on them and when their shoes or clothing would begin to look pretty
shabby he would say to Lyda, "Looks like our boy (or our girl) needs a pair
of shoes or boots" and he would take them to the store always to return with
the new shoes or whatever they had needed. Then when they attended college
he would say, "The boy needs a car" or "Our little girl needs something to
drive back and forth in," and off they'd go to find a good used car. When
mission time came, as usual part of the finances came from Walter and Lyda.
When Lynn was debating about going he didn't know how he could possibly go
with his dad's finances as they were, but here again Walter was there. He
said to Lyda, "Our little man wants to go and he should go. We'll do all
we can to see he has the means to do so." So that problem was solved.
Lynn said to his mother, "Mom, how can I ever pay them back for all they've

done for me?" His mother answered, "Be a good missionery, that is all the pay they want. Not only did they help rear a wonderful family of nieces and nephews but have started on the second generation who also call them "Grandpa Walter" and "Grandma Lyda."

Walter loved his church and put his whole soul into his work. He thought if a thing was worth doing at all, it was worth doing well. He held various positions in the ninth ward. As Deacon advisor he enjoyed the young fellows and often took them on swimming trips or other interesting activities. He was assistant to Bro. Joe Dunn in the M.I.A. and really learned to love and respect him. He enjoyed working as Superintendent of Sunday School with Bro. Parley Packer and Bro. Austin Jones as assistants. Also, he was assistant to Bro. Jim Woodland with Bro. Willis Ward. He has cherished these friendships through the years. He worked as Chairman of the genealogical committee and did a wonderful work in that capacity. As Chairman of the ward teaching in the ninth ward he was faithful in contacting all the teachers to see that the teaching was done and reports were in on time. At the time of his death he was a home teacher and was equally as faithful in performing his duty. It always upset him so much when other things would interfere with it. He was faithful in all his callings.

Everyone who knew him loved and respected Walter. No unkind thing could ever be said about him. His whole life was spent in doing good for others. You could very well say that his hobbies were loving children and doing good wherever he was. His love and devotion for his wife was admirable and there was nothing too hard for him to do for her if it were possible at all. Everything they did was together. They worked in the garden and flowers for hours together and took pride in the things they did. He loved Lyda's folks as his own and often said they were better than just in-laws to him. He will always be remembered with love and respect by the nieces and nephews he loved so dearly. Even the younger ones will miss him. Walter suffered so very much the past several years. In 1953 he had a severe heart attack and has been under the doctor's care since. In 1961 he had an operation for a bleeding ulcer and had most of his stomach removed. His health has been poor the past two years and has had constant pain for well over a year. Death held no fear for him. His only regret was leaving his beloved wife. How he tried to go on for her sake we'll never know. But he became so tired and worn from the struggle that death came as a blessed relief and all who loved him thank a merciful God who saw fit to call him home where he is free from the pain and hardships of this life and has begun a new work preparing for his loved ones who are left behind. He lived a good life and his reward is assured.

*— Mamie Andersen*

And now in conclusion may I personally add this line
Regarding this dear, kind friend of mine.
There is no question in the mind of anyone here
As to the kingdom you've earned in our heavenly sphere.
For by God's rules your life has been led,
You honored your parents as the commandment said,
And shared willingly of your talent and time,
For cause or loved one you gave your last dime.
So, Walter, we bid you our earthly adieu
And, I'll softly whisper - just for you
A last farewell to Lyda, your darling wife,
"I'll be waiting with a love even greater
in Eternal life."

— Eurilla Dunn.

**PHOTO 354 - LYDA 2ND FROM LEFT AND WALTER 6TH FROM LEFT WITH SAM BLUE IN FRONT, PICTURE TAKEN 1930. LYDA AND WALTER HAVE A V ABOVE THEM.**

## WALTER BEAUREGARD HARRIS

This is taken from the Idaho State Journal, July, 1969 Obituary of

Walter Beauregard Harris 66 of 112 Lou, died early today in Bannock Memorial Hospital following a heart attack.

He was born Sept, 16,1902 at Gaffney, Cherokee County, S.C. to Westley Harris and Nancy Elizabeth Gorden, and moved with his parents to Rock Hill, S.C. when he was three years old. His father died when he was 12 and he began working at odd jobs at sawmills and with farmers until he was 16 and started work in the cotton mills in the summer of 1918.

On Oct, 26,1929 he married Lyda Haney at Greenville, South Carolina, and in June, 1931 they came to Pocatello, Idaho. On Sept 8,1935 he began employment with the Union Pacific Railroad.

He was a high priest in the Ninth Ward, Church of Jesus Christ of Latter-day Saints and had served in many capacities in the ward.

On April 8,1935 he received his endowments in the Salt Lake LDS Temple

Survivors include his wife of Pocatello; a half-brother Theodore Harris, of Rock Hill, S.C. and several nephews and nieces.

Funeral services will be announced by the Manning Funeral Chapel.

### LYDA MELDA HANEY HARRIS

This is taken from the Idaho State Journal, February, 1986 Obituary of

Lyda Melda Haney Harris 77, died Tuesday at her home, 765 Lou Ave.
She was born Jan 20, 1909 to William Crayton and Julia Harvey Haney in Westminster, S.C.

On Oct 26, 1929 she married Walter B. Harris at Greenville, S.C. prior to moving to Pocatello, in June of 1931 where she has resided since. Their marriage was solemnized in the Salt Lake LDS Temple on April 8,1935. Mr. Harris died July 7,1969.

She was an active member of the LDS Church, serving in various positions in her ward and stake.

She is survived by three sisters, Effie McCormack, Pocatello; Roma Miller Sandpoint, Idaho; and Mamie Andersen, Pocatello.

Funeral services will be Saturday at 11 a.m. at the Pocatello LDS 31st Ward Chapel at Chubbuck and Hawthorne Roads with Bishop Dennis Dye officiating. The family will receive friends Saturday from 10 a.m. until service time at the 31st Ward chapel. Arrangements are under the direction of Manning Funeral Chapel. Burial will be in Restlawn Memorial Gardens.

PHOTO 355 – HEADSTONE OF WALTER B AND LYDA M HARRIS -- BURIAL: RESTLAWN MEMORIAL GARDENS, POCATELLO, BANNOCK COUNTY, IDAHO, PLOT: 3W, 44, 7

**John Evins Sanders is the son of Lucinda Harris and John Evins Sanders.**

B. John Evins Sanders was born 1 February 1862, Rock Hill,York, South Carolina and died 30 July 1932, Rock Hill,York,South Carolina. He married Martha Harris, daughter of James and Sarah Jane Ayers Harris sr.[333] He had six children, Robert, William, Joseph, Dora, John -Idle, Robert and Lewis Sanders.

> 1. Robert Lee Jackson Sanders was 21 September 1881, Rock Hill, York, South Carolina and died 29 July 1886, Catawba Indian Reservation., Rock Hill, York, South Carolina.

---

[333] Catawba Branch Records.

2. John William Thomas Sanders was born 8 Sep 1885. He married Nora Alvina Boarch-Brown, daughter of Sallie Brown and a white man named John Boarch.[334] In 1913, he was stabbed, allegedly by John and Early Sanders. They were subsequently arrested. William and Nora had Albert, William and Cleo Blanch Sanders.

**PHOTO 356 – ALBERT HENDERSON SANDERS**

a. Albert Henderson Sanders born 10 October 1904, Catawba, York, South Carolina. He married Vera Louise Blue, daughter of Samuel Taylor and Louisa Canty Blue (1909–1991).

Albert was acting chief in 1958-1962. He was noted as the father of 11 children and a textile worker. He continued the efforts to liberate the Catawba, asserting his position firmly when the time came for termination of the tribe in 1961. Albert also signed a motion allowing Catawba off the reservation (which technically did not exist) to become enrolled.[335] Albert died 16 September 1994, Rock Hill, York, South Carolina.

---

[334] LDS Ancestral File submitted by Albert Sanders.
[335] Brown page 363.

**Charlotte Observer, The (NC) - Sunday, September 18, 1994**
**ALBERT H. SANDERS, FORMER CHIEF, DIES**

The Catawba Indian chief who fought to help tribal members attend Rock Hill public schools has died.

Albert H. Sanders, 89, died Friday night at Piedmont Medical Center and will be buried Monday afternoon at the Church of Jesus Christ of Latter-day Saints Cemetery.

In 1943, Mr. Sanders was instrumental in getting school buses to come onto the reservations to pick up Catawba schoolchildren, said his son Albert H. Sanders Jr. Before then, students had to provide their own transportation.

Sanders said his father led the tribe during the mid-1940s and the late 1950s.

Mr. Sanders wanted his tribal members to have their own homes, to be able to work and to function like everybody else, the younger Sanders said. He wanted the tribe to be free of federal government interference, and Mr. Sanders was pleased with the tribe's current direction, Sanders said.

Mr. Sanders worked until he was 84. He retired from Gold Tex Mills, and his most recent job was as a landscaper at Hobby Acres.

Mr. Sanders left the landscaping company to care for his ailing wife, Vera Louise Blue. They were married for 65 years before she died three years ago, his son said.

"He was a good man and a good provider," Albert Sanders said. "He loved his children." "Even in his last hours," said granddaughter Karen Gregory, "he was making sure his children's needs were met."

He is survived by his sons, Albert H. Sanders Jr. and Randall D. Sanders, both of Rock Hill; daughters, Ms. Ada Sanders, Mrs. Lois Thompson, Mrs. Laura Varnadore, Mrs. Brenda Ball, Mrs. Juanita Campbell, Mrs. Ann Morris, Ms. Marilyn Sanders, all of Rock Hill, Mrs. Leone Watts of Fort Mill; 28 grandchildren, 44 great-grandchildren and 11 great-great-grandchildren.

**PHOTO 357 – HEADSTONE FOR ALBERT H SANDERS AND HIS WIFE VERA L - BURIAL: CHURCH OF JESUS CHRIST OF LATTER-DAY STS CEMETERY -- CATAWBA, YORK COUNTY, SOUTH CAROLINA**

August 18, 1962

First row from bottom l-r:

Marilyn Sanders, Rocky Simmers, Cheryl Mackey-Gordon, Midge Simmers-Brown, Pamela Simmers-Thomas-Hawkins Second row: l-r: Ada Sanders, Francine Doreman, Randall Sanders, Juanita Sanders-Campbell, Beckee Simmers-Garris; Third Row : Leone Sanders-Mackey-Doreman, Albert Sanders, Sr.; Vera Blue- Sanders, Marie Sanders-Simmers

**PHOTO 358 – ALBERT H AND VERA L SANDERS FAMILY IN 1962**

Children of Albert H Sanders and Louisa Canty Blue are:

    1 - Lois Sanders 1924–2008

    2 - Albert Henderson Sanders jr 1926–

    3 - Maria Rebecca Sanders 1928–1985

    4 - Ada Inez Sanders 1931–2002

    5 - Nellie Leone Sanders 1936–1957

    6 - Laurie Sanders 1939–

    7 - Brenda Cornelia Sanders 1941–2013

    8 - Leona Sanders 1941–

    9 - Laura Sanders 1943–

    10 - Marylin Sanders

    11 - Ann Sanders

    12 - Juanita Sanders

    13 - Randall Dean Sanders

b. William Thomas Sanders jr. born 20 February 1907, Catawba, York, South Carolina. He married Verdie Harris, daughter of David and Maggie Price Harris. He died 20 Aug 1946, Rock Hill, York, South Carolina. His children are Pearl Renda, Calvin, W. McClain, Lou Gene Sanders, Mary Caroleen, Andrew Clark, Ruth Mae, and Sandra Darnell Sanders.

**PHOTO 359 – CLEO BLANCH SANDERS**

c. Cleo Blanch Sanders born 20 August 1909, Catawba, South Carolina and died 1 March 1972, Catawba, South Carolina. She married Emory Giles Thomas (1910–1992).

There children are: Beulah Mae Thomas 1929–, Lora Lee Thomas 1930–, Emory Randolph Thomas 1936–2007 Lora Lee Thomas.

**PHOTO 360 – CLEO BLANCH SANDERS ALSO HEADSTONE OF CLEO AND HER HUSBAND EMORY - BURIAL: CHURCH OF JESUS CHRIST OF LATTER-DAY STS CEMETERY -- CATAWBA, YORK COUNTY, SOUTH CAROLINA**

d. Cecil Sanders born January 1914, Catawba, South Carolina and died 9 August 1931, Catawba, York, South Carolina.

e. Ella Lou Sanders born 21 August 1916, Catawba, South Carolina and died 9 August1981, Rock Hill, South Carolina. He married Allen Barnes Canty (1911–1947).

f. Lilly Sanders born 1918 in South Carolina.

**The rest of John Evins and Margaret Jane Harris Sanders follow:**

**PHOTO 361 – JOSEPH HINSTON SANDERS**

3. Joseph Hinston Sanders born 19 July 1886 in Catawba Indian Reservation, Rock Hill North, York, South Carolina and died 13 Feb 1930 in Catawba Indian Reservation, Rock Hill North, York, South Carolina . He married 10 October 1910 Lillie Florence Beck, daughter of Samuel and Araha Powell Beck. [336] They had no children. Joseph served in the armed services in the Mech. 156, Depot Brig.[337]

---

[336] Ibid
[337] Watson page 78.

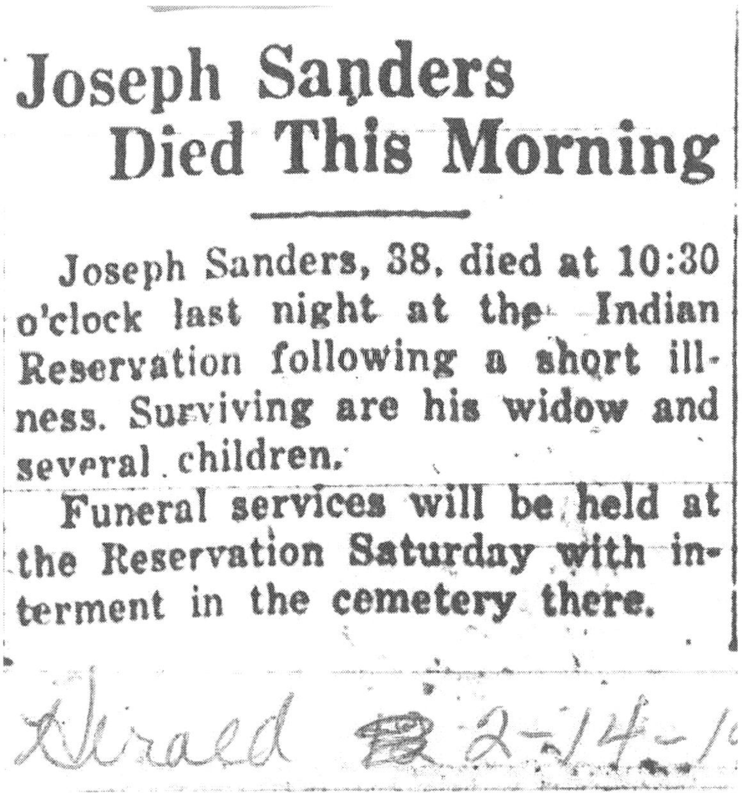

# Joseph Sanders Died This Morning

Joseph Sanders, 38, died at 10:30 o'clock last night at the Indian Reservation following a short illness. Surviving are his widow and several children.

Funeral services will be held at the Reservation Saturday with interment in the cemetery there.

*Herald 2-14-1*

**PHOTO 362 – NEWSPAPER CLIPPING ON DEATH OF JOSEPH SANDERS**

**PHOTO 363 - HEADSTONE OR JOSEPH SANDERS - INSCRIPTION: SOUTH CAROLINA MECH 156 DEPOT BRIG. SON OF JOHN SANDERS AND MARTHA HARRIS SANDERS. HUSBAND OF LILLIE BECK SANDERS BURIAL: CATAWBA INDIAN NATION CEMETERY, ROCK HILL, YORK COUNTY, SOUTH CAROLINA**

4. Dora Sanders born 1890, Rock Hill, York, South Carolina and died before 1910 in Rock Hill, York, South Carolina.

5 Loney Roy Sanders born 25 December 1890, Rock Hill, York, South Carolina and died 25 May 1892, Catawba Indian. Reservation, Rock Hill, York, South Carolina.

**PHOTO 364 – JOHN IDEL SANDERS**

6. John Idel Sanders was born 12 October 1892; he married Arzada Brown, daughter of John and Rachel Wysie George Brown. John served in the armed services and enrolled in 1917. He served on the tribal council in 1952 and was Chief of the Nation in 1954 through 1956. John died August 27, 1973.[338] John and Arzada had eleven children and raised nine of them; two children died young, Blanche and Vivian. The children are: Blanch, Kirk,

---

[338] Catawba cemetery inscriptions.

Catherine, Jack, Thomas, Eula, Fred, William Emory, Roberta, Vivian and Anna Mohave Sanders.

Evening Herald, Aug 29, 1973 pg. 14

# Catawba reservation was intact under reign of Chief Sanders

CATAWBA — John Idle Sanders, 80, who was chief of the Catawba Indians when they had a reservation of more than 3,800 acres, will be buried Thursday. He died Monday at York General Hospital.

Funeral services will be at 4 p.m. Thursday at the Church of Jesus Christ of Latter Day Saints, with burial in the church cemetery.

The church, whose missionaries taught the Indians they belonged to a lost tribe of Israel, maintained a strong influence on the Catawbas during Sanders' lifetime.

Sanders, born Oct. 12, 1892, became tribal elder, then assistant chief, and in 1954 was elected to a two-year term as chief. He had farmed and had been employed in textile and lumber work.

Sanders' two years as chief were spent listening to tribe members arguing among themselves over the dissection and sale of the reservation. The tribe wanted to disband to cut itself free of the federal government and restrictions placed on the Catawbas' land.

The decision to disband the tribe came during the chieftainship of his nephew, Albert Sanders, who succeeded him as chief.

After the tribe disbanded in 1962, there were no more Catawba chiefs, and the tribe, grown from 80 to more than 600 members during one man's lifetime, had scattered all over the country.

As the tribe grew, many of the old customs died out. By 1960 there were no more full-blooded Catawbas, and no one could speak the language, according to historian Douglas Summers.

Family members said Sanders was one of the closest to full-blooded Indians there were left on the reservation when he died.

A new chief was elected last Friday night. He is Gilbert Blue, who was elected at a meeting attended by 60 tribe members on the reservation.

Sanders lived in his home on the plot of reservation land given him when the tribe disbanded just over ten years ago.

It was the same reservation on which he'd been born 80 years ago, and where he'd married Arzada Brown 61 years ago. It was where his nine children were raised.

**PHOTO 365 – NEWSPAPER CLIPPING – CATAWBA RESERVATION – CHIEF SANDERS**

## John Idel and Rachel' Children:

(a) Blanch D. Sanders born 6 November 1912, Catawba Indian Reservation, York County, South Carolina and died 8 November 1912.[339] Catawba Indian Reservation, York County, South Carolina.

(b) Kirk Sanders was born 10 January 1914, Catawba Indian Reservation, York County, South Carolina and he died 1 June 1945, Catawba Indian Reservation, York County, South Carolina. He married Sarah Lee Harris, daughter of David Adam and Dorothy Price Canty Harris. Kirk had two children, Clara Lee and Dorothy Miriam Sanders.

"Kirk was shot in the arm and abdomen with a .38 caliber pistol in the Friendship Community Tuesday of this week. Jess Harris, his brother-in-law was held in the county jail in York in connection with the fatal shooting. Funeral services will be held Sunday at 3 p.m. at the Church of Latter Day Saints."[340] Sarah Lee Harris Sanders then married Hazel Ayers and had

[339] Ibid
[340] Obituary of Kirk Sanders, Evening Herald, June 2, 1945 page 1

Avery Stuart Ayers. More information on Avery will be found in the Ayers chapter.

(c) Herman Sanders born 16 Jan 1916 Catawba Indian Reservation, York County, South Carolina and died 28 Feb 1916. He's buried in the Brown family plot near his sister Blanche in the old family cemetery.[341]

**PHOTO 366 – CATHERINE SANDERS**

(d) Catherine Sanders was born 11 February 1917, Catawba Indian Reservation, York County, South Carolina and died 12 February 1999, Catawba Indian Reservation, York County, South Carolina. She married Billy Columbus Canty, son of Henry Alonzo and Fannie Harris Canty.

(e) Eula Sanders born 31 August 1919 married William David Watts, son of James Harvey and Gertrude Dye Ayers Sanders.[342] Children would be found in the Watts chapter. Eula died 7 November 1988.[343]

(f) John Jack Sanders born 10 March 1920, he married first Ruth Pyler, and second, he married Minnie, white. He was partially blind by 1958. Jack died 14 June 1975.

---

[341] Fred Sanders Biography in April, 1999, 7lh Generation Catawba Newsletter, hereafter referred to as Fred Sanders Biography..

[342] 1920 census of York County and 1953-61 membership rolls.

[343] Fred Sanders Biography.

(g) Thomas McCloud- Sanders born 27 January 1924 married Virgie, white.

**PHOTO 367 – EARLY FRED SANDERS**

(h) Early Fred Sanders born 10 April 1926, Catawba Reservation, York, South Carolina and died 5 December 2013, Catawba, South Carolina. He married first Margaret Alberta Blue Medlin, daughter of Fred Nelson Blue, her first husband was surnamed Medlin; Fred married second Judy Leming.

"I was born on the Catawba Indian Reservation on April 10, 1926. My mother is Arzada Brown Sanders who was born 3 July 1896 and died 20 March 1989, the daughter of Rachel George Brown and John

Brown. My father is John Idle Sanders who was born 12 Oct 1892 and died 27 Aug 1973, he was the son of John Sanders and Martha Harris Sanders. I was the eighth child of twelve.

I was born in our home and the neighbors assisted my mom in my birth. At that time, midwives helped deliver babies. There was also a local doctor who came to the reservation to assist with births (Dr. E. G. Hill). There were very few cars, so transportation was by horse and buggy or saddleback, or mule and wagon.

When my mom went into labor late on the evening of April 9, my father was to go and tell Dr. Hill that she was in labor and to ask him to come an assist in my birth. Dr. Hill's home was approximately five-miles from where we lived, but we had no car, so my dad had to walk. However, he was afraid of the dark, so he told my mother that he was going for Dr. Hill but he went outside and stood in the chimney corner until daylight. He did get Dr. Hill, who arrived on April 10th. Dr. Hill put the date he arrived on my birth certificate (April 10th) rather that the date of my birth (April 9th). They named me Early which has caused some confusion about whether I was named after my Uncle Early Brown, or whether I was given this name because of the circumstances of my birth.

I grew up in a small 3-bedroom house that was built by Bill Sanders (my uncle). The house was purchased from Uncle Sanders by my grandfather John Brown, when he was ill and dying from cancer. (He, John Brown, died 20 June 1927 at the age of 59). My grandfather paid Bill Sanders $90.00 for the house and gave it to my mother and father. He did this because he was afraid that after his death, my mother would be homeless and there would be no place for his grandchildren.

I lived in that little house with all of my brothers and sisters. There were four full-size beds: two in the living room and two in the bedroom. My mother and father slept in one bed in the bedroom with the youngest infants. The next youngest children slept in the second bed in the living room and the older children slept in the bedroom. I slept in a bed with three brothers, Jack, Thomas and William. Two at the head of the bed and two at the foot. This little house was very crowded. If you wanted to play, you had to go outside. The kitchen was always used for eating. It had a wood stove and a table. The smaller children usually ate at the same time with our parents. The older children ate last. There were kitchen cabinets which were used for storing food. There weren't many cooking utensils. In the wintertime, many meals were cooked in the fireplace, which conserved the wood supply. We often ate beans, roasted potatoes and corn bread cooked in a large skillet. Turnover bread (white flour, thick) was also cooked in a skillet. We ate a lot of this bread in the winter with beans. People had to spend a lot of their time gathering food for their families. We ate a lot of wild plants, such as "poke salad" and other types of wild greens from the fields and river bottom which would be boiled and which tasted almost like spinach. There used to be a lot of apple, pear and peach trees, as well as fig bushes at the reservation

Times were tough at the reservation. Very few public jobs were available for Catawba's. Most of the work at that time was in agriculture and timber cutting. To feed so many children and to clothe them wouldn't leave enough money to buy a house. It could also have been a lack of trust in his son-in-law to be able to provide for his family.

# Allen Harris Family

There was no electricity. We used kerosene lamps for light at night and wintertime light from the open fireplace. There was no stove. We heated the house with the fireplace. There was no running water. We carried drinking and cooking water from the local springs or the central well by the corner of the road joining old Chief Sam Blue's residence. Most people on the reservation had an outhouse, as we did.

There was no money for toys, so children had to create their own out of things readily available. Old round metal hooks from barrels or boxes, or thrown away tires which could be rolled up and down the road. You took you bath at the river and played with other children there. That's where many people washed their clothes.

I spent a lot of time fishing in the Catawba River. We would catch crayfish out of creeks and use them for bait to catch catfish out of the river. I've had catfish for breakfast many times. We often had black-eyed peas and hot biscuits with fatback (salt pork) for breakfast. We ate a variety of dried beans and peas, mostly raised in gardens on the reservation. Peas and beans would be dried, husked and stored for winter. I ate a lot of potatoes and yams that were raised in the summer and stored in a "potato hack" which was a hole dug in the ground (in the yard). The hole was lined with leaves and pine needles, and then potatoes were placed on top, with additional leaves and pine needles on top of the potatoes. Then it was covered with dirt.

I grew up picking a lot of plums for preserves. There were many plum trees on the reservation. There were also many wild persimmon trees. We spend many days picking wild blackberries, which were used for jams and jellies and pies. It was also a little cash crop which could be sold to the neighbors for money to buy things to help out with the family needs.

I spent many days with Thomas and Jack cutting wood for non-Indian neighbors. Most people cooked with wood stoves then, so they would hire us to cut wood for them. The money we earned was pooled to buy food for the family. Reservation life when I grew up was a caring, sharing extended family. There wasn't time for a lot of selfishness.

There wasn't a lot of medical care available for Catawba families. My mother went on many trips on the reservation to get herbs for medicinal purposes. We gathered tree branches from local trees to make a tea that would soothe infants or children with hives. We gathered a root called yellow root, which was boiled for tea to treat yellow jaundice. If this tea was going to be consumed quickly, no preservative was added to keep it from spoiling. However, if it was going to be kept for a period of time, a little alcohol was added. There were a lot of Catawba children born with yellow jaundice at that time. Willow bark and limbs were cut into small pieces, dried and boiled into a tea. The tea was given to someone with a fever (there was no money to go to a store and buy aspirin.) There were certain people within the community who had the skills of breathing into children with diphtheria and administering other forms of therapy, which saved their lives.

There was very little social service assistance including food, for not only Catawba's, but all people. The U.S. government had agriculture products, which would be distributed as surplus food during that time. The nearest distribution point was at Catawba Junction, which was approximately six miles from the reservation. I used to go to those distribution points and get food for the family when I was very young. We would go as a group of young boys (11 or 12 years old) from the reservation. Some would use a wagon to haul the food back. I rolled a wheelbarrow and we made sure we got there in time to get cornmeal, flour, lard, cheese, beans, potatoes or whatever was being distributed that day. On our way home, we would stop and play along the way. We would climb trees muscadine and grape vines, play in the creek, and we'd finally make it home just before dark.

World War II began on December 7, 1941. Thomas had already left for the military, but he was home when war was declared, stationed at Fort Bragg, NC. Jack also had gone to the army and was stationed at Fort Bragg. When Jack went into the army, you were not allowed to have a family and be in the military. Jack went into the military for economic reasons, even though the pay wasn't much. He was married to Ruth Pyler, but he had no job, so he lied on his application. His wife became concerned when Jack had not sent the money he promised, so she wrote to his company commander and complained. Jack was discharged because he failed to tell them he was married. The army gave him a suit to wear home and put him on a bus. When he arrived in Rock Hill, Jack had no transportation to the reservation, so he did what most Catawba's did at that time, he walked home. Jack gave me the suit which was my first, and which I wore to church. (The military later changes its rules and began drafting people, including married men with families.)

I delivered Grit newspapers (5 cents) and candy on the reservation as a boy, so we knew there was a war, but didn't really understand why. I sold a lot of newspapers on "credit" and would wait until the family had money to pay me.

I was 18 when I joined the army on September 9, 1944. I was assigned to Fort Jackson, SC, for military indoctrination. I had my first physical exam and saw the first dentist. Shortly after that, I was transferred to Camp Wheeler, GA which was near Macon, Ga. There I received infantry basic training in preparation for going to Europe. I went home several times on weekends during my training then I was given a few days to visit my family before being shipped to New Jersey.

Kirk, my oldest living brother, sometimes played the father role to me. We went hunting and fishing together. He was the one who was always there to see me off whenever I was at the reservation visiting. He was the one who went with me to get on the train in Rock Hill when I left for New Jersey military camp just before going to Europe.

It was the first time that I was exposed to different races and classes of people. Once I was inducted into the military, I had to adapt to the people and to the war tactics and survival skills.

When I went into the military, I had my first private bed and my first experience with three consistently scheduled mealtimes. Your 'family' was 150 other members of the group who all ate together.

Even though I had a private bed, the military barracks had one huge, open area for sleeping quarters. I went from sleeping in one bed with three brothers to sleeping in a single bed by myself but probably had as many as 40 people in the same room. This was the first time I had indoor bathing and bathroom facilities.

On my first trip back home (there were several friends from near the reservation with me in basic training), one of my friends had a car and another had a motorcycle. I rode home with Ray Hamilton from Fort Mill, SC (he had a car). It was a huge culture shock going from the reservation into the military and then returning. It opened up for me an understanding of the world outside the reservation.

On my way to New Jersey, I went to Fort Meade, MD. One of the purposes was to run us through gas chambers to make us familiar with potential gases which might be used on the battlefield. We left New Jersey on a troop train and we went to the Brooklyn Bay area at night. Each soldier had approximately 50 pounds of equipment. Basic Combat gear was a gas mask, rifle, raincoat, overcoat and boots, some of which would be turned over to other soldiers in Europe. It was a way of getting supplies over to Europe.

Basic pay for a private in the army was $50.00 a month; this pay was for putting your life on the line for something you didn't know or understand. I gave whatever pay I had left after buying basics (toothbrush, toothpaste, shaving supplies) to my family. I earned extra money by shining shoes and washing other people's clothes on the weekend in the bathhouses.

I experienced discrimination in the military. People who did not respect people of color would use racial slurs or remarks. I was called "Black" as a nickname on several occasions. It got so bad one time when we were in combat in Germany, one particular soldier was consistently calling me "Black or Blackie". There was another Anglo soldier who reacted violently to him and his remark to this man was, "I've heard enough of your mouth. I've heard enough of your insults to Fred. Fred has put up with your disrespect, but I will not. If I hear this disrespect out of your mouth once more, I'm, going to kill you. Don't you forget it. We're at war zone, and we depend on each other for survival. If you can't respect other people for who they are, and if you do it one more time, it will be your last." He stopped calling me Blackie.

We didn't know where we were going. We only knew we were going to a war zone. We boarded the ship at night. After a couple of days at sea, I discovered we were on a British ship that had been converted for hauling troops. It was the Queen Elizabeth. I knew there were a lot of troops because we traded bunks every night, sleeping somewhere else on the ship. I later discovered there were thousands of troops on that ship. The chow line for feeding troops ran 24 hours a day. You only had two meals a day. Restrooms were crowded. They had steel shutters on the decks of the ship which covered all the light during the nighttime. We went to Glasgow, Scotland. The ship was too large to get into the dock, so we scaled down the side of the ship and onto barges which were taken into port. We took a troop train to Southampton, England and several days later took a ship across the English Channel to France. We were picked up at the port and transported to another staging area for a couple of days, then moved into the countryside. We were then sent to the combat area in Holland.

I was assigned to Company C, 407th Infantry Regiment of the 102nd Infantry Division. Company C was captured by the Germans west of Berlin on April 30, 1945. I was not with the Company C when it was captured. I had just returned to the 102n Division Headquarters from a hospital stay in Paris where I had been treated for double pneumonia. I served in Europe for three years, returning home in June of 1948. [344]

## Obituary

Longtime Catawba Indian tribal leader dead at 87
By Jie Jenny Zou

Fred Sanders, a former vice chief for the Catawba Indian Nation and an ardent supporter of Native American rights, died Thursday at the age of 87 after a battle with cancer.

Early Fred Sanders was a leading figure in the Catawba nation's protracted fight for federal recognition, which was realized in a 1993 settlement with local, state and federal governments. He served as vice-chief of the York County-based tribe for two decades, working closely through two different administrations.

Sanders remained active in tribal leadership into his late 80s, serving as a member of the tribe's executive committee after retiring as vice-chief in the early 1990s.

Sanders recalled tough times growing up on the reservation in an autobiographical account published in a 1999 tribal newsletter.

It wasn't until he was 18 and enlisted in the army in September 1944 that he "was exposed to different races and classes of people," had "three consistently scheduled mealtimes," and indoor plumbing.

"It opened up for me an understanding of the world outside the reservation," Sanders wrote of his service, noting that he faced discrimination and racial slurs while he served and could not vote when he returned to the U.S. in 1948.

He lived briefly in Utah before returning to South Carolina in the 1960s, where he would become involved in tribal politics. He later faced opposition from some tribal leadership when Catawba voting practices were legally challenged.

Sanders worked closely with Bill Harris, the current Catawba Indian chief, to improve living conditions and opportunities for tribe members, pushing for greater Native American rights and for the tribe itself.

"We were working from the outside trying to get change," Harris said. "Fred was a person who was able to see two sides to every situation."

Brent Burgin, director of the archives at University of South Carolina at Lancaster, called Sanders a "consummate politician," adding that "he never stopped, he was on the go the whole time."

---

[344] Fred Sanders Biography.

Burgin worked with Sanders to curate the state's largest collection of archival documents created by a Native American. Sanders gathered 40 years' worth of legal, federal and state documents that shed light on tribal politics and history for USC-Lancaster's Native American Studies Archive.

Sanders played a large role in the Catawba Indian Nation's battle to regain federal recognition, which began in 1973 after the tribe's federal status was terminated in 1959. The nation settled its land claims with federal, state and local governments in 1993, giving up rights to portions of land in the state, but regaining federal status along with an economic development grant.

The Catawba Indian Nation remains the state's sole federally recognized tribe with close to 3,000 members.

But the deal that the nation brokered wasn't ideal for Sanders. "He basically felt it was a flawed deal, he thought the Catawba could have gotten a better deal," Burgin said.

Harris said Sanders considered the "limited" agreement "a blessing and a curse," and was constantly vouching for greater self-rule such as the nation's rights to operate its own police force. The tribe is currently locked in a legal battle with the state over gaming rights to operate a casino in York County.

A graveside service will be held in the cemetery behind the Church of Jesus Christ of the Latter-day Saints, Catawba Ward, at 3 p.m. Tuesday.

**PHOTO 368 - EARLY FRED SANDERS WITH WIFE AND CHILDREN AND AS CHIEF**

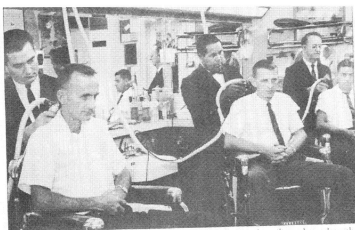

After E. Fred Sanders (also seen on page 43) returned home from the military, he took up the trade of barber. He attended the Salt Lake City Vocational School from 1961 to 1962. He returned to South Carolina in 1964. For a time, he worked at the Thomas Barber Shop in Rock Hill. He is at the center of the photograph. (Courtesy of E. Fred Sanders.)

88

**PHOTO 369 – NEWSPAPER CLIPPING OF EARLY FRED SANDERS IN BARBER SHOP**

**PHOTO 370 - FRED SANDERS AT THE 1973 SHOW POTTERS**

The next child of John Idle and Arzada Brown Sanders is William Sanders.

(i) William Emory Sanders born 7 October 1928, Catawba Indian Reservation, York County, South Carolina and died 5 June 1989, Rock Hill, York, South Carolina. He married a white woman.

(j) Charlotte Roberta Sanders born 19 January 1932, Rock Hill, York, South Carolina. She married Earl H. Honeycutt.

(k) Vivian Sanders born 31 January 1933, [345]South Carolina.

(l) Anna Mohave Sanders born 15 September 1937,[346]South Carolina.

\*\*\*\*\*\*\*\*\*\*\*\*\*\*\*\*\*\*\*\*\*\*\*\*\*\*\*\*\*\*\*\*\*\*\*\*\*\*\*\*\*\*

7. Lewis Ernest Sanders born 18 July 1895, married first on April 22, 1917, Cora Brown, daughter of John and Rachel Wysie George Brown, she died October 9, 1918;[347] he married second Jennie Canty on 25 April 1925, daughter of Frank and Dorothy Price Canty; Lewis married third Minnie Florence Harris on 6 April 1932, the daughter of Benjamin Perry and Mary Dovie George Harris. Lewis's children are Melvin, son of Cora Brown Sanders; Perry, Freddie Grace and Velda are by Minnie Harris. Louis died 5 February 1936.[348]

(a). Melvin Sanders born 23 January 1918, he died 10 October 1918.[349] He died in the influenza epidemic the day after his mother, Cora died.[350]

(b). Perry Sanders born 3 August 1929 married Bobbie, white.

(c). Freddie Grace Sanders born 5 September 1933

(d). Velda Sanders born 1 October 1936[351] in the 1961 roll she is called Velda Sanders Harris.

8. Sarah Ann Sanders born 1897, Catawba Indian Nation, York, South Carolina and death not known.

9. Andrew Behrman Sanders born 10 September 1989, Rock Hill, York, South Carolina and died 27 October 1898, Rock Hill, York, South Carolina

\*\*\*\*\*\*\*\*\*\*\*\*\*\*\*\*\*\*\*\*\*\*\*\*\*\*\*\*\*\*\*

---

[345] Biography of Fred Sanders in April, 1999 7th Generation News.
[346] Membership rolls 1941-1958.
[347] Catawba Cemetery Records.
[348] Catawba Cemetery Records.
[349] Ibid
[350] Ibid
[351] Membership rolls.

**Louis Harris Gordon, the third son of Lucinda Harris, his father was Stell Gordon**.

C. Louis-Lewis Harris Gordon, born in August 1869, Fort Mill, York, South Carolina and he died 13 October 1926, Catawba, York, South Carolina. He worked at the industrial Mill at Rock Hill, South Carolina. Lewis married Sallie Brown (1865-1952), daughter of Margaret Ayers George and Joe Cherry, a white man. Sallie is a sister to Chief Samuel Taylor Blue. Sallie went by the name of Brown; because her father was John William Brown.. Louis-Lewis had two children, Ruth and Lewis Gordon.

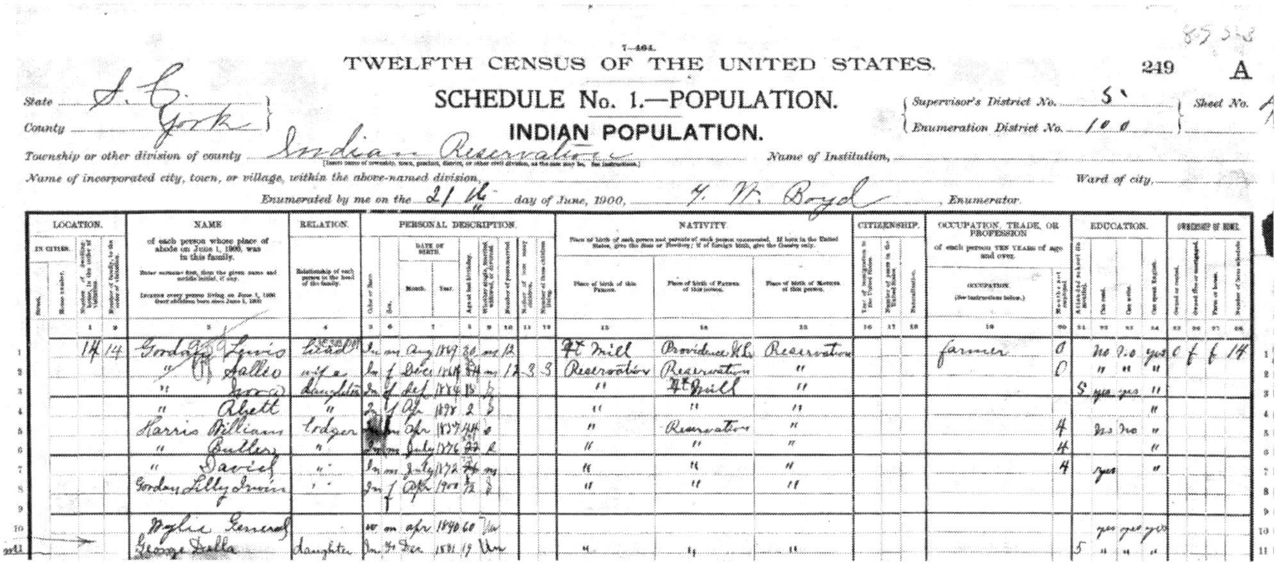

TWELFTH CENSUS OF THE UNITED STATES. 249 A

SCHEDULE No. 1.—POPULATION.

INDIAN POPULATION.

State: S. C.
County: York
Township or other division of county: Indian Reservation
Supervisor's District No. 5
Enumeration District No. 100
Enumerated by me on the 21 day of June, 1900, T. W. Boyd, Enumerator.

| Line | Dwelling | Family | Name | Relation | Color | Sex | Month | Year | Age | Marital | Years married | Children born | Children living | Birthplace of person | Birthplace of father | Birthplace of mother | Occupation | Months not employed | Can read | Can write | Speaks English | Owned/rented | Free/mortgaged | Farm/house | Farm schedule |
|---|---|---|---|---|---|---|---|---|---|---|---|---|---|---|---|---|---|---|---|---|---|---|---|---|---|
| 1 | 14 | 14 | Gordon Lewis | Head | In | m | Aug | 1869 | 30 | m | 12 | | | Ft Mill | Providence N.C. | Reservation | farmer | 0 | no | no | yes | O | F | F | 14 |
| 2 | | | " Sallie | wife | In | f | Dec | 1864 | 34 | m | 12 | 3 | 3 | Reservation | Reservation | " | | 0 | " | " | " | | | | |
| 3 | | | " Nora | daughter | In | f | Sep | 1884 | 15 | S | | | | " | Ft Mill | " | | 5 | yes | yes | " | | | | |
| 4 | | | " Rhett | " | In | f | Apr | 1898 | 2 | S | | | | " | " | " | | | | | " | | | | |
| 5 | | | Harris William | Lodger | In | m | Apr | 1857 | 44 | S | | | | " | Reservation | " | | 4 | no | no | " | | | | |
| 6 | | | " Butler | " | In | m | July | 1876 | 23 | S | | | | " | " | " | | 4 | | | " | | | | |
| 7 | | | " David | " | In | m | July | 1872 | 27 | m | | | | " | " | " | | 4 | yes | | " | | | | |
| 8 | | | Gordon Lilly Irvin | " | In | f | Apr | 1900 | 1/12 | S | | | | " | " | " | | | | | | | | | |
| 10 | | | Wylie General | | W | m | Apr | 1840 | 60 | Wd | | | | | | | | | yes | yes | yes | | | | |
| 11 | | | George Della | daughter | In | f | Dec | 1881 | 19 | Wd | | | | " | " | " | | 5 | " | " | " | | | | |

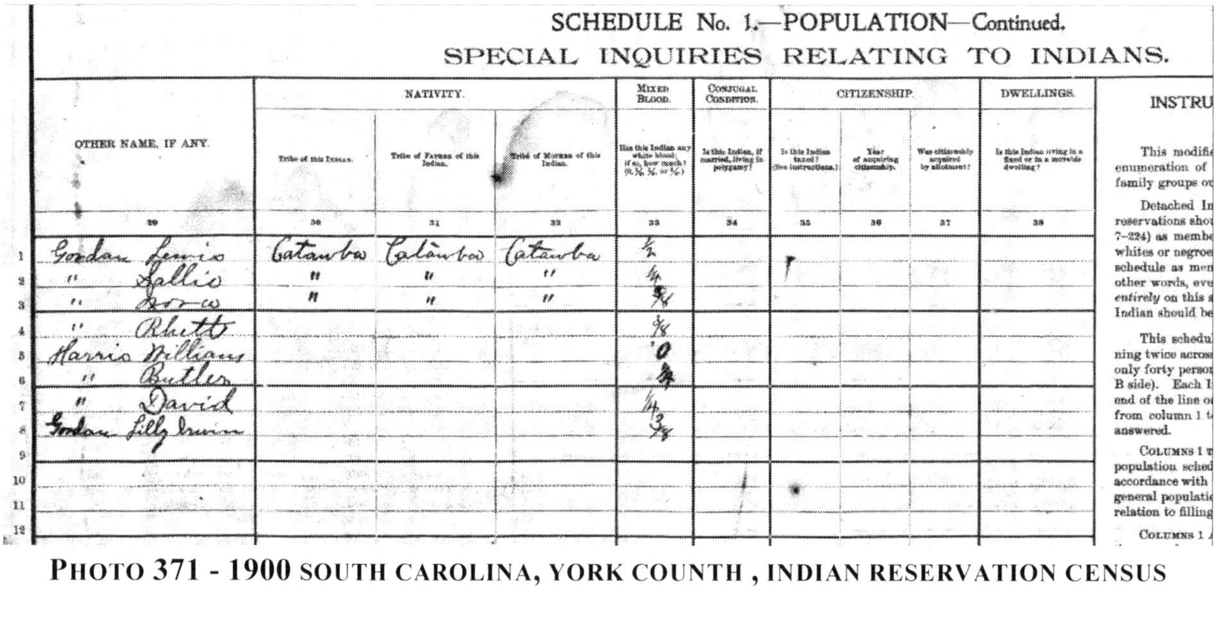

SCHEDULE No. 1.—POPULATION—Continued.

SPECIAL INQUIRIES RELATING TO INDIANS.

| Line | Other name, if any | Tribe of this Indian | Tribe of father of this Indian | Tribe of mother of this Indian | Has this Indian any white blood; if so, how much? | Conjugal condition | Citizenship | Dwellings |
|---|---|---|---|---|---|---|---|---|
| 1 | Gordan Lewis | Catawba | Catawba | Catawba | 1/2 | | | |
| 2 | " Sallie | " | " | " | 1/4 | | | |
| 3 | " Nora | " | " | " | 3/8 | | | |
| 4 | " Rhett | | | | 3/8 | | | |
| 5 | Harris William | | | | 0 | | | |
| 6 | " Butler | | | | [illegible] | | | |
| 7 | " David | | | | 1/4 | | | |
| 8 | Gordan Lilly Irvin | | | | 3/8 | | | |

INSTRU... This modifi... enumeration of... family groups o... Detached In... reservations sho... 7-224) as membe... whites or negroe... schedule as me... other words, eve... *entirely* on this... Indian should be... This schedu... ning twice acros... only forty perso... B side). Each I... end of the line o... from column 1 t... answered. COLUMNS 1 t... population sched... accordance with... general populati... relation to filling... COLUMNS 1...

**PHOTO 371 - 1900 SOUTH CAROLINA, YORK COUNTH , INDIAN RESERVATION CENSUS**

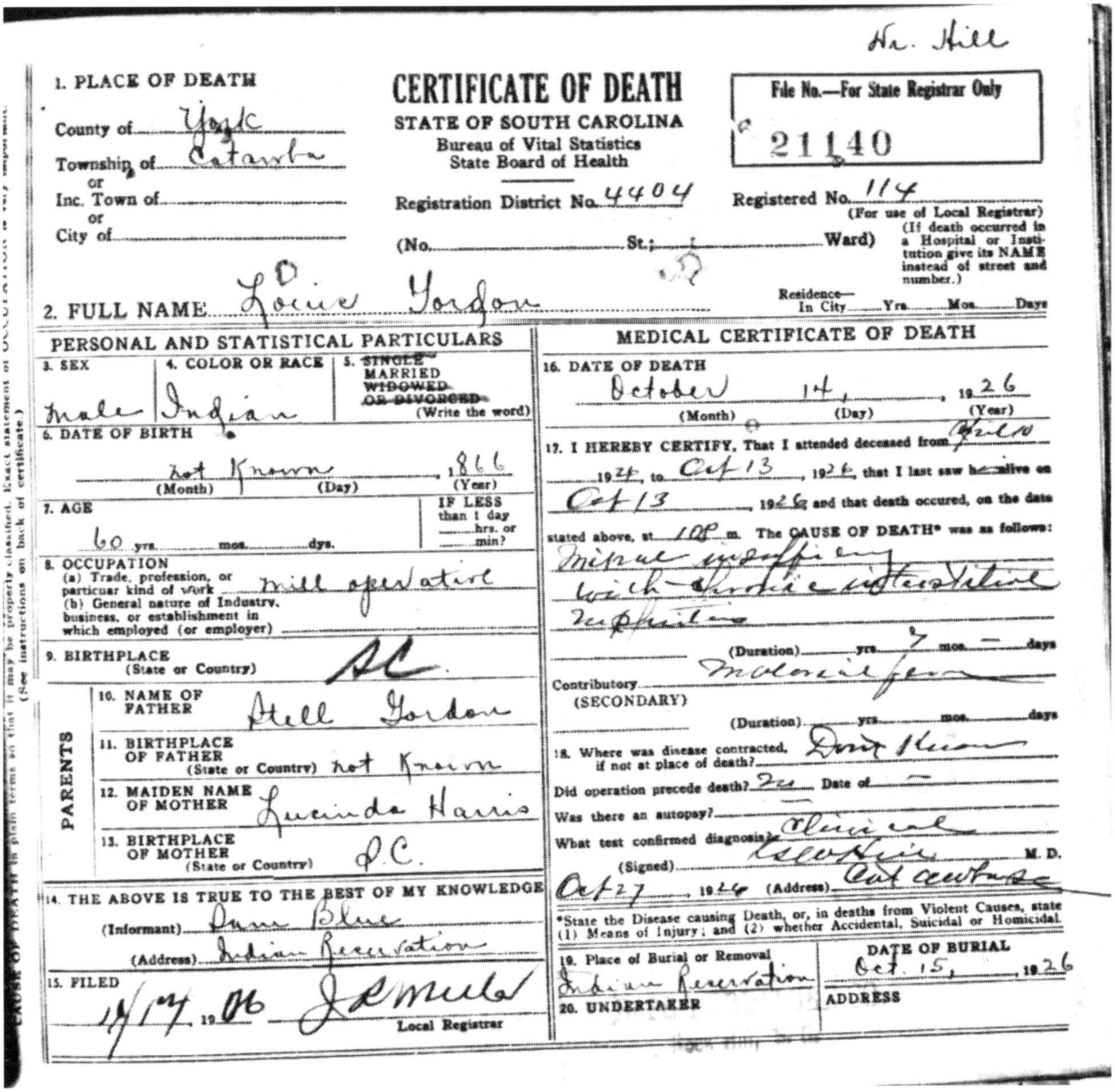

Hr. Hill

1. PLACE OF DEATH
County of York
Township of Catawba
or
Inc. Town of
or
City of

CERTIFICATE OF DEATH
STATE OF SOUTH CAROLINA
Bureau of Vital Statistics
State Board of Health

File No.—For State Registrar Only
21140

Registration District No. 4404
Registered No. 114
(For use of Local Registrar)
(No. St.; Ward) (If death occurred in a Hospital or Institution give its NAME instead of street and number.)

2. FULL NAME Louie Gordon
Residence— In City Yrs. Mos. Days

PERSONAL AND STATISTICAL PARTICULARS

3. SEX male
4. COLOR OR RACE Indian
5. ~~SINGLE~~ MARRIED ~~WIDOWED OR DIVORCED~~ (Write the word)
6. DATE OF BIRTH not Known (Month) (Day) 1866 (Year)
7. AGE 60 yrs. mos. dys. IF LESS than 1 day hrs. or min?
8. OCCUPATION
(a) Trade, profession, or particular kind of work mill operative
(b) General nature of Industry, business, or establishment in which employed (or employer)
9. BIRTHPLACE (State or Country) SC

PARENTS
10. NAME OF FATHER Stell Gordon
11. BIRTHPLACE OF FATHER (State or Country) not Known
12. MAIDEN NAME OF MOTHER Lucinda Harris
13. BIRTHPLACE OF MOTHER (State or Country) S.C.

14. THE ABOVE IS TRUE TO THE BEST OF MY KNOWLEDGE
(Informant) Dave Blue
(Address) Indian Reservation

15. FILED 11/17, 1926 J. R. Mills Local Registrar

MEDICAL CERTIFICATE OF DEATH

16. DATE OF DEATH October 14, 1926 (Month) (Day) (Year)
17. I HEREBY CERTIFY, That I attended deceased from April 1924, to Oct 13, 1926, that I last saw him alive on Oct 13, 1926 and that death occured, on the date stated above, at 10 P m. The CAUSE OF DEATH* was as follows:
Mitral insufficiency with chronic interstitial nephritis
(Duration) yrs. 7 mos. — days
Contributory (SECONDARY) malarial fever
(Duration) yrs. mos. days
18. Where was disease contracted, if not at place of death? Don't know
Did operation precede death? no Date of —
Was there an autopsy?
What test confirmed diagnosis? Clinical
(Signed) [illegible] M.D.
Oct 27, 1926 (Address) Catawba
*State the Disease causing Death, or, in deaths from Violent Causes, state (1) Means of Injury; and (2) whether Accidental, Suicidal or Homicidal.
19. Place of Burial or Removal Indian Reservation
DATE OF BURIAL Oct. 15, 1926
20. UNDERTAKER
ADDRESS

**PHOTO 372 – CERTIFICATE OF DEATH FOR LOUIE GORDON**

a. Ruth Lucinda Gordon was born 29 April 1898, Catawba, York, South Carolina. She was called Rhett. She married John Jefferson Ayers, son of Jefferson Davis and Harriet Berry Ayers.

b. Lewis Ervin Gordon was born 9 April 1900. He married in 1916, Eliza Jane Harris, daughter of Epps and Margaret Elizabeth Harris Harris. He was a grocery clerk. Lewis died on 23 March 1954.

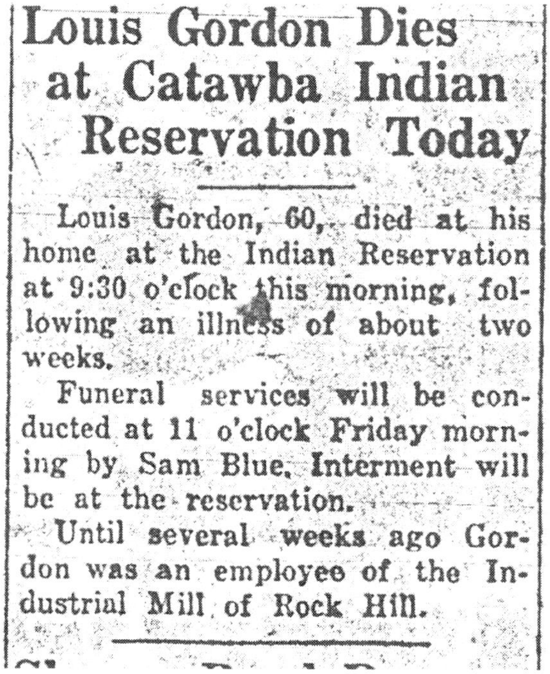

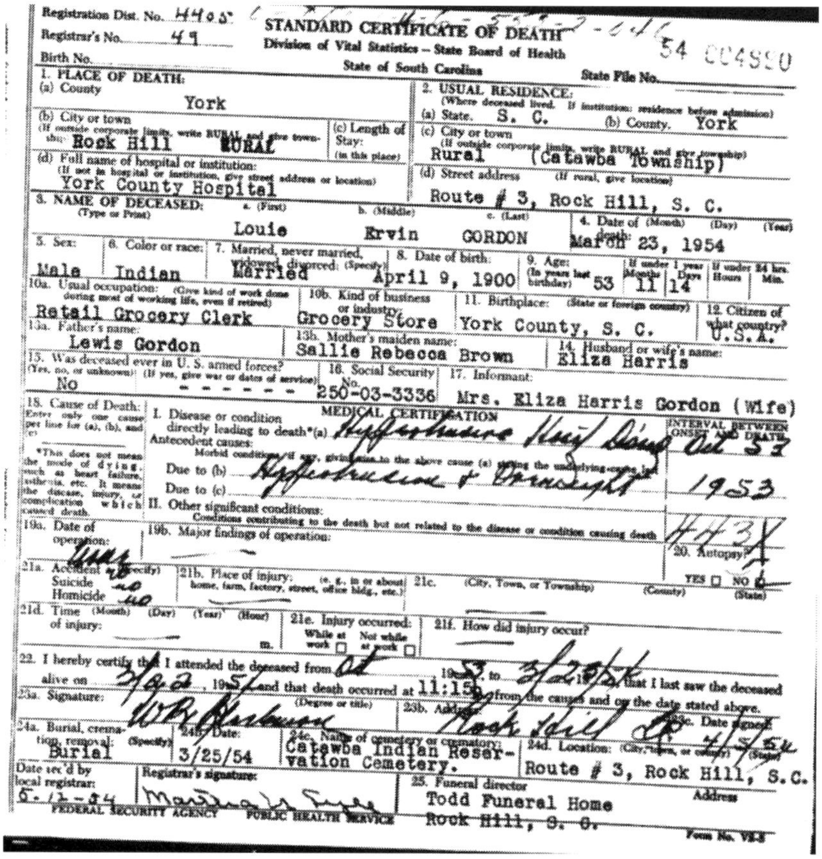

# Louis Gordon Dies at Catawba Indian Reservation Today

Louis Gordon, 60, died at his home at the Indian Reservation at 9:30 o'clock this morning, following an illness of about two weeks.

Funeral services will be conducted at 11 o'clock Friday morning by Sam Blue. Interment will be at the reservation.

Until several weeks ago Gordon was an employee of the Industrial Mill of Rock Hill.

**PHOTO 373 - NEWSPAPER CLIPPING OF DEATH OF LOUIS GORDON**

Registration Dist. No. 4405
Registrar's No. 49
Birth No.

STANDARD CERTIFICATE OF DEATH
Division of Vital Statistics – State Board of Health
State of South Carolina
State File No. 54 004880

1. PLACE OF DEATH: (a) County: York
(b) City or town (If outside corporate limits, write RURAL and give township): Rock Hill RURAL
(c) Length of Stay: (in this place)
(d) Full name of hospital or institution (If not in hospital or institution, give street address or location): York County Hospital

2. USUAL RESIDENCE: (Where deceased lived. If institution: residence before admission)
(a) State. S. C. (b) County. York
(c) City or town (If outside corporate limits, write RURAL and give township): Rural (Catawba Township)
(d) Street address (If rural, give location): Route # 3, Rock Hill, S. C.

3. NAME OF DECEASED: (Type or Print) a. (First) Louie b. (Middle) Ervin c. (Last) GORDON
4. Date of death: (Month) (Day) (Year) March 23, 1954
5. Sex: Male
6. Color or race: Indian
7. Married, never married, widowed, divorced: (Specify) Married
8. Date of birth: April 9, 1900
9. Age: (In years last birthday) 53 If under 1 year: Months 11 Days 14 If under 24 hrs.: Hours Min.
10a. Usual occupation: (Give kind of work done during most of working life, even if retired) Retail Grocery Clerk
10b. Kind of business or industry: Grocery Store
11. Birthplace: (State or foreign country) York County, S. C.
12. Citizen of what country? U.S.A.
13a. Father's name: Lewis Gordon
13b. Mother's maiden name: Sallie Rebecca Brown
14. Husband or wife's name: Eliza Harris
15. Was deceased ever in U. S. armed forces? (Yes, no, or unknown) No (If yes, give war or dates of service) - - - - - -
16. Social Security No. 250-03-3336
17. Informant: Mrs. Eliza Harris Gordon (Wife)

MEDICAL CERTIFICATION
18. Cause of Death: Enter only one cause per line for (a), (b), and (c)
I. Disease or condition directly leading to death*(a) [illegible]
Antecedent causes: Morbid conditions, if any, giving rise to the above cause (a) stating the underlying cause last.
Due to (b) [illegible]
Due to (c)
Interval between onset and death: Oct 53 / 1953
*This does not mean the mode of dying, such as heart failure, asthenia, etc. It means the disease, injury, or complication which caused death.
II. Other significant conditions: Conditions contributing to the death but not related to the disease or condition causing death
19a. Date of operation: [illegible]
19b. Major findings of operation:
20. Autopsy? YES ☐ NO
21a. Accident, Suicide, Homicide (Specify) no
21b. Place of injury: (e. g., in or about home, farm, factory, street, office bldg., etc.)
21c. (City, Town, or Township) (County) (State)
21d. Time of injury: (Month) (Day) (Year) (Hour) m.
21e. Injury occurred: While at work ☐ Not while at work ☐
21f. How did injury occur?
22. I hereby certify that I attended the deceased from Oct 1953 to 3/20/54 that I last saw the deceased alive on 3/22, 1954 and that death occurred at 11:15 from the causes and on the date stated above.
23a. Signature: [illegible] (Degree or title)
23b. Address: Rock Hill SC
23c. Date signed: 4/5/54
24a. Burial, cremation, removal: (Specify) Burial
24b. Date: 3/25/54
24c. Name of cemetery or crematory: Catawba Indian Reservation Cemetery.
24d. Location: (City, town, or county) (State) Route # 3, Rock Hill, S.C.
Date rec'd by local registrar: 5-12-54
Registrar's signature: [illegible]
25. Funeral director: Todd Funeral Home
Address: Rock Hill, S. C.
FEDERAL SECURITY AGENCY PUBLIC HEALTH SERVICE
Form No. VS-3

**PHOTO 374 - CERTIFICATE OF DEATH FOR LOUIE ERVIN GORDON**

**PHOTO 375 – GLADYS GORDON**

(1) Gladys Gordon was born 22 August 1921, married Howard Thomas, white. She had two children, Larry Allen born in 1950 and Louis Scott Thomas born in 1957.[352]

**William Sawyer-Harris was the son of Sarah Lucinda and Sawyer.**

D. William Sawyer-Harris born 1880, Catawba Indian Land and died 26 June 1917, Columbia, South Carolina (died in hospital for the Insane). He was the last child of Sarah Lucinda Harris. He died in a hospital for the insane in Columbia, South Carolina on June 26, 1917.[353]

**PHOTO 376 - CERTIFICATE OF DEATH FOR WILLIAM SAWYER**

---

[352] 1958-61 membership rolls
[353] Blumer page 263 article 2003.

## Chapter 11   Peter Harris Family

I. Chuppepaw[354] -Cuppepaw-Chippapaw[355] —Capt. Johney-John Harris, King of the Catawba was probably born around 1700. He was probably descended from Iscountgonita, since Catawba Chieftains were lineal descendants of one another.

John is the first Harris mentioned in connection with another Catawba King, Iscountgonita, who with John Harris headed the list of eleven of the chief men among the Catawba and Cheraw, around 1739.[356]

Capt. Johnny was a War Captain of the Catawba on August 19, 1735. On October 28, 1738, John Harris, King of the Charraws was commissioned along with Jeamy Harris of Old Sugar Town. His Catawba name was Chuppepaw, Cuppepaw etc. He signed a treaty in 1756 between Virginia and the Catawba, and was headman in December 1757. He also signed the letter from King Hagler, telling of small pox in October 1759.

Chuppepaw-Cuppepaw- Chippapaw --Capt. Johney-John Harris, King of Catawba probably born around 1700, his son was Capt Jamey or Pickahassakehe . His Mark follows:

II. George Harris probably born around 1750 listed on addendum of Drennan's Pay bill of 1780.

III. Capt Jeamy Harris of Old Sugar Town, Capt Jeamy of Sugar Town (Capt. Sugar Jamy) and Big Jamey, were probably all names for James Harris. He was probably born around 1720, thus about 50 during the Revolutionary War. He probably had a son also called Capt. Sugar Jamey.

Capt. Jeamy -?? Jemmie  (Harris)-Pickahassakehe of Sugar Town probably born around 1710.  His son is Wateree Jemmie.  His Mark follows:

---

[354]Watson page 31
[355] Blumer page 49 article 384.
[356] Merrell page 235.

A. Capt. Jeamy -? Jemmie (Harris)-Pickahassakehe of Sugar Town[357] probably born around 1710, mentioned until 1759

    1. Wateree Jemmie-Captain (Sugar) Jenny - Capt. Sugar Jamy (Harris) probably born around 1730, his mark follows: He served in the Revolutionary War, and signed the 1759 petition from Hagler.

    Wateree Jemmie-Captain (Sugar) Jenny - Capt.  Sugar Jamy
    (Harris) probably born around 1730, his marks follows:  1765 letter 1759 Petition

    B. Jesse Harris received payments for tracts within Indian lands between 1808 and 1809.

IV. Peter ThusSeeWontSee or Thus Saw Wontree[358] Harris - Peter Harris was born in 1752, and died 6 December 1823 at Fort Mill, SC.[359]  He supposedly was orphaned by the smallpox epidemic and raised by the Spratts. He is buried in the Spratt graveyard. He received rents for lands on the East Side of the Catawba River between 1808 and 1829. Capt. Peter or ThusSawWontsee- Peter Harris applied for a pension for Revolutionary War service on December 6, 1822.[360] He gave the name of Broad River to Dr. Flannagan, as his birthplace.

An appeal written in 1843 by William Crafts for Old Peter Harris:

    "I am one of the lingering survivors of an almost extinguished race. Our graves will soon be our only habitation. I am one of the few stalks which still remain in the field after the tempest of the Revolution is passed. I fought the British for your sake. The British have disappeared nor have I gained by their defeat. I pursue the deer for subsistence; the deer are disappearing and I must starve. God ordained men for the forest and my ambition is the shade, but the strength of my arm decays and my feet fail me in the chase. The hand which fought the British for your liberty is now open for your relief. In my youth I bled in battle that you might be independent; let not my heart in my old age bleed for the want of your

---

[357] Merrell, page 126.
[358] Merrell page 126
[359] Wesley White listed under full-bloods
[360] Blumer page 117 article 870.

commiseration."[361] He also told about how the Catawba had captured a gun in the battle at Stono.[362] He kept that gun as long as he lived.

He married, according to some sources, Betsy Dudgeon or Prissy Bullen. It is most likely that both were his women. Prissy Bullen would be related to Jamey Bullen, and Betsy Dudgeon would be related to John Dudgeon.

His will states that his rents go to "Betsy Harris, during her lifetime, and after her death, her son, (William) if he out lived her."[363] According to Spratt, Prissy Bullen was the mother of David Harris.[364] He was also called D. Bullin.

Prissy bequeathed all her rents to John Genet Brown, except for a small bit that James Miller and James Moore had, for a little boy.[365] Betsy Dudgeon Harris had a son, I believe that this child was William Harris, who married Sally Ayers, and was a headman around 1839.

Peter went on tour to England after his service in the Revolutionary War. He survived a small pox epidemic about 1759, and was left an orphan to be raised by Thomas Spratt. He received rents in 1813, and was an interpreter on a petition of headmen dated November 28, 1815.[366] He signed a petition in 1821 as Captain Peter Harris.

When Peter was dying, he told the story of his one regret in his life. That in the Revolutionary War, Cornwallis' army was traveling through the area. As a British soldier knelt at the spring to drink, having laid his gun aside, Peter had killed him. He considered this act the act of a coward.

**PHOTO 377 – BACK OF HEADSTONE OF PETER HARRIS - BURIAL: SPRATT GRAVEYARD, FORT MILL, YORK COUNTY, SOUTH CAROLINA**

---

[361] Merrell page 218
[362] Merrell page 560
[363] Watson page 31
[364] Watson page 31.
[365] Watson page 32
[366] Watson page 31

Peter was the father of at least three children, William Harris born around 1800, David Harris born 1805 and Polly Harris born 1814. Polly later became Polly Harris Ayers, then either Polly Otis-Oders or Polly Harris Ayers Tims. Therefore, Peter and Betsy Dudgeon had William Harris; and Peter and Prissy Bullen had David Harris, and Polly Harris could have belonged to either or neither one

A. William Harris, born around 1800 married Sally Ayers, born 1799[367] the daughter of General Jacob Ayers. William succeeded General Jacob Ayers around 1837. In 1838, after the death of Jacob Ayers and John Ayers, William and Sally sold the lands in Kings Bottoms.

Kings Bottoms was considered sacred, and possibly the burial place of the old Kings.

After this sale, all the lands of the Catawba were in the hands of the whites.[368] Ex-Governor Allston named Sally as a model mother in 1860. William appears to have died shortly after 1839, when he stopped signing leases.

1. Nancy Harris, born May 1835,[369] married John 'Mush' Harris, son of David Harris and Nancy George.[370] Nancy was one of five Catawba women who were named as model mother of the year. She is also listed as a Confederate Widow up to 1896. Her children will be found under John 'Mush' Harris.

2. Absolem-Epp Harris was born 1840.[371] In June 19, 1875, he received from the Indian Agent R. L. Crook under Ep. and under Absolem Harris; he received $10.00 on April 10. In 1881, he received $6.66. I believe that under the name Ephaso,[372] he received $2.00 on July 29, 1875.

Epp kept the Ferry at some point; Mrs. Dunlap mentions him and a Sanders as keeping it in 1899. He married first Mary George, daughter of Little Patsy George;[373] second, Martha Jane White, daughter of George and Peggy Quash- Mursh White, this was her first marriage.[374] Epp Harris supposedly served in the Confederate army during the Civil War. He died July 9, 1916. Epp and Martha Jane White Harris had one daughter.

a. Margaret Elizabeth Harris, born August 15,1879. Margaret married James Harris Jr. as his second wife, son of James and Sarah Jane Ayers Harris.

---

[367] Catawba census of 1849
[368] Blumer pages 146-151
[369] Catawba Branch Records and Census records.
[370] Catawba Branch Records.
[371] Ibid
[372] This name was probably just a white mistake, the names of Indians didn't matter much.
[373] Watson pages 53 & 54.
[374] Patterson genealogy.

B. David Harris born 1805 and married Nancy George, born 1809, the daughter of William and Old Nancy Canty George, she was called Little Nancy George in the 1849 census.[375] David was a Captain in the Catawba government in the years 1838-1839. By 1840, he was a Colonel. He was one of the signers of the Nations Ford Treaty in 1840. Another treaty lists him as Major David Harris.[376] In 1847, he was in North Carolina; in 1849 he was back in Greenville District, South Carolina. He also was connected with the Echota Mission in North Carolina.[377] He signed a petition in 1850 for land in Greenville, South Carolina. David Harris, John Joe and Sam Scott were among those Catawba who promised to join the others in Haywood, North Carolina. The first two had families, Sam Scott had none.

"These 3 men were the most trifling, lazy and in temperate Indians belonging to the Tribe. There are several women and children attached to them by relationship and similarity of habits."[378] According to Hutchison, "I furnished them with flour, others with meat and other necessaries. They reached Yorkville in three or four days, had one gun among them, which they pledged in York for fifty cents to buy liquor with, and finally went off without it. They left York and went about 20 miles to the edge of Lincoln Co, where liquor was plenty and still-houses common."[379]

David is alive in the 1854 census, so he had to have died after that.

**PHOTO 378 – HEADSTONE FOR JAMES THOMAS HARRIS**

---

[375] Catawba Branch records.
[376] Brown page 306
[377] 1849 census.
[378] Brown page 312.
[379] Brown page 310

1. James Thomas Harris, born 1828,[380] York County, South Carolina and he died 23 May 1874, Catawba Indian Reservation, Richland, South Carolina. He married Sarah Jane Ayers, daughter of Rebecca Marsh and Edmund Ayers.[381] She was born 31 July, 1829.[382] James was chief after Allen Harris died in 1859. He also served as chief in 1887-1889.

He enlisted in Company H. of the 12th Regiment, along with his brother John. He was a cook, and was wounded at Sharpsburg on September 17, 1862. He was paroled as a prisoner of war on May 16, 1864 in Charlotte, North Carolina.

Either James jr. or James sr. received money from the Indian Agent R. L. Crook in 1881, for $13.32.

**Civil War: Yorkville Enquirer**:

The Indian Land Guards were organized for Confederate service at Rock Hill on 8/3/1861. On August 8th the Yorkville Enquirer ran the following account and list of members:

This District has a voting population of 2500, not more but often less, and now has in the field four large organized companies, besides those who have gone to the assistance of neighboring Districts and of N.C.

We know that the South Battalion of the 46th Regt of S.C.M., has 120 men or more in the field, belonging to companies gone from the state and N.C. It now reports a company for the war.

As this company (The Indian Land Guards) has not yet obtained a hundred names, others will be received until the company is full.

Sarah had stated that she had eight children, with three living in 1910 and only seven are accounted for. Infant Harris, James Thomas Harris, Martha Jane Harris, Anthony "Andy" Harris, Mattie Harris, David Adam Toad Harris, Isabella Harris

     a. child born before 1853.

---

[380] 1849 census
[381] Catwaba Branch Records.
[382] Watson page 36.

**PHOTO 379 - JAMES THOMAS HARRIS**

b. James Thomas Harris Jr. born May 1858[383] Rock Hill, York, South Carolina and died 31 August 1912, Catawba Indian Reservation, South Carolina. He married first Fannie Whitesides, daughter of Thomas Whitesides and Eliza Scott.[384] They had no children. Fannie is dead by 1900; James married second Margaret Elizabeth Harris born 15 August 1879, South Carolina and died 8 December 1926, York, South Carolina, daughter of Absolem or Epp and Martha Jane White Harris.[385]

Wes White describes James JR as 5 foot, 6 inches tall. White also states that James could "speak the language very little." James was Chief of the Nation in the years 1885, 1889-1894, 1896-1898,[386] and in 1896 he became the first chief to bring suit against the state of South Carolina over the Treaty of Nation Ford. He was also the founder of the Catawba Indian School. While he was Chief, in March 1887, he visited the Governor, Richardson, in an attempt to bar 20 Catawba living outside of SC from receiving a share of the $800.00 appropriation.[387]He was one of the first four converts to the Church of Jesus Christ of Latter Day Saints. He and his wife Fannie were baptized 1883 along with Fannie's sister Mary Jane and her husband James Henry Watts and James Patterson.[388] James operated a ferry across the Catawba River, according to Joseph Willey in 1883-85. He resided in Vicksburg, Mississippi during an illness in 1888. James died August 31, 1912.

---

[383] Catawba branch Records.
[384] Patterson-Canty genealogy
[385] Watson page 39 & 40.
[386] Blumer pages
[387] Blumer page 196
[388] Pinkney Head journal.

**PHOTO 380 – HEADSTONE FOR JAMES T HARRIS –**

**Inscription:**    Died age 54 years. Son of James Harris and Sarah Jane Ayers Harris. Chief of Catawba Nation 1885 & 1889-1894 & 1896-1896. He was the first Chief to bring suit against South Carolina over the Treaty of Nation Ford. Founder of Catawba Indian School in 1896.  James Thomas Harris died 23 May 1874 Margaret Harris.

**PHOTO 381 - MARGARET HARRIS**

Margaret Elizabeth Harris Harris – Burial: Catawba Indian Nation Cemetery Rock Hill, York County, South Carolina

Margaret Harris and James Thomas Harris had seven children: Jesse, Jacob, Eliza, Georgia, John Thomas, Robert and George Furman Harris.

(1) Jesse Allen Harris, born 15 April 1899, Catawba, York, South Carolina and died 19 November 1977, Catawba, York, South Carolina. He married 7 January 1942, Jennie Canty Sanders, daughter of Frank and Dorothy Price Canty.[389] In 1934, Jesse was the first person on the scene of the "accidental" death of Henry Canty. Jesse Harris was charged with shooting and killing Kirk Sanders in 1945. This was his half-sister Sarah's husband He was sentenced to 4 years for manslaughter on November 28, 1945. On June 231958, Jesse shot George Humphrey with a 4-10 Shotgun. He was charged with assault and battery with intent to kill. He received a 7-year sentence. Jesse and Jennie were divorced and he was in the penitentiary in 1958.

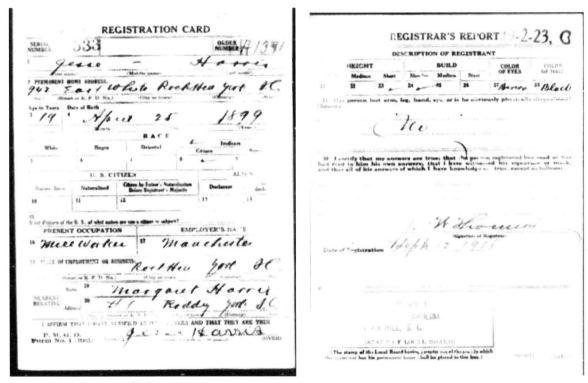

**PHOTO 382 – WWI REGISTRATION CARD FOR JESSE ALLEN HARRIS**

(2) Jacob Harris born 1900, Catawba, York, South Carolina. He passed away before 1910, Catawba, York, South Carolina.

---

[389] Catawba Branch Records.

**PHOTO 383 - ELIZA JANE HARRIS**

(3) Eliza Jane Harris, born April 30, 1902, married Louis-Lewis Ervin Gordon, son of Lewis and Sallie Brown Gordon. She died November 15, 1960. She was a potter. Children will be found under Gordon.

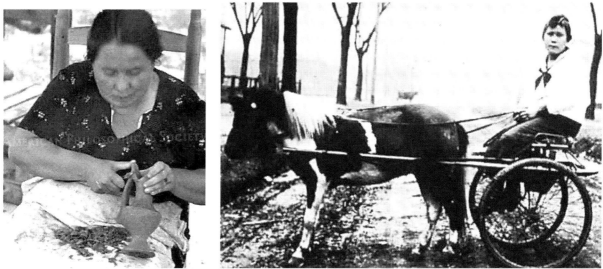

**PHOTO 384 – ELIZA JANE HARRIS -1ST MAKING POTTERY – 2ND IN A BUGGY**

**From the Missionary Journal of Mary Barus**

"A dream of seeing the Indians

Another night I dreamed we were at our journeys end a house full of the Indians were out to meet us. I heard them singing a song where two voices led and in duett (sic) and the rest joined in chorus. I also saw very plainly four indian women.

Jesus Lover of my soule (sic)

I also told Orlando this dream & that I was sure I could recognize them if I ever saw them. Both these dreams or manifestations were proven to my satisfaction to have been given me by the spirit of the Lord for sure enough after we arrived at the Indian Nation the first night there were the people I had seen assembled. Only three of the women were there but I saw the fourth one a few days after. Their features were familiar when I met them. They were sisters Watts, Blue, Gordon & Brown. They sang many songs that night but they did not sing "Jesus Lover of my soule (sic)" with duett (sic) and chorus till I taught it to them & I recognized it just as soon as they sang it as the one I had heard in my dream. This was a very strong testimony to me and I thanked my heavenly Father for the same. These dreams were a source of comfort to me since I of course dreaded the thoughts of taking our family among the Indians. My idea of an Indian was of course the ones I had seen who wore their long unkept (sic) hair – male & female – and with blankets & moccasins.

I was thoroughly surprised tho to find a people speaking the English language & natural songsters –"

**PHOTO 385 – GEORGIA HENRIETTA HARRIS**

(4) Georgia Henrietta Harris, born 29 July 1905, Catawba, South Carolina and died 30 January 1997, Dallas, Paulding, Georgia, United States. She married William Douglas Harris, on April 23, 1927, son of James David and Maggie Price Harris.

"I was born on July 29, 1905 in Lancaster County, South Carolina, not far from the Catawba reservation. At that time, my father was a county paid ferryman on the river. The ferry provided the only way to cross the river from Lancaster and York Counties. No bridge existed until years later. Our family consisted of my parents James and Margaret Harris, my grandparents, Epp and Martha Jane Harris and my sister Eliza and brother Jesse. I had two brothers, Thomas and Robert Lee, who were younger than me, but they died in July 1912, only five days apart. Dad died just six weeks later, and a second brother Furnman was born four months and seven days later.

Life among the Catawbas at that time was hard. Crowded onto a small reservation, most of our people managed as subsistence farmers. Like the other men in our tribe, my dad farmed, and he kept a garden to provide our family with produce. We also had two cows, some chickens and four hogs. These provided us with milk, eggs and pork for the winter months. In 1912, we also had two mules in addition to the other livestock. After my father's death, mother sold a mule and some hogs because she was unable to care for them. These were difficult years for us, and mother had to work hard to provide for her four children so she rented the farm out on halves, and she and Jesse did all the farming and got half of what was gown. Back then, the Indians made pottery during the summer months, but my mother didn't work in clay at this time, for she spent all her time farming. Mother didn't make pottery, until I was grown.

# Peter Harris Family

When I came of school age, I attended our Catawba School on the Reservation. It had two rooms and offered the Indians most of their educational opportunities. Then, when I was eight years old, my grandfather, Epp Haris took us to live at Cherokee, North Carolina (about 1913) and I went to school there for one year. We moved back home to the reservation on July 4, 1915.

Pottery making among the Catawba Indians has always been closely linked to the economy of each family. As the financial situation changed, the amount of pottery produced increased or decreased. In our family, the pottery grew in importance when my father died in 1912 and in 19016 when my grandfather died. We all joined in our efforts to support the family. Whenever we could, my mother my grandmother, sister Eliza and I all worked in the clay and sold our pottery as best we could.

Martha Jane Harris, my grandmother, was one of the most talented Catawba potters. Some of my earliest memories are of my grandmother climbing down into the clay hole to get the best clay of "gold" as she called it. At times the hole would be so deep I could barely see the top of her head. During these early years, I did not work in clay but watched my elders; and in watching, although I did not know it at the time, I learned from them. Sometimes we children would play at making things in the clay and then smash our handiwork. It was not time for us to take the task seriously.

My grandmother had several pipe molds so we could produce pipes quickly. Although they are about ninety years old, I still use her pipe molds today. Whenever she had several dozen pipes, grandmother would cross the Catawba River and walk to Van Wyck to sell her handiwork. Once, when I was a young girl, I accompanied her on a selling trip. We crossed the river in a boat and then walked to Van Wyck where she was able to sell some but not all of her pipes. We then decided to walk to Catawba Junction where we finally met with success and exchanged her handiwork for money and bought our groceries. When we finally walked home to the reservation, I was exhausted. My grandmother's generation of Indians was accustomed to walking, and I had to work hard to keep up with her pace. Sometimes my mother and grandmother would go off in a wagon and sell pottery to the farmers in exchange for produce, but I was too young to go along. My brother Jesse often drove the wagon for them.

During all these years, I was observing my mother and grandmother at work and absorbing their methods of construction the pottery and shapes they commonly built. When I was old enough to want to see an apiece through the entire process from the digging of the clay to burning, mother and grandmother were right there to instruct me in the proper methods. I learned to do all the work from bending the pipes our people are so famous for to building the various pots from headed pieces, gypsy pots, umbrella stands, peace pipes, loving cups, wedding jars, plain bowls, footed bowls, cupid pots, and I could go on and on listing the various things we made and sold. My pottery looked very much like my mother's pottery and our tradition goes back in that fashion for many generations.

When I was 21 years old, I married a member of my tribe, William Douglas Harris, and we set up housekeeping and raised two sons. During this period, I continued to make pottery to sell and often sold it to dealers who liked my work. Once I was asked for a complete set of dishes, and I even made sets of cups and saucers. Even though I was on my own, I was still learning from my grandmother, and I was also teaching my sister-in-law Nola Harris. The two of us often worked together in making up pottery orders, and Nola also makes pottery in the tradition of my grandmother Martha Jane (White) Harris.

**News**

HONOR. In 1997, the National Endowment for the Arts named Georgia Harris a National Heritage Fellow. The award honors master folk and traditional artists whose achievements are recognized as important contributions to our nation's traditional arts heritage. Harris, who passed away between the time the fellowship was announced and the date of the White House awards ceremony, was a Catawba Indian and native of Lancaster, South Carolina.

**PHOTO 386 - GEORGIA HENRIETTA HARRIS WITH HER POTTERY**

**PHOTO 387 –GEORGIA HENRIETTA HARRIS AND HER SISTER ELIZA JANE**

**PHOTO 388 – HEADSTONE FOR GEORGIA H HARRIS AND HUSBAND – BURIAL CHURCH OF JESUS CHRIST OF LATTER-DAY STS CEMETERY, CATAWBA, YORK COUNTY, SOUTH CAROLINA Charlotte Observer, The (NC) - Saturday, February 1, 1997 -- DALLAS, GA –**

Mrs. Georgia Harris Harris 91, died Jan. 30, 1997, in Dallas, GA.

Funeral was at the Church of Jesus Christ of Latter Day Saints - Catawba Ward, officiated by Bishop Scott Garbett. Burial was in the church cemetery.

Mrs. Harris, a native of Lancaster, SC, was the daughter of the late James Thomas and Margaret Elizabeth Harris. Mrs. Harris was a member of the Church of Jesus Christ of Latter Day Saints - Dallas Branch, Dallas, GA. She was a retired licensed practical nurse at York County General Hospital, and a committee person on the Catawba Indian Arts and Crafts

She traveled and demonstrated the art of pottery making all over the country; including the Smithsonian Institute in Washington, DC, the SC State Museum in Columbia, and the Atlanta Historical Center in Atlanta, GA. Pieces of her art have been sold all over the world.

She attended the Cherokee Indian Reservation schools and received her LPN license from Lancaster Memorial Hospital.

Mrs. Harris was the widow of Douglas Harris is survived by her two sons, Floyd Harris of Dallas, GA, and Dewey Harris of Benton, KY; one brother, Furman Harris of York, SC; nine grandchildren; 18 great-grandchildren; and three great-great-grandchildren.

PHOTO 389 – HEADSTONE FOR JOHN THOMAS HARRIS -- INSCRIPTION: SON OF JAMES HARRIS AND MARGARET HARRIS.--BURIAL:  CATAWBA INDIAN NATION CEMETERY, ROCK HILL,  YORK COUNTY, SOUTH CAROLINA

(5) John Thomas Harris, born July 30, 1905, Catawba Indian Reservation, Rock Hill South Carolina and died June 10, 1912.[390] Catawba Indian Reservation, Rock Hill South Carolina

PHOTO 390 – HEADSTONE OF ROBERT LEE HARRIS --INSCRIPTION: SON OF JAMES HARRIS AND MARGARET HARRIS.  -- BURIAL: CATAWBA INDIAN NATION CEMETERY, ROCK HILL,  YORK COUNTY, SOUTH CAROLINA

---

[390] Catawba cemetery records.

(6) Robert Lee Harris, born August 16, 1910, Catawba Indian Reservation, Rock Hill South Carolina and died July 15, 1912.[391] Catawba Indian Reservation, Rock Hill South Carolina

**PHOTO 391 – GEORGE FURMAN HARRIS**

(7) George Furman Harris, born January 7, 1913, Catawba, York, South Carolina and died 5 June 2006 , Rock Hill, York, South Carolina. He married March 30, 1931, Bertha Mae George, daughter of Moroni P. James Joseph and Hattie Millings George.4 See her picture at the end of this chapter, along with her grandson William Harris.

**PHOTO 392 - GEORGE FURMAN HARRIS IN THE GARDEN**

---

[391] Ibid

**PHOTO 393 - HEADSTONE FOR GEORGE F HARRIS -- BURIAL: GRANDVIEW MEMORIAL PARK - ROCK HILL, YORK COUNTY, SOUTH CAROLINA**

\*\*\*\*\*\*\*\*\*\*\*\*\*\*\*\*\*\*\*\*\*\*\*\*\*

c . Martha Jane Harris, born 25 December 1861, Rock Hill, York, South Carolina and died 18 December 1898, South Carolina. She married John Evins Sanders (1862-1932) and their children are:

1. Robert Lee Jackson Sanders (1881-1886)
2. John William Thomas Sanders(1885-1946)
3. Joseph Hinson Sanders, 1886–1930
4. Dora Ann Sanders, 1888–1908
5. Loney Roy Sanders, 1890–1892
6. John Idle Sanders, 1892–1973
7. Lewis Ernest Sanders, 1895–1936
8. Sarah Ann Sanders, 1897–
9. Andrew Behrman Sanders, 1898–1898

More information on these children under John Evins Sanders.

d. Anthony "Andy" Harris, born 1862, South Carolina and died around 1920, in South Carolina.

e. Mattie Harris born 1871, South Carolina, death unknown.

# Peter Harris Family

**PHOTO 394 – DAVID ADAM TOAD HARRIS**

f .David Adam Toad Harris born 15 June 1872, Catawba Indian Reservation, Rock Hill South Carolina and died 1 September 1930, Rock Hill, York, South Carolina,.

David married first Elizabeth Jane (Lizzie) Watts-Patterson, daughter of James Patterson and Nancy Watts. He married second Margaret Della George, daughter of Taylor and Emily Cobb Ayers George; and third Dorothy Minerva Price Canty, (a white woman who was first married to Frank Canty).

David Adam took the name Toad, meaning in the Catawba language, One Toad. From an interview on Catawba, Nola Campbell a Catawba: Nola Campbell: How Toad got his name. "Nola: That's my grandfather." Florence Harris "He was a big fat fellow ever since he was a kid." Nola, Yes I remember how chubby and fat he was. Nola, he called everybody hot toes, and they called him Toad." According to Furman in 1894, "he was a clean shaved, rather striking looking young red man, not quite 22 is the largest farmer among the Catawba."

In 1897, when some were trying to eject Mrs. Dunlap as the teacher of the Catawba school, he wrote the following response:

"This trouble is through half-white. There was no trouble between the white people and the Indians until those half-white Indians came as committee. They give lots of trouble to those who do not know what is best for our tribe. Mrs. Dunlap tries very hard to stop whiskey and she has done some good. She also tries to stop those white men coming in the Nation to ruin our young girls, who have made nice wives for our young men in the Nation. Those are the ones who try very hard to get Mrs. Dunlap to leave, so they can carry on their wicked ways."

He was chief during the years 1906-1917, and was a "good compassionate leader".

David took over running the ferry on September 17, 1916.

In February 1917, David Adam was accused of shooting his second wife, Della George Harris. Della was the accuser; however, in November of 1917, he was acquitted of the murder.[392]

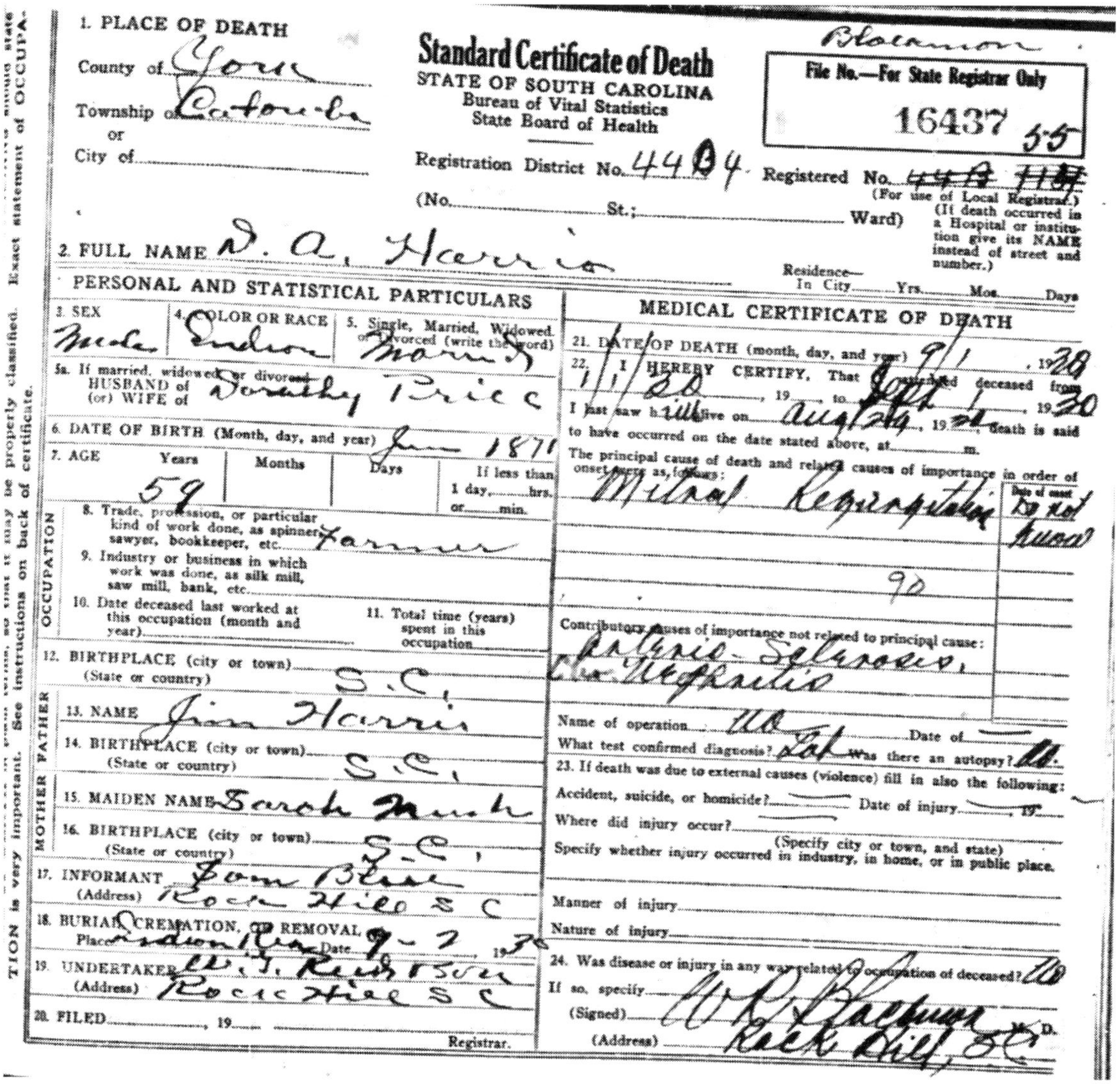

Standard Certificate of Death
STATE OF SOUTH CAROLINA
Bureau of Vital Statistics
State Board of Health

File No.—For State Registrar Only 16437

1. PLACE OF DEATH
County of York
Township of Catawba
or City of
Registration District No. 4404 Registered No.
2. FULL NAME D. A. Harris

PERSONAL AND STATISTICAL PARTICULARS
3. SEX Male
4. COLOR OR RACE Indian
5. Single, Married, Widowed, or Divorced (write the word) Married
5a. If married, widowed or divorced HUSBAND of (or) WIFE of Dorothy Price
6. DATE OF BIRTH (Month, day, and year) Jan 1871
7. AGE Years 59
8. Trade, profession, or particular kind of work done, as spinner, sawyer, bookkeeper, etc. Farmer
9. Industry or business in which work was done, as silk mill, saw mill, bank, etc.
10. Date deceased last worked at this occupation (month and year)
11. Total time (years) spent in this occupation
12. BIRTHPLACE (city or town) (State or country) S.C.
13. NAME (Father) Jim Harris
14. BIRTHPLACE (city or town) (State or country) S.C.
15. MAIDEN NAME (Mother) Sarah Much
16. BIRTHPLACE (city or town) (State or country) S.C.
17. INFORMANT Tom Blue (Address) Rock Hill S C
18. BURIAL, CREMATION, OR REMOVAL Place Indian Res. Date 9-2 1930
19. UNDERTAKER W. J. Roddey Son (Address) Rock Hill S C
20. FILED 19 Registrar.

MEDICAL CERTIFICATE OF DEATH
21. DATE OF DEATH (month, day, and year) 9/1 1930
22. I HEREBY CERTIFY, That I attended deceased from 1/1/30, 19 to Sept 1, 1930
I last saw him alive on Aug 29, 1930 death is said to have occurred on the date stated above, at m.
The principal cause of death and related causes of importance in order of onset were as follows: Mitral Regurgitation
Contributory causes of importance not related to principal cause: Arterio Sclerosis, Chr. Nephritis
Name of operation no Date of
What test confirmed diagnosis? Lab Was there an autopsy? no
23. If death was due to external causes (violence) fill in also the following:
Accident, suicide, or homicide? Date of injury 19
Where did injury occur? (Specify city or town, and state)
Specify whether injury occurred in industry, in home, or in public place.
Manner of injury
Nature of injury
24. Was disease or injury in any way related to occupation of deceased? no
If so, specify
(Signed) W. R. Blackmon M.D.
(Address) Rock Hill, S.C.

**PHOTO 395 – CERTIFICATE OF DEATH FOR DAVID A HARRIS**

[392] Blumer page 261,263,264.

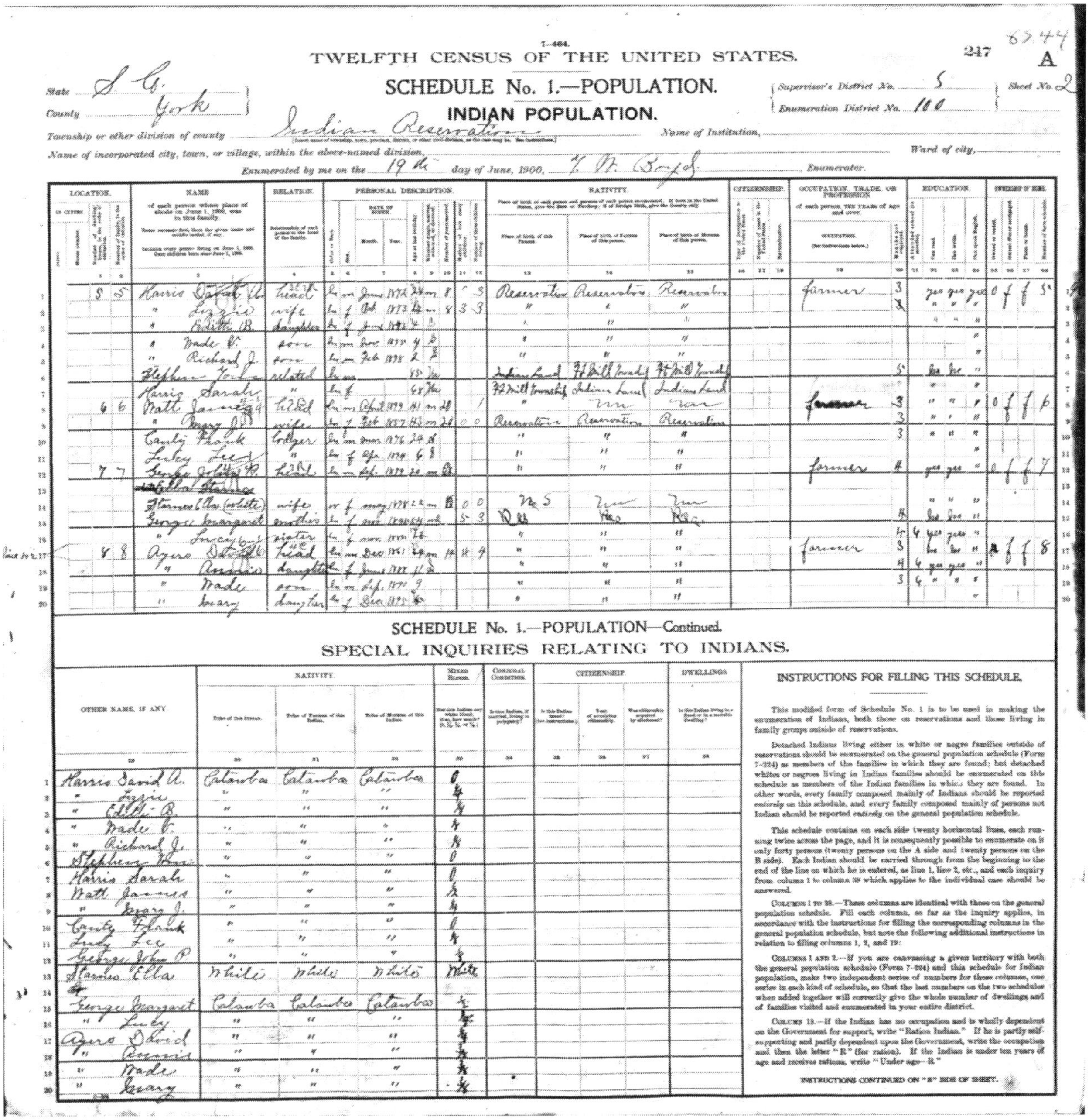

**PHOTO 396 – 1900 US CENSUS, YORK COUNTY, SOUTH CAROLINA**
First wife of David Adam "Toad" Harris

Lizzie Jane Watts-Patterson born 23 April 1874, Catawba Reservation, Rock Hill, York, South Carolina and died February 1917, Catawba, York, South Carolina . Their children are:

**PHOTO 397 – EDITH BERTHA HARRIS**

1. Edith Bertha Harris, born 13 June 1893, Catawba, York, South Carolina and died 12 June 1985, Rock Hill, York, South Carolina. She married Early Mortan Brown, son of John William and Rachel Wysie George Brown.

**PHOTO 398 - EDITH BERTHA HARRIS**

**PHOTO 399 - HEADSTONE OF EDITH BERTHA HARRIS BROWN, BURIAL - CHURCH OF JESUS CHRIST OF LATTER-DAY STS CEMETERY -- CATAWBA, YORK COUNTY, SOUTH CAROLINA**

2. Wade V. Harris, born November 1895, Catawba Reservation, South Carolina and died 1905 Catawba Reservation, South Carolina. He died from complications of a small pox vaccination.

**TOP EDITH BERTHA RIGHT IS LAVINIA HARRIS
BOTTOM IS ARTEMIS HARRIS BOTTOM IS CORA BROWN**

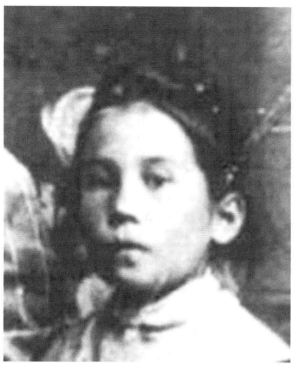

**PHOTO 400 – LAVINIA M HARRIS**

3. Lavinia M Harris, born 18 November 1896, Catawba Indian Nation, York, South Carolina and died 25 July 1916, South Carolina, United States. She married Herbert Blue (1898-1979) they had a daughter  Betssie Mae Blue ( 1916-1916).

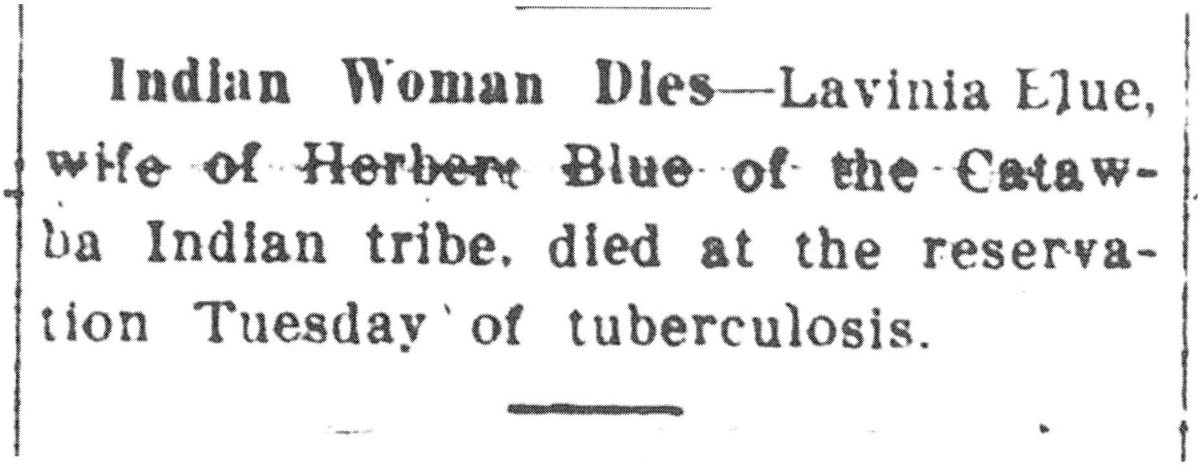

Indian Woman Dies—Lavinia Blue, wife of Herbert Blue of the Catawba Indian tribe, died at the reservation Tuesday of tuberculosis.

**PHOTO 401 – NEWSPAPER CLIPPING OF DEATH OF LAVINA HARRIS BLUE**

FORM NO. 16.

**CERTIFICATE OF DEATH**
STATE OF SOUTH CAROLINA
Bureau of Vital Statistics
State Board of Health

File No.—For State Registrar Only
37651

1. PLACE OF DEATH

County of _York_

Township of _Catawba_
or
Inc. Town of _____ Registration District No. _4404_
or
City of _____ (No. _____ St.; _____ Ward)

Registered No. _53_
(For use of Local Registrar)

(If death occurred in a Hospital or Institution give its NAME instead of street and number.)

2. FULL NAME _Lavinia Blue_

Residence
In City _____ Yrs. _____ Mos. _____ Days.

**PERSONAL AND STATISTICAL PARTICULARS**

| | | |
|---|---|---|
| 3 SEX | 4 COLOR OR RACE | 5 SINGLE, MARRIED, WIDOWED, OR DIVORCED. (Write the word) _Married_ |
| _Female_ | _Indian_ | |

6 DATE OF BIRTH _____, 1 1896
(Month) (Day) (Year)

7 AGE _20_ yrs. _____ mos. _____ dys.

If LESS than 1 day. _____ hrs. or _____ min.?

8 OCCUPATION
(a) Trade, profession, or particular kind of work _Housekeeper_
(b) General nature of Industry, business, or establishment in which employed (or employer) _____

9 BIRTHPLACE
(State or Country) _South Carolina_

PARENTS

10 NAME OF FATHER _David Harris_

11 BIRTHPLACE OF FATHER (State or Country) _South Carolina_

12 MAIDEN NAME OF MOTHER _Lillie Harris_

13 BIRTHPLACE OF MOTHER (State or Country) _South Carolina_

14 THE ABOVE IS TRUE TO THE BEST OF MY KNOWLEDGE

(Informant) _Ben D. Harris_

(Address) _____

15 Filed _7/26/_, 1916 _J. R. Mills_
LOCAL REGISTRAR

**MEDICAL CERTIFICATE OF DEATH**

16 DATE OF DEATH _July_ _25_, 1916
(Month) (Day) (Year)

17 I HEREBY CERTIFY, That I attended deceased from _July 13_ 1915 to _July 25_, 1916, that I last saw her alive on _23_ July 1916 and that death occurred, on the date stated above, at _ _ _ m. The CAUSE OF DEATH was as follows:

_Tuberculosis_

(Duration) _1_ yrs. _____ mos. _10_ dys.
Contributory (SECONDARY) _Puerperal sepsis_

(Duration) _____ yrs. _2_ mos. _10_ dys.

(Signed) _Geo Hill_ M. D.

_July_ 1916. (Address) _Catawba_

*State the Disease Causing Death, or, in deaths from Violent Causes, state (1) Means of Injury; and (2) whether Accidental, Suicidal or Homicidal.

18 LENGTH OF RESIDENCE (For Hospitals, Institutions, Transients, or recent Residents

At place of death _____ yrs. _____ mos. _____ dys.
In the State _____ yrs. _____ mos. _____ dys.

Where was disease contracted,
If not at place of death?
Former or usual Residence _____

19 Place of Burial or Removal. _Indian Reservation_

DATE OF BURIAL _7 26_ 1916

20 UNDERTAKER _W. J. Reed_ ADDRESS _Rock Hill SC_

**PHOTO 402 – CERTIFICATE OF DEATH FOR LAVINIA HARRIS BLUE**

**PHOTO 403 – RICHARD JACKSON HARRIS**

4. Richard Jackson Harris born 13 February 1897, Roddey, York, South Carolina and died 4 February 1985, Catawba Indian Nation, York, South Carolina. He married Nancy Cornelia Harris (1899–1975). They had one son:

Alfred Neal Harris (1920–1994). He then married Cora Ida Harris (1904–1983) and they had two Sons: Wilburn Harris (1922–1996) and Melvin Howard Harris (1924–2010).

**PHOTO 404 – HEADSTONE FOR RICHARD J HARRIS - CHURCH OF JESUS CHRIST OF LATTER-DAY STS CEMETERY - CATAWBA, YORK COUNTY, SOUTH CAROLINA**

**PHOTO 405 – FANNIE HARRIS**

5.  Fannie Harris born 6 July 1900,  Catawba Indian Reservation, Rock Hill, York, South Carolina and died 15 December 1951, York, South Carolina. She married Alonzo George Canty (1905–1979). Their children will be in the Canty chapter.

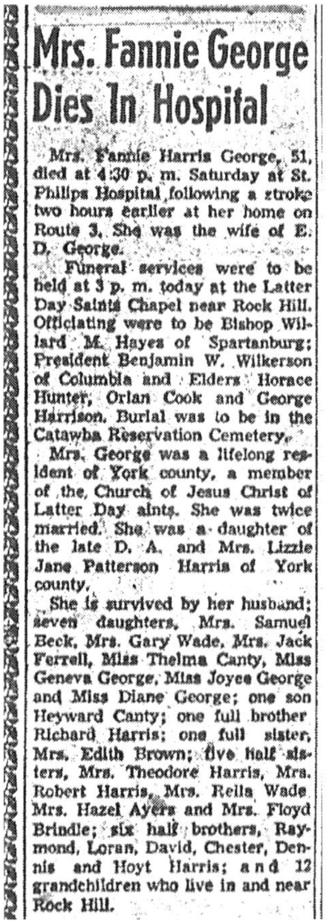

## Mrs. Fannie George Dies In Hospital

Mrs. Fannie Harris George, 51, died at 4:30 p. m. Saturday at St. Philips Hospital following a stroke two hours earlier at her home on Route 3. She was the wife of E. D. George.

Funeral services were to be held at 3 p. m. today at the Latter Day Saints Chapel near Rock Hill. Officiating were to be Bishop Willard M. Hayes of Spartanburg; President Benjamin W. Wilkerson of Columbia and Elders Horace Hunter, Orlan Cook and George Harrison. Burial was to be in the Catawba Reservation Cemetery.

Mrs. George was a lifelong resident of York county, a member of the Church of Jesus Christ of Latter Day Saints. She was twice married. She was a daughter of the late D. A. and Mrs. Lizzie Jane Patterson Harris of York county.

She is survived by her husband; seven daughters, Mrs. Samuel Beck, Mrs. Gary Wade, Mrs. Jack Ferrell, Miss Thelma Canty, Miss Geneva George, Miss Joyce George and Miss Diane George; one son Heyward Canty; one full brother Richard Harris; one full sister, Mrs. Edith Brown; five half sisters, Mrs. Theodore Harris, Mrs. Robert Harris, Mrs. Rella Wade, Mrs. Hazel Ayers and Mrs. Floyd Brindle; six half brothers, Raymond, Loran, David, Chester, Dennis and Hoyt Harris; and 12 grandchildren who live in and near Rock Hill.

**PHOTO 406 – NEWSPAPER CLIPPING FROM THE HERALD**
**(15-17-51) PAGE 4 – DEATH OF FANNIE GEORGE**
Herald - 12/17/51- page 4

Second wife of David Adam "Toad" Harris was Margaret Della George

**PHOTO 407 – MARGARET DELLA GEORGE**

Margaret Della George born 4 December 1879, Catawba Indian Reservation, Rock Hill, South Carolina and died 28 February 1917, Catawba Indian Reservation, Rock Hill, York, South Carolina.

They had seven children listed below.

**PHOTO 408 – CERTIFICATE OF DEATH FOR MARGARET DELLA GEORGE HARRIS**

David Adam and Margaret Della George Harris's children:

1. Hoyt Sidney Harris born 8 November 1901, Catawba Nation, York, South Carolina and died 19 March 1955 age 54, Catawba, York, South Carolina. He married twice: Ruthie Carolina Harris (1915–1935) and Emiline Harris.

**PHOTO 409 – HEADSTONE AND GRAVE MARKER FOR HOYT SIDNEY HARRIS - BURIAL: CATAWBA INDIAN NATION CEMETERY, ROCK HILL, YORK COUNTY, SOUTH CAROLINA**

Inscription:     Son of Chief David A. Harris and Della George Harris. Husband of Emeline Harris.

Second marker of metal: Hoyt Sidney Harris, 1901-1955. [Son of Chief David A. Harris and Della George Harris; husband of Emeline Harris Harris; farmer.

**PHOTO 410 - ISABELLE HARRIS**

2.Isabelle Harris born 7 February 1904, Rock Hill, York, South Carolina and died 15 March 1989, Rock Hill, York , South Carolina. She married Robert H. William Harris (1897–1956) son of Benjamin Perry and Mary Dovie Cornelia George.

**PHOTO 411 -  HEADSTONE FOR ISABELLE HARRIS GEORGE – BURIED IN CHURCH OF JESUS CHRIST OF LATTER-DAY STS CEMETERY -  CATAWBA, YORK COUNTY, SOUTH CAROLINA**

3. Dennis Harris born 4 August 1907, Rock Hill, York, South Carolina and died 14 September 1973, Lexington, South Carolina.

**From Thomas Blumer**: "He was going home and walked along a rail road tressell. When the train came, he had to jump off it. He broke his leg and wasn't found for at least 24 hours. He died of that injury."

### U.S., Social Security Death Index, 1935-2014

Name   Dennis Harris
SSN    248-34-6114
Last Residence - Rock Hill, 29730, York, South Carolina
Born    4 Aug 1907
Died    Sep 1973
State (Year) SSN issued        South Carolina - Before 1951

### Web: Richland County, South Carolina, Obituary Index, 1892-2000

Name   Dennis Harris
Death Place     Rock Hill
Publication Title        The State
Publication or Record Date    15 Sep 1973
Publication or Record Place    Richland, South Carolina, United
          States
Household Members         Name   Age
Dennis Harris

**PHOTO 412 – CHESTER GILBERT HARRIS**

4.Chester Gilbert Harris born  15 August 1909,  Catawba, York, South Carolina and died 30 December  1970, Columbia, Richland, South Carolina. He had two wives: Margaret

Lurene Munn (1921–1976) and their children - Sylvia A Harris (1940– ) and Dwayne Harris. Wife: Cornelia L Hair (1908–1974)

Burial: Amaker-Jeffcoat-Harley Family Cemetery
North, Orangeburg County, South Carolina

## Madsen's observations

Chester Gilbert Harris is mentioned by Brigham D Madsen in his book *Against the Grain*, the following are Madsen's observations about Chester.

In addition to one month with the in- active missionary, I spent another month with James Simmons, a former football player, from Brigham Young University; two months with Clint Adair, a cowboy and rancher from Luna, New Mexico; and four months with Chester G Harris, a full-blooded Catawba Indian from Greenville, South Carolina. At other times I would work with a newly arrived elder for a week or two while waiting for a good place to assign him. I very much enjoyed my labors was Simmons, Adair, and Harris.

Chester G Harris and about 300 of the remnants of the once mighty Catawba nation formed the branch of the LDS church at Greenville under the leadership of Harris's uncle, Chief Blue, who according to Harris and other members of the tribe, was gradually becoming " white and delight some " as prophesied in the book of Mormon. Harris believed this promise with all his heart and proved to be a very effective missionary and speaker for the Mormon cause. He had practically no money or means of getting any; because I felt that I could keep him going financially and also because of my interest in his people, I selected him as a companion for about four months.

In September 1935 he and I undertook to proselyte without purse or scrip in Robeson County, the home of a few thousand Lumbee Indians. These people, a mixture of whites and Indians, claimed descent from Sir Walter Raleigh's lost colony of Roanoke Island and had formally been known as Croatans. Harris was roly-poly, only 5 foot four in contrast to my six-foot four, he was an ever smiling, fun-loving, and hard-working missionary. During our work together I usually gave a short introduction explaining the purposes of our church with a brief description of the Book of Mormon. Then Harris would take over for about 50 minutes giving an impassioned recital of the wrongs perpetrated by white people in the US government on the American Indians, the broken promises and the forgotten and treaties. During his sermons, he would be transformed his eyes would flash and his audience would see a real Indian orator fighting for his people. We nearly always had turn away crowds because many North Carolinians had never seen a real live American Indian. One preacher listened to our sermon to an Indian audience, and then congratulated us on the truthfulness of our message.

The only time I traveled extensively without purse or scrip in North Carolina was when Harris and I were companions. Perhaps my most important contribution to the church in eastern North Carolina was building two chapels.. I convinced Pres. Kirkham that he would see in new Chapel in short order if the mission would help with the financing. He agreed, and on November 6, 1935 I delivered a set of ready-made church plans to a brother Barnhill, the only Mormon carpenter in the town he had agreed to work for minimum wage to help construct the building. He, Harris and I began on November 19 and had it ready to meet in exactly 2 months later. When Barnhill didn't show up to work, Harris and I would work alone. Once when Harris became so ill he had to go to the hospital, I worked by myself for two days. On January 19 we held our first meeting in the new building. I proudly wrote " we had about 50 out. Harris and I preached up a storm. Apostle Melvin J Ballard dedicated the Chapel on June 1. This ends the remembrances of Madsen about Chester Harris.

**PHOTO 413 - ELDER BRIGHAM MADSEN (6FT4 AND CHESTER HARRIS (5FOOT 4)**

PHOTO 414 - ELDER CLINTON ADAIR AND ELDER CHESTER HARRIS

PHOTO 415 - CHESTER HARRIS WITH WIFE AND CHILDREN SYLVIA AND DWAYNE

**PHOTO 416 – CHESTER HARRIS**

**U.S., Social Security Death Index, 1935-2014**
Name   Chester Harris    --              SSN -- 249-07-0015
Last Residence -  Columbia, 29205, Richland, South Carolina
         Born   15 Aug 1909  -   Died   Jan 1970
State (Year) SSN issued -- South Carolina - Before 1951

**PHOTO 417 –FLOYD RAYMOND HARRIS**

5.Floyd Raymond Harris born 17 November 1913, Catawba Indian Reservation, Rock Hill South Carolina and died 23 January 1952, Catawba Indian Reservation, Rock Hill, South Carolina. He married Nola Louella Harris (1918-2001) and they had seven Children.

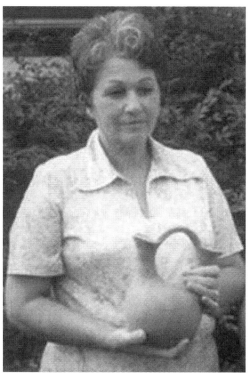

**PHOTO 418 - NOLA LOUELLA HARRIS 1918-2001 WIFE OF FLOYD RAYMOND HARRIS**

ORIGINAL

APPLICATION FOR HEADSTONE OR MARKER
(Please make out and return in duplicate)

CHECK TYPE REQUIRED (See Instructions attached)
- [X] UPRIGHT MARBLE HEADSTONE
- [ ] FLAT MARBLE MARKER
- [ ] FLAT GRANITE MARKER
- [ ] BRONZE MARKER (NOTE RESTRICTIONS)

| | |
|---|---|
| ENLISTMENT DATE | 4-18-44 |
| DISCHARGE DATE | 12-11-45 |
| SERIAL No. | 34 858 208 |
| PENSION No. | XC - 15 416 072 |
| EMBLEM (Check one) | [X] CHRISTIAN [ ] HEBREW [ ] NONE |
| NAME (Last, First, Middle Initial) | HARRIS, Floyd R. |
| STATE | S. C. |
| RANK | PFC |
| COMPANY | Co.A 5th Inf. |
| U. S. REGIMENT, STATE ORGANIZATION, AND DIVISION | |
| DATE OF BIRTH (Month, Day, Year) | Nov.17,1913 |
| DATE OF DEATH (Month, Day, Year) | Jan. 23, 1952 |
| NAME OF CEMETERY | Indian Reservation Cemetery, |
| LOCATION (City and State) | York County, South Carolina |
| SHIP TO (I CERTIFY THE APPLICANT FOR THIS STONE HAS MADE ARRANGEMENTS WITH ME TO TRANSPORT THE STONE FROM THE FREIGHT STATION TO THE CEMETERY) | Mrs. Nola H Harris / Mrs. Nola Harris (SIGNATURE OF CONSIGNEE) |
| NEAREST FREIGHT STATION (City and State) | Rock Hill, South Carolina |
| POST OFFICE ADDRESS OF CONSIGNEE | Route 3, Rock Hill, S. C. |

DO NOT WRITE HERE
FOR VERIFICATION FEB 5 1952
ORDERED PROCTOR, VT. 17 MAR 1952
B/L
SHIPPED 6572063 6536221

I certify this application is submitted for a stone for the unmarked grave of a veteran.
I hereby agree to assume all responsibility for the removal of the stone promptly upon arrival at destination, and properly place it at the decedent's grave at my expense.

Mrs. Nola H. Harris 2-1-52
APPLICANT'S SIGNATURE DATE OF APPLICATION
Route 3, Rock Hill, S. C.
ADDRESS (Street, City, State)

OQMG FORM 623 REV 15 APR 47 COLUMBUS, MISS. 5 AUG 1952 IMPORTANT—Complete Reverse Side 16—11453-6 GPO

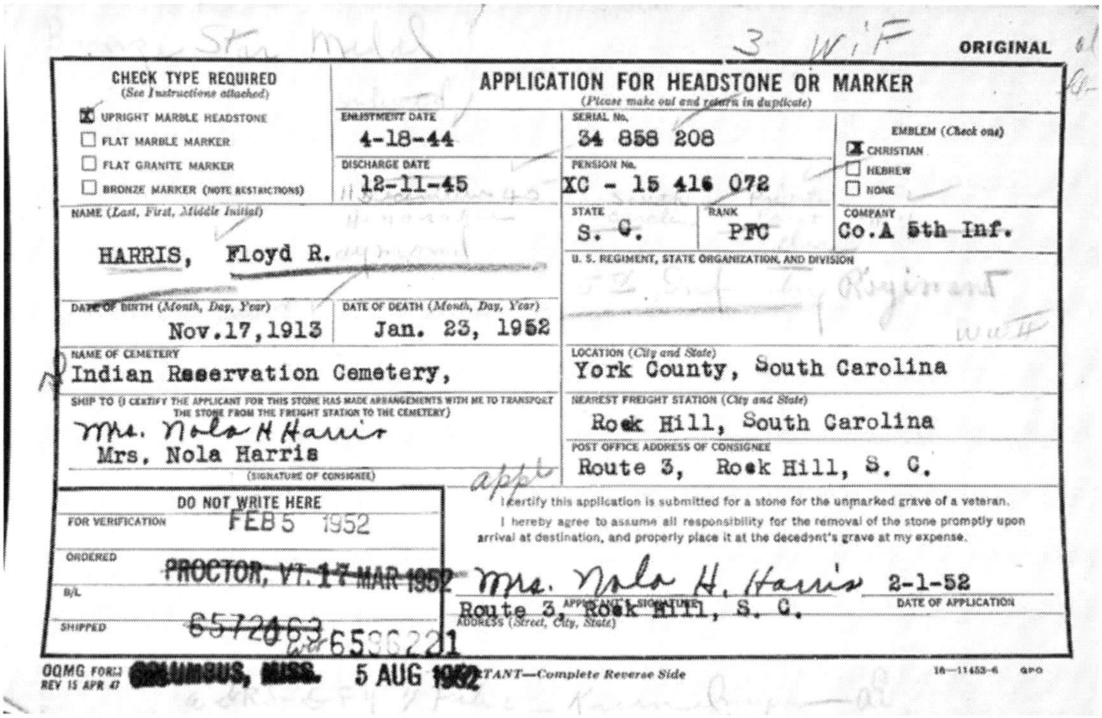

**PHOTO 419 - HEADSTONE APPLICATION FOR FLOYD R HARRIS**

# Raymond Harris, Ex-Catawba Chief, Dies In Hospital

Floyd Raymond Harris, 38, chief of the Catawba Indians from July 1946 until July 1950, died late last night at St. Phillps Hospital following an illness of three months.

Funeral services will be conducted at 3 oclock Friday afternoon at the Church of Jesus Christ of Latter Day Saints Chapel on the Catawba Reservation. Elder Benjamin W. Wilkerson of Greenville, first counselor of State Churches of Jesus Christ of Latter Day Saints. will officiate. He will be assisted by Elder Cook of Salt Lake City. Utah, supervisory elder of traveling missionaries. Graveside military services will be conducted in the Catawba Reservation Cemetery.

Harris was the son of the late David A. and Della George Harris. His father was also a former Chief of the Catawba Indians. Harris, a World War II veteran, served in the European Theater with the Third Army, 71st Division. He was overseas 20 months.

Surviving are his wife, the former Nola Louella Harris of Route 3; three daughters, Betta Lou, Della E., and Deborah Harris, four sons, Carl E., Grady C., Martin R., and W. Leon Harris; three brothers, Hoyt and Dennis Harris of Route 3 and Chester Harris of Columbia; three half-brothers. Richard, Loran and David Harris of Route 3; two sisters. Mrs. Isabelle Harris and Mrs. Adtmis Harris of Route 3, and three half-sisters, Mrs. Edith Brown, Mrs Sara Ayers and Mrs. Florence Wade, also of Route 3.

The body was to be taken from Todd and Garris Funeral Home to the home of his sister, Mrs Adtmis Harris on Route 3, at noon today.

**PHOTO 420 – NEWSPAPER CLIPPING OF FLOYD RAYMOND HARRIS**

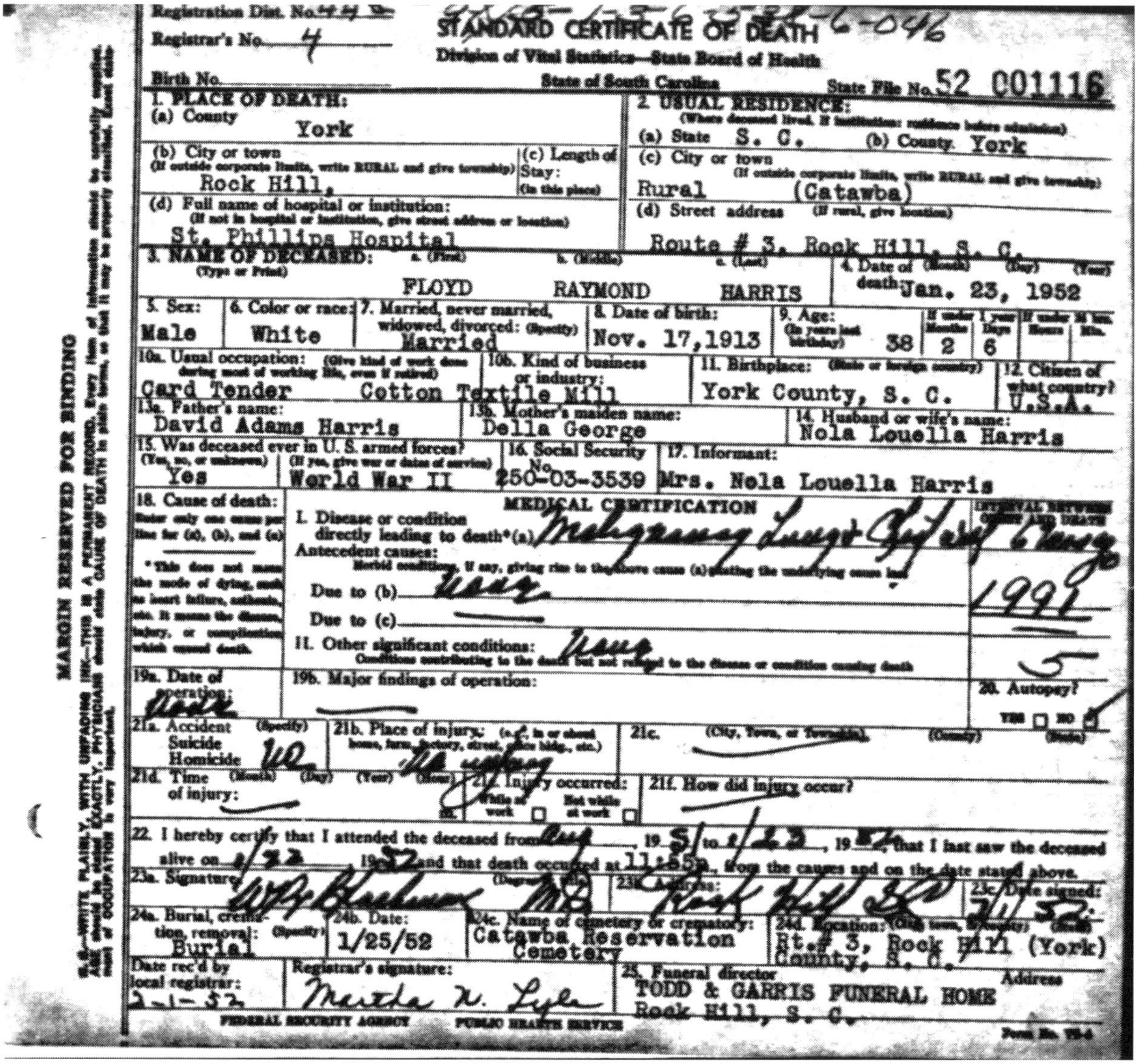

Registration Dist. No. 44
Registrar's No. 4
Birth No.

STANDARD CERTIFICATE OF DEATH
Division of Vital Statistics—State Board of Health
State of South Carolina
State File No. 52 001116

1. PLACE OF DEATH: (a) County York
(b) City or town Rock Hill,
(c) Length of Stay:
(d) Full name of hospital or institution: St. Phillips Hospital

2. USUAL RESIDENCE: (a) State S. C. (b) County York
(c) City or town Rural (Catawba)
(d) Street address Route # 3, Rock Hill, S. C.

3. NAME OF DECEASED: FLOYD RAYMOND HARRIS
4. Date of death Jan. 23, 1952
5. Sex: Male
6. Color or race: White
7. Married, never married, widowed, divorced: Married
8. Date of birth: Nov. 17, 1913
9. Age: 38 2 6
10a. Usual occupation: Card Tender
10b. Kind of business or industry: Cotton Textile Mill
11. Birthplace: York County, S. C.
12. Citizen of what country? U.S.A.
13a. Father's name: David Adams Harris
13b. Mother's maiden name: Della George
14. Husband or wife's name: Nola Louella Harris
15. Was deceased ever in U. S. armed forces? Yes World War II
16. Social Security No. 250-03-3539
17. Informant: Mrs. Nola Louella Harris

18. Cause of death: MEDICAL CERTIFICATION
I. Disease or condition directly leading to death (a) Malignancy Lungs
Due to (b) none
Due to (c)
II. Other significant conditions: none
19a. Date of operation: none
19b. Major findings of operation:
20. Autopsy? No
21a. Accident Suicide Homicide no
21b. Place of injury:
21c.
21d. Time of injury:
21e. Injury occurred:
21f. How did injury occur?

22. I hereby certify that I attended the deceased from 19 to 19 52, that I last saw the deceased alive on 1/23 1952 and that death occurred at 11:55 from the causes and on the date stated above.
23a. Signature: M.D.
23b. Address: Rock Hill S.C.
23c. Date signed: 2/1/52
24a. Burial, cremation, removal: Burial
24b. Date: 1/25/52
24c. Name of cemetery or crematory: Catawba Reservation Cemetery
24d. Location: Rt. # 3, Rock Hill (York) County, S. C.
Date rec'd by local registrar: 2-1-52
Registrar's signature: Martha N. Lyle
25. Funeral director: TODD & GARRIS FUNERAL HOME, Rock Hill, S. C.

MARGIN RESERVED FOR BINDING

FEDERAL SECURITY AGENCY PUBLIC HEALTH SERVICE

**PHOTO 421 – CERTIFICATE OF DEATH FOR FLOYD RAYMOND HARRIS**

**Third wife of David Adam "Toad" Harris was:**

Dorothy Minerva Price born 1893, South Carolina and died 22 May 1961, Columbia, Richland, South Carolina. Their children are:.

**PHOTO 422 – SARAH LEE HARRIS**

1.Sara Lee Harris born 2 August 1919, Rock Hill, York, South Carolina and died 25 November 2002. She was married twice: Kirk Sanders (1914–1945). They had a daughter  Claire Lee Sanders (1941–2004)  and then she married  Hazel Ervin Ayers (1925 - 2000).  They had two children:   Avert Stuart Ayers ( 1947– ) and Hazel Ervin Ayers jr (1949–1949).

**Sarah Lee Harris Sanders Ayers**
**State, The (Columbia, SC) - Wednesday, November 27, 2002**

WEST COLUMBIA - Services for Sarah Harris Ayers, 83, will be held at the Church of Jesus Christ of Latter-Day Saints, Catawba Ward, Reservation Road, Route 3, Rock Hill, conducted by Bishop Tom Cornwell, with burial in the church cemetery. The family will receive friends from 7-9 tonight at the Church of Jesus Christ of Latter-Day Saints, West Columbia Ward, and from 1-2 p.m. Friday at the Church of Jesus Christ of Latter-Day Saints, Catawba Ward, Rock Hill. Memorials may be made to S.C. Arts Commission or Alzheimer's Association.

Mrs. Ayers, widow of Foxx Ervin Ayers, died Monday, November 25, 2002. Born in Rock Hill, she was the daughter of the late Chief David "Toad" Harris and Dorothy Minerva Price Harris. She was a member of the Church of Jesus Christ of Latter Day Saints and an Artist in Residence at the S.C. Arts Commission. She was the recipient of several awards during her lifetime. She was honored at the Kennedy Center in Washington as 1980 American Indian Artist of the Year. Other awards included the S.C. Native American Artist of the Year, the 1989 S.C. Folk Heritage Award and the 2002 Governor's Commission on Women of Achievement Nominee.

Surviving are her daughters and sons-in-law, Claire and Roosevelt Wilson of Columbia, Dot and Paul Frary of Warrenton, Va.; son and daughter-in-law, Avery S. and Linda Ayers of Columbia; sister, Florence Wade of Rock Hill (Catawba Reservation); six grandchildren, seven great-grandchildren. She was predeceased by a son, Hazel E. Ayers Jr., and 12 brothers and sisters.

Spouses:    Hazel Ervin Ayers (1925 - 2000)  ---    Kirk Sanders (1914 - 1945)

 Children:   Claire Lee Sanders Wilson (1941 - 2004)  and   Hazel Ervin Ayers (1949 - 1949)

**PHOTO 423 - GRAVE MARKER FOR SARAH LEE HARRIS AYERS - BURIAL: CHURCH OF JESUS CHRIST OF LATTER-DAY STS CEMETERY -- CATAWBA, YORK COUNTY, SOUTH CAROLINA**

**PHOTO 424 – FLORENCE REBECCA HARRIS**

2. Florence Rebecca Harris born 28 April 1922, Catawba, York, South Carolina and died 12 April 2017 in Rock Hill, York, South Carolina. She married first Elbert Garce: (Her mother slept between them and the marriage didn't take. This story by Donald Williams). This marriage ended in Divorce, both married someone else and had children. Her second husband was Esmerilla Rella-Rilla Wade (1917–1963). They had six children:

**Mrs. Florence Harris Wade, 94, passed away on Wednesday, April 12, 2017 at Rock Hill Post Acute Care Center.**

The funeral will be held at 2pm on Saturday, April 15, 2017 at the Church of Jesus Christ of Latter Day Saints - Catawba Ward with Bishop Bob Trimnal officiating. Burial will be in the church cemetery.

Born in Rock Hill, Mrs. Wade was the last of fourteen children born to the late Chief David A. "Toad" Harris and the late Dorothy Price Harris and the oldest member and matriarch of the Catawba Nation. She was also preceded in death by her husband of 55 years, Rella Wade; her son, Connie Steve Wade; and her daughter, Joy Porter. She retired from J.P. Stevens and then retired from Springs Industries. She was a master potter and taught pottery to the Catawba children as well as demonstrated in the public schools. She enjoyed having the children around her and answering all their questions. She was the 2011 recipient of the Jean Laney Harris Folk Heritage Award; she worked tirelessly to help promote the Catawba culture with dancing and pottery making; and she was a census gatherer for the Catawba Nation. She was a woman of great virtue and morality and was a servant of the community. She was very dedicated and loyal to her family and her church, Church of Jesus Christ of Latter Day Saints - Catawba Ward. She was her grandchildren's favorite cook and a avid Clemson Tiger fan in support of her son who was a mid 1960 Clemson star player.

Surviving are her daughter, Frieda Shrake of Rock Hill; her granddaughter, whom she raised, Melissa Shrake Harris; seven grandchildren; twelve great-grandchildren; and two great-great-grandchildren.

> 3. James Loran Harris born 10 June 1924, Catawba, South Carolina and died 5 August 1958, Catawba, South Carolina.
>
> He was married twice: Edith Frances Canty (1924–2010) and Pauline Angela Wade (1920–1987).

**Obituary from find a grave**

Birth: May 10, 1924       Death: Aug. 5, 1958

Loran Harris, South Carolina, PFC SVC BTRY, 80 Field Arty BN, World War II, June 10, 1924-August 5, 1958. (Son of Chief David A. Harris and Dorothy Price Harris; house painter.)

Inscription: South Carolina PFC SVC BTRY 80 Field Arty BN World War II. Son of Chief David A. Harris and Dorothy Price Harris

Burial: Catawba Indian Nation Cemetery

WWI WWII ✓ KOREA

ORIGINAL

**APPLICATION FOR HEADSTONE OR MARKER**
(See attached instructions. Complete and submit original and duplicate)

1. NAME OF DECEASED—LAST—FIRST—MIDDLE (*Print or type*): HARRIS, Loran ✓
2. ENLISTMENT DATE (*Month, Day, Year*): 11-24-42 ✓
3. DISCHARGE DATE (*Month, Day, Year*): HONORABLE 1-22-46 ✓
4. SERVICE NO.: 34 515 259 ✓
5. PENSION OR VA CLAIM NO.: 15 418 297
6. STATE: S. C. ✓
7. GRADE: Pvt. PFC. ✓
8. MEDALS: ✓
9. BRANCH OF SERVICE, COMPANY, REGIMENT, AND DIVISION OR SHIP: ARMY ✓ 29th Replacement Depot SVC BTRY 80FA BN
10. DATE OF BIRTH (*Month, Day, Year*): 6-10-24 ✓
11. DATE OF DEATH (*Month, Day, Year*): 8-5-58
12. EMBLEM (*Check one*): ☒ CHRISTIAN (*Latin Cross*) ☐ HEBREW (*Star of David*) ☐ NONE
13. CHECK TYPE REQUIRED: ☒ UPRIGHT MARBLE HEADSTONE ☐ FLAT MARBLE MARKER ☐ FLAT GRANITE MARKER ☐ FLAT BRONZE MARKER
14. SHIP TO (*Name and address of person who will transport stone or marker to cemetery*): Hazel Ayers, R#3, Rock Hill, S. C.
15. FREIGHT STATION: Rock Hill, S. C.
16. NAME AND LOCATION OF CEMETERY (*City and State*): Indian Reservation, R#3, Rock Hill, S. C.
17. THE APPLICANT FOR THIS STONE OR MARKER HAS MADE ARRANGEMENTS WITH ME TO TRANSPORT SAME TO THE CEMETERY.
SIGNATURE: Hazel E. Ayers DATE: 10-1-58

DO NOT WRITE HERE
RECEIVED: OCT 30 1958
VERIFIED:
B/L: WY-7929929 DEC 5 1958
ORDERED: COLUMBUS MARBLE WORKS, COLUMBUS, MISSISSIPPI

18. NAME AND ADDRESS OF APPLICANT (*Print or type*): Mrs. Dorothy P. Harris, Route 3, Rock Hill, S. C.
19. This application is submitted for a stone or marker for the unmarked grave of a deceased member or former member of the Armed Forces of the United States, soldiers of Union and Confederate Armies of the Civil War.
I hereby agree to accept responsibility for properly placing the stone or marker at the grave at no expense to the Government.
10 NOV 1958
SIGNATURE OF APPLICANT: Mrs. Dorothy (his X mark) Harris DATE: 10-1-58

DA FORM 1 JUN 57 1815 EDITION OF 1 AUG 56 IS OBSOLETE. IMPORTANT—Reverse Side Must Be Completed. 16—11453-11 GPO

Witnesses: Reedie H. Sanders, York S.C.; Martha Harris, R#3, Rock Hill, SC

**PHOTO 425 - HEADSTONE APPLICATION FOR LORAN HARRIS**

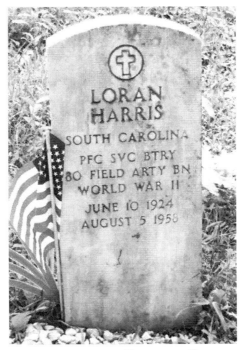

**PHOTO 426 – HEADSTONE FOR LORAN HARRIS -- BURIAL: CATAWBA INDIAN NATION CEMETERY, ROCK HILL, YORK COUNTY, SOUTH CAROLINA**

4. David Adam Harris Jr born 12 July 1927, Catawba, South Carolina and died 13 September 1988, Catawba, South Carolina.

He was married twice:   Martha Sarah Bryson (1931–2007) and Betty Ellen Swecker (1938–2008).

**Obituary from Find a Grave**: Birth: Jul. 12, 1927 Death: Sep. 13, 1988 Charlotte Observer, The (NC) - Thursday, September 15, 1988 CATAWBA LEADER David Adams Harris Jr., 61, a Catawba Indian Council member, died 13 September 1988, at Piedmont Medical Center after a long illness. In the late 1970s, Harris led a dissident group of Catawba's who broke with tribal leadership and opposed creating a federal reservation to settle the tribe's land claim. The dissidents favored individual cash payments. Tribal leaders later settled their internal dispute. His daughter, Connie Scott of Hernando, Fla., said, "He wanted each Indian to be equal and to get an education." His objective in seeking the cash settlement, she said, was "to accomplish better living conditions" for the Catawba's. Harris and his supporters made several trips to Washington in the late 1970s and early 1980s to meet with Interior Department officials and to appear at congressional hearings. Robert Jones of Rock Hill, an attorney for the Catawba tribe, said, "David was a very proud person, very conscious of his heritage as a Catawba and concerned for their future." Harris was born and raised on the Catawba Indian Reservation, son of the late David A. Harris Sr., a former chief. He was a general contractor with a painting and wallpapering business. Harris became a member of the Catawba Tribal Council in 1977 and remained an active member until his death. His funeral is Friday at the Church of Jesus Christ of Latter-day Saints, Catawba Ward, with Bishop Kenneth Harris and Melton Osborne officiating. Burial will be in the church cemetery. Survivors are his wife, Mrs. Betty Ellen Swecker Harris; sons, David S. Harris, Brian A. Harris, both of Rock Hill, John R. Harris of Lancaster, Gary L. Anderson of Gastonia; daughters, Mrs. Connie Scott of Hernando, Fla., Charlene Melech of Mobile, Ala., Katherine Boulder of Fort Smith, Ark., Linda Weber of Kershaw; stepdaughters, Mrs. Amanda Sisk of Rock Hill, Mrs. Peggy Geppie of Baltimore; sisters, Mrs. Florence Wade, Mrs. Isabel George, both of Rock Hill, Mrs. Sara Ayers of Columbia; 30 grandchildren; one great- grandchild. ==============================
This obituary omits his mother, she was a white woman, Dorothy Minerva Price.
Information provided by: Judy Canty Martin

**PHOTO 427 – HEADSTONE FOR DAVID ADAM AND BETTY SWECKER HARRIS – BURIAL IN CHURCH OF JESUS CHRIST OF LATTER-DAY STS CEMETERY - CATAWBA, YORK COUNTY, SOUTH CAROLINA**

**Daughter of James Thomas Harris and Sarah Jane Ayers**

g. Isabella Harris born about 1876, South Carolina – death unknown

**Second Son of David Harris-Bullin and Nancy Quash-Marsh is John "Mush" Harris**

2. John "Mush"[393] Harris was born 1831, Catawba, York, South Carolina, and died 1874, Catawba, York, South Carolina. He married first Jenny Ayers;[394] second Nancy Harris, daughter of Sallie Ayers and William Harris. John served in the Civil War. He enlisted in Company H, 12th South Carolina Infantry at Camp Pemberton, SC, with his brother James. They both were cooks. John was wounded at Sharpsburg on September 17, 1862, and taken prisoner and exchanged in May 1863. He was then sent to Richmond, VA. He was retired on September 7, 1865.[395] Brown stated that he was Chief, in the years 1928-30, however John Harris died in 1874. Robert Lee Harris stated in his narrative to Scaife that his father had been chief. In 1871, John Harris received $280.20 from the Indian Agent. In addition, in 1871, he wrote to Governor Scott, requesting that the appropriation be held up, until the council could decide the best way to spend the money.

John Harris – who had visited the Choctaw Nation in 1860 as part of the Catawba delegation, took part in the battle of Antietam on September 17, 1862. While engaged in the fight there he was shot through one of his legs and when it appeared that he might fall

---

[393] 1863 petition on behalf of John R. Patton, Indian Agent.
[394] Watson page 27 & 28, verifies first name Jenny. A Jenny Ayers signed a petiton in 1847 but disappears by 1849.
[395] Civil War Records of John Harris

into the hands of the enemy he begged his comrades to kill him rather than permit this to happen. He was sent to a hospital in Frederick, Maryland, and took part in the exchanged of prisoners in 1863. In 1864 he was in the Invalid Corp. John Harris was chief to the Catawba from 1869 to 1871.

On May 13, 1862, the third Catawba contingent, including three men, enlisted in Company G, Fifth South Carolina Infantry:

John Harris was Chief in a Petition of 1872: March 8, 1872 to Governor Scott.

"Chief John Harris recalls his 1871 visit to Columbia and his complaints over the Catawba agent's actions." He requested that Solomon Harris of Lancaster be made the Agent. John Harris, Epp Harris, James Harris, Betsy Harris and Susannah Harris signed the petition. Therefore, if John Harris were Chief it would have to have been a short rule in about 1871-72.

John had six children, William, Angeline, John, Fanny, Robert Lee and Benjamin

Perry Harris. John died around 1874.

**PHOTO 428 - WILLIAM (BILLY BOWLEGS) HARRIS**

a. William (Billy Bowlegs) Harris, born 1857, died around 1925. William appears as chief around 1905-06. In 1881, William was tried and convicted of Assault and

Battery with intent to kill Taylor George sentenced to 30 days in jail.[396] In 1939, Speck made the following statement, and there is no explanation for it. He stated that "Billy Harris used to bite his tongue so the dead would not come back and bother us."[397] My explanation is that many cultures do not speak of the dead, the Navajo for instance will not speak the dead person's name for fear that person will haunt them. Obviously, the Catawba had the same sort of superstition. Billy collected money from the agent R. L. Crook in 1881, in the amount of $6.66.

In 1887, William along with Benjamin and James Harris were sent to Columbia to investigate their rights and to seek redress for the injustice of the Treaty of 1840.[398] He took the name Billy Bowlegs, after one of the most famous Seminole Indian Chiefs. He was reported to have had 14 children; however, Dr. Wesley White stated that he did not marry. Billy spoke at the dedication of The Catawba Monument, in 1900.

"Thank ladies for much big trouble done been take to give Indians good dinner. Catawba's never fight against white man but once since creation; never fight no more against him. Wish to thank everybody for all kindness. Takes grit for Indian to make speech. No more take up time. Much Thank.".

b. Angeline Harris, born around 1858, Catawba Indian Nation, York, South Carolina : Death Before 1900.

c. Thomas Wesley Harris born 14 October 1858, Rock Hill, York, South Carolina and died 24 October 1915, South Carolina.

d. John Harris born 1862, , Catawba Indian Nation, York, South Carolina and had died 1900.

e. Fanny Harris born 1865 Catawba Indian Nation, York, South Carolina and died before 1900.

---

[396] Yorkville Enquirer, June 30, 1881 page 2 & 3 and Circuit Court records, November 3, 1881 page 2.
[397] Watson page 35.
[398] Blumer 196.

**PHOTO 429 – ROBERT LEE (RED CLOUD) HARRIS**

f. Robert Lee Harris was born 15 September 1867, Catawba, South Carolina and died 11 November 1954, Rock Hill, South Carolina. Robert was called Red Cloud at the Corn show of 1913. He married first Betsy Harris, daughter of Allen and Rhoda George Harris. There were no children. Robert married second Martha E. Collins Thatcher, white, Robert Lee married third Nettie Harris Owl, daughter of Nancy Harris and Thomas Kilpatrick, as her second husband. Robert Lee was one of the first converts to the LDS Church in 1884.

In his own words, "I was born on the reservation. My father was John Harris who later was chief of the tribe. Until I was six or seven years old, I spoke only the

Catawba language. Then I started going to school and learned English. When I was a boy there were less than 100 on the reservation of course there were more full blooded Catawba then than now. The reservation was covered with big trees then. There was no special house for the chief; he lived just as the others did. The native costumes were used when there were dances. The Catawba wore one eagle feather. I lived on the reservation for about 27 years. Then I lived in this neighborhood and in Washington for a year and in Oklahoma for seven months. I traveled with a show called Daniel Boone on the Trail for one season and took part in a part of the play in which Indians were shown attacking Daniel Boone.

We traveled in Indiana, Kentucky, Ohio, West Virginia, Maryland, Virginia, North Carolina, South Carolina, Georgia, Tennessee, Mississippi, Alabama, Arkansas, Louisville (Louisiana?), Texas and Oklahoma.

The Catawba have always been a Democratic tribe. They practiced woman suffrage before the white men knew America existed. Women always have been free in the Catawba nation.

They might hold any office, though by custom males have always been chiefs. Robert Lee Harris was listed as Chief in 1895,1939-1940, and was a carpenter.

Robert Lee's version of the migration of the Catawba from the North to the Catawba River:

"Once upon a time the Catawba numbered many thousand braves. However, the smallpox killed many people. This was the first smallpox epidemic the Indians had known and they were afraid. They held a council and decided that perhaps the evil spirit which caused the disease could be lost if the people all moved at night. Some agreed to leave; some elected to stay in the village. A large group departed silently after dark-between the two suns- taking with them their possessions. They were to break twigs to mark the trail if the others decided to follow. But the others did not follow and those who left the village were never seen again." [399]

Robert Lee served in the military in World War II. He once was called the last full-blooded male of the tribe.

After touring with the Daniel Boone show, he played the role of an Indian Chief with the Tennessee Opera Company that toured most of the U.S. Robert Lee died 8 November 1954[400]

---

[399] Ward, page
[400] Watson page 31

# Corn Exposition

The group was led by Robert Lee Harris who had traveled with the Daniel Boone Troupe. He was spoken of as a potter of unusual talent. Under Harris's lead, the Indians danced the graceful and yet highly dramatic Wild Goose Dance, one of the most popular dances at the Yap Ye Iswa Festival celebrated on the reservation the Saturday after Thanksgiving. They also danced the wildly vibrant Bear Dance. This dance was discontinued in the 1920s and today is being revived by Monty and Anna Branham. Monty has written a new Bear Dance Song in Catawba. A small but growing number of Catawba Indians know how to perform this ancient show stopper of a Catawba dance.

Unfortunately two dances performed at the Corn Exposition are no longer danced by the Catawba and their patterns have been lost. The first was the Fox Chase Dance organized by a man called Standing Bull. It was probably learned by Robert Lee Harris during his Daniel Boone Troupe days and was not traditionally Catawba. The second was the Catawba War Dance organized by Robert Lee Harris.

The news coverage of the Catawba participation in the Corn Exposition is filled with superlatives. One article The Record newspaper was entitled, "The Catawba Are Star Number." So successful was the Exposition in general that it was extended for an additional week. Photographer Blanchard recorded the event in photos and one is reproduced here. Of the 22 Catawba Indians who took part in the Corn Exposition, only seven can be identified with any certainty today:  Robert Lee Harris, John Brown, Rachel Brown, Rosie Harris Wheelock, Doris Wheelock, Edna Wheelock, and Richard Harris.

**Story contributed by - Tom Blumer**

**PHOTO 430 - FOUR PICTURES OF ROBERT LEE HARRIS**

Inscription: on headstone. --- Chief of Catawba Nation 1895 & 1939-1940. Son of John Harris and Nancy George Harris. Husband of Martha Collins Thatcher.
 Burial: Catawba Indian Nation Cemetery, Rock Hill, York County, South Carolina

**PHOTO 431 - CATAWBA INDIAN NATION CEMETERY WHERE ROBERT LEE HARRIS IS BURIED**

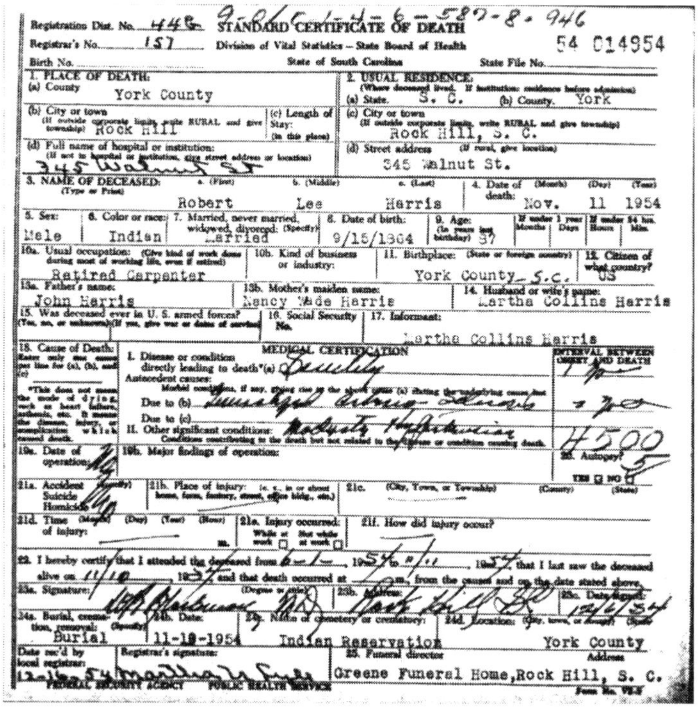

**PHOTO 432 - CERTIFICATE OF DEATH FOR ROBERT LEE HARRIS**

(1) Winona Harris born 20 January 1927, child of Martha E. Collins and Robert Lee Harris married. Morris, white.[401] Died, 2004 • DeSoto Texas.

g. Benjamin Perry Harris, born 1869, Catawba Indian Reservation, Rock Hill South Carolina and died 15 December 1930, Rock Hill, York, South Carolina. He married Mary Dovie George (1874-1972), daughter of Taylor and Emily Cobb Ayers George.[402]

**On March 29, 1897, the Rock Hill Herald reported; —**

"The suit in question is for the ejectment of the present occupants, and on this question the Nation is largely divided. The tribe has no headman now, but a committee composed of Lewis Gordon, Sam Blue and Ben Harris, appointed by J. M. Simpson, Indian Agent, claim to be the controlling power on the grounds. Two of these Indians, Lewis Gordon and Sam Blue are half white, Ben Harris is full blood."

This is was in reference to the Indian Agent attempting to terminate the services of Mrs. R. E. Dunlap and eject she and her husband from the reservation. In response, David Adam Harris wrote:

"This trouble is through half-white. There was no trouble between the white people and the Indians, until those half-white Indians came as committee."

At the dedication of the Catawba Monument in Fort Mill, South Carolina, July 31, 1900, Benjamin spoke, somewhat reluctantly, it appears. He said: "love was the greatest thing in the world; illustrated the love of God in creation and providence. While other things fail love lasts until the millennium. Mortals attain much in life by love. Paul says completion only beyond where ear not hear nor eye not see. Love makes the Indian a friend of the white man. The Catawba's never took part against him but helped him in all life, in all wars, in the Revolution, and they sent 20 braves to the Confederate war. Love prompted White and Spratt to build monument to the Confederate Indians. Much Thank them good men. Indian love them. If white man had done Indian justice like White and Spratt good many of them would have been educated and able to make good speech. Was glad Indian is now getting education. Fifty years from now if wanted, Catawba he make good speech as white man. Much thank to people for love shown us. My forefathers show love by fighting and give life; I show love try to make a speech. All Indians Grateful. Long remember this day."

Since Ben was teaching a night class for adults in 1897 and continued teaching for a good many years, drawing money from the appropriations until as late as 1912,1 think he was not quite as uneducated as he portrayed himself. I have always believed that the Catawba were a lot smarter and understood more than they let on. By 1915, Ben had enough authority in the LDS Church, that he Performed the marriage ceremony of Lavinia Harris and Herbert Blue. Benjamin Perry Harris died December 16, 1930.

[401] Catawba membership rolls
[402] Watson page 38 & 39.

**In the missionary journal of Sister Mary Barrus she states:**

"Bro Ben Harris a full-blooded Catawba – with brains enough for a senator or lawyer - was teaching the school when we came. He had never been to school, but self educated.  He is a great reader & thinker and was doing his best to get the children to read & write and spell correctly."

"Ben Harris is a very intelligent man and is studious in his habits in every way. He is very witty and clever. Like Bro Blue he has a good understanding of the gospel but Bro Ben had the advantage since Bro. Blue could not read much."

"Ben Harris was quite a leader – one of the 5 chiefs"

"He had a family of about 10 children. His wife did the best she knew how. Some of them were bright – some only medium. He was a good speaker and conversationalist. He had a brow like Webster and a rare ability to remember what he read. Tho self educated he taught the school after we went home. When Thayer was born he proved his wit & humor. It was on Sunday. At Sunday school and some one told him there was another indian on the reservation born this morning. He answered Jesus was born in a stable but that's no signe he was a donkey.

Ben like most of the Indians was a good singer and never wearied of singing songs of Zion.

He was quite choice of speech and like the other Indians he used no slang or profanity. Speaking of a farmer near the reservation Ben said he was so lazy he hired a (negro) to bat his eyes for him"

**PHOTO 433 – CERTIFICATE OF DEATH FOR BEN HARRIS**

**He had 9 children**

Sallie Hester, Robert W., Nancy Cornelia, Martha, Carrie I., Benjamin Joseph, Irene E., Minnie F., a son named Marsella (this name was taken from the census, the writing is poor)

**PHOTO 434 - SALLIE HESTER HARRIS**

a. Sallie Hester Harris, born April 28, 1895, Catawba, York, South Carolina and died 21 November 1990, Rock Hill, York, South Carolina.
She was one of the students of the school of Mrs. Dunlap.

On August 11, 1919, it was reported in the newspaper that Sallie had married Alto Winth on August 9, 1919. She later married William Harrison Wade, who was white.[403] White states she had earlier married two Catawba, one named George and one named Saunders.

Sally's children are Pauline, Esmerilla, Reola, Viola, Gary, William and Pauline or Christine Wade

---

[403] April Maria Branch Wade genealogy

b. Robert H. William Harris, born 15 August 1897, Catawba Indian Reservation, Rock Hill South Carolina and died 13 July 1956, Catawba Indian Reservation, Rock Hill South Carolina. He married Isabell Harris, daughter of David Adam and Margaret Delia George Harris. Robert served in World War I.[404]

Burial: Catawba Indian Nation Cemetery, Rock Hill, York County, South Carolina

Serial No. 146 Registration No. 124a

REGISTRAR'S REPORT 39-2-23, B

1 Name in full Robt William Harris (Age in yrs.) 21

2 Home address Roddy, S.C.

3 Date of birth Aug 15th, 1897

4 Where were you born? York Co, SC USA

5 I am 1. A native of the United States.

6 If not a citizen, of what Nation are you a citizen or subject?

7 Father's birthplace York Co, S.C.

8 Name of employer Farm — Place of employment Indian Nation

9 Name of nearest relative Ben Harris — Address of nearest relative Indian Nation York Co SC

10 Race—White, Negro, Indian, or Oriental (Strike out words not applicable)

I affirm that I have verified above answers and that they are true.

Robert W. Harris (Signature or Mark of Registrant.)

P. M. G. O. Form 1 (blue) REGISTRATION CARD.

If person is of African descent, tear off this corner.

1 Tall / Medium / Short — Slender / Medium / Stout (Strike out words not applicable)

2 Color of eyes Black — Color of hair Black

3 Has person lost arm, leg, hand, eye, or is he palpably physically disqualified (specify)? No

I certify that my answers are true; that the person registered has read his own answers; that I have witnessed his signature, and that all of his answers of which I have knowledge, are true, except as follows:

(Signature of Registrar.)

Aug 24 1918 (Date of Registration.)

LOCAL BOARD. NO. 1
YORK CO. SOUTH CAROLINA
ROCK HILL, S. C.

(Stamp of Local Board.)

(The stamp of the local board having jurisdiction of the area in which the registrant has his permanent home shall be placed in this box.)

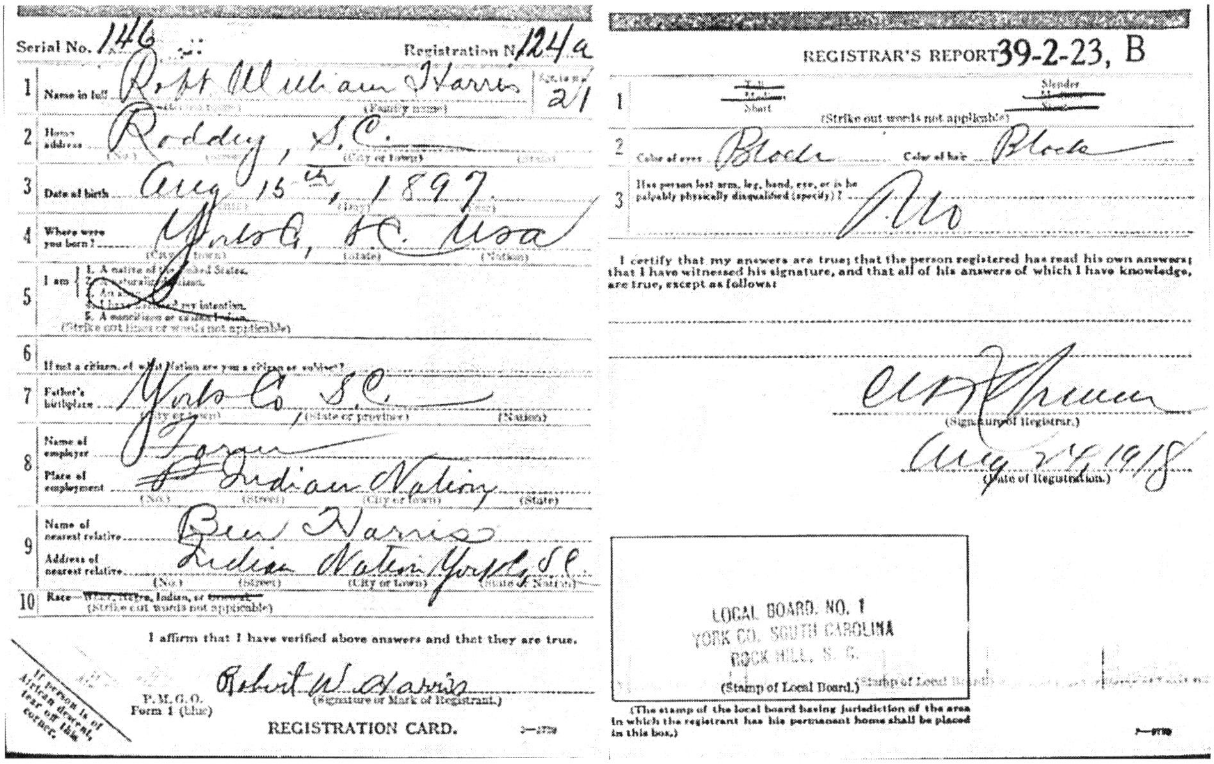

**PHOTO 435 – WWI REGISTRATION CARD FOR ROBERT WILLIAM HARRIS**

[404] Ibid

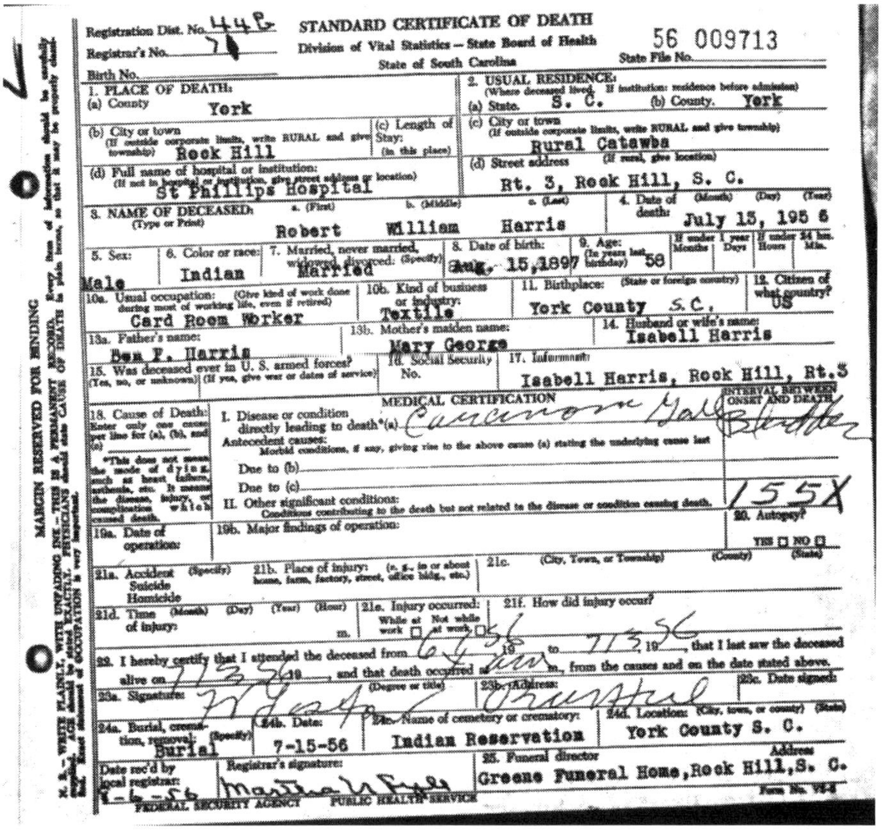

Registration Dist. No. 44 B

STANDARD CERTIFICATE OF DEATH
Division of Vital Statistics — State Board of Health
State of South Carolina

Registrar's No. 7

56 009713

State File No.

1. PLACE OF DEATH:
(a) County York
(b) City or town (If outside corporate limits, write RURAL and give township) Rock Hill
(c) Length of Stay: (in this place)
(d) Full name of hospital or institution: (If not in hospital or institution, give street address or location) St Phillips Hospital

2. USUAL RESIDENCE: (Where deceased lived. If institution: residence before admission)
(a) State S. C. (b) County York
(c) City or town (If outside corporate limits, write RURAL and give township) Rural Catawba
(d) Street address (If rural, give location) Rt. 3, Rock Hill, S. C.

3. NAME OF DECEASED (Type or Print)
(a) (First) Robert (b) (Middle) William (c) (Last) Harris

4. Date of death: (Month) (Day) (Year) July 15, 1956

5. Sex: Male
6. Color or race: Indian
7. Married, never married, widowed, divorced (Specify) Married
8. Date of birth: Aug. 15, 1897
9. Age: (In years last birthday) 58
If under 1 year / If under 24 hrs. Months Days Hours Min.

10a. Usual occupation: (Give kind of work done during most of working life, even if retired) Card Room Worker
10b. Kind of business or industry: Textile
11. Birthplace: (State or foreign country) York County S.C.
12. Citizen of what country? US

13a. Father's name: Ben F. Harris
13b. Mother's maiden name: Mary George
14. Husband or wife's name: Isabell Harris

15. Was deceased ever in U. S. armed forces? (Yes, no, or unknown) (If yes, give war or dates of service) No.
16. Social Security No.
17. Informant: Isabell Harris, Rock Hill, Rt. 3

MEDICAL CERTIFICATION

18. Cause of Death:
I. Disease or condition directly leading to death (a) Carcinoma Gall bladder
Antecedent causes: Morbid conditions, if any, giving rise to the above cause (a) stating the underlying cause last
Due to (b)
Due to (c)
II. Other significant conditions: Conditions contributing to the death but not related to the disease or condition causing death.

20. Autopsy? YES ☐ NO ☒

19a. Date of operation:
19b. Major findings of operation:

21a. Accident Suicide Homicide (Specify)
21b. Place of injury: (e. g. in or about home, farm, factory, street, office bldg., etc.)
21c. (City, Town, or Township) (County) (State)
21d. Time (Month) (Day) (Year) (Hour) of injury:
21e. Injury occurred: While at work ☐ Not while at work ☐
21f. How did injury occur?

155X

22. I hereby certify that I attended the deceased from 6-4-56 to 7-5-56 that I last saw the deceased alive on 7-5-56 and that death occurred at 7:00 a.m. from the causes and on the date stated above.
23a. Signature
23b. Address (Degree or title)
23c. Date signed

24a. Burial, cremation, removal (Specify) Burial
24b. Date 7-15-56
24c. Name of cemetery or crematory: Indian Reservation
24d. Location: (City, town, or county) (State) York County S. C.
25. Funeral director Greene Funeral Home, Rock Hill, S. C. Address

Date rec'd by local registrar 8-6-56
Registrar's signature Martha Faile

FEDERAL SECURITY AGENCY    PUBLIC HEALTH SERVICE    Form No. VS-5

**PHOTO 436 - CERTIFICATE OF DEATH FOR ROBERT WILLIAM HARRIS**

**PHOTO 437 – HEADSTONE FOR NANCY CORNELIA HARRIS HARRIS - BURIAL: CHURCH OF JESUS CHRIST OF LATTER-DAY STS CEMETERY, CATAWBA, YORK COUNTY, SOUTH CAROLINA**

c. Nancy Cornelia Harris, born 17 October 1899, Catawba Indian Reservation, York, South Carolina and died 17 February 1975, Rock Hill, York, South Carolina. She married Richard Jackson Harris (1897-1985), son of David Adam and Lizzie Patterson Harris.

**U.S., Social Security Death Index, 1935-2014**
Name  Nancy Harris -- SSN       248-38-9212
Last Residence       Rock Hill, 29730, York, South Carolina
Born    17 Oct 1899 -- Died  Feb 1975
State (Year) SSN issued       South Carolina - Before 1951

Nancy's headstone and her Social Security give a different year for her birth.

**PHOTO 438 – HEADSTONE FOR MARTHA HARRIS -- BURIAL: FOREST HILLS CEMETERY, ROCK HILL, YORK COUNTY, SOUTH CAROLINA - PLOT: SECTION 2**

d. Martha Harris born 14 January 1902, Catawba Indian Nation, York, South Carolina and died 11 May 1983, Rock Hill, York. South Carolina. She married Isaac J Johnson (1893-), an Eastern Cherokee.

**PHOTO 439 - HEADSTONE FOR CARRIE OR CORA IDA HARRIS**

e. Carrie or Cora Ida Harris, born 17 April 1904, Catawba, York, South Carolina and died 23 June 1983, Rock Hill, York, South Carolina. She married Richard Jackson Harris, son of David Adam and Lizzie Patterson Harris. Children will be found in their father's genealogy earlier in this chapter.

**PHOTO 440 - HEADSTONE FOR BENJAMIN JOSEPH HARRIS - BURIAL: CHURCH OF JESUS CHRIST OF LATTER-DAY STS CEMETERY, CATAWBA, YORK COUNTY, SOUTH CAROLINA**

f. Benjamin Joseph Harris, born 15 April 1906, Rock Hill, York, South Carolina and died 9 May 1967, Rock Hill, York, South Carolina. He married Maggie H. a white woman. No children

Benjamin Joseph Harris, son of Benjam Perry and Dovie George Harris. -- Race: American Indian, citizen (American) Nativity State or Country: South Carolina State of Residence: South Carolina County or City: York

Enlistment Date: 2 Oct 1942 Enlistment State: South Carolina Enlistment City: Fort Jackson Columbia. Branch: Branch Immaterial - Warrant Officers Branch Code: Branch Immaterial - Warrant Officers, Grade: Private, Grade Code: Private -- Term of Enlistment: Enlistment for the duration of the War or other emergency, plus six months, subject to the discretion of the President or otherwise according to law: Component: Selectees (Enlisted Men) Source: Civil Life -- Education: Grammar school -- Marital Status: Divorced, without dependents - Height: 68 - Weight: 134.

**PHOTO 441 - MARTHA, CARRIE IDA AND BENJAMIN JOSEPH HARRIS**

g. Irene Evelyn Harris, born 1908, Catawba Indian Nation, York, South Carolina . She married Hoyett Harris born 1901, Catawba Indian Nation, York, South Carolina.

**PHOTO 442 – MINNIE FLORENCE HARRIS**

h. Minnie Florence Harris, born 23 December 1909, Rock Hill, South Carolina and died 24 June 1979, Rock Hill, York, South Carolina. She married first Louis Ernest Sanders, son of John and Martha Harris Sanders; second David Spencer Harris, son of Wesley and Nancy Harris.

**Her children are given here because of the confusion between the two fathers.**

i. Alford Harris, born 1920, Rock Hill, South Carolina .

B. Jesse Harris, born 1832.[405] Catawba Reservation, South Carolina.  Jesse had two children according to the 1854 census, no record has been found. He is the son of David Harris-Bullin 1801-1854 and Nancy Quash-Marsh 1800- .

---

[405] 1849 & 54 Census.

**Older Reservation Photograph**

Ladies Relief Society taken beside the Mormon Church. Back row, left to right first two unidentified, possibly Emma Brown_ Lula Beck_ possibly Bertha Hariss Unidentified. Front row l-r 3rd from left Louisa Blue and mother in law Margaret George Brown  Abt 1900

## Chapter 12   Head Family

I.      **Robert Henry Head** was born in December of 1841; the son of an un-known man named

Head and Lucy Quash Mursh. He had 2 half-sisters, Emily Cobb Ayers George and (Margaret Peggy Jane Watts) McLonah-Marsh George; 3 half-brothers, John Gandy, and James Harvey and William David Watts. Lucy was the daughter of John Mursh and Betsy Quash-Scott. John was a Pamunkey Indian from Virginia, his brother Robert also fathered children by Betsy Quash-Scott.[406] The family story is told that Robert Henry came home just once, to see his son and wife.

He died soon afterwards. His Civil War record reads: "Robert Henry Head, enlisted at Lightwood

Knot Springs, May 13, 1862 into Company G, 5th South Carolina Infantry, His name appears on register of Effects of Deceased Soldiers, turned over to Quarter Master, 1863, aged 21." He enlisted with Robert Crawford and Peter Harris. Robert Crawford also did not come back to Catawba after the war. "Robert Henry was sent on Furlough on September 21, 1863 from the Hospital at Williamsburg, Virginia. He is listed as among those who died of wounds or disease. Robert Henry Head married Sarah Ann Louisa Evans-Canty born 1 July 1845, Catawba Nation, South Carolina and died 29 December 1919, Kirtland, San Juan, New Mexico, daughter of Chancy Evans and Peggy Canty. Sarah was the only child that can be traced to Peggy Canty, and Peggy's parentage is not known. It is possible she might be a daughter of Major Lewis Canty and Sally Ayers, daughter of Major Ayers, the well-known Headman of the Catawba. After the death of Robert Henry, Sarah married John Alexander Tims in Catawba, South Carolina on 27 June 1886 by Elder Heber Wright, prior to their migration to the West. Sarah died in 1919 and is buried in Kirtland, New Mexico.

Only 1 child can be positively identified.   Pinkney Henry Head

---

[406] Catawba Indian census 1849-1880, Catawba Branch Records and Head Genealogy, as well as Marsh-Mursh-Mush genealogy.

**PHOTO 443 - ROBERT HENRY HEAD SON OF LUCY MARSH**

**PHOTO 444 – SARAH ANN EVANS – CANTY- HEAD WIFE OF ROBERT HENRY AND DAUGHTER OF PEGGY CANTY**

## Robert's Civil War Records

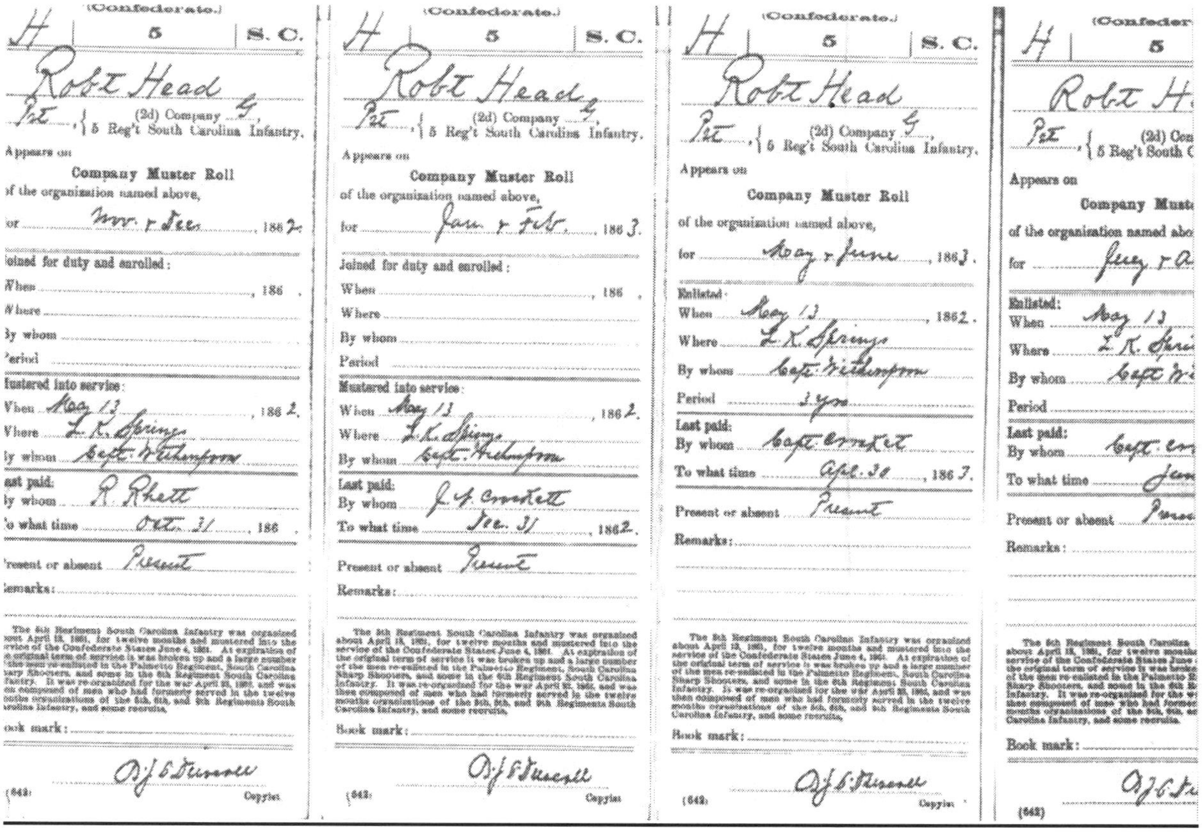

(Confederate.)
H | 5 | S. C.
Robt Head
Pvt, (2d) Company G, 5 Reg't South Carolina Infantry.
Appears on Company Muster Roll of the organization named above,
for Nov. & Dec., 1862.
Joined for duty and enrolled:
When ......, 186 .
Where ......
By whom ......
Period ......
Mustered into service:
When May 13, 1862.
Where L. K. Springs
By whom Capt. Witherspoon
Last paid:
By whom R. Rhett
To what time Oct. 31, 186 .
Present or absent Present
Remarks:

The 5th Regiment South Carolina Infantry was organized about April 13, 1861, for twelve months and mustered into the service of the Confederate States June 4, 1861. At expiration of the original term of service it was broken up and a large number of the men re-enlisted in the Palmetto Regiment, South Carolina Sharp Shooters, and some in the 6th Regiment South Carolina Infantry. It was re-organized for the war April 22, 1862, and was then composed of men who had formerly served in the twelve months organizations of the 5th, 6th, and 9th Regiments South Carolina Infantry, and some recruits.

Book mark: ......
(642) O. J. G. Russell, Copyist.

(Confederate.)
H | 5 | S. C.
Robt Head
Pvt, (2d) Company G, 5 Reg't South Carolina Infantry.
Appears on Company Muster Roll of the organization named above,
for Jan. & Feb., 1863.
Joined for duty and enrolled:
When ......, 186 .
Where ......
By whom ......
Period ......
Mustered into service:
When May 13, 1862.
Where L. K. Springs
By whom Capt. Witherspoon
Last paid:
By whom J. G. Crockett
To what time Dec. 31, 1862.
Present or absent Present
Remarks:

The 5th Regiment South Carolina Infantry was organized about April 13, 1861, for twelve months and mustered into the service of the Confederate States June 4, 1861. At expiration of the original term of service it was broken up and a large number of the men re-enlisted in the Palmetto Regiment, South Carolina Sharp Shooters, and some in the 6th Regiment South Carolina Infantry. It was re-organized for the war April 22, 1862, and was then composed of men who had formerly served in the twelve months organizations of the 5th, 6th, and 9th Regiments South Carolina Infantry, and some recruits.

Book mark: ......
(642) O. J. G. Russell, Copyist.

(Confederate.)
H | 5 | S. C.
Robt Head
Pvt, (2d) Company G, 5 Reg't South Carolina Infantry.
Appears on Company Muster Roll of the organization named above,
for May & June, 1863.
Enlisted:
When May 13, 1862.
Where L. K. Springs
By whom Capt. Witherspoon
Period 3 yrs
Last paid:
By whom Capt. Crockett
To what time Apl. 30, 1863.
Present or absent Present
Remarks:

The 5th Regiment South Carolina Infantry was organized about April 13, 1861, for twelve months and mustered into the service of the Confederate States June 4, 1861. At expiration of the original term of service it was broken up and a large number of the men re-enlisted in the Palmetto Regiment, South Carolina Sharp Shooters, and some in the 6th Regiment South Carolina Infantry. It was re-organized for the war April 22, 1862, and was then composed of men who had formerly served in the twelve months organizations of the 5th, 6th, and 9th Regiments South Carolina Infantry, and some recruits.

Book mark: ......
(642) O. J. G. Russell, Copyist.

(Confeder...
H | 5
Robt H...
Pvt, (2d) Co... 5 Reg't South C...
Appears on Company Must... of the organization named abo...
for July & A...
Enlisted:
When May 13
Where L. K. Spri...
By whom Capt. W...
Period ......
Last paid:
By whom Capt. Cr...
To what time Jun...
Present or absent Pres...
Remarks:

The 5th Regiment South Carolina ... about April 13, 1861, for twelve months ... service of the Confederate States June ... the original term of service it was broke... of the men re-enlisted in the Palmetto R... Sharp Shooters, and some in the 6th R... Infantry. It was re-organized for the w... then composed of men who had former... months organizations of the 5th, 6th, an... Carolina Infantry, and some recruits.

Book mark: ......
(642) O. J. G. ...

**PHOTO 445 – ROBERT'S CIVIL WAR RECORDS**

## U.S., Registers of Deaths of Volunteers, 1861-1865

**Colored G – J year 1864**

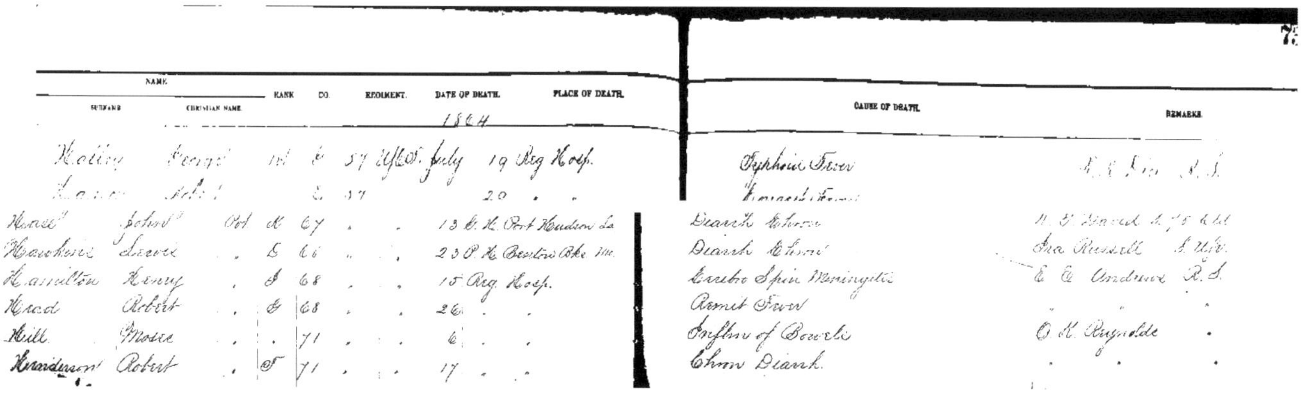

| Surname | Christian Name | Rank | Co. | Regiment | Date of Death 1864 | Place of Death | Cause of Death | Remarks |
|---|---|---|---|---|---|---|---|---|
| Holley | George | Pvt | E | 57 U.S.C.I. | July 19 | Reg Hosp. | Typhoid Fever | |
| [illegible] | [illegible] | | E | 57 | 20 | " | [illegible] | |
| Howell | John | Pvt | K | 67 | " | 13 G. H. Port Hudson La | Diarrh Chron | |
| Hawkins | Lewis | " | D | 66 | " | 23 P. H. Bestons Bke Mi. | Diarrh Chron | Ira Russell S. U.V. |
| Hamilton | Henry | " | I | 68 | " | 15 Reg. Hosp. | Cerebro Spin Meningetis | E. E. Andrews R. S. |
| Head | Robert | " | G | 68 | " | 26 " | Remit Fever | " |
| Hill | Moses | " | | 71 | " | 6 " | Inflm of Bowels | O. K. Reynolds " |
| Henderson | Robert | " | F | 71 | " | 17 " | Chron Diarrh | " |

**PHOTO 446 - U. S. REGISTERS OF DEATH OF VOLUNTEERS, 1801-1865**

1860 US Census South Carolina

Page No. 61

SCHEDULE 1.—Free Inhabitants in _____ in the County of _York_ State of _So Car_ enumerated by me, on the _24_ day of _July_ 1860. _W H Drennon_ Ass't Marshal

Post Office _Fort Mill_ .                                                                    3

| 1 | 2 | 3 The name of every person whose usual place of abode on the first day of June, 1860, was in this family | 4 Age | 5 Sex | 6 White, black, or mulatto | 7 Profession, Occupation, or Trade of each person, male and female, over 15 years of age | 8 Value of Real Estate | 9 Value of Personal Estate | 10 Place of Birth, Naming the State, Territory, or Country | 11 | 12 | 13 | 14 Whether deaf and dumb, blind, insane, idiotic, pauper, or convict |
|---|---|---|---|---|---|---|---|---|---|---|---|---|---|
| | | William Sanders | 13 | M | | | | | " " | | | | |
| 518 | 518 | Brown Watt | 49 | M | | Farmer | | 300 | Can D | | | | |
| | | Lucy Watt | 40 | F | | Dom | | | N. C. | | | | |
| | | R H H Head | 18 | M | | Out farmer | | | " " | | | | |
| | | Emily Eliz Head | 16 | F | | Out Dom | | | " " | | | | |
| | | Peggy Jan Head | 14 | F | | | | | " " | | | | |
| | 2 | John Randolph Head | 12 | M | | | | | " " | | | | |
| | | Nancy Catton Watt | 5 | F | | | | | " " | | | | |
| | | Jas H Watt | 2 | M | | | | | " " | | | | |
| | | W D Watt | 2/12 | M | | | | | " " | | | | |
| | | John L Timms | 14 | M | | | | | " " | | | | |
| 519 | 519 | J J White | 53 | M | | Farmer | 1252 | 4777 | " " | | | | |

No. white males, _19_   No. colored males, _1_   No. foreign born, ___   No. blind, ___   No. idiotic, ___   No. convict

No. white females, _20_   No. colored females, _1_   No. deaf and dumb, ___   No. insane, ___   27382 62282   No. paupers, ___

**PHOTO 447 – 1800 US CENSUS FOR SOUTH CAROLINA, YORK COUNTY**

**PHOTO 448 – PINKNEY HENRY HEAD AND WIFE**

A.      **Pinkney Henry Head** was born 26 October 1862.  Pinkney taught school on the Reservation for a time, around 1884, according to his journal. Elder Joseph Willey baptized him in Catawba on March 16, 1884, along with William George, and Robert Harris,[407] service on mission.

Pinkney married Martha Jane Patterson, born on 21 November 1868, daughter of James Goodwin and Elizabeth Missouri White Patterson. They were married By Elder Heber Wright on 17th February 1886 in South Carolina. Pinkney and Alonzo Canty had been courting the two Patterson girls, and Alonzo and Henrietta Patterson were married the same day, on the John Black farm. Elder Heber Wright married Alexander Tims and Sarah Ann Evans-Canty Head on June 27, 1886. "February 28, 1887 Left Spartanburg, SC at am, bound for Zion. March 5. 1887. I then arrived to the San Louis Stake of Zion with a company of 140 Saints in which my mother and wife and one child, step-father and father in law, and two of his small children.  All making 8 souls." [408]

On November 28, 1889, Pinkney began helping the Catawba in South Carolina with their attempts to have the government pay what they owed the Catawba. He wrote numerous letters, even one to the President of the United States in his attempts. The Catawba were successful, to a point in obtaining a settlement in 1943, in which Pinkney helped a great deal. He and the other Catawba were left off the rolls, and because by 1943, the older Canty's were dead, as were the Pattersons, no one knew that anything could be done to have the Western

Catawba included on the rolls. Pinkney was to die shortly after, never receiving credit for his work for the Catawba tribe.

## Pinkney H. Head (aka"Pink") and Wayne Keith Head
By Wayne Head

Memory can often be like cheap glass, it can allow a distorted view of an object; the memories of others, passed down like heirlooms, can be like stained glass, pieces of opaque glass each carrying its own stain, or prejudice, or coloration.

I offer to you a stained glass image of my great grandfather, as I am relying on the" memories, recollections, and stories of his daughters, son, grandchildren and historical documents. And to farther stain this glass these are my memories of these memories, stories, recollections unaided by notetaking audio, or videotaping.

He was born on the Catawba Nation to Catawba parents. Early in his life his twenty-one year old father died as a Confederate soldier, no one has ever known where his body was laid. No headstone exits to mark his resting place.

---

[407] Catawba Branch Records and Joseph Willey Diary
[408] Journal of Pinkney Henry Head.

Pink's mother did not remarry until after Pink had reached adulthood. His father, and other Catawba men, joined the Confederacy after a white man came to the Nation and threatened to come back with cohorts to raze the village unless many Catawba men and boys fought for the South (Some family members' oral history tell that this visit included a clear threat that if all Catawba men and boys did not join the Confederate Army that the whites would kill all Catawba women and children.)

The man, mother later married, was his father's cousin and a fellow Confederate soldier.[409] Pink kept a diary. His memoirs tell us that he was a teacher at Catawba (at a time when many were illiterate) and a Mormon missionary to the Cherokee. He left Catawba in 1887 (leaving on a train from Spartanburg, South Carolina) and moved to the San Luis Valley, Colorado as a Mormon. He farmed in Colorado and left there in the late 1890s for San Juan County, New Mexico. When he left Colorado he owned two farms. His family's first home in New Mexico was a dugout in the Hammond Ditch area. His daughter Helen was born m in Aztec, New Mexico in 1904. They settled on a 160 acre farm near the confluence of the San Juan and Animas Rivers in Farmington, New Mexico. This farm was Indian Grant Land.

Pink was co-owner of the first dairy in Farmington, New Mexico. He once petitioned the government to allow him and his family to live with the Ute people on the Unitah Reservation near Roosevelt, Utah. The national B.I.A. policy at the time was once an Indian leaves his reservation to keep him off reservations in order to force him to become "mainstreamed" as white people. The B.I.A. denied Pinkney and the five family member's requests to be permitted to join the Utes even though the Utes had granted their permission for such relocation onto Ute lands.

Pinkney was very active in trying to reach a settlement with the federal government for the Catawba Nation, in trying to have his children and grandchildren entered on the tribal rolls. He even wrote the President of the United States asking for help for the Catawba people. His daughters told me that he wrote well and I would enjoy his writings if they hadn't been lost. His writings were found years later in the possession of a granddaughter and I am awed to think that my great grandfather expressed himself so well and knew where to go to be heard. The problem was that he lived in world deaf to an Indian's words, concerns, and dreams.

---

[409] Alec Tims

 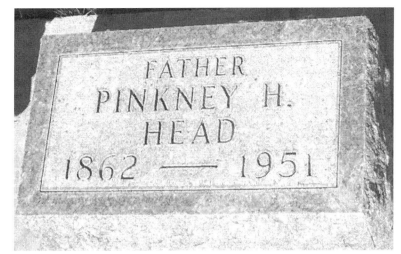

**PHOTO 449 - PICTURE OF PINKNEY HENRY HEAD AND HEADSTONE OF PINKNEY 1862-1951 – BURIED AT KIRTLAND CEMETERY - KIRTLAND, SAN JUAN COUNTY, NEW MEXICO**

**PHOTO 450 – MARTHA JANE PATTERSON HEAD WIFE OF PINKNEY HEAD AND MARTHA WITH TWO OF HER DAUGHTERS – DORTHY AND MARY**

**PHOTO 451 – HEADSTONE FOR MARTHA JANE PATTERSON HEAD - BURIED AT KIRTLAND CEMETERY -KIRTLAND, SAN JUAN COUNTY, NEW MEXICO**

# County Mom Real Pioneer

**By DONNA JENNINGS**
**Daily Times Staff**

A gentle-voiced, white-haired little lady, who has witnessed much living in her 100 plus years, can qualify with honors as San Juan County's unofficial Mother of the Year.

Mrs. Martha Jane Head, her face unlined by the passage of time and attired in a crisp white-trimmed p i n k dress, greeted this visitor at her quiet home on S. Butler, just prior to Mother's Day with a smiling,

"Won't you please sit down awhile?"

Still spry and in reasonably good health, Mrs. Head, a true poineer of the New Mexico area, reached her 100th birthday l a s t November. During that time she raised 12 children, four of whom she has outlived.

When she was a young 65 years old, Mrs. Head began motherhood duties all over again when she took a 13 month old granddaughter to raise. Only a little while later, a daughter died and Mrs. Head again took young children as her own to care for until they reached adulthood.

Today, the descendants of Mrs. Head include eight children, seven of whom are still living in this area; 20 grand children; 30 great-grandchildren and three great-great grandchildren!

A native of South Carolina, Mrs. Head and her late husband, Pinckney H. Head, whom she married when she was 18, became part of the romantic tradition of the Old West when they joined a wagon train from South Carolina to the Mississippi River.

From there they continued their journey by train into the San Luis Valley of Colorado.

In 1903, the Heads and their - then - five children loaded their possessions in a prairie schooner and came to San Juan County settling first at Hammond, then Aztec and eventually in a small farm in Farmington.

Pinckney Head died in 1951 and Mrs. Head continued to raise her family and subsequent grandchildren.

Today she lives quietly at her home near the peacefulness of the sun-splashed mesas with two daughters, Mrs. Helen C. Hayes and Dorothy Head, on the peninsula.

Up until just recently, she would wander down to the nearby river and spend many hours rite pasttime

bration

416

2758: (1890) (Coth)

Santford. P.O.
Conejos Co. Col.

Mr Teller. U.S Senator,
Washington

November 28. 1889

Dear Sir: Having a matter in view Concerning our peopel I write you to let you know that our peopel lays some claim on the government for Serves In the Revlationary War and for 15 miles Square of land In the State of South Carolina on Catauba Rivn and allso I think In the State of North Carolina on the Yadcan Rivn these things Have not Bin look up I came West to look up up lands for our peopel you will greatly obleg us In going to the Indians Department Office of the U.S and examine the Indian Record or Record of the Indians, you will be paid for your serce, if success as made this is in en favor of the Catauba Indian Tribe Which is Now located in York County South Carolina one of our men was In Washington in 1885 But did Not get at the busness the Right way I dont think, His Name was James Harris Plean writ soon and let me know if you will except of this or not

By respectfully yours,

P.H. Head. Catauba Indian

## Pinkney's Work Speaking of Native Languages

Pinkney freighted with his sons to Gallup, New Mexico using horse and wagon teams. At least two of his sons spoke fluent Navajo. Each summer a Navajo family led by a man named Pete, would camp near what is now known as Head Canyon, across the river from the Head farm. These two families would get together occasionally for meals and such.

## Catawba Language Spoken Here

Pinkney spoke Catawba fluently; Martha Jane Patterson Head did not speak the language well since she hadn't been raised on the Nation. He was heard by his daughters to speak Catawba with his mother (Sarah Ann Evens Head Timms), Martha Jane Patterson Head (wife) and his Catawba in-laws (James and Elizabeth Patterson) on occasion.

## Distant Memories

George Head JR recalls Pinkney in his old age standing, facing the bluffs in Farmington, remarking on all the wagons in the wagon train, more and more each year he said. Pinkney H. Head was buried in Kirtland, New Mexico in family plot; teacher, missionary, civil rights activist, father, son, husband, dairy man, farmer, orphan, Catawba, tribal leader, husband, and father.

## Even in Death Pinkney's Life Long Works on Behalf of the Catawba People Continues

Pinkney H. Head's prolific writings throughout his life time and his continuing pursuit for justice have created a social, historic, familiar, political, and legal record that impacts federal and state laws almost fifty years after his death in a small, New Mexico town. Prior to the Catawba Settlement Act of 1993, the Native American Rights Fund (Boulder, Colorado) had a team of lawyers relying in part upon the historic writings of Pinkney in order to provide a legal documentation trail of the Catawba people's diligence to protect Catawba treaty rights. In fact the U.S. State Congress in both the US House and the US Senate accepted documentation that Pinkney H. Head had doggedly pursued the protection and preservation of the Catawba Tribal interests for over fifty years of his life.

It is difficult to say whether or not the historic Catawba Land Settlement Act of 1993 would have been successful or not had Pinkney Head not been a man of determination, honor, dedication, and commitment to the rights of all Catawba's. With absolute certainty it can be stated that there would have been significant historic legal gaps in the present day legal efforts of the current Catawba generation's legal work had Pinkney not been the kind of man that he was. Indeed the Catawba Tribe's lawsuit submitted in federal court would have had an historic hurtle (or gap) to overcome without his writings. Missing from the Nations pleas to Congress would have been the historic efforts of Pinkney Head had he not been a man on a mission to protect the rights of all Catawba's.

# Head Family

Regretfully, Pinkney H. Head a known Catawba in his own life time through the Catawba Nation and the Ute Nation, the States of South Carolina, Colorado, and New Mexico, and the federal government was not listed on the federal Catawba Tribal Rolls of 1943.

Yet, the Catawba Nation and the federal government have had no difficulties in claiming the writings and history of Pinkney as a "known Catawba" as recently as the Catawba Land Settlement Act of 1993. Now, Pinkney's remaining living daughter, Helen Head Hayes (Colorado) is still seeking the justice of tribal recognition that her father sought. Joining with her are Pinkney's grandchildren and great-great grandchildren. It is a gift that Pinkney wanted his descendants to have.

In part, it was his drive for fairness, honor, and justice that has been passed down from his generation to the future generations that has given many of those in the future generations to also be determined to pursue the hill and rightful place of all Catawba's on the Federal and Tribal Catawba Membership Rolls of the 1990s.

Pinkney Head was a man, born over a century ago, but his duty to his tribesmen, his family, and to justice extends and impacts thousands of people well beyond his death. In fact, in the larger picture of things one can say that Pinkney Head's mark of pursuing Catawba treaty rights has impacted the entire United States of America as his voice —through his writings — was heard in the great halls of the United States Congress in the summer of 1993. His words will forever be recorded and passed on to those who read the Catawba Tribal history and the legal battles for justice of past harms to the Catawba's.

And, so by traditional belief Pinkney Head's words, his writings, and actions will be impacting others for seven generations into the future. He has left for us the means to carry on his efforts. One in which honor and determination with family and tribe matters. Being Catawba matters. And, determination matters. Pinkney has taught us that one should never, ever quit. No matter how hard the hurtles in life, no matter how painful the injustice, never, ever quit.

And perhaps if one doesn't win the battle the next generation will prevail, or the next, or the next. One's work may be but the foundation upon which the next generation will be able to work from. All Catawba's everywhere — whether enrolled or not-enrolled — owe a great deal to Pinkney Head. He is deserving of the honor of a great elder and statesman of the Catawba Nation.

Pinkney grew up without a father, was raised in a hostile community in which Indians were treated poorly and denied basic civil rights, he was raised on the Catawba. Nation in poverty, he joined the LDS Church, migrated with his new wife to start a new life in safety, built his first home in Colorado with 7,000 adobe bricks, worked hard and owned two farms, moved to New Mexico, obtained a homestead of 160 acres, continually maintained his ties with the Nation — never giving up his identity as Catawba, had a son murdered without justice being served, was a co-owner of a dairy, hauled freight, spoke English, Catawba, and Navajo languages, raised a large family, and was married to Martha Jane Patterson the bride from his youth.[410]

**Martha's history will be found under James Goodwin Patterson.**

"While Head's earlier attempts at gaining recognition and benefits for his people had failed, he was slightly more successful in New Mexico. Here he was able to make the Dawes General Allotment Act of 1887 work in his favor. Recognized by the federal government as an "Indian of the Catawba tribe or band," he was able to secure a federal land allotment of one hundred and sixty acres along the San Juan River in 1908. As the certificate of allotment indicates, this was considered federal trust land, "allotted…for the period of twenty-five years, in trust for the sole use and benefit of said Indian," after which it would be conveyed in fee simple to Head or his legal heirs. This was in accordance with the federal policy of allotment, most famously associated though not originating with the Dawes Act of 1887. It is interesting to note that while Head was recognized as "an Indian of the Catawba tribe or band," which apparently qualified him for an "Indian" land allotment, the allotted land was obviously not located on the Catawba reservation or any American Indian reservation for that matter"

From a dissertation written by Stan Thayne of Chapel Hill, North Carolina

**Pinkney Henry and Martha Jane Patterson Head's children were Sarah, Rosey, Lucy, Hattie, Heber, Nellie, Willard, George, Helen, Harry, Mary and Gladys Head.[411]**

**PHOTO 452 – SARAH JANE HEAD**

---

[410]  7th Generation News , vol 3.
[411]  Head genealogy courtesy various Head family members,

1. Sarah Jane Head born 28 December 1886 in South Carolina, married Edward James Francis Slaughter born 29 November 1886 and died Dec 1965, Arizona. She died July 1910 and is buried in Kirtland, San Juan, New Mexico.

**PHOTO 453 – HEADSTONE FOR SARAH JANE HEAD SLAUGHTER - BURIED: KIRTLAND CEMETERY, KIRTLAND, SAN JUAN COUNTY, NEW MEXICO**

**PHOTO 454 – HEADSTONE FOR ROSIE LEE HEAD -- BURIAL: SANFORD CEMETERY, SANFORD, CONEJOS COUNTY, COLORADO, PLOT: 2141-A**

2. Rosey Head born 17 June 1889 died in 1891 in Sanford, Colorado of Scarlet Fever. She is buried in the Sanford Cemetery.[412]  Sanford Cemetery Record.  Father was Pinkney Henry Head, Mother was Martha Jane Patterson Head.

**PHOTO 455 - LUCY MYRTLE HEAD**

3. Lucy Myrtle Head born 28 April 1891, married Manoel (Manuel) Marcelino, an American born son of Portuguese immigrants and they moved to Brazil, in 1913. On route, Manuel died in October 1942. Lucy died in Ibipora, Brazil on 13 June 1976, and is buried there. She had 4 children: Paul Victor, Olga Victoria, Guilherme Alberto, and Eduardo Marcelino.

**PHOTO 456 – LUCY MYRTLE HEAD PASS PORT**

---

[412] Ibid.

**Lucy Myrtle Head Marcelino's children**

a. Paul Victor Marcelino, born 1913, Brazil

b. Olga Victoria Marcelino, born 5 January 1915, Borebi, São Paulo, Brasil – died 6 April 1965, Maringá, Paraná, Brasil. She married João Peralta (1907–1977). The had the following children, Lucia Peralta,   Nelson Peralta 1939–1939 , João Peralta 1934–1934.

PHOTO 457 -  JOÃO PERALTA AND OLGA VICTORIA MARCELINO FAMILY, LUCIA, NELSON AND JOÃO PERALT

PHOTO 458 - LUCIA PERALTA DAUGHTER OF OLGA V MARCELINO PERALTA

**PHOTO 459 - GUILHERME ALBERTO MARCELINO**

c. Guilherme Alberto Marcelino, born 20 September 1917, Lençóis Paulista, Lençóis Paulista, São Paulo, Brazil – died 26 July 1999

> Guilherme found one of Lucy's books; it was the Book of Mormon. He read it and then went looking for the church. He didn't find one so he became active in building up a church. He was even considered to be called a patriarch; however he had not married up to that point. He married late in life however; he was ill and couldn't fulfill the calling.

d. Eduardo Marcelino, born 13 October 1926, Sao Paulo, Brazil – died 8 May 1974, Sao Paulo, Brazil

**PHOTO 460 – HATTIE MAE HEAD**

4. Hattie Mae Head was born 16 January 1893. She was married March 3, 1915 to Frank McClure, an Engineer. He was instrumental in getting some of the Head and Canty boys involved in working in the high steel industry, building high rise buildings in Phoenix, Arizona, and bridges around the west. Hattie died February 25, 1985; she and Frank had no children.[413]

**PHOTO 461 – HEBER JACKSON HEAD**

5. Heber Jackson Head born 15 February 1895, he married Mabel Bentley. Sometimes, his death eclipses his life. According to his brother in law and others who knew him, he was a kind, wonderful man. He worked in Colorado and sent money home to his mother, to help with their expenses. He worked the high steelwork during the 20's or 30's on bridges and buildings, traveling from job to job with the Canty boys and his brother George. They were helped, or steered into this

---

[413] Information from Wayne Head.

occupation by Frank McClure, an engineer, who married Hattie Head. The Mountain States Telephone Company, which was headquartered, also employed Heber in Gallup, New Mexico.

**PHOTO 462 – GRAVE MARKER FOR HEBER JACKSON HEAD  - BURIED AT SANFORD CEMETERY –
SANFORD, CONEJOS COUNTY, COLORADO**

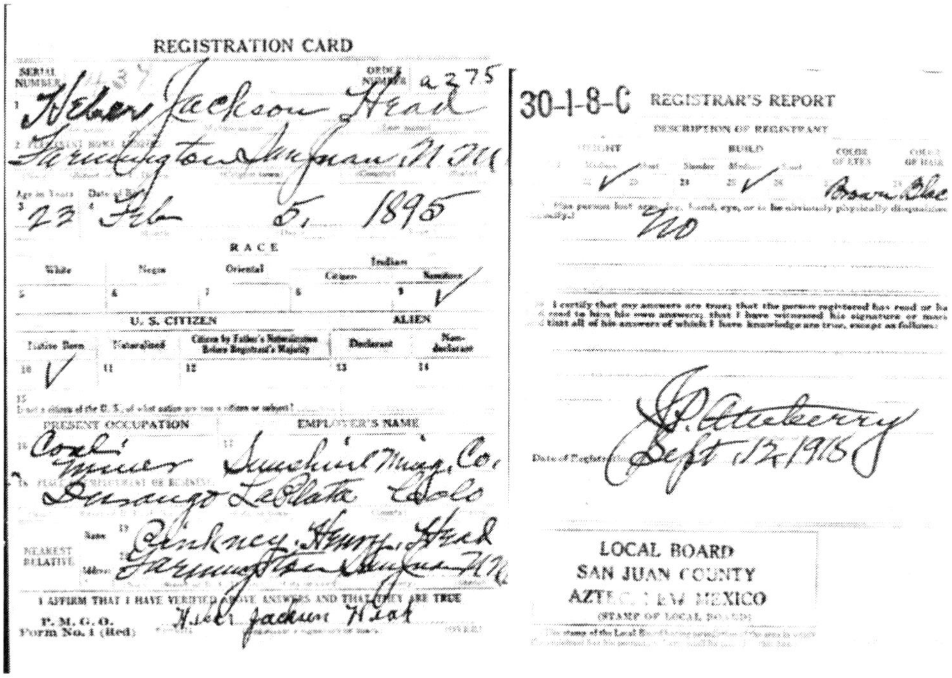

**PHOTO 463 – WWI REGISTRATION CARD FOR HEBER JACKSON HEAD**

**State of Colorado**
**Division of Vital Statistics**
No. **321**

**MARRIAGE RECORD REPORT**

County **ALAMOSA**

Husband's Name **HEAD, HEBER J.** Age **24** Race **W**

Wife's Name **BENTLEY, MABEL** Age **18** Race **W**

Place of Marriage **ALAMOSA COLO** Date **8-19-19**

Name of Official who Performed Ceremony **J A STANSFIELD**

Title **MIN** Address **ALAMOSA COLO**

Reported by

Address

**PHOTO 464 - MARRIAGE RECORD REPORT FOR HEBER J HEAD AND MABEL BENTLEY**

The story of the death of Heber is so tragic, and still painful to any that read it, especially the children and grandchildren. It is not my intention to hurt them, only to let this story enlighten the other readers and family members, for history's sake, "Lest We Forget." Heber died near midnight on Christmas, December 1929 near Antonito, Colorado. Heber, his wife Mabel and his two children, Jack and Barbara, ages 3 and 5, and his brother Harry, were traveling from Farmington, New Mexico to visit Mabel's father Fred Bentley in Sanford, Colorado, Near Antonito, the Head vehicle was involved in a fender-bender. The night was cold, as most Christmas nights are in the San Luis Valley of Colorado, and the windows were partly coated from the frost. After the collision, Heber offered to pay for any damage to the other car, but the boy driving it refused to talk any sort of settlement, saying he was going to have Heber arrested.

(This is my theory, that after being confronted with the gang of boys, and being near Antonito, Heber must have believed that the safest thing for them to do is be on their way. He was not running away, just moving to safety for his young children and wife were with him. Personally, this is the action I would take in this situation.)

"They were about 3 miles from Antonito and the Deputy Sheriff John King and a large group of men overtook their car. Mabel stated, My husband is very dark, like an Old Mexico Mexican and one of the group started yelling at him in Spanish. He stopped him and said he didn't know Spanish, to talk "United States." He then stepped around in front of the car with the officer, his hands in the pockets of his overalls."

"The fellow drew away and the officer stepped up and said, We'll not have any rough stuff here," and my husband answered "Don't worry, there'll not be any trouble." He thrust his hands further into his pockets, (trying to illustrate that he did not intend to fight.) Without warning, the officer fired his gun at Heber, point blank. They were in the front of the car, and Mabel, the two children and Heber's brother Harry could see clearly.

The Deputy stated at the inquest that was held that Head had reached for his hip pocket as the officer tried to arrest him. Exactly what he would have been arrested for, is certainly unclear to me, 70 years later. He had an accident, offered to pay for any damage, and did not attempt to flee, did not have a weapon, and offered no resistance. King insisted that he believed Heber was reaching for a gun and that he had struck Heber on the side of the head, and the gun discharged accidentally. Dr. C. A. Davlin stated that the only bruises visible on his face were abrasions, such as might be caused by his falling face forward, on the graveled road. No bruises were visible on the left side of his face, where Officer King stated he had struck him with the barrel of the gun, when it discharged.

Officer King was taken into custody, after Pinkney came from Farmington, New Mexico to protest the murder. Pinkney charged that King "did feloniously, willfully and of his malice aforethought, kill and murder Heber." In spite of large crowd of Kings friends present at the hearings, on December 30, a coroner's jury found that the charges were substantiated by testimony. The District Attorney in Alamosa stated that he would prosecute King. The family has been unable to find any more information, the notes on the proceedings and the results of the trial, if there was one, are unknown. A good many of the old records have burned in the Conejos County Court House when in burned in the 1980's, and so far, I have not found any more information as to whether or not King was even tried.

A final note to this tragedy is the last paragraph of the December 27, 1929 article entitled, "Widow Says Heber Head Was Shot Down In Cold Blood By Deputy King, <u>Looked Like Indian. The dead man had the physical characteristics of the typical Indian. His cheekbones are high, his chin pointed and his hair is jet black. He is dark skinned and while slightly built appears to have been exceptionally well muscled.</u>"

What point this last entry was trying to make, escapes me, perhaps that because he was an Indian, it was justified, the old "The Only Good Indian is a Dead Indian." There is no way of knowing the intent of the report.

**PHOTO 465 – WILLARD HENNRY HEAD**

6. Willard Henry Head, born September 9, 1897, married Mabel Otis. Willard worked as a road maintainer on the Navajo reservation, and spoke fluent Navajo. He used to run the road grader, sometimes towing a trailer, when the roads became impassable in the wet times of the year. He also worked on the Million Dollar Highway, between Silverton and Ouray, Colorado. Later in his life, he farmed and raised fruit in Kirtland, New Mexico.

**PHOTO 466 – HEADSTONE OF WILLARD HENRY HEAD AND WIFE MABEL OTIS.**

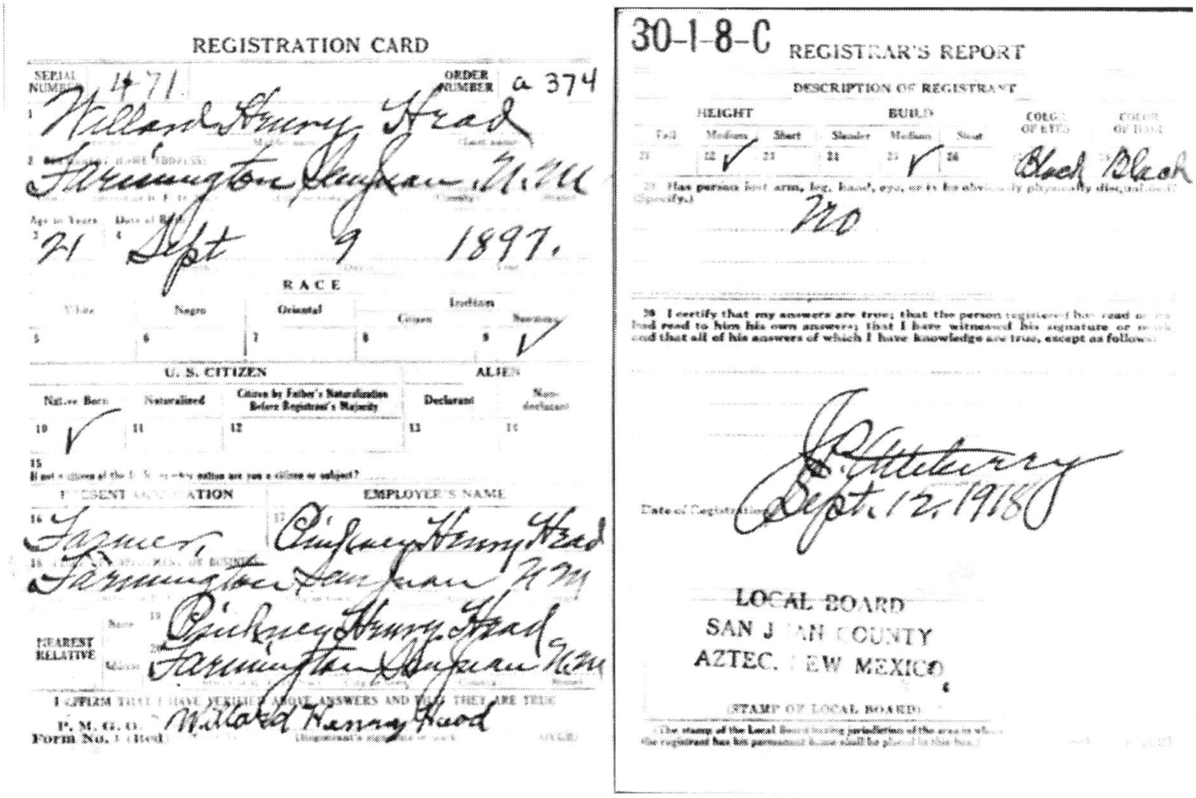

REGISTRATION CARD

SERIAL NUMBER 1471 ORDER NUMBER a 374

1 Willard Henry Head

2 Farmington San Juan N.M.

Age in Years 21 Date of Birth Sept 9 1897

RACE

Indian: Noncitizen ✓

U. S. CITIZEN: Native Born ✓

PRESENT OCCUPATION: Farmer EMPLOYER'S NAME: Pinkney Henry Head

Farmington San Juan N M

NEAREST RELATIVE: Pinkney Henry Head, Farmington San Juan N.M.

I AFFIRM THAT I HAVE VERIFIED ABOVE ANSWERS AND THAT THEY ARE TRUE

P. M. G. O. Form No. 1 (Red) Willard Henry Head

30-1-8-C REGISTRAR'S REPORT

DESCRIPTION OF REGISTRANT

HEIGHT: Medium ✓ BUILD: Medium ✓ COLOR OF EYES: Black COLOR OF HAIR: Black

Has person lost arm, leg, hand, eye, or is he obviously physically disqualified? No

I certify that my answers are true; that the person registered has read or has had read to him his own answers; that I have witnessed his signature or mark, and that all of his answers of which I have knowledge are true, except as follows:

Date of Registration Sept. 12, 1918

LOCAL BOARD SAN JUAN COUNTY AZTEC, NEW MEXICO

(STAMP OF LOCAL BOARD)

**PHOTO 467 – WWI REGISTRATION CARD FOR WILLARD HENRY HEAD**

## WILLARD HENRY HEAD

By Agnes Head Palmer, of Farmington, New Mexico

My father, Willard Henry Head, was the sixth child of Pinkney and Martha Jane Patterson Head. He was born September 9, 1897 in Sanford, Colorado. The Head family moved to San Juan County in the early 1900s and eventually settled south of Farmington on the banks of the San Juan River. As a youngster, Willard and several of his siblings were sent to Fort Lewis boarding school in Colorado. For Lewis is now a four-year college located in Durango, Colorado but began as an army post and later became an Indian boarding school. Daddy had unpleasant memories of the experience and told of being hungry and running away from the school several times. Apparently, since the children were so unhappy at Fort Lewis, there out of state schooling was ended. A funny exchange occurred one day when I took Aunt Hattie Head McClure to a doctor's appointment. A Navajo lady from Shiprock, who had also attended boarding school, recognized Hattie. She came over and shook Hattie's hand and said, "It's good to see you, my old college chum." Referring to Fort Lewis' status. Willard inherited his family's love of storytelling, music, animals, and fishing. He had a terrific sense of humor and his stories were always spiced with his special humor. It was great fun to listen to the stories he and his family told when they got together.

# Head Family

In April of 1932 Willard married Mable Otis and worked for a time as a trader on the Navajo reservation. When the family expanded to include my older brother, Otis and I, he went to work for the Bureau of Indian Affairs maintaining the dirt roads on the Navajo reservation. We first located at Crownpoint, New Mexico where a second daughter, Charlene, was born. We then moved to Kayenta, Arizona where Otis and I started school in a one-room schoolhouse. The first grade class consisted of me another Navajo, Herbert Claw. For a short time during World War II, Daddy followed defense work and we lived briefly in California and Nevada. Because of the frequent moves required by defense jobs, Willard returned to the Bureau of Indian Affairs job and we lived in Tuba City, Arizona at the edge of the Hopi reservation and then moved to Shiprock, New Mexico.

When we resided in Arizona, many roads were trails with small stacks of stone to mark the route. To get to Kayenta, we had to cross numerous small washes and sand dunes. Once when Grandmother Martha Head was with us, we all slept on the bank of a wash because it was running too high to cross. If a windstorm came up and covered the road with sand, Daddy would drive until we became stuck in the sand. Then he would get out a big tarp, dig the sand away from the wheels and drive across the tarp and into the sand until we became stuck again. This process was repeated until we were clear of the sand.

During his early employment with the Bureau of Indian Affairs, Willard would pull a small trailer behind a road grader and live away from the family all week. He had a large collection of pottery pieces and arrowheads that he found while blading roads in remote areas of the reservation. He would take magazines with him and distribute them to his Navajo friends along the way. I have two special memories of this time — once I stowed away in the grader, planning not to be found until we were too far for me to be taken back — it didn't work, I was discovered! The other was when my mother was ill and Daddy took my brother, sister, and me with him in his little trailer. As he told the story Charlene drank all his canned milk and I fell in a sheep trough and got soaked. If Otis got into any trouble, it wasn't reported.

In 1947, Willard and Mable bought a farm in Fruitland, New Mexico. They raised alfalfa and fruit and had a small fruit stand. Willard continued to work in Shiprock for several more years and then was employed as a heavy equipment operator for El Paso Natural Gas Company.

While we lived on the farm, Daddy found an abandoned calf above the ditch near our house. He brought it home and with TLC, it survived. Some months later the calf died. When Daddy told about the calf s death he said it proved that rustling did not pay.

Willard played the guitar and if coaxed would sing. He would sometimes play with other musicians for dances at the community hall. He also enjoyed sports, especially Softball and baseball. When we were growing up every, summer weekend, found us at the ball field watching softball games. His favorite team was the Navajo men from Shiprock. They would travel in the back of a flatbed truck on their way to a game in Farmington and when they passed our house they would honk and yell, "come on Willard, let's go to the game."

After selling the farm and moving to Farmington, Willard and Mable bought season tickets to attend the Connie Mack World Series, an amateur baseball event, and attended every year. Later in life they took up bowling and participated on a senior bowling league. In the spring of 1973, Willard was diagnosed with cancer. He died three months later, on August 13th. In his obituary he was remembered as a quiet, kind man, always ready to help someone in need. He was an avid reader, loved to go to the movies and spend time with his family.[414] His children are Otis Head, Agnes and Charlene Head

**PHOTO 468 - HEADSTONE OF NELLIE ANN HEAD CLIFTON -- BURIAL: SUNSET MEMORIAL PARK ALBUQUERQUE, BERNALILLO COUNTY, NEW MEXICO, PLOT: SEC 7, LOT 17**

7. Nellie Ann Head born 11 September 1899 married Robert Hoy Clifton died during an epidemic or either Typhoid or Typhus when her children were young and Martha and Pinkney raised them. She had three children, Robert, Mildred and Dorothy.

---

[414] Agnes Head Palmer.

**PHOTO 469 – GEORGE JESTON HEAD**

8. George Jeston Head, born July 5, 1901, married Amy Pearl Bentley. George led an interesting life. He was an assistant Game Warden, and also did some Taxidermy work. He-was a fireman on the Denver and Rio Grande Western Railway, between Chama, New Mexico and southern Colorado, when it was a working railroad, instead of a tourist attraction. He worked on the Boulder Dam project, which was later called Hoover Dam, as did his cousin Elbert Garcia-Garce, although they most likely never knew the other was there. He was a high steelworker, working with Lazell and Buck Canty during the 20's or 30's. They traveled around the west, building bridges, and several high rise buildings in Phoenix, Arizona. He spoke fluent Navajo, as did his father, and served as an interpreter for the Navajo Police. "

**George and Amy Bentley Head had eight children: James, Amy, George, Keith, Naomi, Leona, Vera, and Larry Head.**[415]

---

[415] Picture and genealogy courtesy Wayne Head.

**PHOTO 470 – HEADSTONE FOR GEORGE J HEAD –
BURRIED AT GREENLAWN CEMETERY - FARMINGTON,
SAN JUAN COUNTY, NEW MEXICO**

**PHOTO 471 - HELEN CATHERINE HEAD**

9. Helen Catherine Head, born February 29, 1904, married Whitey Hayes. Helen, acted in a silent movie called The Love of a Navajo, which was filmed near Farmington. When I began this project, my dad and I visited Helen, Mary, Dorothy and Hattie at their home in Farmington. Helen even sent me a prized possession, a picture of her mother when she was young. I had it copied, and sent her back copies. Several years later, when this project was further along, Helen and Mary and Wayne Head met with Dr. Russ Judkins and Raymond Harris and I, and taped interviews for his

book. Helen sent me a picture of her mother that I have used in this book, it also appeared in the Farmington Newspaper, when I was in need of help finding all the rest of the Head family. This was also my first meeting with Wayne Head.

**PHOTO 472 – HEADSTONE FOR HELEN CATHERINE HEAD HAYES - BURIAL: SHERIDAN MUNICIPAL CEMETERY, SHERIDAN, SHERIDAN COUNTY, WYOMING - PLOT: BLOCK 100 LOT 8**

Helen C. Hayes Former Sheridan resident Helen C. Hayes, 97, died Sunday, July 15, 2001, in Castle Rock, Colo. Visitation is 9-11 a.m. Thursday at Kane Funeral Home. A graveside service is 11 a.m. in Sheridan Municipal Cemetery. Ms. Hayes was born Feb. 29, 1904, in Aztec, N.M., to Pinkney and Martha (Patterson) Head. She enjoyed fishing and playing cards. She loved to work and was involved with her grandchildren. She was preceded in death by 11 siblings. Survivors include her daughter, Carol (George) Acker of Simla, Colo.; three grandchildren; and four great-grandchildren. In lieu of flowers, memorials may be made to the Sheridan Church of Jesus Christ of Latter-day Saints in care of Kay Roush, First Federal Savings Bank, Box 6007, Sheridan, WY 82801.

**PHOTO 473 – PINKNEY HARRY HEAD**

10. Pinkney Harry Head, born January 12, 1907, married Stella Dell Bentley. Harry was a boxer in his younger days. He lost an eye in a bout, when something was thrown into his face. He was considered a good boxer until this injury forced him to quit. He remained near the old Pinkney Head place on Butler Avenue, in Farmington, New Mexico until his death. Harry died 16 October 1989, and is buried in Kirtland, NM.

Pinkney Head jr. born July 25, 1930, he had 6 children, married Beverly.

## State of Colorado
### Division of Vital Statistics
## MARRIAGE RECORD REPORT

County ....Alamosa....

Husband's Name ....Head Harry.... Age ..22.. Race ...white..

Wife's Name ....Bentley Stella.... Age ...17.. Race ....white....

Place of Marriage ....Alamosa, Alamosa County.... Date ..1/4/30..

Name of Official who Performed Ceremony ....Rev. Gil Traveller....

Title ..Methodist Minister.... Address ....Alamosa, Colorado....

Reported by....................Virginia Mae Pond....

45    Address ....................Alamosa, Colorado....

**PHOTO 474 – HARRY HEAD AND STELLA BENTLEY – MARRIAGE RECORD REPORT**

**PHOTO 475 – HEADSTONE FOR PINKNEY HARRY HEAD AND HIS WIFE STELLA BENTLEY HEAD -
BURIAL:  KIRTLAND CEMETERY,  KIRTLAND,  SAN JUAN COUNTY,  NEW MEXICO**

**PHOTO 476 – MARY EVELYN HEAD HODGSON**

11. Mary Evelyn Head Hodgson born December 26, 1909, she died 19 December 1991 and is buried in Kirtland, NM. She married Vernon Dale Hodgson 1907-1969.

**PHOTO 477 – HEADSTONE FOR MARY E HEAD HODGSON – BURIED AT KIRTLAND CEMETERY KIRTLAND, SAN JUAN COUNTY, NEW MEXICO**

**PHOTO 478 - DOROTHY GLADYS HEAD**

12. Dorothy Gladys Head born February 11, 1912, Farmington, San Juan, New Mexico unmarried, died 23 June 1985 Farmington, San Juan, New Mexico. She is buried in Kirtland San Juan County, New Mexico

**PHOTO 479 - HEADSTONE FOR DOROTHY GLADYS HEAD -- BURIAL: KIRTLAND CEMETERY, KIRTLAND, SAN JUAN COUNTY, NEW MEXICO**

## Chapter 13   Joe Family – Prow – Frow

King Prow-Joe, was probably born around 1730, ruled 1762-1794.  It is said that he owed his position as Eractasswa to a meeting of 42 Catawba head men in 1765, which was referred to as Election of a Catawba King.[416]

Shortly after he was crowned, he and some warriors went to Charles Town to help in the capture of runaway slaves who were threatening trouble in the swamps at Pon Pon. The Catawba were so feared as warriors that slaves, when hearing the Catawba were coming after them, gave up without a fight.[417] "The Indians-partly by the terror of their name and their diligence and singular sagacity in pursuing Enemies through such thickets soon dispersed the runaway Negroes, appended several and most of the rest of them chose to surrender themselves to the attack of an Enemy so dreaded and so difficult to be resisted or evaded."[418]

It was the custom of the white government men to give the Catawba presents when they had sent for the Catawba. This grew to be a custom, the whites would send for the Catawba and ask them to do a little favor, like catch some escaped slaves, or fight the Cherokee, or whatever the colonists needed. In return, and in my estimation, in payment for these services, gifts were given to the Catawba. These gifts then became a serious matter, and occasionally the Catawba came without invitation, (how terrible.) They expected gifts then and the whites were appalled, although it was their customs (the whites), the Catawba were observing.

In 1768, after hearing the whites little sermon about how the Indians "  must not expect gifts unless they were sent for," King Prow left with powder, shot, rum and paint and a saddle for himself. The next year he also obtained four muskets, 25 pounds of powder and 50 pounds of lead and 5 gallons of rum. When he asked for shirts in 1771, he got the same sermon, and left with "powder and shot and a little paint, but the Indians must remember that when they came to town without being sent for, they must not expect any presents."[419] Now the whites were really put out that these "savages" had the audacity to ask for presents when the colonists had not even sent for them. In other words, if the white colonists needed something and it was their idea to have the Catawba come to town; it was all right to give them presents. However, for the Catawba to have the audacity to come without an invitation or call was just too much.

Prow even once complained in 1773 of white hunters using light at night to hunt.[420]

---

[416] Brown page 252
[417] SC Council, Journal XXXII, 442-443, letter signed by King Prow.
[418] Ibid
[419] Merrell pages 205 & 206.bid.
[420] Blumer, page 75.

On April 12, 1775, King Prow sent the following letter to Lord Dunmore, denying the rumor that Catawba had taken part in the Battle of Point Pleasant as allies of the hostile Indians.

**"Honourable Sir:**

I take the Hbl Liberty of interrupting you in order to inform you of a malisious report that have been raised in order to shorten the chain of friendship that have long subsisted between our brothers the white people & us. We are informed that it is reported there was a number of our people in the battle that the Virginian forces under your Excelencys Command had with the Shawnes and that there was several of our people killed in assisting against the white people, but Sir, I can assure you that the report are intirely false. Our people were all at home but one and he informs me that at the time of the battle he was in North Carolina. It would be verry unreasonable for a child to kill a father or one brother another and this must be the case if we should offer to murder the white people, It is from them all our benefits flow our apperral, guns and amonition are all procured from them and our Nation are in the midst of them. So that if we should insence them we must inevitable wholely perish but we hope your excelency will not listen to any report that will darken the bright chain or interupt the good harmony that have been so long subsisted between our brother the white people and us. Sir I assure you it is the great desire of our people to live amongst the white people in peace and uninimity. We have had offers which appeared adventagious from other Nations but our love for the white people made us contemn (condemn) them and continue in the land aloted us by the great King. Our uneasiness was so great that we thought the only method was to inform your Excelency and we got one of our brothers a white man to write from our mouth what was the desire of our hart in regard of our friends and have sent it by two of our people, viz: Capt. Haris and Doctar John and I humbly beg you would use them well and if your esteem is not shortened favr me with a small acknowledgment of two yards of blue cloth and I shall ever hold you fast by the right hand.

Prow, Cataba King." [421]

Prow ruled in 1762 and abdicated in 1794. Among the toasts at the Bastille, celebration was the following: "King Prow, May all kings who will not follow his example follow that of Louis XVI." (Louis XVI was beheaded in the Revolution in France.) An explanation for the toast to King Prow was that he was a man of mean capacity and incapable of governing, and he was accused of doing nothing more than eating their food. He voluntarily resigned his crown of cornshucks to keep the people from shedding each other's blood because there were so few of them left.

General New River succeeded him.

Prow is listed on Drennan's paybill as Jove-Joue. After the American Revolution, the title King was abandoned and military titles were used instead. In addition, the practice of handing down leadership in families was abandoned, and the future leaders were elected. The Catawba were reduced in numbers due to drunkenness and laziness. The young women, according to Smyth, were self-inducing abortions, with the aids of medicinal herbs, and were not having large families.

---

[421] SC Council, Journal, XXXIV

I. John Joe, probably born around 1795, was most likely the son of King Prow-Joe. It is too unlikely that there were a great many Joes around at the time. John received rents from 1818 to 1824. He signed leases as Lt. John Joe from 1827 to 1829. He was living in 1840 and had a family because he signed the 1840 treaty of Nation Ford as Major John Joe.

Because Hutchinson described him as lazy and intemperate that was most probably the cause of his death. John signed a petition of 1840 as Captain John Joe, but died supposed by intemperance by July 1843. He married Caty Scott, born 1799.10 There are only two children attributed to Caty; they are Eliza Scott Canty and

Joseph Joe. More information will be found under Scott for Eliza, and in Genealogy of the Western Catawba under Scott and Canty, since she had children by both Franklin Canty and Thomas Whitesides.

> A. Eliza Scott-Joe born 1826 married first Franklin Canty; and second Thomas Whitesides. Her children were George Washington Canty and two who must have died in early childhood, Mary Jane Whitesides, John Alonzo Canty (he took her married name) and Fannie Whitesides. Evidently, Eliza died young, because in 1860, Caty Joe was raising her grandchildren, which would be these children. Children will be found under Chapter 4, Canty and in Genealogy of the Western Catawba.

> B. Joseph Joe born around 1840, alive at least until after 1854."[422]

II. Gemmima Joe, Billy Brown's rents went to Gemmima, the stepdaughter of Billy's Wife.[423]

III. Jenny Joe, born 1806, disappears after 1849.[424] Unknown family.

IV. Mary Joe probably born around 1800, no more is known, she signed a petition in 1848 in North Carolina and was connected with the Methodist church at Echota in 1849, but does not appear on the 1849 census of adults. In the Plat Book, there is a Mary Scott, who is most likely the same person as Mary Joe.[425]

---

[422] 1854 census.
[423] Watson page 59 & 60.
[424] 1849 census.
[425] Ibid

**PHOTO 480 - MIDDLE BACK LULA BLUE BECK AND THEN LUCY LEOLA WATTS BLUE AND LUCY GEORGE STARNES NEXT TO HER L-R -- ABT 1918**

# Chapter 14   Kegg Family

I. William-Billy Cagg was probably born around 1750 and died between 1780 and 1792. It is possible that these Keggs were Pamunkey, as indicated in one document. The Kegg's later went to live among the Cherokee. Billey Kegg appears on Drennan's Paybill of 1780, but not on the 1792 Petition.[426]

II. John Cagg-Kegg probably born around 1750 and died soon after 1792. He was a Captain in the Catawba council in 1792. He appears on Drennan's paybill for Revolutionary Service in 1780 and probably died soon after 1792.[427] This is most likely the father of Jamey-James Kegg.

A. General Jamey -James Kegg[428] was born 1783.[429] He was Pamunkey, according to Hutchinson. He was 55 at the time he took over as chief or general in 1840. He married Jinney Scott, daughter of William- Billy Scott and Sally Scott-Toole NewRiver.

When he took the leadership capacity as Chief, he did not have the support of the tribe; however, he continued to try to get help for removal. He remarked that "When the Catawba were a strong people, and the state weak, they came to her support: and now when the State was strong and the Catawbas weak, she ought to assist them.[430] His idea was for the state to give each Catawba the money to buy his own land, and by having the title in their individual name, the Catawba would be subject to laws and taxes, but entitled to the privileges and immunities of citizens.[431] He even went to Raleigh to lobby for removal. Then in 1842, he worked for admittance into the Cherokee Nation. He also wanted to marry his women to the Cherokee and then by custom the children would become Catawba, and strengthen the tribe.[432] This was met with problems; one of which was the fact that the Cherokee still had men named Catawba Killer etc., and that the Cherokee thought the Catawba had bad habits.

By 1849, it had become apparent that Catawba were not willing to move.

From the journal of Pinkney Head: dated January 1886, "We went back to Bird Town and while there we went to James Kagg (Kegg) house. He was one of the tribe of Catawba's. I had a long chat with him."

One visitor to Keggs home told of the Catawba men exhibiting their archery skills at the dinner table, by having someone throw up coins into the air and shooting at them with their bows and arrows.[433]

---

[426] Brown page 268 & 289.
[427] Ibid
[428] Brown, pase 307.
[429] 1849 census.
[430] Brown pages 308 & 309.
[431] Brown page 309.
[432] Ibid
[433] Brown page 315.

Richard Springs described him as "more than ordinary by nature, wrote a good hand, but could not resist the besetting evil-spirits—he said to me one day, his ancestors name was Hogshead but it had been reduced to Kegg, he expected it would be brought down to a quart and pint bottle."[434] One time he traded his horse for a blind one, when asked why, he replied: "You take the horse I swapped—ride him one mile- one leg won't go." When he purchased a Negro woman, he was asked why, his answer was: "To be called Master." His idea was that one day the Negro would own the land.[435] These statements better illustrate the conclusion I have made, that the Catawba were not as dumb as people thought, and they have their own process of reasoning that whites cannot understand. It also says that the Catawba did not tell everything they knew to researchers.

Jamey Kegg purportedly served in the Civil War, as he is pictured in a group of Cherokee, who served in the Confederate Army, in North Carolina;[436] however, he died in the fall of 1852, returning from Charleston, and is supposed to be buried there.[437]

1. Phillip Kegg born 1815[438] married Cynthia born 1818. Phillip became a leader of a band of Catawba who removed to the southwest.[439]

   a. Infant born around 1851. Possibly another James Kegg.

2. Betsy Kegg born 1820, her Cherokee name was Quatsie or Quatsy. She married

Da-Wee-Gun-skar-lee-skior Will a Cherokee. They had three children. Betsy probably died near the birth of her child William.

   a. Rebecca Jane born 1839, Indian name Qua-gar-gee-nee or Wogi-jean-nih. She married Lewis Gibson a black man. They had a son Solomon and a daughter Eliza born in 1863 at Soce Creek, Jackson County, and NC. Eliza married second David Taylor.

   b. James born 1841 in Swain Co, NC.

   c. William born 1844 died about 1860.

3. Susy Kegg born 1827 died in Haywood, North Carolina in 1852.

III. Betsy Kegg born around 1790 married John Ayers around 1816, thus becoming Betsy

Kegg now Betsy Ayers, according to the Indian agent, Hugh White.[440] Any children will

---

[434] Brown page 314.

[435] Brown page 314-15

[436] Ibid

[437] Ibid

[438] Although Phillip is listed as having been born in 1826 in the 49 census, it is pointed out by Watson that it is unlikely that he was this young. See Watson pages 64-65.

[439] Ibid

be found under Ayers.

IV. Nanny-Nancy Kegg born around 1780, married and had children by January 1819. She is connected with the Harris family, perhaps the Nancy Harris who, with Sam Evans, had Allen Harris born 1813.[441] Nancy was probably dead by January 1819, when Billy Ayers was paid for her children.[442]

V. Barbara Barbary Kegg born around 1830 married William P. Brown.

A. Alabama Brown born 20 April 1850 in Halls, GA, married Thomas D. Scott born 3 April 1838 in Lawrence, Tennessee.

1. Emma R. Scott born 12 Dec. 1869 Haralson, Ga. Married Nobel Fogg.

2. Barbara Scott born 16 July 1869, Ga.

3. Mary Scott born 16 Mar 1874

4. Robert R. Scott born 30 Aug. 1876

5. Albert N. Scott born 26 Aug. 1879

6. John T. Scott born 2 Sept. 1887 died November 1916

7. Callie Ann Scott born 2 June 1888 in Manassa, Colorado died 9 November 1918.

Information comes from the Manassa, Colorado Ward Records, and is given here, only because of the Kegg connection. Thomas Scott must have been white. None of the Barbary Kegg information has been proven.

---

[440] Merrell page 236.
[441] Ibid
[442] Watson pages 60-62.

**Photo 481 - From Travis Blue**
L-R BACK ROW: MARCILLE CABANISS, MAXINE & RALPH SIMMONS, FLETCHER & SALLY BECK,
IDLE & ARZADA SANDERS, LEABORNE & ARTHUR WHITESELL –
L-R FRONT ROW: FORRREST CABANISS, WILLIE & NOLA CAMPBELL, DOUGLAS & GEORGIA
HARRIS, HERBERT & ADDIE MAE BLUE

## Chapter 15   Kennedy Family

I. Captain Kelly— John Kellian-John Celliah, I believe they are all the same. Captain John Kennedy, and John Celliah are both mentioned in Drennan's pay bill in different parts of the bill; however, they are most likely both the same person, probably born around 1720. The family would have taken their surname name from Captain Quitin Kennedy, a white man. He participated in Grant's Cherokee Campaign with King Hagler and 19 Catawba men on May 25, 1761 at Beaver Dams.₃ Kennedy is also mentioned in connection with a peace meeting involving Captain French, who met at Pine Tree Hill, around 1761.

He also signed the letter, along with 31 other Catawba, asking for redress from the SC House of Representatives in 1792. He also was involved with Jenny Patterson and Patrick Redhead, in the selling to Negroes, for which he nearly paid with his life in 1793. For more information see Patrick Redhead. John married first, wife unknown.

I believe that Betsey Kennedy who was probably born around 1720, and was alive at least from 1813-1816, and possibly to 1824, was John's second wife. She would have been a Betsy-Betsey Ayers Scott Canty, daughter of Jacob Ayers and Ms. Hagler; her first husband was John Scott; her second husband was Major George Canty; and her third husband was John Kennedy.

A. Johnston Kennedy alive from 1812 to 1820, received rents on the Carter Place.

B. Richardson Kennedy is alive at least as early as 1813. He married Nancy Brown, daughter of John Genet Brown; she was alive as early as 1815, but dead by 1825. He received rents on the Mill Place.[443] A child rents paid to Nancy George for this child. It is possible that this child may have been called Brown, taking the mothers name, rather than the fathers for there is no other mention of any Kennedy's in Catawba.

---

[443] 3 Watson page 67.

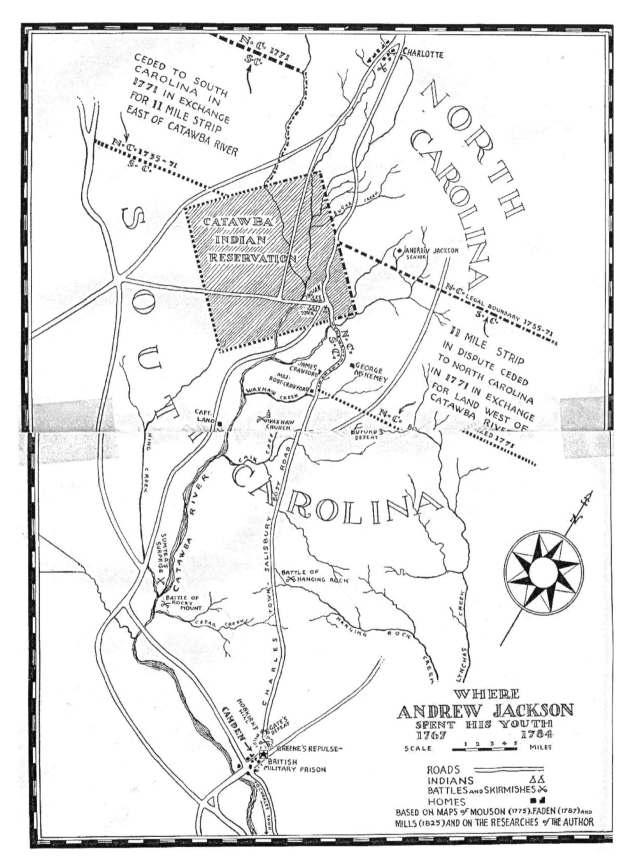

Map Catawba Indian

## Chapter 16   Marsh – Mursh – Mush Family

Robert Mush-Mursh-Marsh, born 1758.[444]   He was a Pamunkey Indian from Virginia.[445]   He was a student at William and Mary in 1769, so this birth year may have been even earlier than 1758.   He wrote and signed the petition of 1798, and was perhaps the headman.[446]

He enlisted in the Virginia Continental Army in 1776 in the 15th Regiment under Colonel Maryson for 3 years and afterwards for the war in the Company commanded by Capt. Gray and was afterwards transferred to the 11th Regiment and then to the 9th Regiment of the same Line.

The declaration of Robert Mursh a native of Virginia and one of the Pamunkey tribe of Indians and now a citizen of and resident in York District in the state of South Carolina, made in pursuance of the provisions of the Act of Congress of the 18th, March, 1818, entitled "An Act to provide for certain persons engaged in the land and naval service of the United States on the Revolutionary War.   The Declarant saith that he enlisted as a common soldier in the Army of the United States in the war of the Revolution in the latter part of the year 1776 and in the early part of the year following he joined the 15th Virginia Regt. of Continental Troops.   Col. Mason attached to the Company commanded by Capt. James Gray at Williamsburg and shortly after joined the main army at Meadowbrook in New Jersey.   That shortly after he joined the Regt. the command of it disolved on Col. James --- and under his command he fought at the battles of Brandywine and Germantown in the Brigade commanded by Genl. Woodford.   The declarant further saith that having served in the Regiment for something more than two years he reenlisted in the Continental Army in the service of the United States during the war; and was attached to a Regiment formed out of the remnants of the 7th and 15th commanded by Col. Rupert-- Col. Ben--- Ball denominated the 7th Regiment of the Virginia Continental Line.   Capt. William Mosely and that with this Regiment he marched to Charleston, where he remained until that place surrendered to the British and was among the prisoners of war and remained in that situation about fourteen months when he was carried to Jamestown and exchanged and then joined a Regiment commanded by Col.--- Capt. Kirkpatrick, the number of which Regiment is not now recollected.   The command of this, Regiment was afterwards assigned to Col. Posey and with this Regt. he marched to Ebenezer in Georgia when they joined the army of Genl. Wayne and that he continued with this army until after the place where he was regularly discharged from the service and that this discharge was delivered at the Land office and farming his military warrant of his bounty of land so that he has it not now to exhibit.   The declarant further saith that he is now about sixty years of age and has resided continually from his birth of the present day in the United States that he is poor and feebly and in consequence of his reduced circumstances stands in need of the assistance of his country for support.   Signed Robert Marsh.

State of North Carolina, Lincoln County.   This day personally before me a Justice of the Peace for said county came Vincent Allen and made oath in due form of law and saith that Robert Marsh a private in

---

[444] Marsh-Mursh-Mush Genealogy.
[445] Roundtree Dorothy, Pocahontas's People pages 170 & 171.
[446] Ibid.

Capt. Kirkpatricks Company formerly in Colonel Phebickers Regiment but marched out under Colonel Posey to Ebenezer in the State of Georgia then was joined by Gen. Wayne and the said Vincent Allen further saith that he knew the said Robert Marsh to have faithfully performed his tour of duty as a Continental in the Revolutionary War on or about the year 1782 and that he was regularly and honorably discharged about the close of the war as I believe and further the said Vincent Allen saith not, sworn to before me this 8th day of October 1818. Signed Henry C. and Vincent Allen." [447]

Robert married Elizabeth born around 1763.[448] Elizabeth was also supposed to be a Pamunkey Indian. She was last known alive in 1850.[449] He died in York County, South Carolina on December 7, 1837. The couple was married according to Pamunkey tradition on 1 October 1782 or 7 August 1783 and after becoming Christians, they were remarried in 1796 by Jack Mills, pastor of the Baptist Church at King William, Virginia.[450]

He was described as a "large and somewhat corpulent warrior." Another author, Robert Milling, described him as "over 6 feet high and raw boned." [451]

Robert moved his family to Chester County.[452] "Rev. R. Mursh left the Nation, time not stated, bought 80 acres of land in the edge of NC, five miles above Rbt. Mills where he spent the remnant of his days. He died there, his wife also, they are buried there and there is a stonewall around their greaves. " [453]

" Robert preached at the Hopewell Baptist Church, the Second Sunday, January 1815. Rev. Marsh was preaching, although at that distance I heard him distinctly. His voice was rather melodious. When I entered the church and took a full view of him he appeared to be an old man dressed in home spun, he used natural gestures and was quite eloquent. These men had great hopes of civilizing and Christianizing the Catawba Indians. They got a young man by the name of James ?? to teach a school for the Indians. This school was on the eastern side of the Catawba River, on the edge of Lancaster County. This schoolhouse answered the place of a church, where Rev. Rooker, McCreary and Mush often preached. After a few years, the school was disbanded. Rev. Mush traveled with Rooker visiting other areas. I have always understood from the Rev. McCreary that Mush's wife was a Catawba Indian, and like the rest of the Catawba's not much influenced by the religion of her husband. " [454]

Robert had a large family, and was considered quite industrious. He purchased the right to lease 50 acres of Indian land from a man named William Pettus. This was a verbal agreement, and the land was described as very poor, broken, sold for a price of three dollars per acre. The land obviously never supported the family. On October 1820, his estate consisted of four cow bells, hogs, two horses, two cows, tools four chairs, a table, trunk, Dutch oven, two pots and a frying pan, one bun, several books,

---

[447] Copy of original in possession Judy Canty Martin.
[448] Patterson genealogy.
[449] Watson pages
[450] Watson, page
[451] Draper letter from Stinson dated July 4, 1873.
[452] Merrell page 606.
[453] Draper letter from Stinson dated July 4, 1873.
[454] Draper Manuscripts, pages 45-48 of Photostatted copy in possession of Judy Canty Martin.

three augers and a knife, four barrels, furniture and fifty acres of poor land. He also had a crop of corn, amounting to 130 bushels.[455] Robert died on 7 December 1837.

I. Kity Mursh, born 16 August 1784 in Plmunkey Indian Reservation, King William, King William Co, Virginia USA, died young in 1790 in, Virginia.[456]

II. John Mursh, born May 6, 1786 married Betsy Quash-Scott born 1789.[457] John fought in the War of 1812. From G. L. Stinson's letter to Lyman Draper in 1873:

"His children must have all been grown before the War of 1812. John was a soldier in Camp at Charleston. He was noticed very much by the soldiers as an active and intelligent fellow. He was stationed as a sentinel somewhere on this Island. General Youngblood came riding by him----- past him. John stopped him, made him dismount and mark time until the Corporal took him in charge of the Guards."[458]

John was refused the right to vote and took it to court. The court decided against him, and he carried it to the Appeals Court. The opinion of the court delivered, stated that "from the papers before him, the res. John Marsh a Pamunkey Indian was a man of good moral character, that during the Revolutionary War he served in the Army of the United States in Virginia under the command of General Washington himself." (This influence may have induced his son John to enter the army in defense of SC. in the war of 1812). The judge stated that it was much to be regretted that there were no exceptions for services rendered the country or worth, but the Constitution was peremptory that he being an Indian was not entitled to the privilege of a citizen. The case was decided in the year 1829.[459] John died around 1855, according to G. S. Stinson in a letter to Draper dated 1873.

John and Betsy had five children: Rebecca, Lucy, Nancy, Delphi and John Marsh.[460]

**PHOTO 482 – HEADSTONE FOR REBECCA MARSH GEORGE -**

[455] Watson, pages 71 & 72.
[456] Marsh genealogy
[457] Patterson genealogy and Marsh genealogy.
[458] Stinson letter of 1873.
[459] Ibid.
[460] Patterson genealogy.

A.  Rebecca Marsh, born 1815,[461] Rock Hill, York, South Carolina and she died 20 January 1882, Catawba Indian Reservation, South Carolina, According to her tombstone. I believe that in R. L. Crook's account of money paid out, he called her Betty George. Betty George received $13.50 on April 10, 1875.   She is listed directly below John Scott and Little John Scott. A Betty George also received $5.00 on July 29 of the same year.[462]   Rebecca was married first.  Major John Scott Sr. who was born around 1814 and died around 1826.   They had one child, John.   Rebecca married 2nd an unknown man named McClansh had John James; she married 3rd Edmund Ayers and had Sarah J. Ayers and Margaret Ayers;  her 4th marriage was to Zachariah Anthony Taylor George and she had two other George children with him.

> 1.  John Scott, born 1826.[463]   John collected money from the Indian Agent R. L. Crook on April 10, 1875 in the amount of $10.00.[464]   Chief John Scott acted as leader of the small tribe during the Civil War.  He operated a gristmill and a ferry at Land Ford.  (Chief Samuel Taylor Blue stated that he "had an uncle who was Chief; his name was John Scott."[465]
>
> > Reasons:
> > > 1. It cannot be from his father's side, because they were white
> > > 2. It is on his mother's side
> > > 3. Chief Blue stated it himself.
>
> > 1.  Margaret-Ayers George had a half-brother named John Scott.
> >
> > Conclusion, Margaret Ayers, born 12 Nov 1845 must have been Samuel Taylor Blue's mother, also known as Margaret George because she was the stepdaughter of Anthony George.  Actually, her father was Edmund  Ayers.  Speck confirms this by stating that John Scott was Margaret Brown's half-brother.  He also stated that Patsy George was her aunt.  Patsy was the sister of Anthony George, and Margaret most often referred to Anthony as her father.) [466]
> >
> > > John Scott was the great grandson of the Reverend Robert Marsh. Patsy Mush-Mursh George, his aunt, lived with him around 1873.   He married a white woman named Colours? [467]
> > >      John Scott – Fought in the battles of Kingston and Goldsboro (December 1862) and was discharged on February 3, 1863. He served as

461    1849 Catawba census.
462    Agents Accounts of Payment to the Catawba 1875.
463    1849 Catawba census.
464    Agents Account of 1875.
465    Brown, page 330 and 349 where Samuel makes the statement himself.
466    Merrell page 259 information from Speck's Catawba Kinship Texts page 572.
467    Stinson letter of 1873.

454

chief of the Catawba for several terms during the balance of the war and into the 1880's

John Scott was listed in the 1849 Census of the Catawba.

See more information under Scott.

Rebecca and an unknown man had:

2. John James McClansh?? born around 1828, died young. (his father is unknown) [468]

Rebecca Marsh and Edmund Ayers had two daughters:

3. Sarah Jane Ayers, born 1829 and died 1917. She married James Harris sr. [469] The children will be found under Harris, Peter.
4. Margaret Ayers-George, born May 1838, Catawba Indian Nation, York, South Carolina and died 9 August 1922, (Catawba Res.) Rock Hill, York, South Carolina. She married John William Brown Jr, Joe Cherry and Samuel Blue. [470] Children will be found under Blue and Brown

Rebecca Marsh and Anthony (Taylor Anthony- Zacariah Taylor) George, born 1799: Their children were:

5. Zachariah Taylor George, born 1824
6. Nelson George born around 1825 [471]

The birth years and ages are as they appear in records, however, it looks like the George children were born before the others. Rebecca was with Anthony George throughout the Catawba census, **until his death.**

---

[468]  Stinson letter to Draper pages 280-283.
[469]  Catawba Branch Records.
[470]  Catawba Branch Records.
[471]  Ibid.

**PHOTO 483 - LUCY MARSH**

B. Lucy Marsh, born November 3, 1817.[472] She died 4 September 1902 in Harmony, Utah.[473] Lucy is called Lucinda Watts in April 1875, and on the 10th, she received $22.50 from the Indian Agent Crook, in 1881, she received $13.32 under Lucy Watts. Lucy and Evan Watts were very instrumental in the Mormon Missionary movement in the late 1880's. It was in their home that Elder Charles Robison died.

"Got to Mr. Watts at 8 am. We walked 35 miles. We found Brother Robison very sick. He was very glad to see us. We anointed him with oil and administered to him. Pres. Easton and myself set up with him till twelve o'clock. He was in much pain slept one hour. The next day we took him to Rock Hill to Br. Smiths. Got a light wagon and took him to the depot at three fifteen we took the train. It created quite an excitement at the station. Elder Miller and myself got off at Fort Mills 8 miles from Rock Hill. Staid to Sister Bunches.

The next morning started to headquarters, walked 25 miles, found Br. Robison very low. He was in great pain all day. He said he wanted to go home. He asked us if we would get

---

472     Catawba Branch Records.
473     Watts Family genealogy from Thora Wright.

456

a team and wagon and take him to the depot. Elder Easton went to the station and telegraphed to President B. H. Roberts to know what to do about taking him home. He waited but could not get any answer to his dispatch.

25th, he was in great pain all day and gradually sinking. He had the hiccups and was still pleading for us to take him home.

Brother Miller and McKay set up with him the first part of the night. We anointed and administered to him and prayed for him by day and by night but his time had come. At twelve o'clock Brother Davidson and myself got up. He had took the change for the worse to all appearance. The pain had left him he was dieing. Bro. Davidson went over to Bro. Moses Gordon to wake up the Elders. He died at ten minutes to two on the 26th. He died without a strugle." [474]

Lucy had 6 children: Robert Henry Head, father unknown; Emily Cobb by John D. Cobb a white man; Margareth J. McLonah by Robert McLonah a white man; John Gandy by Thomas Gandy, a white man; and James and William David Watts by Evan Watts, another white man. She married, according to the LDS Church, Evan Watts.

1. Robert Henry Head, born 1841 married Sarah Ann Louisa Evans-Canty, daughter of Chancy Evans and Peggy Canty. He died in the Civil

   War. [475] Their only child Pinkney Henry and his descendants will be found under Head in Genealogy of the Western Catawba.

   > a. Pinkney Henry Head born 26 October 1862, he married Martha Jane Patterson, daughter of James Goodwin and Elizabeth Missouri White Patterson. Pinkney and Martha had 12 children, Sarah, Rosie, Lucy, Hattie, Heber, Nellie, Willard, George, Helen, Harry, Mary and Dorothy. More about them will be found in the Head chapter.

Lucy Mush-Marsh and John D. Cobb probably from the white family of C. E. Cobb who signed the incorporation of Rock Hill petition in 1868 had Emily. John was born 1815 in York Dist. His white family was Lucinda wife, born 1820 York; 1. Mary born 1844; 2.Martha born 1845; 3. Elizabeth born 1849; his mother Martha Cobb born 1786. [476]

---

[474]   Joseph Willey Diary or Journal.
[475]   Catawba Branch Records, LDS IGI and Head Genealogy.
[476]   1850 census York County, SC.

**PHOTO 484 – EMILY ELIZABETH COBB**

2. Emily Elizabeth Cobb, born December 9, 1843.[477] She married first, Jefferson Ayers; second Taylor George, she died July 17, 1925.[478]

See children under George and Ayers. The children and spouses will be found under the respective father's family. Emily had eight children, two by Jefferson Davis Ayers, and six by (Zachariah) Taylor George.

Briefly, Emily's children follow, more will be found under their fathers, Ayers and George.

(a). Jefferson Davis Ayers, born December 21, 1861, sometimes called Epperson George such as in 1880 census. His children will be found under Ayers.[479] He married a white woman named Harriet Berry.

(b). L. C. Alice Ayers born 17 December 1866,[480] called Alice George by Watson. She married Wesley Harris, son of Lucinda Harris and John "Mush" Harris. She is dead by 1895, and had no children.

(c) Mary Jane George born 13 July 1869.

(d) Minnie Hester George born September 21, 1871. She married Samuel Taylor Blue. Her children will be found under Blue.

---

[477]    Catawba Branch Records.
[478]    Obituary of Emily George in 1925.
[479]    1880 census of Catawba transcribed by Dr. Wes White lists him as Epperson. Birth from Catawba Branch Records.
[480]    Catawba Branch Records.

(e). Rachel Wysie George born August 27, 1874. She married John William Brown. Her children will be found under Brown

(f) Mary Dovie George born 23 May 1874 and died 12 September 1972. She married Benjamin Perry Harris. Her children will be found under Peter Harris.

(g) Margaret Della George born December 4, 1879. She married David Adam Harris as his second wife. Her children will be found under David Adam Harris.

(h)Moroni James Joseph George born August 21, 1884. He married white, Hattie J. Millings. His children will be found under George.[481]

**Lucy Marsh and Robert McLonah or McLure, white, had:**

3. Margaret Jane McClure, also known as Peggy Jane Marsh, and Peggy Jane McClure, born August 21, 1845.[482] She married first . Robert Crawford, who served in the Civil War, and who was causality. Peggy Jane then married second William George, son of Nelson and Sarah Ayers George as <u>his</u> second wife.

From the Missionary Journal of Mary Barus

"Old sister Brown told us soon after we came of a dream she had three years before we came. In this she saw this same house and our family going over to it. she had related this to her son Bro Blue & he verified it to us."

---

[481]     Ibid
[482]     Ibid

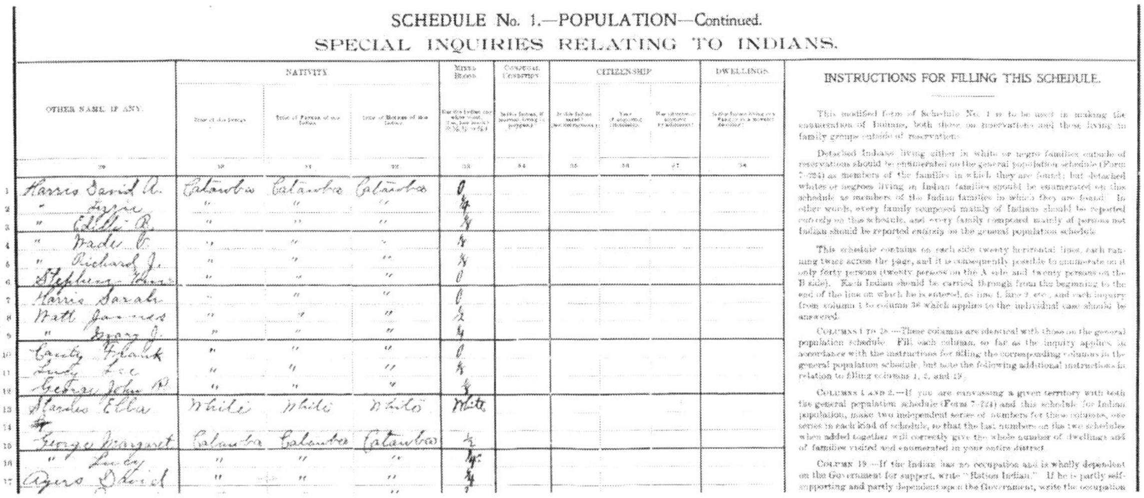

**PHOTO 485 - 1900 US CENSUS OF YORK COUNDY, SOUTH CAROLINA - MARGARET GEORGE**

1900 Census, Margaret George, living with Daughter Ella and Lucy. Age 54 years, she was a widow, and had 5 children with 3 still living. Her and her parents all born on the Indian Reservation, York County, South Carolina. She states that she is ½ white.

Margaret Peggy Jane had three children, by two different husbands.

Bettie Elizabeth Crawford, John Pierce Nelson George, Lucy, Jane S. George.

More information about the George children will be found in the George Chapter. Her child with Bob Crawford is given here.

(1) Mary  Bettie Elizabeth Crawford born 2 January 1861, Catawba Reservation, Rock Hill, York, South Carolina and died 17 August 1941, Catawaba, York, South Carolina. She married Thomas Wylie Estridge 1810–1880 they had no children. She raised the two Watts brothers.

Transcript

Baptized 19 Mar 1885 by Joseph Willey, confirmed by Joseph Willey Detail

Catawba Branch Records, page 208

According to Dr. Thomas Blumer, he calls her Betsy Crawford Harris from his book Catawba Indian Pottery, 2003.

Joseph Willey calls her Betty Estridge, when he baptized her on 19 Mar 1885.

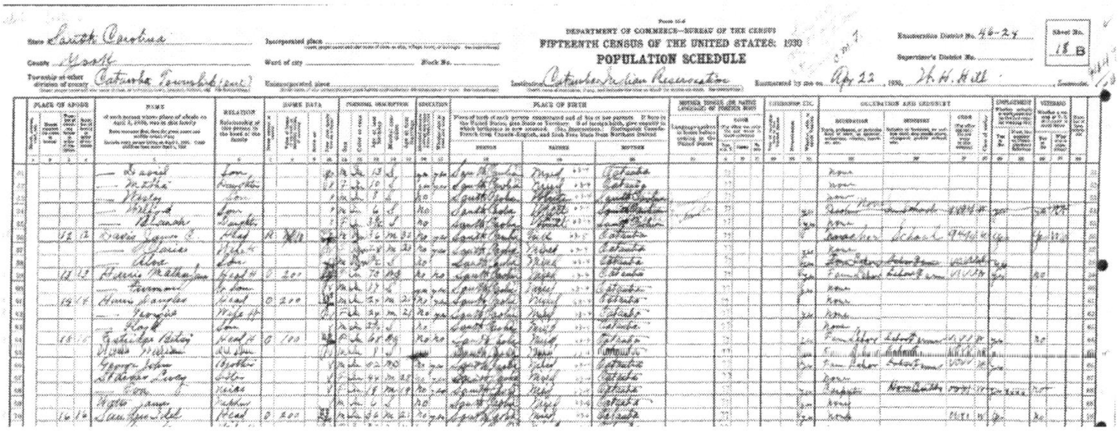

**PHOTO 486 - 22 APRIL 1930 US CENSUS, CATAWBA INDIAN RESERVATION, YORK, SOUTH CAROLINA:**

Name  Betsy Estridge -- Age in 1930,  68 --  Birth Year abt 1862 --  Gender  Female
Race  Indian --  Birthplace South Carolina --  Marital Status  Widowed
Relation to Head of House  Head --  Homemaker?  Yes
Home in 1930 Catawba, York, South Carolina --  Map of Home  Catawba, York, South Carolina --
Institution  Catawba Indian Reserveation --  Dwelling Number  15
Family Number  15 --  Home Owned or Rented  Owned --  Home Value  100
Radio Set  No --  Lives on Farm  No --  Attended School  No
Able to Read and Write  No ---  Mother's Birthplace  Catauba --
Able to Speak English  Yes --  Occupation  Farm Labor --  Industry  Farm
Class of Worker  Wage or salary worker
Employment  Yes --
Household Members  Name  Age
Betsy Estridge  68 --  William Watts  9 adopted son --  John George  52  brother --
Lucy Staines  44  sister --  Eva Staines  19  niece --  James Watts  6  nephew.

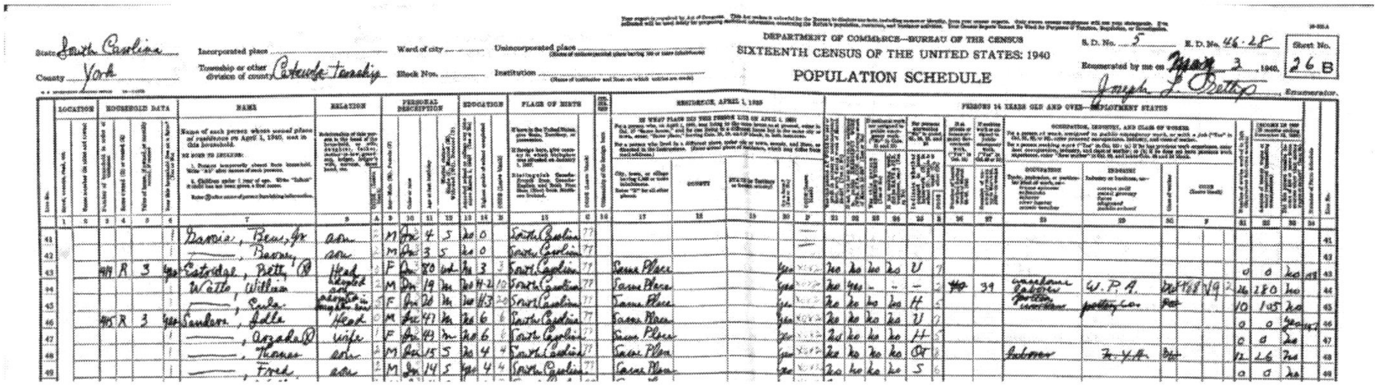

**PHOTO 487 - 3 MAY 1940 US CENSUS, CATAWBA TOWNSHIP, YORK, SOUTH CAROLINA:**

Name   Bertty Estridge   --   Respondent        Yes  --  Age  80  --
Estimated Birth Year  abt 1860  --  Gender  Female   --   Race        Indian
Birthplace        South Carolina  --  Marital Status    Widowed
Relation to Head of House    Head  --   Map of Home in 1940      Industrial Aragon Mills, York, South
Carolina  --   Street   Catawba Indian Reservation
Farm   Yes  --   Inferred Residence in 1935  Industrial Aragon Mills, York, South Carolina
Residence in 1935     Same Place  --   Resident on farm in 1935   Yes
Sheet Number 26B  --   Number of Household in Order of Visitation        414
House Owned or Rented       Rented  --   Value of Home or Monthly Rental if Rented    3
Attended School or College   No  --   Highest Grade Completed    Elementary school, 3rd grade
Weeks Worked in 1939        0  --   Income 0  --   Income Other Sources  No
Household Members    Name         Age
Bertty Estridge        80  --   William Watts        19  adopted son
Eula Watts    20   adopted daughter in law

### Web: Greenville County, South Carolina, Obituary Index, 1914-1992

Name  Mary Elizabeth Estridge
Birth Date       abt 1861  --  Age      Age 80
Death Date     Abt 1941  --  LocationRock Hill
Publication Date        18 Aug 1941
Household Members  --  Name        Age
Mary Elizabeth Estridge

 In 1870, a household made up of William Whitesides, age 24, a white man and Peggy age 40, Indian, Jane aged 16, Nancy aged 10 and what looks like Benj. a female, aged 5.  This is Peggy White and 2 of her children, Martha Jane and Nancy, and I believe the other child to be Bettie.   The child does not appear in the 1880 census or on the known lists, more research needs to be done to find her. In the Dunlap letters around 1890, there is the notation that John Sanders has run off with Betsy Crawford.

Joseph Willey, the Mormon missionary, baptized a Betsy Crawford.  It is possible that this woman is the Betsy Crawford, although since she is not found in anything else Catawba, it is more likely Willey and John Sanders' Betsy Crawford is white.

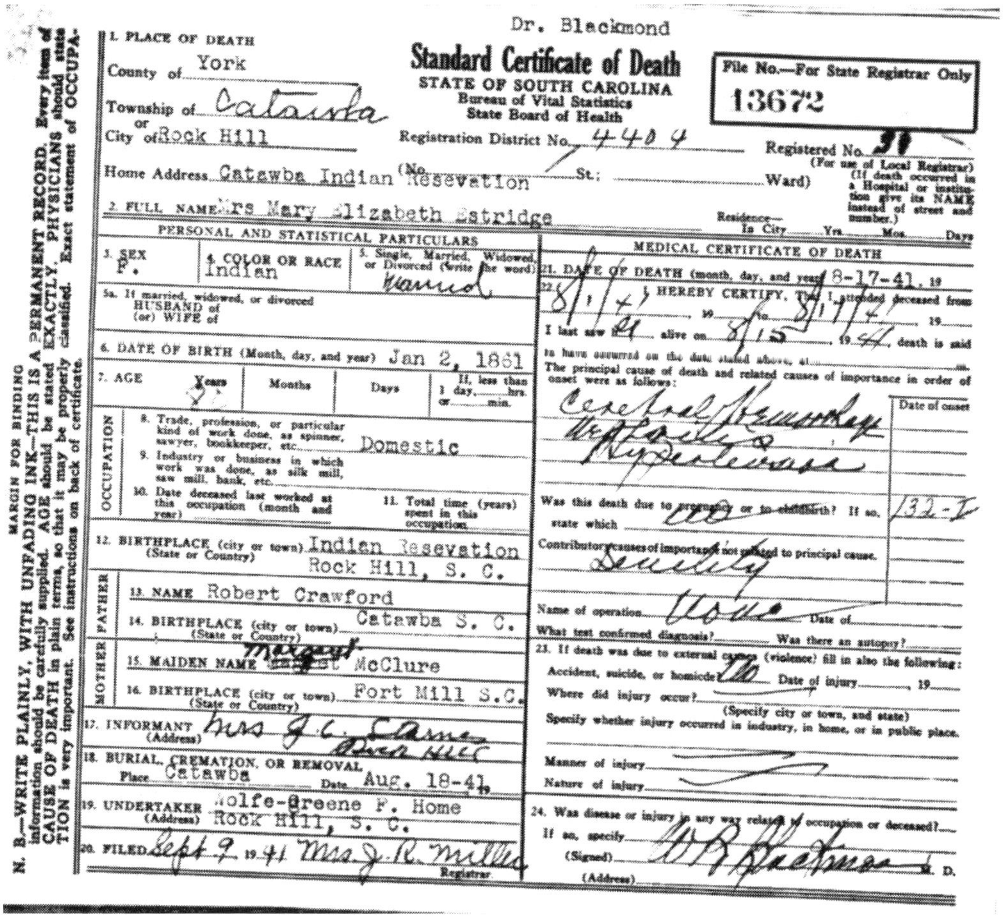

N. B.—WRITE PLAINLY, WITH UNFADING INK—THIS IS A PERMANENT RECORD. Every item of information should be carefully supplied. AGE should be stated EXACTLY. PHYSICIANS should state CAUSE OF DEATH in plain terms, so that it may be properly classified. Exact statement of OCCUPATION is very important. See instructions on back of certificate.

MARGIN FOR BINDING

Dr. Blackmond

**Standard Certificate of Death**
STATE OF SOUTH CAROLINA
Bureau of Vital Statistics
State Board of Health

File No.—For State Registrar Only
13672

1. PLACE OF DEATH
County of York
Township of Catawba
or
City of Rock Hill
Registration District No. 4404
Registered No. 31
(For use of Local Registrar)
Home Address Catawba Indian (No. Reservation St.; Ward)
(If death occurred in a Hospital or institution give its NAME instead of street and number.)

2. FULL NAME Mrs Mary Elizabeth Estridge
Residence—In City Yrs. Mos. Days

PERSONAL AND STATISTICAL PARTICULARS

3. SEX F.
4. COLOR OR RACE Indian
5. Single, Married, Widowed, or Divorced (write the word) Married
5a. If married, widowed, or divorced HUSBAND of (or) WIFE of
6. DATE OF BIRTH (Month, day, and year) Jan 2, 1861
7. AGE Years [illegible] Months Days If, less than 1 day, hrs. or min.

OCCUPATION
8. Trade, profession, or particular kind of work done, as spinner, sawyer, bookkeeper, etc. Domestic
9. Industry or business in which work was done, as silk mill, saw mill, bank, etc.
10. Date deceased last worked at this occupation (month and year)
11. Total time (years) spent in this occupation

12. BIRTHPLACE (city or town) (State or Country) Indian Reservation Rock Hill, S. C.

FATHER
13. NAME Robert Crawford
14. BIRTHPLACE (city or town) (State or Country) Catawba S. C.

MOTHER
15. MAIDEN NAME Margaret McClure
16. BIRTHPLACE (city or town) (State or Country) Fort Mill S.C.

17. INFORMANT (Address) Mrs J. C. [illegible] Rock Hill
18. BURIAL, CREMATION, OR REMOVAL Place Catawba Date Aug. 18-41 19
19. UNDERTAKER (Address) Wolfe-Greene F. Home Rock Hill, S. C.
20. FILED Sept 9 19 41 Mrs J. R. Miller Registrar

MEDICAL CERTIFICATE OF DEATH

21. DATE OF DEATH (month, day, and year) 8-17-41, 19
22. I HEREBY CERTIFY, That I attended deceased from 8/1/41, 19 to 8/17/41, 19
I last saw her alive on 8/15, 19 41, death is said to have occurred on the date stated above, at m.
The principal cause of death and related causes of importance in order of onset were as follows: Cerebral Hemorrhage [illegible] & Hypertension
Date of onset
Was this death due to pregnancy or to childbirth? If so, state which no 132-I
Contributory causes of importance not related to principal cause. Senility
Name of operation None Date of
What test confirmed diagnosis? Was there an autopsy?
23. If death was due to external causes (violence) fill in also the following: Accident, suicide, or homicide no Date of injury, 19
Where did injury occur? (Specify city or town, and state)
Specify whether injury occurred in industry, in home, or in public place.
Manner of injury
Nature of injury
24. Was disease or injury in any way related to occupation or deceased?
If so, specify
(Signed) W. B. Blackmon M. D.
(Address)

**PHOTO 488 - CERTIFICATE OF DEATH FOR MARY ELIZABETH ESTRIDGE**

(4) John Pierce Nelson George, born 20 September 1879 married Ella Starnes 1878-1909, white woman. Second he married Catherine Hester Harris 1889-1922. He died 8 September 1950, Rock Hill, York County, South Carolina

(5). Lucy Jane George born 1 November 1885, Catawba, York, South Carolina and died 9 February 1960, York, South Carolina. More information will be found under the George's. [483]

**Lucy Marsh and Thomas Gandy, a white man had one child:**

4. John Gandy, born July 17, 1850 married Mary C. ?? died November 5, 1886. John received from the Indian Agent R. L. Crook on April 10, 1875 the sum of $10.00, and in 1881, he received $6.66.

(1) Emma Jane Gandy, born June 20, 1884 [484]

---

483 Ibid
484 Catawba Branch Records.

**Lucy Marsh then married Evans Watts, a white man, according to Draper's informant, Patsy Brown George. It could be Eben Watts instead of Evan. The family removed to Utah.**

5. James Harvey Watts, born April 8, 1858.[485] James received money from the Indian Agent R.L. Crook in 1881 in the amount of $13.32. He married first Mary Jane Whitesides, daughter of Thomas Whitesides and Eliza Scott Canty, there were no children.[486] He had a child by a white woman Ella Shaw who abandoned them, Livy Leola was that child. Mary Jane raised her as her own. He married second Gertrude Dye Ayers. James Harvey died March 25, 1926.[487] See his children and more information in the Watts Chapter.

6. William David Watts born May 23, 1860, married Nancy Christine Wats, daughter of James A. Watts and Carolotta Tomson. They removed to Harmony, Utah. See the children under Watts. Nancy had a child previously with James Patterson, that child will be found in the Patterson Chapter, and with David Adam Harris because she was his first wife.[488]

C. Nancy Quash-Mush-Marsh born May 7, 1820, married Jim Sanders born December 25, 1824. She died May 29, 1863.[489] Jim was most likely white, he was not a Catawba.

1. Margaret Elizabeth L. Saunders born May 24, 1842. She married Peter Harris. Children will be found under Harris. Briefly, her children are given here, more information will be found in the Peter Harris Chapter.

(a). Edward Harris, born 1855, died young.

(b). Edward Harris, born March 5, 1867.

(c). James David Harris, born July 26, 1871.

(d). Taylor Butler Harris, born July 3, 1876

(e). Gus Howard Harris, born June 27, 1879. [490]

2. John Evins Sanders, born ca 1845, married Sarah Lucinda Harris, born 1840. John married, or ran away with a Betsy Crawford according to the Dunlap letter. She might be the Bettie Elizabeth Crawford, daughter of Robert Crawford, Civil War Soldier and Nancy Quash, making them closely related. Nothing more is written. In the 1910 census, he is with a Leola Watts, a white woman.

See children under Sanders-Harris, Lucinda.

---

[485] Ibid
[486] Canty and Watts genealogy. Joseph Willey also speaks about Jane Watts. She was found on the old LDS IGI.
[487] Obituary of James Watts.
[488] Patterson-Watts genealogy.
[489] Patterson genealogy.
[490] Catawba Branch Records.

3.  William Thomas Sanders, born ca 1847.[491]   Elder Joseph Willey baptized William Thomas Sanders, on   March 15, 1885.  William had a child with an Elizabeth Cobb, who was probably white.

(a)  John Sanders born September 8, 1884. [492]

D.  Delphi – (Philadelphia) Marsh, born 1822, married Howard Bunch.[493]   She had no children, although Joseph Willey baptized a person that he     called Ellen Bunch in March of 1884.  The Elders stayed in the home of "Sister Bunches" many times. Delphi received money from Indian Agent R.L. Crook on April 10, 1875 in the amount of $4.50,  and in 1881, she received $6.66.  She is one of the signers of a petition in 1863 to keep J. R. Patton from being drafted into the Civil War.  Delphia lived on the land of her grandfather Robert Mush-Marsh. [494]

E.  John Marsh, Born ca 1825, he either married or was involved with Polly Harris Ayers     He had eight children only one of whom follows.

1.  Mary E. born 7 February 1848 in Wait Co. Georgia.  She may have married a Whiteside. [495]

III. Robert Alexander Mush-Marsh, born March 2, 1788 in King William County, VA married Betsy Quash-Scott -Mush daughter of Quash who fought in the Revolution.     Betsy also had children with his brother John.  In 1806, this family became members of the Flint Hill Baptist Church in York District, South Carolina. [496]

1.  Rachel Marsh, born 1819 in Catawba, and John Alexander Tims, a white man had:
a.  Maggie Tims, born 1843 died between 1844 and 1845.

b.  Bishop Tims, born about 1844 died young

c.  Theodore Tims, born about  1845 died young
d.  John Alexander Tims, born July 15, 1845,[497] married first Martha Ann Cottsky-Scott, daughter of Betsy Mush Scott; and second Sarah Ann Evans-Canty Head, daughter of Chancy Evans and Peggy Canty.[498]   John Alexander removed to Sanford, Colorado in 1885 and is buried there with Martha Ann.  More information will be found under Tims.

---

491    Patterson genealogy.
492    Catawba Branch Records.
493    Patterson-Marsh genealogy.
494    Watson page 72
495    LDS IGI.
496    Marsh genealogy and Watson page 72.
497    Marsh-Tims genealogy, Catawba Branch Records, and Patterson genealogy listing children.
498    Catawba Branch Records.

a. Rachel Jane Tims Harris was born 30 April 1866 in Catawba, and died 6 March 1946, Sanford, Conejos, Colorado. She married Hillary Harris, son of Nancy Harris and unknown Kilpatrick, a white man.[499] Hillary left his family, and eventually married again in Oklahoma, where he died.[500] The children of Rachel and Hillary are found under Tims and Harris.

b. Robert Harvey Tims born 30 October 1877. Harvey moved with the family to Sanford, Colorado, where he died in 1904, unmarried. See his picture under Tims.[501]

2. Robert Marsh, born May 14, 1825, married first Betsy Hunnicutt born 1831;[502] Betsy later married William George and John Scott. Robert then married second Susannah Harris, daughter of Allen and Rhoda Harris, who was born in 1847. Robert died of wounds he received in the Civil War on August 28, 1864.[503]

        a. Robert Marsh born December 18, 1846.[504]

        b. ??

        c. George Marsh, born 1863, idiotic, raised by Susannah's second husband Samson Owl.[505]

C. Margareth-Peggy Quash-Mursh-Marsh born 17 June 1827, married a white man named George White and had 6 children: Elizabeth Missouri, Robert, Elvinia, Martha Jane, Henrietta and Nancy A. White. More information will be found under Marsh-White in Western Catawba.[506]

IV. Sarah Marsh, born March 29, 1790 in King William County, VA. She married Jamey Brown.[507] No children have been attributed to them. A Sarah Mush signed the petition of 1748, indicating she was the head of the household.

V. James Marsh, born March 13, 1792, died while a small child.

VI. Philadelphia Marsh, born February 5, 1794, died in infancy.

VII. Elizabeth- Betsy Marsh, born November 14, 1796 in King William County, married John Houghland.[508]

---

[499] I believe that this is Thomas Kilpartick, mentioned in the will of his father Alexander Kilpatrick, the Indian trader.

[500] Wanda Williams Genealogy.

[501] Catawba Branch Records, Head genealogy and Sanford Cemetery Inscriptions.

[502] Patterson genealogy, verified by a petition requesting Patton not be called to serve in the Civil War lists Susannah Mush in 1863.

[503] Civil War Record of Robert.

[504] 1854 census of the Catawba.

[505] 1880 census of the Catawba from Dr. White.

[506] Patterson genealogy written by Elizabeth and James Patterson.

[507] Ibid

1. John Hougland born May 16, 1822
2. Elijah Hougland born 8 May 1823
3. Stephen F. Hougland born 18 November 1826
4. Mary Hougland born 20 July 1827
5. Vinia Hougland born 16 March 1829
6. Robert A. Hougland born 25 November 1830
7. Catey Hougland born 9 June 1932
8. Nancy Elizabeth Hougland born 21 Jan 1834.

VIII.  Patsy Marsh, born July 28, 1798 in King William County, died young.

IX.  Rhoda Mush-Marsh born 21 February 1800, still living with her father in 1820.   She was last known to be alive in 1850.[509]

---

[508]    Marsh genealogy.
[509]    Page out of the Bible of Robert Mush-Mursh-Marsh.

Figure 2 Catawba Branch (picture from Tom Blumer)

## Chapter 17   Nettles Family

`John Nettles was probably born around 1750 and died round 1812. He was sent to the college of William and Mary in Virginia along with Robert Mush a Pamunkey Indian. They were sent because they were supposed to be "promising." They were kept there for five or six years and given all the schooling of the white population.[510]  Mary Nettles most likely John's wife, she may have been white, because she went to visit her brother in Tennessee, according to a letter dated 1874 in the Draper Manuscripts.[511]  Templeton Black said of him, "Nettles was the finest dancer he ever saw preform."[512]

John once appeared in white attire, riding with a Major Carr and reviewed the militia at a battalion muster. He was awarded this honor because of his service in the Revolution. Although he was educated, upon return to the Nation, he got what I would call, Catawba amnesia. (My dad had it, he could not remember much, unless he wanted to remember.) John reverted to Catawba ways. He was once found drunk and lying in the street. When chastised for this action, he took the professors to the window and pointed out at a hog walking in the street. "Take that hog and wash him clean and as the weather is warm it might be very agreeable; but let him go, and he will lie down and wallow in the first mud-hole he comes to, for he is still a hog."[513] While the white education was thought to be the best thing for him, it did not prepare him to be a Catawba.

John served as an interpreter for the whites; however the Catawba did not trust him to interpret for them. While he could read and write, he was never known to have had a book except the Testament. John later became a headman with the rank of Major. He signed leases from 1808 to 1832. John reportedly married and had a respectable family, although I have not found them yet.

---

[510] Brown pages 312, 313.
[511] Draper Manuscripts, page 8 of copies in possession Judy Canty Martin.
[512] Brown page 271.
[513] Brown page 313

## Chapter 18   New River or Newriver Family

General NewRiver or New River according to the Draper manuscript was born around 1740. This is probably incorrect and associated with the time period when "Newcomer" took the name "NewRiver." A more appropriate birth estimate is probably about 1720; he served as Chief in 1794. He married Sally Scott-Toole, daughter of King Hagler's daughter and white Indian Trader Matthew Toole, a white man.[514] The General took the name NewRiver after he killed a great Shawnee chief in battle in 1732.

He was very brave, and served in the Revolutionary War, and is first on the List of Captain Drennan. He served in the Snow Campaign of 1775 where Col. Richard Richardson's forces at 96 recaptured the gunpowder that was intended for the Cherokee.

The General, according to R. A. Springs, was "more than ordinary," and held his power through his wife and the respect the few Catawba had for her. In 1786, he presented a petition on behalf of his people to save their hunting rights.

"We your Petitioners, therefore Humbly pray that your Honers out of your great goodness would put a stop to such a glaring breach of Humanity and gratitude, and grant us such privileges of hunting in this state, as in your wisdom you shall think fitt, and we your petitioners as in duty bound shall every pray."

While Governor Moultrie was sympathetic, the petition was referred to a committee and the Catawba hunting rights were affirmed by a resolution of the House, the situation probably never changed much.[515]

The story was told of the General sucking snake venom from James Spratt, son of Kanawha Spartt that saved James' life. The General gave the Spratt's the land on the reservation. (This is just one version of who gave the land on die reservation to the Spratts.) General New River even borrowed Thomas Spartt's horse at one time. The General rode the horse hard and Spratt beat him for this infraction. The irony was that later Spratt killed the same horse, doing exactly what he had beaten General New River for doing.

The General was described by Elkhana Watson in fairly admirable fashion, "his face showed powerful traits of mind and character" while Watson's other description of the Indians was not that generous.

Reverend Thomas Coke, the Methodist preacher, described him as: " a tall, grave old man, (who) walked with a mighty staff in his hand: Round his neck he wore a narrow piece (I Think) of leather, which hung down before and was adorned with a great variety of bits of silver. He also had a silver breastplate. Almost all the men and women wore silver nose-rings hanging from the middle gristle of the nose, and some of them had little hearts hanging from the rings."[516]

The General died in 1804 at Kings Bottom. More about Sally New River will be found in the Hagler Chapter. See the section entitled Chiefs for any more information.

---

[514] Recollections of Thomas D. Spratt.
[515] Brown pages 279 & 280.
[516] Brown page 288.

**PHOTO 489 - GENERAL NEWRIVER (HIS SHIRT WAS WHITE AND HIS ROB WAS OF A DEEP BLUE WITH GOLD TRIM)**

## Chapter 19   Patterson Family

I. Tom Patterson probably born around 1720, signed a petition 24 November 1792, and died in 1815.[517]

II. Daniel Patterson probably born around 1770, alive in May 1824, married Harriet Brown, daughter of Billy Brown she probably died before April 1824 because Daniel collected her rents in 1824. He apparently died after April of 1824.[518]

III. Jamey Patterson probably born around 1770 was alive in 1821 to 1832.[519] Captain Jamey Patterson signed a lease in November 1821. In June 1825, and in July of 1827, he signed leases as Captain James. The very next lease signed in July he signed as Colonel James Patterson, and the next one he signed as Captain again. In September of 1828, he signed one as Lt. James Patterson; however, the next lease is signed as Captain Patterson again and all through 1828, he alternated between Captain and Lieutenant. He signed his last lease in November of 1832, so we can presume he died there about. In 1824, he willed his rent money to Patsey Patterson, who was most likely his wife.

IV. Jenny Patterson,  probably born around 1770. She, along with Patrick RedHead and John Kennedy, were prosecuted in Lancaster County Court for trading with Negroes once on 28 March 1793. [520]

The Commissioners spared them the punishment, which was death. The Commissioners appealed to Governor William Moultrie and the following proclamation was made:

"Whereas I have received information from the Agents appointed to take care of the Rights of the Catawba Indians that a Prosecution has been commenced against several of the said Indians in the Court of the County of Lancaster, to Wit, Patrick Redhead, Jenny Patterson and John Kennedy for trading with Negroes and that it is apprehended that the said Court intends to inflict Corporal Punishment on them. Now know ye that in consideration of the said Indians being Free People and under the protection of this State I do by these Presents pardon and release said Indians from any Judgment or punishment whatever which has been or may be ordered to be inflicted on them by the said Court of which all concerned are to take due Notice and govern themselves accordingly."

Governor Moultrie signed this proclamation March 28, 1793.

Jenny Patterson was most likely the mother of Virginia-Jenney Patterson; however Virginia's father is unknown

> A. Virginia-Jinney-Jenney Patterson born 1818[521]  "married" John S. Sitgreaves,[522] a white landowner. John signed the Memorial, dated July 31, 1840, where the citizens of Indian Land agreed to the proposed treaty of 1840, known as the Treaty of Nation Ford.

---

[517] Watson page 74.

[518] Indian Plat books.

[519] Watson page 75.

[520] Watson page 75

This memorial reminded the legislature that "Lease-holders are all purchasers, many of them at a high rate, varying from ten to sixteen dollars per acre, and yet subject to a yearly rent." John was joined by Archibald Whyte, R. A. Springs, A. S. Starr and James Moore. Only one child of Virginia can be identified, Martha Patterson. All the following genealogy is from the <u>Patterson Genealogy</u> and <u>Genealogy of the Western Catawba</u>. Only one child has been identified and Virginia-Jenny has only been found on the 1849 census. While the birth years are so close, we can assume that Jenney was actually born earlier, about 1810 or so.

1. Martha Patterson born 1 January 1828, died 9 Aug 1879.[523]  Martha received allotments on 12 November 1869, 19 March 1870, 12 July 1870, and 8 August 1876.

The man for whom she had the child was Laban Chappell son of John and Grace Goodwin Chappell, a white man of a very prominent family.

**PHOTO 490 – JAMES GOODWIN PATTERSON**

a. James Goodwin Patterson was born in 8 November 1849,[524] he married Elizabeth Missouri White, daughter of George and Peggy Margareth- Marsh-Quash White.

On July 1868, James Patterson signed a petition asking that James morrow replace Thomas Whitesides as Indian Agent.[525]

---

[521] 1849 census

[522] Patterson genealogy.

[523] Ibid

[524] Ibid

[525] Letter to Governor R. K. Scott, from the Catawba Indians.

He collected funds in, 1869, in the amount of $27.50; in 1871 hereceived a total of $200.00 from P. J. O'Connell, the Agent, and again on June 19, 1875 in the amount of $2.00. In 1881 he received from the agent W. M. Whyte, $53.28 and in 1883 was living off the reservation but collected funds. In 1877, James signed a petition and collected rents on Catawba lands.[526]  Family tradition says he even served in the Civil War, for two weeks as a water boy, before running home, he was only 12 at the time! [527]

**PHOTO 491 - ELIZABETH MISSOURI WHITE PATTERSON**

**PHOTO 492 – HEADSTONES FOR JAMES PATTERSON (1849-1931) AND ELIZABETH PATTERSON (1849-1934)**

---

[526] Reports and Resolutions of South Carolina pages 552 & 553.
[527] Story from Cynthia Walsh.

**Joseph Willey, one of the first Mormon missionaries to the Nation writes:**

"After singing they said they wished us to hold prayers. We done so after prayers one of the leading Indians, Bro. Patterson applied for baptism. He said he wished to be baptized on the 11th of November. The Indians called us there (their) preachers and the white people called us the Indian preachers. Next morning we bore our testimony to them and paid our fair (fare) which was 1.00 and went to Mr. Pattersons.

There we married five couples which had been living together but was not married. One couple had lived together 30 years. We married them. We had considerable spirit. We eat com bread and butter- milk for the wedding supper it was very cold and stormy. We went over the river and got our mail, went to Bro. Pattersons, staid two days and nights with him. His wife applied for baptism." [528] "We forwarded to the Desert News for books to organize a Sunday School among the Indians. June 1, 1884, Held meeting at or near Bro. William Watses in a house that had fixed for that purpose. Elders J. J. Humphreys, myself and M. Humphrey being present we appointed another meeting at the 4th, at the same place and requested all the Saints to be present as we was going to organize a Branch of the Church. We organized a Branch of the Church of Jesus Christ of Later Day Saints and set Bro. James Patterson apart to Preside over the Branch. It was called the Rock Hill Branch. The Saints numbered 31 in all, 25 of the number was Lamanites." [529]

So in 1884 James Goodwin Patterson, joined the Church of Jesus Christ of Latter Day Saints, and was the first Catawba to seek baptism. James then helped hide the missionaries and led the group until 1885, when his son-in-law, Alonzo Canty was made branch president. During the persecution of the Mormons in South Carolina, he and James Watts, husband of Mary Jane Whitesides, son of Evan and Lucy Quash-Marsh Watts, helped guide the missionaries through the swamps to avoid the mobs. When angry anti-Mormon mobs sought to hurt the missionaries, it was to the house of James and Elizabeth Patterson that they fled and were hidden, on at least one occasion. The Patterson's even took care of the missionary that had been shot. [530]

According to (Magdalene) Mae Garcia Croasmun, "It all started when 2 missionaries visited my grandfather while he was plowing in the field. He told them he didn't have time to listen to their message, but to go to the house and my grandmother would listen to them. So they went up to the house and was introducing the Gospel to my grandmother when in came grandfather, saying he was curious as to what they had to say. They fully accepted the message and were baptized shortly. At that time, my grandmother was either expecting a child, or just had a child, but she wanted to be baptized so they broke the ice on the river so she could be baptized.

One incident I recall hearing my grandma tell about was, one evening while the missionaries were at their home, a group of masked men rode up on horses and wanted to see the D missionaries. Grandpa spoke to them from the inside, but they informed him they "didn't want you, Mr. Patterson", they only wanted the

---

[528] Elizabeth Missouri White, daughter of George and Margareth-Peggy Quash-Mursh-Marsh White.

[529] Elder Joseph Willey Diary.

[530] Patterson Genealogy.

Elders. After a while the Elders began talking to them from the inside, finally venturing to the window and then outside. One by one the men rode off, leaving the 2 Elders alone.

My grandpa came first, bringing my mother (Abbie and her youngest sister, Maud, by train). Mom was approximately 5 years old and Aunt Maud was 2 or 3. The 2 young ones got to go then because they didn't have to pay train fare for them. Grandpa went to Manassa, where there were other Mormons there for the same reason. Then later when Grandpa found work, he sent for the rest of the family.

My grandparents saved up enough money to go to the Salt Lake Temple. They were in the sealing room, waiting for the services to begin when a man came in and sat down and addressed by grandpa as such, "Brother Patterson, I'm so glad you and Sister Patterson were able to come to the temple". Grandpa said he didn't recall meeting him before and the man said he would sometime. Then grandpa turned and asked grandma if she knew him, which she said no. Then he turned again to address the man and he was gone. They always thought he was one of the three Nephite Prophets." [531]

James was a small man, with a big mustache. He always wore the same hat, creased in four ways. He was soft-spoken and very spiritual. He did not curse, although he could when the occasion demanded it. Pete Canty, grandson of James, said that when he even said "Damn", it scared him to death.

James was a farmer in South Carolina, raising among other things, cotton. On more than one occasion, the family picked cotton for a living. He continued to be active in the LDS Church, becoming the Branch President of the Los Cerritos Branch, in 1896 [532] after their arrival in Colorado. He became the janitor of the LDS Church, after they arrived in Sanford, and was so employed until he became unable to work.

Quinn Morgan told of a time when Dudley Carr was deathly ill. He was asked if he wanted a Priesthood blessing, and who did he want to give him the blessing, he replied "James Patterson and Brother DePriest". James and Brother DePriest gave the blessing, asking that the sickness be placed upon them. One of them had to be helped to leave the place and the other had to be bed ridden. Dudley was made whole again.

### The following is the Patriarchal Blessing of James G Patterson:

"Fox Creek Branch, Manassa Ward, San Luis Stake of Zion, July 8, 1896. A Patriarchal Blessing by James C. Berthelsen, to James Patterson born November 8, 1849.

Brother Patterson, in the name of the Lord Jesus Christ, and by authority from him, I have placed my hands upon your head to confer a blessing upon you. Your Heavenly Father has ever held his kind hand over you, for he knew your labor before you came here, and you were given the privilege to come upon the earth in this dispensation to stand as a Savior for your Kindred who in darkness and who have been cursed through their rebellion and disobedience to God.

---

[531] Mae Garcia Croasmun genealogy, received from Cynthia Walsh.

[532] Jensen, Andrew; Church Chronology: A Record of Important Events Pertaining to the History of the Church of Jesus Christ of Latter Day Saints: Salt Lake City, UT; Deseret News; 1899; page 448.

Your spirit is calm and gentle and when the voice of the true Shepherd sounded in your ears you accepted it with gladness. You obeyed its laws and emigrated to Zion. And God has seen your devotion in the midst of your many trials and he has now caused his almighty power to surround you that you should not fall by the wayside. But you shall live to see your sons and daughters take the responsibility of man and woman hood and see your people embrace the Gospel by the tens of thousands and you shall yet be a leader in the Church of Christ among your brethren.

For your spirit possess all the leading qualifications aided by the Holy Ghost, you are a chosen descendent of Israel, heir to the Holy Priesthood, entitled to all the blessings in the house of God.

Your last days on this earth shall be the choicest ones, through your increased knowledge you shall live to see your race of people subdue this nation and give the power of government unto the Apostles and Prophets of God.

And then shall none of the scourges nor the weapons of war, not of the destroying elements shall ever hurt you, and when the Lord has seen your fidelity, and proved you upon this earth, call you unto the other world, there to be a strong preacher of righteousness with power from God to the convincing of innumerable hosts.

You are destined to be a representative of your race, numbered among the hundred and forty thousand. You shall be white as snow, blessed with every beauty and grandeur, even as the chosen Son of God, clothed in white as a token of innocence and purity. And you shall see your wife and your sons and daughters become the recipients of the Heavenly gifts, and your children's' children shall follow in your footsteps down through many generations until they cannot be counted by numbers. And all those whose duty it will be to honor and respect you and to bless you that you started this work. The Angels are keeping records of you and because of your faithfulness it shall go before to judgment and your reward shall await you, even that of King and Priest, after the Celestial order of heaven.

This blessing I confer upon you by the gift and power of God, and in the name of Jesus Christ, Amen."

**Elizabeths' Patriarchal  Blessing follows;**

"San Luis Stake, Fox Creek Branch, Manassa Ward, 8th of July 1896. Patriarchal

Blessing of Elizabeth M Patterson born September 3 1849 of George White and

Margareth Marsh.

Sister Elizabeth, in the name of Jesus Christ, having received the power of

Heaven to seal and bless his obedient children upon the earth, for you are entitled to these blessings because of your obedience, for you have been chosen in connection with your husband to raise a standard of Salvation for your kindred and people, to open the prison doors by performing the ordinances of baptism and sealing which can be attended to upon the earth. And this is your privilege to become a mother of nations, and to start a record in the House of God which by revelation shall trace you back to Laman and Lemuel, through the tribes of Manassa, and clear back to Father Adam.

You shall be found among the obedient and blessed, receiving every honor ever conferred upon the daughters of God, and when you are called forward in the morning of resurrection and again be united with your husband and children and share with your husband an everlasting joy and name to be handed down in honor throughout endless ages of eternity.

I bless you with health and life as long as your heart desires to live with the Holy Ghost as your constant companion to cite you to the blessings of which I have spoken and maintain the faith.' I seal the blessing of the protecting hand of God against all destroying power and bless you with the spirit to bring back your children, to command them to work in the ways of God, and the power of faith for their good, which shall be visible on them the promotion of their faith, your kindred in the other worked are ever praying for you, that you may remain faithful. And theirs and your prayers are heard for you shall maintain the faith midst your experiences here. I seal upon you which are after the Patriarchal order, I holding that Priesthood and power the Lord he does acknowledge by labors, fulfill the promises now made to you. I seal these blessings in the name of Jesus, Amen."

Elizabeth was also a great cook, and when she became blind, about 20 years before her death, she managed to continue her life as if there were nothing wrong with her. "shortly after their (Grandpa and Grandma's) return from the temple, grandma took a severe headache which lasted for 3 days, then she lost her sight completely. We now believe that she had cataracts, for which there was no treatment at the time. She never complained of her loss of vision, she would sing quite often, "Oh see the light upon the hill." A wire was hung between the house and the outhouse to help her negotiate between the two. She had everything in place in her kitchen, knowing exactly where the things were, and she continued to cook, until her death. 'She also continued to piece together quilt blocks, and could even match them. One has to assume that she had a bit of help with the matching. She also had a trick to putting pillow cases on the pillows, she sowed a button on the open end, so her fingers could find it and know which end to put the pillow into.

She was a very independent and faithful woman. She was asked at a Stake Conference how she could remain faithful even though she was blind. Her reply was simply that she "could see the truth, and that was all she needed to see."

She was a faithful member of the LDS Church, her entire life. When the Elders in South Carolina were in hiding, they hid in the Patterson house, and one can imagine they enjoyed her cooking while they were there.

Both James and Elizabeth died and are buried in Sanford, Colorado. More about Elizabeth's family will be found in the White chapter, more will be found on Nancy Christina in the Wats chapter. More on the children and parents will be found in Genealogy of the Western Catawba. The Children given here are just Pattersons, the children of James Patterson.

(1). Jane Lizzie Patterson-Watts, born 23 September 1874, The daughter of James Goodwin Patterson and Nancy Cristina Wats, she married David Adam Harris, son of James and Sarah Jane Ayers Harris, as his first wife. Lizzie died after 1900.

Lizzie had Edith, Lavina, Richard and Fannie Harris. Their information will be found in the Peter Harris chapter, under James Harris Sr and then to David Adam Harris.

**This is the family James Goodwin Patterson and Elizabeth Missouri White**

## Father  James Goodwin PATTERSON

| | | |
|---|---|---|
| Birth | 8 Nov 1849 | , Chester, South Carolina |
| Residen | 1900 | Marital Status: Married Relation to Head of House: Head; Sanford, Conejos, Colorado |
| Residen | 1910 | Marital Status: Married Relation to Head of House: Head; Precinct 14, Conejos, Colorado |
| Residen | 1920 | Marital Status: Married Relation to Head of House: Head; Sanford, Conejos, Colorado |
| Residen | 1930 | Sanford, Conejos, Colorado |
| Death | 7 Sep 1931 | Age at Death: 81; Sanford, Conejos, Colorado |
| Burial | 9 Sep 1931 | Sanford, Conejos, Colorado, United States |
| | | |
| Marriag | 24 Jul 1868 | Catawba Reservation, York, South Carolina |
| Father | Laban CHAPPELL (1821-1862) | |
| Mother | Martha PATTERSON (1827-   ) | |
| Other spouse | Nancy Christina WATS (1855-1926) | |
| Marriag | abt 1883 | Catawba Indian Reservation, York, South Carolina |

## Mother  Elizabeth Missouri WHITE

| | | |
|---|---|---|
| Birth | 3 Sep 1849 | Catawba Reservation, York, South Carolina, United States |
| Residen | 1900 | Marital Status: Married Relation to Head of House: Wife; Sanford, Conejos, Colorado |
| Residen | 1910 | Marital Status: Married Relation to Head of House: Wife; Precinct 14, Conejos, Colorado |
| Residen | 1920 | Marital Status: Married Relation to Head of House: Wife; Sanford, Conejos, Colorado |
| Residen | 1930 | Marital Status: Married Relation to Head of House: Wife; Sanford, Conejos, Colorado |

| Death | 14 Jul 1934 | Sanford, Conejos, Colorado, United States |
|---|---|---|
| Burial | 16 Jul 1934 | Sanford, Conejos, Colorado, United States |
| Father | George D WHITE (1807-1858) | |
| Mother | Margareth Peggy Quash Mush MARSH (1827-1874) | |

## Children

### F  Martha Jane PATTERSON

| Birth | 21 Nov 1868 | Catawba Reservation, York, South Carolina |
|---|---|---|
| Residen | 1900 | Sanford, Conejos, Colorado |
| Residen | 1910 | Farmington, San Juan, New Mexico |
| Residen | 1920 | Farmington, San Juan, New Mexico |
| Death | 5 May 1971 | Age at Death: 102; Farmington, San Juan, New Mexico |
| Burial | 29 May 1971 | Kirtland, San Juan, New Mexico, United States |
| Spouse | Pinkney Henry HEAD (1862-1951) | |
| Marriag | 17 Feb 1886 | John Black Place, Spartanburg, South Carolina |

### F  Georgia Henrietta PATTERSON

| Birth | 4 Jul 1870 | Catawba Reservation, York, South Carolina |
|---|---|---|
| Residen | 13 Jun 1900 | Sanford, Conejos, Colorado |
| Residen | 1910 | Marital Status: Married Relation to Head of House: Wife; Precinct 14, Conejos, Colorado |
| Residen | 1920 | Marital Status: Married Relation to Head of House: Wife; Sanford, Conejos, Colorado |
| Death | 27 Feb 1925 | Sanford, Conejos, Colorado |
| Burial | 28 Feb 1925 | Sanford, Conejos, Colorado |
| Spouse | John Alonzo CANTY (1859-1938) | |
| Marriag | 17 Feb 1886 | John Black Place, Spartanburg, South Carolina |

### F  Tarsabell-Isabell PATTERSON

| Birth | 24 Jun 1872 | Catawba Reservation, York, South Carolina |
|---|---|---|
| Residen | 1900 | Marital Status: Single Relation to Head of House: Daughter; Sanford, Conejos, Colorado |
| Residen | 1920 | Sanrafael, Conejos, Colorado |
| Residen | 1930 | Mogote, Conejos, Colorado |
| Burial | Mar 1949 | Sanford, Conejos, Colorado |
| Death | 22 Mar 1949 | Sanford, Conejos, Colorado |
| Spouse | 1. John E. KING (   -   ) | |
| Marriag | 3 Sep 1892 | |
| Divorce | | |
| Spouse | Jose Pablo GALVEZ (1860-1932) | |
| Marriag | Oct 1905 | Conejos, Colorado |

| F | Lula Ann PATTERSON | | |
|---|---|---|---|
| | Birth | 10 Oct 1874 | Catawba Reservation, York Co., South Carolina |
| | Residen | 1910 | Age in 1910: 34Age in 1910: 24; Marital Status: Married; Relation to Head of House: Wife; San Rafael, Conejos, Colorado |
| | Residen | 1920 | Age: 44Marital Status: Married; Relation to Head of House: Wife; Sanrafael, Conejos, Colorado |
| | Death | 5 Jun 1929 | Age at Death: 54; Mogote, Conejos, Colorado |
| | Burial | 6 Jun 1929 | Fox Creek, Conejos County, Colorado |
| | Spouse | Julio E VALDEZ (1885-1930) | |
| | Marriag | 15 Nov 1894 | |

| F | Eldora Lavinia PATTERSON | | |
|---|---|---|---|
| | Birth | 11 Feb 1877 | Catawba Nation, South Carolina |
| | Chr | 1885 | Catawba Reservation, York, South Carolina |
| | Residen | 1910 | Age in 1910: 32Marital Status: Married; Relation to Head of House: Wife; San Rafael, Conejos, Colorado |
| | Residen | 1920 | Age: 43Marital Status: Married; Relation to Head of House: Wife; Sanrafael, Conejos, Colorado |
| | Residen | 1930 | Age: 52Marital Status: Married; Relation to Head of House: Wife; Mogote, Conejos, Colorado |
| | Residen | 1935 | Los Pinos, Conejos, Colorado |
| | Residen | 1 Apr 1940 | Age: 63Marital Status: Married; Relation to Head of House: Wife; Los Pinos, Conejos, Colorado, United States |
| | Burial | Oct 1969 | Sanford, Conejos County, Colorado |
| | Death | 5 Oct 1969 | Age at Death: 92; Mogote, Conejos, Colorado |
| | Spouse | Ephemenio GARCIA (1873-1947) | |
| | Marriag | 16 Dec 1895 | Conejos, Colorado |

| F | Maggie Emma PATTERSON | | |
|---|---|---|---|
| | Birth | 24 Mar 1879 | Alamosa, Alamosa, Colorado |
| | Burial | Jan 1893 | Sanford, Conejos, Colorado |
| | Death | 22 Jan 1893 | Sanford, Conejos, Colorado |
| | Marriag | | |

| F | Elizabeth Abby Ellen PATTERSON | | |
|---|---|---|---|
| | Birth | 18 Mar 1882 | Catawba Reservation, York, South Carolina |
| | Burial | Jan 1963 | Sanford, Conejos, Colorado |
| | Death | 19 Jan 1963 | Alamosa, Alamosa, Colorado |
| | Spouse | William Thomas BEALS (1878-1949) | |
| | Marriag | 1 Mar 1898 | Conejos County, Colorado |
| | Divorce | | |
| | Spouse | Refugio or Joseph Rufus GARCIA (1865-1933) | |

| | | | |
|---|---|---|---|
| | Marriag | 28 Mar 1904 | Conejos County, Colorado |
| **F** | **Maud Mary PATTERSON** | | |
| | Birth | 14 Feb 1884 | Catawba, South Carolina, United States |
| | Residen | 1920 | Age: 35Marital Status: Married; Relation to Head of House: Wife; Sanrafael, Conejos, Colorado |
| | Residen | 1930 | Age: 46Marital Status: Married; Relation to Head of House: Wife; Mogote, Conejos, Colorado |
| | Death | 28 Mar 1973 | Age at Death: 89; Mogote, Conejos, Colorado |
| | Burial | Apr 1973 | Sanford, Conejos, Colorado |
| | Civil | | Colorado |
| | Spouse | Eleseo GALVEZ (1866-1936) | |
| | Marriag | 25 Oct 1897 | Conejos, Conejos, Colorado, United States |
| **M** | **James Moroni Heber PATTERSON** | | |
| | Birth | 25 Mar 1887 | Spartanburg County, South Carolina |
| | Residen | 1900 | Age: 13Marital Status: Single; Relation to Head of House: Son; Sanford, Conejos, Colorado |
| | Burial | Aug 1903 | Sanford, Conejos, Colorado |
| | Death | 22 Aug 1903 | Age: 16; Sanford, Conejos, Colorado |
| | Marriag | | |
| **M** | **Joseph Brigham PATTERSON** | | |
| | Birth | 1 Jan 1890 | Manassa, Conejos, Colorado |
| | Death | 28 Jan 1890 | Age: 0; Manassa, Conejos, Colorado |
| | Burial | 30 Jan 1890 | Manassa, Conejos, Colorado, United States |
| | Marriag | | |
| **M** | **Henry Alonzo PATTERSON** | | |
| | Birth | 29 Jan 1891 | Sanford, Conejos, Colorado |
| | Residen | 1900 | Age: 9Marital Status: Single; Relation to Head of House: Son; Sanford, Conejos, Colorado |
| | Death | 14 Mar 1909 | Age: 18; Sanford, Conejos, Colorado |
| | Burial | 16 Mar 1909 | Sanford, Conejos, Colorado, United States |
| | Marriag | | |

**Children of James Goodwin Patterson and Elizabeth Missouri White.**

**PHOTO 493 – MARTHA HANE PATTERSON**

(2).Martha Jane Patterson, born 21 November 1868. She married Pinkney Henry Head, son of Robert Henry and Sarah Ann Evans-Canty Head. They had Sarah, Rosey, Lucy, Hattie, Heber, Nellie, Willard, George, Helen, Pinkney Henry jr., Mary and Dorothy Head. Martha died in May 1971. More about Pinkney and Robert Henry Head will be found in the Marsh chapter, since the mother of Robert Henry was Lucy Quash-Marsh. More about her children will be found in Head chapter.

**PHOTO 494 – GEROGIA HENRIETTA PATERSON**

(3). Georgia Henrietta Patterson born 4 July 1870. She married John Alonzo Canty-Whitesides. Rhett died 21 February 1925 in Sanford, Colorado of yellow jaundice. She had Wilford, John Henry, Eddie Archie, William

Franklin, Lazell and Alma Canty. More about this family can be found in the Canty and Scott chapters because the Catawba way was to take the mother's maiden name, which was Scott, so in reality, John Alonzo should have been either Scott or Whitesides. He took his mother's married name of Canty.

**PHOTO 495 – HEADSTONE OF GEORGIA H PATTERSON AND J ALONZO CANTY -- BURIED AT SANFORD CEMETERY - SANFORD, CONEJOS COUNTY, COLORADO**

"February 29th 1884, My companion led two young women down in the waters of baptism,viz. Marthy and Heneretta Patterson, confirmed them at Bro. Evans Watts and we blessed two of Bro. Pattersons' children, Eldora and Emma Patterson I. being the Mouth on Emma. This was the first child I ever blessed."[533]

I know little about her, except some of the things that she cooked, for instance, her beans with dumplings. She was also soft-spoken and evidently long suffering, because she raised 5 of the most rowdy boys in Sanford. [534]

Rhett married the young returned missionary, John Alonzo Canty, on the same day and the same place that her sister Martha married Pinkney Head. They all were married in the John Black Place, in Spartanburg South Carolina on February 17,1886

She died of Yellow Jaundice on February 21, 1925 in Sanford Colorado and is buried in Sanford Cemetery. Her descendants will be found in the Canty Chapter.

\*\*\*\*\*\*\*\*\*\*\*\*\*\*\*\*\*\*\*\*\*\*\*\*\*\*\*\*\*\*\*\*\*

---

[533] Joseph Willey Diary
[534] Memories of Alma (Pete) Canty.

**PHOTO 496 - ISABELL PATTERSON AND A PICTURE OF HER HEADSTONE – BURRIED AT SANFORD CEMETERY - SANFORD, CONEJOS COUNTY, COLORADO**

4). Isabell Patterson born 24 June 1872. She married first. John E. King, they were divorced; second Pablo Galvezand died 22 March 1949. She `James Clander, Annie and Rose Marie Galvez.

**From the Clark Missionary journal**

"Went to S. S. in morning after which I went to James Harris and had dinner and went to R. H. to go as far as Charlotte (North Carolina) with Tersey Patterson to see her off all right. Started from Rock Hill abt. 5 p.m. arrived at Charlotte abt. 6 p.m. Put up at Snyder House and I went and looked around the town and about seven the sounds of more than half a dozen Church bells warning people of meeting. I attend the 2nd Presybterian Church occupying seat in gallery directly opposite the minister."

(a). Joseph Heber Galvez, born 19 March 1907, a twin to James Clander died in infancy.

**PHOTO 497 - JAMES CLANDER GALVEZ**

(b). James Clander Galvez, who was born in 19 March 1907. He married Ada Janette Velasquez, who had two children by a previous marriage. Clander was a government trapper during the depression, and later a ranch hand, died in Sanford, Colorado.

**Children of James Chandler Galvez**

      (1).  Grace Velazquez Galvez 1923–

      (2).  Jack Emzy Galvez 1925–

      (3).  John Clander Galvez 1927–1948

      (4).  Howard Galvez 1930–2009

      (5).  Alice Barbara Janet Galvez 1934–2003

      (6).  Shirley Bell Galvez 1936–1937

      (7).  Robert Kenneth Galvez 1938–

      (8).  Pauline Crisanta Galvez 1940–2013

      (9).  Pearl Annette Galvez 1944–2014

      (10). Opal Georgette Galvez 1944–


**Howard Galvez the 4th child**

**PHOTO 498 – HOWARD GALVEZ**


(4). Howard Galvez, born 24 March 1930, Sanford, Conejos, Colorado, and he died 25 December 2009, La Jara, Colorado.

### Howard Galvez by Wayne Head

"Howard Galvez, Sr. was born in Nortonville, Colorado (north of Sanford, Colorado), March 24, 1930. He is the great-grandson of James and Elizabeth Patterson, the grandson of Isabell Patterson and Pablo Galvez, and the son of Clander and Janette Galvez. He entered basic training at Ft. Riley, Kansas for his military duties in the United States Army during the Korean War. From Ft. Riley he was sent to Okanawa, Japan where he was informed that he had "volunteered" to go to Korea.

Upon arrival in Korea he was issued ten rounds of ammunition. He was wounded in Korea and recouped in Japan. While there he met one brother there before being sent back to Korea. He also served two tours of service in Germany and was then sent back to Korea. There he injured his knees and was medically retired from the military.

Howard served in the U.S. Army during the Korean War from November 1949 to August 1962 and was a Sergeant 1 st. Class. He won a combat infantry badge, the Purple Hear and Bronze Star, and the Korean Service Medal with Five Stars. His Bronze Star Citation reads: "Citation for the Bronze Star, Private 1st Class Howard Galvez, Infantry of the Army of the United states, a member of Company M. 35th Infantry.

"On 15 February 1951 near Yong Dong Po, Korea, Private 1st Class Galvez was guarding a 75-mm recoilless rifle position. At about 2300 hours a small force of North Koreans infiltrated our lines. PFC Galvez saw an American soldier fighting with an enemy soldier so he ran through a hail of enemy lire in a determined effort to be of some aid to his comrade. PFC Galvez managed to kill the North Korean Soldier, thereby saving his comrade from possible death. PFC Galvez in saving his fellow soldier was wounded by a hand grenade. Disregarding his wounds he returned to his position and remained there until it was possible for him to be relieved. PEG Galvez's valorous action and his outstanding courage during this action reflect great credit on himself and the military service. [535]"

> (c). Annie Eleanor Galvez: born 5 June 1910, Sanford, Colorado and died 22 April 1994, La Jara, Colorado
>
> (d). Rose Marie Galvez: born 3 June 1914, Colorado and
>
> died 12 December 1990, Alamosa, Alamosa, Colorado

> \*\*\*\*\*\*\*\*\*\*\*\*\*\*\*\*\*\*\*\*\*\*\*\*\*\*\*\*\*

---

[535] 7th Generation News

**PHOTO 499 LULA PATTERSON**

(5). Lula Patterson was born 10 October 1874. Lula married Joe E Valdez on 15 November 1894. She died 5 June 1929, Her children are:

Harry Valdez 1906–1920
Lila Valdez 1908–1986
Julio Henry Valdez 1911–1989
Gladys Elizabeth Valdez 1913–1983

State of Colorado
Division of Vital Statistics No. #93
MARRIAGE RECORD REPORT

County Conejos

Husband's Name Valdez, Jose E. Age 40 Race White

Wife's Name Patterson, Lula M Age 17 Race White

Place of Marriage San Rafael, Colorado Date 11/15/1894

Name of Official who Performed Ceremony Albert Jacobs

Title An Elder Address Capulin, Colorado

Reported by

Address Antonito, Colorado

Columbia Press, Denver—50M—5-39

**PHOTO 500 – MARRIAGE RECORD REPORT FOR JOSE E VALDEZ AND LULA M PATTERSON**

**PHOTO 501 – ELDORA LININIA PATTERSON**

(6). Eldora Livinia "Dora"Patterson, born 11 February 1877, in Catawba South Carolina and died She died 5 October 1969 Dora married Ephemino Garica (1872-1947) on 16 December 1895.  They had 10 children:

Margaret "Maggie" Garcia Ruybal 1901–1977
Mary Ellen Helen Garcia 1903–1982
Genevive Genorrva "Maud" Garcia 1905–1969
Alfred Garcia 1907–1999
Emma Garcia 1910–
Joseph Garcia 1911–1944
Henry F. Garcia 1915–1990
Samuel Garcia 1917–1984
James Epimenio Garcia 1917–1967
 Philip Garcia 1921–1993

**PHOTO 502 – HEADSTONE FOR ELDORA PATTERSON AND HUSBAND EPIMENIO GARCIA – BURIED SANFORD CEMETERY – SANFORD, CONEJOS COUNTY, COLORADO, PLOT: 2719-A**

(7). Maggie Enma Pattersoa, born 24 March 1879, York County, South Carolina – died 22 January 1893, Sanford, Conejos, Colorado – buried, Sanford Cemetery

**Elder Joseph Willey writes:**

"February 29th, 1884, My companion led two young women down in the waters of baptism, viz. Marthy and Henerena Patterson, confirmed them at Bro. Evans Watts and we blessed two of Bro. Patterson's children, Eldora and Emma Patterson. I being the mouth on Emma This was the first child I ever blessed."

**PHOTO 503 – HEADSTONE FOR MAGGIE EMMA PATTERSON – BURIED AT SANFORD CEMETERY, SANFORD, CONEJOS COUNTY, COLORADO**

**PHOTO 504 – ELIZABETH ABBIE ELLEN PATTERSON**

(8). Elizabeth Abbie Ellen Patterson born 18 March 1882. She married first. William Thomas Beals, divorced after being abandoned with two little boys; married second Rufus Garcia. Rufus had two children when they married. Abbie lost her little Willie and raised

Arthur and the Rufus's child as well as the children the two shared. She had: Joseph Arthur Beals 1899–1986 and James Willie Beals 1901–1919: then, George Henry Garcia 1905–1995, Joseph Willey says

"Sunday 9th 1884, held Sunday school at Bro. Watts. There blessed two (more) of Bro. Patterson's children, namely Abby & Maude Mary Patterson. I being mouth on Abby."[536]

Abbie was one of two children James Patterson brought to Colorado in the first migration; Maud was the other, according to Mae Garcia Croasmun.

Axthur Beals born April 1898, he is now deceased. 678

William (Willie) Beals born 1901 and died 1919 in an influenza epidemic.

Abbie lived through the South Carolina earthquake, when she was about 5 years old. It rattled the farm equipment and ground, and the family thought the mobs were coming..

More about the earthquake comes from a book entitled A City Without Cobwebs^ a History of Rock Hill. South Carolina.

"On the 31st of August, 1886, Rock Hill was shaken by an earthquake. It occurred at ten o'clock at night on a Tuesday. There was a low rumbling sound, like distant thunder. The first shock the earth trembled and the houses swayed and the windows rattled and dishes were broken. The shock was so severe that lamps were placed on the floors to avoid starting fires. This first shock was the most severe, it came from the southwest and continued for 30 seconds. The second shock came ten minutes later but did not last so long. The third shock was felt a few minutes before two o'clock in the morning. Many of the people were sure they heard Gabriel's horn when the steam whistle of the Old Mill was blown. Damage was slight in Rock Hill, one chimney, belonging to John Ratteree had been shortened some three or four feet when it lost bricks. The stores lost many goods packed in crockery, and many widows were broken. One story is told of a former slave named Dick Latta had been taught to play the violin, and played for many events. During that night, he had been playing for a dance,

---

[536] Elder Joseph Willey Diary.

**PHOTO 505 – HEADSTONE FOR ELIZABETH ABBIE PATTERSON AND HUSBANE RUFUS GARCIA --
BURIAL: SANFORD CEMETERY, SANFORD, CONEJOS COUNTY, COLORADO, PLOT: 1021-A**

**Abbie's thirteen Children:**

**Her two children from William Thomas Beals (1878-1949);**

**PHOTO 506 – JOSEPH ATHUR BEALS**

a. Joseph Arthur Beals born 6 December 1899, La Isla, Conejos, Colorado and died 4 June 1986, Tarrant County, Texas. He married Annie Ruth Mabe (1903–1986).

**Texas Death Index, 1903-2000**

Name: Joseph Beals  --   Death Date:4 Jun 1986
Death County:  Tarrant     --     Gender:  Male

**U.S., Social Security Death Index, 1935-2014**

 Name:  Joseph Beals  SSN:  464-01-7217
Last Residence: 76106 Fort Worth, Tarrant, Texas
BORN: 16 Dec 1899
Last Benefit:   76106, Fort Worth, Tarrant, Texas, United States of America   Died:
Jun 1986
State (Year) SSN issued:       Texas (Before 1951)

**PHOTO 507** **HEADSTONE FOR JAMES WILLIE BEALS AND HARVY 1917-1922 - BURIAL: SANFORD CEMETERY, SANFORD, CONEJOS COUNTY - COLORADO, PLOT: 1022-A**

b. James Willie Beals born 7 August  1901, La Isla, Conejos, Colorado and died 19 March 1919,  Sanford, Conejos, Colorado.

**Sanford Cemetery Record.**

In an early cemetery record his name was recorded asames as Willie Garcia) (1901-1919)  He died of the Flu.

**Abbie's children by Rufus Joseph Garcia (1865-1933);**

**PHOTO 508 – GEORGE HENRY GARCIA**

c. George Henry Garcia born 15 January 1905,      Mogote, Conejos, Colorado and died 11 January 1995,  La Jara, Conejos, Colorado.

### U.S., World War II Army Enlistment Records, 1938-1946

Name:    George H Garcia            Birth Year:    1905
Race:      American Indian, citizen (American)
Nativity State or Country:        Colorado        State of Residence: Colorado
County or City:  Conejos
Enlistment Date:  3 Aug 1942  --  Enlistment State:    Colorado
Enlistment City:  Pueblo
Branch Code:    Branch Immaterial - Warrant Officers
Grade:    Private                Grade Code:   Private
Term of Enlistment:      Enlistment for the duration of the War or other emergency, plus six months, subject to the discretion of the President or otherwise according to law
Component:      Selectees (Enlisted Men)
Source:    Civil Life
Education:      Grammar school
Civil Occupation:      General farmers
Marital Status:    Divorced, with dependents
Height:    64

Weight:      121

**U.S., Social Security Applications and Claims Index, 1936-2007**

Name: George Henry Garcia          [George H Garcia]

SSN:  522280722          Gender:  Male          Race:  Hispanic (Latino)

Birth Date:     15 Jan 1905

Birth Place:     Sanford, Colorado          [Sanford|]

Death Date:     11 Jan 1995

Father:          Rufus Garcia

Mother:          Abbie E Patterson

Citizenship or Alien Status:   U.S. citizen.

Claim Date:     10 Jul 1964

Type of Claim:          Duplicate SSN - change or replacement.

Additional Information:          Duplicate request; evidence of identity only submitted.

Notes: 30 Apr 1987: Name listed as GEORGE HENRY GARCIA; 08 Jul 1964: Name listed as GEORGE H GARCIA


**U.S., Department of Veterans Affairs BIRLS Death File, 1850-2010**

Name   George Garcia          Gender          Male

Birth Date          15 Jan 1905          Death Date          11 Jan 1995

SSN     522280722          Branch 1          ARMY

Enlistment Date 1          18 Aug 1942                    Release Date 1          4 Feb 1943

**PHOTO 509  -  GEORGE HENRY GARCIA**

**Garcia Keeps Everyone Smiling**

Conejos County Citizen January 29, 1993      68°

By Lucy Salazar                    Correspondent

Conejos County's George Garcia, affectionately known as an old timer and early settler there, has fallen on hard times with a severe illness. He was recently admitted to the Conejos County Hospital Long Term Care Unit

Garcia was born in Sanford on Jan. 15, 1905, to Abby and Rufus Garcia, the oldest of 10 children, including five boys and five girls. Half of his siblings are still living. Two sisters live in Pueblo and one sister lives in Idaho. His two remaining brothers live in.Utah and S. Carolina.

Garcia had a freak accident when he was just 5 years old while watching a baseball game, as a batter    broke bat and a splinter flew off and hit him in the left eye and blinding him on that side, He    said, "it never slowed, him down.'

When he was 17, his father took sick and George had to take over helping to run the farm and raise his younger brothers and sisters. He said that "it was a lot of work, but he would do it all over again."

The only break from farming occurred during World War II when he served a few years in the Army. He had many friends. One of his hobbies was to go snake-hunting for rattlers on the Rio Grande by Los Sauces.

He said there were, and still continue to be, several large dens in that area. He had a hook fashioned    on the end of a pole that he would use to catch the snakes. Then he'd pin them down while he cut off their rattles with a shovel. One day he caught 118. He never used their meat  or skins. He would never would touch them. He would put them in a pile and leave them by the river.

He also loved to fish and his favorite spot was at Bear Lake, though it was a hard spot to get to. The fishing and scenery was the best up there. He said, "it was so beautiful that postcards could have been made from the pictures." His biggest fish that he caught out of Bear Lake was a 6 1/4-pound rainbow trout.

George also taught himself to play the harmonica- as a young man. he mostly played for his own enjoyment. About 25- years ago, he played for a program at the Mormon Pioneer Days.

His favorite hobby was his garden, which was the biggest one in Sanford for many years. He grew both vegetables and flowers. Every year he would plant over 100 gladiolas as well as poppies, and sweet peas. (Most years he had the first sweet pea to bloom in the area, jcm) Also he had different kinds of apple trees. Since coming to the Long Term Care Unit, George has made many people, including staff and visitors, and other residents smile with his stories, his jokes and his much loved Harmonica.

The staff appreciates George for his kind and quiet manner, And of course for his quick, witty, sense of humor."

**Garcia Keeps Everyone Smiling**

# *George H. Garcia, 89*

LA JARA - George H. Garcia, 89, of Sanford, died Jan. 11, 1995, at the Conejos County Hospital in La Jara.

Mr. Garcia was born on Jan. 15, 1905, in Mogote, Colorado, the son of Joseph Rufus and Abbie Ellen (Patterson) Garcia.

A member of the Church of Jesus Christ of Latter Day Saints, Mr. Garcia served his country in the United States Army during World War II, and was a farmer throughout life.

He is survived by two brothers, Elbert Garce of Smithfield, Utah, and Guy Garcia of Rock Hill, S.C.; three sisters, Viola Schneider of Pueblo West, Dorothy Ong of Pueblo, Martha Riedel of Hagaman, Idaho, as well as several nieces and nephews.

He was preceded in death by his parents and several brothers and sisters.

Funeral services will be held Saturday, Jan. 14, at 2 p.m. from the Sanford Ward Chapel of the Church of Jesus Christ of Latter Day Saints. Interment will follow in the Sanford Cemetery. Friends who wish may call Saturday from 1 p.m. until service time in the Relief Society Room of the church.

Butler-Showalter Chapel is handling the arrangements.

**PHOTO 510 - NEWSPAPER CLIPPING FOR DEATH OF GEORGE H GARCIA – AGE 89 SANFORD CEMETERY RECORD.**

Father was Joseph Rufus Garcia; Mother was Abbie Ellen (Patterson) Garcia.
Burial:  Sanford Cemetery, Sanford, Conejos Count Y, Colorado
Plot: 1021-B

**PHOTO 511 - LABAN RUFUS GARCIA**

d. Laban Rufus Garcia born 21 November 1906, Sanford, Conejos, Colorado and died 12 July 1990, Utah.

### U.S., World War II Army Enlistment Records, 1938-1946

Labon R Garcia   Birth Year 1906   Race   White,
Citizen   Nativity State or Country        Colorado
State of Residence:  Colorado,  County or City: Conejos
Enlistment Date -3 Jul 1942   Enlistment State;  Colorado.  Enlistment City –Pueblo  --
Branch ; Branch Immaterial - Warrant Officers
Branch Code   Branch Immaterial - Warrant Officers
Grade  Private          Grade Code     Private
Term of Enlistment     Enlistment for the duration of the War or other emergency, plus six months, subject to the discretion of the President or otherwise according to law
Component     Selectees (Enlisted Men)               Source          Civil Life
Education      Grammar school
Civil Occupation        Farm hands, general farms
Marital Status  Single, with dependents
Height 62
Weight          128

FAREWELL TESTIMONIAL

*Honoring*
ELDER LABON GARCIA

*called to serve in the*
MEXICO MISSION

Church of Jesus Christ
Latter-Day Saints

*Enter Mission Home October 28*

SANFORD WARD                                    OCTOBER 20, 1963

§ PROGRAM §

| | |
|---|---|
| Opening Song — "I'll Go Where You Want Me to Go Dear Lord" | |
| "It May Not Be On A Mountain High" | |
| Prayer | William Canty |
| Sacrament Song | Page 125 |
| Remarks | Bishop Albert Mortensen |
| Song | Judy Westbrook and Co. (Nancy Morgan, Joyce Smith) |
| Speaker | Ed Canty |
| Musical | Becky and Karla Westbrook |
| Response | Labon Garcia |
| Song | Judy Westbrook and Co. (Nancy Morgan, Joyce Smith) |
| Prayer | Kenneth Jones |

**PHOTO 512 - ELDER LABON GARCIA – SANFORD WARD 20 OCTOBER 1963**

## LABON R. GARCIA

### LABON RUFUS GARCIA
NOVEMBER 21, 1906
JULY 12, 1990

### SERVICES
SANFORD WARD CHAPEL
CHURCH OF JESUS CHRIST OF LATTER DAY SAINTS
SATURDAY, JULY 14, 1990     1:30 P.M

PRESIDING & CONDUCTING     .BISHOP DENNIS Q. MORTENSEN
FAMILY PRAYER. . . .          . .        ELBERT GARCE
INVOCATION    .                          MIKE JOHNSON
"I'LL GO WHERE YOU WANT ME TO GO"     JOYCE VALENTINE
REMARKS . . .    .   .      BISHOP DENNIS Q. MORTENSEN
OBITUARY  . . . . .    .   .   .         STEVEN SMITH
"LAY MY HEAD BENEATH THE ROSE".     . . . .
                         CHUCK AND GENIA RASMUSSEN
SPEAKER. . . . . . .  . .  . . . . .   .   .  PHIL REYNOLDS
"GOIN' HOME". . . . . .JUDY PARISH, NANCY MORGAN, ELVA KREPS
BENEDICTION. . . . .  . . . . . . . .   . . .  KEITH SMITH
ORGANIST. . . . . . .   . .  . . . . .   . .  . . .JANET MORGAN

### PALLBEARERS
JAMES H. SMITH                    DUWAYNE CORNUM
HARVEY HOLMAN                     VERNELL MORGAN
DAVID OTTESON                     JEROME JOHNSON

### HONORARY ESCORTS
JONATHAN SMITH                        DEWEY DYER
ERIC MEDINA                        DEREK MORTENSEN

### USHERS
JOE HOLMAN                        GEORGE SHAWCROFT

### CONCLUDING SERVICE
DEDICATION. . . . . . . . . . . . . . . . . . . . . . . . .ELBERT GARCE
SANFORD CEMETERY
MILITARY HONORS BY AMERICAN LEGION POST 72
LA JARA, COLORADO

### LABON R. GARCIA

A service is planned Saturday for Sanford resident Labon R. Garcia, 83, who passed away at his home July 12.

He was born Nov. 21, 1906, in Sanford to Joseph and Abbie Garcia.

He was a retired farmer and a member of the Church of Jesus Christ of Latter Day Saints.

He was preceded in death by two sisters, Mae Croasmun in 1987, and Stella Erickson, in 1983.

Survivors include four brothers, all Garcia, including George, Sanford, Elbert, Smithfield, Utah, Guy, Rock Hill, S.C., and Ben, Pueblo; three sisters, Viola Schneider, Pueblo, Dorothy Ong, Pueblo, and Martha Riedel, Sumner, Wash.; and several nieces and nephews.

A funeral service will be held at 1:30 p.m. Saturday, July 14, in the Sanford Ward Chapel, Church of Jesus Christ of Latter Day Saints.

Burial will be in the Sanford Cemetery.

Friends may call this afternoon and evening at the Butler-Showalter Chapel in Manassa, and tomorrow [July 14] from 12:30 p.m. until service time at the Sanford Relief Society.

Arrangements are by Butler-Showalter Funeral Home.

PHOTO 513 – HEADSTONE FOR LABON GARCIA  - SANFORD CEMETERY RECORD.   FATHER WAS JOSEPH RUFUS GARCIA; MOTHER WAS ABBIE ELLEN (PATTERSON) GARCIA.
BURIAL:  SANFORD CEMETERY, SANFORD, CONEJOS COUNTY,  COLORADO PLOT: 1755-A

**PHOTO 514 - ELBERT HORACE GARCIA**

e. Elbert Horace Garce born 18 February 1909, Sanford, Conejos, Colorado and died 26 January 2002, Jordan Valley Hospital, West Jordan, Utah. He married Florence Rebecca Harris and they divorced. Then he married Edna Earl Tuck (1915–2015).

**PHOTO 515 – ELBERT GARCIA AND HIS WIFE EDNA**

Elbert Horace Garcia was born 18 February 1909. Elbert also went to South Carolina, when Guy, Ben and Pete Canty went, during or right after the depression. He married Florence Rebecca Harris, daughter of David Adam and Dorothy Price Canty Harris a white woman, Florence and Elbert's marriage "didn't take" as he told told the author and they were divorced. He attended Haskell Institute, and became an Engineer and in the Army during Worle1 War 11. He changed his name to Garce, because, he said, he got tired of being called chili and having to fight. Evidently, his mixture of Catawba, Hispanic and white, left him with problems of racial identity for the outsiders, like it did most of the rest of the Western Catawba. Elbert has been active in the LDS church all his life. He has given many many talks and has always been very proud of his Catawba heritage. Elbert then married Edna Earle Tuck and they have three children. Their son David writes in AICAE Newsletter: "In 1886, a group of five Catawba families (40%of the tribal members of the Catawba Nation led by my great-grandfather and great-grandmother, with their five little girls, left all they could not carry with them and moved to southern Colorado. As many of you know and have felt the same discrimination getting ahead materially, was not easily achieved for them. Grandmother's third of 4 surviving children was my dad. He completed his studies at the Haskell Institute, in the early 1930's, then began working for the civilian conservation Corps and continued the tradition of financially supporting his family. My mother and dad met and married during World War II and dad began his career working for the Bureau of Reclamation as a Civil Engineer, on the Boulder Dam, while mom taught school and began raising my two sisters. In 1955 while my family was in Cordova, Alaska, and dad was working on the roadway project, I was born. Education, my parents thought was the key to a better way of life and understanding other people. When my parents retired in 1971,we moved to a little town in northern Utah where I finished high school and completed my bachelor degree in Landscape Architecture from Utah State University in 1980. Elbert has always been active in the church and served in several Branches, including Valdez, Alaska and Chama, New Mexico. He was instrumental in opening several branches of the Church.

Elbert, Edna, David,    1930 United States Federal Census

Elbert Garcia/Garce in Independence Day Parade
Grand Lake, Colorado -- 1945

**PHOTO 516 – ELBERT GARCIA IN PARADE - 1945**

*1941*

**PHOTO 517 - ELBERT GARCIA ON THE RIGHT MILITARY UNIFORM**

Elbert Garce here poses dressed in his regalia. He was often called upon to speak on the plight of the Indians, family history, and the Catawba Indian Nation. He addressed audiences in universities, high schools, the Rotary, Lions, Elks, Moose, American Legion, and the Veterans of Foreign Wars. He gave well over 450 such talks. (Courtesy of David Garce.)

**PHOTO 518 - NEWSPAPER CLIPPING OF ELBERT GARCIA**

Elbert Garce joined the army in World War II in 1941. He was promised that as an Indian, he would do no guard duty or KP. He soon discovered that promises made to Indians are not kept and was given guard duty. On one very cold night, he used his Native American ingenuity and abandoned his post, got in a nearby car, turned on the engine, and enjoyed the warmth of the heater. He was injured in training and given a medical discharge in 1942. (Courtesy of David Garce.)

**PHOTO 519 - NEWSPAPER CLIPPING OF ELBERT GARCIA – MILITARY**

**PHOTO 520 NEWSPAPER CLIPING OF ELBERT, DAVID, EDNA IN BACK –
MARY RUTH AND ELLEN IN FRONT**

Elbert Garce is here on the job as a Field Inspection Engineer for the Bureau of Reclamation. He worked for the Bureau for 29 years. This job was on the Flaming Gorge Dam. He also worked on Boulder Dam, Nevada; the Shasta Dam, California; the Grand Coolee Dam, Montana; and Blue Mesa Dam, Colorado. He retired in 1969 and died in 2002. (Courtesy of David Garce.)

**PHOTO 521 – NEWSPAPER CLIPPING OF ELBERT GARCIA, (FIELD INSPETION ENGINEER)**

**Obituary**

Elbert H. "Chief Garce

Tue, Jan 29, 2002 00:00:00

SMITHFIELD, Utah - Elbert H. "Chief Garce, born on February 18, 1909, in Sanford, Colorado, passed away peacefully on Saturday, January 26, 2002 at the Jordan Valley Hospital in West Jordan, Utah, due to complications of pneumonia. He was bom to Abbie and Rufus and was preceded in death by his brothers, George, Labon, Ben, Guy, Harvey, Art, Willis, and Juan, and his sisters, Flossie, Magdalene, and Stella. He is survived by his wife of 58 years, children Ellen and Darrell Andersen, Mary and Wesley Pettingill, and David and Patty Garce, as well as nine grandchildren, two great-grandchildren with one on the way. He also has three surviving sisters, Viola Schneider, Dorothy Ong, and Martha Riedil. He and Edna Earle Tuck were married in San Francisco and were later sealed together in the Cardston, Alberta Temple. He was always proud of his Catawba Indian heritage and legacy that and his grandparenf's left for his family. Their baptism, while still on the Catawba Indian Reservation in Rock Hill, South Carolina, and their membership in the Church of Jesus Christ of Latter-day Saints, was a source of strength to him and his family.

He worked for the various agencies and departments of the Federal Government on many large reclamation projects from Alaska to Arizona during his professional career yet balanced his work with active church and civic duties, while always putting his family first. Among his many church callings included are Stake Missionary, and Branch President. He loved the outdoors and was an avid fisher, hunter, and camper. He cared for all people and loved the companionship of his many friends. During his later years, he especially enjoyed daily visits with his friends at Angie's Cafe. Funeral services will be held at 11 a.m. on Thursday, January 31 st, 2002 at the Smithfield Ninth Ward Chapel at 155 West 400 North. There will be a viewing from 10 a.m. to 10:45 a.m. prior to the funeral service. Interment will be at Memorial Estates, 6700 South Redwood Road, in West Jordan, Utah at 3 p.m. on the same day. Flowers may be sent to Allen-Hall Mortuary, 35 East Center Street, Logan, Utah.

**Abbie and Rufus's children continue with Ben and Guy Garcia**

**PHOTO 522 - BEN E RICH GARCIA**

f. Ben E Rich Garcia born 22 December 1910, Sanford, Conejos, Colorado and died 7 October 1991, Pueblo, Pueblo, Colorado. He married Fannie Minerva Irene Beck (1918–2013). They had three children Ben, Bonnie and Calvin.

PHOTO 523 - BEN, IRENE, CAL AND JAN GARCIA

PHOTO 524 - HEADSTONE FOR BEN E AND IRENE B GARCIA -- BURIAL: IMPERIAL MEMORIAL GARDENS, PUEBLO, PUEBLO COUNTY, COLORADO - PLOT: LAST SUPPER

**PHOTO 525 - EDWARD GUY GARCIA**

g. Edward Guy Garcia born 15 September 1912, Sanford, Conejos, Colorado and died 1 Octiber 2000, Catawba Reservation, South Carolina. He married Bettie Juanita Blue

**U.S., Social Security Death Index, 1935-2014**
Name: Edward G. Garcia
SSN: 524-09-0883  Last Residence:
29730 Rock Hill, York, South Carolina
BORN:        15 Sep 1912  -  Died:        1 Oct 2000
State (Year) SSN issued:      Colorado (Before 1951)

**PHOTO 526 - R-L ROY BROWN FRONT GUY GARCIA, HAROLD THATCHER**
**BABY IS GENE BLUE**

Guy was born in 1912 in Sanford, Colorado, the son of Rufus and Abbie Patterson Garcia. He married Betty Juanita Blue. He and Betty resided in the Catawba Nation, SC for the rest of his life.
Burial:  Catawba Indian Nation Cemetery
Rock Hill, York County, South Carolina

**PHOTO 527 -  MAE MAGDALINE GARCIA**

 h. Mae Magdaline Garcia born  21 September 1914, Sanford, Conejos, Colorado and died 31 March 1987, Pueblo, Pueblo, Colorado. She married John Thomas Croasmun (1910–1980).
Burial:  Imperial Memorial Gardens
Pueblo, Pueblo County, Colorado, Plot: Resthaven Section

i. Harvey Garcia born  28 July 1917, Sanford, Conejos, Colorado and died 26 October 1922, Sanford, Conejos, Colorado.
Burial:  Sanford Cemetery, Sanford, Conejos County, Colorado, Plot: 1022-B

**PHOTO 528 - VIOLA ELIZABETH GARCIA**

j. Viola Elizabeth Garcia born 12 April 1919, Sanford, Conejos, Colorado and died 11 October 2004, Pueblo, Pueblo, Colorado. She married Herbert Henry Schnieder (1921–2001).

**PHOTO 529 - VIOLA E GARCIA AND HUSBAND HERBERT HENRY SCHNIEDER**

**2 Colo Nurses Land In Japan**

Two Colorado nurses are among the first 85 American Army nurses to set foot on the Japanese homeland.

They are Second Lt. Mary Flores of Denver and Second Lt. Viola Garcia of Sanford, members of the nursing contingent of the 42d General Hospital, which has lived out the Pearl Harbor slogan of "On to Tokyo."

With a total of 600 persons in the unit, included are physicians and surgeons, administrative officers, dietitians, physiotherapists and Red Cross workers.

This will not be the unit's first experience in handling prisoners of war, as this hospital cared for 74 American survivors of a torpedoed Japanese prison ship last October.

Lt. Flores

**PHOTO 530 - NEWSPAPER CLIPPING - VIOLA E GARCIA AND LT. FLORES**

**A Nurse's Journey**

By Minority Nurse Staff | Mar 30, 2013 | Magazine, Minority and Community Health, Native American Nurses, Veterans in Nursing

For Native American nurses, many of their stories have been lost to the past. Scholars have generally paid scant attention to the lives and deeds of rural minority women, and few articles have been written about the early education of Native American nurses and their contributions to health care. The people of the Catawba Indian Nation use storytelling to keep their culture and the memory of their heroes alive. Consider this one such story, one such hero.

The Sage Memorial Hospital School of Nursing, known simply as "Sage Memorial," operated from 1930–1953. It was the only nursing school ever opened for the sole purpose of educating Native American women as nurses.[1] One of these nurses was Viola Elizabeth Garcia, a graduate of the Class of 1943.[2] Viola's life illuminates the struggles for education common among the women who attended Sage Memorial. Her contributions and experiences as a World War II nurse demonstrate the hardships encountered and outstanding contributions made by many of her fellow alumna.

**Ganado**

By law and custom, most nursing schools were segregated by race before the passing of the Civil Rights laws of the 1960s. From the 1880s through the 1960s, most schools of nursing were comprised of either all white or all African American student bodies, leaving few opportunities for Native Americans, Asian Americans, or Hispanic Americans to obtain a nursing education.

The Board of National Missions of the Presbyterian Church was unique in its efforts to address this inequality. In 1901, the National Presbyterian Church opened the Ganado Mission on Navajo Nation land, in the northeast quadrant of Arizona, near the New Mexico, Colorado, and Utah borders, in the community of Ganado.

After a church and school were successfully operating at the Mission, the home missionaries turned their attention to health care.[3] In 1929, Dr. Clarence Salsbury and his wife, Nurse Cora Salsbury, took over the mission work at Ganado. One of their first priorities was expanding the antiquated 12-bed hospital into a modern facility of 150 beds, an operating suite, a delivery suite, and a laboratory. This new hospital was named Sage Memorial Hospital after one of its largest benefactors and was accredited by the American College of Surgeons.

In order to staff the hospital with nurses, as well as to provide skilled employment opportunities for Native American women, the Salsburys opened Sage Memorial Hospital School of Nursing in 1930. [4]

The school opened while naysayers proclaimed no Native American woman would ever be up to the academic task of completing a Nightingale-based nursing education program. They also claimed these women, given their culture, would not be willing to interact with the sick or dying. Sage Memorial graduates proved these assumptions wrong.

Dr. Salsbury felt training Native American nurses was crucial. "They would be able to understand the patients as no white personnel ever could," he said.[1] Sage Memorial started small, with an entering class of two Navajo women: Adele Slivers and Ruth Henderson. They both graduated three years later and passed the Arizona State Board of Nursing Examinations. Their graduation exercises in 1933 were a festive event with scripture readings, vocal duets, a piano solo, and a pinning ceremony. Dignitaries including the Arizona governor, an Arizona State Board of Nursing member, and one of the chief Navajo medicine men praised the graduates and the school during the proceedings.[3]

As word and reputation of the school expanded among minority communities, the student body increased in number and diversity. By 1943, students from 28 tribes, including the Navajo, Kiowa, and Catawba; students who identified as Eskimo, Hawaiian, Spanish American, Cuban, and Mexican; and one Japanese student from a relocation camp were either enrolled or graduates of Sage Memorial.[6] By all accounts, this unique experiment in multicultural education was a success.

In the 1930s and 1940s, such training and cultural exchange among Native Americans and other minority women was not found anywhere else in the United States. The nurses developed a camaraderie and commitment to their work that consistently earned them the highest marks on state licensing exams. The students lived in interracial cooperation while learning the nursing arts and sciences. The school's stellar reputation drew the attention of white applicants—who were denied consideration because they had access to many other schools of nursing.[1]

## Viola Elizabeth Garcia

Viola Elizabeth Garcia was born on April 12, 1919, in Sanford, Colorado, a poor, rural Mormon community home to approximately half the members of the Catawba Nation. Viola's family was financially impoverished, but rich in family and culture. The older brothers, George and Labon, left school after completing the fourth and fifth grade to help their ailing father support the large family. Viola's father was ill for much of her young life and died when Viola was only 11 years old, leaving behind 10 children for his wife to support.

Viola completed the ninth grade in Sanford, but due to the Great Depression, the public high school was closed. For the next three years, Viola tried desperately to complete her high school education by repeatedly applying for admission to the Bureau of Indian Affairs Haskell Boarding School in Lawrence, Kansas. Finally, she was admitted at 18 years old and completed her high school diploma in 1940 at the age of 21. Viola's classes focused on cooking skills, sewing, home care, and arts. As graduation neared, she was offered full-time employment as a cook's assistant on the Apache reservation in New Mexico, but Viola was determined to continue her education.[2]

With the guidance of the staff at Haskell Boarding School, Viola applied to several nursing programs but was only admitted to Sage Memorial. One such rejection stated that she was too old at 21 years of age to begin the nursing program. There was also a concern, as World War II loomed and U.S.-Japan relations became strained, that her Native American features would appear Japanese and frighten patients.[6]

The head mistress of Haskell wrote in a reference letter about Viola, "Whatever Viola decides to do, she does." Several months after Viola enrolled at Sage Memorial, Dr. Salsbury personally wrote the Haskell headmistress asking if she had any other students like Viola, and if so, to please send them to his school.[6]

**Studying at Sage Memorial**

Applicants to Sage Memorial had to be unmarried high school graduates between 18–30 years of age. Their applications had to be accompanied by a health certificate, as well as four character references, with one being their pastor. Tuition was $100 for the first year with additional fees of $1 for laboratory courses, $0.50 for library use, and $3.50 for health fees. The hospital provided room, board, and laundry services. In addition to their course work, students tended the hospital floors eight hours a day, six days a week. However, students had time to relax outside of their rigorous classroom and clinical schedules, enjoying picnics, parties, movies, and glee club, as well as mandatory gym class and chapel.[4]

Although Viola was accepted to Sage Memorial, she was not sure that she could afford the tuition, fees, and living expenses. As the months progressed, Dr. Salsbury procured the funds to pay for all her education expenses except for personal items she needed to bring with her.6 According the 1940 catalog, all students had to supply for themselves the following: a bag for soiled clothing, rubbers or galoshes, toiletries, two fountain pens (one for red ink and one for blue), a watch with a second hand, an alarm clock, two standard-size loose-leaf notebooks, a napkin ring, and coat hangers.[4] Viola's eldest brother, George, gave her an entire month's wages so she could buy the required watch with the second hand sweep. With her determination and supplies in tow, Viola began her three-year long education at Sage Memorial.[6]

Over the next three years, Viola and her fellow students not only studied the nursing curriculum but also spent many clinical hours on the hospital floors. They made and rolled their own patient bandages and folded disposable patient trash bags and slippers out of newspapers. Third-year students were expected to help teach the lower-level nursing students. Viola not only learned the nursing skills that she would use throughout her life, but she developed a deep devotion and admiration for the Navajo people. She even taught herself to speak Dine, the Navajo language.[6]

**A nurse in practice**

Though Viola grew up in the rural, remote, and poor town of Sanford, she was surprised to learn that her new community at Ganado was even more so. Patients were brought to the hospital on horseback and buckboard wagons, and sometimes by rattling old vehicles over rutted and narrow dirt roads. Many roads were so rough and rocky that they were impassable in wet and winter weather. The nursing students were expected to go on home visits with the nursing staff to the homes of the Navajo people, traditional dwellings known as hogans.[7] They made these visits in buckboard wagons. Viola would write back to her mentor at Haskell Board School that these hogans were "loving and cozy homes."[6]

Viola viewed success as the ability to provide for herself, and she felt her education was essential to achieving that level of self-reliance. Viola studied hard and was the 1943 class valedictorian. She was awarded a set of surgical instruments for her academic success.

In 1943 Viola took her Arizona nursing boards and returned home to Colorado to await the results. She had been worried because she did not have an additional $75 to retake the nursing board examination if she failed. One day a letter arrived addressed to Viola Garcia, R.N., and she knew she had passed. In fact, Viola received the highest test score in the entire state of Arizona. Viola's academic and nursing success, however, was common among the students who graduated from Sage Memorial.

**World War II**

Not long after graduating from nursing school, Viola found herself working in Denver, Colorado, when President Roosevelt delivered an ominous speech. While the war efforts in Europe were drawing to a close, battles were still raging in the Pacific, and there might be a need to draft nurses into the military. Viola was told that if she volunteered for military service, she could select her location of duties. In January 1944, she enlisted in the United States Army Nurse Corps, requesting no surgical duties or overseas assignments. Within weeks of her enlistment, she was assigned to Camp Carson (now, Fort Carson, Colorado Springs, Colorado) in the surgical suite where she assisted with amputations from the war-wounded returning from the bitter winter campaign in Europe under General Patton. There were endless mounds of amputated ears, fingers, toes, hands, feet, arms, and legs that filled the air with putrid smells. Viola approached her supervisor and informed her of what she had requested: "No surgery and no overseas duties." She was promptly informed, "Honey, you are in the Army now."[6]

Step Back in Time The curriculum at Sage Memorial Hospital was based on the National League for Nursing Education criteria, accredited by the Arizona Board of Nursing Examiners. But what was nursing school in Viola Garcia's day really like? Around 1940, courses required for graduation at Sage Memorial included: First-Year Courses: Basic sciences, professional adjustments, nursing arts of bandaging, massage and personal hygiene, nutrition, cookery, pharmacology and therapeutics, aseptic techniques, and nursing care of conditions involving respiratory, circulatory, gastro-intestinal, endocrine, and muscular-skeletal systems Second-Year Courses: Medical-surgical nursing; nursing conditions of the eye, ear, and reproductive tract; and communicable diseases such as tuberculosis, gonorrhea, syphilis, obstetrics, diet therapy, and social problems in nursing Third-Year Courses: Psychiatric, pediatric, emergency, and public health nursing, along with another course in professional adjustment

Within a few months, First Lt. Viola Garcia shipped out from Camp Carson to Los Angeles, where she, along with 600 other nurses, embarked on the largest U.S. Army Hospital Ship at the time, the USAHS Marigold, with an unknown destination. After two weeks, the ship arrived in Hawaii, and 300 of the 600 nurses disembarked, but Viola's group remained on board. After leaving Hawaii, ship's public address system announced their destination: Tokyo, still a heavy battle area as the war in the Pacific raged on. "My heart just dropped, I was so frightened," Viola recalled. The U.S. military was fighting Japanese troops on many Pacific Islands and an invasion of the Japanese mainland was thought to be imminent. The costs in human life for both sides would be high.[6]

The ship was under the command of General Douglas McArthur, who over saw the military operations in the Pacific. The 300 nurses in Viola's grouping were to be part of the U.S. invasion actions in Japan. Military leaders expected heavy casualties among those nurses during the invasion operations; the 300 nurses left behind in Hawaii would be their replacements.

Under international rules of combat, hospital ships were not to be attacked at sea, and thus were to be lit up at night and clearly marked with a red cross. Not long out at sea, the Japanese attacked one such marked ship, and the Marigold was immediately ordered to go into complete darkness. As the lights were put out, those in surgery raced to cover the windows of surgeries in progress. A frightening silence fell upon the crew as the Marigold steamed along in darkness on its way across the Pacific.

The Marigold stopped in the Philippines, and the nurses were allowed to disembark for a few days before the ship went to Japan. While docked there, however, the United States dropped the atomic bombs on Japan, and World War II was brought to a close. Yet, the Marigold continued on to Tokyo, but this time with a different mission. The USAHS Marigold was the first U.S. ship to enter Yokahoma Bay after the Japanese ended the war, and it was in Tokyo Bay where General McArthur accepted the formal surrender of the Japanese on the USS Missouri. That day the sea was filled with ships and the air was filled with flyover planes celebrating the end of the Second World War.

**Rebuilding in Tokyo**

Over the next eight months, Viola was stationed in Tokyo at the 42nd General Hospital. She treated survivors of the Bataan Death Camp and Corregidor Island (a military stronghold in the Philippines). The hospital had five surgical rooms that had been stripped of all equipment by the Japanese at the end of the war. They were filled with soot and rubble. Several Army nurses ranking higher than Viola were assigned the task of restoring these rooms to their full function. According to Viola, none of the higher-ranking nurses could deal with such an overwhelming task;

each time, Viola was asked to "fill in." After a third nurse was left in tears at the monumental task, Viola was asked to take on the responsibilities as acting head surgical nurse.[6]

Viola walked into surgical suites devoid of the equipment necessary for performing operations—no surgical tables, no IV stands, no surgical tools. She remembered entering the rooms: "I just wanted to cry too and said to myself, 'Oh Lordy, what am I going to do?'" But Viola went on to do what she had always done—she rolled up her sleeves and got to work. Viola called in her military crew and ordered them to wash and scrub all the rooms from top to bottom. When that was done, she began looking for equipment for her surgical rooms, including salvaging items from the hospital ship.6 She even taught herself to speak Japanese, just as she learned to speak Dine as a nursing student.

First Lt. Garcia's work in Tokyo was supported by her own ethic of care, as well as the training she received at Sage Memorial Hospital School of Nursing. From those days following the war until her death in 2004, Viola continued caring for others, marrying Herbert Schneider, another member of the U.S. Army, and raising three daughters. Her legacy, one of determination and pride, compassion and grace, lives on.

## References

1. Salsbury, C.G., & Hughes, P. (1969) The Salsbury Story. Tucson: The University of Arizona Press. 152–153.

2. People of Catawba official website, "Life of Viola Schneider." Cynthia Walsh. http://www.catawba-people.com/viola_schneider_eulogy.htm. (Accessed 2011).

3. Trennart, R. (2003). "Sage Memorial Hospital and the Nation's First All-Indian School of Nursing." The Journal of Arizona History, vol. 44, 353.

4. Prospectus of School of Nursing, (Ganado, Arizona: Sage Memorial Hospital, n.d), 1-11; Presbyterian Historical Society, Philadelphia, Pennsylvania: Ganado Mission Records.

5. "Excerpts from Statement re: School of Nursing, Sage Memorial Hospital, Ganado, Arizona sent in on January 3, 1939." Document from Ganado Mission Records, Presbyterian Historical Society; Philadelphia, Pennsylvania.

6. Viola Garcia, personal comm. with author.

7. Salsbury, C.G. (1932). "Medical Work in Navajoland." The American Journal of Nursing, 32(4), 415.

Posted by Cynthia Schnieder Walsh

**PHOTO 531 - DOROTHY ELLEN GARCIA**

k. Dorothy Ellen Garcia born 12 August 1922, Sanford, Conejos, Colorado and died 5 October 2010, Pueblo, Pueblo, Colorado. She married Lee Foy Ong (1922–1987).

**Obituary: n Memory of Dorothy E Ong**

Dorothy Ellen Ong, 88, passed away October 5, 2010. Dorothy is preceded in death by her husband, Lee F. Ong. She is survived by her sister, Martha Riddell; daughters, Jennifer Adachi and Lonnie DeLonge; 4 grandchildren and 2 great-grandchildren. Dorothy was a member of Latter-Day Saints Church. Graveside service, at 10:00 AM, Monday, October 11, 2010, at Imperial Memorial Gardens.

**PHOTO 532 - DOROTHY ELLEN GARCIA AND HUSBAND LEE F ONG**

**PHOTO 533 – MARTHA GARCIA**

l. Martha Garcia born 24 June 1924, Sanford, Conejos, Colorado and died 1 December 2012, Idaho Falls, Idaho. She married William Reidel (1917–2002).

**PHOTO 534 – BONNIE ESTELLA GARCIA**

 m. Bonnie Estella Garcia born 25 November 1926, Sanford, Conejos, Colorado and died 7 January 1983,  San Francisco, California.She married Lloyd Perry Erickson (1923–1977).

 "San Franciso's Mission district is a little poorer today because of the loss of a woman described by her neighbors as having a "heart of gold" who died under what homicide detectives say were somewhat suspicious circumstances.

Police were called Saturday to an apartment building at 301 I Mission St. near Army Street to investigate the death of Stella Erickson, 56, owner of the Modern

Bait and Tackle Shop half a block away and, according to a friend a local Good Samaritan.

"She knew everybody in the neighborhood," said Jim Carter, the manager of Erickson's bait shop" Erickson, known to the neighborhood residents as Bennie, was discovered by a neighbor. She was lying crumpled on the concrete patio behind the multi-story apartment house she lived in. Homicide Inspector Marvin Dean said police have not come to any conclusion about the likelihood of foul play. She was always in a good mood, always jolly. George Salamy"a businessman in the area said, Everybodyi n the whole area knew her. She was well loved." Bonnie would always help charity drives and people were always coming to her to ask her to give them credit or a loan, and she always came through for them, and was repaid. Bonnie got a bigger kick out of helping people than anything else."

It has never been determined exactly what killed Stella, nor has anyone been charged with her death, foul play is suspected by the family. There were odd circumstances surrounding her death and the wills which left her very successfull business to employees."[537]

**PHOTO 535 – MARY MAUD PATTERSON**

(9). Mary Maud Patterson, was born 14 February 1884, Blacksburg, Cherokee, South Carolina, and died 28 March 1973, Mogote, Conejos, Colorado. She married Elseco Galvez on 25 October 1897. Maud did not bear any children, but did take care of some of her sister Lula's children, after Lula died. She also

---

[537] Article from Laban Garcia

adopted Fred Galvez Jr. Maud outlived her husband, and lived on the south side of the Conejos River, and just west of Mogote, Colorado. She always said that there were no rattle snakes at her home, because snakes did not swim (which was obviously wrong, because snakes, even rattle snakes, swim well.) Maud and Abbie were fairly close, not just in age, but they used to get together often. Pete Canty and Guy Garcia used to play cards with the two old ladies. Of course the boys always tried to cheat, and always got caught, because the two old ladies always won the games. These two boys, once put a picture of an ugly, wrinkled old woman in a picture frame, and tried to pass it off as some of their relatives. They nearly convinced

Abbie and Maud, but were caught, and had to confess.

**PHOTO 536 - GRAVE MARKER FOR MARY MAUD PATTERSON GALVEZ (1884-1973)**

**PHOTO 537 - JAMES MORONI HEBER PATTERSON - BURIAL: SANFORD CEMETERY, SANFORD, CONEJOS COUNTY, COLORADO,**

(10). James Moroni Heber Patterson, was born 25 March 1887, in Spartanburg, South Carolina. He was born during the mini-Mormon exodus of the Catawba. The Mormon's were enduring a great deal of persecution. "The whites just didn't want the Mormons to get established. Some Indian women had children by white men. They came in here to find the Indian women because they couldn't get out and ramble. That was the only reason the whites came in here. They soon found that they couldn't keep the Indians from becoming Mormons. I don't think any of the whites around here belong.

"James Moronic died in Sanford on 22 August 1903. Cause of death is unknown at the present time.

**PHOTO 538 - JOSEPH BRIGHAM PATTERSON**

(11). Joseph Brigham Patterson, born 1 January 1890, Manassas, Conejos, Colorado and died 28 January 1890, Manassas, Conejos, Colorado. A Catawba Indian was the son of James Goodwin and Elizabeth Missouri White Patterson. The Patterson's were part of a group of southern Saints that came with Elder John Morgan in 1887. The rest of the family is buried in Sanford, Colorado.  Joseph Brigham Patterson Burial: Old Manassa Cemetery, Manassa, Conejos County, Colorado

**PHOTO 539 - HENRY ALONZO PATTERSON**

(12). Henry Alonzo Patterson: born 29 January 1891, Sanford, Conejos, Colorado and died 29 January 1909, Sanford, Conejos, Colorado. Henry was the last chance to pass the Patterson name on.  This ends the family of James Goodwin and Elizabeth Missouri White Patterson.

**PHOTO 540 - HEADSTONE FOR HENRY A PATTERSON**

**PHOTO 541 -- MAUDE, ABBIE, DORA, BELL AND MARTHA PATTERSON DAUGHTERS OF JAMES GOODWIN PATTERSON**

Photos courtesy Cynthia Schneider Walsh, daughter of Viola Garcia Schneider.

**Neighbors**

Guy Garcia

Rock Hill

Guy Garcia, a youthful 86 just last week, braces his weight with two of his somewhat famous hand carved walking sticks and does a little Catawba dance.

He glances up with a mischievous grin lo make sure potential observers caught his act

His family and neighborhood children are familiar with this impish sense of humor. It's what drew them to his small Indian Trail home nestled among oaks, maples and an assortment of other indigenous trees.

"A lot of children have climbed that tree," said his daughter Barbara Talley, pointing to a bean tree in the front yard. Swings and other vestiges of children's visits still dot the property. The barbecue grill, where every Saturday Garcia and his family cooked the brim fish he snared in a nearby pond, still sits beside the house..This is my favorite spot," he said, resting in his chair swing under a graybeard tree. He has a terrific view of hummingbirds visiting his feeders and passing cars whose drivers offer him a wave.

"The graybeard smells real sweet," he said as he inhaled.

Beside him are walking ticks that have made him well known among the Catawba's. Visitors can buy them for $25 at the Catawba Cultural Center, but Garcia has given them away to hundreds of crippled and elderly people in this area and across the country.

"If people are hurt or crippled, I take my sticks to them, "he said.'.'. He searches the woods for a dogwood bent to resemble the shape of a snake. Then he devotes several hours to carving it, removing all of the bark except for athat which will coil along the stick like a snake. ,

Many have fangs created from Native American beads strung on leather. Some are festooned with pheasant and peacock feathers bellac adds the finishing touch.

Garcia's mother was raised on the reservation, but married and moved to Colorado, where her son was born.

In 1938, Garcia returned to the reservation to discover his Catawba roots. He met Betty, the granddaughter of Chief Sam Blue.

"The love bug caught me right quick," he said. "I came back in 1939 and we got married."

He and Betty raised their daughters Barbara and Marlene on the reservation and now have six grandchildren, five great grandchildren and two step great grandchildren.

He sits in his swing and waits for the children to visit His health is tailing, but on a good day, he still plays hide and seek with them or drops a few coins on the ground and exclaims, "Oh, look what I found!"

And he loves to make up stories to tell them: Sometimes he will even share his stories with adult visitors.

"Anyone is welcome to drop by and look at my sticks,," he said.

# A few tidbits

Born: Sept 15, 1912, in Sanford, Colo.

Occupation: Retired housepainter, a job that took him up and down the east coast as far as Labrador.
Owned Beaver Robbins
Paint Company until he retired.
Favorite book: The Bible.

Favorite meal: Fried chicken
with mashed potatoes and gravy.

' If you could invite anyone to dinner, who would it be?:
"Somebody who wouldn't eat too much," he quipped. "No, my granddaughter Micheie Atkinson. She lived with us all her life until she got married."

Favorite story: The one he
concocted about how he was
spawned from a Scudebaker hubcap. Or maybe the one about how he to
his girlfriend Falling Rock in the mountains and had to post signs on the highway saying, "Watch for falling rock."

Person most admires: "Beside, my wife, my daughters"

Proudest accomplishment:
"My family. That comes first.  Then my socks.'*
Any regrets?: "I'd do the same thing. I'd marry the same woman and
 I'd still paint.  I love open spaces. I'm satisfied.

## Chapter 20 Quash Family

I. Quash - Capt. Quash- was born around 1758. He married Betsy Scott, said to be an Englishwoman. The Patterson genealogy has always called her an English woman. It is very possible that Betsy who married the father was English. This Elizabeth-Betsy was Catawba, with her father being Quash and the mother a Scott.[538]

These are the progenitors of the Quash-Mush-Marsh family in Catawba.[539]

Quash served in the Revolutionary War. The Catawba usually fought as a unit, under the leadership of white commanders The only occasion that this was not the case, was in 1780, 1781, 1782 when a company of 41 men joined with General Sumter. They were led by Capt. Thomas Drennan. Quash is listed on Drennan's paybill.[540]

Quash married and his grandchildren still retained the name Quash on the 1849 census. The one identifiable child listed in the Patterson is Betsy Quash-Scott. If the mother was surnamed Scott, Betsy would have taken either surname.[541]

Quash[542] -Capt. Quash- Robert Quash born 1758, married Betsy Scott. They are the progenitors of a major portion of the present Catawba tribe. His mark follows

A. Betsy Quash-Scott was born in 1789. She married first John Mush-Mursh-Marsh, son of Robert and Elizabeth Mush-Marsh, Pamunkey Indians he died and Betsy married second Robert Alexander Mush-Mursh-Marsh,(around 1817) a brother of John Mush-Mursh-Marsh. Betsy had nine children: Kity, John, Robert Alexander, Sarah, James, Philadelphia, Elizabeth-Betsy, Patsy and Rhoda. More about this family will be found in the Marsh Chapter. [543]

---

[538] Draper Manuscripts call her Betsy Quash, Patterson genealogy says Scott.

[539] Patterson genealogy.

[540] Brown pages 265-70.

[541] 1849 Catawba census.

[542] Drennan's paybill.

[543] Mush-Mursh-Marsh genealogy found in Rountree.

## Group Photo

Photo 542 - LEFT half of the Catawba Branch 1926

Photo 543 -- right half if the Catawba Branch 1926

## Chapter 21   Red Head or Redhead Family

I. Red Tick- Red Button- Capt- Red Head [544] - Billy Redhead, was probably born around 1710.
In May 1760, he was a Headman, and stated his nation is ready for war against the Cherokee.[545]
Because King Hagler was ill. Red Tick was to take Hagler a gold gorget, the color of the sun and a Silver plate, the color of the moon- The gorget was supposed to be a symbol of leadership. Red
Tick stated mat the Catawba wanted to remove from Pine Tree Creek, for the people were not friendly to them. His term was "exceeding cross with them."

While the Catawba were attempting peace with the Cherokee and Iroquois, Capt RedHead, who attended the Albany peace conference with King Hagler. went to Chota in 1771, and received a string of white beads from the Cherokee.[546]
He appears on Drenan's Pay Bill as Billey Redhead 44 days and 22 pounds, for service in the Revolutionary War- He also appears on the list for which there is no voucher for Revolutionary War Service, both dated 1783-4.

II Patrick Redhead, a brother of Billy, at least as old as he being an adult during the Revolutionary War.[547]
In 1793, Patrick along with Jenny Patterson and John Kennedy were prosecuted in Lancaster County Court for trading with Negroes. The Commissioners spared them the punishment, which was death. The Commissioners appealed to Governor William Moultrie and the following proclamation was made:

"Whereas I have received information from the Agents appointed to take care of the Rights of the Catawba Indians that a Prosecution has been commenced against several of the said Indians in the Court of the County of Lancaster- to Wit, Patrick Redhead, Jenny Patterson and John Kennedy for trading with Negroes and that it is apprehended that the said Court intends to inflict Corporal Punishment on them. Now7 know ye that in consideration of the said Indians being Free People and under the protection of this State I do by these Presents pardon and release said Indians from any Judgement or punishment whatever which has been or may be ordered to be inflicted on them by the said Court of which all concerned are to take due Notice and govern themselves accordingly." This proclamation was signed March 28,193 by Governor Moultrie-

Jinney Redhead [548]

John Redhead

Prissy Redhead

[544] Brown page 257
[545] Blumer page 60
[546] Petition of 1792
[547] Ibid
[548] Merrell page 233

Sus- Redhead is Susan Redhead.

Widow Redhead[549]

Sally Redhead born 1779,[7] she removed to Choctaw 1851-53.

Molly or Polly Redhead born 1809[550] (a son John Rooker Redhead born around 1840 if he survived this long, the son of Reverend John Rooker)- The Redheads removed to Choctaw.

A Catawba Warrior (Captain Redhead?). 1771. Artist unknown Joseph Brevard Kershaw Papers South Caroliniana Library

**PHOTO 544 -- CAPTAIN RED HEAD**

---

[549] Brown, City Without Cobwebs page 297.
[550] 1849 Census of Catawba

## Chapter 22   Scott Family

I.   Siman meaning Persimmon-was John Scott. He was probably born around 1730, making him an elder of sorts, due to the short life span of people in those days. James most was likely his brother. He was called General John Scott in the Draper Manuscripts, dated July 27, 1874. [551] John was used as an interpreter for the whites. He appeared on a voucher for Revolutionary War services, as "John Scott, 1 hog." [552]

\*\*\*\*\*\*\*\*\*\*\*\*\*\*\*\*\*\*\*\*\*\*\*\*\*\*\*\*\*\*\*\*\*\*\*\*\*\*\*\*\*\*\*\*\*\*\*\*\*\*\*\*

II.   James Scott was probably born around 1740. Both Jamey and John Scott acted as interpreters for a meeting held at the Quareterhouse with King Hagler, where scalps were brought and presents were received for them. Commissions were given to King Hagler and Captain Ayers at this meeting on September 12, 1761.

III.   Captain William-Billy Scott, born around 1750, married King Hagler's daughter. He was originally thought to have been white; however, law required that four Catawba sign their land leases and he began signing in 1808 and continued until August 13, 1817. He began signing the leases as Captain William Scott.[553] He did not sign anything between 1808 and 1813. William- Billy began signing them again in June 1813 and continued signing as Captain until August of 1817 when he became a Major[554] He did not sign leases after that date, so he most likely died around 1817, he would have been around 70 years of age. William had children; Jacob, Sally, Jenny and perhaps Samuel and Katy Scott. Samuel and Katy are not proven children of William.

A. General Jacob Scott, born 1770, because he was about 55 in 1858 when he died. He was the son of King Hagler's daughter and William (Billy) Scott. General Scott accompanied King Hagler in 1761, requesting pay for a prisoner Hagler had taken in a war against the Cherokees. Lieutenant Governor Bull gave them money for the prisoner.

Jacob served as chief after the death of King Hagler in August of 1763. Jacob also appears on Drennan's pay bill for Revolutionary War service as Jacob Scott, 52 days and 26 pounds. He also appears on a list for service, for which there is no voucher.[555]

He was rather tall and straight and very dark. Elkana Watson in 1735 called him New River, alias Scott, because he was the half-brother of Sally New River. Of course, Watson did not

---

[551] Brown page 214.

[552] Drennan's pay bill, Brown page 269.

[553] Blumer page 84 article 667.

[554] Blumer pages 84-106.

[555] Drennan's paybill, Brown pages 268 & 269

take in account the fact that Sally's maiden name was Scott-Toole, her father was Matthew Toole, and her stepfather William Scott.

In 1817, Jacob and Thomas Brown, Henry Whyte and Col. Jacob Ayers signed leases.

B. Sally Scott-Toole born around 1780 married first Little Aleck-Allik; [556] and second General New River. A Sally Scott appears in the Plat Book, no other information is available. More information will be found in the Hagler Chapter. Sally was the mother of at least two children, Jane Allik and Jacob Scott. It is possible that Samuel and Caty Scott were also her children.

1. Jane Allik born around 1776, her father was Little Alik-Allik-Alec of the Revolutionary War. Nothing more has been found to date.

2. Jacob-Jack (John?) Scott born ca 1790 died ca 1825. He married Betsy Ayers born 1789, daughter of General Jacob Ayers.

a. John Jacob Scott born 1814 served in the Civil War. His record states:

"December 9, 1861. Company K. 17th South Carolina Infantry" he enlisted with Jefferson Ayers, William Canty.

John was wounded at Manassas and listed on last muster roll in February 1863. He also served as Chief in 1863, when most of the young men were away in the war. For several years after the war, according to official records, there was no chief; however, it seems that someone always acted as a chief, while that information was not always known by the whites around them. Chief Samuel Blue acknowledged his Uncle John Scott as being a former chief. Living conditions were pitiful; however, being isolated from the rest of the state left the remnant of the Catawba at peace.

John signed the 1868 Petition requesting James Morrow be named Indian Agent, as Thomas Whitesides did not want to serve further.

He married Rebecca Quash Mursh, daughter of John and Betsy Scott Marsh. They had John Scott Jr.

(1). Little John Scott, born 1826, called Jr. Both John SR and John Jr. signed the 1868 petition requesting that James Morrow replace Thomas Whitesides as Indian agent. A note: the person writing the entry spelled Scott, Skott.

---

[556] Merrell, page 546.

C. Jenny Scott born around 1785 married Jamey -James Kegg born 1785. The Children will be found under Kegg.

D. Major Samuel Scott, born 1799, signed the Treaty at Nations Ford in 1840 and disappears after 1849. He is described as "one of the most trifling and lazy, intemperate Catawba" by Hutchinson. He went on to say, "Many like Sam Scott, for instance would take a bottle of whiskey for their whole year's rent and many white men would do business with them in that way until it became an intolerable disgrace to the country."

In spite of these facts, Sam Scott was listed as Major Sam Scott and signed leases beginning in 1827 as one of the Headmen under General William Harris, along with Captain Edmund Ayers and Col. John Ayers, and continued through 1839. Scott also signed the treaty of Nations Ford in 1840.

This also must be the Sam Scott who killed a Catawba woman named Canty. He fled to the Cherokee where he remained for six or 7 years. Eventually he returned to his people, but was always sober and armed. He went to Columbia with a group and got drunk. When he sobered up, he realized that he was in danger. Finally, he became a drunk again. One day when he was lying drunk along the road, a party of Catawba came by, among them a daughter of the woman who was slain, a girl of 14. She gathered a large rock and crashed his skull with it. The others took him into the shade by a house and left him there. He lived for several days. According to Merrell, page 235, this happened in the mid nineteenth century between the 1849 and 1854 censuses.

E. Caty-Katy Scott, born 1799, becomes Caty Joe before 1849. She is probably a sister of Major Sam Scott. Ex-governor Allston named her mother of the year in 1860, along with several other Catawba women. "An old Indian say 80 to 90 years old (who) is raising some grandchildren." This was most likely the Whitesides children, so something had happened to Eliza Scott Canty by 1860; however, an Eliza Scott is mentioned as teaching school with Mrs. Dunlap in the Indian Agents report of 1861

Caty-Katty signed the petition for John R. Patton in 1863 and did not receive any allotments after 1869 so was probably dead by then.

1. Eliza Scott, born 1826. Eliza taught school, along with a Mrs. Dunlap, in the agent's report of 1861. Eliza married in 1840, Franklin Canty, born 1826. She had three children by 1854, one of which was George Washington Canty, presumably all by Franklin Canty. Eliza died sometime after 1869.

a. George Washington Canty born January 16, 1851 in Union County, South Carolina. He married Mary Jane Elizabeth (M. J. E. -Betsy Mush-George) who was born 1857, daughter of William and Betsy Mush George. A Bio will be found under Southern Canty's since George went by Canty.

b.  unknown

c.  (Children not known, but living with Eliza in the 1854 census.) She then had three children by the white Indian agent, Thomas Whitesides for seven children.

d.  Mary Jane Whitesides born 13 February 1855 married James Henry Watts, son of Lucy Quash-Marsh and Evan Watts. No children were born to Mary Jane. Mary Jane died 8 November 1910.

"Feb. 26 1884, one of the Laminates Jane Watts was very sick with cramps in her stomach. She wished me to administer to her which I did and she got well immediately which was a great testimony to her and to me.

March 19, 1884. After meeting one sister Mary Jane Watts, who had come ten miles to meeting took very sick. We administered to her according to her request. She grew weaker and weaker. We set up with her that night. She grew even weaker the next night, some thirty Lamanites set up with her. We prayed for her, day and night. There was something wrong inwardly. Her Bro. and sister who was not of our faith sent for three doctors who was very bitterly opposed to us and our teachings. Two of the doctors gave her up and said there was no hope of her recovery and said "Them Mormon Elders says they can heal the sick " and said she would be a corpse in twenty-four hours. We administered to her and started 10 miles to get some clean clothes. We had not been there long when they sent us word she was still no better. We started back at 8 PM and walked until midnight to get back, taking a small Indian boy 14 years old to pilot the way. When we arrived we found her on the mend. The house was filled with her friends and relatives. We again administered to her and in two days she was around the house."

**From the Missionary Journal of Mary Barus**

"A dream of seeing the Indians
Another night I dreamed we were at our journeys end a house full of the Indians were out to meet us. I heard them singing a song where two voices led and in duett (sic) and the rest joined in chorus. I also saw very plainly four Indian women.
Jesus Lover of my soule (sic)
I also told Orlando this dream & that I was sure I could recognize them if I ever saw them. Both these dreams or manifestations were proven to my satisfaction to have been given me by the spirit of the Lord for sure enough after we arrived at the Indian Nation the first night there were the people I had seen assembled. Only three of the women were there but I saw the fourth one a few days after. Their features were familiar when I met them. They were sisters Watts, Blue, Gordon & Brown. They sang many songs that night but they did not sing "Jesus Lover of my soule

(sic)" with duett (sic) and chorus till I taught it to them & I recognized it just as soon as they sang it as the one I had heard in my dream. This was a very strong testimony to me and I thanked my heavenly Father for the same. These dreams were a source of comfort to me since I of course dreaded the thoughts of taking our family among the Indians. My idea of an Indian was of course the ones I had seen who wore their long unkept (sic) hair – male & female – and with blankets & moccasins.

I was thoroughly surprised tho to find a people speaking the English language & natural songsters –"

e.    John Alonzo Canty born 9 November 1858 married Georgia Henrietta Patterson, daughter of James Goodwin and Elizabeth Missouri White Patterson. John Alonzo died 1 February 1939 in Sanford, Colorado. His descendants will be found in the Patterson chapter and in Genealogy of the Western Catawba. They had Wilford, John Henry, Eddie, Wilford, Lazell and Alma Canty. The John Alonzo Canty family continues in the Canty Chapter.

f. Fannie Whitesides born 9 November 1858, twin sister to John Alonzo, she married James Harris jr. on 16 May 1884. Fannie died between 1885 and 1900.

"Sunday March 16 1884, there was a woman by the name of Whitesides said she understood her Bible and she wished to have a talk with me. They gathered around to hear the argument. I find her so clost she became excited and unreasonable and her relative took her away. They were disgusted with her."

"There was one couple married and baptized that day about 10 o'clock instant. Namely James Harris and Fanny Whitesides in the same stream I was baptized in."

**The other child Caty-Katy Scott Joe had was Joseph Joe.**

2. Joseph Joe, born around 1850. Joseph Joe does not appear after the 1854 census, nor does he appear in the Plat Book, although there is a Jamey Joe, who could be Joseph Joe. Names were not so important to the Catawba as they were to the whites who wrote the records. Betsy Scott born 1831, married first Robert Marsh-Mush JR, son of Robert Mush-Marsh and Rebecca Quash, then she becomes Betsy Mush in the 1849 census. The father of Martha Ann is William Clisky or Cottsky, evidently a white man, however Betsy was married second to John Scott JR, son of John Scott and Rebecca Quash-Marsh, at the time of the birth of Martha Ann, so she is sometimes called Martha Ann Scott.

**PHOTO 545 - HEADSTONE FOR MARTHA ANN KALISKIE – SCOTT TIMS - BURIAL: SANFORD CEMETERY, SANFORD, CONEJOS COUNTY, COLORADO, PLOT: 3046-B**

a. Martha Ann Kaliskie -Scott, born 14 February 1848 in Jackson, South Carolina., married John Alexander (Alec) Tims, son of John Alexander Tims, a white man, and Rachel Quash- Mursh, a Catawba. This marriage evidently ended before 1886, when Alec married Sarah Ann Evans-Canty Head, widow of Robert Henry Head. They all moved to Sanford, Colorado, where Martha died and he and Ann buried there in 1946. More information will be found in the Tims Chapter and in Genealogy of the Western Catawba.

## Chapter 23   Stephens - Stevens Family

Big Stephen, if there is a Little Stephen, more than likely there was a Big Stephen.[557]

I. Little Stephen was probably born around 1750 and he served in the Revolution.[558]

   A. Lewis Stephens was born in 1802.[559]  He was a Lieutenant in the Tribal Government in 1837. Lewis married Harriot Canty, the daughter of Lewis Canty.[560]

   Only three children can be identified.

      1. Joseph Stevens born 1818.[561]

      2. Polly Stevens born 1824.[562]

      3. Thomas Stevens born 1831 in Charleston, South Carolina.[563]  He received funds from the Indian Agent W. M. Whyte in 1881 in the amount of $6.66.[564]  He also signed a petition requesting that J. R. Patton be exempt to duty with the State Troops during the Civil War in October 1863. Thomas signed the petition of 1877 requesting that Agent Crook be replaced with Whyte. Thomas helped Jim Watts keep the Cureton Ferry, according to the Dunlap Letter, dated February 1902. He died December 14, 1905, freezing to death while trying to visit his wife's grave in Lancaster. According to Sallie Harris Wade, "he was a good old man." He was about the size of Guy Garcia, (he apparently always seemed old to her, and of course, she was 10 years old when he died.) He stayed around David Adam Harris's mom, Sarah Jane Ayers. Sallie had heard that he was her (Sarah Jane Ayers Harris) brother, (however; Watson's research did not find this to be true. That does not mean Sarah was not at least a half-sister or some other relation to Tom.) He was staying with the Harris family when he crossed the river to go to Lancaster County. He left the Nation in the evening and walked to where Bull Waters is now and he stayed all night with Uncle Jim and Aunt Jane.[565]

   It was raining the next morning and they tried to talk Tom out of going on, and to wait until the rain stopped, since it was January and very cold. He went on, saying he intended to see his wife's grave, and telling them it would be the last trip he would make. He stopped at a Plyler's house to get warm, and was refused entry. He walked on about 2 miles and got in

---

[557] Watson pages 53-55.
[558] He is listed on Drennan's paybill.
[559] Catawba Branch Records.
[560] Watson pages 53-55.
[561] 1849 census.
[562] Ibid
[563] Ibid
[564] Whyte's accounting of payments to Catawba.
[565] James and Sarah Jane Ayers Harris.

the muddy ditch. He could not get out and when he was found, he had his hands up on the bank and froze in the position. Sallie stated that if he had been given a place to warm up, he probably would not have frozen to death."[566]

  a. John Stevens born around 1840, he received $4.50 from R. L.
  Crook on April 10, 1875. He might have been born in Lancaster Co.

B. Polly Stephens born ca 1803 married Isaac White (her will 1818).[567]

C. William or Billy Stephens born ca 1804 living from 1823 to 1824.[568]

---

[566] Watson page 79.
[567] Watson page 79.
[568] Ibid

## Chapter 24   Tims Family

John Alexander Tims, born 1810, South Carolina and died 1870, Jackson, Lincoln, Louisiana, United States. He was a white man, married Rachel Quash-Mursh, a Catawba, daughter of Robert and Betsy Quash- Marsh.[569] Together they had four children, only one child reached maturity.

1. Maggie Tims, born 1843, Catawba Reservation, York, South Carolina and  died between 1844 and 1845.[570]

2. Bishop Tims, born about 1844, Catawba, South Carolina and died 1845, Catawba, South Carolina.

3. Theodore Tims, born about 1845, Catawba, South Carolina and died 1846, Catawba, South Carolina.

**PHOTO 546 – ALEC JOHN ALEXANDER TIMS**

4. Alec John Alexander Tims, born 15 July 1845, Chester, Chester County, South Carolina and died 20 April 1941, Sanford, Conejos, Colorado

Alec married Martha Ann Kaliskie -Scott the daughter of Robert Cottsky or Klisky, a white man and Betsy Mush Scott and a step daughter of Little John Scott hence the two different names.[571] This marriage ended before 1884.

Alec married second in Catawba, South Carolina, and Sarah Ann Evans-Canty Head, daughter of Chancy and Peggy Canty Evans and widow of a Civil War soldier Robert Henry Head. Alec served in the Civil War, along with most of the rest of the Catawba men.

---

[569] Patterson Genealogy.

[570] LDS IGI

[571] Martha's father was white, Cottsky or Klisky and she occasionally used her stepfather's name of Scott.

John Alexander Tims, enlisted December 9, 1861. Was wounded at the second battle of Manassas (August 30, 1862). He returned to duty on January 1863 and fought at the trenches in front of Petersburg and in the battle of Petersburg (July and August 1863). He remained in the trenches at Petersburg until February 1865. In 1880 he attended his company's reunion.

The second group of Catawba Joined Company H, Twelfth South Carolina Infantry, on December 20, 1861. It consisted of two brothers: Alec, as he was called was wounded at Manassa 2nd in on or near August 29, 1862. He was a member of the Lacy Guards, guarding Fort Lacy the list was published January 30, 1862. This list indicated that Alec was with the 17th South Volunteers, under L. P. Sadler, commanding the guard at Fort Lacy. He served with Jefferson Ayers and William Canty.

Three years later he emigrated to Sanford, Colorado, where his descendants are members of the Colorado Catawba Band.

From Evan's Brigade Headquarters, in Kinston, North Carolina on January 20, 1863, he was listed as Absent Without Leave from Company K, and the list included Jefferson Ayers as well as Alec Tims. From the dates, it appears that these men went to duty at Fort Lacy, and were listed as AWOL. He also could have been in hospital or recovering from wounds received at Manassa. He was listed on the last muster roll in February 1863.[572]

John A. Tims signed the 1868 petition requesting that James Morrow replace Thomas Whitesides as Indian Agent.[573] He signed a petition in 1868 as Chief, asking that William Whyte replace Crook as Indian Agent.

Alec and Sarah were frequent hosts to the LDS missionaries that were sent to the Catawba Nation and to the South.

Elder Joseph Willey writes in his journal or diary of his mission the following account.

"August 28th, 1884. Walked 17 miles to Mr. Tims. There Prest J. J Humphreys had sent one of the Saints to tell us it would not be safe for us to come any farther in the daytime but to come in the night.

That night he had received a notice from eight men who came with it, which reads as follows:

"August 23, 1884

Notice, Messrs Willey, Humphreys, Humphrey, We the peaceable citizens of this surrounding country have been pained to learn that you three men professing to be Mormon missionaries have taken up your quarters with an ignorant class of our people and are

---

[572] Civil War Record of Alec Tims, and news clippings.
[573] Petition to Governor R. K. Scott, Governor of South Carolina from the Catawba Indians dated July 15, 1868.

denominating doctrines among them calculated to disorganize human society and adverse to the peace and wellbeing of our people and country. To the laws and dignity of the State, now therefore these presents are to civilly and peaceably request and command you to vacate the State and to return no more among us and you are hereby allowed five days to obey this order to peaceably absent yourselves from the State without hurt or molestation but if you are found within the limits of the State after the expiration of that time you may charge consequences to disobedience to this order. We are going to be rid of you."

Capt of the mob, Wm. Kithcart, Wm. Carethers, Charles Harrison, Paul Harrison, Alexander Millens, Clarence Cotter.

The names of the rest of the mob we did not get. This notice had been received while we was gone and the 5 days was up. Prest Humphreys was afraid we would run in there hands unknowingly. We learned he was staying in the woods nights. "

"September 1, 1884. We left our hiding place in the woods at Bro. Georges and moved to Mr. Tims and stayed in the loft of his stable. Mr. Tims brought us food 3 times a day. We wrote a letter to Prest. Humphreys to know what to do as we did not think it safe to be seen by our enemies."

**Pinkney Head, stepson of Alec, and son of Sarah Tims writes in his journal:**

" Brother Joseph Willey and Bro. Humphrey traveled sometime in the southern part of South

Carolina trying to open up new fields but failed to do so on account of mobs and had to return back to York County. They came to our house about 10 o'clock in the night. The mobs was ragin at the same time there also so they was compelled to hide up a little season. They staid in the stable loft at our house were often unsettled by our neighbors after while the Elders was there but they did not no where the Elders was. They thought they had left the country. One morning Brother George Canty came to our house and was surprised to see Elders there and to hear them say they had been there all the time."

**Pinkney in telling this story is speaking about the Alec and Sarah Head Tims home.**

"On the 16th of May, Elders Cragun and F. A. Fraughton came back to stay with us all the summer season. They had been there one week and one day there was about 12 men came when I was teaching school. The Elders was there with me in the house and one of the men came to the door and called for Elder Cragun. Elder Fraughton went out to talk with them, they gave the Elders a petition that had about 33 names signed to it, telling them they had to leave the country. The told them that they were citizens of the United States and thought they had a right to stay in the country as any other citizen. They gave the Elders 6 days to leave the place, but the Elders did not pay any attention to it much, they stayed on. On the night of the 25th of May there was 32 men came on the Elders at our house about 10 o'clock. They came running up to the house, Elder Cragun had just taken off his shoes to retire to bed when he heard the noise. Someone said run, and Elder Cragun made his escape out of the north door and ran for the woods, which was about 30 yards. While on his way to the woods there was about 25 or 30 shots fired at him, one shot just grazed him on the chin. Elder F. A. Fraughton had no chance to get out and the mob came in about 8 of them caught Elder Fraughton and led him away and gave him 50 lashes with hickory switches and turned him loose charging him to leave the country. The next day he came back to our house, then we all looked for Elder Cragun for about 2 hours before we found him. Both staid in the woods the rest of the night and next morning came to the house and got breakfast."

Alec and his second wife, Sarah moved with his first wife other family members to Sanford, Colorado in the year 1886. He died in 1941and is buried in Sanford with his first wife Martha, who died in 1906. Along with his daughter and son, Rachel Jane Tims Harris and Robert

The Mormom missionaries stayed at the home of Alec and Sarah Head Tims many times. Many singing times and meetings were held in their home.

Alec signed a petition as Chief, and more can be found in <u>Genealogy of the Western Catawba</u>.

Alec married second Sarah Ann Evans-Canty Head; daughter of Chancy and Peggy Canty Evans and widow of a Civil War soldier named Robert Henry Head.[574]

## ALEXANDER TIMS: CIVIL WAR SERVICE

Compiled by Wayne Head

Alexander Tims born July 15, 1845, to John Alexander Time and Rachel Marsh. He enlisted in The Confederate Army, Company K, 17th South Carolina Infantry on December 9, 1861. He was wounded at Manasas and a second wound was received on August 29, 1862. He was last listed on a muster roll on February 1, 1863. Alexander Tims enlisted along with William Canty, John Scott, and Jefferson Ayers.

My grandfather, George J. Head, Sr. told me that Grampa Time told him that two things he recalled from the Civil War was seeing all the white tents, lined up in rows, and the bugle playing revelry each morning

Raymond Harris related to me that his great-grandfather, Grandpa Tims told him two things from the war. One was that the Civil War was a rich man's war and a poor man's fight. The other was in response to a question if he shot anyone in the war. He said that he and a fellow were exchanging shots and he quit shooting. The Yankee soldier must have thought he'd hit Alec Tims, and he "peered around his tree, Grandpa Tims said that fella never shot at anyone ever again." Alex Tims name is on a statute dedicated to Catawba soldiers at Ft. Mills, South Carolina.***

"1 had the privilege of knowing my great-great grandfather, John Alexander Timms and his daughter (my great grandmother Rachel Timms Harris). As a little girl, my parents and 1, on many occasions went to

---

[574] Head genealogy.

visit our Catawba relatives. I remember my great-great grandfather Timms sitting by the pot-bellied stove with a shawl around his shoulders wearing his Confederate cap, which he rarely took off. He would ask me to dance for him, clap his hands and laugh. The more he would clap, the more I would dance. I loved to hear him laugh.

John Alexander Timms lived to be just over 90 years old. His daughter Rachel, took care of her father. She was a hardworking and caring woman. She wore long dresses with long sleeves and an apron. Her gray hair was combed back in a bun. She always smelled so good, like the soap she made. Rachel married Hillary Harris and had three children, Josiah Hillard Alexander, Roy Allen, Evelina and Ellis Nelson; all born in Rock Hill, South Carolina. My grandfather was Josiah Alexander or commonly referred to as Bosco Harris. Bosco married and had four children, Ruby, Harvey, (my father), Raymond and Odell. Bosco's first wife died as a young woman.

My father was seven years old when he went to live with his grandmother Rachel. She called him "Son" and I know my father loved her as his mother.

My father Harvey told stories about Chief Sam Blue coming to visit the families in Kirtland, New Mexico. As a young boy, he remembered the excitement of the families awaiting the arrival of their leader. My father said Chief Sam Blue arrived in Kirtland by horse drawn wagon from Gallup, New Mexico. I can still hear the excitement in my father's voice as he speaks of Chief Blue)" This account was written for the Catawba 7th Generation News in 1998 by Virginia (Jenny) Harris Tattershall.

More can be found in the Marsh chapter, as well as Canty and Scott and in Chiefs of the Catawba.

**PHOTO 547 - RACHEL JANE TIMS HARRIS**

A. Rachel Jane Tims Harris was born April 30, 1866 in Catawba, and died in Sanford, Colorado. She married Hillary Harris, son of Nancy Harris and Thomas Kilpatrick, a white man. Hillary left his family, and eventually married again in Oklahoma, where he died. The children of Rachel and Hillary Harris.

**PHOTO 548 - ROBERT HARVEY TIMS**

B. Robert Harvey Tims born 30 October 1877. He died unmarried in 1904 and is buried in Sanford Colorado, along with his mother, father and sister Rachel Tims Harris.[575]

**PHOTO 549 - TIMS FAMILY PICTURE 1937**

---

[575] Sanford Colorado cemetery inscriptions.

## Chapter 25   Watts Family

I. James A. Wats-Watts, a white man was born around 1833 married Charlotte or Carolotta Naomi Thompson-Tomson, born around 1837. [576]   It is possible that Charolotte-Carolotta was a descendant of John Thompson of the Revolutionary War; however, no other record exists of Thompsons after that one disappeared.

    A.  Nancy Christine Wats was born 25 August 1855. [577]   She married first James Goodwin Patterson, son of John S. Sitgreaves (white) and Martha Patterson, (Catawba) and together they had a daughter, Lizzie Jane Patterson-Watts. [578]   Nancy married second Robert Detan or Deyton, and together they had two children. (I am unsure of the spelling of the father's name.)[579] Nothing is known of Robert Detan.  Their two children were Lena Dayton born 21 December 1876, York, South Carolina and died 12 September 1887, York, South Carolina and Lillie Deyton born 1880, nothing more..

Nancy then married third William David Watts, son of Evan and Lucy Quash-Marsh Watts and they removed to Utah.   Nancy died 24 April 1926 in Cedar City, Iron County, Utah.[580]

More will be found in <u>Genealogy of the Western Catawba</u> and in the Peter Harris chapter. In all Nancy had 9 children, Lizzie Patterson -Watts, Lena Detan, Lillie Detan, Henry Watts, Lauri Lizzie, Katy H., William, Allie May, and Vaun Willard Watts.

    1. Lizzie Jane Patterson born 23 September 1874 married David Adam Harris, son of James SR and Sarah Jane Ayers Harris.  Lizzie was the first of his three wives.  Her children can be found in the Peter Harris chapter, under David Adam Harris.[581]

    2. Lena Laura Watts-Detan born 21 December 1875. Elder Joseph Wiley baptized Lena on March 9, 1884:she died 12 September 1887.

    3. Lillie Detan born 1880 in York, South Carolina.


\*\*\*\*\*\*\*\*\*\*\*\*\*\*\*\*\*\*\*\*\*\*\*\*\*\*\*\*\*\*\*\*\*\*\*\*\*\*\*\*\*\*\*\*\*\*\*\*\*\*\*\*\*\*\*\*\*\*\*\*\*\*\*\*\*\*\*\*\*\*\*\*\*\*

    I.  Evans-Eben Watts, white, born 13 May 1817 in Lancaster County, South Carolina.[582] Evan was the son of William D. or William H. Watts and Elizabeth Madis or Martin.  He married Lucy Quash-Marsh, born November 3, 1817, daughter of Robert and Betsy Scott Marsh.[583]

---

[576]    LDS Ancestral File.
[577]    Ibid
[578]    LDS Branch Records.
[579]    Ibid
[580]    Catawba Branch Records.
[581]    Patterson Genealogy.
[582]    1920 census Iron County, Utah.

Briefly, the children of Lucy Quash-Marsh-Mush are found here, she had six children: Robert Henry Head, Emily Cobb, Margaret McLonhan, John Gandy, James Harvey Watts and William David Watts.[584]

## U.S. Civil War Soldiers, 1861-1865

Name   Evans Watts -- Side  Confederate --Regiment State/Origin -- South Carolina
Regiment       6th Regiment, South Carolina Reserves (90 days 1862-63) -- Company    G
Rank In        Private -- Rank Out  Private
Film Number  M381 roll 33 -- Other Records        6th Regiment, South Carolina Reserves (90 days 1862-63)

August 1882, anti-Mormon sentiments are aroused and Reverend White directs actions. Elders Henry Miller and C. E. Robison left southeasterly to Rock Hill and to Lancaster County, but they were treated coldly by the white population and returned to Catawba.[20]

June 3, 1882, Elder Robison became sick with chills and fever in the home of Evan and Lucy Quash-Mush [21] Watts. Evan was a white man, married to a Pamunkey-Catawba woman, Lucy Quash-Mush; they had two boys together. Lucy had several grown children, including Pinkney Head's father Robert Head. Elder Robisonn died there in the presence of Elder Joseph Willey on September 25, 1882. [22]

The following is found in Joseph Willey's Diary. It shows just how deeply the family was committed to the new religion, The Church of Jesus Christ of Latter

A.  James Harvey Watts, born 8 April 1858, Catawba Indian Reservation, York County, South Carolina and died  21 March 1926, Catawba Reservation, York, South Carolina. He first married Ella Shaw a white woman they had a daughter Lucy Leola Watts (1892-1969).[585] Lucy married Frederick Nelson Blue (1889-1980) and their family is in the Blue Chapter. Ella Shaw abandoned them and James married (second) Mary Jane Whitesides (1855-1910) they had no children but she raised Lucy Leola as her own. James third wife was Gertrude Dye Ayers (1892- ), step daughter of Davis Ayers and Harriet Berry.[586] Gertrude was alive in 1926 when James passed away but was not found on the 1930 census. Their two sons William David and Clifford Ordell Watts was living with Betsy Estridge on the 1930 census.

---

[583]    LDS Ancestral File.
[584]    Catawba census records.
[585]    Patterson genealogy.
[586]    Obituary of James Watts.

**JAMES HARVEY WATTS**

"President John Morgan wrote that it would be well, if possible for the Elders to come in here and organize a branch. He desired the Elders to use their own judgement about coming. Accordingly on July 31, 1885, Elders W. E. Bingham and W. G. Cragun walked about 30 miles part of the distance through the woods and after night, they staid all night at Mr. Bailey Barkers. Next day, Brothers James Patterson and James Watts, piloted them through the woods for about 15 miles so they arrived in the nation without it being known in the country round about. They spent part of a day and two nights in the woods while they remained in the Nation." [587]    from the Ministry of John Morgan

James Harvey Watts died March 21, 1926.   More will be found in <u>Genealogy of the Western Catawba</u>, and in the Marsh chapter.  James had two children, William David Watts and James Clifford Odell Watts.

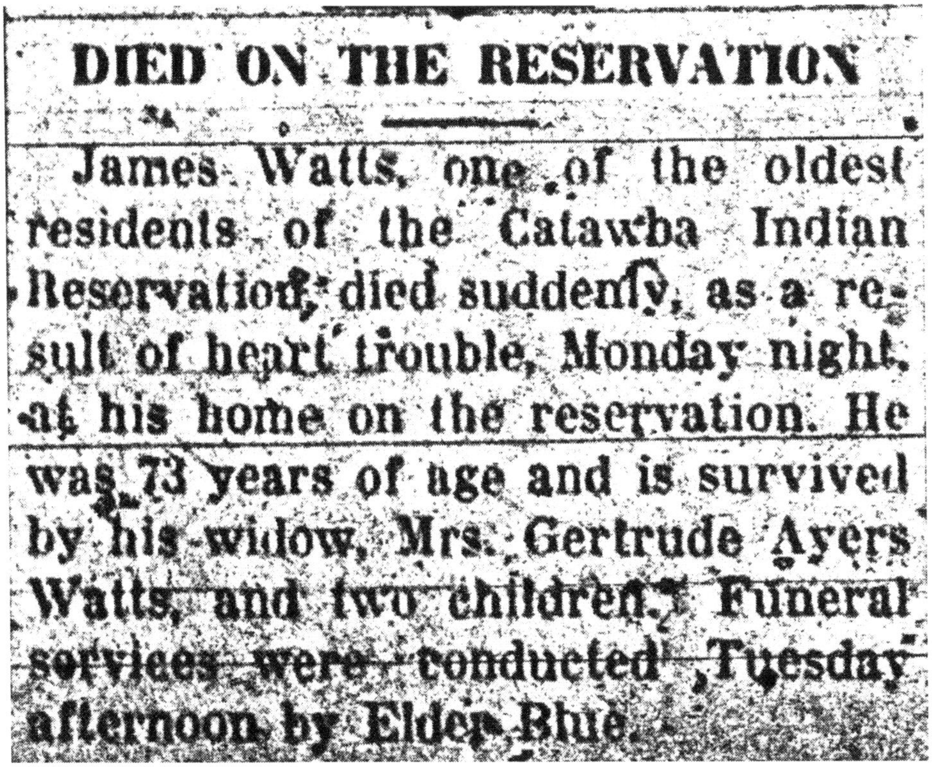

**DIED ON THE RESERVATION**

James Watts, one of the oldest residents of the Catawba Indian Reservation, died suddenly, as a result of heart trouble, Monday night, at his home on the reservation. He was 73 years of age and is survived by his widow, Mrs. Gertrude Ayers Watts, and two children. Funeral services were conducted Tuesday afternoon by Elder Blue.

**PHOTO 550 – NEWSPAPER CLIPPING OF DEATH OF JAMES HARVEY WATTS**

**From the thesis of Jerry D Lee 1976 at BYYU**

"the indians were also impressed with the elders ability to heal the sick several members of the tribe witnessed remarkable healings among the whites as well as 60 indians one of the first converts mr james henry wats was

sick in bed and he wished us to administer to him and we did so the next day he was able to go to work he said it was a great testimony to him and he demanded baptism.

---

[587]    LDS History of Southern States Mission, Film #001983.

# Catawba Reservation Resident Passes at Home There Suddenly

One of the oldest residents of the Catawba Indian Reservation, James Watts, passed away last night at his home on the reservation, death resulting from heart complications. He was apparently in good health, going about his regular duties yesterday and on his return to his home late yesterday afternoon collapsed and never regained consciousness. He was 73 years of age.

The deceased is survived by a wife, Mrs. Gertrude Watts, who is the step-daughter of Davis Ayers, also of the reservation. He also leaves two children.

Funeral services were conducted this afternoon at the reservation by Elder Blue. Interment was in the reservation cemetery.

PHOTO 551 - NEWSPAPER CLIPPING OF DEATH OF JAMES WATTS

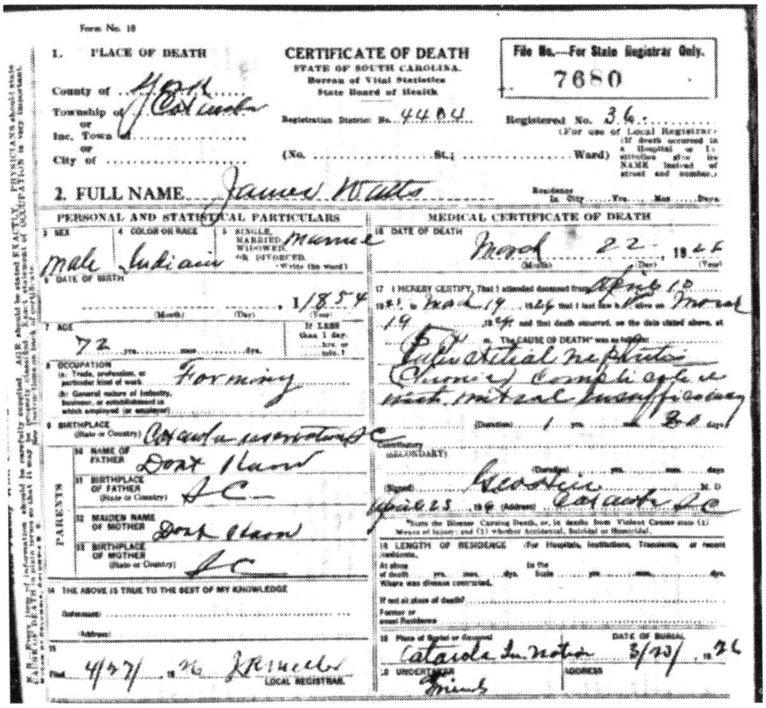

Form No. 18

1. PLACE OF DEATH

CERTIFICATE OF DEATH

STATE OF SOUTH CAROLINA.

Bureau of Vital Statistics

State Board of Health

File No.—For State Registrar Only. 7680

County of York

Township of Catawba

or Inc. Town of

or City of

Registration District No. 4404

Registered No. 36

(For use of Local Registrar)

(No. St.; Ward)

2. FULL NAME James Watts

Residence in City yrs. mos. dys.

PERSONAL AND STATISTICAL PARTICULARS

3 SEX male

4 COLOR OR RACE Indian

5 SINGLE, MARRIED, WIDOWED, OR DIVORCED (Write the word) married

6 DATE OF BIRTH (Month) (Day) 1854 (Year)

7 AGE 72 yrs. mos. dys.

8 OCCUPATION (a) Trade, profession, or particular kind of work Farming

(b) General nature of industry, business, or establishment in which employed (or employer)

9 BIRTHPLACE (State or Country) Catawba reservation SC

PARENTS

10 NAME OF FATHER Dont Know

11 BIRTHPLACE OF FATHER (State or Country) SC

12 MAIDEN NAME OF MOTHER Dont Know

13 BIRTHPLACE OF MOTHER (State or Country) SC

14 THE ABOVE IS TRUE TO THE BEST OF MY KNOWLEDGE

(Informant)

(Address)

15 Filed 4/27 19 26 J R Mullen LOCAL REGISTRAR

MEDICAL CERTIFICATE OF DEATH

16 DATE OF DEATH March 22 1926 (Month) (Day) (Year)

17 I HEREBY CERTIFY, That I attended deceased from April 10 1925 to March 19 1926 that I last saw h alive on March 19 1926 and that death occurred, on the date stated above, at

The CAUSE OF DEATH was as follows:

Interstitial nephritis

Chronic complicated with mitral insufficiency

(Duration) 1 yrs.

CONTRIBUTORY (SECONDARY)

(Duration) yrs. mos. days

(Signed) Geo Strait M.D.

April 23 1926 (Address) Catawba SC

*State the Disease Causing Death, or, in deaths from Violent Causes state (1) Means of Injury; and (2) whether Accidental, Suicidal or Homicidal.

18 LENGTH OF RESIDENCE (For Hospitals, Institutions, Transients, or recent residents.)

At place of death yrs. mos. dys. In the State yrs. mos. dys.

Where was disease contracted,

If not at place of death?

Former or usual Residence

19 Place of Burial or Removal Catawba Indian Nation DATE OF BURIAL 3/23/ 1926

20 UNDERTAKER Friends ADDRESS

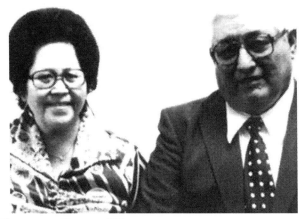

**PHOTO 552 -- CERTIFICATE OF DEATH FOR JAMES WATTS**

Children of James Harvey Watts

**PHOTO 553 - WILLIAM DAVID WATTS AND HIS WIFE EULA SANDERS WATTS**

1. William David Watts born 26 July 1920, Lancaster, South Carolina and died 14 September 1978, Salt Lake City, Salt Lake, Utah. He married Eula Sanders, daughter of John Idle and Arzada Brown Sanders.

**PHOTO 554 – HEADSTONE OF WILLIAM DAVID WATTS - BURIED AT SALT LAKE CITY CEMETERY
SALT LAKE CITY, SALT LAKE COUNTY, UTAH,**

2. James Clifford O'Dell Watts born 25 May 1923, York County, South Carolina and died 2 April 2002, Knoxville, Knox, Tennessee. He married a white woman, Mary. The 1943 roll has Starnes written above Clifford's name.[588]

**PHOTO 555 – WILLIAM DAVID WATTS**

B. William David Watts, born May 22, 1861 in Catawba, South Carolina and died 20 October 1933 in Cedar City, Iron, Utah. He married Nancy Christine Wats, daughter of James Wats and Carolotta Naomi Thompson, first wife of James Goodwin Patterson. He had six children. More about them will be found in <u>Genealogy of the Western Catawba</u> and earlier in this chapter under Nancy Christina Watts, and in the Marsh chapter.[589]

---

[588]    Ibid
[589]    Mauna Woodbury Genealogy.

**PHOTO 556 – NANCY CHRISTINE WATTS (1855-1926) WIFE OF WILLIAM DAVID WATTS**

**PHOTO 557 – HEADSTONE FOR WILLIAM DAVID WATTS AND NANCY C WATTS – BURIED AT CEDAR CITY CEMETERY - CEDAR CITY, IRON COUNTY, UTAH**

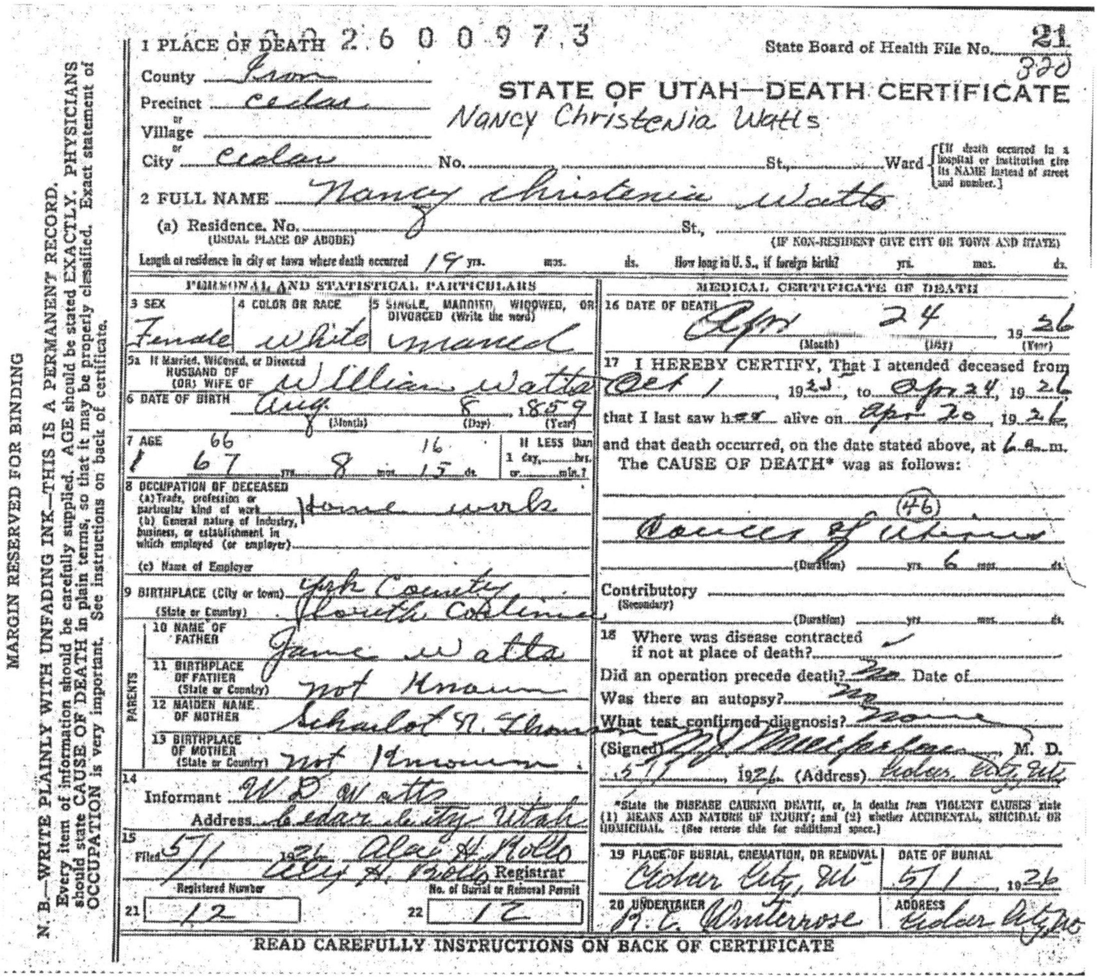

1 PLACE OF DEATH 2 6 0 0 9 7 3 — State Board of Health File No. 21 / 330

STATE OF UTAH—DEATH CERTIFICATE

County Iron
Precinct Cedar
Village
City Cedar
Nancy Christenia Watts

2 FULL NAME Nancy Christenia Watts
(a) Residence. No. — St.
Length of residence in city or town where death occurred 19 yrs.

PERSONAL AND STATISTICAL PARTICULARS

3 SEX Female | 4 COLOR OR RACE white | 5 SINGLE, MARRIED, WIDOWED, OR DIVORCED married
5a If Married, Widowed, or Divorced HUSBAND OF (OR) WIFE OF William Watts
6 DATE OF BIRTH Aug 8 1859
7 AGE 66 16 / 67 yrs. 8 mos. 15 ds.
8 OCCUPATION OF DECEASED Home work
9 BIRTHPLACE York County, North Carolina
10 NAME OF FATHER Jame Watts
11 BIRTHPLACE OF FATHER not Known
12 MAIDEN NAME OF MOTHER Scharlot N. Thomas
13 BIRTHPLACE OF MOTHER not Known
14 Informant W D Watts
Address Cedar City Utah
15 Filed 5/1 1926 Alex H Rollo, Registrar
21 12 | 22 12

MEDICAL CERTIFICATE OF DEATH

16 DATE OF DEATH Apr 24 1926
17 I HEREBY CERTIFY, That I attended deceased from Oct 1, 1925, to Apr 24, 1926, that I last saw her alive on Apr 20, 1926, and that death occurred, on the date stated above, at 6 a.m.
The CAUSE OF DEATH was as follows:
(46) Cancer of Uterus — 6 mos.
Contributory
18 Where was disease contracted if not at place of death?
Did an operation precede death? no
Was there an autopsy? no
What test confirmed diagnosis? None
(Signed) M. J. Macfarlane, M. D.
5/1 1926 (Address) Cedar City Utah
19 PLACE OF BURIAL, CREMATION, OR REMOVAL Cedar City, Utah | DATE OF BURIAL 5/1 1926
20 UNDERTAKER R. C. Winterrose | ADDRESS Cedar City Utah

READ CAREFULLY INSTRUCTIONS ON BACK OF CERTIFICATE

MARGIN RESERVED FOR BINDING
N. B.—WRITE PLAINLY WITH UNFADING INK—THIS IS A PERMANENT RECORD.

**PHOTO 558 – CERTIFICATE OF DEATH FOR NANCY CHRISTINE WATS WATTS**

This from Angelfire "the older Watts couple just about have to be buried in New Harmony? "These are stories told about William David Watts Born: 22 May 1861 and Nancy Christina Watts Born: 25 Aug 1855 as told by their Granddaughter."

About 20 years ago (approx. 1985) I went to New Harmony, Utah where William David and Nancy Christina Watts lived and visited with an old lady there who was almost 100 years old. She remembered the Watts family really well. She even still had a crush on Henry, William David and Nancy Christina Watts' son…after all these years. She told me how handsome and manly he was.

She remembered Lucy Marsh Watts (William David's Mother) as an old lady sitting on the porch—smoking a corn cob pipe. She also remembered when Nancy Christina saved her own daughter Allie May's life. There had been a Diphtheria epidemic, and a lot of the children there were dying. Allie was ill and the Doctor came and told them that she had Diphtheria, and there was nothing he could do for her. He said that she was going to die and he started to leave. Nancy stopped him insisting that he do something…there had to be something he could do. She told him that she couldn't lose another child. So, the Doctor said that the only treatment there was to do was to cut Allie's throat and pull the membrane out that was suffocating her. He wouldn't do the surgery himself and left. So, in desperation, Nancy sterilized a hunting knife in the open flame of the coal stove. With William David holding the child down on the kitchen table...Nancy cut her throat and pulled the membrane out, saving her life. Then she sewed Allie's throat back together. When I asked how the old lady knew this, she said her and the neighbor kids sat on the back steps and watched.

An old gentleman that I talked to their remembered stories about "Billy" Watts (William David) delivering the mail. I remember stories about Billy having asthma so bad while on his route, that he had to hold on to the fence posts to catch his breath.

**This next story was handed down from different family members:**

After Nancy Christina died, the Mormon Bishop tried to get William to marry a widow he had picked out for him in the town. William David refused to marry her, and for that he was ex-communicated...for not following the counsel of his Bishop. It was then that William moved to Cedar City, Utah.

My daughter and I went to New Harmony recently (2004) to look for Evan and Lucy's (William's parents) grave. We meticulously went through every headstone row by row, and couldn't find it. A cement headstone we saw with no markings on it could be it.

**Children of William David Watts and Nancy Christina Watts**

**PHOTO 559 - HENRY JAMES EVAN WATTS**

1. Henry James Evan Watts born 11 November, 1884 in York, Spartanburg, South Carolina and died 20 June 1957 in Granite, Salt Lake County, Utah.

**PHOTO 560 -  LYONA SPROUL WIFE OF HENRY JAMES EVAN WATTS**

He married 21 October 1912 in Cedar City, Iron, Utah, United States to  Lyona Sproul b 1893 - d 1982. They had 10 children

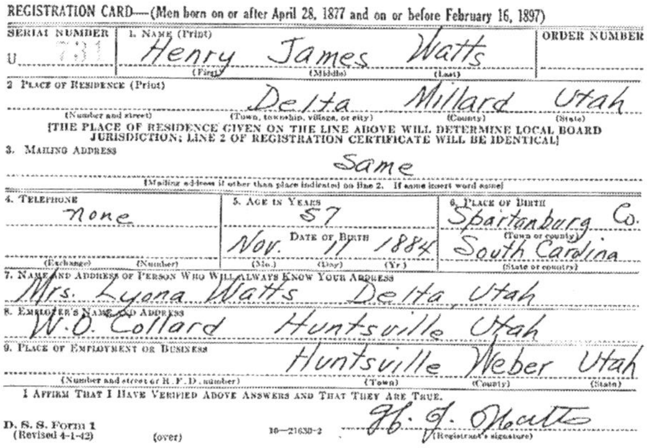

**PHOTO 561 – WWII REGISTRATION CARD FOR HENRY JAMES WATTS**

**Henry James Watts in the Utah, Select County Marriages, 1887-1937**

Name: Henry James Watts        Gender:    Male      Age: 27

Birth Date:     1885

Marriage Date:          21 Oct 1912        Marriage Place:   Iron, Utah, United States

Spouse:        Lyona Sproul

FHL Film Number:    484842

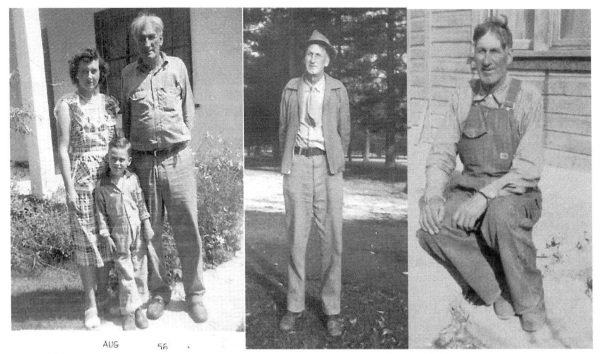

**PHOTO 562 – JAMES HENRY EVANS WATS WITH DAUGHTER AUG 1956 – 2 OTHER PICTURES OF JAMES WATTS**

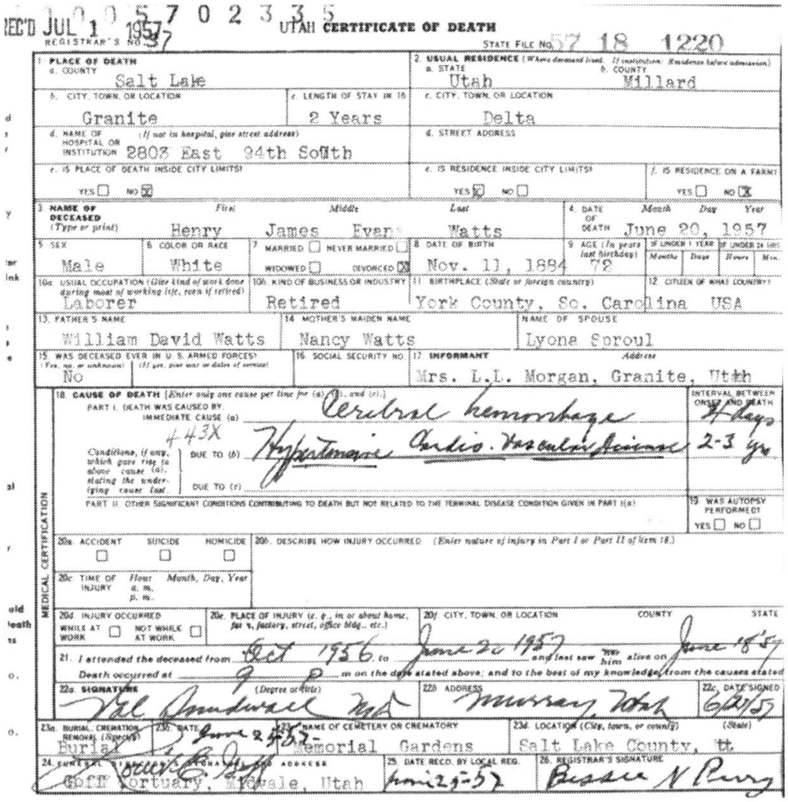

REC'D JUL 1 1957 100057023335
REGISTRAR'S NO. 57
UTAH CERTIFICATE OF DEATH
STATE FILE NO. 57 18 1220

1. PLACE OF DEATH a. COUNTY Salt Lake
b. CITY, TOWN, OR LOCATION Granite
c. LENGTH OF STAY IN 1b 2 Years
d. NAME OF HOSPITAL OR INSTITUTION (If not in hospital, give street address) 2803 East 94th South
e. IS PLACE OF DEATH INSIDE CITY LIMITS? YES ☐ NO ☒
2. USUAL RESIDENCE (Where deceased lived. If institution: Residence before admission) a. STATE Utah b. COUNTY Millard
c. CITY, TOWN, OR LOCATION Delta
d. STREET ADDRESS
e. IS RESIDENCE INSIDE CITY LIMITS? YES ☒ NO ☐
f. IS RESIDENCE ON A FARM? YES ☐ NO ☒
3. NAME OF DECEASED (Type or print) First Henry Middle James Evans Last Watts
4. DATE OF DEATH Month Day Year June 20, 1957
5. SEX Male
6. COLOR OR RACE White
7. MARRIED ☐ NEVER MARRIED ☐ WIDOWED ☐ DIVORCED ☒
8. DATE OF BIRTH Nov. 11, 1884
9. AGE (In years last birthday) 72
10a. USUAL OCCUPATION (Give kind of work done during most of working life, even if retired) Laborer
10b. KIND OF BUSINESS OR INDUSTRY Retired
11. BIRTHPLACE (State or foreign country) York County, So. Carolina
12. CITIZEN OF WHAT COUNTRY? USA
13. FATHER'S NAME William David Watts
14. MOTHER'S MAIDEN NAME Nancy Watts
NAME OF SPOUSE Lyona Sproul
15. WAS DECEASED EVER IN U. S. ARMED FORCES? No
16. SOCIAL SECURITY NO.
17. INFORMANT Mrs. L.L. Morgan, Granite, Utah
18. CAUSE OF DEATH PART I. DEATH WAS CAUSED BY: IMMEDIATE CAUSE (a) Cerebral hemorrhage — INTERVAL BETWEEN ONSET AND DEATH 4 days
DUE TO (b) 443X Hypertensive Cardio-Vascular Disease — 2-3 yrs
DUE TO (c)
PART II. OTHER SIGNIFICANT CONDITIONS CONTRIBUTING TO DEATH BUT NOT RELATED TO THE TERMINAL DISEASE CONDITION GIVEN IN PART I(a)
19. WAS AUTOPSY PERFORMED? YES ☐ NO ☐
20a. ACCIDENT ☐ SUICIDE ☐ HOMICIDE ☐
20b. DESCRIBE HOW INJURY OCCURRED (Enter nature of injury in Part I or Part II of item 18.)
20c. TIME OF INJURY Hour a.m. p.m. Month, Day, Year
20d. INJURY OCCURRED WHILE AT WORK ☐ NOT WHILE AT WORK ☐
20e. PLACE OF INJURY (e.g., in or about home, farm, factory, street, office bldg., etc.)
20f. CITY, TOWN, OR LOCATION COUNTY STATE
21. I attended the deceased from Oct 1956 to June 20 1957 and last saw him alive on June 18 57
Death occurred at 9 P.m. on the date stated above; and to the best of my knowledge, from the causes stated
22a. SIGNATURE (Degree or title) Val Sundwall MD
22b. ADDRESS Murray, Utah
22c. DATE SIGNED 6/21/57
23a. BURIAL, CREMATION, REMOVAL (Specify) Burial
23b. DATE June 22 57
23c. NAME OF CEMETERY OR CREMATORY Memorial Gardens
23d. LOCATION (City, town, or county) (State) Salt Lake County, Ut
24. FUNERAL DIRECTOR ADDRESS Goff Mortuary, Midvale, Utah
25. DATE RECD. BY LOCAL REG. June 25-57
26. REGISTRAR'S SIGNATURE Bessie N Perry

**PHOTO 563 - CERTIFICATE OF DEATH FOR HENRY JAMES EVANS WATTS**

Henry James Evan Watts

My Great Grandfather, Henry James Evan Watts, was born Nov. 11, 1884 in York, South Carolina. He lived there until he was nine years old. He moved with his folks to the west and settled in New Harmony, Utah. Later on he moved with his folks to Cedar City, Utah.

He went to school in Cedar City to learn to read and write. As he grew older he drove mail from Cedar City to New Harmony. He took great pride in his team of horses. He loved to dance and was asked to call for all the dances there in New Harmony. They square danced alot and as he would dance as he called.

In 1912 he married my Great Grandmother, Lyona Sproul. They lived in Cedar City for about one year. Then they moved to Delta, Utah. There they lived in a boarded up tent and he worked at odd jobs. He got a job herding sheep. And when he wasn't herding sheep he worked in the hay fields or dug ditches, anything to make a living.

They eventually built a home, a small one at first. It burned down. The second one a little larger. It also burned down. The third one larger still. It did not burn down.

In 1923 he and a friend won a trophy cup for pitching horse shoes. The next year they won it again. They were told if they won one more time they could keep it. But that year they could not go the state fair so they didn't get to keep it. Great Grandpa was over six feet tall and he walked like a million dollars. So straight and at an even pace. He was also an excellent butcher, something he took great pride in. He could make jerky and often did for his family. He loved his children, many times he laughed 'till tears came to his eyes over the games the children played. Great Grandpa died June 20, 1957.

**PHOTO 564 – HEADSTONES FOR HENRY JAMES WATTS AND WIFE LYONA S WATTS - BURIED LARKIN SUNSET GARDENS CEMETERY - SANDY, SALT LAKE COUNTY, UTAH**

| **Father  Henry James Evan WATTS** | | |
|---|---|---|
| Birth | 11 Nov 1884 | York, Spartanburg, South Carolina, United States |
| Residence | 1900 | Age: 15Marital Status: Single; Relation to Head of House: Son; Harmony, Washington, Utah |
| Residence | 1910 | Age in 1910: 25Marital Status: Single; Relation to Head of House: Son; Cedar, Iron, Utah |
| Residence | 1930 | Age: 45Marital Status: Married; Relation to Head of House: Head; Delta, Millard, Utah |
| Residence | 1935 | Delta, Millard, Utah |
| Residence | 1 Apr 1940 | Marital Status: Married Relation to Head of House: Head; Delta, Millard, Utah |
| Death | 20 Jun 1957 | Granite, Salt Lake, Utah, United States |
| Burial | 25 Jun 1957 | Sandy City, Salt Lake, Utah, United States |
| Residence | | Millard, Utah |
| Marriage | 21 Oct 1912 | Iron, Utah |
| Father | William David WATTS (1860-1933) | |
| Mother | Nancy Christina WATS (1855-1926) | |
| **Mother  Lyona SPROUL** | | |
| Birth | 29 Apr 1893 | Washington, Washington, Utah, United States |
| Residence | 1935 | Delta, Millard, Utah |
| Residence | 1 Apr 1940 | Marital Status: Married Relation to Head of House: Wife; Delta, Millard, Utah |
| Death | 5 May 1982 | Sandy City, Salt Lake, Utah, United States |
| Burial | 8 May 1982 | Delta, Millard, Utah, United States |
| Father | Andrew SPROUL (1869-1960) | |
| Mother | Eveline CHIDESTER (1868-1946) | |
| **Children** | | |

| F | Katie WATTS | |
|---|---|---|
| | Birth | 19 Jul 1913 | Cedar City, Iron, Utah, United States |
| | Death | 2 Mar 1995 | Sandy City, Salt Lake, Utah, United States |
| | Burial | 7 Mar 1995 | Sandy, Salt Lake, Utah |
| | Spouse | Leonard Levern MORGAN (1908-1986) |
| | Marriage | 6 Mar 1934 | Fillmore, Millard County, Utah |

| F | Thora WATTS | |
|---|---|---|
| | Birth | 16 Dec 1916 | Delta, Millard, Utah |
| | Blessing | 4 Mar 1917 | Delta Ward, Deseret Stake, L.D.S. Church |
| | Residence | 1920 | Delta, Millard, Utah, United States |
| | Death | 14 Sep 2002 | Age at Death: 85; Sandy, Salt Lake, Utah, United States of America |
| | | 16 Sep 2002 | United States |
| | Burial | | Granite, Salt Lake, Utah, United States |
| | Spouse | Lymon Neal WRIGHT (1914-1982) |
| | Marriage | 3 Apr 1937 | Salt Lake City, Salt Lake, Utah, United States |

| M | Henry Arshell WATTS | |
|---|---|---|
| | Birth | 29 Oct 1918 | Delta, Millard, Utah |
| | Residence | 1920 | Marital Status: Single Relation to Head of House: Son; Delta, Millard, Utah |
| | Residence | 1930 | Delta, Millard, Utah |
| | Residence | 1935 | Delta, Millard, Utah |
| | Residence | 1 Apr 1940 | Marital Status: Single Relation to Head of House: Son; Delta, Millard, Utah |
| | Death | 24 Oct 1958 | Ventura, California |
| | Burial | | Ventura, Ventura County, California, United States of America |
| | Spouse | Frances Lucille WOLF (1910-1958) |

| F | Erva Sharree WATTS | |
|---|---|---|
| | Birth | 25 Apr 1920 | Delta, Millard, Utah |
| | Residence | 1930 | Delta, Millard, Utah |
| | Death | 7 Jul 2006 | Age at Death: 86; Kingsville, Ashtabula, Ohio |
| | Burial | 12 Jul 2006 | North Kingsville Village, Ashtabula, Ohio, United States |
| | Cemetery | | Greenlawn Memory Gardens, North Kingsville Village, Ashtabula, Ohio, United States |
| | Spouse | Alfred W MEYER (1910-1988) |
| | Marriage | 6 Sep 1936 | Beaver, Utah, United States |

| M | David Ardell WATTS | |
|---|---|---|
| | Birth | 4 Sep 1922 | Delta, Millard, Utah, United States |
| | Residence | from 1930 to 1940 | Delta, Millard, Utah |
| | Residence | 1942 | Age: 20; Millard County, Utah |
| | Arrival | 27 Aug 1943 | New York, New York |

| | | | |
|---|---|---|---|
| Residence | 1959 | Salt Lake City, Utah | |
| Residence | 1960 | Salt Lake City, Utah | |
| Death | 28 Jun 1986 | Salt Lake City, Salt Lake, Utah, United States | |
| Burial | | Sandy, Salt Lake County, Utah, United States of America | |
| Departure | | Mobile Via New York | |
| Spouse | Anna Colleen HAMMOND (1929-2009) | | |
| Marriage | 5 Oct 1946 | | |
| Spouse | Edna Velma RYMER (1923-2010) | | |
| Marriage | 20 May 1943 | Salt Lake City, Salt Lake, Utah, United States | |

| F | **Eveline WATTS** | | |
|---|---|---|---|
| Birth | 19 Aug 1924 | Delta, Millard, Utah, United States | |
| Residence | 1930 | Marital Status: Single Relation to Head of House: Daughter; Delta, Millard, Utah | |
| Residence | 1935 | Delta, Millard, Utah | |
| Residence | 1 Apr 1940 | Marital Status: Single Relation to Head of House: Daughter; Delta, Millard, Utah | |
| Death | 4 Oct 2014 | Hydesville, Humboldt, California, United States | |
| Burial | 9 Oct 2014 | Fortuna, Humboldt, California, United States of America | |
| Spouse | Lawrence HORTON (1915-1974) | | |
| Marriage | 2 Sep 1943 | Salt Lake City, Salt Lake, Utah, United States | |

| M | **William Wilford Sproul WATTS** | | |
|---|---|---|---|
| Birth | 7 May 1926 | Cedar City, Iron, Utah, United States | |
| Chr | 7 Nov 1926 | Delta, Millard, UT | |
| Residence | 1930 | Age: 3Age: 3 10/12; Marital Status: Single; Relation to Head of House: Son; Delta, Millard, Utah | |
| Residence | 1935 | Delta, Millard, Utah | |
| Residence | 1 Apr 1940 | Marital Status: Single Relation to Head of House: Son; Delta, Millard, Utah | |
| Residence | 1943 | Age: 17 | |
| Death | 8 Dec 1977 | Age at Death: 51; Salt Lake City, Utah | |
| Burial | | Centerville, Davis, Utah, United States | |
| Spouse | Vena Irene GALE (1929-2003) | | |
| Marriage | | Salt Lake City, Salt Lake, Utah, United States | |

| F | **Maurie WATTS** | | |
|---|---|---|---|
| Birth | 29 Feb 1928 | Cedar City, Iron, Utah, United States | |
| Residence | 1930 | Marital Status: Single Relation to Head of House: Daughter; Delta, Millard, Utah | |
| Residence | 1935 | Delta, Millard, Utah | |
| Residence | 1 Apr 1940 | Marital Status: Single Relation to Head of House: Daughter; Delta, Millard, Utah | |

| | | | |
|---|---|---|---|
| Death | | | |
| Burial | | | |
| Spouse | Cyrel Hubert NAGEL (1920-2001) | | |

**F** | **Sharron WATTS** | | |

| | | |
|---|---|---|
| Birth | 10 Dec 1933 | Delta, Millard, Utah |
| Death | 22 Jun 1934 | Delta, Millard, Utah |
| Burial | 24 Jun 1934 | Delta, Millard, Utah, United States |
| Marriage | | |

**M** | **Donald Myron WATTS** | | |

| | | |
|---|---|---|
| Residence | 1935 | Same Place, , |
| Birth | 25 Jul 1937 | Delta, Millard, Utah |
| Residence | 1 Apr 1940 | Marital Status: Single Relation to Head of House: Son; Delta, Millard, Utah |
| Death | 16 Apr 2012 | Taylorsville, Salt Lake, Utah, United States |
| Obituary | 17 Apr 2012 | Utah, United States |
| Burial | | Moroni, Sanpete, Utah, United States |
| Spouse | Luetta Joy NIELSEN (1936-2012) | |
| Marriage | 22 Apr 1955 | Salt Lake City, Salt Lake, Utah |

The 10 children of Henry James Evan WATTS and Lyona SPROUL WATTS:

Photo 565 - Katie (1913-1995)　　-- Thora (1916-2002)　　--　　Henry Arshell (1918-1958)

Erva Sharree Watts 1920–2006   -   David Ardell Watts 1922–1986

**PHOTO 566 – EVELINE (1924 – 2014)**

William Wilford Sproul Watts 1926–1977 - Maurie Watts 1928–) - Sharron Watts 1933–1934

**PHOTO 567 - DONALD MYRON  (1937-2012)**

**PHOTO 568 – LAURI LIZZIE WATTS**

2. Lauri Lizzie Watts born, 29 September 1888, York, Spartanburg, South Carolina and died 18 October 1910, Cedar City, Iron County, Utah. She married Wilbur Everett Dow

They had two children:

a. Wilber E Dow, born 11 Feb 1904, Pioche, Lincoln, Nevada, United States, married Jessie Morrill (born 1908) 5 Jan 1926, Beaver Co., Utah

b. Grace Elva Dow, born 27 Aug 1909, Pioche, Lincoln, Nevada, United States, died 9 Apr 1980 Los Angeles, California.

Burial: Cedar City Cemetery, Cedar City, Iron County. Utah, Plot: C-20-1-4

**Utah, Select Marriages, 1887-1966**

Name Laura Lizzie Watts Gender - Female, Marital Status Single Age 19
Birth Date 1888 -- Marriage Date 25 Jun 1907 Marriage Place New Harmony, Washington, Utah -- FHL Film Number 484842 Reference ID P218
Household Members -- Wilbur Everett Dow , Laura Lizzie Watts

State Board of Health File No. 34

STATE OF UTAH—DEATH CERTIFICATE.

THIS CERTIFICATE MUST BE FORWARDED BY LOCAL REGISTRAR TO THE STATE BOARD OF HEALTH, SALT LAKE CITY, ON OR BEFORE THE 5TH OF THE FOLLOWING MONTH, AFTER FIRST HAVING BEEN PROMPTLY REGISTERED.

060

| | |
|---|---|
| PLACE OF DEATH<br>County of Iron<br>Precinct of Cedar City<br>City, Town or Village of Cedar City<br>Street and No. 1000780 | Full Name of Deceased: Lora E. Lizzy Watts Dow<br>Former or Usual Residence: Pioche<br>How long resident at place of death: Six Weeks |
| PERSONAL AND STATISTICAL PARTICULARS<br>Sex: Female<br>Color: White<br>Date of Birth: September 29 1889<br>Age: 22 years, months, 20 days<br>Single, Married, Widowed, or Divorced: Married<br>Birthplace (State or country): So. Carlina<br>Name of Father: William David Watts<br>Birthplace of Father (State or country): So Carlina<br>Maiden Name of Mother: Nancy Christina Watts<br>Birthplace of Mother (State or country): So. Carlina<br>Occupation: none<br>THE ABOVE STATED PERSONAL PARTICULARS ARE TRUE TO THE BEST OF MY KNOWLEDGE AND BELIEF<br>(Informant) Wm D. Watts<br>(Address) Cedar City<br>Place of Burial: Cedar City<br>Date of Burial: Oct 20 - 1912<br>Undertaker: [illegible]<br>Address: Cedar City Utah | MEDICAL CERTIFICATE OF DEATH<br>Date of Death: Oct. 18 1912<br>I HEREBY CERTIFY, That I attended deceased from Oct 7th 1912 to Oct 18 1912, that I last saw her alive on Oct. 18 1912, and that death occurred, on the date stated above, at 4:30 A. M. The CAUSE OF DEATH was as follows:<br>Chief Cause: Typhoid<br>Where Contracted: Cedar  Duration 12 Days<br>Contributory (if any)<br>Where Contracted  Duration  Days<br>(Signed) Ernest Green M. D.<br>Date Oct 19 1912 (Address) Cedar City<br>Filed Nov. 1 1912 E. Schuppman Registrar<br>21  21 |

(OVER)

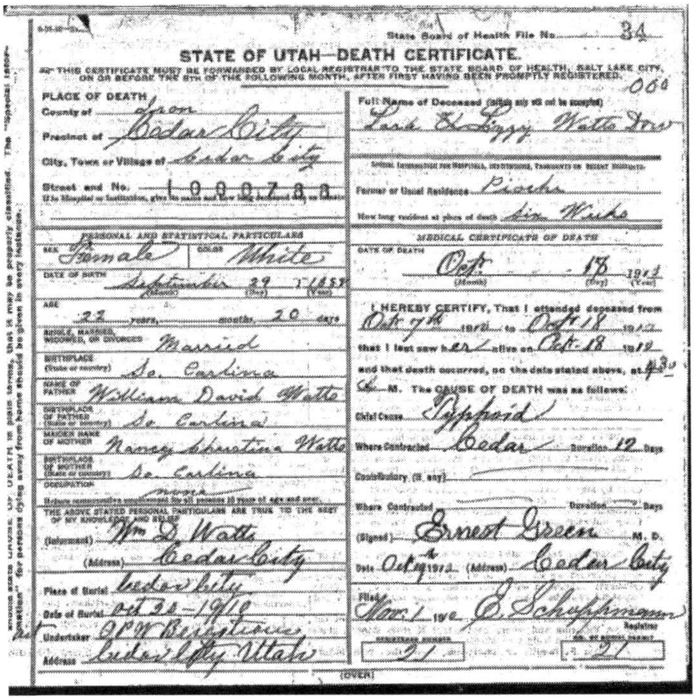

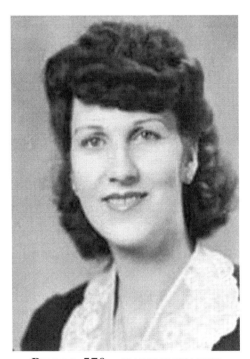

**PHOTO 569 - CERTIFICATE OF DEATH FOR LAURI LIZZIE WATTS DOW**

**PHOTO 570 – KATY H WATTS**

3. Katy H. Watts born 11 June 1891, New Harmony, Washington, Utah, United States and died 27 April 1912, New Harmony, Washington County, Utah, United States. She married Edward Llewellyn Hooper (1884-1944), 13 Dec 1911, Iron, Utah, United States

**Katie and husband Edward L Hooper had one Child:**

Leroy J. Hooper, 1912-1973

4. William Redd Watts born 8 May 1893, New Harmony, Utah and died 4 August 1893, Cedar City, Utah

Allie May Watts
(McDonald)

**PHOTO 571 - ALLIE MAY WATTS**

5. Allie May Watts born 27 May 1895, New Harmony, Washington, Utah, United States and died 6 June 1966.

She married Lamont Alexander Mcdonald (1893-1972) in 19 Nov 1913, Parowan, Iron, Utah. FHL Film Number 484842, Reference ID P322

**PHOTO 572 – HEADSTONE FOR ALLIE MAY WATTS MCDONALD -- BURIAL: CEDAR CITY CEMETERY, CEDAR CITY, IRON COUNTY, UTAH**

They had seven children:

Thressa Mcdonald 1915–1999

Maxine Mcdonald 1919–1961

Virginia McDonald 1921–1995

Sylvia Billie McDonald 1924–1940

La Wanna McDonald 1929–

Mauna Ray (Monty) McDonald 1934–

**PHOTO 573 - ALLIE MAY WATTS MCDONALD'S HUSBAND LAMONT ALEXANDER MCDONALD AND FIVE OF THEIR DAUGHTERS.**

**PHOTO 574 - VON WILLARD WATTS**

6. Von Willard Watts, born 13 December 1898 New Harmony, Iron, Utah and died 25 MAR 1965, Provo, Utah, Utah.

He married, Elizabeth Imlay (1906-1979) on 12 May 1924, Iron, Utah

They had one child:     John Wadkins Watts

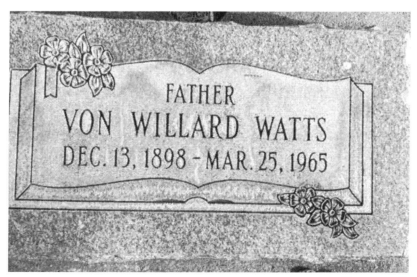

**PHOTO 575 - HEADSTONE FOR VON WILLARD WATTS - BURIED AT PROVO CITY CEMETERY**

## PROVO, UTAH COUNTY, UTAH
## Group Photo

Catawba Branch

## Chapter 26  White Family

I. Henry White -Lieutenant Henry White, probably born around 1760. He signed leases as Lieutenant Henry White beginning in 1808. In 1816, he stopped signing and did not sign any of the August 1817 leases. He began signing again in May 1817 and going through May 21, 1819. He then began signing as just Henry White, then in August of that year, he again signs as Lieutenant Henry White. He last signed leases in 1819.[590] He also appears on Capt. ThoTnas Drennan's Pay Bill for Revolutionary War service, "#8, Henry White, 52 days, 26 pounds" and on the list for which there is no voucher.[591] Judging from his last signing, he probably died sometime after 1819. He signed a lease, giving David Hutcheson land in 1817, along with Thomas Brown, Jacob Scott and Jacob Ayers.

Henry White [592] -Lieutenant Henry White, probably born around 1760. He signed a lease, giving David Hutcheson land in 1817, along with Thomas  Brown, Jacob Scott and Jacob Ayers.  His mark follows:

II. George White -Watciktci or Wiktcikci-eagle,[593] a nickname, was probably born around 1760, is listed on Drennan's Pay bill for Revolutionary War service, "#37, George White, 10 days, 5 pounds." He is also listed on the list for which there was no voucher as "George White, horse lost at Sumter's defeat (Fishing Creek) who also asserts that he was 80 days."[594]

George was a headman of the Catawba in 1796, signing first Major George White, along with Captain John Delo, Captain Billy Redhead, James Scott and Patrick Brown. All had seen service in the Revolutionary war with him, except for James Scott. This George White was not the George White who married Margareth Marsh; however, he and Henry most likely took the name of White after the family of our George White, as they were quite prominent in the area.

---

[590] Blumer, by year of signing, includes quite a few pages.
[591] Brown pages 268 & 269
[592]     Brown pages 268 & 269.
[593] Virginia Magazine XIII. January 1906, notes on pages 228n and 229n.
[594] Brown pages 268 & 269.

George White was born April 10, 1807 and died July 10, 1858.[595] He married Margareth (Peggy) Quash Mush-Marsh, born June 17, 1827, daughter of Robert Alexander and Betsy Scott-Quash. George was a white man. George and Peggy Quash-Marsh White, had six children.

Peggy died September 10, 1874. Margareth-Peggy their six children are: Elizabeth Missouri, Robert, Elvinia, Martha Jane, Henrietta and Nancy A.White.[596]

PHOTO 576 - ELIZABETH MISSOURI WHITE

A. Elizabeth Missouri White, born September 3, 1849, died 1934 in Sanford, Colorado. Children will be found in the Patterson chapter in <u>Genealogy of the Western Catawba</u>.

Briefly the children were; Martha Jane, Georgia Henrietta, Isabell, Lula, Eldora, Maggie, Abbie, Mary Maud, James Moroni Heber, Joseph Brigham and Henry Alonzo Patterson

---

[595] Patterson genealogy.
[596] Ibid

**PHOTO 577 – HEADSTONE FOR ELIZABETH PATTERSON WHITE**

B. Robert White, born July 3, 1850 in Catawba, South Carolina, died May 8, 1858.

C. Elvinia White, born March 18, 1852, died February 11, 1861

D. Martha Jane White, born 1854, married Absolum (Epp) Harris, son of Sally Harris, as his second wife. Jane White received money, in 1879. Margaret married as his second wife, James Harris JR, born 1858; his first wife was Mary Jane Whitesides.[597] Martha and James had seven children, and they will be found in the Peter Harris Chapter. Briefly the children were Jesse, Jacob, Eliza, Georgia, John Thomas, Robert and George Furrnan Harris.

E. Henrietta White was born in 1858 she died on August 18, 1858.

F. Nancy A. White, born 1861. On April 10, 1875, she received $4.50 and in 1881, she received $19.98 from the Indian Agent R. L. Crook. She married Allen Alston Harris. Nancy had two children; the father of Peggy is unknown. Evidently, Allen Harris was the father of Rosa.

> 1. Peggy Jane White born January 1878,[598] She was sometimes called Whitsides. She married Calvin Deperry Rogers 1877–1944 in 1892 in South Carolina. In 1900 they were living in Georgia and by 1910 they were in Florida. Calvin died in Florida. Haven't found when or where Peggy died. According to the 1910 census they had 6 children with 5 living. Only 5 have been identified: Lula Rogers 1893–, Angie or Oza Rogers 1896–, Minnie Rogers 1897–, Rosa Rogers 1900– and James "Jimmy R" Rogers 1903–

---

[597] Catawba Branch Records.
[598] 1880 census of York County

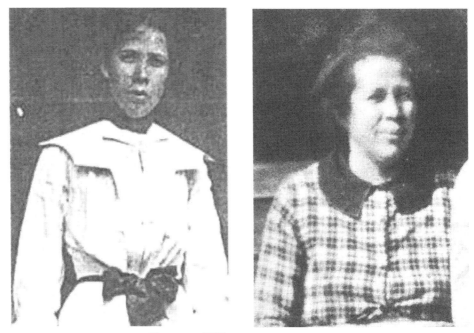

**PHOTO 578 - ROSA HARRIS**

2. Rosa Harris was born in July 1879. She married an Onieda Indian named Archie Wheelock. Rosa attended Carlisle Industrial School in the years 1895- 1903 where she evidently married Archard Baldwin on 14 November 1903, York, South Carolina. Rosa was a noted potter; she even operated a studio in Washington DC.[599] She died 19 June 1935, Richland, South Carolina.

**PHOTO 579 - ROSIE HARRIS WHEELOCK AND DAUGHTER DORIS, THE BABY IS EDNA WHEELOCK**

---

[599] Evening Herald, May 15, 1985 page 2.

Standard Certificate of Death
STATE OF SOUTH CAROLINA
Bureau of Vital Statistics
State Board of Health

File No.—For State Registrar Only 10975

1. PLACE OF DEATH
County of RICHLAND
Township of
or
City of COLUMBIA
Registration District No. 38-A
Registered No. 631
Residence (If not same) ROCK HILL S.C.
(No. BAPTIST HOSPITAL St.; Ward)

2. FULL NAME ROSIE HARRIS WHEELOCK

PERSONAL AND STATISTICAL PARTICULARS
3. Sex FEMALE
4. Color or Race INDIAN
5. Single, Married, Widowed, or Divorced (write the word) MARRIED
5a. If married, widowed, or divorced HUSBAND of (or) WIFE of ARCHIE WHEELOCK
6. DATE OF BIRTH (Month, day, and year) JULY 1879
7. AGE 54 Years
8. Trade, profession, or particular kind of work done, as spinner, sawyer, bookkeeper, etc. DOMESTIC
9. Industry or business in which work was done, as silk mill, saw mill, bank, etc.
10. Date deceased last worked at this occupation (month and year)
11. Total time (years) spent in this occupation
12. BIRTHPLACE (city or town) (State or country) S.C.
13. NAME (FATHER) ALLEN HARRIS
14. BIRTHPLACE (city or town) (State or country) S.C.
15. MAIDEN NAME (MOTHER) NANCY WHITESIDES
16. BIRTHPLACE (city or town) (State or country) S.C.
INFORMANT SAM BLUE
(Address) ROCK HILL S.C.
BURIAL, CREMATION, OR REMOVAL Place INDIAN RESERVATION Date 6-20-35
UNDERTAKER J.W. McCORMICK INC.
(Address) COLUMBIA S.C.
FILED July 15 1935 [illegible], Registrar

MEDICAL CERTIFICATE OF DEATH
21. DATE OF DEATH (month, day, and year) June 19, 1935
22. I HEREBY CERTIFY, That I attended deceased from May 16, 1935, to June 19, 1935
I last saw her alive on June 18, 1935; death is said to have occurred on the date stated above, at 2:30 a.m.
The principal cause of death and related causes of importance in order of onset were as follows: [illegible]
Contributory causes of importance not related to principal cause: Pancreatic [illegible] secondary infection
Name of operation Drainage of Pancreatic [illegible]
What test confirmed diagnosis? Operation. Was there an autopsy? yes
23. If death was due to external causes (violence) fill in also the following:
Accident, suicide, or homicide? Date of injury 19
Where did injury occur? (Specify city or town, and state)
Specify whether injury occurred in industry, in home, or in public place
Manner of injury
Nature of injury
24. Was disease or injury in any way related to occupation of deceased?
If so, specify
(Signed) [illegible] M.D.
(Address) Columbia S.C.

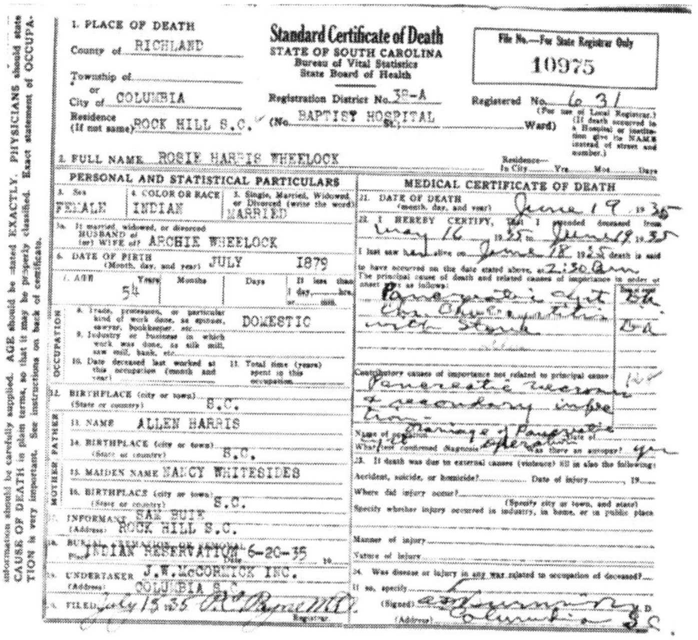

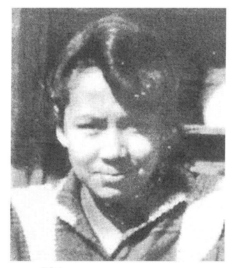

**PHOTO 580 - CERTIFICATE OF DEATH FOR ROSIE HARRIS WHEELOCK**

**PHOTO 581 – DORIS BELLE WHEELOCK**

a. Doris Belle Wheelock was born 14 January 1905. She married Samuel Andrew Blue, son of Samuel Taylor and Louisa Canty Blue. Doris died in 14 May of 1985.[600] Briefly the children are: Mildred born 1922, Betty Juanita was born 1924, Lillian born 1925, Harvey was born 1930 and Andrew Gene born 1938.[601] More about the children will be found in the Blue chapter. She was a great Catawba potter.

[600] Ibid
[601] Membership rolls.

**PHOTO 582 - THREE PICTURES OF DORIS BELLE WHEELOCK**

**PHOTO 583 - HEADSTONE FOR DORIS WHEELOCK BLUE – BURRIED AT CHURCH OF JESUS CHRIST OF LATTER-DAY STS CEMETERY --CATAWBA, YORK COUNTY, SOUTH CAROLINA**

**PHOTO 584 -- EDNA MAE WHEELOCK**

b. Edna Mae Wheelock was born 14 May 1911.. She married Alton Ramsey Thatcher (1907–1976). They had two children:  Margaret Peggy Elizabeth Harris (1923–1984) and Harold Lloyd Thatcher (1929–1986). She married Roy Brown, son of John William and Rachel Wysie George Brown on May 23, 1931. They had no children. They raised Margaret and Harold.  Edna died in September 1985.[602]

In the 1943 roll, Peggy and Harold Thatcher, the children of Cora George Thatcher were living with the Browns.

**PHOTO 585 – TWO PICTURES OF EDNA MAE WHEELOCK THATCHER AND ONE WITH ARCHIE AND ROSA HARRIS WHEELOCK**

---

[602] Obituaries, Evening Herald, September 11, 1985 page 2.

**PHOTO 586 - 1910 US CENSES OF THE INDIAN POPULATION**

Thirteenth Census of the United States 1910 – Indian Population- 20th of April James and Elizabeth Patterson, married 42 years, first marriage for both, they had 12 children with 7 living at this time. They were Catawba, their fathers were white and their mothers were Catawba, so they were ½ white and ½ Catawba.

**PHOTO 587 - FOUR GENERATION PICTURE OF ELIZABETH MISSOURI WHITE PATTERSON**

Four generation picture, Elizabeth Missouri White Patterson, with her son-in-law John Alonso Canty on the left, her grandson Eddie Archie Canty on the right and her great grandson (Eddie's son) Eddie William "slim" Canty

**PHOTO 588 – TWO PICTURES OF MARTHA JANE WHITE-HARRIS AND ONE OF MARTHA AND HUSBAND EBSOLOM EPP HARRIS**

## MARTHA JANE HARRIS, A MASTER CATAWBA POTTER -RIDGE FROM THE 19TH TO THE 21ST CENTURY
### by Dr. Thomas J. Blumer

On July 4, 1936, a summer rain descended on the reservation. The roads were nearly impassable. A handmade pine coffin lay in the back of a mule-drawn wagon. A small procession of mourners walked behind the wagon to the old cemetery. A tremendous sorrow stayed with witness Faye Robbins. She was equally impressed by the door to the deceased's cabin, left open to the rain.

Faye asked her mother why the door was left ajar. The answer was simple: So the soul of Martha

Jane Harris could escape the house and go to the next life. Faye was too young to come under

Martha Jane's artistic influence, but this amazingly talented potter impressed the Catawba on many levels, even though her funeral cortege.

Martha Jane Harris was born in May of 1860. She was the daughter of Peggy George and George White. Times were far from normal. When Martha Jane was just seven months old, South Carolina seceded from the Union. In the following months, all of the able bodied Catawba men joined the Confederate cause. Peggy White and the other Catawba women were left responsible for the economic survival of the Catawba Nation.

With the men off on the war front in Virginia, the women stepped up their pottery production. But an evil is always turned to good by the workings of the Creator, and one of the positive results of this destructive war was that Martha Jane grew up surrounded by the influences of the Catawba pottery tradition. Her opportunities to leave the reservation were few. They consisted of pottery peddling trips with her mother Peggy George White and occasional visits to the clay holes. Little did anyone know that these hard times would produce a great Catawba Indian potter. At the height of yet another economic disaster, Reconstruction, she married Epp Harris, a Catawba pipe maker of tremendous skill. Their only child, Margaret, was born in 1879. The struggling family made a living from pottery, and Epp Harris also ran a ferry across the Catawba River from the reservation to Lancaster County. Around 1890, the family took their pet dog Penny and went north to Virginia to visit Martha Jane's Pamunkey relatives. While in Virginia, they introduced several Catawba shapes to the Pamunkey and left a lasting imprint on this tradition. Until quite recently, one of Epp's shoe pipes was kept by the Pamunkey as a relic of the Harris family's visit. They were so poor that when they returned home (ca. 1892), the trio walked the railroad tracks. Family tradition says that Penny made it home but wore her toenails out on the railroad ties. They slept under beds of leaves to the side of the tracks.

Martha Jane Harris saw the possible benefits of tragedy twice in her life. She owed her pottery making skills to the poverty of the Civil War and Reconstruction years. Then in 1912 her daughter's husband, Chief James Harris, died leaving Margaret with four young children to raise without the social benefits of our times. Martha Jane naturally led the family in pottery making. Martha Jane understood the importance of education. She supported the first Catawba Indian School built by her son-in-law, Chief James Harris, in the 1890s. She realized this modest educational effort was the key to Catawba survival. She struggled to see that her grandchildren had _98 the best education available to them. In 1913 the Harris family move to Cherokee so Margaret's children could attend the Cherokee Boarding School.

When Epp Harris died in 1916, Martha Jane's pottery became even more crucial to the family's economic survival. She produced Catawba smoking pipes and sold them for $1.00 a dozen in Van Wyck. She also insured the survival of the pipe tradition by making molds for her fellow potters.

It would not be until the late 1980s that Martha Jane's skill as a mold maker would Be equaled by contemporary potter Earl Robbins.

Perhaps her greatest pottery masterpiece was purchased by William Simpson of Rock Hill. Today this vessel is part of the Simpson Collection and is housed in the Catawba Nation Archives. A large water jar with two handles, it may be studied by requesting an appointment from tribal archivist

**Bille Anne McKeller.**

Master Potter Martha Jane also was celebrated for her gardens. She raised chickens and was always generous with what little she had. A proud woman, she maintained her sense of dignity and when peddling pottery would not accept rags in barter. She was a respected quilter, midwife and assisted in laying out the dead. It is significant that she referred to good clay as "the gold."

Martha Jane Harris is a legendary figure among the Catawba. She is remembered for her large vessels of graceful form. Her work can be studied at the Catawba Nation Archives, the Smithsonian Institution in Washington, the Museum of the American Indian — Heye Foundation, and the Schiele Museum in Gastonia, North Carolina. Today the New Generation Master Catawba potters emulate the work of Martha Jane Harris. She in effect has become an artistic bridge between the excellence of the 19th century and the burst of artistic energy, often called a Catawba Renaissance, currently being experienced in the Nation. Today's potters follow in Martha Jane Harris's footsteps and those of her primary students: Georgia Harris and Nola Harris Campbell.

A. Margaret Elizabeth Harris, more can be found under William Harris, she married James Harris Jr.

## Documents

Catwaba Indian National Cemetery, Rock Hill, York County, South Carolina


Church of Jesus Christ of Latter-day Sts Cemetery, Catawba, York County, South Carolina

\*\*\*\*\*\*\*\*\*\*\*\*\*\*\*\*\*\*\*\*\*\*\*\*\*\*\*\*\*\*\*\*\*\*\*\*\*\*\*\*\*\*\*\*\*\*

Reprinted here are extracts from several of the primary sources which were used in the preparation of this genealogy, and which are essential to any future genealogical work on the tribe. The selection criterion was that sources had to be unavailable in print or in microfilm, or nearly so, *and* of paramount importance to Catawba genealogy. The 1780 and 1792 name lists, the cemetery transcript, and the 1943 tribal roll have never been published, while the 1849 and 1853 name lists were South Carolina state publications which survive today only as single copies in the South Carolinians Library.

## The Revolutionary pay list of 1780

On 21 June 1783 Thomas Drennan submitted a "Pay bill for Capt Thomas Drennans company of Catawba Indians under the comand of Genrl Thomas Sumpter in the State of South Carolina Servis—for the year 1780 and discharge[?] in the year 1781." It lists the following people.

1 Genrl New River
2 John Brown
3 Robbin
4 Willis—decesd killed @ Rock Mt
(his wife & child alive)
5 Suggar Jamey
6 Pintree George
7 [Jno] Morrison
8 Henry White
9 John Cagg
10 [Capt] Quash
11 Littel Mick
12 Patrick Readhead
13 Billey Williams
14 Big Jamey
15 Billey Cagg
16 John Connar
17 Docter John
18 Chunkey Pipe
19 Capt Petter
20 Billey Otter

21 Littel Aleck
22 (Colo) John Eayrs
23 Petter Harris
24 Jacob Eayrs
25 Billey Readhead
26 John Tompson
27 Joue
28 Pattrick Brown
29 George Cantey
30 Jacob Scott
31 Bobb
32 James Eayrs
33 Littel Stephen
34 Littel Charley
35 John Celliah [Kelliah]
36 Petter George
37 George White
38 Jack Simmons
39 Billey Scott
40 Young John
41 Tom Cook

White Men. Mathew Brown, Michael Delou, Ralph Smith

An attached unnumbered list entitled "List of those Indians who did service which cannot be vouched for" is very similar. It omits those people numbered 4, 12, 14, 16, 17, 18, 28, 29, 32, 33, 38, and 40 on the other list, as well as the "white men." It adds the information given in brackets above under numbers 7, 10, 22, and 35. It also lists the following additional Catawbas:

Jammy Jo[mes?]
Gilber[ ]
Capt Redhead [= #12 above?]
Tom Cross

George Harris
Chickesaw Jimmy
John Nettles [= #17 above?]

Source: "Pay bill for Capt Thomas Drennans company of Catawba Indians..." Comptroller General's Accounts Audited, 3931-A, South Carolina Department of Archives and History.
My reference: M02.

\*\*\*\*\*\*\*\*\*\*\*\*\*\*\*\*\*\*\*\*\*\*\*\*\*\*\*\*\*\*\*\*\*\*\*\*\*\*\*\*\*\*\*\*\*\*\*\*\*\*\*\*\*\*\*\*\*\*\*\*\*\*\*\*\*\*\*\*\*\*\*\*\*\*

## *The Catawba petition of 1792*

On 24 November 1792 the Catawbas submitted a petition to the South Carolina House of Representatives, signed by the thirty-one Catawba men listed below. Except for John Nettles, each signed with their mark.

Genl New River
Collo John Ears
Major John Brown
Capt Peter
Capt Jacob Scott
Capt Thos Cook
Capt Jammy
Capt John Scott
Capt John Cagg
Jammy Bullen
Jammy Ears
Peter George
George White
Pinetree George
Billey Williams
Jacob Ears
Billey Scott
John Kennedy
Patrick Dickson
Pinetree Robbin
Tom Patterson
John Nettles
George Canty
John Yong
Billy Readhead
John Ears
John Kelley
John Deloe
Billy Ears

Gilbert George
Chickeshaw Jammy

Source: Petition of "the Chief and head men of Cataba Nation...," 24 Nov. 1792, South Carolina General Assembly Petitions, 1792, #26, South Carolina Department of Archives and History. My reference: G1792.
\*\*\*\*\*\*\*\*\*\*\*\*\*\*\*\*\*\*\*\*\*\*\*\*\*\*\*\*\*\*\*\*\*\*\*\*\*\*\*\*\*\*\*\*\*\*\*\*\*\*\*\*\*\*\*\*\*\*\*\*\*\*\*\*

## *The Catawba "census" of 1849*

After the treaty of Nation Ford in 1840 the Catawbas were not settled on a new reservation, as the treaty implied they would be; rather they dispersed across North and South Carolina, some going to the Cherokees in North Carolina. The "census" of 1849 stems from an attempt by B.S. Massey to account for all of them. It consists of three separate lists, all of which are reproduced below. Many Catawbas appear on more than one list.

Church at Echota Mission
To minister to the Cherokee people living in the area of present-day Jackson County, the Holston Conference of the Methodist Episcopal Church of the South established the Echota Mission along Soco Creek. In 1841 Reverend D. Ring became the mission's first pastor. Eventually several native preachers served the congregation. After attending one of the worship services, Charles Lanman reported that Cherokee worship was very similar to the worship of white Christians only that the service was done in Cherokee. He found the congregation to be neatly dressed and worshipping according to the Methodist custom, with the exception of singing hymns with more wild excitement.
 The mission established a school in 1850. Reverend Ulrich Keener, who had previously served as minister to the mission in 1847 to 1848, became the first resident superintendent of the school. He held the position until his death in 1856. Keener's original cabin still stands next to the Cherokee United Methodist Church in the Soco Community of Cherokee. The cabin is the oldest architectural structure at a Cherokee site in North Carolina.
References:
John R. Finger, The Eastern Band of Cherokees, 1819-1900 (1984)
Richard Price, Holston Methodism: From Its Origin to the Present Time (1913)
Barbara R. Duncan and Brett H. Riggs, Cherokee Heritage Trails Guidebook (2003)
Vicki Rozema, Footsteps of the Cherokees (2007)


 EXHIBIT A. List of the Catawbas in connection with the Church at Echota Mission.
SHOAL CREEK CAMP GROUND, Sept. 17th, 1849.

Mr. MASSEY,

Dear Sir : At your request I furnish you with the number and names  of the Catawbas, in connection with the Methodist Episcopal Church South,  at the Echota Mission, viz :
William Morrison,      John Scott,

| | |
|---|---|
| Mary Morrison, | John Hart, |
| Betsy Hart, | Lewis Stevens, |
| Nancy George, | Allen Harris, |
| Polly Stevens, | Rhoda Harris, |
| Cinthy Kegg, | Franklin Canty, |
| Betsy Brown, | David Harris, |
| Harriet Stevens, | Polly Harris, |
| Molly Red Head, | Patsy George, |
| Sally Red Head, | Ginny Ayres, |
| Rebecca George, | Mary Joe, |
| Rachel Brown, | Thomas Morrison, |
| Caty Joe, | John Morrison, |
| Eliza Canty, | Jefferson Ayres, |
| Sally Harris, | Jane Harris, |
| Ginny Joe, | John Brown. |
| Esther Scott, | |

Males, 11.   Females, 22.   Total, 33.

Very respectfully yours, &c.

U. KEENER, Preacher in Charge.

\*\*\*\*\*\*\*\*\*\*\*\*\*\*\*\*\*\*\*\*\*\*\*\*\*\*\*\*\*\*\*\*\*\*\*\*\*\*\*\*\*\*\*\*\*\*\*\*\*\*\*\*\*\*\*\*\*\*\*\*\*\*\*\*\*\*

*Accounts of the Catawba at Qualla Town*

*Accounts of the Catawba Indians, due W. H. Thomas, at Qualla Town.*

*Rosa Ayrs, $143 221/2*
*Jenny Ayrs, 18 301/2*
*Elizabeth Ayrs, 43 221/2*

| | |
|---|---|
| Rosa Ayrs, | $143 22 ½ |
| Jenny Ayrs, | 18 30 ½ |
| Elizabeth Ayrs, | 43 22 ½ |
| Mary Ayrs, | 31 29 ½ |
| Margaret Ayrs, | 19 72 ½ |
| Frankey Brown, | 71 77 ½ |
| Elizabeth Brown, | 81 25 |
| William Brown, | 6 00 |

# Documents

| | |
|---|---|
| William George, | 73 47 ½ |
| Anthana George, | 123 55 |
| Patsey George, Anthaney's Daugher, | 143 27 ½ |
| Mary George, | 5 45 ¼ |
| Nancy George, | 8 78 ¾ |
| David Harris, | 67 13 ½ |
| Salley Harris, | 61 02 ½ |
| John Harris, | 3 00 |
| Jinny Joe, | 33 08 ¼ |
| Katy Joe, | 15 12 ½ |
| Franklin Kanty, | 83 77 ¼ |
| Philip Kegg, | 46 87 ½ |
| Dr. James Kegg, | 4 83 ¼ |
| Susan Kegg, | 37 78 ¾ |
| William Morrason, | 42 42 |
| Polla Readhead, | 22 65 |
| Easter Scott, | 1 00 |
| Lewis Stephens, | 66 13 ¼ |
| Polly Stephens, | 25 |
| John Scott, | 51 79 ¼ |
| | $1,306 22 |

\*\*\*\*\*\*\*\*\*\*\*\*\*\*\*\*\*\*\*\*\*\*\*\*\*\*\*\*\*\*\*\*\*\*\*\*\*\*\*\*\*\*\*\*\*\*\*\*\*\*\*\*\*\*\*\*\*\*\*\*\*\*\*\*\*\*\*\*

*A List of Names of Catawba Indians, residing in North Carolina, Haywood County, Cherokee Nation.*

| MALES. | AGE. | MALES. | AGE. | |
|---|---|---|---|---|
| James Kegg, | 66 | Jessey Harris, | 17 | |
| Phillip Kegg, | 22 | William Morrison, | 33 | |
| Billey George, | 33 | John Hart, | 30 | |
| Lewis Stephens, | 46 | Peter Harris, | 14 | |
| Thomas Stephens, | 18 | James Harris, | 16 | |
| Antoney George, | 50 J | John Harris, | 18 | |
| Total, | | | | 12 |
| Male children under 10 years of age, | | | | 12 |

| FEMALES. | AGE. | FEMALES. | AGE. |
|---|---|---|---|
| Nancey George, | 44 | Susy Kegg, | 21 |
| Rebeccah George, | 36 | Cyntha Kegg, | 30 |
| Harriot Stephens, | 44 | Mary Ayers, | 21 |
| Margaret Ayers, | 18 | Mary Ayers, | 12 |

| | | | |
|---|---|---|---|
| Betsey Ayers, | 19 | Salley Readhead, | 60 |
| Salley Harris, | 43 | Polly Stephens, | 24 |
| Frankey Brown, | 27 | Sally Ayers, | 50 |
| Rosey Canty, | 36 | Salley George, | 35 |
| Julia Ann Ayers, | | | |
| (a cripple,) | 15 | | |

Total, 17

Female children under 10 years of age, 15

Total at Qualla Town, Cherokee Nation, Haywood County, North Carolina,

Females, 32

Males, 24

## NUMBER IN SOUTH CAROLINA.

*Greenville District.*

| MALES. | AGE. | MALES. | AGE. |
|---|---|---|---|
| Franklin Canty, | 23 | John Scott, | 23 |
| John Brown, | 12 | David Harris, | 40 |
| Billey Brown, | 20 | | |

Total males, 5

Male children under 10 years of age, 2

| FEMALES. | AGE. | FEMALES. | AGE. |
|---|---|---|---|
| Polley Ayers, | 35 | Betsey Mush, | 18 |
| Eliza Canty, | 23 | Patsey George, | 30 |
| Caty Joe, | 50 | Rachel Brown, | 35 |
| Jane Ayers, | 18 | Esther Brown, | 28 |
| Jinny Joe, | 43 | Polly Readhead, | 40 |
| Mary George, | 18 | Betsey Hart, | 26 |
| Patsey George, | 48 | Peggey Canty, | 20 |

Total females, 14

Female children under 10 years of age, 6

Total males, 7

586

Total females,                                                    <u>20</u>
                                                                  27


*Chester District.*

| MALES. | AGE. | MALES. | AGE. |
|---|---|---|---|
| Allen Harris, | 35 | Robert Mush, | 19 |
| Sam Scott | 50 | | |

Total,                                                            3

Male children under 10 years of age,                              3

| FEMALES. | AGE. | FEMALES. | AGE. |
|---|---|---|---|
| Rody Harris, | 19 | Nancey George, | 70 |
| Jiney Patterson, | 30 | Little Nancy George, | 24 |
| Martha Patterson, | 18 | | |

Total,                                                            5

Female children under 10 years of age,                            2

Total in Chester District, males,                                 6
Total in Chester District, females,                               7


*York District, in their old homes.*

| FEMALES. | AGE. | FEMALES. | AGE. |
|---|---|---|---|
| Betsey Quash, | 60 | Peggy Quash, | 25 |
| Susey Quash, | 35 | Rachel Quash, | 30 |
| Delphy Quash, | 32 | Polley Ayers, | 35 |
| Nancey Quash, | 37 | | |

In the District of York, total                                    7
Females under 10 years,                                           4
Males under 10 years,                                             <u>3</u>
                                                                  14

------

In South Carolina,                                                54
In North Carolina,                                                56

Total of Catawbas in both States,            110

Source: Appendices A, B, and C of *Correspondence relative to the Catawba Indians, Embracing Gov. Seabrook's Letter to the Special Agent and Commissioners appointed by him.* Columbia: I.C. Morgan, State Printer. Also in: *Reports and Resolutions of the General Assembly of the State of South-Carolina* (Columbia, 1849), pp. 249-270. My reference: C1849.

\*\*\*\*\*\*\*\*\*\*\*\*\*\*\*\*\*\*\*\*\*\*\*\*\*\*\*\*\*\*\*\*\*\*\*\*\*\*\*\*\*\*\*\*\*\*\*\*\*\*\*\*\*\*\*\*\*\*\*\*

## Massey's 1853 list of Catawbas

B.S. Massey was in charge of distributing provisions—salt, flour, bacon, lard, blankets, shoes, and so forth—to indigent Catawbas throughout the year 1853. He submitted a report to the state of South Carolina, organized by recipient, listing the date and composition of each payment. Extracted below are the names of each recipient; the first date they were supplied; if they received provisions on more than one date, the last date they were supplied; and the page number of their entry in Massey's report.

| Page | Name | First supplied | Last supplied |
|---|---|---|---|
| 7 | Polly Ayres | 3 Feb. | 1 Oct. |
| | Old Nancy George | 21 Feb. | 22 April |
| 8 | Little Nancy George | 21 Feb. | 22 April |
| | Eliza Canty & 3 ch. | 3 Feb. | 11 Nov. |
| | Rachel Brown & son John | 3 Feb. | 4 Nov. |
| 9 | Allen Harris, wife Roda, & 2 ch. | 1 Feb. | 4 Nov. |
| | Lucinda Harris | 10 May | 4 Nov. |
| 10 | Billey George, wife, & 2 ch. | 14 Feb. | 11 Nov. |
| 11 | Robert Marsh, wife, & 3 ch. | 14 Feb. | 9 Nov. |
| | Lucy Marsh & 4 ch. | 14 Feb. | 9 Nov. |
| 12 | Peggy White & 3 ch. | 14 Feb. | 9 Nov. |
| 13 | Jesse Harris, wife, & 2 ch. | 14 Feb. | 9 Nov. |
| 14 | Betsy Brown & 2 ch. | 23 Jan. | 23 June |
| | Little Patsy George & 1 ch. | 23 Jan. | 4 Nov. |
| | Old Patsy George 23 | Jan. 4 | Nov. |
| 15 | Joseph Joe | 1 Feb. | 17 Nov. |
| | Sally George & 3 ch. | 29 Jan. | |
| | John Harris & wife Jinny | 28 Jan. | 11 Nov. |
| | Absalem Harris | 7 March | 5 Oct. |
| 16 | Sallie Harris | 1 Feb. | 15 June |
| | Nancy Harris | 15 April | 12 May |

| | | | |
|---|---|---|---|
| | Anthony George | 14 Feb. | |
| | William Brown | 31 Jan. | 4 Nov. |
| 17 | Mary Brown & 2 ch. | 6 June | 4 Nov. |
| | Nancy Sanders & 3 ch. | 16 May | 9 Nov. |
| | Esther Brown & 3 ch. | 14 Feb. | 31 Oct. |
| 18 | Jimmy Harris, wife, & 1 ch. | 14 Feb. | 4 Nov. |
| | Caty Joe | 14 Feb | 4 Nov. |
| 19 | Jefferson Ayers | 23 Jan. | 31 Oct. |
| | Peter Harris | 31 Jan. | 2 Nov. |
| | Rachel Tims & 3 ch. | 14 Feb. | 9 Nov. |
| 20 | Rebecca George & 4 ch. | 14 Feb. | 4 Nov. |
| 21 | Davy Harris & wife | 14 Feb. | 4 Nov. |
| | Peggy Canty & 3 ch. | 14 Feb. | 4 Oct. |
| 22 | John Scott 28 | Jan. | 4 Nov. |
| | Betsy Marsh | 17 Feb. | 4 Nov. |
| 23 | Mary Ayres | 10 Feb. | |

Source: Massey, B.S. *Report to the Governor of South Carolina on the Catawba Indians.* Columbia: R.W. Gibbes & Co., State Printers, 1854. My reference: Massey 1854.

\*\*\*\*\*\*\*\*\*\*\*\*\*\*\*\*\*\*\*\*\*\*\*\*\*\*\*\*\*\*\*\*\*\*\*\*\*\*\*\*\*\*\*\*\*\*\*\*\*\*\*\*\*\*\*\*\*\*\*\*

Accounts of the Catawba at Qualla Town

Accounts of the Catawba Indians, due W. H. Thomas, at Qualla Town.

Rosa Ayrs, $143 22 1/2
Jenny Ayrs, 18 30 1/2
Elizabeth Ayrs, 43 22 1/2
Mary Ayrs, 31 29 1/2
Margaret Ayrs, 19 72 1/2
Frankey Brown, 71 77 1/2
Elizabeth Brown, 81 25
William Brown, 6 00 William George, 73 47 1/2
Anthana George, 123 55 Patsey George, Anthaney's Daugher, 143 27 1/2
Mary George, 5 45 1/4
Nancy George, 8 78 3/4
David Harris, 67 13 1/2
Salley Harris, 61 02 1/2
John Harris, 3 00
Jinny Joe, 33 08 1/4

Katy Joe, 15 121½
Franklin Kanty, 83 77¼
Philip Kegg, 46 87½
Dr. James Kegg, 4 83¼
Susan Kegg, 37 78¾
William Morrason, 42 42
Polla Readhead, 22 65
Easter Scott, 1 00
Lewis Stephens, 66 13¼
Polly Stephens, 25
John Scott,        51 79  ¼
$1,306 22

# BIBLIOGRAPHY

Genealogy of the Western Catawba / by Judy Canty Martin:
 Martin, Judy Mae Canty, 1946---Call Number: M243.621 M381g 1998

My father's people: a complete genealogy of the Catawba nation / by Judy Canty Martin
Martin, Judy Mae Canty, 1946- --   Call Number: M243.621 M381m 2002

Missionary journals: journal or diaries of two LDS missionaries to the Catawba Indians (Joseph Willey
and Catawba Pinkney Head) / transcribed and footnoted by Judy CantyMartin
Call Number: M256.08 M6785 1995

Ancestra File, Church of Jesus Christ of Latter Day Saints, Family History Department, Salt Lake City,
Utah, 1995.

Baker, Steven G, The Historic Catawba Peoples: Exploratory Perspectives irrEthnohistory and
Archaeology. Department of History, University of South Carolina, Columbia, SC, 1975.

Blumer, Thomas J., Bibliography of the Catawba, Native American Bibliography, Series No. 10, Tlie
Scarecrow Press Inc. Metuchen, N.J., & London, 1987.

_____ Catawba Indian Reservation Cemetery, 1980.

Brown, Douglas Summers, The Catawba Indians. The People of the River. University of
South Carolina Press, Columbia, 1966.

# Bibliography

_____, City Without Cobwebs. Rock Hill. South Carolina. University of South Carolina Press, Columbia, no date.

Brown, Douglas Summers, A City without Cobwebs, A History of Rock Hill South Carolina

Canty Genealogy; Genealogical Information and news-clippings from family members compiled by Judy Canty Martin, unpublished manuscript. Original genealory from John Alonzo and Georgia Patterson Canty's genealogy book.

Harris Genealory, Genealogical collected from descendants of Hillary Harris, and Lillie Susan Harris Ballard. Wanda Williams responsible for Lillie Susan Harris Ballard genealogry, Hillary Harris information from Bobby Jon Harris, Don Murray, Donna Tanner and other members the of families.

Head, Pinkney Henry, Mv Mission to the Cherokee, 1884, unpublished, transcribed by Judy Canty Martin, 1997.

Head, Pinkney H., Missionary Journal, 1885, Transcription of original document by Judy Canty Martin, 1995, unpublished manuscript.

Head Genealory, Genealogical Inforniation from members of the Pinkney and Martha Patterson family, compiled by Judy Canty Martin, unpublished manuscript.

Hudson, Charles M., The Catawba Nation, Department of Sociology and Anthropology, University of Georgia, Athens, Georgia, University of Georgia Press, 1970.

International Genealogical Index, Family History Department, Church of Jesus Christ of Latter-Day Saints, Salt Lake City, Utah, 1995 version.

Jenson, Andrew, Encyclopedic History of the Church of jesus Christ of Latter Day Saings, Desert News Publishing Co. Salt Lake City, Utah, 1941

Martin, Judy Canty, Catawba Census 1847-1920, unpublished manuscript, 1995.

Merrell, James H, The Indians' New World. Catawba and Their Neighbors from European Contact through the Era of Removal. Early American History and Culture, Williamsburg, Virginia, University of North Carolina Press, Chapel Hill and London, 1989, two volumes.

Merrell, James H., As Long As the Waters Flow. Native Americans in The South and the East. Winston-Salem, North Carolina, John F. Blair,

Merrell, James Hart, Natives in a New World: The Catawba Indians of Carolina, 1650-1800, Parts 1 and 2, University Microfilms International, Johns Hopkins University, 1982.

Patterson Genealory compiled by Judy Canty Martin, transcription of original information collected from family members. Original Patterson genealogy from James and Elizabeth Missouri White Pattersons' own book, unpublished manuscript.

Romney, Marion G., The Power of God Unto Salvation, Speeches of the year, Provo, Utah, Extension Publications, Brigham Young University, 1960 pp. 6-7.

Rountree, Helen C., Pocahontas' People, The Powhatan Indians of Virginia, Through Four Centuries, University of Oklahoma Piess, Norman and London, 1990.

Speck, F. G. & Carr, L. G, Catawba Folk Tales From Chief Sam Blue. New York, Columbia University Press, 1934.

Ward, Bob,The Children of King Hagler, The Catawba Press, Rock Hill, SC. 1940.

Watson, Ian M., Catawba Indian Genealogy, The Geneseo Foundation and Department of Anthropology, State University of New York at Geneseo, 1995.

White, Wesley D., Jr., The Catawba Indians 1975: report to the Center for the Study of Man at the Smithsonian Institution, Washington, D.C. 1975.

Willey, Joseph, Journal of Mission,1885,Transoription of original document by Judy Canty Martin, 1995, unpublished manuscript.

Willey, Joseph, Elder, Church of Jesus Christ of Latter-Day Saints, Missionary Journal, unpublished, transcribed by Judy Canty Martin, 1997

_____, Catawba Indians 1975-1981: Revision of White, 1975.